DICTIONARY OF FOREIGN PHRASES
AND CLASSICAL QUOTATIONS

DICTIONARY OF FOREIGN PHRASES AND CLASSICAL QUOTATIONS

COMPRISING 14,000 IDIOMS, PROVERBS, MAXIMS MOTTOES, TECHNICAL WORDS AND TERMS, AND PRESS ALLUSIONS FROM THE WORKS OF THE GREAT WRITERS IN

LATIN	FRENCH	ITALIAN
GREEK	GERMAN	SPANISH
	PORTUGUESE	

ALPHABETICALLY ARRANGED, WITH ENGLISH TRANSLATIONS AND EQUIVALENTS

EDITED WITH NOTES BY

HUGH PERCY JONES, B.A.

NEW AND REVISED EDITION

JOHN GRANT: BOOKSELLERS: LTD
31 GEORGE IV. BRIDGE
EDINBURGH

Reprinted . 1963

PRINTED IN GREAT BRITAIN BY
OLIVER AND BOYD LTD., EDINBURGH

PUBLISHERS' NOTE.

In presenting this New Dictionary to subscribers and the public, the publishers desire to draw attention to one important respect in which it differs from its predecessor, "Deacon's Dictionary of Foreign Phrases." Although the price of the present work is only about double that of the former, it contains nearly ten times as much information. It forms, in fact, the largest collection of Quotations, Proverbs, etc., which has hitherto been brought together in a single volume.

CONTENTS.

———◆———

INTRODUCTION.

"Omne tulit punctum, qui miscuit utile dulci."

IN an age when we are said to suffer from a superfluity of dictionaries of every kind, it may seem that an apology is required for the production of a New Dictionary of Foreign Quotations.

It is, therefore, necessary to explain that the present volume owes its existence to the extraordinary success of a book which, although far smaller both in size and design than the present work, had a somewhat similar aim. The book alluded to is " Deacon's Dictionary of Foreign Phrases," a little volume—now out of print—which was intended to assist those who, in these days when scarcely a single column of a newspaper is without a foreign phrase, find such a dictionary almost as much a necessity as a convenience.

That such a book was something more than the long-felt want of advertisement was amply proved by the fact that it speedily passed through several editions.

The success of " Deacon's Dictionary of Foreign Phrases " has encouraged the belief that there is room for a more ambitious work which, while preserving all the advantages of its predecessor, would, by the enlargement of its scope, deserve the approval of a wider circle of readers. It is true that the addition of innumerable quotations and the complete revision of the whole have left little resemblance in the present volume to the former one, but all that has been proved useful is carefully retained.

It is, perhaps, scarcely necessary to demonstrate to anyone who has the most superficial acquaintance with the English writers of to-day, whether they be those who address the public through the medium of the Press or of the bookseller, that it is becoming more and more common to seize upon some happy quotation from a foreign tongue in order, if not to point a moral, at least to adorn their tale. The writings of the Press constantly contain allusions and references which presuppose some knowledge of foreign languages and literature on the part of both the writer and reader. The same may be said of our public speakers. Although it has ceased to be a habit in the House of Commons for honourable members to denounce one another in a phrase borrowed from Lucan or Virgil, and although Prime Ministers do not now imitate the example of Walpole, and make guinea bets about the correctness of a quotation with leaders of the Opposition, still a happy phrase from the treasury of the classics is often found to be no mean ally in enforcing an argument.

Nowadays we are all citizens of Cosmopolis, and we do not hesitate to import a phrase, even if clothed in a strange dress, should it serve our purpose better than the more familiar words of our mother tongue. It might be thought by some that this borrowing from languages not our own is sometimes carried to excess. Still, the fact remains that very many phrases from foreign languages have become part of our own literary currency. For example, how common is the use of such Latin phrases as : *Deus ex machinâ; Quantum mutatus ab illo; Nolo episcopari; Non possumus; Pro bono publico; Tempus fugit; Cui bono? De mortuis nil nisi bonum*, and countless others. Such French phrases as *Bon chien chasse de race ; Vogue la galère ;*

Autres temps, autres mœurs; Du sublime au ridicule; Point d'argent, point de Suisse; Such Italian phrases as *Vedi Napoli e poi mori; Se non è vero, è ben trovato; Dolce far niente,* etc., etc.

At the same time, while these and numerous other phrases are in common use, it must not be forgotten that a large number of the reading public—indeed, an ever-increasing multitude—are often in doubt as to the meaning of the commonest phrases of this kind. A great majority have never had the opportunity of cultivating any language other than their own, while, in the present day, technical education has very properly diverted the attention of many from the study of languages to what is of more immediate practical utility. Such people, when confronted by a quotation from a foreign language, may be tempted to exclaim with Berchoux, *Qui nous délivrera des Grecs et des Romains?* A confession of ignorance is always unpleasant, and it is for the convenience of those troubled ones that this book is primarily designed.

Nevertheless, it must not be thought that the object of this work is merely to help those to whom such common expressions as, shall we say? *Après moi le déluge,* or *Vox populi, vox Dei,* present difficulties. The intention has been rather to deserve to the full the motto which has been set at the head of these prefatory remarks. The collection and translation of common phrases is the contribution to the *utile* of the design. Let me now proceed to show how far an effort has been made to mingle the *dulce* of quotations, chosen for their beauty, with the *utile* of hackneyed expressions.

To the many phrases which, either because they are commonly employed by English writers, or because they are very familiar to those who are acquainted with the language from which such phrases are taken, have an obvious claim to inclusion, a large number of longer quotations has been added. These have been selected chiefly on the ground that they have become " winged-words " in the languages whence they have sprung ; that is to say, they are well-known to all who have an intimate knowledge of the literature of those languages. In some few cases passages have been selected on account of their own intrinsic merit, apart from any popularity they may have gained.

Furthermore, it is hoped that all lovers of proverbs will find in these pages an adequate number of those sententious sayings which, perhaps better than anything else, illustrate a nation's peculiar habit of thought. It will, doubtless, be interesting to many to find the same or a similar proverb possessed by many nations, a fact which may well be taken to confirm the good knight Don Quixote's view, that proverbs are true, being opinions extracted from the same experience. Wherever a proverb, or proverbialism, requires explanation, the literal translation has been given in brackets, while the explanation or English equivalent follows afterwards. The same plan has been pursued with many of the idiomatic phrases.

I will now deal with each section separately.

Paradoxical though it may seem, the Latin section has given the greatest difficulty, because quotations from that language are most frequent. For, in addition to the many **Latin.** Latin legal phrases which are in common use, there are an enormous number of short quotations which are, so to speak, shreds from the fabric of a well-known passage of a Latin author. These passages are so familiar to those who are themselves well versed in the literature of the Romans that a word or two quoted from them becomes a finger-post to the entire passage. But I fear that to the average man the information that *virginibus puerisque* is a quotation from Horace, or that *cacoëthes scribendi* are words of Juvenal, would not materially add to his respect for the genius of these writers. It may be given to a few, to apply a phrase of Horace, to recognise a poet even in his dismembered limbs, but such people are, I imagine, in a minority. In these cases, therefore, the name of the author, from whom such a quotation has been taken, is sometimes omitted; but if the full passage is also familiar as a quotation, the full text will be found in the alphabetical order of its first letters, with the name of the author appended. Such an arrangement has, of course, disadvantages, but the advantages are equally obvious. If the long form alone of the quotation were given, it would necessitate the addition of very full indexes to enable the diligent inquirer to discover in what long passage the short quotation is buried, and he would then be left unaided to thresh out the meaning of the shorter phrase. Experience has shown that such indexes, however sufficient they may be for the man who has a good acquaintance with the foreign language quoted, are of little service to the man who has no such equipment. Moreover, we live in days when time means money, and few are disposed to spend time over the scrutiny of an index, when they can gain the same information with less labour.

The arrangement adopted has the further advantage of giving both the popular and the correct form of a quotation. Thus *Non ignara mali, miseris succurrere disco* will be also found in its popular, but incorrect, form of *Haud ignara mali*, etc. Sometimes, too, the popular sense given to brief excerpts from the Latin is different from the meaning of the original. For example, *Noli me tangere*, which is the Vulgate version of the risen Christ's "Touch me not!" addressed to the Magdalene, is now commonly used to indicate a threatening attitude. Again, Horace's *Vestigia nulla retrorsum* and Virgil's *O fortunatos nimium, sua si bona norint* are often applied in a way not meant by the poets. Consequently, the plan followed admits of giving the now generally accepted interpretation of these phrases without doing open violence to the authors of them.

When, however, the author's name has been attached to a **quotation**, every attention has been paid to the correctness of both the Latin and the interpretation. In one case of a familiar passage, *Facilis descensus,* et seq., one line has been omitted, but this has been done in deference to a long-established custom and also to the fact that the line is rather a parenthesis than an integral part of the sentence.

It may be noted that, while many of the more popular law maxims are included in this section, several which often find a place in dictionaries of phrases have been omitted. This has been done because a large number of such phrases are of no interest to the general public, while their meaning is not infrequently so obscure as to require one learned in the law to explain them. Even lawyers themselves, unless rumour lies, have been known to hold serious, not to say costly, differences of opinion upon the subject.

I fear that some people, on seeing that more than fifty pages of this book are devoted to Greek quotations, will be **Greek.** inclined to exclaim : *Que diable allait-il faire dans cette galère?* Greek has, unfortunately, ceased to be popular as a subject for study. " What is the use of Greek ? " —a question often put to long-suffering pedagogues by their charges—is now more often heard from the lips of those whose age ought to have given them more wisdom. But, as in the past :

> " Græcia capta ferum victorem cepit, et artes
> Intulit agresti Latio " —

so we may be permitted to hope that Greek literature is only receiving a temporary rebuff. At any rate, the attack made upon it in one of the ancient seats of learning was repulsed, and this, perhaps, may be taken as a happy augury for the renewal of interest in the literature which contains the noblest thoughts written in the noblest language.

In making a selection of Greek quotations, a difficulty is caused by an *embarras de richesse*, for there are an immense number of passages which might reasonably be included on the ground of merit.   Still, it is hoped that the quotations selected are fairly representative, and are sufficient to show what pithy sayings we owe to the Greek writers.   Many of these are well known in a Latin or English dress.   For instance, such popular sayings as : " Call a spade a spade ! "   " Speak no ill of the dead ! "   " Nothing in excess ! "   " Those whom the gods love, die young ! "   " Life is short, Art is long," can all be traced to Greek sources.

It is true that we seldom hear Greek quoted nowadays ; but this is a fault that may be remedied.   I am told that, within recent years, an alderman has been heard to adorn his speech with excerpts in the language of Sophocles.   Why should not this wholesome infection spread even to our Lord Mayors ?   I can conceive of nothing that would be more in harmony with the spirit of a civic feast than the recitation of an ode of Anacreon.

The Greek quotations are, for the most part, given exactly as written by their authors.   A few passages have been slightly altered in their structure where absolutely necessary ; that is to say, when a few words or lines have been taken from a passage too long to quote in its entirety.

Every effort has been made to include in this section as many as possible of those French words and phrases which are to be **French.** found in the newspapers, periodicals, and novels of to-day.   It must be owned, however, that it is a difficult task to keep pace with the constant influx of French words and idiomatic expressions into our language, as this Gallic invasion continues to make such great advances.

A very large number of literary quotations will also be found in this portion of the book.   They have been chosen carefully, and it is believed that none of the best-known passages have been omitted.   A considerable number of authors has been drawn upon, and both the old and the modern writers are re-presented.   For example, by the side of extracts from the

Chevalier Balzac, La Rochefoucauld, Molière, etc., will be found passages from such moderns as Paul Bourget, Emile Zola, and Edmond Rostand. The great writers of maxims and reflections, such as La Rochefoucauld, La Bruyère, and Vauvenargues, have been laid under heavy contribution; for these pithy sayings, both for the knowledge of human nature they show and for their terseness of expression, must commend themselves to every age. The apothegms of Vauvenargues are especially noteworthy on account of their loftiness of thought.

The remark has often been made, that in France many men have owed their reputation to the coining of smart sayings, and it is an undoubted fact that no nation possesses a larger number of memorable phrases which have been uttered on historic occasions. These remain fixed in the memory even when the events that occasioned them are forgotten, and so numerous are they that Mr. Max O'Rell is not very wide of the mark in declaring that " the history of France might be written between quotation marks." Many of these sayings are as well known in England as in France. Phrases like : *L'Etat c'est moi ; C'est magnifique, mais ce n'est pas la guerre ; Tout est perdu fors l'honneur ; De l'audace, encore de l'audace ; Nous avons changé tout cela ; J'y suis, J'y reste ; La Garde meurt et ne se rend pas,* are on the lips of all.

When we consider the authenticity of many of these historic sayings we are on dangerous ground. M. Fournier, in his books *L'Esprit des Autres* and *L'Esprit dans l'Histoire*, holds the brief of *Advocatus Diaboli* against their acceptance. From him we learn that Louis XIV. probably never exclaimed *L'Etat c'est moi;* that Francis I. did not write, in the hour of defeat, *Tout est perdu fors l'honneur;* and, worst of all, that the credit of the immortal *La Garde meurt et ne se rend pas* is due, not to the courage of the soldier Cambronne, but to the inventiveness of the journalist Rougemont. Reading M. Fournier's onslaughts upon cherished popular traditions, one is inclined to regret his passion for truth at all hazards. Popular prejudices are stubborn things to grapple with. We know that the Duke of Wellington himself denied that he ever uttered the words " Up Guards, and at 'em," at Waterloo. But these words are still accepted as historical by the great majority of people, and similarly, M. Fournier notwithstanding, faith in the authenticity of many of those French sayings will be difficult to destroy.

This section owes much to Büchmann's *Geflügelte Worte,*
German. wherein are collected the " winged words" taken from the literatures of various countries.

The German portion of that book is, as is natural, the most complete, and is most useful because it contains the extracts from authors that are most often quoted by Germans themselves. A very large portion of the passages selected for this Dictionary are taken from the writings of Goethe and Schiller, but other authors of repute have not been neglected. German writers are, as a rule, too verbose to be a prolific source of supply for the collector of concise maxims ; but several examples of the aphorisms of Schopenhauer and Lichtenberg are given. Several of the most famous sayings of Bismarck, who was a phrase-maker as well as a maker of empires, will also be found recorded. Some of these, such as *Nach Canossa gehen wir nicht. Macht geht vor Recht,* and *Eisen und Blut* have almost become part of our own language.

From the most widely-known works of the classic writers, the *Divina Commedia* of Dante, the *Gerusalemme* of Tasso, and
Italian. Ariosto's *Orlando Furioso,* many extracts have been made. Petrarch and Boccaccio do not lend themselves so readily to brief quotations, and the latter is, therefore, but meagrely represented. Of the maxims contained in the works of Guicciardini and Machiavelli numerous examples are given. It will be noticed that, as an inditer of Machiavellianisms, if such a word may be coined, the latter is disappointing. To

xviii   INTRODUCTION.

judge from his writings, Machiavelli's code of ethics appears to
have obtained a worse reputation than it merits.

Many of the pretty conceits to be found in *Il Pastor Fido* of
Guarini are included, although it is an open question whether
some of these are not merely glosses on Petrarch and other
writers rather than due to Guarini himself. So much for the
older writers. The more modern ones, as Metastasio, Monti,
Alfieri, Manzoni, Pellico, etc., have provided many of the quotations. The Italian proverbs are, in general, excellent specimens
of popular adages neatly expressed, and are well worth perusal.
A very full list of Italian musical terms is also given in this
section. It may seem somewhat banal to find selections from
Dante sandwiched between the prosaic directions that are found
on a musical score. These terms, however, have been included
on the ground of practical utility. The insertion of them proved
to be an acceptable feature in "Deacon's Dictionary of Foreign
Phrases," and on that account they have been retained in the
present volume.

The comedies of Calderon and Lope de Vega, as well as those
of Tirso de Molina, have supplied many of the Spanish quotations.

Spanish.   Baltasar Gracian and Antonio Perez, the two great
writers of maxims, the former terse though some-
times obscure, the latter occasionally trivial but always clear,
have been often drawn upon. Numerous selections have also
been made from the writings of Cervantes. Of the more modern
writers, Yriarte and Campoamor are most frequently quoted.

It will be seen that a large proportion of the Spanish section
is taken up by proverbs. This is explained when we consider
the high place that sayings of this kind—the *refranes, adagios,*
and *proverbios*—hold in the estimation of the people of Spain.
If France may be said to be the land of the *bon mot,* assuredly
Spain is the country of proverbs. Probably no nation possesses
a greater number of sententious sayings, and nowhere is the
study of them more diligently cultivated. Around the subject an

extensive literature has grown, and continues to grow, for the Spaniards take a warm pride in the numerous wise saws that abound in their language. Whether the Moorish strain in his blood is responsible for the Spaniard's love of sententious sayings we need not inquire. It is sufficient to say that many of their proverbs are so full of practical wisdom as to deserve our close study. It has been well said, too, that without doubt the purest Spanish is to be found in these proverbs, and for that reason alone they are attractive to the student. Sancho Panza has made most of us acquainted with many of the wise sayings current in Spain. Indeed, honest Sancho is not a Sam Weller. His maxims are not peculiarly his own, for he often merely repeats the adages popular among his countrymen.

Some of the Spanish proverbs are histories in brief. We may learn something of the misrule of the monarchs of Spain from *Allá van leyes do quieren reyes,* of the terrors of the Inquisition from *Con el Rey y la inquisicion chiton!* while *El diablo está en Cantillana* reminds us that Don Juan, the prototype of all gay deceivers, was something more than a fiction of dramatists and poets.

Needless to say, it has not been possible to cull more than the choicest flowers from the abundant stores of the proverbs of Spain. The best, and all of the widest application, have been diligently collected.

The proverbs included in this section will show that the inhabitants of Portugal are not far behind their neighbours in **Portuguese.** practical wisdom. The fact that Camoens is the only Portuguese writer to be quoted by name, might lead the uninitiated to think that writers in Portugal have something in common with snakes in Iceland. This is not the case, but many Portuguese writers of eminence have chosen the sonorous Castilian as their medium of expression in preference to using their own native tongue.

In conclusion, the Editor feels very conscious of the truth of

Ab initio.

From the beginning; from the very first.

Ab integro *or* de integro.

Afresh, anew.

Ab irato.

(From an angry man.)   Unfair; unprovoked.*

Abnormis sapiens.

(Wise by natural good sense.)   A born philosopher.

Ab officio et beneficio.

(From his office and benefice.)   Suspended from his duties.†

Ab origine.

From the origin; from the commencement.

A bove majori discit arare minor.

(The young ox learns how to plough from the older.)   As the old cock crows, the young cock learns.

Ab ovo.

(From the egg.)   From the earliest commencement.

Ab ovo usque ad mala.

(From the egg to the apples.)   From beginning to end.‡

Abscissio infiniti.

(Cutting off the infinite.)   The exclusion of everything but the point under consideration.

Absens heres non erit.

(The absent will not be heir.)   Out of sight, out of mind.

Absentem lædit, cum ebrio qui litigat.
     — *Publius Syrus*

(He that enters into dispute with a man in drink, wrongs the absent.)   The man, not being in his sober senses, is practically absent.

Absentem qui rodit amicum,
Qui non defendit, alio culpante solutos
Qui captat risus hominum famamque dicacis,
Fingere qui non visa potest, commissa tacere
Qui nequit, hic niger est : hunc tu Romane caveto.—*Horace.*

He that shall rail against his absent friends,
Or hears them scandalized, and not defends;
Sports with their fame, and speaks whate'er he can,
And only to be thought a witty man;
Tells tales and brings his friends in disesteem;
That man's a knave ;—be sure beware of him.—*Creech.*

Absente reo.

In the absence of the accused.

Absit invidia.

(All envy apart.)   Take it not amiss.

Absit omen.

(Evil omens apart.)   May no portent of evil be attached to the words I say

Absque sudore et labore nullum opus perfectum est.

Without sweat and toil no work is perfect.

Abstinete, sustinete.

Forbear and bear.

Absurdum est ut alios regat, qui seipsum regere nescit.

(It is absurd that a man should rule others, who cannot rule himself.) Self-control is the most necessary qualification of a leader of men.

---

* An action is said to be performed *ab irato* when we wish to signify that it is unprovoked, and, on that account, not to be taken too seriously.
† The technical term for the suspension of a clergyman by his bishop, on account of some irregularity or misconduct.
‡ Eggs formed the first course of a Roman's dinner, and fruit the dessert.

Abundans cautela non nocet.

(Plenty of caution hurts nobody.) Safe bind, safe find.

Ab uno disce omnes.

(From one learn all.) From a single instance learn the nature of the whole.

Ab urbe condita.

From the founding of the city (Rome).*

Abusus non tollit usum.

Abuse is no argument against the use of anything.

Acceptissima semper Munera sunt, auctor quae pretiosa facit.
— *Ovid.*

(Gifts are always most valued when the giver is dear to us.) Rich gifts seem poor when givers prove unkind.
— *Shakespeare.*

Accipere quam facere injuriam praestat.
—*Cicero.*

It is better to receive than to inflict an injury.

Acclinis falsis animus meliora recusat.
—*Horace.*

The mind inclined to falsehood rejects the nobler course.

Acerbus et ingens.

Fierce and mighty.

Acerrima proximorum odia.— *Tacitus.*

The hatred of those who are our nearest kin is the most grievous to endure.

Acherontis pabulum.—*Plautus.*

(Food for Acheron.) Food for death.†

Acribus initiis, incurioso fine.— *Tacitus.*

(Alert in the beginning, negligent in the end.) Too much zeal often leads to carelessness. Slow and steady wins the race.

A cruce salus

Salvation from the cross.

Acta deos nunquam mortalia fallunt.
— *Ovid.*

The deeds of men never escape the eyes of God.

Actum est de republica.

(It is all over with the commonwealth.) The country is in danger.

Actum ne agas.

(Do not do what is done.) Let well alone.

Actus Dei nemini facit injuriam.

(The act of God does wrong to no one.) No person can be held legally responsible for an event due to divine agency.

Acum in meta fœni quaerere.

To look for a needle in a bundle of hay.

A cuspide corona

(A crown from the spear.) A kingdom won by the sword.

Ac veluti magno in populo quum sæpe coorta est
Seditio, sævitque animis ignobile vulgus;
Jamque faces et saxa volant; furor arma ministrat;
Tum pietate gravem ac meritis si forte virum quem
Conspexere silent, arrectisque auribus adstant;
Iste regit dictis animos, et pectora mulcet.— *Virgil.*

And as in a mighty throng of men, when some tumult has arisen, and the rabble has been roused to fury; firebrands and stones fly this way and that, since rage finds weapons. Anon, if they chance to see among them a man whose probity and merits give him influence, silence takes them, and they hearken attentively to his counsel; he diverts their angry thoughts with his words, and soothes their savage rage.

* The Romans reckoned all dates from 753 B.C., the year when, according to tradition, Rome was built by Romulus and Remus *Ab urbe condita* is usually expressed by the letters A. U. C.

† Acheron, the river of Woe, was one of the seven streams which were supposed to flow round the lower world.

Ad amussim.

(By the plumb-line.)   Correct in every particular.

Ad arbitrium.

At pleasure; at will.

Ad astra per ardua.

(To the stars through difficulties.)   To win eternal renown in spite of all opposition.

Ad calamitatem quilibet rumor valet.
—*Publius Syrus.*

(Any rumour is good enough to use against the unfortunate.)   Give a dog a bad name and hang him.

Ad Calendas Græcas.

(At the Greek Calends.)   When two Sundays come in one week.*

Ad captandum vulgus.

To catch the rabble; to tickle the ears of the mob.

Ad clerum.

To the clergy.

Ad damnum adderetur injuria.—*Cicero.*

That would be adding insult to injury.

Addecet honeste vivere.

It much becomes us to live honourably.

Addendum.

Something to be added.

Adde parum parvo, magnus acervus erit.

(Keep adding little to little, and soon there will be a great heap.)   Many littles make a mickle.

A Deo et Rege.

From God and the King.

Adeo in teneris consuescere multum est.—*Virgil.*

(So strong is custom in youthful minds.)   Just as the twig is bent, the tree's inclined.—*Pope.*

A Deo lux nostra.

Our light cometh from God.

Ad eundem (gradum).

To the same degree (rank).†

Ad extremum.

To the extremity; at last.

Ad finem.

To the end; finally.

Adhibenda est in jocando moderatio.
—*Cicero.*

(There should be a limit observed in joking.)   Jokes should not exceed the bounds of good taste.

Ad hoc.

For this purpose; unto this end.

Adhuc sub judice lis est.

The case is not yet decided.

Ad infinitum.

To infinity; without limit or end.

Ad interim.

In the meanwhile.

Ad internecionem.

To extermination.

Adjuvante Deo labor proficit.

With God's help, work prospers.

Ad libitum.

At pleasure.

Ad literam.

(To the letter.)   Minutely exact.

Ad majorem Dei gloriam. (A.M.D.G.)

For the greater glory of God.

Ad mensuram aquam bibit.

(He drinks water by measure.)   Penny wise and pound foolish.

Ad nauseam.

(To produce sickness.)   To produce a feeling of disgust.

---

* The Calends was the name given by the Romans to the first day of each month. As this was a usage peculiar to the Romans, to say that something will happen on the Greek Calends is an emphatic way of saying " never."
† Graduates of one university are allowed, under certain circumstances, to take a corresponding degree to that which they hold in another university. Thus, a Master of Arts of Oxford could obtain the same degree at Cambridge without further examination.

Adolescentem verecundum esse decet.
— *Plautus.*

Modesty is a becoming ornament to a young man.

Ad perditam securim manubrium adjicere.

(To throw the helve after the hatchet.) To give up all hope.

Ad perpetuam rei memoriam.

For the perpetual remembrance of the thing.

Ad pœnitendum properat, cito qui judicat.— *Publius Syrus.*

(He that comes too quickly to a decision is fast on the road to repent.) Marry in haste and repent at leisure.

Ad populum phaleras, ego te intus et in cute novi.— *Persius.*

(Show your trappings to the common folk; I know you inside and out.) Your hypocrisy may impose on others, but I know your real character.

Ad præsens ova cras pullis sunt meliora.

(Eggs to-day are better than chickens to-morrow.) A bird in the hand is worth two in the bush.

Ad quod damnum.

To what damage.*

Ad referendum.

To be further considered.

Ad rem.

To the thing, point, purpose.

Adscripti glebæ.

(Attached by law to the soil.) Originally a class of Roman serfs.

Adsiduus usus uni rei deditus et ingenium et artem sæpe vincit.
— *Cicero.*

(Constant attention to one subject frequently produces better results than mere natural ability and skill.) Practice makes perfect. Genius is an infinite capacity for taking pains.

Ad summam.

In short; in a word.

Adulandi gens prudentissima laudat sermonem indocti, faciem deformis amici.— *Juvenal.*

The crafty race of flatterers praises the conversation of an uneducated boor and the features of an ugly friend.

Ad unguem.

To the nail; to a T; to a nicety.†

Ad unum omnes.

All to a man; everybody without exception.

Ad usum Delphini.

(For the Dauphin's use.) An expurgated book.‡

Ad utrumque paratus.

Prepared for either event; ready for good or ill fortune.

Ad valorem.

According to value.§

Adversa virtute repello.

By courage I repel adversity.

Adversis etenim frangi non esse virorum.— *Silius Italicus.*

Brave men ought not to be overcome by adversity.

Adversis major, par secundis.

Superior to adversity, equal to prosperity.

---

* A writ issued to ascertain whether the granting of a privilege to some district, such as the right of holding a fair, is likely to prove detrimental to the interests of any portion of the inhabitants of that district.

† Horace speaks of a man *factus ad unguem,* meaning a "perfect gentleman." The origin of the expression is the practice of sculptors testing the smoothness of marble by passing their finger-nail over it, just as makers of billiard balls test them by rubbing the ivory against the sensitive nerves of the cheek.

‡ This was the title of a celebrated edition of classic authors, which was prepared for the use of the Dauphin by order of Louis XIV.

§ A tariff *ad valorem* is the imposition of certain duties on imported goods, the rate of duty being fixed on the commercial value of these imports.

Adversus solem ne loquitor

(Do not speak against the sun.) Do not argue against a fact which is clear as daylight.

Ad vivum.

(To the quick.) To the life.

Advocatus Diaboli.

The Devil's advocate.*

Ægis fortissima virtus.

Virtue is the strongest shield.

Ægrescit medendo.

(The disease grows worse by attempts to heal it.) The remedy is worse than the disease.

Ægri somnia.

The empty visions of a sick man.

Æneadum genetrix, hominum divomque voluptas,
Alma Venus, cæli subter labentia signa
Quæ mare navigerum, quæ terras fru-giferentis
Concelebras, per te quoniam genus omne animantum
Concipitur visitque exortum lumina solis :
Te, dea, te fugiunt venti, te nubila cæli,
Adventumque tuum, tibi suavis dædala tellus
Summittit flores, tibi rident æquora ponti,
Placatumque nitet diffuso lumine cælum.
—*Lucretius.*

Mother of the Æneadæ, darling of men and gods, increase - giving Venus, who, beneath the gliding signs of heaven, fillest with thy presence the ship-carrying sea, the corn-bearing lands, since through thee every kind of living thing is conceived, rises up and beholds the light of the sun. Before thee, goddess, flee the winds, the clouds of heaven ; before thee and thy advent ; for thee earth manifold in works puts forth sweet-smelling flowers ; for thee the levels of the sea do laugh, and heaven propitiated shines with outspread light.†— *Munro.*

Æquam memento rebus in arduis
Servare mentem, non secus in bonis
Ab insolenti temperatam
Lætitiâ.—*Horace.*

In times of adversity remember to preserve equanimity, and equally in prosperous moments restrain excessive joy.

Æqua tellus
Pauperi recluditur,
Regumque pueris.—*Horace.*

The impartial earth is opened alike for the pauper and the children of the rich and noble.

Æquitas sequitur legem.

(Equity follows the law.) The rules of equity modify the strict letter of the law by taking into account the circumstances of the case.

Æquum est,
Peccatis veniam poscentem reddere rursus.—*Horace.*

It is right that the man who asks pardon for his own faults, should be willing to pardon others.

Æra nitent usu ; vestis bona quærit haberi ;
Canescunt turpi testa relicta situ.
—*Ovid.*

Brass shines by use ; a good garment ought to be worn ; deserted houses soon fall into ruin and decay.

---

* When it is proposed to add a new name to the list of saints, the Roman Catholic Church appoints a person to examine and oppose the claim. This individual is known as the *Advocatus Diaboli.* Hence the term is applied to anyone who supports an unrighteous course of action.

† These are the opening lines of the *De Rerum Naturâ*, the famous poem in which Lucretius expounds his theory of the creation of the world. The poet invokes Venus, the Goddess of Love, as being the chief motive power in the universe. She is called "Mother of the Æneadæ," because the Romans claimed descent from her, through Æneas, the Trojan hero.

Ære perennius.

More enduring than bronze; everlasting.*

Ærugo animi, robigo ingenii.—*Seneca.*

(The rust of the mind is the blight of genius.) A mind not used is a mind abused.

Æs alienum.

(Money belonging to another.) Debt.

Æs debitorem leve; grave inimicum facit.—*Publius Syrus.*

(A small debt produces a debtor; a heavy one an enemy.) Lend and lose; so play fools.

Æsopi ingenio statuam posuere Attici,
Servumque collocarunt æterna in basi,
Patere honoris scirent ut cunctis viam.
        —*Phædrus.*

The Athenians erected a large statue to Æsop and placed him, though a slave, on a lasting pedestal: to show that the way to honour lies open indifferently to all.

Ætatis suæ.

Of his or her age.

Æthiopem lavare (*or* dealbare).

(To wash a blackamoor white.) To lose one's labour.

Afflatus.

(A breathing on.) Inspiration; the divine afflatus.

Afflavit Deus et dissipantur.

God sent forth his breath, and they are scattered.†

A fonte puro pura defluit aqua.

(From a clear spring clear water flows.) A man is generally known by the company he keeps.

A fortiori.

(With stronger reason.) If one horse can pull a cart, *a fortiori* ten horses can do it more easily.

A fronte præcipitium, a tergo lupi.

(A precipice in front, wolves behind.) Between the devil and the deep sea.

Agenda.

Things (business) to be done.

Age quod agis.

(Do what you are doing.) Mind the business you have in hand.

Agnosco veteris vestigia flammæ.
        —*Virgil.*

(I feel the symptoms of the former flame.) Having loved once before, I know the symptoms.

Agnus Dei.

The Lamb of God.‡

Ah, quam dulce est meminisse!

What joys doth memory give!

Albæ gallinæ filius.

(The son of a white hen.) A man born with a silver spoon in his mouth.§

Alcinoo poma dare.

(To give fruit to Alcinous.) To carry coals to Newcastle.‖

Alea jacta est.

The die is cast.¶

---

* See *Exegi monumentum.*
† This was the inscription on the medal which was struck by the order of Queen Elizabeth, to commemorate the defeat of the Spanish Armada.
‡ The name given to part of the office for the burial of the dead in the Roman church, Agnus Dei being the opening words of one portion of the service.
§ It is related that an eagle dropped a white hen into the lap of Livia, the wife of the Emperor Augustus, and this was accepted as a favourable omen.
‖ Alcinous, King of Corcyra (the modern Corfu) possessed such fertile orchards, so tradition says, that their excellence became proverbial.
¶ The words of Julius Cæsar when he led his army across the Rubicon, an action tantamount to a declaration of civil war.

Aleator, quanto in arte est melior, tanto est nequior.—*Publius Syrus*.

(The better the gambler, the greater the knave.) Success in gambling is not a good recommendation for honesty.

Alere flammam.

To feed the flame ; to add fuel to the fire.

Alias.

(Otherwise.) At another time.

Alibi.

(Elsewhere.) In law the plea of a person who alleges that he was in some other place than that stated in the charge.

Aliena vitia in oculis habemus, a tergo nostra sunt.—*Seneca*.

(The vices of others we keep in our eyes, our own on our back.) We see the mote in our brother's eyes, but do not observe the beam in our own.*

Alieni appetens, sui profusus.— *Sallust*.

Covetous of the possessions of others, and prodigal of his own.†

Alii sementem faciunt, alii metentem.

(Some do the sowing, and others the mowing.) One beats the bush, and another catches the bird.

Aliorum medicus, ipse ulceribus scates.

(The physician of others, you yourself are full of sores.) Physician, heal thyself.

Aliquando bonus dormitat Homerus.

(Even the good Homer sometimes nods.) The greatest writers are occasionally prosy.

Aliquis malo sit usus ab illo.

Some advantage may come of that evil.

Alitur vitium vivitque tegendo.— *Virgil*.

Vice thrives and lives by concealment.

Aliud nihil est agendum.

There is no more to be done.

Alium silere quod voles, primus sile.
— *Seneca*.

(If you wish another to keep your secret, first keep it yourself.) Speech is silver, silence is golden.

Alma mater.

(A foster mother.) Generally applied to a University.

Alta sedent civilis vulnera dextræ.
—*Lucan*.

Deep are the wounds that civil strife inflicts.

Alterâ manu fert lapidem, panem ostentat alterâ.—*Plautus*.

(In one hand he carries a stone, while in the other he shows a piece of bread.) A treacherous fellow. One who carries fire in one hand and water in the other.

Alter ego.

Another self.

Alter ipse amicus.

A friend is a second self.

Alterius non sit, qui suus esse potest.

Let no man be the hireling of another if he can be his own master.

Altiora peto.

I seek higher things, a higher life.

* The writings of Seneca contain so much that resembles the teachings of Christianity that he has been regarded as a Christian writer. His sentiments, however, present the loftiest ideals of the Stoic school of philosophy. He had the misfortune to be the preceptor of Nero, which only proves the best teachers do not produce the best pupils.
† So the historian describes Catiline, the Thistlewood of Roman history. The phrase is now applied to political adventurers by their opponents.

Altius ibunt qui ad summa nituntur.

They will rise highest who strive for the highest place.

Alumnus.

(A nursling; foster-child.) The students of a college or university are said to be its *alumni*, foster-children.

Amabilis insania.

An amiable madness; a pleasing illusion.

Amantes sunt amentes.

(Lovers are madmen.) Love and pride stock Bedlam.

Amantium iræ amoris integratio est.
　　　　　　　　　—Terence.

The quarrelling of lovers is the renewal of love.

Amare et sapere vix deo conceditur.
　　　　　　　— Publius Syrus.

To love, and to be wise at the same time, is scarcely possible even for a god.

Ama tanquam osurus. Oderis tanquam amaturus.

(Love as though you might hate. Hate as though you might love.) Do not run to extremes either in love or hatred.*

Amat victoria curam.

(Victory loves care.) Victory and prudence are close friends.

A maximis ad minimos.

From the greatest to the least.

Ambigendi locus.

Room for doubt; dubious.

A mensâ et toro.

(From table and bed.) A legal formula to indicate a divorce.

Amica pax, magis amica veritas.

I love peace, but I love truth even more.

Amicitia sine fraude.

Friendship without deceit.

Amicum perdere est damnorum maximum.

To lose a friend is the greatest of all losses.

Amicus certus in re incertâ cernitur.
　　　　　　　　　—Ennius.

(A sure friend is made manifest in a doubtful matter; when one is in difficulty.) A friend in need is a friend indeed.

Amicus curiæ.

(A friend of the court.) A person who gives an opinion or contributes information on the invitation of the judge, although not otherwise engaged in the cause.

Amicus humani generis.

A friend of the human race.

Amicus Plato, amicus Socrates, sed major veritas.

Plato is my friend, Socrates is my friend, but truth is greater.†

Amicus usque ad aras.

A friend even to the altars—to the last extremity.

Amicus vitæ solatium.

A friend is the comfort of life.

Amissum quod nescitur non amittitur.
　　　　　　　—Publius Syrus.

(The loss that is not known, is no loss at all.) What the eye does not see, the heart does not grieve for.

Amor et melle et felle est fecundissimus.—*Plautus.*

Love is very rich both in honey and in gall.

---

* This precept, the truth of which is somewhat dubious, is apparently of Greek origin, for Sophocles puts the same idea into the mouth of a character in one of his tragedies.
† The author of this phrase is unknown, but the idea is expressed by Aristotle.

Amor gignit amorem.

(Love begets love.)   Love is the load-stone of love.

Amor magnus doctor est.
—*St. Augustine.*

Love is a great teacher.

Amor patitur moras.

(Love endures delays.) Love is a sweet tyranny.

Amor patriæ.

The love of our country.

Amor timere neminem verus potest.
—*Seneca.*

(True love can fear no one.)   Perfect love casteth out fear.

Amoto quæramus seria ludo.—*Horace.*

A truce to jesting ; to serious matters let us now give our attention.

Anceps forma bonum mortalibus.
—*Seneca.*

Beauty is a doubtful boon.

Anguillam caudâ tenes.

(You hold an eel by the tail.) You have caught a Tartar.

Anguis in herbâ.

(A snake in the grass.)   A hidden danger.

Aniles fabulæ.

Old women's tales ; prosy nonsense.

Animadverto, enim, etiam deos ipsos, non tam accuratis adorantium preci-bus, quam innocentiâ et sanctitate laetari.—*Pliny the Younger.*

I perceive that the gods themselves are propitiated, not so much by the prayers of their worshippers, as by singleness and holiness of life.

Animi labes nec diuturnitate vanescere nec amnibus ullis elui potest.—*Cicero.*

Stains that affect the soul are not ob-literated by time, nor can rivers of water wash them away.

Animo et fide.

By courage and faith.

Animo imperabit sapiens, stultus serv-iet.—*Publius Syrus.*

A wise man will be the master of his passions, a fool their slave.

Animo non astutiâ.

By valour, not by craft.

Animula, vagula, blandula
Hospes, comesque corporis !
Quæ nunc abibis in loca,
Pallidula, frigida, nudula,
Nec, ut soles, dabis joca.

Dear little fleeting soul of mine ; my sometime guest and comrade ! Now whither wilt ?   To what unknown climes wilt thou go, so pale, and cold, and tiny as thou art, forgetting thy former playful ways, a stranger now to mirth.*

Animum curis nunc huc nunc dividit illuc. — *Virgil.*

This way and that the anxious mind is torn.

Animum fortuna sequitur.

(Fortune attends on courage.) Fortune gives her hand to a bold man.

Animum picturâ pascit inani.—*Virgil.*

And with the shadowy picture feeds his mind.

Animum rege, qui, nisi paret, imperat.
—*Horace.*

Rule your passions, or they will rule you.

Animus lætus bene afficit vultum.

A merry heart maketh a cheerful coun-tenance.

Animus meminisse horret luctuque re-fugit.

My heart shudders at the remembrance, and shrinks from the thought.

* The celebrated verses which the Emperor Hadrian addressed to his soul, as he was approaching death. The Latin is very beautiful, but anything like an adequate translation is hopeless.

Animus non deficit æquus.

A well-balanced (firm, courageous) mind is not wanting.

Animus quod perdidit optat, Atque in præteritâ se totus imagine versat.—*Petronius Arbiter.*

The heart always yearns for what it has lost, and employs itself in dreaming of days that are gone.

An nescis longas regibus esse manus ? — *Ovid.*

Dost thou not know that kings have long arms ? *

Anno ætatis suæ.

In the year of his (or her) age.

Anno Christi.

In the year of Christ.

Anno mundi (A.M.).

In the year of the world.

Annosa vulpes non capitur laqueo.

(An old fox is not caught in a trap.) Old birds are not to be caught with chaff.

Anno urbis conditæ (A.U.C.).

In the year from the building of the city (Rome).†

Annus mirabilis.

A year of wonders (1666). Name of a poem by Dryden.

Anser, apis, vitulus populos et regna gubernant.

(Goose, bee, and calf rule the kingdoms of the world.) Pen, wax, and parchment govern the world. "The pen is mightier than the sword."‡

Ante barbam doces senes.

(You teach old persons before your beard has come.) Jack Sprat would teach his granny.

Ante bellum.

Before the war.

Ante omnia.

Before all things. In the first place.

Ante senectutem curavi ut bene viverem ; in senectute, ut bene moriar. — *Seneca.*

Before I was old I was careful to live well; when I was old, to die well.

Ante tubam trepidat.

(He trembles before the trumpet sounds.) He cries before he is hurt.

Ante victoriam ne canas triumphum.

(Do not celebrate a triumph before the victory.) Do not shout until you are out of the wood.

Antiquitas quo propius aberat ab ortu et divinâ progenie, hoc melius ea fortasse, quæ erant vera, cernebat. — *Cicero.*

The ancients saw more clearly, perhaps, what was really true, inasmuch as they were nearer to the beginning and divine origin of creation.§

A numine salus.

Salvation (health, bodily, or spiritual) comes from the Deity.

Aperto vivere voto.

To live with undisguised prayers ; to pray for nothing that you would not wish others to know.

Apologia pro vitâ suâ.

A defence of the conduct of his life.‖

---

* This saying is not so true as it was when the ruler of Rome was the master of the whole civilised world, whose anger none could escape.
† See note on *Ab Urbe.*
‡ This saying is of mediæval origin.
§ This seems to be the origin of Bacon's aphorism "*Antiquitas sæculi juventus mundi*"— "Antiquity was the youth of the world." He is thought, however, to have derived it from Giordano Bruno.
‖ The title given by Cardinal Newman to his autobiography.

A posse ad esse.

From possibility to realization.

A posteriori.

(From the latter.)   An argument from effect to cause.

Apparent rari nantes in gurgite vasto.
— *Virgil.*

A few appear swimming here and there in the seething surf.*

Appetitus rationi pareat.—*Cicero.*

Let your desires be ruled by reason.

A priori.

(From the former.)   Arguing from cause to effect.

Aptissima omnino sunt arma senectutis, artes, exercitationesque virtutum, quæ in omni aetate cultæ cum multum, diuque vixeris, mirificos efferunt fructus, non solum quia nunquam deserunt, ne in extremo quidem tempore aetatis, verum etiam quia conscientia bene actæ vitæ, multorumque benefactorum recordatio jucundissima est.—*Cicero.*

The best armour of old age is an early life well spent in the practice and exercise of virtuous deeds.   For when you are advanced in years your previous good actions bring a great reward, seeing that your habits of virtue still abide with you even in extreme old age.   Moreover, the consciousness of a well-spent life and the memory of many kind actions is in itself a very sweet consolation.

Aquæ furtivæ suaves sunt.

Stolen waters are sweet.

Aquam a pumice nunc postulas.
— *Plautus.*

You wish to get water out of a stone.

Aqua profunda est quieta.

Still waters run deep.

Aqua regia.

(Royal water.)   A mixture of nitric and muriatic acids capable of melting gold or platinum.

Aquila non capit muscas.

(An eagle does not catch flies.)   A goshawk beats not at a bunting.

Aranearum telas texere.

(To weave spiders' webs.)   To elaborate feeble arguments ; to split hairs.

Arbiter bibendi.

(The ruler of the drinking.)   The master of the feast among the ancients gave directions when to fill the cups.†

Arbiter elegantiarum.

An authority on matters of elegance or taste.

Arcades ambo,
Et cantare pares, et respondere parati.
— *Virgil.*

Arcadians both, well matched in singing, each ready to cap the other's verse.‡

Arcana imperii.

(The mysteries of government.)   State secrets.

Arcanum demens detegit ebrietas.

(Insane intoxication discloses a secret.) *In vino veritas.*   What soberness conceals drunkenness reveals.

Arcus nimis intensus rumpitur.

(A bow too much kept on the stretch breaks.)   A bow long bent at last waxeth weak.

---

* A favourite quotation when a critic wishes to say a book contains some good things among much inferior stuff.
† This *arbiter* was not necessarily the giver of the feast. The choice was decided by casting dice.   One of the duties of the position was to decide the proportion of water to be mixed with the wine, for to drink wine neat was considered the act of a profligate.
‡ The meaning that Byron, in "Don Juan," attaches to *Arcades ambo* is "blackguards both," and this is now their usual connotation.

Ardua molimur : sed nulla, nisi ardua, virtus.—*Ovid.*

We essay a difficult task ; but there is no merit save in difficult tasks.

Arenæ mandas semina.

(You are sowing the sand.) You waste your toil. You are ploughing the sand.

Arena sine calce

(Sand without lime.) A work that will not endure.

Argillâ quidvis imitaberis udâ.

(You may mould soft clay into any shape you please.) Young minds are easily impressed. Best to bend while it is a twig.

Argumentum ad absurdum.

An argument intended to prove the absurdity of an opponent's argument.

Argumentum ad crumenam.

An argument to the purse ; an appeal to interest.

Argumentum ad hominem.

(Argument to the man.) Argument deriving its force from the situation of one's opponent.*

Argumentum ad ignorantiam.

Argument founded on one's opponent's ignorance of facts.

Argumentum ad invidiam.

An argument appealing to low passions.

Argumentum ad judicium.

An argument to the judgment.

Argumentum ad misericordiam.

An argument appealing to one's pity.

Argumentum ad populum.

An appeal to the people.

Argumentum ad verecundiam.

(An argument to the modesty.) An appeal to the sense of decency.

Argumentum baculinum.

The argument of the staff or stick ; conviction by force.

Arma accipere.

(To receive arms.) To be created a Knight.

Arma dare.

(To give arms.) To create a person a Knight.

Arma tuentur pacem.

(Arms maintain peace.) To be ready for war is the best protection against it.

Arma virumque cano.—*Virgil.*

Arms and the man I sing.†

Arrectis auribus.

With ears erect ; pricking one's ears ; on the alert.

Ars æmula naturæ.—*Apuleius.*

Art is the rival of nature.

Ars est celare artem.

(It is true art to conceal art.) A fine work of art is effective, but does not make apparent the processes by which the effect has been arrived at.

Ars longa, vita brevis.

(Art is long, life is short.) Art is long and time is fleeting.—*Longfellow.*

Ars prima regni posse te invidiam pati. —*Seneca.*

The first qualification of a ruler is the ability to endure unpopularity.

Arte perire suâ.

(To perish by one's own machinations.) To be caught in one's own trap.

---

* The popular illustration of this is the advice to a barrister : " If you have a bad case to defend, abuse the plaintiff's attorney."
† The opening words of Virgil's *Æneid.*

Artium magister (A.M.).

Master of Arts (M.A.).

Asinum tondes.

(You are shearing an ass.)   Great cry, and little wool.

Asinus ad lyram.

(An ass at the lyre.)   An awkward fellow; a sow to a fiddle.

Asinus asino, et sus sui pulcher.

(An ass seems a beauty to an ass, and a pig thinks a pig to be a lovely creature.)   Men are inclined to think that their own geese are swans.

Asinus in unguento.

(An ass among perfumes.)   A bull in a china shop.

Aspera ad virtutem est via.

It is a difficult road that leads to virtue.

Asperius nihil est humili cum surgit in altum.—*Claudian.*

(Nothing is more trying than a low-bred fellow who has reached eminence.)   Set a beggar on horseback and he will ride to the devil.

Aspiciunt oculis superi mortalia justis.
—*Ovid.*

The gods survey the acts of men with the eyes of justice.

Assentatio, vitiorum adjutrix, procul amoveatur.—*Cicero.*

Let flattery, the attendant on vice, be altogether spurned by friends.

Assidua stilla saxum excavat.

A steady drop hollows a stone.

Assiduus in oculis hominum fuerat, quæ res minus verendos magnos homines ipsâ satietate facit.—*Livy.*

Being continually seen by his fellows, he wearied them, and this fact makes even great men less venerated than they ought to be.)   Familiarity breeds contempt.

Audaces (*or* audentes) fortuna juvat.

Fortune favours the bold.

Audi alteram partem.

(Hear the other side.)   There are two sides to every question.

Auditâ querelâ.

(The complaint being heard.)   The plea of the defendant having been heard.*

Augescunt aliæ gentes, aliæ minuuntur;
Inque brevi spatio mutantur sæcla animantum,
Et, quasi cursores, vitai lampada tradunt.—*Lucretius.*

Some nations rise to power in the world, while others decline, and in a short space of time the peoples suffer change and decay, and, like runners in a race, hand the torch of life to those that succeed them.†

Aula regis.

The king's court.‡

Aura popularis.

(The popular breeze.)   The darling of the public is said to be borne along by the *aura popularis.*

Aurea mediocritas.

(The golden mean.)   The happy medium between excess in either direction.

---

* The name of the writ giving a defendant leave to appeal.
† *Quasi cursores.* A reference to the Greek torch race, in which several companies of men took part, the prize being given to the line of runners who succeed in passing the torch from hand to hand most quickly.
‡ In early times the members of the King's court accompanied their master wherever he went, and had certain judicial functions assigned to them, from which originated the court of King's or Queen's Bench.

Auream quisquis mediocritatem
Diligit, tutus caret obsoleti
Sordibus tecti, caret invidendâ
Sobrius aulâ.—*Horace.*

Whoever loves the golden mean, avoids
in safety the squalor of an old house,
while, in the enjoyment of moderation, he escapes the unpopularity that
dogs those who dwell in palaces.

Aurea nunc vere sunt sæcula; pluri-
mus auro
Venit honos : auro conciliatur amor.
                                — Ovid.

The present time is the true golden
age ; for nowadays the highest
honours are sold for it, and even
love yields to gold.*

Aurea rumpunt tecta quietem,
Vigilesque trahit purpura noctes.
O si pateant pectora ditum
Quantos intus sublimis agit
Fortuna metus!—*Seneca.*

Golden palaces break the rest, and regal
splendour brings sleepless nights.
Could the hearts of the rich be seen,
what fears does prosperity excite
within them !

Aureo hamo piscari.

(To fish with a golden hook.) Money
makes the mare to go.

Auribus tenere lupum.

(To hold a wolf by the ears.) To have
caught a Tartar.

Auri sacra fames.

The accursed thirst for gold.

Auro quaeque janua panditur.

A golden key opens any gate.

Aurora musis amica est.

(The Dawn is the friend of the Muses.)
The morning is the best time for the
student.

Aut amat, aut odit mulier.

A woman either loves or hates; is
never neutral in feeling.

Aut Cæsar, aut nihil.

(Either Cæsar or nothing.) Neck or
nothing.†

Aut Cæsar, aut nullus.

(Either Cæsar or nobody.) Not content
with any place under the highest.

Aut insanit homo, aut versus facit.
                                —Horace.

The fellow's mad, or else he is compos-
ing verses.

Aut inveniam viam aut faciam.

(I will either find a way or make one.)
Where there's a will there's a way.

Aut nunquam tentes aut perfice.

(Either never try or accomplish.) Having put your hand to the plough, do
not turn back.

Aut vincere aut mori.

Victory or death.

                  Aut virtus nomen inane est,
Aut decus et pretium recte petit experi-
ens vir.—*Horace.*

Virtue is either a mere name, or else it
is a thing of glory and value which a
man wisely pursues.

Auxilia firma consensus facit.

(Unanimity gives strength.) Union is
strength.

Auxilium ab alto.

Help from on high.

Auxilium non leve vultus habet.—*Ovid.*

A good face is a good recommendation.

Ave, Cæsar, morituri te salutant.

Hail, Cæsar, those who are about to
die salute thee.‡

* The sovereignty of money is a truism known to every age.   Philip of Macedon, father of
Alexander the Great, used to say that he could capture any town, if it were possible to drive
to the gates of it an ass laden with silver, with which to bribe some of the defenders.
  † This inscription was found inscribed on the bust of one of the Roman Emperors, who all
adopted the name Cæsar as a title.
  ‡ The gladiators' address to the Emperor when they entered the arena.   It is frequently
quoted to illustrate an act of desperate courage.

A verbis ad verbera.

From words to blows.

A verbis legis non est recedendum.

(The words of a statute must be strictly adhered to.) Judges must interpret the laws literally.

Avia Pieridum loca.

The Muses' lonely haunts.

Avidis natura parum est.—*Seneca.*

The bounty of nature is too little for the greedy man.

A vinculo matrimonii.

From the bond of marriage.

Avito viret honore.

He flourishes upon ancestral honours.

Barbæ tenus philosophi.

(Philosophers as far as the beard.) People who have the pretence of knowledge without the reality.

Basis virtutum constantia.

Firmness is the foundation of the virtues.

Beati possidentes.

(Happy, fortunate are they who are in possession.) Possession is nine points of the law.

Beatissimus is est, qui est aptus ex sese, quique in se uno sua ponit omnia.

He is the happiest man, who depends upon himself, and is entirely self-reliant.

Beatus ille, qui procul negotiis,
Ut prisca gens mortalium,
Paterna rura bubus exercet suis,
Solutus omni fenore ;

Neque excitatur classico miles truci,
Neque horret iratum mare ;
Forumque vitat, et superba civium
Potentiorum limina.—*Horace.*

Blessed is the man who, far from the business of the town, ploughs with his own oxen his ancestral fields, with mind free from all cares about money. This was the life of the ancient race of men. Such an one is not like the soldier, roused by the bugle's loud note, nor does he fear the angry main ; he shuns the law courts and the proud portals of the rich.

Bella detestata matribus.—*Horace.*

Wars, the dread of mothers.

Bella, horrida bella !—*Virgil.*

Wars, horrid wars !—*Dryden.*

Bella suscipienda sunt ob eam causam, ut sine injuriâ in pace vivatur.
        —*Cicero.*

Wars are to be undertaken in order that we may live in peace without suffering wrong.

Bello flagrante.

During hostilities.

Bellum internecinum.

A war of extermination.

Bellum nec timendum nec provocandum.—*Pliny the Younger.*

War ought neither to be dreaded, nor provoked.

Belua multorum capitum.

(The many-headed monster.) The multitude ; King Demos.

Bene est tentare.

(It is as well to try.) Nothing venture, nothing have.

Benefacta male locata, malefacta arbitror.—*Ennius.*

Benefits bestowed upon the undeserving are no kindness.

Beneficia tacite danda sunt.

(Benefits should be given silently.) Let not your right hand know what your left hand doeth.

Beneficium accipere, libertatem est vendere.—*Publius Syrus.*

(To accept a kindness is to sell one's freedom.) He that goes a-borrowing goes a-sorrowing.

Beneficium non in eo quod fit aut datur constitit, sed in ipso facientis aut dantis animo : animus est enim qui beneficiis dat pretium.—*Seneca.*

A benefit consists not in that which is done or given, but in the spirit in which it is done or given ; for it is the spirit in which a kindness is done, that makes it valued.

Bene qui latuit, bene vixit.—*Ovid.*

(He who has lived unknown to the world has lived well.) Who lives obscurely, lives securely.

Bene si amico feceris, ne pigeat fecisse.
—*Plautus.*

If you have conferred a favour upon your friend, repent not of having done so.

Benigno numine.

By the favour of heaven ; by the favour of Providence.

Benignus etiam dandi causam cogitat.
—*Publius Syrus.*

The benevolent man always seeks an excuse for charity.

Bibamus, moriendum est.—*Seneca.*

(Let us drink, for die we must.) Let us eat, drink, and be merry, for to-morrow we die.

Bibliotheca.

A library.

Bis dat qui cito dat.

He gives twice who gives in a trice.

Bis peccare in bello non licet.

To blunder twice is not allowed in war.

Bis pueri senes.

(Old men are twice children.) Bodily and mentally.
Last stage of all is second childish-ness.—*Shakespeare.*

Bis vivit qui bene.

He lives twice who lives well.

Bœotum in crasso jurares aere natum.
—*Horace.*

You could swear it had its birth in Bœotia's sluggish air.*

Bonâ-fide.

In good faith.

Bona opinio hominum tutior pecuniâ est.

A good name is better than riches.

Boni pastoris est tondere pecus non deglubere.—*Suetonius.*

(It is the duty of a good shepherd to shear his sheep, not to flay them.) Taxation should be imposed with due discretion.

Bonis nocet. quisquis pepercerit malis.
—*Publius Syrus.*

He hurts the good who spares the bad.

Bonis quod bene fit haud perit.
—*Plautus.*

(A benefit done to the good is never lost.) Cast thy bread upon the waters.

Bonitas non est pessimis esse meliorem.
—*Seneca.*

To be better than the worst, is not goodness.

Bonus arator agricultione se oblectat, cultu sæpe defatigatur, culturâ dites-cit.—*Cicero.*

(A good husbandman takes delight in agriculture ; he is often wearied with his labours, but by culture he gets rich.) The labour we delight in physics pain.—*Shakespeare.*

Bonus atque fidus
Judex honestum prætulit utili.
—*Horace.*

A good and faithful judge prefers honesty to expediency.

* The damp air of Bœotia was supposed to be the cause of the dull wits of its inhabitants. Still the country produced Pindar and Epaminondas.

Bonus dux bonum reddit comitem.

(A good leader makes a good follower.) A good master makes a good servant.

Bos lassus fortius figit pedem.

(The tired ox treads surest.) Slow and sure wins the race.

Bovi clitellas imponere.

(To put a pack saddle on an ox.) To impose a duty on one not fit to discharge it.

Breve et irreparabile tempus vitæ est omnibus.— *Virgil.*

To everybody life is short, nor can it be recovered.

Breves haustus in philosophiâ ad Atheismum ducunt, largiores autem reducunt ad Deum.— *Bacon.*

Small draughts of knowledge lead men to Atheism, but deeper draughts bring them back to God.

Brevi manu.

With the short hand. Off-hand ; summarily.

Brevis esse laboro, obscurus fio.
                                    —*Horace.*

In trying to be concise, I become obscure.*

Brutum fulmen.

(A harmless thunderbolt.) A vain menace. Empty vessels sound the loudest.

Cacoethes scribendi.

An itch for writing.

Cadit quæstio.

(The question falls to the ground.) There is an end of the discussion.

Cæsarem vehis et fortunam ejus.

You carry Cæsar and his fortunes.†

Cætera desunt.

(The remainder is wanting.) The rest (of the speech, poem, &c.) is wanting.

Cæteris paribus.

Other things being equal.

Calamitas virtutis occasio est.—*Seneca.*

(Misfortune is the test of a man's merit.) Calamity is a man's true touchstone.
                                    —*Beaumont and Fletcher.*

Callida junctura.

(Skilful or clever joining of literary composition.) Cunning workmanship.

Calumniare fortiter, et aliquid adhærebit.

(Slander stoutly, and something will stick.) Throw plenty of mud, and some of it will stick.

Camelus desiderans cornua etiam aures perdidit.

(The camel desiring horns, lost its ears as well.) Be thankful for small mercies.

Candida pax.

White-robed peace.

Candide et constanter.

Frankly and firmly.

Cane pejus et angue.

Worse than a dog or a snake.

Canes timidi vehementius latrant.

Timid dogs bark the loudest.

Cantabit vacuus coram latrone viator.
                                    —*Juvenal.*

(The penniless wayfarer will sing before the robber.) The poor man has little to lose.

---

* So Mr. John Morley says of Tacitus, " Beyond almost anybody, he suffered from what a famous writer of aphorisms in our time has described as ' the cursed ambition to put a whole book into a page, a whole page into a phrase, and the phrase into a word.' "

† In 48 B.C. Julius Cæsar was caught in a squall, while sailing in a small vessel off the coast of Illyria. Tradition says that he encouraged the frightened pilot with the remarks given above.

Capax imperii, nisi imperasset.
— *Tacitus.*

He would have been thought capable of governing if he had never come to the throne.*

Capias.

(You may take.)   A writ for arresting a debtor.

Capiat qui capere possit.

(Let him take who can.)
The simple plan,
That they should take who have the power,
And they should keep who can.
- *Wordsworth.*

Captantes capti sumus.

(We catchers are caught.)   The biter is bitten.

Caput mortuum.

(A dead head.)   The residuum left by a process of chemical analysis; a worthless person.

Carendo discimus quam cara amiserimus.
— *Seneca.*

We learn the value of a thing when we have lost it.

Carent quia vate sacro.   (See *Vixere fortes.*)

Because they lack the inspired poet's aid.

Caret initio et fine.

It wants both beginning and end.

Caret periculo, qui etiam tutus cavet.
— *Publius Syrus.*

He is best secure from dangers who is on his guard, even when he seems safe.

Cari sunt parentes, cari liberi, propinqui, familiares : sed omnes omnium caritates patria una complexa est ; pro quâ quis bonus dubitet mortem oppetere, si ei sit profuturus ? — *Cicero.*

We love our parents, we love our children, our relatives, and our friends : but the love of our native land embraces all these affections : for his country, therefore, what good patriot would refuse to endure death, if, by so doing, he could confer any benefit upon it ?

Caritate, benevolentiâque sublatâ, omnis est e vitâ sublata jucunditas.
— *Cicero.*

When affection and kindly feeling are removed, all sweetness is taken away from life.

Carpe diem quam minime credula postero. — *Horace.*

(Enjoy the present day, trusting as little as possible to what the morrow may bring.)
Gather ye rosebuds while ye may,
Old Time is still a-flying.— *Herrick.*

Cassis tutissima virtus.

(Virtue is the safest helmet.)   An honest man has nothing to fear.

Castigat ridendo mores.

(It corrects faults by laughing at them.)   When preaching has failed to reform a man, try a little ridicule.†

Casus belli.

(An occasion for war.)   Something that causes or justifies war.

---

* This is the verdict of Tacitus on the character of Galba, the Roman general who wrested the sovereign power from Nero, but was assassinated in A.D. 69, the fatal year that saw three Roman Emperors, all of whom met with a violent death.   Galba had too many virtues and too few graces to make a successful ruler of a turbulent nation.
† The French poet Santeuil's description of the true function of comedy.

Catulæ dominas imitantes.

(Puppies imitating their mistresses.) High life below stairs.

Caudæ pilos equino paulatim oportet evellere

(You must pluck out the hairs of a horse's tail one by one.) Little strokes fell great oaks.

Causa causans.

(The cause that causes all other things.) The Great First Cause ; the Supreme Being.

Causa latet, vis est notissima.—*Ovid.*

The cause is secret, but the effect is known.—*Addison.*

Caveat.

Let him take care, or look out.

Caveat emptor.

(Let the purchaser beware.) The buyer must take the risk.*

Cavendum est ne major pœna quam culpa.—*Cicero.*

Care must be taken that the punishment does not exceed the crime.

Cave tibi cane muto et aquâ silente.

Be on your guard against a silent dog and still water.

Cedant arma togæ.—*Cicero.*

(Let arms yield to the gown.) Let military power yield to the civil authority.†

Celerius occidit festinata maturitas.

(Forced ripeness falls away more quickly.) Premature development of one's powers ends in an early grave.

Celsae graviore casu decidunt turres.

(Lofty towers fall down with heavier crash.) The highest tree hath the greatest fall. Climb not too high, lest the fall be the greater.

Censor morum.

Censor of morals.

Cereus in vitium flecti, monitoribus asper.—*Horace.*

(The young man) is as wax to the bent of vice, but unbending to its reprovers.

Cernit omnia Deus vindex.

An avenging God marks all things.

Certa amittimus, dum incerta petimus. —*Plautus.*

We lose what is certain, while we pursue uncertainties.

Certamina divitiarum.—*Horace.*

Struggles of riches, or after wealth ; to strive to be richer than others.

Certiorari.

(To be made more certain.) A writ to call up the records of an inferior court.

Certis rebus certa signa præcurrunt. —*Cicero.*

(Certain events are preceded by certain signs.) Coming events cast their shadows before.

Certum est quia impossibile est.

It is true, because it is impossible.‡

Certum voto pete finem.—*Horace.*

Seek to limit your desires.

---

* The law requires that the purchaser must show reasonable care, in buying anything, to find out that the vendor has the right to dispose of it. Otherwise, he has no legal title to the property bought.

† The toga was the garment worn by Roman citizens when taking part in any civil business. Hence it is frequently used in the sense of the civil, as opposed to the military authority.

‡ The celebrated remark of Tertullian. The apparent improbability of the truth of the supernatural is to be regarded, considering the limitations of our understanding, rather as an argument for than against its credibility. See also *credo quia absurdum.*

Cervæ luporum præda rapacium
Sectamur ultro, quos opimus
Fallere et effugere est triumphus.
—*Horace.*

We, like weak hinds, the brinded wolf provoke,
And when retreat is victory,
Rush in, tho' sure to die. — *Oldisworth.**

Cessante causâ, cessat et effectus

Remove the cause, and the effect also ceases.†

Cessio bonorum.

The giving up of one's goods (property, to one's creditors); insolvency.

Chius dominum emit.

(The Chian buys himself a master.) He prepares a rod for his own back.‡

Cicada cicadae cara, formicae formica.

(Tree-cricket is dear to tree-cricket, ant to ant.) Like draws to like. Birds of a feather.

Cineres credis curare sepultos ?

(Think you that the ashes of the dead can be affected by this ?) The dead are unmoved by either the approval or disapproval of the living.

Cineri gloria sera est.—*Martial.*

(Glory paid to ashes comes too late.) If you wish to honour a man, honour him while he is alive.

Circuitus verborum.

A circumlocution ; a roundabout way of expression.

Circulus in probando

(A circle in the proof.) Arguing in a circle. Assuming the conclusion as an argument to prove it.

Citius venit periculum, cum contemnitur.

Danger comes more quickly when it is despised.

Cito enim exarescit lacrima, præsertim in alienis malis. —*Cicero.*

Our tears are soon dried, especially when it is another's trouble we bewail.

Cito maturum, cito putridum.

Soon ripe, soon rotten.

Cito rumpes arcum, semper si tensum habueris.

(You will soon break the bow if you keep it always on the stretch.) He that runs fast will not run long.

Civis Romanus sum.

I am a Roman citizen. §

Civitas ea in libertate est posita, quae suis stat viribus, non ex alieno arbitrio pendet.—*Livy.*

That state alone is free, which rests on its own strength, and does not depend upon the will of another.

Civium ardor prava jubentium.
— *Horace.*

(The wild rage of fellow-citizens ordering evil measures to be pursued.) The man tenacious of purpose fears neither the tyranny of the despot nor of the mob.

Clarior e tenebris.

More bright from obscurity.

* This is part of the famous panegyric on Rome, which Horace puts into the mouth of Hannibal. As the Carthaginian leader was the terror of the Romans during the second Punic War, the lines are more magnificent as a patriotic eulogy than true to fact
† With this maxim Lord Bacon's aphorism may be compared : " the best way of removing seditions is to remove the causes of them."
‡ When Mithridates, King of Pontus, subdued the Chians, he put the government of Chios into the hands of the former slaves of the citizens.
§ The proud boast of a Roman citizen when citizenship was the privilege of a small portion of the world. The boast, however, lost its force when the Roman Emperors made Roman citizenship to be easily gained. Finally, Caracalla made it the universal possession of all his subjects.

Clarum et venerabile nomen | A famous and venerable name.

Cœlitus mihi vires. | My strength is from heaven.

Cœlum non animum mutant qui trans mare currant.—*Horace.* | (Those that beyond sea go, will sadly find,
They change their climate only, not their mind.)—*Creech.*
The mind is its own place, and in itself Can make a heav'n of hell, a hell of heav'n.—*Milton.*

Cœtus dulces valete!—*Catullus.* | Happy meetings, fare ye well!

Cogi qui potest, nescit mcri —*Seneca.* | (The man who can be forced to do anything knows not how to die.) The strong man prefers to submit to death rather than tyranny.

Cogito, ergo sum. | I think, therefore I exist.*

Cognovit actionem. | He (the defendant) has acknowledged the action (or plaintiff's claim.)

Collectanea. | A collection of things; the name of a non-extant book written by Julius Cæsar.

Colluvies vitiorum. | A sink of vices.

Colossus. | A gigantic statue, or figure.†

Colubrem in sinu fovere. | To cherish a serpent in one's bosom.

Comes jucundus in viâ pro vehiculo est. —*Publius Syrus.* | An agreeable companion upon the road is as good as a coach.

Comitas inter gentes. | Courtesy or politeness between nations.

Comitia. | The political assemblies of the Romans.

Commodius esse opinor duplici spe uti. — *Terence.* | (I think it best to have a double hope.) Have two strings to your bow.

Commune bonum. | A common good.

Commune periculum concordiam parit. | A common danger produces unity.

Communia proprie dicere. | To speak with propriety on a hackneyed topic.

Communibus annis. | On the annual average.

Communi consensu. | By common consent.

Communiter negligitur, quod communiter possidetur. | (That is neglected by all, which is possessed by all.) Everybody's business is nobody's work.

Compendia plerumque sunt dispendia. | Short cuts are generally farthest about.

Componere lites. | To settle disputes.

Compos mentis. | In one's senses; of a sound mind.

Concio ad clerum. | A discourse to the clergy.

Concordat. | (A compact.) An agreement made between the Pope and a sovereign.

Concordia discors.—*Lucan.* | (Harmonious discord.) An armed truce; the musical efforts of the untrained amateur.

* This dictum is the basis of the philosophical system of Descartes.
† Any statue larger than life-size was so called, but the best-known was the famous Colossus of Rhodes, a huge figure 90 feet high, which was said to have been set up with one foot resting on each side of the harbour of Rhodes.

Conditio sine quâ non.

(A condition without which the agreement cannot be made.) An indispensable condition.

Conjugium vocat, hoc prætexit nomine culpam.— *Virgil.*

She calls it marriage now ; such name She chooses to conceal her shame.
                                        — *Conington.*

Conscia mens recti famæ mendacia ridet.

A mind conscious of integrity laughs to scorn the lies of rumour.

Conscientia mille testes.

(The conscience is as good as a thousand witnesses.)   When consciences approve none can disapprove.

Consensus facit legum.

(Consent makes law.)   If two persons make an agreement not illegal in its terms, it is as binding as a legal enactment.

Consequitur quodcunque petit.

He attains whatever he attempts.

Consilio et animis.

By wisdom and courage.

Consilio, non impetu.

By deliberation, not impetuosity.

Constantiâ et virtute.

By constancy and virtue.

Consuesse deos immortales, quo gravius homines ex commutatione rerum doleant, quos pro scelere eorum ulcisci velint, his secundiores interdum res, et diuturniorem impunitatem concedere.— *Cæsar.*

The immortal gods, when they wish to punish some men for their sins, sometimes grant them prolonged prosperity and immunity from punishment, in order that when change of fortune comes upon them, they may feel remorse more keenly.

Consuetudinem benignitatis largitioni numerum longe antepono. Hæc est gravium hominum atque magnorum. Illa quasi assentatorum populi, multitudinis levitatem voluptate quasi tittillantium. – *Cicero.*

I esteem a habit of benignity greatly preferable to munificence.   The former is peculiar to great and distinguished persons ; the latter belongs to flatterers of the people, who tickle the levity of the multitude with a kind of pleasure.

Consuetudo pro lege servatur.

(Custom is to be held as law.)   Where there is no law on some point, it is to be decided by usage.

Consuetudo quasi altera natura.
                                    — *Cicero.*

Habit is, so to speak, second nature.

Consule Planco.—*Horace.*

(When Plancus was consul.)   When I was young and foolish.*

Contra bonos mores.

Contrary to good habits ; a breach of the moral law.

Contraria contrariis curantur.

(Diseases are cured by the remedies most unlike them.)   The basis of the allopathic treatment of medicine.

Copia fandi.

A great flow of talk.†

Coram nobis.

(Before us.)   Before the court.

Coram non judice.

(Before one who is not the judge.) Before an irregular tribunal.

---

* The Romans distinguished the years by the names of the consuls who held office in them. Plancus was consul in 42 B.C., when Horace was 23 years of age.

† The phrase is common in Virgil, who uses it rather in the sense of " an opportunity of speaking."

Coram populo.
In the presence of the people; publicly.*

Cornix cornici non effodit oculos.
(A crow does not peck out the eyes of a crow.) Dog does not eat dog.

Corpus delicti.
The whole body or nature of the offence.

Corpus sine pectore.
(A body without soul.) A human clod.

Corrigenda.
Things to be corrected.

Corrumpunt nos mores colloquia prava.
Evil communications corrupt good manners.

Corruptio optimi pessima.
(The corruption of the best is the worst.) The fallen saint is the worst kind of sinner.

Corruptissimâ republicâ plurimae leges.
—*Tacitus.*
When the state is most corrupt, the laws are most numerous.

Cor unum, via una.
One heart, one way.

Coryphæus.
(The leader of the Greek dramatic chorus.) A leader.

Crambe bis cocta, *or* repetita.
(Cabbage twice cooked, or served.) To harp on the same string; the same old story.

Cras ingens iterabimus aequor.
(To-morrow we shall resume our voyage o'er the mighty sea.) Sufficient for the day is the evil thereof.

Cras mihi.
My turn to-morrow.

Credat Judaeus Apella.—*Horace.*
(Let the Jew Apella believe that.) Tell that to the marines.†

Crede Deo.
Trust to God.

Crede quod habes, et habes.
Believe you have it, and you have it.

Credite posteri.—*Horace.*
Believe it, future generations.

Creditur, ex medio quia res arcessit, habere sudoris minimum.—*Horace.*
To write on vulgar themes, is thought an easy task.

Credo quia absurdum est.
I believe it because it is so unlikely.

Credula res amor est.
(Love is a credulous thing.) Love sees no faults.

Credula vitam Spes fovet, ac melius cras fore semper ait.—*Tibullus.*
Hope, ever confident, cherishes life, and always tells to-morrow will be better.

Crescit amor nummi quantum ipsa pecunia crescit.
(The love of money increases as fast as the money itself increases.) The more a man has, the more he desires to have.

Crescit eundo.
It increases as it goes.

Crescit sub pondere virtus.
(Virtue increases under a weight.) Oppression fosters manly determination.

---

* Horace uses the phrase, when he warns the would-be dramatist not to allow a murder to take place in sight of the audience. It was contrary to ancient usage to allow the representation of killing on the stage.
† The Jews were as unpopular among the Romans as they are in certain European countries to-day. The satirists showed them no mercy, and failing to comprehend their religious beliefs, accused them of gross superstition.

Cretâ an carbone notandi ?

(Are they to be marked with chalk or with charcoal ?) Are they wise men or fools ?

Cribro aquam haurire.

(To draw water in a sieve.) To lose one's pains, labour.

Crimen falsi.

The charge of falsehood, or perjury.

Crimen læsæ majestatis.

The charge of high treason.

Crimine ab uno disce omnes.

From one deed of wickedness learn the character of the whole people.

Cristæ surgunt illi.

(His crest rises.) He is cock-a-hoop.

Crux criticorum.

The cross or puzzle of critics.

Crux mihi ancora.

The cross is my anchor.

Cucullus non facit monachum.

(The cowl does not make a monk.) Do not look at the coat, but at what is under the coat.

Cui bono ?

Who will be the better for it ? What good will it do ? *

Cui malo ?

Whom will it harm ?

Cui mens divinior, atque os
Magna sonaturum, des nominis hujus honorem.—*Horace.*

On him confer the poet's sacred name, Whose lofty voice declares the heavenly flame.

Cui multum est piperis etiam oleribus immiscet.

He that has plenty of pepper can season his cabbage well.

Cui peccare licet, peccat minus.

If a man has it in his power to commit a sin, he is less inclined to do so.

Cujusvis hominis est errare, nullius nisi insipientis in errore perseverare.
—*Cicero.*

Every man is liable to err, but it is only the part of a fool to persevere in his error.

Culpam pœna premit comes.

Punishment presses hard upon the heels of guilt.

Cum diis volentibus.

With heaven's help.

Cum grano salis.

With a grain of salt ; with some reserve.

Cum multis aliis, quæ nunc præscribere longum est.

With many others, which it would be tedious to mention now.

Cum privilegio.

(With privilege or license.) A book published by leave of the authorities.

Cum vulpibus vulpinandum.

(When you are with foxes you must act like a fox.) Diamond cuts diamond.

Cunctando restituit rem.—*Ennius.*

By delay he saved the fortunes of the State.†

Cupido dominandi cunctis affectibus flagrantior.—*Tacitus.*

The desire of ruling is stronger than all other human feelings.

Curae leves loquuntur, ingentes stupent.
—*Seneca.*

(Slight griefs find utterance, but great ones are dumb.)
The grief that does not speak
Whispers the o'er-fraught heart, and bids it break.—*Shakespeare.*

* Literally, " for whom for good." The meaning " what good will it do," is not strictly correct, but that is the sense which is usually attached to the phrase.
† This praise was given to Quintus Fabius Maximus, who saved his country by avoiding a pitched battle with Hannibal. The phrase is now usually applied to those who get the better of their opponents by the exercise ot sagacity and caution.

Cura pii Dis sunt.

The good are Heaven's care.

Curia pauperibus clausa est.—*Ovid.*

Parliament keeps its doors closed to the poor man.

Cur in theatrum, Cato, severe venisti ?

(Why have you come to the theatre, Cato, with such a solemn face ? (Sour looks are out of place in scenes of mirth.

Curiosa felicitas.

Careful happiness of phrase.*

Cur me querelis exanimas tuis ?
          —*Horace.*

Why weary me to death with your incessant complainings ?

Currente calamo.

With a running pen; off-hand; a free style of composition.

Curriculum.

A race course; a course of study at school or college.

Currus bovem trahit.

(The coach draws the ox.) To put the cart before the horse.

Curta supellex.

(Small stock of furniture.) A scanty stock of knowledge.

Custos morum.

(The guardian of morals.) A judge or magistrate.

Custos rotulorum.

The custodian of the rolls, or records of judicial trials.

Cutem gerit laceratam canis mordax.

(A snapping cur wears a torn skin.)
Those who in quarrels interpose
Must often wipe a bloody nose.—*Gay.*

Dabit Deus his quoque finem.—*Virgil.*

God will put an end to these troubles also.

Da dextram misero.

Give a lift to a man in misfortune.

Da locum melioribus.

Give place to your betters.

Damnosa quid non imminuit dies ?
          —*Horace.*

What does not wasting time destroy ?

Damnum absque injuriâ.

Loss without legal injury; loss due to legitimate competition.

Damnunt quod non intelligunt.—*Cicero.*

Men condemn what they do not understand.

Dante Deo.

By the gift of God.

Dare pondus fumo.

(To give weight to smoke.) To give importance to trifles. To make mountains of molehills.

Dare pondus idonea fumo.—*Persius.*

(Fit only to add weight to smoke.) The book is absolutely worthless.

Da spatium tenuemque moram : male cuncta ministrat impetus.—*Statius.*

Take time for consideration in all matters; too much haste ill serves the progress of any business.

Data.

Things granted; statements that have been acknowledged to be true.

* This is the criticism of Petronius on the style of Horace, denoting that the latter understood the truth of *ars est celare artem.* The words are now generally translated "a curious felicity," but this is not precisely their original meaning.

Dat Deus immiti cornua curta bovi.

(To the fierce ox, God gives short horns.) God sends a curst cow short horns.* *—Shakespeare.*

Date obolum Belisario.

Give a farthing to Belisarius.†

Dat Galenus opes ; dat Justinianus honores.

(Galen gives riches; Justinian gives honours.) Physicians acquire wealth. Lawyers attain high rank.

Dat veniam corvis, vexat censura columbas.—*Juvenal.*

(The doves are censured, while the crows are spared.) The guilty are left in peace, but the innocent are persecuted.

Davus sum, non Œdipus.

(I am Davus, not Œdipus.) I am a poor, uninstructed, plain man, not a genius. You have applied to the wrong person—I can't help you.‡

De alieno corio liberalis.

(To cut large thongs from another man's leather.) To be very liberal out of another man's pocket.

De asini umbrâ disceptare.

(To dispute about an ass's shadow.) Little things attract light minds.

Debitum naturæ.

The debt of nature; death.

Decies repetita placebit.

(Though ten times repeated, it will please.) A good story cannot be too often told.

Decipimur specie recti.—*Horace.*

(We are deceived by the appearance of what is right.) Fair appearances are necessary to the purposes of deception.

Decipit frons prima multos.

(The first appearance deceives many.) We must eat a peck of salt with a man before we know him.

Decori decus addit avito.

He adds glory to the glory of his ancestors.

Decus et tutamen.

Honour and protection.

Dedecus ille domus sciet ultimus. —*Juvenal.*

The master of the house will be last to know the disgrace that has befallen him.

De die in diem.

From day to day.

Dediscit animus sero, quod didicit diu. —*Seneca.*

(The mind is slow to forget what it has been a long time learning.) Habit is second nature.

De duobus malis, minus est semper eligendum.—*Thomas à Kempis.*

Of two evils always choose the least.

De facto.

In fact, in reality.

De fide et officio judicis non recipitur quæstio.

(No question is allowed concerning the good intention and duty of the judge.) It is illegal to suggest that a judge is administrating the law unfairly, unless undoubted proof exists.

* Sterne expresses the reverse of this idea in " He tempers the wind to the shorn lamb."
† The great general, Belisarius, in his old age was neglected and allowed to beg in the streets by the Emperor Justinian. Gibbon denies the story, but it is useful to point a moral.
‡ Davus was the usual name given to the faithful slave in Roman comedies, a character much resembling Shakespeare's clowns.

De fumo in flammam.

(Out of the smoke into the flame.) Out of the frying-pan into the fire.

Degeneres animos timor arguit.—*Virgil.*

Fear convicts degenerate souls.

De gustibus non est disputandum.

(There is no disputing about tastes.) Everyone to his liking.

Dei gratiâ.

By the grace of God.

Dei memor, gratus amicis.

Mindful of my God and grateful to my friends.

De jure.

By right in law.

De lanâ caprinâ rixari.

(To wrangle about goat's wool.) To split straws.

Dele.

Erase.

Delectando pariterque monendo.

By pleasing while instructing. *Omne tulit, &c.*

Delenda est Carthago.

Carthage must be destroyed.*

Deliberandum est diu, quod statuendum semel.

What can be decided only once, should be long pondered over.

Deliberat Roma, perit Saguntum.

(Rome deliberates, Saguntum perishes.) While the doctors are deliberating the patient dies.†

Delirium tremens.

(Trembling delirium.) The delirium with trembling, a brain disease of great drunkards.

Delphinum natare doces.

(You are giving swimming lessons to a dolphin.) You are teaching your granny to suck eggs.

De lunatico inquirendo.

A writ to a commission to inquire whether a person is or is not a lunatic.

De male quaesitis gaudet non tertius hæres.

(A third heir seldom enjoys property dishonestly got.) Ill gains go apace.

Deme supercilio nubem.

Remove the cloud from your brow; smooth out those wrinkles.

De minimis non curat lex.

The law does not regard trifles.

Demitto auriculas ut iniquæ mentis asellus.—*Horace.*

I make my ears droop, like an ass of a stubborn disposition.

De mortuis nil nisi bonum.

(Of the dead nothing but good.) Let nothing be said of the dead but good.‡

Denique cœlum.

Heaven at last.§

De non apparentibus et de non existentibus eadem est ratio.

(The reasoning is the same as to things that are not seen, and things that do not exist.) What is not apparent must be considered as non-existent.

---

* This was the constant advice of Cato the Elder to the Roman Senate. The destruction of Carthage and Corinth, her two great commercial rivals, are considered to be Rome's worst political crimes. The words are now used to signify a war fought out to the bitter end. Carthage was destroyed in the year 147 B.C.
† The Romans allowed their allies, the Saguntines, to perish while they were discussing how to rescue them.
‡ A saying often attributed to Solon, the Athenian law-giver and statesman, but Chilo, another of the Greek Sages, is the real author of it.
ł The battle-cry of the Crusaders.

De novo.

Anew; afresh.

Deo dignus vindice nodus.

A knot worthy of a god to unloose it; a supreme difficulty.*

Deo duce, ferro comitante.

God being my leader, and my sword my companion.

Deo et regi fidelis.

Loyal to God and my sovereign.

Deo favente.

With God's favour.

Deo gratias.

Thanks to God.

De omnibus rebus et quibusdam aliis.

Concerning everything and other matters.†

De omni re scibili et quibusdam aliis.

Concerning every known thing and a few things in addition.

Deo, non fortunâ.

From God, not fortune.

Deo, patriæ, amicis.

For my God, my country, and my friends.

Deo volente (D. V.)

God being willing.

De paupertate tacentes plus poscente ferent.—*Horace.*

(They who are silent concerning their poverty will receive more than those who beg.)‡

De pilo pendet.

(It hangs by a hair.) The affair is in a critical condition.§

Deprendi miserum est.—*Horace.*

It is wretched to be found out.

De profundis.

Out of the depths.

De quibus certus es, loquere opportune.

Speak at the right moment, and on those subjects that you are master of.

De quibus ignoras tace.

Hold your tongue about things that you know nothing about.

Desideratum (*pl.* desiderata).

A thing desired, much wanted.

Desine fata deûm flecti sperare precando. —*Virgil.*

Cease to think that prayers can alter the fixed decrees of Heaven.

Desinit in piscem mulier formosa superne. —*Horace.*

(A woman beautiful above, ends in the tail of a fish.) A bad literary style presents similar incongruities.

Desipere in loco.

To unbend on occasion.

Destrictus ensiscui super impiâ
Cervice pendet, non Siculæ dapes
Dulcem elaborabunt saporem,
Non avium citharæque cantus
Somnum reducent.—*Horace.*

Sicilian dainties will have no delightful flavour for the man over whose impious neck ever hangs the naked sword; the songs of birds and of the lyre will not restore his sleep.‖

Desuetudo omnibus pigritiam, pigritia veternum parit.—*Apuleius.*

Disuse produces sloth, and sloth incapacity.

Desunt cætera.

The remainder is wanting; the quotation is incomplete.

Desunt inopiæ multa, avaritiæ omnia.

The poor man needs much, the miser desires everything.

---

* See *Deus ex machinâ.*
† A description of books that err on the side of being too diffuse.
‡ A popular but doubtful statement
§ The sword that Dionysius, tyrant of Syracuse, suspended over the head of Damocles, was held in position by a hair. Hence the proverbial phrase.
‖ A reference to the experience of Damocles. See *De pilo pendet.*

Deteriores omnes sumus licentiâ.

We are all the worse for uncontrolled liberty of action.

Detrahere aliquid alteri, et hominem hominis incommodo suum augere commodum, magis est contra naturam, quam mors, quam paupertas, quam dolor, quam cætera quæ possunt aut corpori accidere, aut rebus externis. — *Cicero.*

To detract anything from another, and for one man to multiply his own conveniences by the inconveniences of another, is more against nature than death, than poverty, than pain, and the other things which can befall the body, or external circumstances.

Detur digniori.

Let it be given to the most deserving.

Detur pulcriori.

Let it be given to the fairest.

Deum cole, regem serva.

Worship God and serve the king.

Deus aut bestia.

(A god or a beast.) The nature of man is either godlike or bestial.*

Deus est qui regit omnia.

There is a God who rules all things.

Deus est summum bonum.

God is the chief good.

Deus ex machinâ.

(A god out of a machine.) A person or thing that saves the situation in a crisis.†

Deus gubernat navem.

God is the pilot of the ship.

Deus nobis hæc otia fecit.

God made us these comforts.

Deus providebit.

God will provide.

De vitâ hominis nulla cunctatio longa est. — *Juvenal.*

When the life of a man is at stake, no delay is too long.

Dextras dare.

To shake hands as a pledge of confidence.

Dicenda bona sunt bona verba die.

(Good words should be spoken on a good day.) The better the day, the better the deed.

Dicenda tacendaque calles.

Thou clearly knowest when to speak, and when to keep silent.

Dictum de dicto.

Report upon hearsay.

Dictum sapienti sat est.

A word is enough to the wise man.‡

Diem perdidi.

I have lost a day.§

Dies adimit aegritudinem hominibus.

Time assuages the griefs of men.

Dies datus.

(A day given.) The day appointed for hearing a law-suit.

Dies faustus.

A lucky day.

Dies infaustus.

An unlucky day.

Dies iræ.

The day of wrath.‖

Dies non.

(A day on which judges do not sit.) A day on which legal proceedings cannot be taken.

---

* One of the dicta of Aristotle.

† This was a favourite stage-trick of the Greek tragedian, Euripides. Whenever the plot of the play seems hopelessly involved, some divine person is introduced, borne down from above, to clear up all difficulties.

‡ More familiar in the incorrect form *Verbum sap.*

§ The Emperor Titus is said to have exclaimed, *Diem perdidi,* when he had allowed a day to pass in which he had done no gracious act.

‖ The opening words of a familiar Latin hymn.

Difficile est proprie communia dicere.

(It is difficult to speak of common topics in an appropriate manner.) The cleverest speakers are those who can make hackneyed subjects interesting.

Difficile est satiram non scribere.

(It is difficult not to write satire.) It is difficult to refrain from lashing the follies and sins of society.

Difficilia quæ pulcra.

The best things are the most difficult to attain.

Difficilis, facilis, jucundus, acerbus et idem,
Nec tecum possum vivere, nec sine te.
— *Martial.*

In all thy humours, whether grave or mellow,
Thou'rt such a touchy, testy, pleasant fellow;
Hast so much wit, and mirth, and spleen about thee,
There is no living with thee, nor without thee.—*Addison.*

Digito monstrari, et dicier · Hic est.
— *Persius.*

(To be pointed at by the finger, and have it said : " There he is.") The joy of notoriety.

Digna canis pabulo.

(The dog is worth her keep.) It is an ill dog that deserves not a crust.

Dignum laude virum Musa vetat mori.
— *Horace.*

(The Muse forbids the death of those who are truly great.) The poet makes their name immortal.

Dignus vindice nodus.

A difficulty that requires the intervention of another to solve it. *Deus ex machinâ.*

Dii benefecerunt, inopis me quodque pusilli
Finxerunt animi, raro et perpauca loquentis.—*Horace.*

Thank Heaven, that made me of an humble mind ;
To action little, less to words inclined.

Dii laboribus omnia vendunt.

(The gods sell everything for labour.) Without pains, no gains. No mill, no meal.

Dii majores.

The greater gods.

Dii penates.

(Household gods.) The guardians of the hearth and home.

Dilationes in lege sunt odiosae.

Delays in law are odious.

Diluculo surgere saluberrimum est.

It is very healthy to rise at daybreak.

Di meliora.

Heaven send better times.

Dimidium facti, qui bene cœpit habet.

Well begun is half done.

Dimidium plus toto.

(The half is more than the whole.) The half obtained with safety is better than the whole which we have to incur risk to obtain.

Dimidium scientiæ, prudens quæstio.

Wise investigation is the half-way house to knowledge.

Di nos quasi pilas homines habent.
— *Plautus.*

The gods hold us mortals as balls in their hands.

Diruit, ædificat, mutat quadrata rotundis.

(He pulls down, he builds up, he changes square things into round.) He is always capriciously altering things.

Dis aliter visum.

(To the gods it seemed otherwise.) Man proposes, God disposes.

Disce docendus adhuc, quæ censet amiculus, ut si
Cæcus iter monstrare velit ; tamen aspice si quid
Et nos quod cures proprium fecisse, loquamur.—*Horace.*

Yet hear what an unskilful friend can say :
As if a blind man should direct your way ;
So I myself, though wanting to be taught,
May yet impart a hint that's worth your thought.

Discere docendo.

To learn through teaching.

Discessionem facere.

To divide the House.

Discipulus est prioris posterior dies.

(Each succeeding day is the scholar of the preceding.) The experience of one day is a guide for the conduct of the next.

Discum audire quam philosophum.

(To listen to a quoit rather than to a philosopher.) To prefer trifles to serious talk.

Disjecta membra.

Scattered limbs, or members.*

Distrahit animum librorum multitudo.

(A multitude of books distracts the mind.) Indiscriminate reading is unprofitable to the mind.

Diu apparandum est bellum, ut vincas celeriter.— *Publius Syrus.*

You ought to make long preparations for war, in order that you may more quickly conquer.

Diversos diversa juvant.

Different things please different men.

Dives qui fieri vult, et cito vult fieri.

He that wishes to become rich, also wishes to become so quickly.

Divide et impera.

(Divide and govern.) The despot maintains his own position by playing one rival faction against another.

Divina natura dedit agros, ars humana ædificavit urbes.—*Varro.*

(God gave us the country, the skill of man has built the town.) God made the country, and man made the town.
—*Cowper.*

Divina particula auræ.

The Divine spirit (in man).

Docendo disco.

I learn by teaching others.

Doce ut discas.

Teach, that you may learn.

Doctrina sed vim promovet insitam,
Rectique cultus pectora roborant :
Utcumque defecere mores,
Dedecorant bene nata culpæ —*Horace.*

Yet the best blood by learning is refined,
And virtue arms the solid mind ;
Whilst vice will stain the noblest race,
And the paternal stamp efface.
— *Oldisworth.*

Dolium volvitur.

(A cask is easily moved.) A weak man is easily turned.

Dolus versatur in generalibus.

(Fraud lurks in generalities.) Be definite.

Domine, dirige nos.

O Lord, direct us.

---

* Horace speaks of the *disjecti membra poetæ*,—"the limbs of the dismembered poet"—saying, that you can appreciate the greatness of good poets, even in short quotations from their works.

Domino (*or* Deo) optimo maximo (D.O.M.).
To the Lord God, the supreme and mighty ruler of the world.*

Dominus illuminatio mea.
The Lord is my light.

Dominus providebit.
The Lord will provide.

Dominus videt plurimum in rebus suis.
The master has the keenest eye in his own affairs.

Domus et placens uxor.
A house and pleasing wife.

Donec eris felix, multos numerabis amicos :
Tempora si fuerint nubila, solus eris.
                    —*Ovid.*
While you are prosperous you will have plenty of friends ; but when your sky is cloudy, you will be left to yourself.

Dono dedit *or* Dat, donat, dicat.
(He gave *or* gives, presents, dedicates.) An inscription often written in presentation books before the name of the giver.

Dormit secure, cui non est functio curae.
(He who has no anxious duties, sleeps well.) Far from court, far from care.

Dos est magna parentium virtus.
The virtue of parents is a great dowry.

Dramatis personæ.
(The persons of the drama.) The characters.

Duabus ancoris fultus.
Duabus niti ancoris.
(To ride at two anchors. To be in harbour.) To have two strings to one's bow.

Duabus sellis sedere.
(To sit in two saddles.) To hold with the hare and run with the hounds. To play a double game.

Ducit amor patriæ.
The love of country leads me.

Dulce oellum inexpertis.
War is magnificent to those who never tried it.

Dulce domum.
(Sweet homeward.)†

Dulce est desipere in loco.--*Horace.*
(It is sweet to unbend on proper occasions.) To play the fool, to lay aside one's wisdom and gravity. A little nonsense now and then is relished by the wisest men.

Dulce et decorum est pro patriâ mori.
It is sweet and glorious to die for one's country.

Dulce et decorum est pro patriâ mori :
Mors et fugacem persequitur virum,
Nec parcit imbellis juventae
Poplitibus timidoque tergo.—*Horace.*
How bless'd is he who for his country dies,
Since death pursues the coward as he flies ;
The youth in vain would fly from fate's attack
With trembling knees and terror at his back.—*Swift.*

Dulce quod utile.
What is useful is sweet.

Dulce ridentem Lalagen amabo,
Dulce loquentem.—*Horace.*
I shall continue to love my sweetly smiling and sweetly speaking Lalage.

---

* This is the motto of the Benedictine Order, which is familiar owing to the fact that the abbreviated form of it is written on the label of the famous Bénédictine liqueur. This liqueur is manufactured at Fécamp, in Norman ly.
† The opening words of the Winchester College song, given at end of term.

D

Dulces moriens reminiscitur Argos.
—*Virgil*.

(And, as he dies, his thoughts revert to his beloved Argos.) The dying man thinks of the home of his childhood.

Dulcis et alta quies, placidæque simillima morti.—*Virgil*.

Sleep calm and deep, most like to tranquil death.

Dum deliberamus quando incipiendum, incipere jam serum fit.—*Quintilian*.

(While we are considering when to begin, it is already becoming too late to begin.) While the doctors deliberate the patient dies.

Dum fata sinunt, vivite læti.—*Seneca*.

(Be merry while fate permits.) Eat, drink, and be merry, for to-morrow we die.

Dum fortuna fuit.

As long as fortune lasted.

Dum loquor, hora fugit.—*Ovid*.

Time is flying while I speak.

Dummodo risum
Excutiat sibi, non hic cuiquam parcet amico.—*Horace*.

(Provided he can raise a laugh, he will not spare the feelings of a friend.) Better waste your wit than lose your friend.

Dum relego, scripsisse pudet.

While I am reading my compositions over again, I am ashamed of having written them.

Dum spiro, spero.

Whilst I breathe, I hope.

Dum tacent, clamant.

(Though they keep silence, they cry aloud.) Their silence speaks louder than words.

Dum vires annique sinunt, tolerate labores :
Jam veniet tacito curva senecta pede.
—*Ovid*.

Work hard while you have youth and strength; for soon weak old age will creep on you with silent tread.

Dum vita est, spes est.

While there is life, there is hope.

Dum vitant stulti vitia, in contraria currunt.

(While striving to shun one vice, fools run into its opposite) Fools are ever in extremes.

Dum vivimus, vivamus.

Whilst we live, let us live.

Duo cum faciunt idem, non est idem.

(When two persons do the same thing, it is not the same thing.) No two persons do the same thing in an exactly similar manner.

Duo parietes de eadem fidelia dealbare.

(To whitewash two walls from one pot.) To kill two birds with one stone.

Duos qui sequitur lepores, neutrum capit.

(He that follows two hares, catches neither.) Too many irons in the fire.

Duplici spe uti.

(To have a double hope.) To have two strings to one's bow.

Dura mater.

The outer membrane covering the brain.

Dura molli saxa cavantur aquâ.

(Hard stones are hollowed by soft water.) Continual droppings will wear away a stone.

Durante bene placito.

(During our good pleasure.) The conditions under which certain official positions are given by the Crown.

Duro flagello mens docetur rectius.

(By scourging the mind is trained aright.) Suffering is a stern teacher, but a good one.

Durum telum est necessitas.

Necessity is a hard weapon.

Dux femina facti.

(A woman was the originator of the deed.) There's a woman at the bottom of it.—Cherchez la femme.

Dux vitæ ratio.

The guide of life is common sense.

Ea libertas est, quæ pectus purum et firmum gestitat.—*Ennius*

(True liberty consists in the possession of a pure and steadfast heart.)
If I have freedom in my love
And in my soul am free,
Angels alone that soar above,
Enjoy such liberty.—*Lovelace*.

Eamus quo ducit fortuna.

Let us go where fortune leads.

Eandem cantilenam recinere.

To keep on singing the same old song.

Ea sub oculis posita negligimus : proximorum incuriosi, longinqua sectamur.—*Pliny the Younger*.

(We neglect the things that are before our eyes, and, taking no interest in what is within reach, we go in quest of everything remote.) We ignore the beauties of our own land and are too eager to visit foreign countries, because distance lends enchantment to the view.

Ecce homo.

Behold the man.*

Ecce iterum Crispinus!

(Lo, Crispin again!) I revert to the topic I have dealt with so often already.

Ecce signum.

Behold the sign ; here is the proof.

Editio princeps.

A first edition of a book.

Effodiuntur opes irritamenta malorum. —*Ovid*.

Riches, which are incentives to evil courses, are dug out of the ground.

E flammâ petere cibum.—*Terence*.

(To snatch food from the flames.) To be utterly desperate.†

Ego de caseo loquor, tu de cretâ respondes.

(I talk of cheese, and you of chalk.) We are at cross-purposes.

Ego et rex meus.

My king and I.

Ego illam periisse puto cui periit pudor. —*Plautus*.

I consider the woman who has lost her modesty, lost indeed.

Egomet mihi ignosco.—*Horace*.

(I myself pardon myself.) I am on the best of terms with myself.

Ego nec studium sine divite venâ
Nec rude, quid possit, video ingenium :
  alterius sic
Altera poscit opem res, et conjurat
  amice.—*Horace*.

I neither see what art can do without natural talent, nor natural talent without artistic training ; each requires the aid of the other, and united they assist one another to reach the desired goal of success.

* The words of Pilate to the Jews at the trial of Christ. Hence pictures representing the Saviour wearing the crown of thorns, bear this title.
† The Romans used to throw food on the funeral pyres, where the bodies of the dead were burning. Only starving folk would be likely to wish for this food.

Ego spem pretio non emo.—*Terence.*   (I am not giving cash for hopes.)   No pig in a poke for me.

Ego sum rex Romanus et super grammaticam.   I am the king of the Romans, and am superior to rules of grammar.*

Egregii mortalis altique silenti.   A man of uncommon silence and reserve.

Eheu! fugaces labuntur anni!   Alas! the years glide fleeting by.

Eheu fugaces, Postume, Postume, Labuntur anni; nec pietas moram Rugis et instanti senectæ Afferet, indomitæque morti.—*Horace.*   Alas! friend Postumus, the fleeting years glide away; nor will reverence towards the gods stay the advance of wrinkled old age, or of invincible death.

Ejusdem farinæ.   (Of the same flour.)   Of the same kidney.

Ejusdem generis.   Of the same kind, or sort.

Elephantem ex muscâ facis.   (You are making an elephant out of a fly.)   You are making a mountain out of a mole-hill.

E libris *or* ex libris.   From the books of; part of the library of.

Elixir vitæ.   (The quintessence of life.)   A cordial or potion that prolongs life.

Emeritus.   A veteran who has received his discharge.   A title of honour given to some professors in certain universities, &c.

Emollit mores, nec sinit esse feros.   (Learning) softens manners, and does not permit men to be rude.

Empta dolore docet experientia.   (Experience bought by pain teaches us a lesson.)   A burnt child dreads the fire.

E multis paleis paulum fructus collegi.   (From much straw I have gathered but little fruit.)   Much cry and little wool.

Ens rationis.   A creature of reason.

Eodem collyrio omnibus mederi.   (To cure all diseases with the same salve.)   To play the quack.

Eo magis præfulgebat, quod non videbatur.—*Tacitus.*   (He was all the more impressive, because he was not seen.)   He was conspicuous by his absence.

Eo nomine.   On this account; for this cause.

Epicuri de grege porcus.   (A hog from the drove of Epicurus.)   A glutton.

Episcopatus non est artificium transigendæ vitæ.—*St. Augustine.*   (The office of bishop is not a mere device for passing life.)   It is the duty of a bishop to set an example of diligence to his subordinates.

Epithalamium.   Song or poem delivered at a marriage.

E pluribus unum.   One out of many.

---

* The reply of the Emperor Sigismund, at the Council of Constance, to the cardinal who ventured to correct the Emperor's Latin.

Erectos ad sidera tollere vultus.

(To raise their countenances boldly to the stars.) To hold up their heads like free men.

Ergo.

Therefore.

Ergo sollicitæ tu causa, pecunia,vitæ es,
Per te immaturum mortis adimus iter.
                              —*Propertius.*

Money, thou art the cause of the anxieties of life, and through thee we go down to the grave before our time.

Eripuit cœlo fulmen sceptrumque tyrannis.

He snatched the lightning from heaven and the sceptre from the tyrants.*

Errare est humanum.

To err is human.

Errare malo cum Platone.

(I prefer to be in the wrong in Plato's company.) Follow the wise few rather than the vulgar many.

Esse oportet ut vivas, non vivere ut edas.— *Cicero.*

We ought to eat in order to live, not live in order to eat.

Esse quam videri.

To be, rather than seem to be.

Est brevitate opus, ut currat sententia.
                              —*Horace.*

Let brevity dispatch the rapid thought.

Est deus in nobis.— *Ovid.*

(God is within us.) Ye are the temples of the Holy Ghost.

Est mihi namque domi pater, est injusta noverca.

For at home I have a father and an unjust stepmother.

Est modus in rebus ; sunt certi denique fines,
Quos ultra citraque nequit consistere rectum.— *Horace.*

(There is a medium in all things ; there are, in fact, certain bounds, on either side of which rectitude cannot exist.) Extremes of any kind are liable to lead to bigotry and tyranny.

Est natura hominum novitatis avida.
                              —*Pliny the Elder.*

It is the nature of a man to long for novelty.

Estne Dei sedes nisi terra et pontus et aer
Et cœlum et virtus ? Superos quid quærimus ultra ?
Jupiter est quodcunque vides,quocunque moveris.— *Lucan.*

Is there any dwelling of God save the earth, the sea, the air, the heavens, and virtue ? Why, then, do we seek a God beyond ? The Deity is to be found in everything your eyes can see, and in every place whither your feet can go.

Esto perpetua.

Be thou perpetual.†

Esto, ut nunc multi, dives tibi, pauper amicis.— *Juvenal.*

Adopt the popular plan ; keep your riches for yourself, and be niggardly to your friends.

Est pii Deum et patriam diligere.

It is the part of a good man to love God and his country.

Est proprium stultitiæ aliorum cernere vitia, oblivisci suorum.

It is a peculiarity of fools to perceive the faults of others, but to forget their own.

---

* These words appeared on the medal struck in honour of Benjamin Franklin, when he was the Ambassador of the United States of America to France. The former part of the inscription refers to Franklin's scientific discoveries, the latter to his successful efforts in promoting the independence of his country.
† The dying words of Father Paul Sarpi, expressing a hope for the future prosperity of Venice, his native state.

Est quædam flere voluptas ;
Expletur lacrimis egeriturque dolor.
—*Ovid*.

There is a kind of pleasure in weeping, for grief is assuaged and removed by tears.

Est quoque cunctarum novitas carissima rerum.

Novelty is the most delightful of all things.

Esurienti ne occurras.

(Do not encounter a hungry man.) *Durum telum necessitas.*

Et cætera.

And the rest ; and so on.

Et decus et pretium recti.

Both the ornament and the reward of uprightness.

Et ego in Arcadiâ.

(I, too, have been in Arcadia.) I am an idealist.

E tenui casâ sæpe vir magnus exit.

(From an humble cottage a hero often springs.)

Et hoc genus omne.

(And everything of the kind.) All this sort of thing ; persons of this class.

Etiam oblivisci quod scis interdum expedit.

It is sometimes expedient to forget, to fail to recollect, what you know.

Etiam sapientibus cupido gloriæ novissima exuitur.—*Tacitus*.

(The love of fame is the last weakness which even the will puts off.) That last infirmity of noble minds.
      —*Milton*.

Etiam si Cato dicat.

(Even if Cato were to say so.) Even if a man as truthful as Cato were to tell me, I should not believe it.

Et nunc et semper.

Now and ever.

Et qui nolunt occidere quenquam, posse volunt.—*Juvenal*.

Even those who do not wish to kill another would gladly have the power to do so.

Et sceleratis sol oritur.— *Seneca*.

(The sun shines even on the wicked.) He maketh the sun to rise on the evil and on the good, and sendeth rain on the just and on the unjust.
      —*St. Matthew*.

Et sequentia.

And what follows.

Et servata fides perfectus amorque ditabunt.

Tried faith and perfect love will enrich.

Et sic de similibus.

And so of similar things.

Et tu, Brute.

You, too, Brutus.*

Et vitam impendere vero.

To stake one's life on the truth.

Eundem calceum omni pedi induere.

(To put the same shoe on every foot.) Every shoe fits not every foot.

Everso succurrere sæclo.

(To succour the down-thrown age, or times.) To be a saviour of society.

Ex abusu non arguitur in usum.

No argument against the use of a thing can be drawn from the abuse of it.

Ex acervo.

Out of a heap.

Ex adverso.

From the opposite side ; in opposition.

* The traditional dying words of Cæsar, when Brutus stabbed him. There seems to be no real evidence that these words were ever spoken, and, like Wellington's " Up guards and at 'em," they belong to the category of things that ought to have been said.

Ex animo. — Heartily, sincerely.

Ex arenâ funiculum nectis. — (You are for making a rope of sand.) You are engaged in an impossible task.

Ex auribus cognoscitur asinus. — An ass is known by his ears.

Ex capite. — Out of one's head; from memory.

Ex cathedrâ. — (From the chair.) With authority, real or supposed.*

Excelsior. — Higher; aiming at higher achievements.

Exceptio probat regulam. — The exception proves the rule.

Exceptis excipiendis — The due exceptions being made.

Excitari non hebescere. — To be spirited, not inactive.

Ex concesso. — From what has been granted, or admitted (by an opponent).

Excursus. — A sally; a digression; a special disquisition.

Ex dono Dei. — By or from the gift of God.

Exeat. — (Let him depart.) The leave given for temporary absence from a school or college.

Exeat aulâ
Qui vult esse pius; virtus et summa potestas
Non coeunt.—*Lucan.* — Let him who would be virtuous shun the courts of kings; for virtue and regal power seldom go hand in hand.

Exegi monumentum ære perennius
Regalique situ pyramidum altius;
Quod non imber edax, non Aquilo impotens
Possit diruere, et innumerabilis
Annorum series, et fuga temporum.
             —*Horace.* — I have raised a monument more enduring than one of brass, and loftier than the pyramids of kings; a monument which shall not be destroyed by the consuming rain, nor by the mad rage of the north wind, nor by the countless years and flight of ages.†

Exemplaria Græca
Nocturnâ versate manu, versate diurnâ.
             —*Horace.* — (Study diligently the writings of the Greeks both day and night.) Give your days and nights to the Greek authors.

Exempli gratia (e.g. *or* ex. gr.). — By way of example.

Exemplo plus quam ratione vivimus. — We live more by example than by reason.

Exemplumque Dei quisque est in imagine parvâ — (Every man is in a small degree the image of God.) God made man after his own image.

Exercitatio optimus est magister. — (Practice is the best master.) Practice makes perfect.

Exeunt omnes. — All retire.

Ex fide fortis. — Strong through faith.

Ex granis fit acervus. — (Many grains make a heap.) Every little helps.

* A cathedral is so called because it contains the *cathedra*, the throne, or official chair of the bishop of the diocese.

† Horace concludes the third book of his Odes with this proud prophecy of the permanent quality of his work, intending it to be his last word as a poet. He was afterwards induced to add a fourth book to the Odes.

Ex hoc malo proveniat aliquod bonum.	From this evil some good may issue.
Ex hypothesi.	According to the hypothesis; according to the supposition assumed to be true.
Exigitur enim jam ab oratore etiam poeticus decor.—*Tacitus.*	An orator is expected to have a poetic style of diction.
Exigui numero, sed bello vivida virtus. —*Virgil.*	Small in number, but full of courage in war.
Ex illo fluere ac retro sublapsa referri. —*Virgil.*	From that time the fortunes failed and took a backward course.
Exitus acta probat.	(The issue proves deeds.) All's well that ends well. The evening crowns the day.
Ex longinquo.	From a great distance.
Ex mero motu.	Of his own accord; spontaneously.
Ex nihilo nihil fit.	Nothing comes of nothing.*
Ex officio.	By virtue of his office.
Exordium.	An introduction; the opening words.
Exoriare aliquis nostris ex ossibus ultor. —*Virgil.*	May some avenger arise from my bones.†
Ex parte.	On one side only.
Ex pede Herculem.	(Hercules from his foot.) Judge of the whole from a part, as you can guess the size of Hercules from seeing only his foot.
Expende Hannibalem; quot libras in duce summo invenies.—*Juvenal.*	Weigh the dust of Hannibal. How many pounds will you find in that great leader? ‡
Experientia docet.	Experience teaches.
Experientia stultorum magistra.	Experience is the mistress of fools.
Experimentum crucis.	(The experiment or trial of the cross.) A bold and dangerous experiment.
Experto crede.	(Trust one that has tried.) Believe one that has had experience.
Expertus metuit.	(Having had experience, he feared it.) The burnt child dreads the fire.
Explorant adversa viros.	Adversity tries men.
Ex post facto.	From something done afterwards; retrospective.

---

* The dictum of Lucretius, who, in his *De Rerum Naturâ*, declares the world to have been created by the fortuitous union of atoms falling from space.

† The poet puts these words into the mouth of Dido, the Carthaginian queen, who utters them when she is deserted by her lover, Æneas. Virgil thus makes the victories of Hannibal over the descendants of Æneas to be an act of poetic justice. These words have been quoted on many historic occasions. They were uttered by Diego Leon, the Spanish General, who was shot by order of Espartero in 1841, to the soldiers who carried out the execution. Mr. Gladstone in the House of Commons also quoted these words with great effect in his notable speech on the Reform Bill of 1866.

‡ *Compare:—*
　　　　　　"Imperial Cæsar, dead and turned to clay,
　　　　　　Might stop a hole to keep the wind away;
　　　　　　O, that that earth, which kept the world in awe,
　　　　　　Should patch a wall to expel the winter's flaw."
　　　　　　　　　　　　—*Shakespeare.*

Ex professo.

Professedly.

Ex proposito.

By design ; of set purpose.

Ex quovis ligno non fit Mercurius.

(An image of Mercury cannot be made out of every piece of wood.) You cannot make a silk purse out of a sow's ear ; or a horn of a pig's tail.

Extant recte factis præmia.

The rewards of good deeds endure.

Ex tempore.

Without premeditation ; without preparation ; off-hand.

Extra muros.

Beyond the walls.

Extrema gaudii luctus occupat.

(Grief follows close upon joy.) No joy without annoy.

Extremis malis extrema remedia.

(Extreme evils require extreme remedies.) Desperate diseases require prompt remedies.

Ex ungue leonem.

By his claw one knows the lion. *Ex pede Herculem.*

Ex uno disce omnes.

From one you may learn all.

Ex utrâque parte.

On both sides.

Ex voto.

According to vow, in consequence of a vow.

Fabas indulcet fames.

(Hunger sweetens beans.) To the hungry man everything is sweet.

Faber compedes, quas fecit ipse, gestet.

Let the smith himself wear the fetters he forged.

Faber est quisque fortunæ suæ.

(Every man is the architect of his own fortune.) Fortune helps those that help themselves.

Facetiæ.

Jests ; witty and pleasant sayings.

Facetiarum apud præpotentes in longum memoria est.

(The powerful have long memories for jests.) Laugh with a king, but never at him.

Facies tua computat annos.—*Juvenal.*

(Your face shows your years.) There is no need to ask your age.

Facile est imperium in bonis.—*Plautus.*

It is an easy task to rule good men.

Facile est inventis addere.

(It is easy to add to things invented.) To improve an invention.

Facile princeps.

The acknowledged chief ; an easy first

Facilis descensus Averno,
Sed revocare gradus superasque evadere ad auras
Hoc opus, hic labor est.—*Virgil.*

The descent to the nether world is easy, but to retrace one's steps thence and to regain the air above, this is the toil, this the laborious task.

Facilius crescit quam inchoatur dignitas.—*Laberius.*

(It is easier to add to a dignity when won, than it is to gain it in the first instance.) Nothing succeeds like success.

Facinus, quos inquinat, æquat.

Guilt places on a level those whom it contaminates.

Facis de necessitate virtutem.
    — *St. Jerome.*

You are making a virtue of necessity.

Facit indignatio versum.

(Indignation produces the verse.) Anger makes even dull wits bright. Glowing coals sparkle oft.

Factotum.

A do-all, a general agent, servant, or deputy.

Fac ut sciam.

Tell me.

Fæx populi.

The dregs, scum, of the people.

Fallentis semita vitæ.—*Horace.*

(Path of declining days.) The course of an obscure, humble life.

Fallitur egregie quisquis sub principe credit
Servitium ; nunquam libertas gratior exstat
Quam sub rege pio.—*Claudian.*

In truth they err who think, if monarch's sway
Doth rule the land, 'tis slavish to obey ;
For good kings' subjects have their liberty,
And, more than all men, they are truly free.

Falsi crimen.

A charge of forgery.

Falsus in uno, falsus in omni.

False in one point, false in every point.

Famæ damna majora quam quæ aestimari possint.

(Injuries to reputation are too great to be estimated.)
Good name in man and woman, dear my lord,
Is the immediate jewel of their souls.
     —*Shakespeare.*

Famæ laboranti non facile succurritur.

(It is not easy to repair a character when falling.) Give a dog a bad name and hang him.

Fama malum quo non aliud velocius ullum.—*Virgil.*

Nothing travels more swiftly than scandal.

Famam extendere factis.

To extend one's fame by deeds.

Fama semper vivit.

Fame lives for ever.

Fare, fac.

Speak and act.

Fare quæ sentias

Speak what you think.

Farrago libelli.

The hotch-potch, or miscellaneous contents of the little book.

Fasces.

A bundle of rods and an axe, carried before the highest Roman magistrates, and indicating their power to scourge and behead criminals.

Fasciculus.

A small bundle, packet, parcel.

Fas est ab hoste doceri.

It is allowable to learn even from an enemy.

Fata obstant.

(The Fates oppose.) The thing is impossible.

Fata volentem ducunt, nolentem trahunt.

The Fates lead the willing, and drag the unwilling.

Fatetur facinus, qui judicium fugit.

He that shuns judgment acknowledges his crime.

Fato prudentia major.

Wisdom is stronger than fate.

Favete linguis.

(Favour with your tongues.) Avoid uttering any ill-omened word to interrupt the religious rite. Maintain a holy silence.

Fax mentis incendium gloriæ.

The passion of glory is the torch of the mind.

Felices sequeris, Mors, miseros fugis.
—*Seneca.*

Death, thou pursuest the fortunate, but leavest the wretched in their misery.

Felices ter et amplius
Quos irrupta tenet copula, nec, malis
Divulsus quærimoniis,
Supremâ citius solvet amor die.
—*Horace.*

Thrice happy they, whom an indissoluble union binds together, and whom love, unimpaired by angry complainings, does not separate before the last day.

Felicitas habet multos amicos.

(Happiness has many friends.) In time of prosperity friends will be plenty.

Feliciter sapit, qui alieno periculo sapit.
— *Plautus.*

(That man gets experience in a pleasant fashion, who gains it from another's dangers.) Better learn frae your neighbours' scathe than frae your ain.

Felicium multi cognati.

Rich people have many relations.

Felix est qui sorte suâ contentus vivit.

Happy is the man who lives content with his own lot.

Felix qui nihil debet.

(Happy he who owes nothing.) Out of debt, out of danger.

Felix qui potuit rerum cognoscere causas,
Atque metus omnes et inexorabile fatum,
Subjecit pedibus, strepitumque Acherontis avari.—*Virgil.*

Happy is the man who has been able to learn the causes of created things, and has put under his feet all fears and unyielding Fate, and has heeded not the noise of Death's devouring stream.

Felix se nescit amari.—*Lucan.*

(A prosperous man does not know that he possesses friends.) Adversity tests friendships.

Felo de se.

(A felon upon himself.) A suicide.

Feræ naturæ.

Of a wild nature.

Fere libenter homines id, quod volunt, credunt.—*Cæsar.*

People are generally willing to believe that a thing is true, when they wish it to be so.

Fere totus mundus exercet histrionem.
—*Petronius Arbiter.*

Almost the whole world practises the art of acting.
   All the world's a stage,
And all the men and women merely players.—*Shakespeare.*

Feriunt summos fulmina montes.

(Thunderbolts strike the tops of mountains.) Huge winds blow on high hills.

Ferrum ferro acuitur.

Iron sharpens iron

Fervet olla, vivit amicitia.

(While the pot boils, friendship endures.) The man who gives good dinners has plenty of friends.

Fervet opus.

The work thrives.

Fessus viator.

A weary traveller.

Festina lente.

(Hasten slowly.) Forward, but not too fast.*

Festinatio tarda est.

(Haste is slow.) The greater hurry the worse speed. He who is hasty fishes in an empty pond.

Fiat.

(Let it be done.) A peremptory order.

Fiat Dei voluntas.

God's will be done.

Fiat experimentum in corpore vili.

(Let the experiment be tried on a worthless body.) Try your skill in gilt first, and then in gold.

Fiat justitia ruat cœlum.

Let justice be done though the heavens should fall.

Fiat lux.

Let there be light.

Ficta omnia celeriter, tanquam flosculi decidunt, nec simulatum potest quidquam esse diuturnum.—*Cicero.*

Everything that is false, like short-lived flowers, quickly perishes, nor can anything that is untrue endure for a long time.

Ficta voluptatis causa sint proxima veris.—*Horace.*

(Fictions to please should wear the face of truth.)

To hold, as 'twere, the mirror up to nature ; to show virtue her own feature, scorn her own image, and the very age and body of the time his form and pressure.— *Shakespeare.*

Ficus ficus, ligonem ligonem vocat.

He calls figs figs, and a spade a spade.

Fide abrogatâ, omnis humana societas tollitur.—*Livy.*

If you abolish confidence between man and man, every human bond of union is broken.

Fide et amore.

By faith and love.

Fide et fiduciâ.

By faith and confidence.

Fidei coticula crux.

The cross is the touchstone of faith.

Fidei defensor (F.D.).

Defender of the Faith.

Fidelius rident tuguria.

(The laughter in cottages is the most genuine.) Free from greatness, free from care.

Fidem qui perdit perdere ultra nil potest.—*Publius Syrus.*

He who loses his good faith, has nothing further to lose.

Fide, non armis.

By faith, not by arms.

Fides ante intellectum.

(Faith before intellect *or* understanding.) The pupil must accept without questioning his master's instructions.

Fides et justitia.

Fidelity and justice.

Fides non timet.

Faith has no fear.

Fides Punica.

Punic (or Carthaginian) faith; treachery.†

Fides servanda est.

We must keep our plighted word

Fides unde abiit, eo nunquam redit.
—*Publius Syrus.*

Trust, when once lost, never returns.

---

* A favourite maxim of Augustus Cæsar.
† The Romans were very fond of accusing the Carthaginians of perfidy, an accusation in which there appears to have been as little truth as there is in *Perfide Albion*, which our Gallic neighbours are pleased to apply to us.

Fidus Achates. | (Faithful Achates.)   A faithful friend.*
Fidus et audax. | Faithful and intrepid.
Fieri curavit (F.C.). | (Caused it to be made.)   A common inscription added to the name of the person who has designed some monument or other edifice.
Fieri facias (Fi. Fa.). | (Cause it to be done.)   A writ empowering a sheriff to levy execution on the goods of a debtor.
Figulus figulo invidet, faber fabro. | (The potter envies the potter, the blacksmith the blacksmith.) Two of a trade never agree.
Filius nullius. | A son of nobody; a bastard.
Finem respice. | Look to the end.
Finis coronat opus. | The end crowns the work.
Finis Poloniæ. | The end of Poland.†
Fit via vi. | Force finds a way.
Flagrante bello. | During hostilities.
Flagrante delicto. | In the commission of the crime; red-handed.
Flamma fumo est proxima.—*Plautus.* | (Flame is smoke's kinsman.)   There is no smoke without fire.
Flamma per incensas citius sedetur aristas.—*Propertius.* | Sooner could flames be quenched when they spread among the standing corn.
Flebile ludibrium. | A deplorable mockery; deriding an estimable thing.
Flectere si nequeo superos, Acheronta movebo.—*Virgil.* | If I cannot influence the gods of heaven, I will stir up Acheron itself.   If Heaven refuses help, I will seek the powers of Hell, in order to accomplish my purpose.
Flecti, non frangi. | To be bent, not to be broken.
Floreat Etona! | May Eton flourish!
Floriferis ut apes in saltibus omnia libant.—*Lucretius.* | As bees taste of every flower that blooms within the glades.
Fluvius cum mari certas. | (You, a river, are contending with the ocean.)   You are imitating the ways of those richer than yourself.
Fœnum habet in cornu, longe fuge. | (He has hay on his horn; keep at a safe distance.)   Like a dangerous animal; as an angry bull.‡
Fons et origo. | The source and origin.
Fons malorum. | The fountain, source of evils.
Forma bonum fragile est. | (Beauty is a blessing easily lost.)   Beauty is only skin-deep.
Forma flos, fama flatus. | Beauty is a flower, Fame a breath.

---

* The constant companion of Æneas, the Trojan hero in *The Æneid.*
† Kosciusko is said to have exclaimed *Finis Poloniæ,* when he was captured by the Russians in 1794, but he denied ever uttering these words.
‡ The Romans, to warn passers-by, fastened a wisp of hay on the horn of a dangerous bull.

Formam quidem ipsam, Marce fili, et
tanquam faciem honesti vides : quæ
si oculis cerneretur, mirabiles amores
(ut ait Plato) excitaret sapientiæ.
—*Cicero*

Formidabilior cervorum exercitus duce
leone quam leonum cervo.

Forsan et hæc olim meminisse juvabit ;
Durate, et vosmet rebus servate secundis.—*Virgil.*

Forsan miseros meliora sequentur.

Fortem posce animum.

Fortem posce animum, mortis terrore
carentem,
Qui spatium vitæ extremum inter munera ponat,
Naturæ.—*Juvenal.*

Fortes fortuna juvat.

Forti et fideli nil difficile.

Fortior est qui se, quam qui fortissima
mœnia vincit.

Fortis cadere, cedere non potest.

Fortis et constantis est non perturbari
in rebus asperis, nec tumultuantem
de gradu dejici, ut dicitur.—*Cicero.*

Fortis et fidelis.

Fortiter in re.

Fortitudine et prudentiâ.

Fortitudo et justitia invictæ sunt.

Fortunæ cetera mando.

Fortunæ filius.

Fortuna favet fatuis.

Fortuna multis dat nimis, satis nulli.
—*Martial.*

Fortunam velut tunicam, magis con-
cinnam proba, quam longam.
—*Apuleius.*

Fortuna, nimium quem fovet, stultum
facit.

You see, my son Marcus, virtue as if it
were embodied, which if it could be
made the object of sight, would (as
Plato says) excite in us a wonderful
love of wisdom.

An army of stags led by a lion is more
formidable than an army of lions led
by a stag.

Perhaps it may one day be a pleasure to
remember these sufferings ; bear up
against them, and reserve yourself for
more prosperous days.

Perhaps better days may be in store for
the unfortunate.

(Pray for a strong will.) O well for him
whose will is strong.—*Tennyson.*

Pray for a strong will, and a heart so
fearless of death, that it will count
the closing hours of life among the
gifts of Nature.

Fortune helps the brave.

Nothing is difficult to the faithful and
brave.

(More valiant is he that conquers himself than he that takes the most
strongly fortified city.)   He that
ruleth his spirit is better than he that
taketh a city.

The brave may fall, but cannot yield.

A man of firm and courageous character ought not to be over-anxious in
critical times, nor ought he to allow
himself to be jostled and knocked
off the step, as the saying goes.

Brave and trustworthy.

With firmness in action.

By fortitude and prudence.

Fortitude and Justice are invincible.

(I commit the rest to Fortune.)   I cannot think of any better precautions
or arrangements.

A child of fortune ; a favourite son of
fortune.

Fortune favours fools.

Fortune gives too much to many,
enough to none.

Judge your fortune as you judge a
coat ; look not at the size of it, but
see that it fits.

When Fortune caresses a man too much,
she makes him a fool.

Fortuna opes auferre, non animum, potest.

(Fortune can take away wealth but not courage.) A man of strong mind rises superior to all the changes of fortune.

Fortuna sequatur.

Let fortune follow. Good luck to the project !

Fortunatos nimium, sua si bona norint!

Only too happy were they but sensible of the blessings they enjoy !

Fortuna vitrea est ; tum, cum splendet, frangitur.—*Publius Syrus.*

Fortune is made of brittle glass ; when it shines the most, it is shattered.

Fragrat post funera virtus.

Virtue smells sweet after death.

Frangas non flectes.

You may break, you cannot bend me.

Frange, miser, calamos, vigilataque prœlia dele.—*Juvenal.*

(Break your pens, poor wretch, and destroy the records of your sleepless toil.) Advice to the would-be poet starving in his garret.

Fraus est celare fraudem.

It is a fraud to conceal a fraud.

Frons prima decipit multos.

(The first view deceives many.) Second thoughts are best.

Fronti nulla fides.

(There is no trusting to appearances.) All that glitters is not gold.

Fruges consumere nati.

Men born to consume the fruits of the earth.

Frustra laborat qui omnibus placere studet.

He labours in vain who tries to please everybody.

Frustra vitium vitaveris illud
Si te alio pravum detorseris.—*Horace.*

It is vain for you to shun one vice, if in your depravity you rush into another.

Fugaces labuntur anni.

The years glide fleeting on.

Fugam fecit.

He has absconded.

Fuge magna; licet sub paupere tecto
Reges et regum vitâ præcurrere amicos.
         — *Horace.*

Shun greatness ; in the poor man's cottage one may live more happily than princes and friends of princes ever do.

Fugiendo in media sæpe ruitur in fata.

By fleeing, men often rush right on their fate.

Fugit hora.

The hours fly.

Fuimus.

(We have been.) We are no more ; our day is over.

Fuit Ilium.

Troy *has* been—is no more.

Fulgente trahit constrictos Gloria curru
Non minus ignotos generosis.—*Horace.*

Chain'd to her shining car, Fame draws along
With equal whirl the great and vulgar throng.

Fulmen brutum.

(Harmless thunderbolt.) A vain threat.

Fumus et opes strepitusque Romæ.

The smoke, wealth, and din of Rome.

Functus officio.

Having performed his office.

Fundamentum enim est justitiæ fides.
         —*Cicero.*

(Fidelity is the foundation of justice.) The faithful observing of pledges.

Fungar inani munere.

I will discharge a fruitless task.

      Fungor vice cotis, acutum
Reddere quæ ferrum valet, exsors ipsa secandi.—*Horace.*

I play the whetstone ; useless, and unfit
To cut myself, I sharpen others' wit.
         —*Creech.*

Funiculis ligatum vel puer verberaret. | Even a child may beat a man that's bound.

Furor fit læsa sæpius patientia. | (Patience if too often abused becomes madness.) Fear the anger of a patient man.

Furor loquendi. | An enthusiastic eagerness for speaking.
Furor scribendi. | A mania for writing.

Galeatum sero duelli pœnitet. —*Juvenal.* | (When you have got your helmet on, it is too late to refuse to fight.) Look before you leap.

Gallus in suo sterquilinio plurimum potest. | Every cock crows loudest on his own dunghill.

Gaudetque viam fecisse ruinâ.—*Lucan.* | And he rejoices to have made his way by ruin.*

Gaudet tentamine virtus. | Virtue rejoices in trial.
Generosus nascitur non fit. | The gentleman is born and not made.
Genius loci. | The genius of the place ; the protecting spirit.

Genus est mortis male vivere.—*Ovid.* | An evil life is a species of death.

Genus immortale manet, multosque per annos
Stat fortuna domus, et avi numerantur avorum.—*Virgil.* | Th' immortal line in sure succession reigns, The fortune of the family remains, And grandsires' grandsons the long list contains.—*Dryden.*

Genus improbum. | A knavish race.
Genus irritabile vatum. | The irritable race, or tribe, of poets.
Gladiator in arenâ consilium capit. | (The gladiator having entered the lists is taking advice.) *Galeatum sero.* Look before you leap.

Gloria est consentiens laus bonorum, incorrupta vox bene judicantium de excellenti virtute. — *Cicero.* | True glory is the unanimous approbation of good men, for their praise is not bought with money, and they alone are able to estimate real merit at its proper value.

Gloria in excelsis Deo. | Glory to God in the highest.
Gloria Patri. | Glory to the Father.
Gloria virtutis umbra. | Glory is the shadow of virtue.
Gradu diverso, via una. | The same way by different steps.
Græcia capta ferum victorem cepit, et artes Intulit agresti Latio.—*Horace.* | Greece subdued, captivated her uncivilised conqueror, and imported her arts into unpolished Latium.†
Græculus esuriens, in coelum jusseris, ibit.—*Juvenal.* | (Tell a hungry Greek to go to heaven, he'll attempt it.) A starving man will promise anything.‡

* The description originally applied to Cæsar, but aptly fits the career of any of the successful political adventurers.
† Rome owed its literature and art almost entirely to the Greeks, who were the models and instructors of the Romans in artistic matters. Even the writing of satire, which the Romans claimed as peculiarly their own, probably owed much to the writers of Greek comedies
‡ Rome, in the days of the Cæsars, was thronged with Greek freedmen and adventurers, who would stoop to anything in order to gain a living.

Grammatici certant, et adhuc sub judice lis est. – *Horace.*

The grammarians disagree, and the matter in dispute is still under consideration.

Grata superveniet, quæ non sperabitur, hora.

The hour that is not hoped for will be delightful when it arrives.

Grata testudo.

The welcome lyre.

Gratia ab officio, quod mora tardat, abest.

(There are no thanks for a kindness which has been delayed.) He loses his thanks, who promiseth and delayeth.

Gratia gratiam parit.

(Kindness produces kindness.) One good turn deserves another.

Gratias agere.

To give thanks.

Gratior et pulcro veniens in corpore virtus.

Even virtue is more fair, when it appears in a comely person.

Gratis anhelans, multa agendo, nihil agens.—*Phædrus.*

Out of breath to no purpose, and very busy about nothing.

Gratis dictum.

Mere assertion.

Gratulor quod eum, quem necesse erat diligere, qualiscunque esset, talem habemus ut libenter quoque diligamus.—*Trebonius.*

I rejoice that the man, whom it was my bounden duty to love, whatever his character might be, is so worthy that my inclination bids me love him.

Gravamen.

The thing complained of; what weighs most heavily against the accused.

Graviora quædam sunt remedia periculis.
　　　　　—*Publius Syrus.*

Some remedies are worse than the diseases.

Gravis ira regum semper.

The anger of kings is always severe.

Grex totus in agris unius scabie cadit.

(A whole flock perishes in the fields from the scab of one sheep.) A rotten sheep affects the whole flock.

Gula plures quam gladius perimit.

Gluttony kills more than the sword.

Gustus elementa per omnia quærunt Nunquam animo pretiis obstantibus.
　　　　　　　　　— *Juvenal.*

(From all the elements they seek choice dainties, and no expense debars them from purchasing the viands they desire.) The description of the gourmands of every age.

Gutta cavat lapidem non vi sed sæpe cadendo.

The drop hollows the stone not by its force but by constant dropping.

Gutta fortunæ præ dolio sapientiæ.

(A drop of fortune is better than a cask of wisdom.) An ounce of fortune is worth a pound of forecast.

Habeas corpus.

(You may have the body.) A writ for delivering a person from imprisonment.

Habeas corpus ad prosequendum.

You may have the body in order to prosecute.

Habemus confitentem reum.—*Cicero.*

We have before us a person accused, who pleads guilty.

Habent sua fata libelli.

Books have their own destiny.

E

Habeo te loco parentis.

Habet.

Habet et musca splenem.

Habet in adversis auxilia, qui in secundis commodat.—*Publius Syrus.*

Habet natura ut aliarum omnium rerum sic vivendi modum; senectus autem peractio ætatis est tanquam fabulæ. Cujus defatigationem fugere debemus, præsertim adjunctâ satietate.
         — *Cicero.*

Hac mercede placet.

Hæc olim meminisse juvabit.—*Virgil.*

Hæc studia adolescentiam agunt, senectutem oblectant, secundas res ornant, adversis perfugium ac solatium præbent, delectant domi, non impediunt foris, pernoctant nobiscum, peregrinantur, rusticantur.—*Cicero.*

Hæ nugæ in seria ducent mala.
         —*Horace.*

Hærent infixi pectore vultus. -- *Virgil.*

Hæret lateri lethalis arundo.

Hæreticis non est servanda fides.

Hæ tibi erunt artes; pacisque imponere morem,
Parcere subjectis et debellare superbos.
         —*Virgil.*

Hanc veniam petimusque damusque vicissim.—*Horace.*

Hannibal ad portas.

Haud facile emergunt, quorum virtutibus obstat,
Res angusta domi.—*Juvenal.*

I love or regard you as a parent.

He has it; he is hit.*

(A fly even has its anger.) Even a worm will turn at last.

He who lends in the day of his prosperity, finds help in his day of adversity.

Life, as well as all other things, hath its bounds assigned by nature; and its conclusion, like the last act of a play, is old·age, the fatigue of which we ought to shun, especially when our appetites are fully satisfied.

I am satisfied with these conditions.

To remember these things hereafter will be a pleasure.

These studies (literary pursuits) employ youth, give pleasure to old age, make prosperity more prosperous, are a refuge and a solace in sorrow, amuse us when at home, do not hinder us in our duties abroad, make our nights less lonely, and in our travels and sojournings are our constant companions.

These trifles will lead to serious evils.

Her looks were deep imprinted in his heart.

The deadly spear-shaft sticks to his side.

(No faith should be kept with heretics.) That is, with such as claim to think on religious matters for themselves, and refuse the teaching of Roman Catholicism.

This will be thy task; to give the nations peace, to spare the humbled and crush the rebellious.†

(We grant this concession ourselves, and receive in return.) Give and take is a right policy to follow.

(Hannibal is at the gates.) We are in imminent danger.‡

(Those people do not easily emerge from obscurity whose abilities are cramped by narrow means at home.) Slow rises worth by poverty oppressed.

---

* The cry of the spectators when a gladiator received a fatal blow.
  i In these words Virgil describes the imperial destiny of Rome.
  ‡ The name of Hannibal had been such a terror to the Romans, that *Hannibal ad portas* became a proverb indicating that the country was in peril. Cicero uses the words in one of his diatribes against Antony, whom he regarded as a public enemy.

Haud ignara mali, miseris succurrere disco.

Not ignorant of misfortune, I learn to succour the unfortunate.

Haud ignota loquor.

I speak of well-known events.

Haud passibus æquis.

Not with equal steps.

Helluo librorum.

(A glutton of books.)　A book-worm.

Heredis fletus sub personâ risus est.

The weeping of an heir is laughter under a mask.

Heu quam difficile est crimen non pro dere vultu !—*Ovid.*

How in the looks does conscious guilt appear !—*Addison.*

Hiatus valde deflendus.

A gap, or deficiency, much to be regretted.

Hibernis ipsis Hiberniores.

More Irish than the Irish themselves.

Hic amor, hæc patria est.—*Virgil.*

My heart is there, for there's my native land.

Hic et ubique.

Here, there, and everywhere.

Hic finis fandi.

Here was an end to the discourse.

Hic funis nihil attraxit.

(This line has taken no fish.)　The attempt is a failure.

Hic jacet.

Here lies.

Hic murus aeneus esto, Nil conscire sibi, nullâ pallescere culpâ. —*Horace.*

(Be this a brazen wall about thee, to be conscious of no guilt, to turn pale at no charge.) Conscious innocence.*

Hic niger est : hunc tu, Romane, caveto. —*Horace.*

That man is a knave : Roman, beware of him.

Hic nigræ succus loliginis, hæc est Ærugo mera.—*Horace.*

This is the essence of malice, this is pure jealousy.

Hic patet ingeniis campus.—*Claudian.*

Here is a field open to talent.

Hinc illæ lacrimæ.

Hence those tears.

Hinc subitæ mortes atque intestata senectus.—*Juvenal.*

(Hence arise sudden deaths, and an intestate old age.)　The results of a profligate life.

Hirundinem sub eodem tecto ne habeas.

(Do not have a swallow under the same roof.)　Beware of fair-weather friends.

Hoc erat in votis.

This was my wish.

Hoc est Vivere bis, vitâ posse priore frui. —*Martial.*

The present joys of life we doubly taste, By looking back with pleasure to the past.

Hoc indictum volo.

(I wish this unsaid.)　I withdraw the statement.

Hoc maxime officii est, ut quisque maxime opis indigeat, ita ei potissimum opitulari.—*Cicero.*

(It is a most important duty to assist another most, when he most needs assistance.)　A friend in need is a friend indeed.

Hoc opus, hic labor est.

This is the labour, this is the work ; this is the great difficulty.

Hoc sustinete, majus ne veniat malum. —*Phædrus.*

(Endure this evil, lest a greater come upon you).　Better to bear the ills we have, than fly to others that we know not of.—*Shakespeare.*

* Sir Robert Walpole once misquoted these words in the House, and Pulteney wagered a guinea that Walpole's Latin was wrong.　The clerk at the table decided in Pulteney's favour. and the guinea was promptly tossed across the floor of the House.

Hoc volo, sic jubeo, sit pro ratione voluntas.—*Juvenal*.

(I wish this, I order it, let my wish stand for reason.) The fact that I wish it is sufficient argument.

Hodie, non cras.

To-day not to-morrow; without procrastination.

Hodie tibi, cras mihi.

Your turn to-day, mine to-morrow.

Hominem non odi sed ejus vitia.

I hate not the man, but his faults.

Homines ad deos nullâ re propius accedunt, quam salutem hominibus dando.—*Cicero*.

Men resemble the gods in nothing so much as in doing good to their fellow-creatures.

Homines amplius oculis quam auribus credunt.

Men trust their eyes more than their ears.

Homines nihil agendo discunt malum agere.

(By doing nothing, men learn to do ill.) Satan finds some mischief still for idle hands to do.

Homo doctus in se semper divitias habet.

A learned man always has riches within himself.

Homo est sociale animal.—*Seneca*.

(Man is a social animal.) Men were not intended to live alone.

Homo extra est corpus suum quum irascitur.

A man when angry is beside himself.

Homo homini lupus.—*Plautus*.

(Man to man is a wolf.) Man's inhumanity to man makes countless thousands mourn.—*Burns*.

Homo multarum literarum.

A man of great learning.

Homo proponit sed Deus disponit.

Man proposes, God disposes.

Homo, qui erranti comiter monstrat viam,
Quasi de suo lumine lumen accendat, facit
Nihilo minus ipsi lucet, cum illi accenderit.—*Ennius*.

He who shows the right path to one that has gone astray, lights, so to speak, the other's lantern from his own. Yet, though he has given light, his own doth still burn bright.

Homo qui in homine calamitoso est misericors meminit sui.

(A man who is merciful to the afflicted, remembers what is due to himself.) A touch of nature makes the whole world kin.

Homo sum; humani nihil a me alienum puto.—*Terence*.

I am a man, and deem nothing that relates to man foreign to my feelings.

Homo trium literarum.

(A man of three letters.) A thief. Latin *fur*.

Homunculi quanti sunt.—*Plautus*.

What an insignificant creature is man.

Honesta mors turpi vitâ potior.

An honourable death is preferable to a base life.

Honesta paupertas prior quam opes malæ.

(Poverty with honesty is better than ill-acquired wealth.) Honesty may be dear bought, but can never be a dear pennyworth.

Honesta quam splendida.

Respectable things rather than splendid ones.

Honora medicum propter necessitatem.

(Make much of a physician through necessity.) Honour a physician before thou hast need of him.

Honores mutant mores.

Honor fidelitatis præmium.

Honos alit artes.

Horæ
Momento cita mors venit, aut victoria læta.—*Horace*.

Horresco referens.

Horribile dictu.

Hortus siccus.

Hos ego versiculos feci, tulit alter honores.—*Virgil*.

Hostis honori invidia.

Hostis humani generis.

Humano capiti cervicem equinam jungere.

Humano capiti cervicem pictor equinam
Pingere si velit et varias inducere plumas.
Undique collatis membris, ut turpiter atrum
Desinat in piscem mulier formosa superne ;
Spectatum admissi risum teneatis amici ?
Credite, Pisones, isti tabulæ fore librum
Persimilem, cujus velut ægri somnia, vanæ
Fingunter species.—*Horace*.

Humanum est errare.

Humiles laborant, ubi potentes dissident.—*Phædrus*.

Hypotheses non fingo.

Ibidem (*Ibid.*)

Ibi omnis effusus labor.

Id arbitror
Adprime in vita esse utile, ne quid nimis.—*Terence*.

Idem quod (*i.q.*)

Idem sonans.

Id est (*i.e.*).

Id genus omne.

Idoneus homo.

Honours alter manners.

Honour is the reward of loyalty.

Honour nourishes the arts.

In a moment's flight
Death, or a joyful conquest, ends the fight.—*Francis*.

I shudder at the recollection.

Horrible to tell.

A collection of dried plants.

I wrote these versicles, another carried off the credit of them.*

Envy is the bane of honour.

An enemy of the human race.

To put a horse's head on a human body (said of a painter) ; out of character.

If in a picture, Piso, you should see
A handsome woman with a fish's tail,
Or a man's head upon a horse's neck,
Or limbs of beasts, of the most different kinds,
Cover'd with feathers of all sorts of birds ;
Would you not laugh, and think the painter mad ?
Trust me that book is as ridiculous,
Whose incoherent style, like sick men's dreams,
Varies all shapes, and mixes all extremes.
—*Roscommon*.

To err is human.

When the great quarrel, the lowly suffer.

(I do not frame hypotheses.) I make no suppositions ; I concern myself solely with facts.

In the same place.

There all the labour was expended (or wasted).

(I take to be a principal rule of life, not to be too much addicted to any one thing.) Too much of anything is good for nothing.

The same as.

Sounding alike ; having the same sound or meaning.

That is, that is to say.

All persons of that sort.

A fit man ; a man of known ability.

---

* See *Sic vos, non vobis*.

Ignaviâ nemo immortalis factus ; neque quisquam parens liberis ut æterni forent, optavit ; magis ut boni honestique vitam exigerent.—*Sallust.*

No man ever won undying fame by idleness : no parent has ever wished his children never to die, but rather that they should employ their lives in a good and honourable manner.

Ignavis semper feriæ sunt.

(With idlers it is always holiday.) Doing nothing is hard work.

Ignem ne gladio fodito.

(Stir not the fire with the sword.) Put not fat into the fire.

Ignis aurum probat, miseria fortes viros
—*Seneca.*

As fire tests gold, so misery tests brave men.

Ignis fatuus.
Ignoramus.

Will-o'-the-wisp.
(We do not know.) A person who is always pleading ignorance. An ignorant fellow.

Ignorantia legis neminem excusat.
Ignoratio elenchi.

Ignorance of the law excuses no one.
(Ignorance of the refutation.) Missing the point of the argument ; arguing outside the case.

Ignoscas aliis multa, nil tibi.

Forgive many things to others, nothing to thyself.

Ignoscito sæpe aliis, nunquam tibi.
Ignoti nulla cupido.

Forgive others often, thyself never.
(No desire is felt for a thing unknown.) Where ignorance is bliss, 'tis folly to be wise.

Ilium fuit.
Illam, quicquid agit, quoquo vestigia flectit,
Componit furtim, subsequiturque decor.
—*Tibullus.*

Troy has existed, but exists no longer.
Whate'er she does, where'er her steps she bends,
Grace on each action silently attends.

Ille crucem pretium sceleris tulit, hic diadema !

One man receives crucifixion as the reward of his guilt ; another, a crown

Ille mî par esse Deo videtur,
Ille (si fas est) superare Divos,
Qui sedens adversus, identidem te
     Spectat et audit.
Dulce ridentem ; misero quod omnes
Eripit sensus mihi, nam simul te,
Lesbia, adspexi, nihil est super mî.
—*Catullus.*

Peer for the gods he seems to me
And mightier, if that may be,
Who, sitting face to face with thee,
     Can there serenely gaze ;
Can hear thee sweetly speak the while,
Can see thee, Lesbia, sweetly smile,
Joys that from me my senses wile,
     And leave me in a maze.
—*Martin.*

Ille potens sui
Lætusque deget, cui licet in diem
Dixisse, ' Vixi.'—*Horace.*

Happy he
Self-centred, who each night can say,
     My life is lived —*Conington.*

Ille, velut pelagi rupes immota, resistit.
—*Virgil.*

He, like a rock that billows vainly buffet, stood firm.

Illi scelerum suorum conscientia cruciati pœnas dabunt.

(Those who are tortured by the consciousness of guilt will soon be punished.)
Suspicion always haunts the guilty mind ;
The thief doth fear each bush an officer.—*Shakespeare.*

Illotis pedibus ingredi.

(To enter with unwashed feet.) To enter a shrine in that state. To treat holy things with scorn.

Illud maxime rarum genus est eorum, qui aut excellenti ingenii magnitudine, aut præclarâ eruditione atque doctrinâ, aut utrâque re ornati, spatium deliberandi habuerunt, quem potissimum vitæ cursum sequi vellent.
— *Cicero.*

The number is especially small of those, who, either by surpassing genius, or by remarkable erudition and knowledge, or by being endowed with either, have enjoyed the opportunity of deciding what path of life they prefer to follow.

Illuminati.

Enlightened ones; scholars.

Imitatores, servum pecus.

Servile herd of imitators.

Immensa est finemque potentia cœli Non habet, et quicquid Superi voluere, peractum est.—*Ovid.*

The power of heaven is immense and without limit, and whatever the heavenly powers wish, comes to pass.

Immersabilis est vera virtus.

True virtue cannot be overwhelmed.

Imo pectore.

From the lowest breast; from the bottom of one's heart.

Impedimenta.

Things which impede us; luggage; baggage.

Imperat aut servit collecta pecunia cuique.

Money is always either our master or our slave.

Imperator.

Military commander; Emperor.

Imperium et libertas.

Empire and liberty.*

Imperium in imperio.

A government within a government.

Imperium Trajani, rarâ temporum felicitate, ubi sentire quæ velis, et quæ sentias dicere licet.—*Tacitus.*

The reign of Trajan, those rare and happy days, when you may think what you please, and say what you think.

Impotens sui.

(Without power over one's self.) Without self-control; passionate.

Imprimatur.

(Let it be printed.) Authority to publish; approval; assent.

Imprimis.

In the first place.

Impune.

With impunity.

In actu.

In the very act.

In ære piscari ; in mare venari.

(To fish in the air ; to hunt in the sea.) Fish are not to be caught with a birdcall.

In æternum.

For ever.

In amore hæc omnia insunt vitia : injuriæ,
Suspiciones, inimicitiæ, induciæ,
Bellum, pax rursus.—*Terence.*

In love are all these ills : suspicions, quarrels,
Wrongs, reconcilements, war and peace again.—*Coleman.*

In angustiis amici apparent.

Adversity trieth friends.

In arduis virtus.

Virtue in difficulties.

In articulo mortis.

At the point of death.

In banco.

(In bench.) A judge sitting *in banco*, in court, not in chambers.

In bello parvis momentis magni casus intercedunt.—*Cæsar.*

In war, important events are the results of trivial causes.

* One of Lord Beaconsfield's famous expressions.

In caducum parietem inclinare.

(To lean against a falling wall.) Lean not on a reed.

In camerâ.

In chamber; in private.

In capite.

In the head; in chief.

Incerta pro certis deputas.

(You reckon the uncertain as certain.) Don't count your chickens before they are hatched.

Incessu patuit dea.

Her stately walk showed her to be a goddess.

Incidis in Scyllam cupiens vitare Charybdim.

(You fall into Scylla in endeavouring to escape Charybdis.) Out of the frying-pan into the fire.*

Incipe; dimidium facti est, cœpisse. Supersit Dimidium : rursum hoc incipe, et efficies.—*Ausonius.*

Begin; to have begun makes the work half done. Half still remains; again begin this, and you will complete the task.

Incipit effari, mediâque in voce resistit. —*Virgil.*

He begins to speak, but breaks off in the midst of his words.

In cœlo quies.

There is rest in heaven.

In commendam.

In trust for a time.

Increduli odimus.

We are sceptical about it and detest the subject.

Incudi reddere.—*Horace.*

(To return to the anvil.) To reconsider and repolish a literary composition.

Inde iræ.

Hence this anger.

Index expurgatorius.

A list of prohibited books.†

Index rerum.

A student's note-book, or catalogue of reference.

In diem (*or* In horam) vivere.

To live for the day, or the hour; from hand to mouth.

Indocilis pauperiem pati.

A man who has not learnt to endure poverty.

In eâdem conditione.

In the same condition or category; under the same circumstances.

In eâdem re utilitas et turpitudo esse non potest.—*Cicero.*

It is impossible for the same conduct to be both expedient and dishonourable.

In equilibrio.

Equally balanced.

In esse.

(In being.) In a state of existence.

Inest et formicæ bilis.

(Even an ant has a temper.) Even a worm will turn.

Inest sua gratia parvis.

(Little things have their value.) Trifles are not to be despised.

In extenso.

(In full.) Without abridgment.

In extremis.

In extreme difficulties; at the last gasp.

---

* The line of some mediæval writer founded on the account in *The Odyssey,* where Scylla, the rock dwelling of a hideous monster, and Charybdis, a dangerous whirlpool, threatened danger to the ship of Ulysses and his companions. These prodigies were supposed to exist near the Straits of Messina.

† The record of the books forbidden to be read by loyal Roman Catholics is so-called. M. Zola's *Rome,* for example, was recently added to this list by the Pope's advisers.

Infandum, regina, jubes renovare dolorem.— *Virgil.*

(You command me, O queen, to renew an unspeakable grief.) Said by Æneas, with reference to the destruction of Troy, when requested by Dido to relate the history of the downfall of that city.*

In flagrante delicto.

Taken in the act of committing the offence; red-handed.

In flammam flammas, in mare fundis aquas.

(You are adding flame to the flames, and water to the sea.) You are carrying coals to Newcastle.

In flammam ne manum injicito.

(Thrust not your hand into the fire.) Don't run into danger with your eyes open.

In fore.

In prospective.

In formâ pauperis.

(As a pauper.) A term applied to the privilege, whereby a man, without means, can obtain the aid of the law.

In foro conscientiæ.

Before the tribunal of conscience.

Infra dignitatem (*Infra dig.*).

Beneath one's dignity.

Infra tuam pelliculam te contine.

(Content yourself with your own skin.) Do not imitate the ass that puts on the lion's skin.

In futuro.

In the future.

Ingens æquor.

The mighty ocean.

Ingens telum necessitas.

Necessity is a powerful weapon.

Ingentum foribus domus alta superbis Mane salutantum totis vomit ædibus undam.— *Virgil.*

His lordship's palace view, whose portals proud Each morning vomit forth a cringing crowd. – *Warton.*†

Ingenuas didicisse fideliter artes emollit mores, nec sinit esse feros.— *Ovid.*

Faithful study of the liberal arts softens men's manners and polishes their minds.

Ingratum si dixeris, omnia dicis.

(If you say he is ungrateful you say everything.) Gratitude is the least of virtues, but ingratitude the worst of vices.

Ingratus unus miseris omnibus nocet.

One ungrateful man does an injury to all the wretched.

In gremio legis.

In the lap (or bosom) of the law.

In hoc signo spes mea.

In this sign is my hope.

In hoc signo vinces.

In this sign thou shalt conquer.‡

Inhumanum verbum est ultio.— *Seneca.*

Revenge is an inhuman word.

In infinito.

Perpetually.

In initio.

In the beginning.

---

* Quoted by a Westminster boy to Queen Elizabeth, when she asked him how he liked a birching.

† The poor Roman called on his rich patron every morning, and received a dole for his trouble.

‡ The Emperor Constantine is said to have had a vision of a fiery cross, with these words below, τούτῳ νίκα, appearing in the sky. Tradition says that this circumstance led to his conversion to Christianity.

Iniquissimam pacem justissimo bello antefero.

I prefer the hardest terms of peace to the most just war.

Injuriæ addis contumeliam.

You add insult to injury.

Injuriam qui facturus est jam facit.
—*Seneca.*

He who is about to commit an injury has committed it already.

Injuriarum remedium est oblivio.
—*Publius Syrus.*

The best remedy for injuries is to forget them.

In limine

At the threshold.

In loco parentis.

In the place of a parent.

In magnis et voluisse sat est.
—*Propertius.*

(In great enterprises to have attempted is enough.)
The virtue lies
In the struggle, not the prize.
—*Monckton Milnes.*

In mari aquam quærit.

(He is looking for water in the sea.) None so blind as those who will not see.

In medias res.

Into the midst of things.

In mediis rebus.

In the midst of things; in the very heart of the business.

In medio tutissimus ibis.—*Ovid.*

Safety lies in a middle course.

In mortuâ manu.

(In a dead hand.)*

In necessariis unitas, in dubiis libertas, in omnibus caritas.

Unity in things necessary, liberty in things doubtful, charity in everything †

In nocte consilium.

(In the night is counsel.)   Night is the mother of thought.

In nubibus.

In the clouds; befogged.

In nullum avarus bonus est, in se pessimus.

The avaricious man is good to no one, but he is worst to himself.

In occipitio quoque oculos habet.

(He has an eye in the back of his head.) He has an eye behind him; he is a wary fellow.

In oculis civium.

In the eyes of citizens; in the public eye; in public.

In omni labore emolumentum est.

There is profit in all labour.

Inopi beneficium bis dat qui dat celeriter.

He who gives quickly to a poor man confers a double benefit on him.

Inops, potentem dum vult imitari, perit.—*Phædrus.*

The poor man, who tries to imitate the powerful, is lost.

In otio et negotio probus.

(Upright in business and out of business.) Upright in every relation of life.

In ovo.

In the egg; in the inception.

In pace leones sæpe in prœlio cervi sunt.

Lions in peace are often deer in war.

In partibus infidelium.

In infidel (*i.e.*, not Roman Catholic) countries.

In perpetuam rei memoriam.

In perpetual memory of the affair.

In perpetuum.

In perpetuity; for ever.

---

* Property left to ecclesiastical bodies in mediæval times was so called, being inalienable.
† A saying generally attributed to St. Augustine, but not to be found in his extant writings.

In pontificalı

In posse.

In præsenti.

In pretio pretium nunc est; dat census honores,
Census amicitias: pauper ubique jacet.
— *Ovid.*

In primoribus habent, ut aiunt, labris
— *Cicero.*

In procinctu.

In propriâ personâ.

In puris naturalibus.

Inquinat gregios adjuncta superbia mores.

In re.

In rerum natura.

In sæcula sæculorum.

Insanire certâ ratione modoque.

Insanus omnis furere credit ceteros.

In scirpo nodum quæris.—*Plautus.*

In se magna ruunt.

Insignia.

In silvam ligna ferre.

Insita hominibus natura violentiæ resistere.—*Tacitus.*

In situ.

In statu pupillari.

In statu quo.

In statu quo ante bellum.

In te, Domine, speravi.

Integer vitæ scelerisque purus
Non eget arcu.—*Horace.*

Integra mens augustissima possessio.

Intemperans adolescentia effetum corpus tradet senectuti.

In tenebris.

Inter alia.

Inter arma leges silent.

Inter duas sellas, decidium.

Interdum et insanire jucundum est.

In pontificals; in episcopal robes.

In a state of possible existence.

At the present time.

Money is now the most prized thing; a good income can buy both lofty rank and friends, while the poor man is everywhere despised.

They have it, to use the common expression, on the tip of their tongue.

(In readiness.) With loins girded.

In one's own person.

In a state of nudity.

The most excellent characters are ruined by the addition of pride.

In the matter (or estate) of.

In the nature of things.

For ages of ages; for ever and ever.

(To be mad with definite reason and measure.) There is method in his madness.

Every madman thinks everybody else mad.

(You are looking for a knot in a bulrush.) A needle in a bundle of hay.

Great things rush against each other.

Distinguishing marks or badges of rank or honour.

(To carry wood to the forest.) To carry coals to Newcastle.

It is by nature implanted in man to resist oppression.

In the situation; in position; at rest.

In the position of a pupil.

In the former position.

In the same state, posture, or position, as before the war.

In Thee, O Lord, have I trusted.

A man of upright life, and pure from guilt, needs no weapon to defend him.

Integrity is the noblest possession.

An intemperate youth will hand down to old age a worn-out body.

In darkness.

Among other things.

In the midst of arms the laws are silent.

Between two stools one falls to the ground.

It is pleasant to play the fool (to relax one's gravity) at times. *Dulce est desipere, &c.*

Interdum lacrimæ pondera vocis habent.—*Ovid*.

(Sometimes tears have the weight of words.) Tears are sometimes more eloquent than words.

Interdum speciosa locis, morataque recte
Fabula nullius veneris, sine pondere et arte,
Valdius oblectat populum, meliusque moratur,
Quam versus inopes rerum, nugæque canoræ.—*Horace*.

When the sentiments and manners please,
And all the characters are wrought with ease,
Your tale, though void of beauty, force, and art,
More strongly shall delight, and warm the heart ;
Than where a lifeless pomp of verse appears,
And with sonorous trifles charms our ears.—*Francis*.

Interdum stultus bene loquitur.

Even a fool sometimes speaks sense.

Interdum vulgus rectum videt, est ubi peccat.—*Horace*

Sometimes the common people see aright ; sometimes they err.

Inter ignes Luna minores.—*Horace*.

(As shines) the moon among the lesser stars.

Interim.

In the meanwhile.

Inter malleum et incudem.

(Between the hammer and the anvil.) Between the devil and the deep sea.

Inter nos.

Between ourselves.

Inter pocula.

Between cups ; over a glass.

Interregnum.

The time between two reigns.

In terrorem.

As a warning.

Inter silvas academi quærere verum.
—*Horace*.

To search for truth in academic groves.*

In toto.

In the whole ; entirely.

In transitu.

In course of transit.

Intra verba peccare.

To offend in words only.

Intus et in cute.

(Within and in the skin.) Inside and out, thoroughly.

I nunc, et versus tecum meditare canoros.

Go now, and practise by thyself melodious verses.

In utrumque paratus.

Prepared for either event.

In vacuo.

In empty space, or in a vacuum.

Invendibili merci oportet ultro emptorem abducere,
Proba merx facile emptorem reperit, tametsi in abstruso sit.—*Plautus*.

To unsaleable wares it is necessary to try to tempt the buyer ; good wares easily meet with a purchaser, although they may be hid in a corner.

Inveniam viam aut faciam.

(If I cannot find a way I will make one.) I will carry my point at all hazards.

Inveni portum, Spes et Fortuna valete ;
Sat me lusistis, ludite nunc alios.

I've reached the harbour, Hope and Fortune, farewell ; you have made me your plaything long enough ; now mock others †

* The Academus, the famous gymnasium and garden near Athens where Plato taught. Hence originated the name of the Academic school of philosophers.
† Lines written at the end of Le Sage's *Gil Blas*.

In verba magistri.

(To swear by) the words of a master.

In veritate triumpho.

I rejoice in truth.

Invictus maneo.

I remain unconquered.

Invident honori meo; ergo invideant labori, innocentiæ, periculis etiam meis; quoniam per hæc illum cepi.
—*Sallust.*

They envy the distinction I have won; let them, therefore, envy my toils, my honesty, and the dangers I have undergone; for these were the methods by which I gained it.

In vino veritas.

(There is truth in wine; truth is told under the influence of wine.) Drunken folk often speak the truth.

Invisa nunquam imperia retinentur diu.
—*Seneca.*

Unpopular governments are never abiding.

Invita Minerva.

(Minerva being unwilling.) Against one's humour, or inclination; without inspiration.

Ipsa quidem virtus pretium sibi.
—*Claudian.*

Virtue is its own reward.

Ipsa scientia potestas est.—*Bacon.*

Knowledge is power.

Ipse dixit.

(He the master himself, said it.) An authoritative assertion; dogmatism.

Ipse semet canit.

(He sings about himself.) He blows his own trumpet.

Ipsissima verba.

The very words.

Ipso facto.

(By the fact or deed itself.) Obvious from the facts of the case.

Ipso jure.

(By the law itself.) By unquestioned right.

Iracundiam qui vincit, hostem superat maximum.

The man who restrains his anger, overcomes his greatest foe.

Iracundus et ingens.

Angry and huge.

Ira furor brevis est.

Anger is brief madness.

Iram qui vincit, hostem superat maximum.

He that overcomes his anger, conquers his greatest enemy.

Iras et verba locant.—*Martial.*

(Their anger and words they let out on hire.) Eloquence is the stock-in-trade of the legal advocate.

Irrevocabile verbum.

(A word that cannot be called back.) The spoken word cannot be recalled.

Irritabis crabrones

(You will irritate the hornets.) You will bring a hornets' nest about your ears.

Is est honos homini pudico, meminisse officium suum.—*Plautus.*

To be mindful of his duty, is the highest honour of an upright man.

Is mihi videtur amplissimus qui suâ virtute in altiorem locum pervenit.
—*Cicero.*

He seems to me the greatest man, who attains a position of eminence by his own merits.

Istuc est sapere, qui, ubicunque opus sit, animum posses flectere.—*Terence.*

That is true wisdom, to know how to alter one's mind when occasion demands it.

Ita lex scripta est.

Such is the law.

Ita me Dii ament, ubi sim nescio.
     —Terence.

Lord love me, if I know where I am.

Ita sit sane.

Granted ; let it be so.

Ite missa est.

(Go, the service is finished.)   The Mass has been celebrated.

Jacta est alea.

The die is cast.

Jam omnibus in ore est, qui semotus sit ab oculis eundem quoque ab animo semotum esse.—*Erasmus.*

(Everyone now declares that the man who is far removed from their sight, is also far removed from their thoughts.) Out of sight, out of mind.

Jamque opus exegi, quod nec Jovis ira, nec ignes,
Nec poterit ferrum, nec edax abolere vetustas. – *Ovid.*

(Now I have finished a work, which neither Jove's anger, nor fire, nor sword, nor devouring time can destroy.*)

Janitor.

A porter ; door-keeper ; gate-keeper.

Januæ mentis.

Gates of the mind ; entrances for (or sources of) knowledge.

Januis clausis.

With closed doors.

Jejunus raro stomachus vulgaria temnit.
     —Horace.

(A hungry stomach seldom scorns plain food.)   Hunger is the best sauce.

Jesus, hominum Salvator (I.H.S.).

Jesus, the Saviour of mankind.

Jucundi acti labores.

The remembrance of difficulties overcome is delightful.

Judex damnatur, cum nocens absolvitur.
     —Publius Syrus.

The judge is condemned when the guilty is acquitted.

Judex non solum quid possit, sed etiam quid deceat ponderare debet.—*Cicero.*

It is the duty of a judge to consider not only what he has the power to do, but, also, what is his duty.

Jugulare mortuos.

(To stab the dead.)   To show fiendish cruelty.

Juncta juvant.

(Things when joined aid each other.) Union is strength.

Juniores ad labores.

Young men for labours ;   the burden is for young shoulders.

Jupiter ex alto perjuria ridet amantum.
     —Ovid.

(Jove, in heaven, laughs at lovers' perjuries.)
At lovers' perjuries they say Jove laughs.
     —Shakespeare.

Jura publica favent privatæ domui.

(The laws respect the private house.) A man's house is his castle.

Jurare et fallere numen.

To swear and to break one's oath.

Jurare in verba magistri.

To swear to the words of a master ; to say ditto to one.

Juravi linguâ, mentem injuratam gero.
     —Cicero

(I have sworn with my tongue, but I have a mind unsworn.) I feel no constraint to perform my oath.†

---

* Compare Horace's *Exegi monumentum* for a similar last word by the poet on his own career.

† A close translation of a line of Euripides, illustrating the casuistry of the Athenian sophists : 'Η γλῶσσ ὀμωμοχ', ἡ δὲ φρὴν ἀνώμοτος.

Jure divino.
By divine law

Jure humano.
By human law.

Jus belli, ut qui vicissent, iis quos vicissent, quemadmodum vellent, imperarent.— *Cæsar.*
War gives this right, that the conquerors may impose any conditions they please upon those who are vanquished.

Jus civile.
Civil law.

Jus et norma loquendi.
The law and rule of speaking; ordinary usage.

Jus gentium.
Law of nations.

Jus summum sæpe summa est malitia.
—*Terence.*
The rigour of the law is often the hardest injustice.

Justitiæ fundamentum est fides.—*Cicero.*
Honour and fidelity are the basis of justice.

Justitiæ partes sunt non violare homines: verecundiæ non offendere.—*Cicero.*
Justice consists in doing no injury to men; decency in giving them no offence.

Justitiæ soror fides.
Faith is the sister of justice.

Justitia regnorum fundamentum.
Justice is the foundation of kingdoms.

Justitia vacat.
There is no justice in it.

Justum et tenacem propositi virum
Non civium ardor prava jubentium,
Non voltus instantis tyranni,
Mente quatit solidâ.—*Horace.*
The man who is just and firm of purpose is not moved by the zeal of his fellow-citizens when they urge him to evil courses, nor does the lowering brow and threats of a despot shake him from his rock-like resolve.*

Juxta fluvium puteum fodit.
(He is digging a well close by a river.) He is carrying coals to Newcastle.

Labitur et labetur in omne volubilis ævum.—*Horace.*
It rolls, and rolls, and will for ever roll.

Labitur occulte fallitque volatilis ætas
Et nihil est annis velocius.—*Ovid.*
(Time is winged and glides from us, though we see and heed it not. Nothing is swifter than the flight of years.)
Old age creeps on us, ere we think it nigh.—*Dryden.*

Laborare est orare.
(To work is to pray.) He preaches best that lives well.

Labor est etiam ipsa voluptas.
—*Manilius.*
(Toil also is real pleasure.)
The labour we delight in physics pain.
—*Shakespeare.*

Labor limæ ac mora.
(The prolonged labour of the file.) The tedious labour of correcting literary work.

Labor omnia vincit.
Labour overcomes all obstacles.

Laborum dulce lenimen.
Sweet solace of toils.

Lacrimæque decoræ
Gratior et pulchro veniens in corpore virtus.— *Virgil.*
Becoming sorrows and a virtuous mind More lovely in a beauteous form enshrined.

* These lines, so often quoted, may be compared with Tennyson's "O, well for him whose will is strong," *et seq.*

Lacrima Christi — Tear of Christ.*

Lacuna. — A gap; deficiency.

Lapis qui volvitur algam non generat. — (A rolling stone finds no sea-weed.) A rolling stone gathers no moss.

Lapsus calami. — A slip of the pen.

Lapsus linguæ. — A slip of the tongue.

Lares et penates. — Household gods; the guardians of the hearth and home.

Largitio fundum non habet. — Charity has a bottomless purse.

Lateat scintillula forsan. — A small spark may perchance lurk unseen.†

Laterem lavas. — (You are washing a brick.) Washing an unbaked brick; making bad worse.

Latet anguis in herba. — (There is a snake hidden in the grass.) A hidden danger.

Latius regnes avidum domando Spiritum, quam si Libyam remotis Gadibus jungas, et uterque Pœnus Serviat uni.—*Horace.* — You will have a more extensive sway by ruling a greedy disposition, than if you were to unite Africa to Cadiz, and both Carthages (*i.e.*, Spain and Africa) were your slaves.

Latrante uno, latrat statim et alter canis. — (When one dog barks, another at once barks too.) One barking dog sets all the street a-barking.

Laudari a viro laudato. — To be praised by a man who is himself praised.

Laudato ingentia rura, Exiguum colito.—*Virgil.* — (Commend large estates, but cultivate a small one.) You will both avoid giving offence to others, and will insure your own happiness and be free from all anxiety.

Laudator temporis acti. — A praiser, eulogiser, of times gone by.

Laus Deo. — Praise be to God.

Leges juraque servamus. — We keep the statutes and laws; we maintain our laws and rights.

Legimus, ne legantur. — We (reviewers, censors) read books to prevent their being read by others.

Legis constructio non facit injuriam. — (The construction of the law does no wrong.) The law shall not be interpreted so as to cause wrong.

Leone fortior fides. — Faith is stronger than a lion.

Leonem larvâ terres. — (You are for frightening a lion with a mask.) You waste your pains.

Leonina societas. — (A lion's partnership.) A partnership in which one partner takes the lion's share, *i.e.*, the whole, of the profits.

Leve fit, quod bene fertur, onus.—*Ovid.* — A load that is cheerfully borne becomes light.

* This is the name given to a well-known brand of Italian wine, and usually appears in this form: *Lacrima Cristi.*
† The motto of the Royal Humane Society.

Levis est dolor qui capere consilium potest.

It is light grief that can take counsel.

Levitatis est inanem aucupari rumorem.
—*Cicero.*

It is the sign of a weak character to catch at every baseless rumour.

Levius fit patientiâ quidquid corrigere est nefas.—*Horace.*

(Whatever cannot be amended is made easier by patience.) What can't be cured must be endured.

Lex loci.

The law of the place.

Lex mercatoria.

Commercial law.

Lex non scripta.

The unwritten law ; the common law of the country.

Lex scripta.

Statute or written law.

Lex talionis.

The law of retaliation ; an eye for an eye, a tooth for a tooth.

Liber et ingenuus sum natus utroque parente,
Semper ero liber credo, Deo juvante.
—*Grimwald, Duke of Benevento.*

I am free born, as both my parents were, and, by God's help, a freeman I will remain to the end of my life.

Libertas est potestas faciendi id quod jure liceat.

Liberty is the power of doing that which is permitted by law.

Libertas et natale solum.

Liberty and my native land.

Libertas, quæ sera, tamen respexit inertem.—*Virgil.*

Liberty which, though late, at last regarded my helplessness.

Liberum arbitrium.

Free will, or choice.

Licet superbus ambules pecuniâ,
Fortuna non mutat genus.—*Horace.*

Although you walk in all the pride of wealth, your newly found fortune does not change your character.

Ligonem ligonem vocat.

He calls a spade a spade.

Limæ labor.

(The labour of the file.) Polishing literary compositions.

Linguæ verbera.

(The lashings of the tongue.) A sharp tongue is worse than a sharp sword.

Linguam compescere, virtus non minima est.

(To restrain the tongue is not the least of virtues.) Speech is silver, silence is golden.

Linquenda tellus, et domus, et placens
Uxor; neque harum, quas colis, arborum
Te, præter invisas cupressos,
Ullâ brevem dominum sequetur.
—*Horace.*

Thou must leave thy lands, house, and the wife of thy bosom ; nor shall any of those trees follow thee, their short-lived master, except the hated cypresses.*

Lis litem generat.

(Strife begets strife.) One quarrel breeds another.

Lis sub judice.

A case not yet decided.

Lite pendente.

During the trial.

Literæ humaniores.

(Learning of a rather polite nature, of a more humane description.) Greek and Latin classics.

Litera scripta manet, verbum imbelle perit.

The written letter remains, the weak word perishes.

* The lot of the rich man, whom death deprives of all his possessions save the cypress trees, which, being symbolical of death, grew over the graves of the dead, even as the yew tree is to be found in almost every English churchyard.

F

Literati.
Literatim.
Litus ama, altum alii teneant.

Loco citato (*loc. cit.*).
Locum tenens.

Locus in quo.

Locus pœnitentiæ.
Locus sigilli (L.S.).
Locus standi.

Longissimus dies cito conditur.
—*Pliny the Younger.*
Longo sed proximus intervallo.

Longum iter est per præcepta, breve et efficax per exempla.

Lucernam olere.

Lucidus ordo.
Lucri bonus est odor ex re quâlibet.
—*Juvenal.*
Lucrum malum æquale dispendio.

Lucus a non lucendo.

Ludere cum sacris.
Lumenque juventæ purpureum.

Lumina civitatis.
Lupum auribus tenere.
Lupus in fabulâ.

Lupus pilum mutat, non mentem.

Lustrum.
Lusus animo debent aliquando dari
Ad cogitandum melior ut redeat sibi.
—*Phædrus.*
Lusus naturæ.
Lutum nisi tundatur, non fit urceus.

Literary men.
Literally ; letter for letter.
(Love thou the shore, let others possess the deep.) Ambition plagues her proselytes.
At the place or passage quoted.
(One holding the place of another.) A deputy.
(The place in which.) The place where a passage, or incident, occurs.
Place (opportunity) for repentance.
The place of the seal.
A place for standing ; right to appear before a court.
The longest day quickly comes to an end.
(The next, but after a long interval.) A bad second.
(Tedious is the way by precepts, short and effectual by examples.) Example is better than precept.
(To smell of the lamp.) To show signs of laborious composition.
A clear arrangement.
Cash, obtained from any source, smells sweet.
(An evil gain is equal to a loss.) Ill-gotten goods seldom prosper.
(A grove is so called because it excludes the light.) A misnomer ; a ridiculous derivation.*
To trifle with sacred things.
(The purple light of youth.)
The bloom of young desire, and purple light of love.—*Gray.*
Lights of the state ; the leading citizens.
To hold a wolf by the ears.
(The wolf in the fable.) Long looked for, come at last.
The wolf changes his coat, not his disposition.
A space of five years.
The mind ought sometimes to be diverted, that it may return the better to thinking.
A freak of nature.
(Unless the clay be well pounded, no pitcher can be made.)
Industry is fortune's right hand.

---

* The words are commonly used of any absurd derivation or *non sequitur.*

Luxuriant animi rebus plerumque secundis,
Nec facile est æquâ commoda mente pati.—*Ovid*.

The mind grows wanton in prosperity, for it is hard to endure good fortune with calmness.

Luxuria sævior armis.

Luxury more terrible in its ravages than war.

Macte virtute.

(Be strong in virtue.)　Continue in the good course you have taken.

Magis mutus quam piscis.

(More dumb than a fish.)　Silent as the grave.

Magna civitas, magna solitudo.

A great city is a great desert.*

Magna est veritas et prævalebit.

Truth is great and it will prevail.

Magnas componere lites.

To settle great quarrels.

Magna servitus est magna fortuna.
　　　　　　　　—*Seneca*.

A great fortune is a great slavery.

Magnas inter opes inops.

Poor in the midst of great wealth.

Magni nominis umbra.

The shadow of a great name ; the unworthy descendant of a great family.

Magnis tamen excidit ausis.

It was, however, at great undertakings that he failed.

Magno conatu magnas nugas agere.

(Great efforts on great trifles.)　Much cry and little wool.

Magnos homines virtute metimur, non fortunâ.—*Nepos*.

Great men we estimate by their virtue (or valour), not by their success.

Magnum bonum.

A great good.

Magnum est vectigal parcimonia.
　　　　　　　— *Cicero*.

Economy is a great revenue.

Magnum opus.

A great work.

Major e longinquo reverentia.

(Distance increases respect.)　No man is a hero to his valet.

Major famæ sitis est quam virtutis.

The thirst for fame is greater than for virtue.

Malâ fide.

In bad faith.

Mala gallina, malum ovum.

(Bad hen, bad egg.)　Like father, like son.

Mala ultro adsunt.

(Misfortunes come unsought.)　Sorrow comes unsent for.

Male imperando summum imperium amittitur.— *Publius Syrus*.

The greatest empire may be lost by bad government.

Male parta male dilabuntur.

(Ill-got, ill-spent.)　Ill-gotten goods seldom prosper.

Malesuada fames.— *Virgil*.

Hunger that persuades to evil.

Mali exempli.

Of a bad example.

Malo mori quam fœdari.

(I had rather die than be disgraced.)　Death before dishonour.

---

* Originally said of Megalopolis, *i.e.*, the Great City, which Epaminondas, the Theban statesman, founded to be a constant menace to the Spartan power in the south of Greece. The scheme, however, proved a *fiasco*. The words are now used to depict the sense of loneliness that a great city inspires in a friendless man. They are a translation of the line from a Greek comedy : 'Ερημία μεγαλη 'στὶν ἡ Μεγάλη πόλις,—" the Great City is a great wilderness."

Malo nodo malus quærendus cuneus.

For a hard knot a hard tool must be sought.

Malum bene conditum ne moveris.

(Do not disturb an evil that has been fairly buried.) Let sleeping dogs lie.

Malum grave remedium anceps exigit.

Bad diseases need strong remedies.

Malum in se.

(An evil in itself.) A crime against nature.

Malum prohibitum.

A prohibited evil or wrong; a legal, though not, necessarily, a moral crime.

Malum vas non frangitur.

(A worthless vessel does not get broken.) A bad penny is never lost.

Mandamus.

(We command.) A writ from a superior court directing some action on the part of an inferior court.

Manebant vestigia morientis libertatis.

There remained the traces of dying liberty.

Manes.

The shades; ghost of a dead person.

Manet altâ mente repostum.

It (the grievance) remains deeply seated in the mind.

Mania a potu.

Madness caused by drunkenness.

Manibus pedibusque.

With hands and feet; with all one's might.

Manu forti.

With a strong hand.

Manus hæc inimica tyrannis.

This hand is hostile to tyrants.

Manus justa nardus.

The just hand is as precious ointment.

Manus manum fricat et manus manum lavat.

(Hand rubs hand, and hand washes hand.) All men live by another's aid.

Mare clausum.

A sea closed to commerce.

Mare, ignis, et mulier sunt tria mala.

The sea, fire, and woman are three evils.

Mare liberum.

An open sea; open to all.

Mater artium necessitas.

(Necessity is the mother of arts.) Necessity is the mother of invention.

Materia medica.

Substances used in the healing art.

Materiam superabat opus.

The workmanship was better than the materials.

Matre pulchrâ filia pulchrior.

A daughter more lovely than her lovely mother.

Mature fias senex si diu senex esse velis.— *Cicero.*

(Become old betimes if you wish to be old for many years.) Old young, and old long. Adopt the prudent habits of age when you are young if you wish to live long.

Maxima debetur puero reverentia. —*Juvenal.*

The greatest reverence is due to a child.

Maxima illecebra est peccandi impunitatis spes.—*Cicero.*

The greatest incitement to wrongdoing is the hope of impunity.

Maxima pars eorum quæ scimus, est minima pars eorum quæ nescimus.

The most that anyone knows bears but a small proportion to the amount that is to be known.

Maximas virtutes jacere omnes necesse est voluptate dominante.—*Cicero*.

Where pleasure prevails, all the greatest virtues will lose their power.

Maximum remedium iræ mora est.
　　　　　　　　　—*Seneca*.

The best remedy for anger is a little time for thought.

Maximus in minimis.

Very great in trifling things.

Mea maxima culpa.

(Through my very great fault.) The guilt is mine.

Meâ virtute me involvo.—*Horace*.

(I wrap myself up in my virtue.) A good conscience consoles a man in his hours of failure.

Mecum sentit.

He is of my opinion.

Mediocria firma.

Moderation is safe. *Aurea mediocritas*.

　　　　　Mediocribus esse poetis
Non homines, non Di, non concessere columnæ. *Horace*.

(Mediocrity is not permitted in poets, either by the gods, or by men, or by the pillars supporting the booksellers' shops.) No one reads such compositions, and there is no sale for them.

Medio de fonte leporum
Surgit amari aliquid quod in ipsis floribus angat.—*Lucretius*.

(From the midst of the fountain of delight something bitter arises to vex us even amid the flowers themselves.)
Full from the fount of joy's delicious springs
Some bitter o'er the flowers its bubbling venom flings.—*Byron*.

Medio tutissimus ibis.

A middle course will be safest.

Me duce, tutus eris.

Under my guidance you will be safe.

Me judice.

In my opinion.

Meliora sunt ea, quæ naturâ, quam illa, quæ arte perfecta sunt.—*Cicero*.

The works of nature are superior to those which are produced by art.

Meliores priores.

The better, the first; the best men, the first place.

Melius est modo purgare peccata, et vitia resecare, quam in futurum purganda reservare.—*Thomas à Kempis*.

It is better to cleanse ourselves of our sins now, and to give up our vices, than to reserve them for cleansing at some future time.

Mellitum venenum, blanda oratio.

(A flattering speech is honied poison.) A honey tongue, a heart of gall.

Memento mori.

Remember death.

Meminerunt omnia amantes.

Lovers recollect all things; have long memories.

Memorabilia.

(Things worthy of being remembered.) Reminiscences.

Memoria est thesaurus omnium rerum et custos.—*Cicero*.

Memory is the treasury and guardian of all things.

Memoria technica.

An artificial memory; aids to memory.

Memoriter.

By memory.

Mendico ne parentes quidem amici sunt.

(To a beggar not even his own parents are friendly.) Poverty breeds strife.

Mens æqua rebus in arduis.

An even mind in difficulties.

Mens agitat molem.

Mind moves the mass; mind moves matter.

Mensa secunda.
The second course; dessert.

Mens conscia recti.
A mind conscious of rectitude.

Mens divinior.
A soul of diviner cast; an inspired soul.

Mense malum Maio nubere vulgus ait. —*Ovid.*
To marry in May is unlucky, say the common folk.

Mens invicta manet.
The mind remains unconquered.

Mens præscia futuri.
A foreseeing mind.

Mens regnum bona possidet.—*Seneca.*
An honest heart is a kingdom in itself.

Mens sana in corpore sano.
A sound mind in a sound body.

Mens sibi conscia recti.
A mind conscious of uprightness.

Mentis gratissimus error.
A most pleasing hallucination; a sweet reverie.

Meo periculo.
At my own risk.

Mero motu.
Of his own motion, or free will.

Merses profundo, pulchrior evenit. —*Horace.*
Though you plunge it in the deep, it comes forth more splendid still.

Merum sal.
(Pure salt.) Genuine Attic wit.

Metiri se quemque suo modulo ac pede verum est.—*Horace.*
(It is just that every man should measure himself according to his own measure or standard.) A man ought to know his own limitations.

Meum et tuum.
Mine and thine.

Mihi autem videtur acerba et immatura mors eorum, qui immortale aliquid parant. Nam qui voluptatibus dediti quasi in diem vivunt, vivendi causas cottidie finiunt; qui vero posteros cogitant, et memoriam sui operibus extendunt, his nulla mors non repentina est, ut quæ semper inchoatum aliquid abrumpat. —*Pliny the Younger.*
It seems to me that death is always untimely and premature when it comes to those men who are engaged on some immortal work. For those who live from day to day entirely given over to pleasure, terminate the purpose of their life with the close of each day: but those who think of posterity, and strive to win an undying fame by good works, to such death is always premature, for it cuts them off in the midst of some task that they have undertaken.

Mihi cura futuri.
My care is for the future.

Militavi non sine gloriâ.
I served with some distinction.

Minor est quam servus dominus qui servos timet.
A master that fears his servants is inferior to a servant.

Minus aptus acutis Naribus horum hominum.—*Horace.*
Too weak to bear the sneers of such men as these.

Minutiæ.
The smallest details.

Mirabile dictu.
Wonderful to be told.

Mirabile visu.
Wonderful to behold.

Misce stultitiam consiliis brevem. —*Horace.*
Mingle a little folly with your wisdom.

Miserabile vulgus.
A wretched crew.

Miserere nostri.
Have compassion on us.

Misericordia Domini inter pontem et fontem.—*St. Augustine.*
(God's mercy may be found between bridge and stream.) True repentance finds mercy even at the eleventh hour.

Miseris succurrere disco.

I learn to succour the distressed.

Mittimus.

(We send.) Warrant of commitment to prison.

Mobilitate viget, viresque acquirit eundo.
　　　　　　　　—*Virgil.*

It lives by moving, and gains strength as it goes.*

Moderata durant.

(Moderate things endure.) Nothing in excess.

Modica voluptas laxat animos et temperat.—*Seneca.*

Pleasure, taken in moderation, calms and relieves the anxious mind.

Modo et formâ.

In manner and form.

Modo me Thebis, modo ponit Athenis.—*Horace.*

He now places me at Thebes, now at Athens.†

Modus operandi.

Manner of working.

Modus vivendi.

(A method of living.) A compromise between two or more disputants to promote harmony.

Mole ruit suâ.

It is crushed by its own weight.

Molestum est ferre invidiam, sed multo molestius nihil habere invidendum.

(It is hard to endure envy, but much harder to have nothing worth envying.) Better be envied than pitied.

Mollia tempora fandi.

The favourable occasions for speaking.

Mons cum monte non miscebitur.

(Mountain will not mingle with mountain.) Two of a trade seldom agree.

Monstrum, horrendum, informe, ingens cui lumen ademptum.—*Virgil.*

A monster, horrible, unshapely, gigantic, and eyeless.

Monstrum, nullâ virtute redemptum a vitiis.—*Juvenal.*

A monster whose vices were not redeemed by a single virtue.

Monumentum ære perennius.

(A monument more enduring than bronze.)

Mora sæpe malorum
Causa fuit.—*Manilius.*

(Delay was ever the cause of troubles.) Tarrying hath oft wrought scathe.

More majorum.

After the manner of our ancestors.

Mores hominum multorum vidit et urbes.

(He saw the manners and the cities of many peoples.) Far-travelled. Much-experienced.

More Socratico.

After the manner of Socrates; in a dialectical manner.

More solito.

As usual; in the accustomed manner.

More suo.

After his own manner.

"Moriemur inultæ,
Sed moriamur," ait.—*Virgil.*

"None will avenge my death, still let me die," she cried.‡

Mors janua vitæ.

Death is the gate of life.

Mors omnibus communis.

Death is common to all.

Mors potius maculâ.

Death rather than disgrace.

Mors ultima linea rerum est.—*Horace.*

Death is the utmost boundary of wealth and power.

* See *Fama malum.*
† Refers to a dramatist who can make calls upon the imaginations of his audience so artistically that the demand is not perceived.
‡ The words of Dido, when she resolves to commit suicide on hearing that Æneas has sailed for Italy.

Mortui non mordent. (Buried men bite not.) Dead men tell no tales.

Mortuo leoni et lepores insultant. (Even hares insult a dead lion.) Do not kick a man when he is down.

Mortuum flagellas. (You are beating a dead man.) You cannot reform a man when he is dead.

Mos pro lege. Custom (is accepted) for law.

Motu proprio. Of his own accord.

Mucrone suo se jugulat. (He kills himself with his own sword.) He makes a rod for his own back.

Mugitus labyrinthi. (The roaring of the labyrinth.) The vapouring of an inferior poet.*

Mulier cupido quod dicit amanti,
In vento et rapidâ scribere oportet
aquâ.—*Catullus*.
The vows that woman makes to her fond lover, ought to be written on the wind and swiftly-flowing stream.

Multa cadunt inter calicem supremaque labra. There's many a slip 'twixt cup and lip.

Multa docet fames. Hunger teaches many lessons.

Multa gemens. With many a groan.

Multa petentibus multa desunt. (Those who ask much, lack much.) Much would have more.

Multa tuli fecique. Much have I suffered and done.

Multis ille bonis flebilis occidit.
—*Horace*.
He died bewailed by many good men.

Multis terribilis, caveto multos.
—*Ausonius*.
If many fear you, beware of many.

Multitudo medicorum certa mors est ægrotantium. (Too many doctors mean certain death to those who are sick.) Too many cooks spoil the broth.

Multorum manibus grande levatur opus. Many hands make labour light.

Multos in summa pericula misit
Venturi timor ipse mali.—*Lucan*.
The very apprehension of an impending evil has placed many in the greatest peril.

Multum facit qui multum diligit.
—*Thomas à Kempis*.
Who loveth much, doeth much.

Multum in parvo. Much in little; a great deal in a small compass.

Mundus vult decipi, et decipiatur. The world wishes to be deceived, and let it be deceived.

Murus æneus conscientia sana. A sound conscience is a wall of brass.

Mutare vel timere sperno. I scorn to change or to fear.

Mutatis mutandis. The necessary changes being made.

Mutato nomine. Under a changed name.

Mutato nomine de te fabula narratur. Change the name, and the story applies to yourself.

Mutum est pictura poema.—*Horace*. A picture is a poem without words.

* The Labyrinth of Crete and the tale of the Minotaur were the hackneyed topics of the third-rate poets of Rome.

Nam ego illum periisse duco, cui quidem periit pudor.—*Plautus.*

I think that man is lost indeed, who has lost the sense of shame.

Nam historia debet egredi veritatem.
—*Pliny the Younger.*

History ought not to exceed the bounds of truth.

Namque inscitia est
Adversum stimulum calces.—*Terence.*

For it is stupidity to kick against the pricks.

Nam sera nunquam est ad bonos mores via.—*Seneca.*

(It is never too late to choose the path of virtue.) It is never too late to mend.

Nam tua res agitur paries dum proximus ardet.

For your interests are concerned when your neighbour's house is on fire.

Narratur et prisci Catonis
Sæpe mero caluisse virtus.—*Horace.*

It is said that even stern old Cato warmed himself with wine.

Nascentes morimur, finisque ab origine pendet.—*Manilius.*

(From the moment of our birth we begin to die, and the end of our life is closely allied to the beginning of it.) Each moment of existence is a step towards the grave.

Natale solum.

Natal soil.

Natio comœda est.—*Juvenal.*

(It is a nation of actors.) A description of the decadent Greeks.

Natura beatis
Omnibus esse dedit, si quis cognoverit uti.—*Claudian.*

Nature gives all men opportunities to be happy, if they know how to use them.

Naturæ debitum reddiderunt.
—*Cornelius Nepos.*

They paid the debt of nature.

Natura enim in suis operationibus non facit saltum.—*J. Tissot.*

Nature does not proceed by leaps in its working.

Naturalia non sunt turpia.

Natural things are never shameful.

Naturam expelles furcâ, tamen usque recurret.—*Horace.*

(You may drive out nature with a fork, yet it will still come back.) What is bred in the bone will come out in the flesh.

Natus ad gloriam.

Born to glory.

Ne Æsopum quidem trivit.

(He has not so much as thumbed Æsop.) He does not know B from a bull's foot.*

Nebulæ.

Mists ; cloudlets.

Nec amor, nec tussis celatur.

Love and a cough cannot be hidden.

Nec Deus intersit, nisi dignus vindice nodus.—*Horace.*

(Let not a god interfere, unless the difficulty demands his aid.) Do not introduce a divine character into the play unless the necessity really demands it. Do not use strong remedies for trifles.†

Ne cede malis.

Yield not to misfortunes.

Necesse est facere sumptum, qui quærit lucrum.—*Plautus.*

(You must spend money if you wish to gain it.) Nothing venture, nothing have.

---

* *Æsop's Fables* were used as an elementary text-book for the young Roman.
† Compare *Deus ex machinâ.*

Necesse est ut multos timeat, quem multi timent.—*Seneca.*

He whom many fear, must fear many.

Necessitas non habet legem.

Necessity has no law.

Nec forma æternum, aut cuiquam est fortuna perennis.

Beauty fades and fortune abides not; sooner or later death claims its own.

Longius, aut propius, mors sua quemque manet.—*Propertius.*

Nec imbellem feroces
Progenerant aquilæ columbam.
                                    —*Horace.*

Fierce eagles do not beget the timid dove.

Nec lusisse pudet, sed non incidere ludum.—*Horace.*

Not in committing, but in prolonging acts of folly is the shame.

Nec mora, nec requies.

No rest or repose.

Nec pluribus impar.

(Not unequal to many.) A match for the whole world.*

Nec prece nec pretio.

Neither by entreaty nor by bribe.

Nec quærere nec spernere honorem.

Neither to seek nor to despise honour.

Nec satis est pulchra esse poemata, dulcia sunto.—*Horace.*

'Tis not enough a poem's finely writ; It must affect and captivate the soul.

Nec scire fas est omnia.

It is not permitted to know all things.

Nec semper feriet quodcunque minabitur arcus.

(The arrow will not always hit that which it is aimed at.) The best laid schemes o' mice and men gang aft agley.

Nec tecum possum vivere, nec sine te.

I cannot live with you, nor without you.

Nec temere nec timide.

Neither rashly nor timorously.

Nec timeo, nec sperno.

I neither fear nor despise.

Ne cuivis dextram injeceris.

(Don't give your right hand to every one.) Trust not a new friend nor an old enemy.

Nec vixit male, qui natus moriensque fefellit.—*Horace.*

He has not lived ill who has lived and died unnoticed.

Ne depugnes in alieno negotio.

(Don't fight in another's affair.) Let every one settle their own quarrels.

Ne exeat.

Let him not depart.

Nefas nocere vel malo fratri puta.
                                    —*Seneca.*

Consider it wrong to injure even a bad brother.

Nefasti dies.

(Unlucky days.) Days on which the courts do not sit.

Ne fronti crede.

Do not trust to appearance.

Ne glorieris de die crastino, quia nescis quid pariturus sit dies.

Boast not thyself of to-morrow, for thou knowest not what a day may bring forth.

Ne Jupiter quidem omnibus placet.

(Not Jupiter himself can please everybody.) Grumblers are never satisfied.

Nemine contradicente (*nem. con.*).

Without opposition; no one contradicting.

Nemine dissentiente (*nem. diss.*).

No one disagreeing.

Nemo bene imperat nisi qui paruerit imperio.

No man is a successful commander, who has not first learned to obey.

* The motto of Louis XIV. of France.

Nemo fit fato nocens.—*Seneca*.

Fate never drives a man to commit a crime.

Nemo liber est, qui corpori servit.
—*Seneca*.

No one who is a slave to his body, is truly free.

Nemo malus felix.

(No bad man is happy.) There is no peace unto the wicked.

Nemo me impune lacesset.

No one will attack me with impunity.

Nemo mortalium omnibus horis sapit.
—*Pliny*.

No mortal is wise at all times.

Nemo potest nudo vestimenta detrahere.

(No man can strip a naked man of his garment.) Blood cannot be got out of a stone.

Nemo repente fuit turpissimus.
—*Juvenal*.

No man ever became a villain all at once.

Nemo sine vitiis nascitur.

(Nobody is born without sins.) Every man has his faults.

Nemo solus satis sapit.—*Plautus*.

(Nobody is wise by himself.) Two heads are better than one. In a multitude of counsellors is safety.

Nemo tam divos habuit faventes,
Crastinum ut possit sibi polliceri.
—*Seneca*.

Nobody has ever found the gods so favourably disposed to him that he can be sure of another day.

Nemo vir magnus sine aliquo afflatu divino unquam fuit.—*Cicero*.

No man was ever great without some degree of inspiration.

Ne nimium.

Do nothing in excess.

Ne obliviscaris.

Do not forget.

Ne pennas nido majores extende.

(Don't spread your wings beyond your nest.) A proud heart and a beggar's purse will not agree.

Ne plus supra.

Nothing above; the highest type; the chief example.

Ne plus ultra.

Nothing beyond; the greatest extent.

Ne prius antidotum quam venenum.

(Don't take the antidote before the poison.) He that excuses himself, accuses himself.

Ne pueri, ne tanta animis assuescite bella:
Neu patriæ validas in viscera vertite vires.—*Virgil*.

This thirst of kindred blood, my sons, detest,
Nor turn your force against your country's breast.—*Dryden*.

Ne puero gladium.

Do not put a sword in a boy's hand.

Neque mel, neque apes.

(No bees, no honey.) No rose without a thorn.

Neque semper arcum tendit Apollo.

(Nor does Apollo always bend his bow.) Due relaxation is necessary.

Nequicquam sapit, qui sibi non sapit.

To no purpose is he wise who is not wise to his own benefit.

Ne quid detrimenti respublica capiat.

That the state suffer no harm.*

Ne quid nimis.

Go not too far.

---

* The *decretum ultimum* passed by the Roman senate in times of national peril, which gave the chief magistrates, the consuls, full powers to use any means to save the commonwealth. Cicero had these powers given him to defeat the conspiracy of Catiline.

Nescia mens hominum fati sortisque futuræ.—*Virgil*.

(The mind of man is ignorant of fate and future destiny.) We know not what a day may bring forth.

Nescio quomodo inhæret in mentibus quasi seculorum quoddam augurium futurorum ; idque in maximis ingeniis altissimisque animis et existit maxime et apparet facillime. — *Cicero*.

There is, I know not how, in the mind a certain presage, as it were, of a future existence ; this has the deepest root, and is most discoverable in the greatest geniuses and most exalted souls.

Nescis, mi fili quantulâ sapientiâ gubernatur mundus !

Thou knowest not, my son, with how little wisdom the world is governed !

Nescit plebs jejuna timere.

(A starving populace knows no fear.) Hungry flies bite sore.

Nescit vox missa reverti.

The spoken word cannot be recalled.

Ne scuticâ dignum horribili sectere flagello.—*Horace*.

(Do not punish with a scourge a fault which only merits a whip.) Fit the punishment to the crime.*

Ne sus Minervam.

(Let not a pig presume to teach Minerva, the Goddess of Wisdom.) Teach not thy granny to suck eggs.

Ne sutor ultra crepidam.

(Let the shoemaker stick to his last.) Let every one mind his own business.†

Ne verba pro farinâ.

(Don't give me words for meal.) Soft words butter no parsnips.

Nictat oculis suis.

He winks with his eyes.

Nihil ad me attinet.

It is nothing to me.

Nihil ad rem.

Nothing to the point.

Nihil æque gratum est adeptis, quam concupiscentibus.
        —*Pliny the Younger*.

Nothing is so pleasing to you when you have obtained it, as it was when you merely desired it.

Nihil agas quod non prosit.

Do nothing but what may turn to good account.

Nihil amas, cum ingratum amas.
        —*Plautus*.

Love is nothing when unrequited.

Nihil amori injurium est.—*Plautus*.

There is no wrong that love will not forgive.

Nihil debet.

(He owes nothing.) A plea denying a debt.

Nihil dictum quod non prius dictum.

There is no saying which has not been uttered before.

Nihil eripit fortuna nisi quod et dedit.

Fortune takes from us nothing but what she has given us.

Nihil est ab omni parte beatum.
        —*Horace*.

There is no situation (in life) that is in every respect happy.

Nihil est autem tam volucre quam maledictum ; nihil facilius emittitur ; nihil citius excipitur, nihil latius dissipatur.—*Cicero*.

Nothing flies so fast as calumny ; nothing is easier to utter ; nothing more readily listened to, and nothing spreads more widely.

---

* The *scutica* was merely a strap with which schoolboys were beaten. The *flagellum* was like the knout, capable of killing the man who had to submit to it.
† The saying of Apelles, the great painter of the fourth century B.C., to the cobbler who criticised the appearance of some shoes in a picture, and then proceeded to pass his judgment on the painting generally.

Nihil est toto quod perstet in orbe.
Cuncta fluunt, omnisque vagans, formatur imago,
Ipsa quoque assiduo labuntur tempora motu,
Non secus ac flumen.—*Ovid*.

There is nothing in the whole world which abides. All things are in a state of ebb and flow, and every shadow passes away. Even time itself, like a river, is constantly gliding away.
Time rolls his ceaseless course.—*Scott*.

Nihil homini amico est opportuno amicius. —*Plautus*

(Nothing is more welcome to a man than a friend in need.) A friend in need is a friend indeed.

Nihil largiundo gloriam adeptus est.
—*Sallust*.

By bestowing nothing he acquired glory.

Nihil peccat, nisi quod nihil peccat.
—*Pliny the Younger*.

He has no faults, unless to be faultless is considered one.

Nihil quod tetigit non ornavit.

He touched nothing which he did not adorn.

Nihil scire est vita jucundissima.

(To know nothing at all is the happiest life.) Children and fools have merry lives.

Nihil sub sole novi.

Nothing new under the sun.

Nil actum reputans, dum quid superesset agendum.—*Lucan*.

(Thinking that nothing was done while anything remained to be done.) Leaving no stone unturned.

Nil admirari.

To wonder at nothing.

Nil conscire sibi nullâ pallescere culpa.

To be conscious of wrong, to turn pale at no accusation.

Nil consuetudine majus.—*Ovid*.

Nothing is stronger than habit.

Nil dicit.

(He says nothing.) The defendant has no defence.

Nil ego contulerim jucundo sanus amico.—*Horace*.

The greatest blessing is a pleasant friend.

Nil falsi audeat, nil veri non audeat dicere.—*Cicero*.

Let him (the historian) not dare to state anything that is false, or to refrain from stating anything that is true.

Nil fuit unquam
Tam dispar sibi.—*Horace*.

(Nothing was ever so unlike itself.) Made up of naught but inconsistencies.

Nil habet infelix paupertas durius in se,
Quam quod ridiculos homines facit.
—*Horace*.

The greatest disadvantage that poverty possesses is this, that it makes men to be despised.

Nil homine terra pejus ingrato creat.
—*Ausonius*.

(The earth produces nothing viler than an ungrateful man.)
Blow, blow, thou winter wind;
Thou art not so unkind
As man's ingratitude.
—*Shakespeare*.

Nil similius insano quam ebrius.

Nothing is more like a madman than a drunken man.

Nil sine Deo.

Nothing without God.

Nil sine magno.
Vita labore dedit mortalibus.—*Horace*.

(Life has bestowed nothing on man without great labour.) The greatest genius does not succeed without hard work.

Nil tam difficile est, quin quærendo investigari possit.—*Terence.*

Nothing is so difficult that it cannot be accomplished by diligence.

Nimia familiaritas parit contemptum.

Too much familiarity breeds contempt.

Nimium ne crede colori

(Trust not too much to appearances.) A blush may cover deceit.

Nimium premendo litus.

By hugging the shore too closely; keeping out of danger.

Nisi Dominus, frustra.

Unless the Lord is with us, our efforts are vain.*

Nisi prius.

(Unless before.) A writ by which the sheriff is to bring up a jury on a certain day "*unless before*" that day the judges go into the counties to hold assizes.

Nitimur in vetitum semper, cupimusque negata.—*Ovid.*

We always strive after what is forbidden, and desire the things refused us.

Nitor in adversum.

I strive against opposition.

Nobilitas sola est atque unica virtus.
—*Juvenal.*

(Virtue is the only true nobility.)
  Howe'er it be, it seems to me
  'Tis only noble to be good.
            —*Tennyson.*

Nocet differre paratis.

(It is prejudicial to those that are ready, to delay.) Strike while the iron is hot.

Nocturnâ versate manu, versate diurnâ.

Give your days and nights to the study of these authors.

Nolens volens.

Whether he will or not.

Noli me tangere.

Do not touch me.

Nolle prosequi.

To be unwilling to prosecute; stoppage of a suit by the plaintiff or by the Crown.

Nolo episcopari.

I do not wish to be made a bishop.†

Nolumus leges Angliæ mutari.

We are unwilling that the laws of England be changed.

Nomina honesta prætenduntur vitiis.
—*Tacitus.*

Specious names are lent to cover vices.

Nominis umbra.

The shadow of a name.

Non aliter quam qui adverso vix flumine lembum
Remigiis subigit : si brachia forte remisit,
Atque illum in præceps prono rapit alveus amni.—*Virgil.*

So the boat's brawny crew the current stem,
And, slow advancing, struggle with the stream :
But if they slack their hands, or cease to strive,
Then down the flood with headlong haste they drive.—*Dryden.*

Non aliter vives in solitudine, aliter in foro.—*Quintilian.*

Do not live one way in private, and another in public.

---

* The motto of the city of Edinburgh. Some unconscious humourist is said to have rendered it, "You can do nothing here unless you are a Lord."
† The expression has become a proverbial one to indicate mock modesty.

Non amo te, Sabidi, nec possum dicere quare ;
Hoc tantum possum dicere ; non amo te.
—*Martial.*

(I do not love you, Sabidius, but I can't say why ; this only can I say, I do not love you.)
    I do not love thee, Dr. Fell,
    The reason why I cannot tell ;
    But this I'm sure I know full well,
    I do not love thee, Dr. Fell.*

Non compos mentis.

Not of sound mind.

Non constat.

(It is not evident, agreed, settled.) The evidence is not before the Court.

Non convivere licet, nec urbe totâ
Quisquam est tam prope tam proculque nobis.—*Martial.*

What correspondence can I hold with you,
Who are so near and yet so distant too ?

Non cuivis homini contingit adire Corinthum.

It is not every man's fortune to go to Corinth.†

Non deficit alter.

A second is not wanting.

Non domus hoc corpus sed hospitium et quidem breve.—*Seneca.*

This body of ours is not a home, but a place of sojourning, and that for a short time.‡

Non ego ventosæ venor suffragia plebis.
—*Horace.*

I do not hunt for the votes of the common people, which veer with every wind.

Non equidem invideo, miror magis.

Indeed I do not envy, I am surprised rather.

Non est ad astra mollis e terris via.
—*Seneca.*

The ascent to heaven from the earth is difficult.

Non est alter.

There is no other.

Non est, crede mihi, sapientis dicere, vivam.
Sera nimis vita est crastina, vive hodie.
—*Martial.*

It is not, believe me, the part of a wise man to say " I will live."
To-morrow's life is too late, so—live to-day.

Non est inventus.

(He has not been found.) The accused person has not been arrested.

Non est jocus esse malignum.

There is no fun in ill-natured remarks.

Non est tanti.

It is not worth while ; not worth the trouble.

Non est vivere, sed valere vita.
—*Martial.*

For life is only life, when blest with health.

Non exercitus, neque thesauri, præsidia regni sunt, verum amici.—*Sallust.*

Neither armies, nor treasures, but friends, are the surest protection of a king.

Non generant aquilæ columbas.

Eagles do not bring forth doves.

Non hæc in fœdera.

Not into such leagues as these.

Non ignara mali, miseris succurrere disco.—*Virgil.*

Not ignorant myself of misfortune, I learn to succour the distressed.

* Dr. Fell, who was Dean of Christ Church at the end of the seventeenth century, offered to cancel an order of expulsion against Tom Brown, the humorist, if the latter could translate this epigram of Martial on the spur of the moment. The Dr. Fell lines were the unexpected result.
† Corinth, one of the chief commercial towns of the ancients, was notorious for its luxury Only a wealthy man could afford to visit it.
‡ A similar remark is made by Cicero in his *De Senectute.*

Non libet.

Non licet.

Non liquet.

Non magni pendis quia contigit.
—*Horace.*

Non misere quisquam, qui bene vixit, obit.

Non nisi parendo vincitur.—*Bacon.*

Non nobis, Domine.

Non nobis solum sed omnibus.

Non nobis solum sed toti mundo nati.

Non nostrum tantas componere lites.

Non numero hæc judicantur sed pondere.

Non omnia possumus omnes.—*Virgil.*

Non omnis error stultitia est dicenda.

Non omnis moriar.—*Horace.*

Non opus admisso subdere calcar equo.
—*Ovid.*

Non possidentem multa vocaveris Recte beatum.—*Horace.*

Non possumus.

Non res, sed spes erat.

Non revertar inultus.

Non semper erit æstas.

Non semper erunt Saturnalia.

Non sequitur.

Non sibi, sed omnibus.

Non, si male nunc, et olim Sic erit.— *Horace.*

Non sine Dis animosus infans.—*Horace.*

It does not please me.

It is not lawful.

(The case) is not clear ; not proven.

(You do not value it highly because it came incidentally.) A lucky find is not as much valued as money earned.

(The man who has lived aright dies happy.) A good beginning makes a good ending.

(It is only by obedience that the conquest is made.) Nature is beyond all teaching, and we can only control it by obeying its laws.

Not to us, O Lord.

Not for ourselves only, but for all.

Born not for ourselves only, but for the whole world.

It is not our duty to adjust such high disputes.

These things are estimated not by number but by weight.

We cannot all of us do all things.

Not every mistake is to be stigmatised as folly.

(I shall not wholly die.) My works, my poetry will be immortal.

Do not spur a free horse.

You cannot rightly call the very rich man happy.

We cannot.*

(Not performance, but hope.) He was a most promising man, though he did not accomplish anything great.

I shall not return unavenged.

It is not always May.

It will not always be holiday time.†

(It does not follow.) A form of fallacy in which the conclusion states what cannot be justly inferred from the premises.

Not for oneself, but for all.

(Even if you are unfortunate now, some day you may find happiness.) It is a long lane that has no turning.

A child endowed with courage from the gods above.

* A phrase that is used to signify the attitude of the Papacy towards innovations of doctrine.
† The Saturnalia was one of the chief festivals of the Romans, and was celebrated during the month of December. At these festivities even the slaves enjoyed their liberty.

Non subito delenda.

Not to be hastily destroyed.

Non sum qualis eram.

I am not what I was; my character and inclinations have changed.

Non tali auxilio, nec defensoribus istis tempus eget.

The juncture needs not such help or such defenders as you offer.

Nonumque prematur in annum.

Let (your compositions) be kept in your desk for nine years.

Non verbis sed factis opus est.

Deeds not words are needed.

Non vi, sed sæpe cadendo.

(Not by force, but by frequent falling.) Perseverance is essential to success.

Non vultus, non color.

Neither the countenance nor the colour; nothing like it.

Nosce teipsum.

Know thyself.

Noscitur a sociis.

He is known by his associates.

Nos duo turba sumus.— *Ovid.*

We two seem to ourselves a crowd.

Nos patriam fugimus, nos dulcia linquimus arva.

We are fleeing from our country, we are leaving our pleasant fields.

Nosse hæc omnia salus est adolescentulis.

It is good for young men to know all these things.

Nota bene (N.B.).

Mark well.

Novos amicos dum paras, veteres cole.

Whilst you seek new friends, make much of the old ones.

Novus homo.

(A new man.)   One whose family has never held any of the offices of State.

Novus rex, nova lex.

New kings make new laws.

Nuces relinquere.

To abandon one's nuts; to cease to be a child.

Nuda veritas.

(Naked truth.)   Truth's best ornament is nakedness.

Nudis verbis.

In plain words.

Nudum latro transmittit.—*Seneca.*

The robber leaves the beggar alone.

Nudum pactum.

An invalid agreement.

Nugæ canoræ.

Melodious trifles.

Nugis addere pondus.—*Horace.*

To add weight to trifles.

Nugis armatus.

Armed with trifles.

Nulla aconita bibuntur fictilibus.

(No poison is drunk out of earthenware.)   No one would think it worth while to poison a poor man.

Nulla dies mærore caret.—*Seneca.*

(Every day brings its sorrows.)
One sorrow never comes but brings an heir
That may succeed as its inheritor.
                              —*Shakespeare.*

Nulla dies sine lineâ.

No day without a line—without some work accomplished.

Nulla est sincera voluptas.

No joy is unalloyed.

Nulla falsa doctrina est quæ non permisceat aliquid veritatis.

There is no false doctrine but mixes up with itself some element of truth.

Nulla fere causa est, in quâ non femina litem moverit.—*Juvenal.*

There are hardly any disputes but a woman has been at the bottom of them.

G

Nulla lex satis commoda omnibus est, id modo quæritur, si majori parti et in summam prodest.—*Livy*.

No law satisfies the interests of all; the only thing to be considered is, whether it is profitable to the majority of citizens.

Nullâ pallescere culpa.

Not to turn pale on any imputation of guilt.

Nulla unquam de morte hominis cunctatio longa est.—*Juvenal*.

When a man's life is at stake no delay can be.

Nullâ virtute redemtum.

A creature with no redeeming points in his character.

Nulli jactantius mærent, quam qui maxime lætantur.—*Tacitus*.

None mourn with more show of sorrow than those who are especially delighted.

Nullis amor est medicabilis herbis.

Love is not to be cured by any herbs.

Nulli secundus.

Second to none ; first fiddle.

Nullius addictus jurare in verba magistri.—*Horace*.

Not pledged to swear by the words of any master.

Nullius filius.

Nobody's child ; an illegitimate son.

Nullum caruit exemplo nefas.—*Seneca*.

No crime is without precedent.

Nullum est jam dictum quod non dictum sit prius.

(Nothing is said to-day that has not been said before.) There is nothing new under the sun.

Nullum imperium tutum, nisi benevolentiâ munitum.

No government is safe unless fortified by good will.

Nullum infortunium solum.

No misfortune comes alone.

Nullum magnum ingenium sine mixturâ dementiæ fuit.—*Seneca*.

There has never been a great genius without a spice of madness in him.
Great wits are sure to madness near allied.—*Dryden*.

Nullum magnum malum quod extremum est.—*Nepos*.

No evil which is last can be great.

Nullum medicamentum est idem omnibus.

(No medicine is the same for all persons.) One man's meat is another man's poison.

Nullum quod tetigit non ornavit.

He touched nothing which he did not adorn.*

Nullus dolor est quem non longinquitas temporis minuat atque molliat.

There is no grief that length of time does not lessen and assuage.

Nullus est locus domesticâ sede beatior.
—*Cicero.*

No place is so pleasant as one's own home.

Nullus idem est diuturnus et præcox fructus.—*Q. Curtius*.

(Fruit that ripens soon never lasts long.) Soon ripe, soon rotten.

Nullus tantus quæstus, quam quod habes parcere.

(There is no gain so sure as that which results from economising what you have.) A penny saved, is a penny earned.

Numerisque fertur
Lege solutis.—*Horace*.

(And he is borne along in numbers unfettered by laws.) He treats with contempt all poetic rules.†

* Dr. Johnson's epitaph on Oliver Goldsmith.
† The reference is to the Greek poet, Pindar, whose metres were not fully comprehended by Horace. Edmund Burke wittily quoted these words when he saw Wilkes carried on the shoulders of the mob.

Nunc aut nunquam.
Nunc scio quid sit amor.
Nunc tuum ferrum in igni est.

Nunquam ad liquidum fama perducitur.

Nunquam aliud Natura, aliud Sapientia dixit.—*Juvenal.*

Nunquam dormio.

Nunquam minus solus, quam cum solus.
                                    —*Cicero.*

Nunquam non paratus.
Nunquam potest non esse virtuti locus

Nunquam vera species ab utilitate dividitur.—*Quintilian.*
Nusquam tuta fides.

Obiit.
Obiter dictum.
Obscuris vera involvens.
Obscurum per obscurius.

Obseqium amicos, veritas odium parit.
                                    —*Terence.*
Obsta principiis.

Obstupui, steteruntque comæ, et vox faucibus hæsit.—*Virgil.*

Occasio furem facit.
Occasionem cognosce.

Occultæ inimicitiæ magis timendæ sunt quam apertæ.—*Cicero.*
Occupet extremum scabies.
Oculis magis habenda fides quam auribus.
Oculis subjecta fidelibus.

Oculus domini saginat equum.
O curas hominum! O quantum est in rebus inane.—*Persius.*

Now or never.
Now I know what love is.
(Now your iron is in the fire.) Strike while the iron is hot.
Report never shows things in their true light.
(Nature and Wisdom never give contrary advice.) Nature is beyond all teaching.
I never sleep; I am always on the alert.
(Never less alone, than when alone.) To the man absorbed in his studies solitude is no burden.
Never unprepared; aye ready.
There must always be room for virtue; virtue can never be at a discount.
There is nothing that is truly beautiful if it is not also useful.
(Our confidence is everywhere misplaced.) We cannot trust a single person.

He *or* she died.
A thing said by the way.
Concealing the truth in obscure terms.
(One obscure thing by something still more obscure.) Defining an unknown thing in terms equally unknown.
Flattery gains friends, but truth enemies.
(Resist the first beginnings.) Root out an evil before it becomes too strong.
(I was astounded, my hair stood on end, and my voice clave to my throat.) A description of the physical efforts of fear.
Opportunity makes the thief.
(Know your opportunity.) Strike while the iron is hot.
Secret enemies are more to be feared than open hostility.
Plague take the hindmost.
(It is better to trust our eyes than our ears.) Seeing is believing.
(Under faithful eyes.) Fully and carefully examined. Plain as a pikestaff.
The master's eye makes the horse fat.
O the cares of mankind! How much emptiness there is in human affairs.

O curvæ in terris animæ, et cœlestium inanes.—*Persius*.

O souls, in whom no heavenly fire is found ; Flat minds, and ever grovelling on the ground !—*Dryden*.

Oderint dum metuant.

Let them hate provided they fear me.

Oderunt peccare boni virtutis amore.
—*Horace*.

The good, for virtue's sake, abhor to sin.—*Creech*.

Odi et amo, Quare id faciam, fortasse requiris
    Nescio : sed fieri sentio, et excrucior.—*Catullus*.

I hate and I love at the same time. Why I do so, you may desire to know : I cannot tell ; but I feel that it is so, and I am tormented.

Odi profanum vulgus.

I loathe the uncouth vulgar throng.

Odium theologicum.

(Theological hatred.) The hatred among religious folk, engendered by differences of opinion on doctrinal points.

Officina gentium.

The workshop of the nations.

O fortunatam, natam, me consule, Romam !

O happy Rome, when I was consul, born.*

O fortunatos nimium, sua si bona norint.

O happy men, did they but know the blessings of their present lot.

O fortunatos nimium, sua si bona norint,
Agricolas, quibus ipsa, procul discordibus armis,
Fundit humo facilem vietum justissima tellus !—*Virgil*.

O happy, happy husbandmen, did they but know the blessings they possess, for whom, far from the din of war, the kindly earth pours forth an easy sustenance.

Ohe ! jam satis.

(Oh ! that is enough.) My patience is exhausted.

    Oh, si angulus ille
Proximus accedat qui nunc denormat agellum.—*Horace*.

Oh, that that little corner of my neighbour's field, that spoils the symmetry of my land, were given to me.

O imitatores, servum pecus.

O servile herd of imitators.

Oleo tranquillior.

(More smooth than oil.) Soft words break no bones.

Oleum addere camino.

(To pour oil upon the fire.) To add fuel to the flame.

Olim meminisse juvabit.

It will be pleasant to remember these things in after times.

O major, tandem parcas, insane, minori.
—*Horace*.

Thou mighty madman, spare one who is not thy peer—in folly.

O miseras hominum mentes ! O pectora cæca.—*Lucretius*.

How wretched are the minds of men ! How blind their intelligence !

Omne ignotum pro magnifico.
—*Tacitus*.

(The unknown is always thought to be magnificent.) Distance lends enchantment to the view.

Omne in præcipiti vitium stetit.
—*Juvenal*.

Every kind of vice has not reached its highest development.

---

* Juvenal has preserved for us this specimen of Cicero's poetic efforts. The line is nothing to be proud of, and Juvenal truly says that the writer of it might have escaped the swords of his murderers, the creatures of Antony, had he written nothing more. In oratory and philosophy Cicero was pre-eminent among his countrymen, but he seems to have had no claim to be considered a poet.

Omnem crede diem tibi diluxisse supremum.

Believe that each day that dawns on you is your last.

Omnem movere lapidem.

(To leave no stone unturned.) To go the whole hog.

Omne nimium vertitur in vitium.

(Everything in excess becomes a vice.) There may be too much of a good thing.

Omne scibile.

Everything that may be known; everything knowable.

Omnes deteriores sumus licentiâ. —*Terence.*

(Too much license debases us.) Spare the rod and spoil the child.

Omnes eodem cogimur.

We are all driven towards the same quarter (deathwards).

Omnes eodem cogimur; omnium Versatur urnâ, serius, ocius, Sors exitura.—*Horace.*

We are all driven in the same direction; for all the urn of death is shaken, and soon or late the lot of each will come forth.

Omne solum forti patria est.—*Ovid.*

Every soil is a fatherland to a brave man.

Omnes sibi melius esse malunt quam alteri. —*Terence.*

(All men prefer to do good to themselves rather than to another.) Charity begins at home.

Omne tulit punctum, qui miscuit utile dulci.—*Horace.*

(He has gained every vote, who blended the useful with the agreeable.) The writer who can combine instruction with amusement is deserving of praise.

Omnia ad Dei gloriam.

All things are for the glory of God.

Omnia bona bonis.

All things are good with good men.

Omnia bonos viros decent.

(All things are becoming to good men.) Honest men fear neither the light nor the dark.

Omnia fert ætas, animum quoque. —*Virgil.*

Time bears away all things, and the powers of the mind among them.

Omnia inconsulto impetu cœpta, initiis valida, spatio languescunt.— *Tacitus.*

All things commenced with inconsiderate haste, although vigorous at the outset, droop after a time.

Omnia mala exempla bonis principiis orta sunt.

All bad precedents have taken their origin from good beginnings.

Omnia mea mecum porto.

(I carry all my property with me.) My intellect is my best possession.

Omnia mors æquat.—*Claudian.*

Death levels everything.

Omnia non pariter sunt omnibus apta.

All things are not alike suited for all men.

Omnia novit Græculus esuriens.

(A starving Greekling knows everything.) He will undertake any office.*

Omnia præclara sunt rara.

All excellent things are rare.

Omnia profecto cum se cœlestibus rebus referet ad humanas, excelsius magnificentiusque et dicet et sentiet. —*Cicero.*

The contemplation of celestial things will make a man both speak and think more sublimely and magnificently when he descends to human affairs.

* See *Græculus esuriens.*

Omnia serviliter pro dominatione.

To perform every slavish action in order to gain the mastery.

Omnia suspendens naso.

One who turns up his nose at everything; turns everything to ridicule.

Omnia tuta timens.

Fearing all things, even such as are safe.

Omnia vanitas.

All is vanity.

Omnia vincit amor; nos et cedamus amori.—*Virgil.*

Love conquers all things; let us yield to its power.

Omnia vincit labor.

Labour overcomes all things.

Omnibus hoc vitium est.

All have this vice.

Omnibus hoc vitium est cantoribus, inter amicos
Ut nunquam inducant animum cantare rogati,
Injussi nunquam desistant.—*Horace.*

This is a fault common to all singers, that among their friends when asked to sing they never will bring their minds to comply, but when not requested they will never leave off.

Omnibus in terris, quæ sunt a Gadibus usque
Auroram et Gangem, pauci dignoscere possunt
Vera bona, atque aliis multum diversa, remota
Erroris nebulâ.—*Juvenal.*

Look round the habitable world, how few
Know their own good, or, knowing it, pursue?
Now rarely reason guides the stubborn choice,
Prompts the fond wish, or lifts the suppliant voice.

Omnibus notum tonsoribus.

(Every barber knows that.) It is the talk of the town.*

Omnibus se accommodat rebus.

(He suits himself to all conditions.) All is fish that comes to his net.

Omnisque potestas
Impatiens consortis erit.—*Lucan.*

Authority always finds it hard to endure a partner.

Omnium consensu capax imperii, nisi imperasset.

Everybody would have considered him capable of governing, if he had never governed.†

Omnium gatherum.

A miscellaneous collection.‡

Omnium rerum principia parva sunt.
—*Cicero.*

The beginnings of all things are small.

Omnium rerum vicissitudo est.
—*Terence.*

(All things suffer change.)
Even as the mists
Of the grey morn before the rising sun,
That pass away and perish.—*Shelley.*

Onus probandi.

The burden of proving.

O passi graviora.

Ye who have borne e'en greater toils than these.

Ope et consilio.

By help and counsel.

Operæ pretium est.

It is worth while.

Opere in longo fas est obrepere somnum.—*Horace.*

Who labours long may be allowed to sleep.

Operose nihil agunt.

They are busy about nothing.

---

* Barbers were as notorious gossips in ancient times as they are to-day.
† See *Capax imperii.*
‡ *Gatherum* is not a proper Latin word, but is merely Latinised humorously from "gather."

Opinionum commenta delet dies, naturæ judicia confirmat.

Time wipes out the comments of men's opinions, but it confirms the judgments of nature.

Opprobrium medicorum.

(The disgrace of the doctors.) Any disease for which there has not been found any cure.

Optat ephippia bos piger, optat arare caballus.—*Horace.*

(The lazy ox wishes for horse-trappings, and the horse wishes to plough.) We are dissatisfied with what we have, and long for what we have not.

Optimum est pati quod emendare non possis.—*Seneca.*

What cannot be cured must be endured.

Optimum obsonium labor.

Work is the best relish.

Opum furiosa cupido.

The ungovernable lust for riches.

Opus artificem probat.

(The workman is known by his work.) A carpenter is known by his chips.

Opusculum.

A little work (book).

O ! quid solutis est beatius curis ?
Cum mens onus reponit, ac peregrino
Labore fessi venimus larem ad nostrum
Desideratoque acquiescimus lecto.
Hoc est, quod unum est pro laboribus tantis.—*Catullus.*

Oh, what is more delightful than to lay one's cares aside, when the mind puts aside its burden, and we return to our beloved home wearied by distant travel, and rest our limbs on the wished-for bed ? This, this alone, repays us for our grievous toil.

Ora et labora.

Pray and work.

Orandum est ut sit mens sana in corpore sano.

We should pray for a sound mind in a sound body.

Ora pro nobis.

Pray for us.

Orationem concludere.

To end a speech.

Orator fit, poeta nascitur.

The orator is made such by education, but a poet must be born such.

Ore rotundo.

With a round mouth ; volubly ; grandly.

Ore tenus.

By word of mouth ; verbally.

Origo mali.

The origin of evil.

O rus, quando te aspiciam ?

O country, when shall I behold thee ?

O sancta simplicitas.

O blessed simplicity.

O Sancte Pater, sic transit glori mundi.

Holy Father, thus passes away the glory of the world.*

Os homini sublime dedit, cœlumque tueri.
Jussit, et erectos ad sidera tollere vultus.
           — *Ovid.*

He gave to man a lofty countenance, and bade him look to the heavens, and turn his gaze upward to the stars.†

O ! si sic omnia.

Oh ! that he had always done *or* spoken thus.

O tempora ! O mores !

Oh the times ! Oh the manners !‡

O terque quaterque beati.

Thrice, yea, four times happy are they.

---

* The master of the ceremonies, at the installation of the Pope, holds two reeds in his hands. One of these has a candle attached to it, and with this he sets alight the other reed, crying out at the same time, *Sancte Pater, sic transit, etc.*
† Much quoted in reference to the emancipation of slaves.
‡ The exclamation occurs in Cicero's first speech denouncing Catiline.

Otiosis nullus adsistit Deus.

(No deity assists the idle.) God helps those who help themselves.

Otium cum dignitate.

Ease with dignity.

Otium omnia vitia parit.

(Idleness produces every vice.) Satan finds mischief for idle hands to do.

Otium sine dignitate.

Ease without dignity.

Ovem lupo committere.

(To set the wolf to guard the sheep.)

Ovis ovem sequitur.

(One sheep follows another.) Like follows like.

O vitæ philosophia dux! O virtutis indagatrix, expultrixque vitiorum! quid non modo nos, sed omnino vita hominum sine te esse potuisset? tu urbes peperisti: tu dissipatos homines in societatem vitæ convocasti: tu eos inter se primo domiciliis, deinde conjugiis, tum litterarum, et vocum communione junxisti: tu inventrix legum, tu magistra morum, et disciplinæ fuisti: ad te confugimus: a te opem petimus. Est autem unus dies bene, et ex præceptis tuis actus, peccanti immortalitati anteponendus.—*Cicero.*

Philosophy, thou guide of life! Thou searcher after virtue, and banisher of vice! What would not only we ourselves, but the whole life of men, have been without thy aid? It is thou that foundedst cities, gatheredst men in social union; thou that united them together first in dwellings, then in the nuptial tie, then in the pleasures of literature and the interchange of speech: to thee we owe the devising of the laws, and thou didst guide men to righteous ways, and virtuous habits. To thee we come for refuge, from thee we seek for help. One day well spent, according to thy precepts, is preferable to an immortality of sin.

O vita misero longa, felici brevis!
    —*Publius Syrus.*

O life! too long for the wretched, too short for the prosperous.

Pabulum.

Fodder; matter for study, &c.

Pace.

With the favour, leave of.

Pace et bello.

In peace and in war.

Pacem hominibus habe, bellum cum vitiis.

(Be at peace with men, at war with vices.) Peace flourishes when reason rules.

Pacta conventa.

Conditions agreed upon; a diplomatic compact.

Pæte, non dolet.

See, Pætus, it does not hurt.*

Palam mutire plebeio piaculum est.
    —*Ennius.*

For a poor man to speak his mind is a crime worthy of punishment.

Palinodiam canere.

To recant; to make apology.

Palladium.

(Protection; support.) An image of Pallas Athene, carefully preserved at Troy, the safety of the city being supposed to depend on it.

Pallas, quas condidit arces Ipsa, colat; nobis placeant ante omnia silvæ.—*Virgil.*

Let Pallas haunt the cities she has built; let us find our chief pleasure in the forest glades.

---

* Pætus was condemned to suicide by Claudius Cæsar, on the charge of conspiracy. His heroic wife, Arria, first plunged the dagger into her own breast, saying *Pæte, non dolet,* before she handed it to her husband.

Pallida mors æquo pulsat pede pauperum tabernas
Regumque turres.—*Horace.*

(Pale death enters with impartial step the cottages of the poor and the lofty palaces of kings.)
Death's shafts fly thick! here falls the village swain,
And there his pamper'd lord!—*Blair.*

Pallidus irâ.

Pale with rage.

Palmam qui meruit ferat.

Let him who has won the palm bear it.*

Pandectæ.

(The Pandects *or* Digest.) A collection of Roman laws from the writings of Roman jurists, made by the order of Justinian.

Panditur ad nullas janua nigra preces.
—*Propertius.*

No prayers unbar the gates of death.

Panem et circenses.

Bread and the show of the circus.†

Papa alterius orbis.

Pope of a second world.

Par.

Equal; the condition of equality; equal value.

Parce gaudere oportet, et sensim queri; Totam quia vitam miscet dolor et gaudium.—*Phædrus.*

We ought to rejoice sparingly, and bewail with moderation, for the whole of life is but a mingling of pain and joy.

Parcere subjectis, et debellare superbos.
—*Virgil.*

To spare the conquered and subdue the proud.

Parendo vinces.

(You will conquer by obedience.) If you resist nature she will crush you.
—*Maine.*

Parentes objurgatione digni sunt, qui nolunt liberos suos severâ lege proficere.—*Petronius Arbiter.*

Parents are worthy of severe reproof, who are unwilling to use strict discipline in order to train their children well.

Pares cum paribus facillime congregantur.

(Like persons most readily crowd together.) Birds of a feather flock together.

Par est fortuna labori.

(Fortune responds to toil.) No gains without pains.

Pari passu.

With an equal pace; side by side.

Paritur pax bello.

Peace is produced by war.

Par negotiis neque supra.

(Neither above nor below his business.) A mediocre man.

Par nobile fratrum.

A noble pair of brothers.

Par oneri.

Equal to the burden.

Par pari refero.

I return like for like; tit for tat.

Pars minima est ipsa puella sui.—*Ovid.*

(The girl is the least important part of herself.) The amount of her dowry is the point to be considered.

Pars pro toto.

Part for the whole.

Parta tueri debent.

What is gained ought to be maintained.

---

* The motto of Lord Nelson, derived from some Latin verses by Dr. Jortin.
† Juvenal says that the Roman people, once the conquerors of the world, in his time cared for nothing but free doles and spectacular shows.

Parthi quo plus bibunt, eo plus sitiunt.

(The more the Parthians drink, the more thirsty they are.) Ever drunk, ever dry.

Parthis mendacior.

(More lying than Parthians.) A consummate liar.

Particeps criminis.

An accomplice.

Parturiunt montes, nascetur ridiculus mus.

(The mountains are in labour, a ridiculous mouse will be born.) Great cry and little wool.

Parva componere magnis.

To compare little things with great.

Parva leves capiunt animas.

Little minds are caught with trifles.

Parva metu primo, mox sese attollit in auras. —*Virgil.*

Crouching at first through fear, soon it rises boldly in the air.*

Parvi enim sunt foris arma, nisi et consilium domi.—*Cicero.*

Armed forces abroad are of little value, unless there is prudent counsel at home.

Parvum parva decent.

(Humble things become humble men.) The man in a low station never makes himself ridiculous but when his efforts exceed his means.

Pascitur in vivis livor, post fata quiescit. —*Ovid.*

Envy feeds on the living, but after death it is dumb.

Passim.

Everywhere.

Patere legem quam ipse tulisti.

(Observe the law you yourself have made.) Law-makers must not be law-breakers.

Pater ipse colendi haud facilem esse viam voluit.—*Virgil.*

The Father himself decreed that the task of tillage should not be easy.

Pater patriæ.

Father of his country.

Pati necesse est multa mortalem mala. —*Nævius.*

(Man must of necessity suffer many evils.) Man is born to trouble as sparks fly upward.

Patrem sequitur sua proles.

(A son takes after his father.) As the old cock crows, the young one learns.

Patres conscripti.

(Senators, hereditary and elected; Roman senators.) The supreme authority.

Patria cara, carior libertas.

My country is dear, but liberty is dearer.

Patriæ fumus igne alieno luculentior.

The smoke of one's own country is brighter than a foreign fire.

Patriæ infelici fidelis.

Faithful to an unhappy country.

Patriæ pietatis imago.

An image of paternal tenderness.

Patria est communis omnium parens. —*Cicero.*

Our country is the common parent of all.

Patria est ubicunque est bene.

Wherever we find happiness, that is our country.

Patria est ubicunque vir fortis sedem elegerit.

Whatever place a brave man has chosen to dwell in, that is his country.

Patris est filius.

(He is his father's son.) Like father, like son.

* This line refers to the growth of scandal (see *Fama Malum*); it is now commonly applied to the progress of sedition.

Patruæ verbera linguæ.—*Horace.*

The lashes of an uncle's tongue.*

Paucis carior est fides quam pecunia.

(To few persons is loyalty dearer than money.) Most men have their price.

Paucis verbis.

In few words ; in brief.

Paulo post futurum.

(A little past the future.) A name given by Latin grammarians to the future perfect tense.

Pax in bello.

Peace in war.

Pax potior bello.

(Peace is more powerful than war.) Peace has her victories no less renowned than war.

Pax tamen interdum, pacis fiducia nunquam est.—*Ovid.*

Sometimes there is peace, but its continuance is never certain.

Pax vel injusta utilior est quam justissimum bellum.—*Cicero.*

Peace even on hard terms is better than the justest war.

Pax vobiscum.

Peace be with you.

Peccavi.

I have sinned ; I am in the wrong.

Pectus est quod disertos facit.
              —*Quintilian.*

(It is the heart that makes men eloquent.) Out of the fulness of the heart the mouth speaketh.

Pecuniæ obediunt omnia.

(All things yield to money.) Money rules the world. Money makes the mare to go.

Pecuniam in loco negligere maximum est lucrum.

(To spend money freely on proper occasions is the greatest gain.) Nothing venture, nothing gain.

Pejor est bello timor ipse belli.
              —*Seneca.*

The reality of war is less harmful than the constant fear of it.

Penates.

(Roman household gods.) Home.

Pendente lite.

Whilst the suit is pending.

Pendent opera interrupta.—*Virgil.*

The works unfinish'd and neglected lie.

Penetralia mentis.

The inmost recesses of the mind ; the heart of hearts.

Penitus toto divisi orbe Britanni.
              — *Virgil.*

The Britons, a people utterly separated from the rest of mankind.

Pennas incidere alicui.

To clip one's wings ; to take one down a peg.

Per accidens.

(Through accident.) A logical term.†

Per acria belli.

Through the dangers of war.

Per angusta ad augusta.

Through difficulties to honours.

Per capita.

By the head ; individually.

Per contra.

On the contrary ; as a counterpoise.

Percunctatorem fugito, nam garrulus idem est.—*Horace.*

Th' inquisitive will blab ; from such refrain :
Their leaking ears no secret can retain.

---

* Roman uncles had a reputation for giving improving harangues to their relatives. " Don't come the uncle over me " was the protest of a Roman when another was inclined to give him an unwelcome lecture.

† A quality is said to belong to a thing *per accidens,* when it does not arise from the nature of the thing, but from some external circumstance. Thus water is heated *per accidens,* fire burns *per se,* i.e., naturally.

Per damna, per cædes, ab ipso
Ducit opes animumque ferro.
—*Horace.*

Through losses, through wounds, from the steel itself it derives strength and vigour.

Per Deum et ferrum obtinui.

By the help of God and my sword have I kept it.

Peream si falsa loquor.

May I die if I speak what is false.

Pereant amici, dum unâ inimici intercidant.

(Let our friends perish, provided that our enemies fall with them.) We consider nothing but our own interests.

Pereant qui ante nos nostra dixerunt.
—*Donatus.*

Plague take those who have said our smart sayings before we uttered them.

Per fas et nefas.

Through right and wrong ; justly or unjustly.

Perfusus calidâ gelidam timet aquam.

(The man who has been scalded fears cold water too.) A burnt child dreads the fire.

Pericula veritati sæpe contigua.
—*Marcellinus.*

Truth is often attended with danger.

Periculosæ plenum opus aleæ
Tractas et incedis per ignes
Suppositos cineri doloso.—*Horace.*

A work full of risk and danger is that which you are attempting ; you are walking, as it were, on ashes that hide a fire beneath.*

Periculosior casus ab alto.

(A fall from on high is dangerous.) Pride goeth before destruction and a haughty spirit before a fall.

Periculum in morâ.

Danger in delay.

Per incuriam.

Through heedlessness, or negligence.

Perituræ parcere chartæ.

(To spare paper doomed to disappear.) To abstain from scribbling.

Perjuria ridet amantum
Jupiter et ventos irrita ferre jubet.
—*Tibullus.*

At lover's perjuries Jove laughs, and bids the winds disperse such vain triflings.

Per mare per terram.

Through sea and land.

Permissum fit vile nefas.

A privilege is not valued when it has been obtained.

Permitte divis cætera.

Leave the rest to heaven.

Per risum multum possis cognoscere stultum.

(By much laughter you may distinguish a fool.) A fool will laugh when he is drowning.

Per saltum.

By a leap or jump.

Per se.

By itself.

Persona grata

(A welcome person.) A favourite ; a welcome guest.

Persona ingrata.

(An unwelcome person.) An objectionable person ; a person disliked by others.

Persta atque obdura.

Be steadfast and endure.

---

* Words addressed to Pollio, the historian, who was writing a history of the recent civil wars, before the rancour of the opposing parties had quite died away.

Per varios casus, per tot discrimina rerum,
Tendimus in Latium.—*Virgil.*

Through many changes of fortune. and many dangerous experiences, we make for Latium.

Per viam dolorosam.

By the path of sorrow.

Per vias rectas

By straight roads.

Pervigilium.

Watching all night.

Pessimum genus inimicorum laudantes.

Flatterers are the worst kind of enemies.

Petitio principii.

(Begging the question.) The logical fallacy of assuming what has to be proved.

Pia fraus.

(A pious fraud.) Fraud committed for a good object ; a justifiable injustice.

Pietas fundamentum est omnium virtutum.—*Cicero.*

Filial duty is the foundation of all the other virtues.

Placet.

(It pleases.) Decree ; ordinance ; official order.

Planta quæ sæpius transfertur non coalescit.

(A plant often removed cannot thrive.) Watch the kettle and it will never boil.

Plebs.

The common people ; the plebeians.

Pleno jure.

With full authority.

Plenus annis abiit, plenus honoribus.
—*Pliny the Younger.*

He died full of years and honours.

Plerumque gratæ divitibus vices.

Changes are generally agreeable to the wealthy.

Ploratur lacrimis amissa pecunia veris.
—*Juvenal.*

The loss of money is lamented with real tears.

Plura faciunt homines e consuetudine, quam e ratione.

Men do more actions from habit than on reflection.

Plures crapula quam gladius.

Gluttony kills more than the sword.

Plus aloes quam mellis habet.

The bitter overbalances the sweet.

Plus dolet quam necesse est, qui ante dolet quam necesse est.

He grieves more than is needful, who grieves before it is needful.

Plus potest, qui plus valet.— *Plautus.*

(He is the more powerful who is the stronger.) The weakest goes to the wall.

Plus ratio quam vis cæca valere solet.

Common sense can usually effect more than blind force.

Plus salis quam sumptus.

More tasteful than costly.

Plus vident oculi quam oculus.

Two eyes see better than one.

Poëta nascitur, non fit.

The poet is born, not made.

Polliceri montes auri.

(To promise gold mountains.) To make extravagant promises.

Pollice verso.

With thumb turned down.*

Pons asinorum.

(The asses' bridge.) The fifth proposition in Euclid.

---

* When one gladiator in the amphitheatre had another at his mercy, he looked towards the spectators. If they turned their thumbs towards their breast, it was a signal for death.

Populus me sibilat ; at mihi plaudo.
—*Horace.*

(The people hiss me, but I applaud myself.) I care nothing for the opinion of the crowd.

Populus vult decipi, decipiatur.

The people wish to be deceived, let them have their wish.*

Posse comitatus.

(The power of the county.) A *posse* of police is a body of police.

Posse videor.

I appear to be able ; I think I can.

Possunt quia posse videntur.

(They are able because they seem to be able.) They can because they think they can.

Post bellum auxilium.

Aid after the war ; help offered too late.

Post equitem sedet atra cura.—*Horace.*

(Black care sits behind the horseman.) The wealthy man as he rides his horse is still pursued by anxiety.

Posteriores cogitationes sapientiores solent esse.

Second thoughts are usually best.

Post factum nullum consilium.

Advice comes too late when a thing is done.

Post festum venisti.

(You have come after the feast.) You have arrived too late.

Post hoc, ergo propter hoc.

(After this, therefore in consequence of this.) The logical fallacy of treating a subsequent event as undoubtedly a result of a preceding one, although of course it is not necessarily so.

Post nubila Phœbus.

(After cloudy weather comes the sun.) Every cloud has a silver lining.

Post obit.

A bond payable after death.

Post prœlia præmia.

After battles come rewards.

Post tenebras lux.

(After darkness light.) "Joy cometh in the morning."

Post tot naufragia portum.

After so many shipwrecks (we reach) a harbour.

Postulatum (*pl.* Postulata).

A demand ; an assumption required for an argument.

Potentissimus est qui se habet in potestate.

He is most powerful who has himself in his own power.

Potius amicum quam dictum perdere.

Rather to lose a friend than a witticism.

Præfervidum ingenium Scotorum.

The fiery, impetuous disposition of the Scotch.

Præmonitus præmunitus.

Forewarned, forearmed.

Præmunire.

A writ issued against certain offenders, who are thus placed outside the protection of the law, and are liable to forfeiture of goods and to imprisonment.†

* Words attributed to Cardinal Caraffa, legate of Pope Paul IV. Their origin, however, is not certain.

† The name is taken from the first words, *præmoneri* or *præmuniri facias.* " Cause A.B. to be warned to appear."

Præpropera consilia raro sunt prospera.

Over-hasty counsels seldom prosper.

Præsentem mulgeas, quid fugientem insequeris ?

(Milk the cow you have caught, what's the good of following the runaway ?) A bird in the hand is worth two in the bush.

Præstat sero quam nunquam.

Better late than never.

Præteriti anni.

Years past and gone ; bygone days.

Pravis assuescere sermonibus est via ad rem ipsam.

(To hearken to evil conversation is the road to wickedness.) Evil communications corrupt good manners.

Prima caritas incipit a seipso.

(Charity begins with oneself.) Charity begins at home, but should not end there.

Primâ facie.

At first sight ; on a first view, or consideration.

Primo.

In the first place.

Primum mobile.

The primary motive, or moving power.

Primus in orbe deos fecit imor.
—*Statius.*

Fear was the first creator of gods in the world.

Primus inter omnes.

The first among them all.

Primus inter pares.

Chief among equals.

Princeps obsoniorum.

The prince of tit-bits.

Principia.

First principles.

Principia, non homines.

Principles, not men.

Principibus placuisse viris non ultima laus est.—*Horace.*

To please the great is not the smallest praise.—*Creech.*

Principiis obsta. Sero medicina paratur Cum mala per longas convaluere moras.—*Ovid.*

Meet the evil at the outset. Too late is medicine prepared when the mischief has become strong through long delay.

Principis est virtus maxima, nosse suos.
—*Martial.*

To know his own subjects is the chief duty of a ruler.

Priusquam incipias consulito, et ubi consulueris, mature facto opus est.

(Before you begin consider, and when you have well considered, then act with promptitude.) Deliberate slowly, execute promptly.

Privato consensu.

By one's own consent.

Privatus illis census erat brevis, commune magnum.—*Horace.*

(Their private fortunes were but small, but the public wealth was great.) So great was the simplicity of life and true patriotism among our ancestors.

Pro aris et focis.

For our altars and firesides ; for God and country.

Probitas laudatur et alget.

Honesty is praised and freezes ; is left in cold and neglect.

Probitas verus honor.

Honesty is true honour.

Pro bono publico.

For the public good.

Probum non pœnitet.

The honest man does not repent.

Pro confesso.

As if conceded.

Procul, O ! procul este, profani.

Begone, begone, ye profane ones.

Prodigus est natus de parco patre creatus.

(A miserly father has a spendthrift son.) After a great getter comes a great spender.

Pro et con (*for* contra).

For and against.

Profanum vulgus.

The common people.

Pro formâ.

For the sake of form; as a mere formality.

Pro hac vice.

For this turn or occasion.

Proh pudor.

For shame!

Projecere animas.—*Virgil.*

They prodigally threw their lives away. —*Creech.*

Pro libertate patriæ.

For the liberty of one's country.

Pro loco et tempore.

For place and time.

Pronuntiatio est vocis et vultus est gestus moderatio cum venustate. —*Cicero.*

Good delivery is a graceful management of the voice, countenance, and gesture.

Proœmium.

Introduction, preface, prelude.

Pro patriâ.

For our country.

Propositi tenax.

Firm of purpose.

Propria domus omnium optima.

(One's own house is the best of all.) Home is home, be it ever so homely.

Propria persona.

One's own individuality.

Proprio motu.

On one's own motion; of one's own accord.

Pro rata.

In proportion.

Pro rege, lege, et grege.

For the king, the law, and the people.

Pro re natâ.

For a special emergency, or business.

Prosperum ac felix scelus Virtus vocatur; sontibus parent boni; Jus est in armis, opprimit leges timor. —*Seneca.*

Successful crime is given the name of virtue; honest folk become the slaves of villains; might is right; and fear silences the laws.

Pro tanto.

For so much; to that extent.

Pro tempore.

For the time being.

Proxime accessit.

(He came next.) Honourable mention.

Proximus ardet Ucalegon.

(Ucalegon's house, next door, is on fire.) When thy neighbour's house is on fire, be careful of thine own.*

Proximus sed proximus longo intervallo.

Next, but next at a great distance; a bad second.

Prudens futuri.

Thoughtful of the future.

Prudens futuri temporis exitum Caliginosâ nocte premit Deus,   Ridetque, si mortalis ultra   Fas trepidat.—*Horace.*

The issue of the time to be Heaven wisely hides in blackest night, And laughs, should man's anxiety   Transgress the bounds of man's short   sight.—*Conington.*

Publico consilio.

By public consent.

Publicum bonum privato est præferendum.

(The public good is to be preferred to private advantage.) **Privilege must** yield to public interest.

---

* See *Nam tua res agitur, etc.*

Pugnis et calcibus.

With fists and heels ; with all one's might.

Pulvis et umbra sumus.—*Horace.*

We are dust and shadows.

Puris omnia pura.

(Unto the pure all things are pure.) Evil be to him who evil thinks.

Puteus si hauriatur melior evadit.

Drawn wells have sweetest water.

Quadrupedante putrem sonitu quatit ungula campum—*Virgil.*

And galloping with heavy tread the charger shakes and pounds the arid plain.*

Qua ducitis adsum.

Wherever you lead, I am with you.

Quæ amissa salva.

What was lost is safe.

Quæ e longinquo magis placent.

The further fetch'd, the more things please.

Quæ fuerant vitia mores sunt.

What used to be vices are now common manners.

Quæ regio in terris nostri non plena laboris !

What region in the world is not full of our calamities.

Quærenda pecunia primum, virtus post nummos.

Money is the first thing to be sought ; reputation is a secondary consideration.

Quæstio fit de legibus, non de personis.

(The question is confined to the laws, and not to persons.) The law is impartial, considers the respective claims, not the social position, of litigants.

Quæ supra nos nihil ad nos.

(The things above us are nothing to us.) We do not trouble about things beyond our comprehension.

Quæ uncis sunt unguibus ne nutrias.

(Do not foster animals with hooked claws.) He that handles thorns shall prick his fingers.

Qualis ab incepto.

The same as from the beginning.

Qualis artifex pereo.—*Nero.*

What an artist dies in me.†

Qualis rex talis grex.

(Like king, like people.) A good master makes a good servant.

Quamdiu se bene gesserit.

During his good behaviour.

Quam multa injusta ac prava fiunt moribus.

How many injustices and wrongs are enacted through custom.

Quam parvâ sapientiâ mundus regitur.

With how little wisdom is the world governed.‡

Quam prope ad crimen sine crimine.

How near a man may approach to guilt without being guilty.

---

* A famous onomatopœic line, the sound of the words imitating the noise made by a horse galloping over the ground. Similarly, Tennyson suggests the sound of the hoofs of the farmer's horse in the line " But proputty proputty sticks, and proputty proputty graws." And Charles Kingsley in his *Ballad of Lorraine* uses the words " Barum, Barum, Barum, Barum, Barum, Barum, Baree," for the same purpose.

† The exclamation of the Emperor Nero shortly before his death. His love of music and poetry were well known, but whether he possessed any great artistic skill is an open question.

‡ The remark of the Swedish Chancellor, Oxenstiern, to his son.

H

Quam sæpe forte temere eveniunt quæ non audeas optare!
Quandoque bonus dormitat Homerus.
Quandoquidem accepto claudenda est janua damno.—*Juvenal.*

How often do things you dare not hope for happen by mere chance!
Sometimes even good Homer nods.*
(Since the door has to be shut after the theft has been made.) Shutting the stable-door when the horse has been stolen.

Quando uberior vitiorum copia? Quando
Major avaritiæ patuit sinus? Alea quando
Hos animos?—*Juvenal.*
Quando ullum inveniemus parem?
Quanquam ridentem dicere verum
Quid vetat?—*Horace.*
Quanto quisque sibi plura negaverit,
A Deis plura feret.—*Horace.*

When was there a greater abundance of vices? When was the greediness of avarice so great? When had gambling such an attraction?
When shall we find his like again?
And yet, what hinders us from telling the truth in a cheerful fashion?
They that do much themselves deny,
Receive a blessing from the sky.
—*Creech.*

Quantum a rerum turpitudine abes, tantum te a verborum libertate sejungas.—*Cicero.*
Quantum est in rebus inane!

We should be as careful of our words as our actions; and as far from speaking as from doing ill.
(How much emptiness there is in the pursuits of man.) What trifles men pursue!

Quantum libet.
Quantum meruit.
Quantum mutatus ab illo.
Quantum sufficit.
Quantum valeat.

As much as you please.
As much as he deserved.
How changed from what he once was.
As much as is sufficient.
(What it is worth.) Taken for as much as it is worth.

Quare impedit?

Why does he stand in the way, or hinder?

Quare, si fieri potest, et verba omnia, et vox hujus alumnum urbis oleant; ut oratio Romana plane videatur, non civitate donata.—*Quintilian.*

If it can be done, let all your words and pronunciation be such as befits a native of this city; so that your speech may seem to be truly Roman, and not that of a man who is merely Roman by adoption.

Quartâ lunâ nati.

(Born in the fourth moon.) Born under an unlucky star.

Quasi.
Quasi solstitialis herba, paulisper fui:
Repente exortus sum, repentino occidi.
—*Plautus.*
Quem di diligunt adolescens moritur.
Quem pœnitet peccasse, pæne est innocens.—*Seneca.*
Quem vult perdere Jupiter prius dementat.

As if; in a manner.
Brief was my life, as that of grass scorched by the summer sun. Quickly I grew, and just as quickly died.
Whom the gods love dies young.†
He who repents is almost innocent.
Whom God wishes to destroy he first drives mad.

* See *Aliquando Homerus.*
† This familiar expression first appears in a fragment of the writings of the Greek dramatist Menander: " Ον όι Θεοὶ φιλοῦσιν ἀποθνήσκει νέος."

Qui amicus est amat, qui amat non utique amicus est.

He who is a friend loves, but he who loves is not necessarily a friend.

Qui aut tempus quid postulet non videt, aut plura loquitur, aut se ostentat, aut eorum quibuscum est rationem non habet, is ineptus esse dicitur.— *Cicero*.

That man may be called impertinent who considers not the circumstances of time, or engrosses the conversation, or makes himself the subject of his discourse, or pays no regard to the company he is in.

Qui capit ille facit.

(He who applies it to himself is the doer of the deed.) If the cap fits, put it on.

Quicquid agunt homines nostri est farrago libelli.—*Juvenal*.

(Whatever men do forms the miscellaneous matter of my little book.) The ways of mankind is my theme.

Quicquid delirant reges, plectuntur Achivi.—*Horace*.

(Whatever mad freaks their rulers indulge in, it is the Greeks themselves that suffer.) Kings call the tune, but their subjects pay the piper.

Quicquid excessit modum pendet instabili loco.—*Seneca*.

Whatever has exceeded its proper bounds is in a state of instability.

Quicunque turpi fraude semel innotuit, etiamsi verum dicit, amittit fidem.

Whoever has once become known for an act of base deceit, even when he speaks the truth, loses the credit of it.

Quid æternis minorem.
Consiliis animum fatigas ?—*Horace*.

Why with thoughts too deep
O'ertask a mind of mortal frame ?
—*Conington*.

Quidam æternitati se commendari per statuas existimantes, eas ardenter affectant, quasi plus præmii ex figmentis æneis sensu carentibus adepturi, quam ex conscientiâ honeste recteque factorum.—*Marcellinus*.

Some persons, thinking that they can commend themselves to the Eternal One by erecting statues to Him, earnestly devote themselves to these, as if they were likely to obtain more reward from senseless idols of brass than from the consciousness of the righteous performance of honourable deeds.

Quid brevi fortes jaculamur ævo multa.
—*Horace*.

Why do we, in our brief span of life, aim at achieving so much ?

Quid cæco cum speculo ?

(What good is a mirror to a blind man ?) Blind men should judge no colours.

Quid crastina volverit ætas,
Scire nefas homini.— *Statius*.

What to-morrow will bring forth it is not lawful for a man to know.

Quid de quoque viro et cui dicas sæpe caveto.—*Horace*.

Have a care
Of whom you talk, to whom, and what, and where.—*Pooley*.

Quid dulcius hominum generi a naturâ datum est quam sui cuique liberi ?
—*Cicero*.

What is there in nature so dear to man as his own children ?

Qui dedit beneficium taceat; narret, qui accepit.—*Seneca*.

The man who confers a kindness should be silent concerning it; he who receives it should proclaim it.

Qui derelinquunt legem, laudant improbos.

They that forsake the law, praise the wicked.

Quid est somnus, gelidæ nisi mortis imago ?—*Ovid.*

(What is sleep but the image of cold death.)
How wonderful is Death,
Death and his brother Sleep.
—*Shelley.*

Quid leges sine moribus vanæ proficiunt ?—*Horace.*

Where is the good of laws in the absence of morals ?

Quid non mortalia pectora cogis,
Auri sacra fames ?—*Virgil.*

(Accursed thirst for gold, what dost thou not tempt men to attempt ?)
O, cursed hunger of pernicious gold !
What bands of faith can impious lucre hold ?—*Dryden.*

Quid nunc ?

("What now ?")   One curious to know everything is a *quidnunc.*

Qui docet, discit.

He who teaches others, learns himself.

Quid pro quo.

Tit for tat ; a mutual consideration.

Quidquid multis peccatur inultum est.

The guilt that is committed by many passes unpunished.

Quidquid præcipies, esto brevis.

When you lay down a rule, be short.

Quid rides ?

Why do you laugh ?

Quid Romæ faciam ?—*Juvenal.*

What should I do at Rome ?

Quid si cœlum ruat.

(What if the sky should fall.)   If the Thames went on fire.

Quid sit futurum cras, fuge quærere.

Avoid inquiring what is going to happen to-morrow.

Quid tantum insano juvat indulgere dolori ?

What does it avail you to give way so much to unreasonable grief ?

Quid turpius est quam illudi ?

What is more shameful than to be made a fool of ?

Quid verbis opus est ? Spectemur agendo.—*Ovid.*

What need is there of words ? Let us be proved by our actions.

Quid verum atque decens.

What is true and honourable.

Quid verum atque decens curo et rogo, et omnis in hoc sum.—*Horace.*

What right, what true, what fit we justly call,
Let this be all my care—for this is all.
—*Pope.*

Quid voveat dulci nutricula majus alumno,
Quam sapere et fari ut possit quæ sentiat.—*Horace.*

What greater blessing could a woman ask for her nurseling than that he should have wisdom and liberty to declare his opinions.

Qui e nuce nucleum esse vult, frangat nucem.

He that would eat the kernel, must crack the nut.

Quieta non movere.

To let sleeping dogs lie.

Qui facit per alium facit per se.

(What a man does through another, he does through himself.)   He is legally responsible for his agent.

Quî fit, Mæcenas, ut nemo, quam sibi sortem
Seu ratio dederit, seu fors objecerit, illâ
Contentus vivat, laudet diversa sequentes.—*Horace.*

How comes it, Mæcenas, that nobody lives contented with that lot which either his own choice has given him, or chance has brought, but praises the condition of those engaged in different pursuits ?

Qui fugit molam farinam non invenit.

(He who flies from the mill does not get any meal.) Laziness travels so slowly that poverty soon overtakes him.

Qui invidet minor est.

He who envies is the inferior.

Qui jacet in terrâ non habet unde cadat.

(He who lies on the ground has no place from which to fall.)*

Qui male agit odit lucem.

He that does evil hates the light.

Quinctili Vare, legiones redde.

Varus, give me back my legions.†

Qui nescit dissimulare nescit vivere.

He who knows not how to dissemble knows not how to live.

Qui non est hodie cras minus aptus erit.

He that is not fit to-day will be less fit to-morrow.

Qui non libere veritatem pronunciat, proditor est veritatis.

He who does not speak the truth is a traitor to the truth.

Qui non proficit, deficit.

He who does not advance, goes backwards.

Qui non vetat peccare cum possit, jubet.

He that does not forbid wrongdoing, when it is in his power, orders it.

Qui non vult fieri desidiosus, amet.

Let him who does not wish to become indolent fall in love.

Quinquennium.

A period of five years.

Qui pergit ea quæ vult dicere, ea quæ non vult audiet.—*Terence.*

(He who insists on saying what he pleases, will hear that which does not please him.) He that speaks lavishly shall hear as knavishly.

Qui per virtutem peritat, non interit.
—*Plautus.*

The man who dies for virtue's sake, does not really perish.

Quis custodiet ipsos custodes ?
—*Juvenal.*

Who shall guard the guards themselves ?

Quis desiderio sit pudor aut modus
Tam cari capitis ?—*Horace.*

(What shame can there be or what limit in our affection for one so dear ?)

Why blush to let our tears unmeasured fall

For one so dear ?– *Conington.*

Qui semel est læsus fallaci piscis ab hamo.

The fish shuns the bait when the hook has once touched him.) A burnt child dreads the fire.

Qui sentit commodum, sentire debet et onus.

He who feels the advantage ought to feel the burden as well.

Quis fallere possit amantem ?

Who can deceive a lover ?

Qui spe aluntur, pendent non vivunt.

(Those who feed on hope, exist in suspense, they do not live.) Hope deferred maketh the heart sick.

Quis talia fando
Temperet a lacrimis ?—*Virgil.*

Who can relate such woes without a tear ?

Qui sui memores alios fecere merendo.
—*Virgil.*

Men who by their merits have caused others to cherish their memory.

* The reply of Charles I. in his captivity, to the man who had told him that the Parliament were plotting against his life.
† This was the constant lament, according to Suetonius, of the Emperor Augustus after a Roman army under Varus had been annihilated by the Germans, led by the heroic Arminius.

Qui terret, plus ipse timet.

He who awes others, is more in fear himself.

Qui timide rogat, docet negare.

He who asks timidly courts a refusal.

Qui transtulit, sustinet.

He who brought us hither still preserves us.

Qui uti scit, ei bona.

Good things to him who knows how to use them.

Qui vult decipi decipiatur.

Let him that wishes to be deceived be deceived.

Quoad hoc.

As regards this particular matter.

Quo animo ?

With what mind or intention ?

Quocunque modo.

In whatsoever manner.

Quod avertat Deus.

Which may God avert.

Quod cibus est aliis, aliis est venenum.

(What is food for some is poison to others.) One man's meat is another man's poison.

Quod cito acquiritur, cito perit.

Easy come, easy go.

Quod decet honestum est, et quod honestum decet.—*Cicero.*

What is becoming is honourable, and what is honourable is becoming.

Quod defertur non aufertur.

(That which is deferred is not relinquished.) Omittance is no quittance.

Quod erat demonstrandum (Q.E.D.).

Which was to be proved.

Quod erat faciendum (Q.E.F.).

Which was to be done.

Quod est in corde sobrii est in ore ebrii.

(What a man keeps in his heart when sober, he has on his lips when he is drunk.) Drunkards have a fool's tongue.

Quod est violentum, non est durabile.

(What is violent is not lasting.) Extremes seldom last long.

Quodlibet.

Any thing whatever.

Quod licet ingratum, quod non licet acrius urit.—*Ovid.*

What we may do we do not care for, and what we may not do attracts us more keenly.

Quod non vetat lex, hoc vetat fieri pudor.—*Seneca.*

The moral sense forbids a man to do some things, even when there is no law against them.

Quod potui perfeci.

I did what I could.

Quod quisque fecit, patitur : auctorem scelus
Repetit, suoque premitur exemplo nocens.—*Seneca.*

Every man suffers for his actions : crime tracks out its author, and the guilty man is hounded down by his own misdeeds.

Quod satis est, cui contingit, nihil amplius optet.—*Horace.*

Let the man who has enough for his wants, desire nothing more.

Quod si in hoc erro, quod animos hominum immortales esse credam, libenter erro : nec mihi hunc errorem, quo delector, dum vivo, extorqueri volo.
—*Cicero.*

But if I am mistaken in this belief, that the souls of men are immortal, I am happy in my error : nor, while I live, shall it be possible for anyone to root out this opinion from me, as I derive much pleasure from it.

Quod sors feret, feremus æquo animo.

Whatever chance shall bring, we shall bear with a calm and firm mind.

Quod tegitur, majus creditur esse malum.—*Martial*.

If you try to conceal a defect, it is sure to be exaggerated by others.

Quod vide (*q.v.*).

Which see.

Quo fata vocant.

Whither destiny calls me.

Quo jure ?

By what right ?

Quo me cunque vocat patria.

Wherever my country calls me.

Quo mihi fortunam, si non conceditur uti ?—*Horace*.

What use is fortune to me, if I am not allowed to enjoy it ?

Quondam.

Formerly ; former.

Quondam vicimus his armis.

We were once victorious with these arms.

Quo pacto ?

How ? By what means ?

Quorum.

(Of whom.) A sufficient number to form a legal meeting.

Quorum pars magna fui.

In which I bore a great part.

Quos amor verus tenuit, tenebit.—*Seneca*.

He who has once been held by the chains of true love, will never be free.

Quos Deus vult perdere prius dementat.

Those whom God wishes to destroy He first deprives of their senses.

Quota.

Share, proportion.

Quot homines, tot sententiæ.—*Terence*.

So many men, so many minds.

Quot servi, tot hostes.

So many servants, so many enemies.

Quousque tandem abutere patientiâ nostrâ ?—*Cicero*.

How long, pray, will you abuse our patience ?

Quo warranto ?

By what authority ?

Radit usque ad cutem.

(He shaves close to the skin.) He is a near man, he always wants his pound of flesh.

Rara avis in terris nigroque simillima cycno.—*Juvenal*.

A rare bird upon the earth and very like a black swan. A strange prodigy; an unusual event.

Rara fides probitasque viris qui castra sequuntur.

Good faith and probity are rare among such as follow camps.

Raram facit misturam cum sapientiâ forma.—*Petronius Arbiter*.

Wisdom and beauty are rarely united in the same person.

Rari nantes.

Swimming one here another there.

Raro antecedentem scelestum Deseruit pede Pœna claudo.—*Horace*.

Justice, though she halts, has seldom failed to catch the man she pursues.

Rarus sermo illis, et magna libido tacendi.—*Juvenal*.

They speak but seldom, and have a wondrous love of silence.

Ratio et consilium propriæ ducis artes.

Reason and deliberation are the proper qualities of a general.

Rationale.

A statement of reasons ; an exposition of the principles of a subject.

Rebus angustis animosus atque
Fortis appare ; sapienter idem
Contrahes vento nimium secundo
Turgida vela.—*Horace*.

Be brave in trouble ; meet distress
With dauntless front ; but when the gale
Too prosperous blows, be wise no less,
And shorten sail.—*Conington*.

Rebus in angustis facile est contemnere vitam;
Fortiter ille facit, qui miser esse potest.—*Martial.*

In adversity it is easy for a man to despise life, but the truly brave man is he who can endure to be miserable.

Rebus parvis alta præstatur quies.
—*Seneca.*

(To humble folk deep and quiet sleep is given.)
Come, Sleep ; O Sleep ! the certain knot of peace,
The baiting-place of wit, the balm of woe,
The poor man's wealth, the prisoner's release,
Th' indifferent judge between the high and low.—*Sir P. Sidney.*

Recepto
Dulce mihi furere est amico.—*Horace.*

It is pleasant to make merry when a friend has been restored to us.

Recrastinari seges matura non debet.

(A ripe crop must not wait for to-morrow.) Do not put off until to-morrow what you can do to-day.

Recte et suaviter.

Justly and mildly.

Rectus in curiâ.

Upright in the court ; a litigant with an honest cause.

Redintegratio amoris.

The renewal of love.

Redire nescit cum periit pudor—*Seneca.*

Modesty once gone never returns.

Redivivus.

Restored to life ; resuscitated.

Redolet lucernam.

It smells of the lamp ; it is a laboured production.

Reductio ad absurdum.

Reducing an argument to an absurdity.

Regalia.

Badges, marks, or ensigns of royalty.

Regia, crede mihi, res est succurrere lapsis.—*Ovid.*

It is a kingly task, believe me, to help the afflicted.

Regium donum.

A royal gift.

Regum timendorum in proprios greges,
Reges in ipsos imperium est Jovis.
—*Horace.*

O'er men kings hold unquestioned sway,
But Jupiter e'en kings obey.

Re infectâ.

Without accomplishing one's object.

Relictâ non bene parmulâ.—*Horace.*

(Having left my little shield behind.)
Having ingloriously run away.*

Religio loci.

(The religion of the place.) The feeling produced by the sacred or solemn associations of a locality.

Rem acu tetigisti.

(You have touched the thing with a needle.) You have hit the right nail on the head.

Rem, facias rem ;
Si possis recte, si non, quocunque modo rem.—*Horace.*

Get money, get money ; honestly if you can, if not, by any means get money.

Remis velisque.

(With oars and sails.) With might and main.

Renovato nomine.

By a revived name.

* Horace confesses that he ran away at the battle of Philippi, where Octavius (afterwards Augustus Cæsar) and Antony defeated Brutus and Cassius.

Re opitulandum non verbis.

We should help others by deeds, not words.

Repente dives nemo factus est bonus.
—*Publius Syrus.*

No good man ever became suddenly rich.

Reperit Deus nocentem.

(God finds out the guilty man.) God stays long, but strikes at last.

Requiem.

(Rest.) A hymn entreating rest for the dead.

Requiescat in pace (R.I.P.).

May he (or she) rest in peace.

Rerum primordia.

The first elements of things.

Res angusta domi.

Narrow circumstances at home.

Res est ingeniosa dare.—*Ovid.*

(Giving is a noble act.) It is better to give than to receive.

Res est sacra miser.

A person in distress is a sacred object.

Res est solliciti plena timoris amor.

Love is a constant source of fear and anxiety.

Res in cardine est.

(The matter is on the hinge.) The affair is hanging in the balance.

Res judicata.

(A decided case.) A case or point on which judgment has been pronounced.

Respice finem.

(Look to the end.) Look before you leap.

Resurgam.

I shall rise again.

Retinens vestigia famæ.

Maintaining the traces of fame.

Revocare gradum.

To recall (retrace) one's steps.

Rex est, qui metuit nihil
Rex est, qui cupiet nihil.—*Seneca.*

The man who neither fears nor desires anything is truly a king.

Rex regnat sed non gubernat.

(The king reigns but does not govern.) In limited monarchies kings are only figure-heads.

Ridentem dicere verum quid vetat ?
—*Horace.*

(What hinders one from laughing and speaking the truth ?) One may speak the truth without pulling a long face.

Ride si sapis.—*Martial.*

(Laugh, if you are wise.) Mirth and motion prolong life.

Ridiculum acri
Fortius ac melius magnas plerumque secat res.—*Horace.*

Ridicule often decides important matters more effectually and better than severity.

Risu inepto res ineptior nulla est.
—*Catullus.*

Nothing so foolish as the laugh of fools.

Risum teneatis ?

Can you forbear to laugh ?

Rostra.

A raised platform to speak from; tribune.*

Ruat cœlum.

Though the heavens fall.

Rudis indigestaque moles.

(A rough and confused mass.) A state of chaos.

Rus in urbe.

The country in town; a house which combines the pleasures of both.

* The *rostra* was the pulpit or platform in the Forum, from which those who wished to address the popular assemblies spoke. It derived its name from the *rostra*, or ships' beaks, which the Romans had captured at the battle of Antium. The form *rostrum* in this sense is incorrect.

Rusticus exspectat dum defluat amnis ; at ille
Labitur, et labetur in omne volubilis ævum.—*Horace.*

The peasant waits till the river flow past ; but it glides on, and will glide on rolling for ever and ever.

Sacer intra nos spiritus sedet, malorum bonorumque nostrorum observator et custos.—*Seneca.*

A holy spirit dwells within us, that protects us and notes all that is good and evil in us.

Sæpe est sub pallio sordido sapientia. —*Cicero.*

Wisdom is often found under a shabby cloak.

Sæpe intereunt aliis meditantes necem.

Those who set the trap for others often fall into it themselves.

Sæpe stilum vertas, iterum quæ digna legi sint scripturus.

Frequently turn the stilus (re-write your compositions again and again), if you propose to write anything worth reading twice.*

Sæpe viâ obliquâ præstat quam tendere rectâ.

(Often it is better to go by a roundabout way than by the straight road.) Short cuts are often the longest way home.

Sæpius locutum, nunquam me tacuisse pœnitet.

(I frequently regret that I have spoken, but never that I have been silent.) Speech is silver, silence is golden.

Sævis inter se convenit ursis.

Even savage bears agree among themselves.

Sævus tranquillus in undis.

Calm amidst the angry waves.

Sal Atticum.

Attic salt ; wit.

Salus populi suprema est lex.

The welfare of the people is the highest law.

Salvam fac reginam, O Domine.

God save the Queen.

Salve !

Hail ! Welcome .

Salvo jure.

Saving the right ; if the king's rights be not interfered with.

Salvo pudore.

Without offence to modesty.

Sancte et sapienter.

Religiously and wisely.

Sanctum.

A holy (place) ; a private cabinet.

Sanctum sanctorum.

Holy of holies.

Sanitas sanitatum, omnia sanitas.

(Health of healths, all is health.) After " vanity of vanities, all is vanity." The chief concern is health.

Sapere aude.

Dare to be wise.

Sapiens dominabitur astris.

The wise man will govern the stars.

Sapiens ipse fingit fortunam sibi. —*Plautus.*

The wise man fashions his fortune for himself.

Sapientiam ac eruditionem stulti spernunt.

Fools despise wisdom and instruction.

Sapientia primi est stultitiâ caruisse.

The first step to wisdom is to be free from folly.

* The reverse end of the *stilus*, or pen, was flat, and was used to make erasures on the wax writing-tablets

Sartor resartus.

The tailor mended.

Sat cito, si sat bene.

Soon enough if but well enough.

Sat habeo.

I have enough ; I am content.

Satis accipere.

To take security, or bail.

Satis divitiarum est, nil amplius velle.
—*Quintilian.*

Contentment is riches enough.

Satis eloquentiæ, sapientiæ parum.

Sufficient eloquence, but little wisdom.

Satis quod sufficit.

(What suffices satisfies.) Enough is as good as a feast.

Satis, superque.

Enough, and more than enough.

Satis verborum.

Enough of words; you need say no more.

Sat pulchra si sat bona.

(Fair enough if good enough.) Handsome is who handsome does.

Saturno rege.

In the reign of Saturn; in the golden age.

Saucius ejurat pugnam gladiator, et idem Immemor antiqui vulneris arma capit.
—*Ovid.*

The wounded gladiator forswears fighting, and then forgets his former wound and grasps his weapons again.

Saxum volutum non obducitur musco.

A rolling stone gathers no moss.

Scandalum magnatum (Scan. Mag.).

Scandal or slander of great personages.

Scelere velandum est scelus.—*Seneca.*

One crime must be concealed by another.

Scholium.

Annotation ; gloss.

Scienter.

Knowingly.

Scilicet.

That is to say ; to wit.

Scintilla.

A spark.

Scire facias.

"Cause it to be known"; a writ.

Scire quid valeant humeri, quid ferre recusent.

(To know how strong the shoulders are and what they refuse to carry.) To know one's strength and one's weakness.

Scire tuum nihil est, nisi te scire hoc sciat alter.—*Persius.*

Your knowledge is nothing unless others know that you possess it.

Scire ubi aliquid invenire possis, ea demum maxima pars eruditionis est.

To know where you can find anything is the most important part of education.

Scribendi recte sapere est et principium et fons.—*Horace.*

(Knowledge is the basis and source of clever writing.) Sound judgment is the ground of writing well.
—*Roscommon.*

Scribere jussit amor.—*Ovid.*

Love bade me write.

Scribimus indocti doctique poemata passim.—*Horace.*

(All of us everywhere, both taught and untaught, write poetry.)
Those who cannot write and those who can,
All rhyme, and scrawl, and scribble, to a man.—*Pope.*

Secundum artem.

According to art; according to established usage.

Secundum formam statuti.

According to the form of the statute.

Secundum naturam.

According to nature.

Securius divites erimus, si sciverimus quam non sit grave pauperem esse.
— Seneca.

We can enjoy wealth with less anxiety if we have learnt that poverty is not a heavy burden.

Securus et ebrius.

Drunk and free from care.

Securus judicat orbis.

Untroubled the world passes its judgment.

Securus judicat orbis terrarum, bonos non esse qui se dividunt ab orbe terrarum in quacunque parte terrarum.
—St. Augustine.

The calm judgment of the world is that those men cannot be good who, in any part of the world, cut themselves off from the rest of the world.

Se defendendo.

In self-defence.

Sedibus in patriis det mihi posse mori.
—Ovid.

God grant that I may die in my own home.

Sed mihi vel tellus optem prius ima dehiscat
Vel pater omnipotens adigat me fulmine ad umbras,
Pallentes umbras Erebi noctemque profundam,
Ante, pudor, quam te violem aut tua jura resolvam.
Ille meos, primos qui me sibi junxit, amores
Abstulit : ille habeat secum, servetque sepulchro.—*Virgil.*

But first let yawning earth a passage rend,
And let me thro' the dark abyss descend :
First let avenging Jove, with flames from nigh,
Drive down this body to the nether sky,
Condemn'd with ghosts in endless night to lie ;
Before I break the plighted faith I gave ;
No : he who had my vows shall ever have ;
For whom I loved on earth, I worship in the grave.—*Dryden.*

Sed tu simul obligasti
Perfidum votis caput enitescis
Pulchrior multo.—*Horace.*

But thou
When once thou hast broke some tender vow,
All perjured dost more charming grow !

Segnius irritant animum demissa per auras,
Quam quæ sunt oculis subjecta fidelibus.—*Horace.*

The information that we receive through the ears, makes less impression than what our eyes behold.

Semel et simul.

At once and together.

Semel insanivimus omnes.

(We have all once been mad.)   The wisest and best are not immaculate.

Semper ad eventum festinat et in medias res auditorem rapit.—*Horace.*

He always hastens towards the critical part and hurries his listener to the middle of the subject in hand.

Semper avarus eget.

The miser is ever in want.

Semper bonus homo tiro est.—*Martial.*

A good man is always a novice in the ways of the world.

Semper ego auditor tantum ? nunquamne reponam,
Vexatus toties rauci Theseide Codri ?
—Juvenal.

Am I always to be a listener only ? Shall I never answer back when I have been plagued by listening so often to Codrus, getting hoarse by droning out his Theseid ? *

* The often-quoted opening lines of Juvenal's *Satires.*

Semper felix.	Always happy.
Semper fidelis.	Always faithful.
Semper idem (*fem*. eadem).	Always the same.
Semper paratus.	Always ready.
Semperque recentes Convectare juvat prædas, et vivere rapto. —*Virgil.*	A plundering race, still eager to invade, On spoil they live, and make of theft a trade.
Semper, ubique, et ab omnibus.	(Always, everywhere, and by everybody.) Views which have been universally held by all mankind in all times.
Semper vivit in armis.	He ever lives in arms.
Senatus consultum.	A decree of the (Roman) Senate.
Senatus Populusque Romanus (S.P.Q.R.).	The Senate and the Roman People.
Senectus insanabilis morbus est. —*Seneca.*	Old age is an incurable disease.
Senem juventus pigra mendicum creat.	(Youth passed in idleness produces an old age of beggary.) A young man idle, an old man needy.
Seniores priores.	(The older ones first.) Give precedence to age.
Senioribus gravis est inveterati moris mutatio.—*Quintus Curtius.*	(A change of confirmed habits is severely felt by aged persons.) Use is second nature.
Sentio te sedem hominum ac domum contemplarique si tibi parva (ut est) ita videtur, hæc cœlestia semper spectato; illa humana contemnito. —*Cicero.*	I perceive you contemplate the seat and habitation of men; which if it appears as little to you as it really is, fix your eyes perpetually upon heavenly objects, and despise earthly.
Separatio a mensa et toro.	Separation from bed and board.
Sequela.	A consequence or result.
Sequens mirabitur ætas.	Posterity will admire.
Sequiturque patrem non passibus æquis.	(He follows his father, but not with equal paces.) He is not equal in ability to his father.
Sequitur superbos ultor a tergo Deus.	(The avenging God closely pursues the proud.) He hath put down the mighty from their seat.
Sequor non inferior.	I follow, but am not inferior.
Sera in fundo parcimonia.—*Seneca.*	(Economy is useless when all is spent.) To lock the door after the horse is stolen.
Se rebus aliorum immiscere.	(To meddle with other people's business.) To have a finger in every pie.
Seriatim.	In regular order.
Sermo animi est imago.	(Speech is the picture of the mind.) Judge a man's character by his conversation.
Sero sapiunt Phryges.	(The Phrygians are wise too late.) They are wise after the event.
Sero, sed serie.	Late, but seriously.

Sero venientibus ossa.

(The bones for those who come late.) First come first served.

Serum est cavendi tempus in mediis malis.—*Seneca.*

Caution time is over when one is in the midst of evils.

Servabo fidem.

I will keep faith.

Servare modum.

To keep within bounds.

Servetur ad imum, Qualis ab incæpto processerit, et sibi constet.—*Horace.*

(Keep one consistent plan from end to end.) A literary composition ought to be consistent in aim and execution.

Sesquipedalia verba.

Words a foot and a half long.

Si ad honestatem nati sumus, ea aut sola expetenda est, aut certe omni pondere gravior est habenda quam reliqua omnia.—*Cicero.*

If we be made for honesty, either it is solely to be sought, or certainly to be estimated much more highly than all other things.

Sibi non cavere, et aliis consilium dare Stultum est.—*Phædrus.*

It is a fool's part to neglect one's own affairs, and to give advice to others.

Sic.

So; thus.

Si cadere necesse est, occurrendum discrimini.—*Tacitus.*

(If we must fall, let us boldly face the danger.) "How can a man die better than facing fearful odds?"

Sic itur ad astra.

Such is the way to the stars; to immortality.

Sic jubeo.

So I order.

Sic me servavit Apollo.—*Horace.*

Thus Apollo preserved me.*

Sic passim.

So everywhere; in different parts of the book.

Sic totidem verbis.

So in as many words.

Sic transit gloria mundi.

So passes away the glory of the world.

Sicut ante.

As before.

Sic utere tuo ut alienum non lædas.

Exercise your rights in such a manner as not to injure another man's rights.

Sicut in stagno generantur vermes, sic in otioso malæ cogitationes.

As worms are generated in a pool of stagnant water, so evil thoughts spring up in the mind of an idle man.

Sicut mos est nobis.

As is my custom.

Sic vita erat : facile omnes perferre ac pati :
Cum quibus erat cunque una, his sese dedere,
Eorum obsequi studiis, advorsus nemini ;
Nunquam præponens se aliis : Ita facillime
Sine invidiâ invenias laudem.—*Terence.*

His manner of life was this : to bear with everybody's humours ; to comply with the inclinations and pursuits of those he conversed with ; to contradict nobody ; never to assume a superiority over others. This is the ready way to gain applause without exciting envy.

Sic vive cum hominibus, tanquam Deus videat ; sic loquere cum Deo, tanquam homines audiant.—*Seneca.*

Live among men as if the eye of God was upon you ; pray to God as if men were listening to you.

Sic volo, sic jubeo.

So I wish, so I command.

* So Horace expresses his gratitude to the god Apollo, the protecting deity of poets, when he escaped from the clutches of a talkative bore. The expression is now used proverbially to indicate a timely release from any awkward predicament.

Sic vos non vobis.

(Thus you labour, but not for yourselves.) You do the work, and another gets the credit.

Sic vos non vobis nidificatis aves.
Sic vos non vobis vellera fertis oves.
Sic vos non vobis mellificatis apes.
Sic vos non vobis fertis aratra boves.

Thus you, birds, build nests, but not for your own advantage, and also the sheep grow wool, the bees make honey, and the oxen support the ploughs ; but none of them gain profit by their toil.*

Si Deus nobiscum, quis contra nos ?

If God be with us, who shall be against us ?

Si fortuna juvat.

If fortune favours.

Si fractus illabatur orbis
Impavidum ferient ruinæ.—*Horace.*

If the world were to crumble into atoms, the ruins would strike him (the man of firm purpose) undismayed.

Silent leges inter arma.

The laws are silent in the midst of arms.

Si leonina pellis non satis est, assuenda vulpina.

(If the lion's skin is not enough, sew the fox's to it.) Supplement strength by astuteness.

Simia simia est, etiamsi aurea gestet insignia.

(An ape is an ape still, though it wear jewels of gold.) You must not judge a man by his coat.

Similia similibus curantur.

(Like is cured by like.) The basis of the homœopathic system of medicine.

Similis simili gaudet.

(Like delights in like.) Birds of a feather.

Si monumentum requiris, circumspice.

If you seek a monument, look around.

Simplex munditiis.

Simple in thy elegance ; plain in thy neatness.

Sine amore jocisque nil est jucundum.

Without Love and Mirth there is no pleasure.

Sine Cerere et Libero friget Venus.

(Without corn and wine love grows cold.) When poverty comes in at the door, love flies out at the window.

Sine cruce, sine luce.

Without the cross, without light.

Sine die.

(Without a day appointed.) An adjournment for an indefinite period.

Sine dubio.

Without doubt.

Sine ictu.

Without a blow.

Sine invidiâ.

Without envy ; without ill-will.

Sine joco.

Without jesting ; seriously.

Sine odio.

Without hatred.

Sine omni periculo.

Without any danger.

* Virgil, when Bathyllus, a rival, had wrongly claimed a couplet in honour of Augustus, which had been found written on the palace door, wrote on the same door " *Hos ego versiculos feci, tulit alter honores* " and four incomplete lines, beginning *Sic vos, non vobis.* Bathyllus was asked to complete these lines, but failed to do so, when Virgil came forward, supplied the remainder, and vindicated his claim to the first couplet as well.

Sine pennis volare haud facile est.
　　　　　　—*Plautus*.

(It is difficult to fly without feathers.) He would fain fly, but he wants feathers.

Sine quâ non.

(Without which it cannot be done.) An indispensable condition.

Singula de nobis anni prædantur euntes.
　　　　　　—*Horace*.

The advancing years rob us of our pleasures, one by one.

Si non possis quod velis, velis id quod possis.

(If you can't do what you wish, wish to do what you can.) Cut your coat according to your cloth.

Sint Mæcenates, non deerunt, Flacce, Marones.—*Martial*.

Provided there are patrons like Mæcenas, Flaccus, there will not be wanting poets like Virgil.*

Si Pergama dextrâ defendi possent.

(If Troy could have been saved by might.) Everything possible has been attempted to save the situation.

Si quid novisti rectius istis,
Candidus imperti; si non, his utere mecum.—*Horace*.

If you know anything better than these ideas of mine, impart them frankly; if not, use these as I do.

Si quis piorum manibus locus, si, ut sapientibus placet, non cum corpore extinguuntur magnæ animæ, placide quiescas, nosque domum tuam ab infirmo desiderio et muliebribus lamentis ad contemplationem virtutum tuarum voces, quas neque lugeri neque plangi fas est.—*Tacitus*.

If there is any place where the spirits of the righteous dwell, if, as philosophers are disposed to think, souls of the great and good do not perish when their bodies die, mayst thou rest in peace, and call us, thy family, from indulging in vain regrets and womanish tears to the contemplation of thy virtues. These, at least, we have no right to bewail and deplore.†

Si, quoties homines peccant, sua fulmina mittat
Jupiter, exiguo tempore inermis erit.
　　　　　　—*Ovid*.

If Jupiter were to hurl a thunderbolt for every sin that men commit, very soon he would have none to throw.

Siste viator.

(Stop, traveller.) A common inscription on a tombstone.

Sit sine labe decus.

Let honour be stainless.

Sit tibi terra levis.

May the earth lie lightly on thee.

Si vales, bene est.

If you are in good health, it is well.

Si vis me flere, dolendum est
Primum ipsi tibi.—*Horace*.

If you wish me to weep, you must first display grief yourself.

Si vis pacem, para bellum.

(If you desire to maintain peace, be prepared for war.) Strong armaments are the best security for peace.

Si vivere perseverarent.

If they were to persist in living.

---

* Mæcenas, the great minister and adviser of Augustus Cæsar, was the most liberal patron of literary men. He used their skill to glorify the Roman Empire, and to make the rule of the newly-established monarchical system more popular among the Romans.

† The valedictory words of Tacitus to his father-in-law Agricola, whose administration of Britain made a considerable part of that island to be one of the best-ordered parts of the Roman dominions. The view of Tacitus and Seneca with respect to a future life were considerably in advance of those held in the century before, during the latter days of the Republic. At the same time it must not be supposed that Tacitus was in any way affected by the teachings of Christianity, for when he alludes to the spread of Christian doctrines during the first century A.D., he speaks of the new faith with abhorrence, regarding it as a "pernicious superstition."

Si volet usus
Quem penes arbitrium est, et jus, et
  norma loquendi.—*Horace.*

If usage so wills it, which is the arbiter,
  the law and rule of speech.

Socrates quidem cum rogaretur cujatem
  se ipse diceret, mundanum inquit;
  totius enim mundi se incolam et
  civem arbitrabatur.— *Cicero.*

(Socrates, when asked of what country
  he called himself, answered, of the
  world; for he considered himself an
  inhabitant and citizen of the whole
  world.) The world is my parish.
                                    —*Wesley.*

Sola juvat virtus.

Virtue alone assists me.

Sola nobilitas virtus.

Virtue alone is true nobility.

Solent mendaces luere pœnas malefici.
                                    —*Phædrus.*

Liars have generally to suffer for their
  guilt.

Soles occidere et redire possunt:
Nobis cum semel occidit brevis lux,
Nox est perpetua una dormienda.
                                    —*Catullus.*

Suns that set may rise again;
But if once we lose this light,
'Tis with us perpetual night.
                                    —*Ben Jonson.*

Soli lumen mutuari.

(To lend light to the sun.) To carry
  coals to Newcastle.

Solitudinem faciunt, pacem appellant.
                                    —*Tacitus.*

(They make a solitude and call it peace.)
  They remove rebellion by putting the
  rebels to the sword.

Solus et cælebs.

A lone bachelor.

Solventur risu tabulæ; tu missus abibis.
                                    —*Horace.*

Oh, then a laugh will cut the matter
  short:
The case breaks down, defendant leaves
  the court.— *Conington.*

Solvitur ambulando.

The question is resolved by action.

Solvitur risu.

The question is settled by a laugh.

Somno et inertibus horis
Ducere sollicitæ jucunda oblivia vitæ.
                                    —*Horace.*

To taste sweet forgetfulness of the
  anxieties of life in sleep and hours of
  idleness.

Sors tua mortalis, non est mortale quod
  optas.—*Ovid.*

(Thou art mortal in thy destiny, but
  thy aims are those of a god.)   Men,
  though doomed to perish, aspire to
  the imperishable.

Spargere voces in vulgum ambiguas.

To scatter among the people words
  bearing a double meaning.

Spatio brevi
Spem longam reseces: dum loquimur,
  fugerit invida
Ætas: carpe diem, quam minimum
  credula postero.—*Horace.*

Thy lengthen'd hopes with prudence
  bound
Proportion'd to the flying hour;
While thus we talk in careless ease,
The envious moments wing their flight;
Instant the fleeting pleasure seize,
Nor trust to-morrow's doubtful light.
                                    —*Francis.*

Spectemur agendo.

Let us be known by our actions.

Spem pretio non emam.—*Terence.*

(I will not give money for hopes only.)
  I will not buy a pig in a poke.

Sperandum est.

Hope on.

Sperat infestis.

He hopes in adversity.

Spero meliora.

I hope for better things.

ɪ

Spes facit, ut, videat cum terras undique
  nullas,
  Naufragus in mediis brachia jactet
  aquis.
Sæpe aliquem sollers medicorum cura
  reliquit
Nec spes huic venâ deficiente cadit ;
Carcere dicuntur clausi sperare salutem ;
  Atque aliquis pendens in cruce vota
  facit.—*Ovid.*

'Tis Hope that causes the shipwrecked
  mariner to strike out in the midst of
  the waves, even when he sees no land
  in sight. Often when the doctor's
  skill has failed, Hope still lingers
  while life is ebbing. Even the
  prisoner hopes for safety in his prison,
  and the man hanging on the cross
  utters prayers for his release.
Hope springs eternal in the human
  breast,
Man never is but always to be blest.
  —*Pope.*

Spes gregis.
Spes mea Christus.
Spes protracta ægrum efficit animum.
Spes tutissima cœlis.
Splendide mendax.
Splendide mendax et in omne virgo
  Nobilis ævum.

The hope of the flock.
Christ is my hope.
Hope deferred maketh the heart sick.
The safest hope is in Heaven.
Nobly mendacious.
A maiden who nobly told a lie for a
  good cause, and is, thereby, famous
  for all time.
  His honour rooted in dishonour stood
And faith unfaithful kept him falsely
  true.—*Tennyson.*

Spolia opima.

(The choicest spoils.) Spoils won by
  a commander from another, in single
  combat.

Sponte suâ.
Spretæ injuria formæ.
Stans pede in uno.
Stare super antiquas vias, et videre
  quænam sit via recta et bona, et
  ambulare in eâ.
Stat magni nominis umbra.

Unsolicited ; of one's own accord.
The offence of despising her beauty.
Standing on one foot.
To stand on the ancient ways, and to
  see which is the straight and good
  road, and in that to walk.
He stands the shadow of a mighty
  name.

Stat pro ratione voluntas.
Stat sua cuique dies ; breve et irrepara-
  bile tempus
Omnibus est vitæ ; sed famam extendere
  factis,
Hoc virtutis opus.—*Virgil.*
Statu quo.
Status quo ante bellum.
Stemmata quid faciunt ? Quid prodest,
  Pontice, longo
Sanguine censeri pictosque ostendere
  vultus
Majorum ?—*Juvenal.*

Will stands for reason.
Each has his destined time : a span
Is all the heritage of man :
'Tis virtue's part by deeds of praise
To lengthen fame through after days.
  —*Conington.*
As things were before.
The position existing before the war.
(What are the advantages of a long
  pedigree ? What good is it, Pon-
  ticus, to be reckoned of ancient line-
  age and to display the painted faces
  of your ancestors ?)
Kind hearts are more than coronets,
And simple faith than Norman blood.
  —*Tennyson.*

Stet.

Let it stand.

Stet pro ratione voluntas.

Let my will stand for a reason.

Stratum super stratum.

Layer above layer.

Strenua inertia.

Energetic idleness.

Stultorum calami carbones, moenia chartæ.

(Fools use chalk to write with, and walls for paper.) A white wall is a fool's paper.

Stultum est timere, quod vitare non potes.

It is foolish to fear what you cannot avoid.

Stultus spernit eruditionem patris sui.

A fool despises his father's instruction.

Stylo inverso.

With the wrong end of the stylus or pen ; the act of erasing

Sua cuique voluptas.

Every man has his own pleasures.

Suæ quisque fortunæ faber.

Every man is the maker of his own fortune.

Sua munera mittit cum hamo.

(He sends his presents with a hook attached.) A sprat to catch a herring.

Suave mari magno turbantibus æquora ventis,
E terrâ magnum alterius spectare laborem.—*Lucretius.*

'Tis pleasant, when the seas are rough, to stand
And see another's danger, safe at land.

Suaviter in modo, fortiter in re.

Gentle in manner, but resolute in action.

Sub cruce veritas.

Truth under oppression.

Sub divo.

Under the open sky.

Sub ferulâ.

Under the rod.

Sub hoc signo vinces.

Under this sign thou shalt conquer. [See *In hoc signo.*]

Sub Jove.

Under the open sky.

Sub judice.

Under consideration.

Sublatum ex oculis quærimus.

(We miss what we have lost.) When the well is dry we begin to appreciate the value of water.

Sublimi feriam sidera vertice —*Horace.*

With head uplifted I shall tower to the stars.

Sub poenâ.

Under a penalty.

Sub rosâ.

Under the rose ; secretly.

Sub silentio.

In silence.

Substratum.

What lies under an erection ; support.

Successus improborum plures allicit. —*Phædrus.*

The success of the wicked tempts many to imitate them.

Suggestio falsi.

The suggestion of what is false ; putting forward as the fact what one knows to be untrue.

Sui generis.

Of its own kind ; belonging to a class of things peculiar to itself.

Suis stat viribus.

He stands by his own strength.

Summa petit livor.

Envy attacks the noblest.

Summa sedes non capit duos.

(The highest seat will not admit of two.) There is only room for one at a time on the topmost rung of the ladder.

Summum bonum.

The greatest good.

Summum jus, summa injuria.

(The rigour of the law is the rigour of injustice.) The strict enforcement of a law sometimes operates as a great wrong.

Summum nec metuas diem, nec optes.
—*Martial*.

Neither fear death, nor desire it.

Sumptus censum ne superet.—*Plautus*.

(Let not your expenditure exceed your income.) Cut your coat according to your cloth.

Sunt aliquid Manes ; letum non omnia finit.—*Propertius*.

The spirits of the dead do really exist. Death is not the end of everything.

Sunt bona, sunt quædam mediocria, sunt mala plura.—*Martial*.

Some good, more bad, some neither one nor t'other.

Sunt lacrimæ rerum, et mentem mortalia tangunt.—*Virgil*.

(There are tears for human affairs, and mortals' sorrows touch the heart.) The sense of tears in mortal things.
—*Matthew Arnold*.

Suo gladio jugulari.

To be condemned out of one's own mouth ; foiled with one's own devices.

Suo Marte.

By one's own valour.

Suo motu.

On one's own motion ; spontaneously.

Superanda omnis fortuna ferendo est.
—*Virgil*.

Every misfortune is to be overcome by endurance.

Supersedeas.

A writ to stay or set aside proceedings.

Super visum corporis.

Upon a view of the body.

Supplicationes eloquitur pauper, dives autem loquitur aspere.

The poor use entreaties, but the rich speak roughly.

Suppressio veri.

A suppression of the truth.

Supra.

Above.

Surdo loqui.

To talk to a deaf man : to lose one's labour ; to urge a hopeless suit.

Surgit amari aliquid.

(Something bitter rises.) No joy without annoy.

Sursum corda.

Lift up your hearts.

Suspendens omnia naso.—*Horace*.

Turning everything to ridicule.

Suspiria de profundis.

Sighs from the depths.

Suum cuique decus posteritas rependit.
—*Tacitus*.

Posterity pays to every man the honour that is due to him.

Suum cuique pulcrum.

(To every one his own is most beautiful.) The crow thinks her own bird fairest.

Suus cuique mos.

Everyone has his particular habit.

Symposium.

A banquet ; feast ; usually of learned persons.

Tabula rasa.

A blank tablet.

Tædium vitæ.

Weariness of life.

Tam ficti pravique tenax quam nuntia veri.—*Virgil.*

(As ready to spread lies and scandal as to tell the truth.) The character of Rumour.

Tandem fit surculus arbor.

A twig at length becomes a tree.

Tangere ulcus.

(To touch the sore.) To hit the nail on the head.

Tanquam ungues digitosque suos.

(As well as his own nails and fingers.) At his fingers' end; at the tip of his tongue.

Tantæne animis cœlestibus iræ?

Does such anger dwell in heavenly minds?

Tantas componere lites.

To settle so great a quarrel.

Tanti.

Of such importance.

Tanti quantum habeas fis.—*Horace.*

(You are valued by the amount of money you possess.) Money makes the man.

Tanto brevius omne, quanto felicius tempus.— *Pliny the Younger.*

Time passes more quickly in proportion as you are happy.

Tantum religio potuit suadere malorum. —*Lucretius.*

So many evils has superstition been able to arouse.

Tarde, quæ credita lædunt, Credimus.—*Ovid.*

We are slow to believe those things which, if believed, would cause us pain.

Tardus ad iram abundat intelligentia.

He that is slow to anger is of great understanding.

Taurum tollet qui vitulum sustulerit.

(He who has carried the calf will be able to carry the ox.) Custom makes anything easy.

Te judice.

You being the judge.

Telum imbelle sine ictu.

(A feeble weapon thrown without effect.) A weak, useless argument.

Tempestas sequitur serenum.

After calm the storm.

Tempora mutantur, nos et mutamur in illis.

The times change and we change with them.

Temporibus inserviendum.

Time and tide wait for no man.

Temporis ars medicina fere est.—*Ovid.*

Time is a great healer.

Tempus edax rerum.

Time the devourer of all things.

Tempus fugit.

Time flies.

Tempus in ultimum.

To the last extremity.

Tempus omnia revelat.

Time reveals all things.

Tenax propositi.

Tenacious of his purpose.

Teres atque rotundus.

(Polished and round. Round as a ball.) A man of self-control; self-contained.

Terminus ad quem.

(The limit to which.) The end of one's journey or aim.

Terminus a quo.

The limit from which; the starting-point.

Terræ filius.

A son of the soil; a man of mean birth.

Terra es, terram ibis. — Dust thou art, to dust thou shalt return.

Terra firma. — Solid earth ; a firm footing.

Terra incognita. — (An unknown land.) A place or subject of which nothing is known.

Terram cœlo miscent. — (They mingle earth with heaven.) They turn the world upside down.

Tertium quid. — A third something; the result of the union or collision of two forces opposed to one another.

Timeo Danaos et dona ferentes. *— Virgil.* — (I fear the Greeks, even when they offer presents.) A foe is most dangerous when he feigns to be friendly.

Timet pudorem. — He fears shame.

Timidi est optare necem.*—Ovid.* — It is a coward's part to long for death.

Timidi mater non flet. — (A coward's mother does not weep.) He who fights and runs away—.

Timidi nunquam statuere tropæum. — (Cowards never set up a trophy of victory.) Faint heart never won fair lady.

Timor addidit alas.*— Virgil.* — Fear gave him wings.

Timor animi auribus officit.*—Sallust.* — (Fear closes the ears of the mind.) No exhortation moves a coward.

Timor Domini fons vitæ. — The fear of the Lord is the fountain of life.

Toga. — The Roman civil dress.*

Toga virilis. — (The gown of manhood.) The dress that a Roman assumed when he reached manhood, and put off the *toga prætexta*, the garb of boyhood.

Tot homines, quot sententiæ. — So many men, so many minds.

Totidem verbis. — In just so many words.

Toties quoties. — As often as.

Totis viribus. — With all his might.

Toto cœlo. — (By the whole heavens.) Diametrically opposed.

Totum in eo est. — All depends on this.

Totus mundus agit histrionem. — All the world's a stage.

Totus teres atque rotundus. — Complete, smooth, and round.

Traditus non victus. — Betrayed, not conquered.

Transeat in exemplum. — May it pass into an example.

Tria juncta in uno. — Three joined in one.

Tribus Anticyris caput insanabile. *— Horace.* — (A head incurable even by three Anticyræ.) A hopeless lunatic.†

Triste lupus stabulis, maturis frugibus imbres, Arboribus venti, nobis Amaryllidis iræ.*— Virgil.* — The wolf is fatal to the flocks, showers to ripened corn, winds to the trees, the wrath of Amaryllis to me.

Tristis eris, si solus eris.*— Ovid.* — You will be sad if you keep only your own company.

* See note on *Cedant arma.*
† Anticyra was famed for its hellebore, a remedy that the ancients thought cured madness.

Triumpho morte tam vitâ.

I triumph in death as in life.

Troja fuit.

(Troy has been.) Its day is over.

Tros Tyriusque mihi nullo discrimine agetur.—*Virgil.*

(Trojan and Tyrian shall be treated by me with no difference.) I will be quite impartial, as I care for neither side.

Truditur dies die.

One day is pressed onward by another.

Tu ne cede malis, sed contra audentior ito.—*Virgil.*

Yield not to misfortunes, but confront them all the more boldly.

Tunica propior pallio est.

(My coat is nearer than my cloak.) Charity begins at home.

Tu quoque.

(You, too.) A retort, implying that the case of the opposite party is no better than its rival's; each being guilty of the same misdoings.

Tu recte vivis, si curas esse quod audis. —*Horace.*

You live as you ought, if you take care to act up to the reputation you deserve.

Turpe quid ausurus, te sine teste time. —*Ausonius.*

When about to do an evil thing, though there be no other witness, respect thyself and forbear.

Tutor et ultor.

Protector and avenger.

Tutum silentii præmium.

(The reward of silence is sure.) Silence is golden.

Tuum est.

It is your own.

Uberrima fides.

Implicit reliance.

Ubi amici ibi opes.

Where there are friends money is not far to seek.

Ubicumque homo est, ibi beneficio locus est.—*Seneca.*

(Wherever a human being exists, there is an opportunity to do a kindness.) Be ye kind one to another.

Ubi jus incertum, ibi jus nullum.

Uncertainty destroys law.

Ubi libertas, ibi patria.

Where liberty dwells, there is my country.

Ubi mel, ibi apes.—*Plautus.*

(Where there is honey, there are bees.) Where there is an attractive thing to be seen, a crowd is sure to gather.

Ubi mens plurima, ibi minima fortuna.

(Where there is most mind, there is least money.) Philosophers despise wealth.

Ubique.

Everywhere.

Ubi solitudinem faciunt pacem appellant.

(Where they make a solitude, they call it peace.)
Mark where his carnage and his conquests cease,
He makes a solitude and calls it peace.
　　　　　　　　　　　—*Byron.*

Ubi supra

Where above mentioned.

Ultima ratio.

The final reason or argument.

Ultima ratio regum.

(The last reasoning of kings.) Military force.*

* The *ultima ratio*, according to Richelieu, was the fire of artillery, and these words were inscribed on some cannon of Louis XVI.

Ultima semper
Exspectanda dies homini, dicique beatus
Ante obitum nemo supremaque funera
debet.—*Ovid.*

(Each man must wait his latest day of life, and none may we call truly happy until the grave closes over him.) It is impossible to judge a man's prosperity until his life is ended.

Ultima Thule.

(Most distant Thule.) The furthest land or limit.

Ultimatum.

The last proposal before recourse to active hostilities.

Ultimo (ult.).

The preceding month.

Ultimus regum.

The last of the kings.

Ultra vires.

Beyond, in excess of (one's legal) powers.

Una hirundo non facit ver.

One swallow does not make a summer.

Una salus victis, nullam sperare salutem.—*Virgil.*

(The only safety that remains for the conquered is to hope for none.) Despair often gives courage even to the timid.

Unâ voce.

With one voice ; unanimously.

Unguibus et rostro.

(With claws and beak.) With all one's force.

Unguis in ulcere.

A claw in the wound.

Uni navi ne committas omnia.

(Venture not all in one bottom.) Do not put all your eggs in one basket.

Unius dementia dementes efficit multos.

(The madness of one makes many mad.) Folly is catching ; one fool makes many.

Uno animo.

With one mind ; unanimously.

Uno avulso, non deficit alter.

(On the removal of one, another is not wanting.) *Il n'y a d'homme nécessaire.* There is no one so important but the world can go on without him.

Unum et commune periculum, una salus ambobus erit.

There shall be one common danger, one safety for both.

Unus homo nobis cunctando restituit rem ;
Non ponebat enim rumores ante salutem.—*Ennius.*

(One man, by delay, saved the state ; for he cared less for what was said than for the safety of his country.)*

Unus vir nullus vir.

(One man is no man.) A man unaided cannot do much. Two heads are better than one.

Urbem latericiam invenit, marmoream reliquit.

He (Augustus) found the city (Rome) a city of bricks, he left it a city of marble.

Urbi et Orbi.

To the city (Rome) and to the world.†

Urbs antiqua ruit, multos dominata per annos.—*Virgil.*

An ancient city that for ages held imperial sway, falls into ruins.

Urit mature urtica vera.

(The real nettle stings early.) Vicious puppies early show their teeth.

---

* See *Cunctando restituit rem.*
† These were the words that formerly accompanied the benediction which the Pope publicly pronounced on the Catholic world upon certain solemn festivals of the year.

Usque ad aras.

To the very altars : to the last extremity.

Usque ad nauseam.

Even to satiety, to disgust.

Usus et experientia dominantur in artibus.—*Columella.*

Practice and experience are of the greatest importance in all works of skill.

Usus loquendi.

The usage of speech.

Usus promptos facit.

(Use makes men ready.)　　Practice makes perfect.

Ut ameris, ama.

To win love, show love to others.

Utinam populus Romanus unam cervicem haberet.

Would that the Roman people had but one neck.*

Ut infra.

As below.

Uti possidetis.

As you possess ; state of present possession.

Ut nemo in sese tentat descendere, nemo ! Sed præcedenti spectatur mantica tergo. —*Persius.*

(You can never find a man who tries to look into his own conscience. Everyone keeps his eyes fixed on the wallet of the man in front.) We can all see the burden of sins that our neighbour carries, but never our own.

Ut pictura poesis est.—*Horace.*

(Poems like pictures are.)　　The art of the poet is akin to that of the painter.

Ut prosim.

That I may do good.

Ut quisque est vir optimus, ita difficillime esse alios improbos suspicatur.

The better a man is, the less is he inclined to suspect others.

Utrum horum mavis accipe.

Take whichever you prefer ; choose one of two evils.

Ut sæpe summa ingenia in occulto latent.—*Plautus.*

The greatest geniuses are often living in obscurity.

Ut sementem feceris, ita metes.—*Cicero.*

As you have sown, so shall you reap.

Ut supra.

As above ; as above stated.

Ut vidi, ut perii.

The moment I beheld, how I was undone !

Vacuum.

Absolutely empty space.

Vade mecum.

(Go with me.)　A guide ; a handbook.

Væ soli.

(Woe to the solitary man.)
O Solitude ! where are the charms
That sages have seen in thy face ?
　　　　　　—*Cowper.*

Væ victis.

Woe to the vanquished.

Vale.

Farewell.

Valeat quantum valere potest.

Let it pass for what it is worth.

Valete ac plaudite.

Farewell and applaud.

　　　　　　Valet ima summis Mutare, et insignem attenuat deus, Obscura promens.—*Horace.*

(God hath power to change the lowliest with the loftiest, and He maketh the great men weak, bringing to light things hidden in gloom.)　" He hath put down the mighty from their seat."

* Suetonius narrates that Caligula, the maddest of the early Cæsars, made this remark in one of his bloodthirsty moments.

Valvæ.
A folding door; valves.

Vanitas vanitatum. Omnia vanitas.
Vanity of vanities. All is vanity.

Variæ lectiones.
Various readings; different versions of an author's words.

Variatio delectat.
(Variety pleases.) All work and no play makes Jack a dull boy.

Variorum (editio).
An edition with the notes of various writers (*cum notis variorum*).

Varium et mutabile semper femina.
—*Virgil.*
Woman is ever fickle and changeable.

Vates sacer.
Sacred prophet, or poet; an inspired bard.

Vehimur in altum.
We are borne on high; we are carried out into the deep sea.

Velis et remis.
With sails and oars; by every possible means.

Velocem tardus assequitur.
(The slow overtakes the swift.) Slow and steady wins the race.

Velocius quam asparagi coquantur.
(More quickly than you could cook asparagus.) Done in the twinkling of an eye.

Velox consilium sequitur pœnitentia.
(Repentance quickly follows hasty counsels.) Marry in haste and repent at leisure.

Vel prece, vel pretio.
For either love or money.

Veluti in speculum.
As in a mirror.

Venalis populus, venalis curia patrum.
(The people is venal, the senate is venal.) Every man has his price.

Vendidit hic auro patrium.
This man sold his country for gold.

Venenum in auro bibitur. Expertu loquor :
Malam bonæ præferre fortunam licet.
—*Seneca.*
It is in golden cups that poison is found. I speak from experience : the lot of the poor man is preferable to that of the rich.

Venia necessitati datur.—*Cicero.*
(Pardon is granted to necessity.) Necessity dispenses with decorum.

Veni, Creator Spiritus.
Come, Holy Ghost, our souls inspire.

Venienti occurrite morbo.
Meet an approaching disease; combat it on the first symptoms.

Venire facias.
(Cause him to come.) The writ for summoning a jury.

Veniunt a dote sagittæ.
(The darts come from her dowry.) Her money is her chief attraction.

Veni, vidi, vici.
I came, I saw, I conquered.

Ventis remis.
(With wind and oars.) With all one's might.

Ventis secundis.
With prosperous winds.

Ventis verba profundere.
(To pour forth words to the winds.) To speak to deaf ears.

Vento et fluctibus loqui.
(To speak to the wind and the waves. To waste one's words.

Vento vivere.
To live upon wind; to live on air.

Vera gloria radices agit, atque etiam propagatur: ficta omnia celeriter, tanquam flosculi, decidunt, nec simulatum potest quidquam esse diuturnum.
—*Cicero.*

True glory takes root, and even spreads; all false pretences, like flowers, fall to the ground; nor can any counterfeit last long.

Verbatim et literatim.

Word for word, and letter for letter.

Verbosa et grandis epistola.—*Juvenal.*

A huge wordy letter.

Verbum Domini manet in æternum.

The word of the Lord endureth for ever.

Verbum sat sapienti.

A word is enough for a wise man.

Verbum semel emissum volat irrevocabile.—*Horace.*

A word once uttered flies away and can never be recalled.

Vere prius volucres taceant, æstate cicadæ.

(Sooner can birds be silent in spring, and the crickets in summer.) An extreme improbability.

Veritas nihil veretur nisi abscondi.

Truth fears nothing but concealment.

Veritas nunquam perit.—*Seneca.*

Truth never dies.

Veritas odium parit.

Truth begets hatred.

Veritatis absolutus sermo ac semper est simplex.

The language of truth is plain and always simple.

Ver non semper viret.

Spring does not always flourish.

Verso pollice vulgi Quem libet occidunt populariter.
—*Juvenal.*

With thumbs bent back, they popularly kill.—*Dryden.*

Versus.

Against.

Verus et fidelis semper.

Always true and loyal.

Vestibulum domus ornamentum est.

(The hall is the ornament of a house.) First impressions are always the strongest.

Vestigia.

Footsteps, traces.

Vestigia nulla retrorsum.

(There are no backward footsteps.) He has burned his bridges.

Vestigia terrent Omnia te adversum spectantia, nulla retrorsum.—*Horace.*

I'm frightened at those footsteps; every track Leads to your home, but ne'er a one leads back.—*Conington.*

Vetustas pro lege semper habetur.

Ancient custom is always reckoned as a law.

Vexata quæstio.

A vexed question; a moot point

Via media.

A middle course.

Viaticum.

(Provision for the journey.) The Eucharist, when administered to the sick, or to persons unable to go to church.

Via trita, via tuta.

The beaten path is the safe path.

Vice versâ.

The terms being exchanged; the reverse.

Victrix causa deis placuit, sed victa Catoni.—*Lucan.*

(The conquering cause pleased the gods, but the conquered one pleased Cato.) Noble spirits ally themselves to great causes even when there is no hope of ultimate success.*

* Cato killed himself at Utica after the defeat of the Senatorial forces in Africa, 46 B.C., by Julius Cæsar. As a Stoic he chose death rather than submit to a form of government which he regarded as a despotism.

Victrix fortunæ sapientia.

Vide.

Vide et crede.

Videlicet (viz.).

Video meliora proboque, deteriora sequor.—*Ovid*.

Vide ut supra.

Vi et armis.

Vigilate et orate.

Vilius argentum est auro, virtutibus aurum.—*Horace*.

Vincam aut moriar.

Vincere aut mori.

Vincit amor patriæ.—*Virgil*.

Vincit qui patitur.

Vincit, qui se vincit.

Vincit veritas.

Vinctus invictus.

Vinculum matrimonii.

Vir bonus est quis Qui consulta patrum, qui leges juraque servat.—*Horace*.

Vires acquirit eundo.

Virescit vulnere virtus.

Virginibus puerisque.

Viri infelicis procul amici.

Vir pietate gravis ac meritis.

Vir sapit qui pauca loquitur.

Virtus agrestiores ad se animos allicit. —*Cicero*.

Virtus ariete fortior.

Virtus est vitium fugere.

Virtus in actione consistit.

Virtus in arduis.

Virtus incendit vires.

Virtus invidiæ scopus.

Virtus laudatur et alget.—*Juvenal*.

Virtus nec eripi, nec surripi potest unquam.—*Cicero*.

Virtus non stemma.

Virtus probata florescit.

Virtus, recludens immeritis mori Cœlum negatâ tentat iter viâ ; Cœtusque vulgares et udam Spernit humum fugiente pennâ. —*Horace*.

Wisdom conquers fortune.

See.

See and believe.

Namely.

(I see and approve of the better things, I follow the worse.) I know the right, and yet the wrong pursue.

See what is stated above.

By force of arms.

Watch and pray.

Silver is inferior to gold, gold to virtue.

I will conquer or die.

To conquer or to die.

The noblest motive is the public good.

He that can endure overcometh.

He conquers who overcomes himself.

Truth conquers.

Chained but not conquered.

The bond of marriage.

He is the truly good man who observes the decrees of his rulers, and the laws and rights of his fellow-citizens.

It acquires strength in going.

Virtue flourishes from a wound.

For lads and lasses.

Friends keep at a distance from an unfortunate man.

A man whose reputation for probity and good actions has gained him influence.

The man is wise who talks little.

Virtue allures to herself even the boorish minds.

Virtue is stronger than a battering ram.

It is virtue to shun vice.

Virtue consists in action.

Virtue in difficulties.

Virtue kindles the strength.

Virtue is the mark of envy.

Virtue is praised, but is left to starve.

Virtue can neither be taken away nor stolen from a man.

Virtue, not pedigree.

Virtue flourishes in trial.

Virtue, throwing open heaven to those who deserve not to die, directs her course by paths denied to others, and spurns with swift pinion the vulgar throng and the dank earth.

Virtus repulsæ nescia sordidæ
  Intaminatis fulget honoribus ;
  Nec sumit aut ponit secures
  Arbitrio popularis auræ.—*Horace.*

Virtue, which knows no base repulse, shines with untarnished honours ; she neither receives nor resigns the emblems of authority at the will of the fickle populace.

Virtus semper viridis.

(Virtue is always green.)   Virtue never fadeth.

Virtus sub cruce crescit, ad æthera tendens.

Virtue increases under the cross and strives towards heaven.

Virtute meâ me involvo.

I wrap myself up in my integrity.

Virtutem incolumem odimus,
Sublatam ex oculis quærimus, invidi.
                        —*Horace.*

We envy and hate the noble, when they are alive; when they are dead we cease not to despise their loss.

Virtutem videant. intabescantque relictâ.
                        —*Persius.*

In all her charms set Virtue in their eye, And let them see their loss, despair and die.—*Gifford.*

Virtute non viris.

From virtue not from men.

Virtute officii.

By virtue of office.

Virtuti nihil obstat et armis.

Nothing can oppose virtue and courage.

Virtutis amore.

By the love of virtue.

Virtutis laus omnis in actione consistit.
                        —*Cicero.*

(All the merit of virtue consists in action.)

Even so faith, if it hath not works, is dead.—*St. James.*

Virum volitare per ora.

(To flit through the mouths of men.) To pass from lip to lip; to spread like wild-fire.

Vis a tergo.

A propelling force from behind.

Vis comica.

Comic power, or talent.

Vis consilii expers mole ruit suâ.
                        —*Horace.*

(Force unsupported by discretion falls by its own weight.)   Discretion is the better part of valour.

Vis inertiæ.

The power of inertness.

Vis poetica.

Poetic genius.

Visu carentem magna pars veri latet.
                        —*Seneca.*

They that are dim of sight see truth by halves.

Vis unita fortior.

Union is strength.

Vis vitæ.

The vigour of life.

Vita brevis, ars longa.

Life is short and art is long.

Vitæ postscenia celant.—*Lucretius.*

Men conceal the back-scenes of their life.

Vita hominum altos recessûs magnasque latebras habet.—*Pliny the Younger.*

The life of each man contains hidden depths and secret places, unknown to other men.

Vitam impendere vero.

To stake one's life for the truth.

Vita mortuorum in memoriâ vivorum est posita.—*Cicero.*

The life of the dead is maintained in the memory of those who survive them.

Vitam regit fortuna, non sapientia.

It is fortune that governs human life, not wisdom.

Vitanda est improba siren, Desidia.

The wicked siren, Sloth, is to be **shunned.**

Vitaque mancipio nulli datur, omnibus usu.—*Lucretius.*

Life is given to no man as a lasting possession, but merely for use.

Vita, si scias uti, longa est.—*Seneca.*

Life is long, if we know how to use it.

Vitia erunt, donec homines.—*Tacitus.*

(So long as men live, vices will abound.) The heart is deceitful above all things, and desperately wicked.—*Jeremiah.*

Vitiis nemo sine nascitur.

No man is born without his faults.

Vitium fuit, nunc mos est assentatio.

Flattery which was formerly a vice, is now a custom.

Vivamus, mea Lesbia, atque amemus.
                              —*Catullus.*

Let us live and love, my darling Lesbia.

Vivat regina.

Long live the queen.

Vivâ voce.

By the living voice ; orally.

Vive memor leti. Fugit hora : hoc quod loquor inde est.—*Persius.*

Live mindful of death. Time flies; this very word I speak is so much taken from it.

Vivere est cogitare.—*Cicero.*

To live is to think.

Vivere si recte nescis decede peritis.
                              —*Horace.*

If you do not know how to live rightly, submit to those who do.

Vive, vale.

Farewell and be happy.

Vivida vis animi.

The living force of the mind.

Vivit post funera virtus.

Virtue survives the grave.

Vixere fortes ante Agamemnona.

There lived brave men before Agamemnon.

Vixere fortes ante Agamemnona
    Multi ; sed omnes illacrimabiles
    Urgentur ignotique longâ
    Nocte, carent quia vate sacro.
                              —*Horace.*

Many brave men lived before Agamemnon, but all unwept and unknown lie buried in endless night, because they lack an inspired bard to relate their exploits.

Vixi ! et, quem dederat cursum fortuna, peregi. Crastinum si adjecerit Deus, læti recipiamus. Ille beatissimus est, et securus sui possessor, qui crastinum sine sollicitudine expectat. Quisquis dixit " Vixi " quotidie ad lucrum surgit.—*Seneca.*

I have lived and finished the course which Fortune gave me. If God grant us to-morrow, let us receive it joyfully. That man is most truly happy, and complete master of himself, who awaits the morrow without anxiety. Whoever has said, " I have lived," rises daily to live profitably.

Volenti non fit injuria.

No injustice is done to a person by an act to which he consents.

Volo, non valeo.

I am willing, but unable.

Voluptates commendat rarior usus.
                              —*Juvenal.*

Pleasures, when they come rarely, are most enjoyed.

            Vos exemplaria Græca
Nocturnâ versate manu, versate diurnâ.
                              —*Horace.*

Study the Greek literary models by night, study them by day.

Vota vita mea.

My life is devoted.

Vox audita perit, litera scripta manet.

The word that is heard perishes, but the letter that is written abides.

Vox clamantis in deserto.

The voice of one crying in the wilderness.

Vox et præterea nihil.

A voice and nothing more.

Vox faucibus hæsit.	The voice that stuck in the throat.
Vox populi, vox Dei.	The voice of the people is the voice of God.
Vulgo.	Commonly.
Vulgus amicitias utilitate probat. —*Ovid*.	Vulgar people value friendships only for the advantages to be gained therefrom.
Vulgus ex veritate pauca, ex opinione multa æstimat.—*Cicero*.	The great majority of people estimate few things according to the real value of them, most things according to their own preconceived ideas.
Vulneratus, non victus.	Wounded, but not conquered.
Vulnus immedicabile.	An irreparable injury; an incurable wound.
Vultus est index animi.	The face is the index of the mind.
Zephyrus.	A gentle wind; a zephyr.
Zonam perdidit.	He has lost his purse; he is ruined.
Zonam solvere.	(To untie the girdle.) To marry a woman.*

* Roman women wore a *zona*, or girdle, around the loins until they married, as a sign of maidenhood. This was laid aside at the time of marriage, and its removal was, therefore, typical of surrender to marital authority.

Greek.

Ἀβδηρολόγος ἐστὶν ὁ ἀπὸ τῶν Ἀβδήρων ἄνθρωπος.

(Abderite by birth, Abderite by speech.) A boor is known by his talk.*

Ἀγαθὴ δὲ παραίφασίς ἐστιν ἑταίρου. —*Homer.*

The advice that a friend gives is good.

Ἀγαθὴ δ᾽ ἔρις ἥδε βροτοῖσι.— *Hesiod.*

(Rivalry is a blessing to men.) Honest rivalry adds zest to toil.

Ἀγαθοὶ δ᾽ ἀριδάκρυες ἄνδρες.

The good are always prone to tears.

Ἀγαθὸς ὁ θεός· καὶ τῶν μὲν ἀγαθῶν οὐδένα ἄλλον αἰτιατέον, τῶν δὲ κακῶν ἄλλ᾽ ἄττα δεῖ ζητεῖν τὰ αἴτια, ἀλλ᾽ οὐ τὸν θεόν.—*Plato.*

Since God is good, we must regard him as the author of all our blessings ; our misfortunes we must assign to other causes, but never to God.

Ἀγάπα τὸν πλησίον. - *Thales.*

Love thy neighbour.

Ἃ γὰρ ἐπιθυμεῖ ψυχὴ, καὶ πιστεύειν φιλεῖ.— *Heliodorus.*

The mind is always prone to believe what it wishes to be true.

Ἄγει δὲ πρὸς φῶς τὴν ἀλήθειαν χρόνος. —*Menander.*

Time brings the truth to light.

Ἀγευστοὶ καλλίστου καὶ γονιμωτάτου λόγων νάματος, τὴν ἐλευθερίαν λέγω, οὐδὲν ὅτι μὴ κόλακες ἐκβαίνομεν μεγαλοφυεῖς.—*Longinus.*

If we have not tasted of that best and most fruitful source of eloquence, I mean liberty, we are naught but vain babblers of flattering speeches.

Ἀγνώστῳ Θεῷ.

To the unknown God.†

Ἀδελφὸς ἀνδρὶ παρείη.—*Socrates.*

Let each man aid his brother man.

Ἅδης.

Hades ; the abode of the dead.

Ἀδύνατον πολλὰ τεχνώμενον ἄνθρωπον πάντα καλῶς ποιεῖν.—*Xenophon.*

It is impossible for a man who attempts much to do everything well.

Ἁδύ τι τὸ στόμα τοι, καὶ ἐφίμερος, ὦ Δάφνι, φωνά·
κρέσσον μελπομένῳ τεῦ ἀκουέμεν ἢ μέλι λείχειν.—*Theocritus.*

Sweet are thy lips, thy utterances, and lovely thy voice, Daphnis ; it is better to hear thy singing than to eat honey.

Ἀεὶ γεωργὸς εἰς νέωτα πλούσιος. —*Philemon.*

(The farmer is always to be rich the next year.) "Man never is, but always to be blest."

Ἀεὶ κολοιὸς παρὰ κολοιῷ ἱζάνει.

(A jackdaw always sits near a jackdaw.) Birds of a feather flock together.

---

* The boorishness of the people of Abdera was proverbial in ancient times. It was, however, the birthplace of one famous man, the philosopher Democritus.
† The words occur in St. Paul's speech to the Athenians, "For as I passed by, and beheld your devotions, I found an altar with this inscription, To the Unknown God."—*Acts xvii.* 23.

'Αεὶ Λιβύη φέρει τι καινόν.—*Aristotle.*

We are always hearing of some new thing from Africa.

'Αεὶ νομίζονθ' οἱ πένητες τῶν θεῶν.
— *Menander.*

The poor are always thought to be under the special protection of the gods.

'Αεὶ τὰν ποσὶν ὄντα παρατρεχόμεσθα μάταιοι,
κεῖνο ποθοῦντες ὅπερ μακρὸν ἄπωθεν ἔφυ.
—*Pindar.*

(We foolish men ever pass by the things that lie at our feet, while we long for that which is far away.)
'Tis distance lends enchantment to the view.—*Campbell.*

῎Αελπτον οὐδὲν, πάντα δ' ἐλπίζειν χρεών.
—*Euripides.*

Nothing is hopeless, we must hope for everything.

'Αεργοῖς αἰὲν ἑορτά.— *Theocritus.*

Every day is a holiday to people who have nothing to do.

'Αεροβατῶν.

(One who treads the air.) An affected, conceited person ; a wool-gatherer.

'Αετὸν ἵπτασθαι διδάσκεις.

(You are teaching an eagle to fly.) Jack Sprat would teach his grand-dame.

'Αετὸς οὐ θηρεύσει τὰς μυίας.

An eagle will not catch flies.

'Αετοῦ γῆρας, κορύδου νεότης.

An old eagle is better than a young sparrow.

'Αθανάτους μὲν πρῶτα θεοὺς, νόμῳ ὡς διάκειται, τίμα.

First of all, thou must honour the gods as the law ordains.*

Αἱ γὰρ εὐπραξίαι δειναὶ συγκρύψαι καὶ συσκιάσαι τὰς ἁμαρτίας τῶν ἀνθρώπων εἰσίν.— *Demosthenes.*

Success cloaks and obscures the evil deeds of men.

Αἰδεῖσθαι πολιοκροτάφους.

Respect grey hairs.

Αἱ δ' ἐλπίδες βόσκουσι φυγάδας, ὡς λόγος.
καλῶς βλέπουσιν ὄμμασιν, μέλλουσι δέ.
— *Euripides.*

Exiles, the proverb says, subsist on hope.
Delusive hope still points to distant good,
To good, that mocks approach.

Αἱ δὲ σάρκες αἱ κεναὶ φρενῶν
ἀγάλματ' ἀγορᾶς εἰσί.—*Euripides.*

Bodies devoid of mind are like the statues in the market-place.

Αἱ δεύτεραι φροντίδες σοφώτεραι.
—*Euripides.*

Second thoughts are best.

Αἰδὼς δ' αὖ νέον ἄνδρα γεραίτερον ἐξερέεσθαι.—*Homer.*

It is shameful for a young man to question an older one.

Αἰδὼς δ' οὐκ ἀγαθὴ κεχρημένον ἄνδρα κομίζει.—*Hesiod.*

False shame is ever the comrade of the needy man.

Αἰδὼς τοῦ κάλλους καὶ ἀρετῆς πόλις.
— *Demades.*

Modesty is the citadel of beauty and virtue.

Αἰεὶ δ' ἀμβολιεργὸς ἀνὴρ ἄτῃσι παλαίει.
— *Hesiod.*

The man who procrastinates is always struggling with misfortunes.

Αἰὲν ἀριστεύειν.— *Homer.*

Always to excel.

Αἰθίοπα σμήχειν.

To wash an Ethiopian; to wash a blackamoor.

Αἴνει δὲ παλαιὸν μὲν οἶνον,
ἄνθεα δ' ὕμνων νεωτέρων.—*Pindar.*

Give praise to wine that's old, but to poetry that's new.

* The opening line of the Golden Verses of Pythagoras.

K

Αἰνούμενοι γὰρ ἀγαθοὶ, τρόπον τινὰ
μιτοῦσι τοὺς αἰνοῦντας, ἢν αἰνῶσ' ἄγαν.
                              —Euripides.

When good men are praised, they are inclined to hate those who praise them if they are praised beyond their deserts.

Αἰών.

An æon ; a long period of time.

Αἰὼν πάντα φέρει.

Time changes all things.

Ἀκίνητα κινεῖς.

(You are meddling with what should be left alone.)   You play with fire.

Ἄκουε πολλὰ, λάλει καίρια.—Bias.

Listen carefully, speak seasonably.

Ἀκρόπολις.

A citadel ; the ancient citadel of Athens.

Ἀληθεύοντες ἐν ἀγάπῃ.—St. Paul.

Speaking the truth in love.*

Ἁλιεὺς πληγεὶς νοῦν οἴσει.

(The fisherman when stung will learn wisdom.)   The burnt child dreads the fire.

Ἀλλὰ καὶ λέγουσι πάντες ὡς δειλότατόν
ἐσθ' ὁ πλοῦτος.—Aristophanes.

It is a common saying that wealth brings much misery in its train.

Ἀλλ' ἀπ' ἐχθρῶν δῆτα πολλὰ μανθάνουσιν
οἱ σοφοί.—Aristophanes.

Wise men often learn from their enemies.

Ἀλλὰ τὰ μὲν προτετύχθαι ἐάσομεν.
                              —Homer.

We will let by-gones be by-gones.
Let us not burden our remembrances with a heaviness that's gone.
                              —Shakespeare.

Ἀλλὰ τὸ τῆς κυνὸς ποιεῖς τῆς ἐν τῇ
φάτνῃ κατακειμένης.—Lucian.

You are playing the part of the dog in the manger.

Ἀλλ' ἔστ' ἀληθὴς ἡ βροτῶν παροιμία,
ἐχθρῶν ἄδωρα δῶρα κοὐκ ὀνήσιμα.
                              —Sophocles.

The old proverb is true ; the gifts of an enemy are no gifts, but bring mischief.

Ἀλλ' ἢ καλῶς ζῆν, ἢ καλῶς τεθνηκέναι
τὸν εὐγενῆ χρή.—Sophocles.

(A noble man must either live a good life or die a glorious death.)   Death rather than dishonour.

Ἀλλ' οἱ ἀθυμοῦντες ἄνδρες οὔποτε τρό-
παιον ἐστήσαντο.—Eupolis.

(No coward ever set up a trophy.) Faint heart never won fair lady.

Ἄλλοι κάμον, ἄλλοι ὤναντο.

(One does the work, another gets the profit.)   One beats the bush and another catches the bird.

Ἀλλ' οὐ Ζεὺς ἄνδρεσσι νοήματα πάντα
τελευτᾷ—Homer.

(God does not accomplish all that man designs.)   Man proposes, God disposes.

Ἀλλ' οὐκ αὖθις ἀλώπηξ πάγαις.

(A fox is not caught twice in a snare.) The burnt child dreads the fire.

Ἄλλων ἰατρὸς, αὐτὸς ἕλκεσιν βρύων.
                              —Euripides?

(The physician of others, he himself is full of sores.)   He does not see the beam in his own eye.

Ἄλφα καὶ Ὠμέγα.

(Alpha and Omega.)   The first and last letters of the Greek alphabet ; the beginning and the end.

Ἅμα δὲ κιθῶνι συνεκδυομένῳ ἐκδύεται καὶ
τὴν αἰδὼ γυνή.—Hrodotus.

When a woman takes off her clothes, she puts off her modesty too.

Ἅμα ἔπος, ἅμα ἔργον.

No sooner said than done.

* These words were the favourite motto of the late Professor Blackie, and generally appeared on the letters that he wrote to his friends.

'Αμαθία μὲν θράσος, λογισμὸς δὲ ὄκνον
φέρει.—*Thucydides.*

'Αμαρτίης αἰτίη ἡ ἀμαθίη τοῦ κρέσσονος.
—*Democritus.*

'Αμβροσία.

'Αμέραι δ' ἐπίλοιποι μάρτυρες σοφώτατοι.
—*Pindar.*

'Αμφοῖν φίλοῖν ὄντοιν, ὅσιον προτιμᾶν
τὴν ἀλήθειαν.—*Aristotle.*

'Αμφότεροι κλῶπες, καὶ ὁ δεξάμενος, καὶ
ὁ κλέψας.—*Phocylides.*

'Ανάγκη γὰρ τὴν μὲν τῆς πρώτης καὶ
θειοτάτης πολιτείας παρέκβασιν, εἶναι
χειρίστην.—*Aristotle.*

'Ανάγκη οὐδὲ θεοὶ μάχονται.
—*Simonides of Ceos.*

'Ανάγκης οὐδὲν ἰσχύει πλέον.
—*Euripides.*

'Ανάθεμα.

Ἄναξ ἀνδρῶν 'Αγαμέμνων.—*Homer.*

'Αναφαίρετον κτῆμ' ἐστὶ παιδεία βροτοῖς.
—*Menander.*

Ἄνδρες γὰρ πόλις, καὶ οὐ τείχη, οὐδὲ
νῆες ἀνδρῶν κεναί.—*Thucydides.*

Ἄνδρες πόληος πύργοι ἀρήϊοι.—*Alcæus.*

'Ανδρὶ μελετητέον οὐ τὸ δοκεῖν εἶναι
ἀγαθὸν ἀλλὰ τὸ εἶναι, καὶ ἰδίᾳ καὶ
δημοσίᾳ.—*Plato.*

'Ανδρί τοι χρεὼν
μνήμην προσεῖναι, τερπνὸν εἴ τί που πάθοι.
—*Sophocles.*

'Ανδρὸς δικαίου κάρπος οὐκ ἀπόλλυται.

'Ανδρὸς κακῶς πράσσοντος ἐκποδὼν φίλοι.
—*Menander?*

'Ανδρὸς χαρακτὴρ ἐκ λόγου γνωρίζεται.
—*Menander.*

'Ανδρῶν γὰρ σωφρόνων μέν ἐστιν, εἰ μὴ
ἀδικοῖντο, ἡσυχάζειν, ἀγαθῶν δὲ ἀδι-
κουμένους ἐκ μὲν εἰρήνης πολεμεῖν, εὖ
δὲ παρασχὸν ἐκ πολέμου πάλιν ξυμ-
βῆναι, καὶ μήτε τῇ κατὰ πόλεμον
εὐτυχίᾳ ἐπαίρεσθαι μήτε τῷ ἡσυχίῳ
τῆς εἰρήνης ἡδόμενον ἀδικεῖσθαι.
—*Thucydides.*

Ignorance produces rashness, reflection
timidity.

Ignorance of what is better is often the
cause of sin.

(Ambrosia.)   The food of the gods;
anything pleasing to the taste.

Future days are often the best test of
present reputations.

Both are dear to me, but duty compels
me to prefer the truth.*

Both are thieves, he who receives and he
who steals.

The corruption of the best and divinest
form of government must be the
worst.

(Not even the gods can resist necessity.)   Necessity has no law.

Nothing is stronger than necessity.

An accursed thing; a solemn curse.

Agamemnon, king of men.

Education is a possession that none can
take away.

It is not walls, or ships devoid of crews,
but men that make a city.

Brave men are a city's strongest tower
of defence.

A man should endeavour not merely to
appear good, but to be good both in
his public and private life.

If a man has received a kindness from
another, he ought ever to keep it in
grateful remembrance.

The good deeds of a righteous man
perish not.

(When a man is unfortunate, his friends
are hard to find.)   A friend in need, etc.

The character of man is known from his
conversation.

It becomes prudent men to remain quiet
so long as they are not injured, but
courageous men ought to exchange
peace for war as soon as they have
been wronged; when they have
brought the war to a successful issue,
peace may be made with the enemy;
but no one ought to be uplifted un-
duly by success in war, nor should
any submit to injustice because they
are unwilling to sacrifice the calm
delights of peace.

---

* This expression is more familiar in the Latin form, *Amicus Plato, sed major veritas.*

Ἀνδρῶν ἡρώων τέκνα πήματα.

(Sons of heroes are a plague.)   Many a good cow hath an evil calf.

*Ἂν ἔτι μίαν μάχην νικήσωμεν, ἀπολώ-
λαμεν.—*Pyrrhus, King of Epirus.*

Another such victory and we are lost.*

Ἀνὴρ ἀτυχῶν σώζεται ταῖς ἐλπίσιν.
                    —*Menander.*

(Hope saves a man in the midst of misfortunes.)   Hope is the salve for a breaking heart.

Ἀνὴρ γὰρ ἰδιώτης ἐν πόλει δημοκρατου-
μένῃ νόμῳ καὶ ψήφῳ βασιλεύει· ὅταν
δ' ἑτέρῳ ταῦτα παράδῳ, καταλέλυκεν
αὐτὸς τὴν αὐτοῦ δυναστείαν.
                    —*Æschines.*

In a democratic state, the power of voting gives to the individual regal authority; but when he surrenders this privilege to another, he dethrones himself.

Ἀνὴρ δίκαιός ἐστιν οὐχ ὁ μὴ ἀδικῶν,
ἀλλ' ὅστις ἀδικεῖν δυνάμενος, οὐ βούλεται.—*Philemon.*

The just man is not he who merely does not injure another, but he who, having the power to do so, refuses to commit any injustice.

Ἀνὴρ, ὅστις τρόποισι συντακῇ, θυραῖος ὢν,
μυρίων κρείσσων ὁμαίμων ἀνδρὶ κεκτῆσθαι
φίλος.—*Euripides.*

A man of congenial habits, even though he be a stranger, is a better friend to get than ten thousand relations.

Ἀνὴρ ὁ φεύγων καὶ πάλιν μαχήσεται.
                    —*Menander.*

(The man who runs away will fight again.)
        He who fights and runs away,
        May live to fight another day.

Ἄνθρωποι δὲ μάταια νομίζομεν, εἰδότες
οὐδέν·
θεοὶ δὲ κατὰ σφέτερον πάντα τελοῦσι
νόον.—*Theognis.*

Vain are the thoughts of men, and nothing our knowledge; but the gods direct all things according to their will.

Ἄνθρωποι δὲ μινυνθάδιοι τελέθουσιν.
                    —*Homer.*

Men have but a short time to live.

Ἀνθρώποισι πᾶσι μέτεστι γιγνώσκειν
ἑαυτοὺς καὶ σωφρονεῖν.—*Heraclitus.*

To all men it is given to know themselves, and to practise self-control.

Ἀνθρώποισι τὰς μὲν ἐκ θεῶν
τύχας δοθείσας ἐστ' ἀναγκαῖον φέρειν.
                    — *Sophocles.*

Men must endure whatever ills the gods may send.

Ἄνθρωπός ἐστι πνεῦμα καὶ σκιὰ μόνον.
                    —*Euripides.*

Man is but a breath and a shadow.

Ἀνθρώπους μὲν ἴσως λήσεις ἄτοπόν τι
ποιήσας,
οὐ λήσεις δὲ θεοὺς οὐδὲ λογιζόμενος.
                    —*Lucian.*

Probably you will deceive men when you sin, but you will not escape the eyes of Heaven, whatever wiles you may devise.

Ἀνθρώπων ὀλίγον μὲν κάρτος, ἄπρηκτοι
δὲ μεληδόνες
αἰῶνι δ' ἐν παύρῳ πόνος ἀμφὶ πόνῳ,
ὁ δ' ἄφυκτος ἐπικρέμαται θάνατος.
                    —*Simonides of Ceos.*

(Small is the strength of man, unprofit-
able his anxious thoughts; toil follows toil throughout his brief span of life, and death invincible is ever imminent.)
All our yesterdays have lighted fools
The way to dusky death.
                    —*Shakespeare.*

Ἀνίη καὶ πολὺς ὕπνος.—*Homer.*

Too much sleep becomes a pain.

---

* Pyrrhus, King of Epirus, carried on a successful war against the Romans, 281 to 275 B.C., in Sicily and the south of Italy. Badly supported by his allies, however, his victories were too expensive for ultimate success. The above saying is the origin of the expression, "a Pyrrhic victory."

Ἀξία ἡ κύων τοῦ βρώματος.

(The dog is worth its food.) 'Tis a poor dog that deserves not a crust.

Ἀξιώματα.

Admitted propositions: general maxims.

Ἅ οἱ φίλοι τοῖς βασιλεῦσιν οὐ θαρροῦσι παραινεῖν, ταῦτα ἐν τοῖς βιβλίοις γέγραπται.—*Plutarch.*

The advice which their friends dare not give to kings is found written in books.

Ἅπαν διδόμενον δῶρον, εἰ καὶ μίκρον ᾖ, μέγιστόν ἐστιν, εἰ μετ' εὐνοίας διδῷς
— *Philemon.*

Every gift, even though it is small, is valuable if you give it with a kind intention.

Ἅπανθ' ὁ μακρὸς κἀναρίθμητος χρόνος φύει τ' ἄδηλα καὶ φανέντα κρύπτεται·
κοὐκ ἔστ' ἄελπτον οὐδέν, ἀλλ' ἁλίσκεται χὠ δεινὸς ὅρκος χαὶ περισκελεῖς φρένες.
—*Sophocles.*

All strangest things the multitudinous years
Bring forth, and shadow from us all we know.
Falter alike great oath and steeled resolve ;
And none shall say of aught, " This may not be."—*Calverley.*

Ἅπανθ' ὃς ὀργιζόμενος ἄνθρωπος ποιεῖ ταῦθ' ὕστερον λάβοις ἂν ἡμαρτημένα.
— *Menander.*

All things that a man in anger does, in the end are found to have been done amiss.

Ἅπαντ' ἐπαχθῆ πλὴν θεοῖσι κοιρανεῖν.
— *Æschylus.*

Every lot has its hardships except the lordship of heaven.

Ἅπαξ λεγόμενον.

A phrase, that only occurs once in a book ; a rare word.

Ἅπᾶσα δὲ χθὼν ἀνδρὶ γενναίῳ πατρίς.
—*Euripides.*

Every land is a fatherland to the man of lofty courage.

Ἅπας δὲ τραχὺς ὅστις ἂν νέος κράτῃ.
— *Æschylus.*

(Every ruler is severe when he has just mounted the throne) New brooms sweep clean.

Ἅπας ἐρυθριῶν χρηστὸς εἶναι μοι δοκεῖ.
— *Menander.*

Every man who can blush has, me-thinks, some honesty in him.

Ἀπάτης δικαίας οὐκ ἀποστατεῖ θεός.
—*Æschylus.*

God is not opposed to deceit in a righteous cause.

Ἁ πένια τὰς τέχνας ἐγείρει.—*Theocritus.*

Poverty is the mother of the arts.

Ἀπιστοῦνται δ' οἱ λάλοι, κἂν ἀλη-θεύωσιν. — *Plutarch.*

Nobody believes gossiping fools, even when they speak the truth.

Ἁπλοῦς ὁ μῦθος· μὴ λέγ' εὖ· τὸ γὰρ λέγειν
εὖ, δεινόν ἐστιν, εἰ φέροι τινὰ βλάβην.
— *Archelaus.*

Let thy speech be simple, avoid fine speaking ; for fine speaking that produces evil results is a vile thing.

Ἁπλοῦς ὁ μῦθος τῆς ἀληθείας ἔφυ.
—*Euripides.*

The language of the true is always simple.

Ἀποθέωσις.

(Apotheosis.) Deification ; raising a distinguished person to the rank of a god.

Ἅ ποιεῖν αἰσχρὸν, ταῦτα νόμιζε μηδὲ λέγειν εἶναι καλόν.—*Isocrates.*

Consider that those acts which it is disgraceful to perform, are not even fit to be mentioned.

Ἀπόλοιτο πρῶτος αὐτὸς
ὁ τὸν ἄργυρον φιλήσας·
διὰ τοῦτον οὐκ ἀδελφὸς,
διὰ τοῦτον οὐ τοκῆες·
πόλεμοι, φόνοι δι' αὐτόν.—*Anacreon.*

Let the greatest curses light on him who is a slave to lust of gold ! For gold brothers are sacrificed, and parents betrayed. Wars and blood-shed are caused by gold.

'Απορία ψαλτοῦ βήξ.

A cough is the musician's trick to hide his blunder.

'Απ' οὐρᾶς τὴν ἔγχελυν ἔχεις.

(You have got an eel by the tail.) You have caught a Tartar.

'Απροσίκτων ἐρώτων ὀξύτεραι μανίαι.
—*Pindar.*

The longing for unattainable objects is always the keenest.

'Απώτερω ἢ γόνυ κνήμη.

(My shin is not so near me as my knee.) Charity begins at home.

'Αργὸς μὴ ἴσθι, μηδ' ἂν πλουτῇς.
—*Thales.*

Shun idleness, even if you are wealthy.

'Αργυρέαις λόγχαισι μάχε, καὶ πάντα κρατήσεις.

Fight with silver spears, and you will conquer everywhere.*

'Αρετὰ, θήραμα κάλλιστον βίῳ.
—*Aristotle.*

Virtue, the noblest object to be sought in life.

'Αρετὴ δέ, κἂν θάνῃ τις οὐκ ἀπόλλυται ζῇ δ' οὐκέτ' ὄντος σώματος· κακοῖσι δὲ ἅπαντα φροῦδα συνθανόνθ' ὑπὸ χθονός.
—*Euripides.*

(Virtue does not perish when the good man dies, but lives when his body is turned to dust : but when the wicked die, all their glories are buried with them in the clay.)
Each man makes his own statue, builds himself ;
Virtue alone outbuilds the Pyramids.
—*Young.*

Ἄρης δ' οὐκ ἀγαθῶν φείδεται, ἀλλὰ κακῶν.—*Anacreon.*

War slays the brave, but spares the cowards.

Ἄριστον ἀνδρὶ κτῆμα συμπαθὴς γυνή.
—*Hippothoon.*

A sympathetic wife is her husband's best possession.

Ἄριστον μὲν ὕδωρ.—*Pindar.*

(Water is the best.) Water is the greatest of the elements.

Ἄριστον μέτρον.

Moderation is best.

'Αρχὰ πολιτείας ἁπάσης νέων τροφά.
—*Diogenes.*

The education of the young is the proper basis of every state.

Ἄρχειν οὐδενὶ προσήκει, ὃς οὐ κρείττων ἐστὶ τῶν ἀρχομένων.—*Cyrus.*

No one ought to rule, if he is not superior to those whom he rules.

Ἄρχεσθαι μαθὼν ἄρχειν ἐπιστήσῃ.
—*Solon.*

By learning to obey you will learn how to govern.

'Αρχὴ ἄνδρα δείξει.—*Bias.*

Authority will prove a man.) It is impossible to tell a man's character until he has been tried in a position of responsibility.

'Αρχὴ ἥμισυ παντός.—*Hesiod.*

(The beginning is the half of the whole.) Well begun is half done.

'Αρχομένων τῶν νόσων, ἦν τι δοκέῃ κινεῖν κίνει.—*Hippocrates.*

(When diseases begin to show themselves, use active measures at once if the case seems to require it.) Resist the beginnings of evil.

Ἄσβεστος γέλως.—*Homer.*

(Unquenchable laughter.) Homeric laughter.

---

* The reply of the Delphic oracle to Philip of Macedon, father of Alexander the Great. Philip followed the advice, and boasted that he could capture any town if he could manage to convey a bribe to some of the citizens.

'Αστέρας εἰσαθρεῖς 'Αστὴρ ἐμός· εἴθε
　γενοίμην
οὐρανός, ὡς πολλοῖς ὄμμασιν εἰς σὲ
βλέπω.—*Plato Comicus?*

'Ατελέστατα γὰρ καὶ ἀμάχανα
　τοὺς θανόντας κλαίεν
Θανόντος ἀνδρὸς πᾶσ' ἀπολλυτ' ἀπ'
　ἀνθρώπων χάρις.—*Stesichorus.*

Αὐθαδία γὰρ τῷ φρονοῦντι μὴ καλῶς
αὐτὴ καθ' αὑτὴν οὐδενὸς μεῖον σθένει.
　　　　　　　　　　　—*Æschylus.*

Αὔξεται δ' ἀρετά, χλωραῖς ἐέρσαις ὡς
　ὅτε δένδρον ἀΐσσει.—*Pindar.*

　　　　　　　　　Αὐτὰρ ὕπερθεν
νίκης πείρατ' ἔχονται ἐν ἀθανάτοισι
θεοῖσιν.—*Homer.*

Αὐτᾶς ἄκουκα πολλάκις.
　　　　—*Agesilaus, King of Sparta.*

Αὐτὸ δὲ τὸ σιγᾶν ὁμολογοῦντός ἐστί σου.
　　　　　　　　　　　—*Euripides.*

Αὐτόματον.

Αὐτονομία.

Αὐτὸς γὰρ ἐφέλκεται ἄνδρα σίδηρος.
　　　　　　　　　　　—*Homer.*

Αὐτὸς ἔφα.

Αὐτός τι νῦν δρᾶ, χοὕτω δαίμονας κάλει·
τῷ γὰρ πονοῦντι χὠ θεὸς συλλαμβάνει.
　　　　　　　　　　　—*Euripides.*

'Αφορᾶν οὖν δεῖ εἰς τὸν νοῦν, καὶ μὴ εἰς
　τὴν ὄψιν.—*Æsop.*

'Αφροδίσιος ὅρκος οὐκ ἐμποίνιμος.

ᵃΑ ψέγομεν ἡμεῖς, ταῦτα μὴ μιμώμεθα.
　　　　　　　　　　　—*Menander.*

Βάλλ' ἐς κόρακας.

Βαρεῖα δ' ἀστῶν φάτις ξὺν κότῳ.
　　　　　　　　　　　—*Æschylus.*

Βαρὺ φόρημ' ἄνθρωπος εὐτυχῶν ἄφρων.
　　　　　　　　　　　—*Æschylus.*

Βῆ δ' ἀκέων παρὰ θῖνα πολυφλοίσβοιο
　θαλάσσης.—*Homer.*

Why dost thou gaze upon the sky ?
O that I were yon spangled sphere !
Then every star should be an eye
To wander o'er thy beauties here.
　　　　　　　　　　—*Moore.*

Vain it is for those to weep
Who repose in Death's last sleep.
With man's life ends all the story
Of his wisdom, wit, and glory.
　　　　　　　　　　—*Merivale.*

　　　　　　Self-will, by itself,
In one who is not wise is less than
nought.—*Plumptre.*

Noble deeds grow before the eyes of
men, even as a tree waxes great when
watered by the quickening dew.

But the immortal gods hold the
threads of victory in their hands.

I have often heard the nightingale herself.*

(Your silence is in itself an admission.)
Your silence gives consent.

(An automaton.)　A thing that is self-
moved, as a clock, etc.

Autonomy ; self-government.

The sword itself often provokes a man
to fight.

(He himself said so.)　*Ipse dixit.*†

Be active first thyself, then seek the aid
of heaven ; for God helps him who
helps himself.

We ought to consider a man's intelligence, not his outward appearance.

(Lovers' vows are broken with impunity.)　All's fair in love and war.

We ought to avoid in ourselves the
faults that we blame in others.

Away with you ; go and be hanged !

Grievous is the voice of the people
when hatred inspires their words.

A fool in prosperity is a heavy burden
to endure.

And (the old man) in bitter grief paced
along the shore of the loud-roaring
sea.

---

* A reply to one who told him of a musician who imitated and rivalled the nightingale.
† The saying of the Pythagoreans when they quoted the opinion of their teacher on any subject, Αὐτὸς ἔφα, "The Master said so-and-so."

Βίον καλὸν ζῆς, ἂν γυναῖκα μὴ ἔχῃς.
— *Menander.*

(You live happily, if you have no wife.)
When a man's single he lives at his ease.

Βούλονται δ' οἱ πλεῖστοι τὰ φαῦλα δι'
ἀπειρίαν τῶν καλῶν καὶ ἄγνοιαν.
— *Plutarch.*

Most men are knavishly inclined because they have no experience and are ignorant of the blessings of virtue.

Βούλου γονεῖς πρὸ παντὸς ἐν τιμαῖς ἔχειν.
— *Philemon.*

Honour thy parents before all else.

Βοῦς ἐπὶ γλώσσῃ.

(An ox on the tongue.)   A bribe to keep silence.

Βουστροφηδόν.

(Turning in writing like oxen in ploughing.) Writing from left to right, and then from right to left.

Βραδέως ἐγχείρει· ὃ δ' ἂν ἄρξῃ, διαβε-
βαιοῦ.—*Bias.*

Be slow to undertake a thing; but, once undertaken, go through with it.

Βραχεῖα τέρψις ἡδονῆς κακῆς.
— *Euripides.*

Brief is the joy that wicked pleasure brings.

Βράχιστα γὰρ κράτιστα τὰν ποσὶν κακά.
— *Sophocles.*

Even slight sorrows, when they are present with us, are grievous to bear.

Βριάρεος φαίνεται ὢν λαγώς.

(He seems to be a Briareus when he is only a hare.) Great boast, small roast.

Βροτοῖς ἅπασι κατθανεῖν ὀφείλεται,
κοὐκ ἔστι θνητῶν ὅστις ἐξεπίσταται
τὴν αὔριον μέλλουσαν εἰ βιώσεται.
— *Euripides.*

All men must die, and no mortal can tell whether he will live through the coming day.

Βροτοῖς ἅπασιν ἡ συνείδησις θεός.
— *Menander.*

Conscience is to all men a god.

Βρῶμα θεῶν.

(Food for the gods.)   Mushrooms.*

Γαμεῖν ἐκ τῶν ὁμοίων· ἐὰν γὰρ ἐκ τῶν
κρειττόνων, δεσπότας, οὐ συγγενεῖς,
κτήσῃ —*Cleobulus.*

Take a wife from your own rank; for if you marry the daughter of greater folk than yourself, you will find them masters, not kinsmen.

Γαμεῖν ὁ μέλλων εἰς μετάνοιαν ἔρχεται.

(He who would marry is on the road to repentance.) When a man's married his troubles begin.†

Γάμοι δ' ὅσοις μὲν εὖ καθεστᾶσιν βροτῶν,
μακάριος αἰών· οἷς δὲ μὴ πίπτουσιν εὖ,
τά τ' ἔνδον, τά τε θύραζε δυστυχεῖς.
— *Euripides.*

Marriage is a blessed state to men when all things go well with them; but when misfortunes come, both home ties and outside affairs are equally burdensome.

Γάμος γὰρ ἀνθρώποισι εὐκταῖον κακόν.
— *Menander.*

Marriage is an evil that most men welcome.

Γελᾷ δ' ὁ μῶρος, κἄν τι μὴ γελοῖον ᾖ.
— *Menander.*

The fool laughs, even though there is nothing to laugh at.

---

* A saying of Nero.   His mother, Agrippina, was suspected of having given poison to the Emperor Claudius in a dish of mushrooms, and so won the throne for her son, who afterwards showed his gratitude by compassing her death.   The Roman emperors were deified after death. so the mushrooms were indeed food for a god on this occasion.
† An adaptation of a line written by the comic poet Philemon.

Γέλως ἄκαιρος ἐν βροτοῖς δεινὸν κακόν.
—*Menander.*

Ill-timed laughter is an evil thing.

Γένοιτο δ' ἂν πᾶν ἐν τῷ μακρῷ χρόνῳ.
—*Herodotus.*

Length of time may bring anything to pass.

Γέοοντα τὸν νοῦν σάρκα δ' ἡβῶσαν φέρει.
—*Æschylus.*

Old man's brains in a young man's body.

Γέρων ἀλώπηξ οὐκ ἁλίσκεται πάγῃ.

(You can't catch an old fox in a trap.)
You can't catch an old bird with chaff.

Γηράσκω δ' αἰεὶ πολλὰ διδασκόμενος.
— *Solon.*

I grow in learning as I grow in years.

Γλαῦκας εἰς 'Αθήνας.

(Owls to Athens.) Carrying coals to Newcastle.

Γλυκὺ δ' ἀπείροισι πόλεμος. – *Pindar.*

War is sweet to those who never proved it.

Γνῶθι σαυτόν.— *Chilon.*

Know thyself.*

Γυναικὶ κόσμος ὁ τρόπος, κ' οὐ χρυσία.
—*Menander.*

Manner, not gold, is a woman's best adornment.

Γυναικὸς οὐδὲ χρῆμ' ἀνὴρ ληΐζεται
ἐσθλῆς ἄμεινον, οὐδὲ ῥίγιον κακῆς.
Simonides of Amorgos.

Of earthly goods, the best is a good wife ;
A bad, the bitterest curse of human life.

Γυναιξὶ κόσμον ἡ σιγὴ φέρει.—-*Sophocles.*

Silence is a woman's true adornment.

Γυνὴ γὰρ ἐν κακοῖσι καὶ νόσοις πόσει
ἥδιστόν ἐστι.—-*Euripides.*

In the hour of sorrow or sickness, a wife is a man's greatest blessing.

Γυνὴ δ' ἀπόντος ἀνδρὸς ἥτις ἐκ δόμων
εἰς κάλλος ἀσκεῖ, διάγραφ', ὡς οὖσαν κακήν.
— *Euripides.*

If a woman tricks herself out in finery when her husband is away, you may write her down no faithful wife.

Γυνή ἐστι δαπανηρὸν φύσει.

Woman is naturally prone to extravagance.

Γυνὴ πολυτελής ἐστ' ὀχληρόν.
—*Menander.*

An extravagant wife is a plague to her husband.

Δεῖ ἀμέλλητον εἶναι τὴν πρὸς τὰ καλὰ ὁρμήν.—*Nigrinus.*

In an honourable enterprise there must be no delay.

Δεῖ γὰρ τὸν ἄρχοντα σώζειν πρῶτον αὐτὴν τὴν ἀρχήν· σώζεται δ' οὐχ ἧττον ἀπεχομένη τοῦ μὴ προσήκοντος, ἢ περιεχομένη τοῦ προσήκοντος. 'Ο δ' ἐνδιδοὺς, ἢ ἐπιτείνων, οὐ μένει βασιλεὺς, οὐδὲ ἄρχων, ἀλλ' ἢ δημαγωγὸς, ἢ δεσπότης γιγνόμενος, ἐμποιεῖ τὸ μισεῖν, ἢ καταφρονεῖν τοῖς ἀρχομένοις.
— *Plutarch.*

It is the first duty of a ruler to preserve the constitution ; this can be done by maintaining his own rights while not trespassing on the rights of others. For the ruler who surrenders his own prerogatives, or assumes powers not his own, is no longer a king or governor, but a demagogue or a despot, whose subjects either despise or hate him.

Δεῖ καρτερεῖν ἐπὶ τοῖς παροῦσι καὶ θαρρεῖν περὶ τῶν μελλόντων.—*Isocrates.*

We ought to endure patiently our present suffering, and look with confidence to the future.

---

* This famous phrase, attributed also to Thales and to others of the Seven Wise Men of Greece, was inscribed over the entrance of Apollo's temple at Delphi.

Δειλὴ δ' ἐνὶ πυθμένι φειδώ.—*Hesiod.*

(Economy is useless at the bottom.) It is hard to save when you have spent your all.

Δειλοὺς δ' εὖ ἔρδοντι ματαιοτάτη χάρις ἐστίν.— *Theognis.*

To benefit the wicked is a vain and thankless task.

Δεινὰ περὶ φακῆς.

(Terrible talk about lentils.) Much ado about nothing.

Δεινὸν τὸ τίκτειν καὶ φέρει φίλτρον μέγα πᾶσίν τε κοινὸν ὥσθ' ὑπερκάμνειν τέκνων.—*Euripides*

A wonderful thing is motherhood, and great the consolations that it brings to all, so that parents are willing to suffer for their children.

Δεινὸς γὰρ οἶνος, καὶ παλαίεσθαι βαρύς. —*Euripides.*

Wine is a dread foe, and hard to wrestle with.

Δεινὸς Ἔρως.

Love the conqueror.

Δεῖ φέρειν τὰ τῶν θεῶν.—*Euripides.*

We must endure whatever God sends us.

Δέλτα.

(A delta.) Islands formed by the mouths of large rivers, that are shaped like the Greek letter Δ.

Δελφικὴ μάχαιρα.

(A Delphic sword.) A two-edged response.*

Δεύτερος πλοῦς.

(A second voyage.) The next best way ; a second plan if the first one fails.

Δέχεται κακὸν ἐκ κακοῦ αἰεί.—*Homer.*

(One evil always succeeds another.) Misfortunes never come singly.

Διαβολὴ γάρ ἐστι δεινότατον· ἐν τῇ δύο μέν εἰσι οἱ ἀδικέοντες, εἷς δὲ ὁ ἀδικεόμενος. Ὁ μὲν γὰρ διαβάλλων ἀδικέει οὐ παρεόντος κατηγορέων· ὁ δὲ ἀδικέει ἀναπειθόμενος πρὶν ἢ ἀτρεκέως ἐκμάθῃ. —*Herodotus.*

Slander is a most dreadful thing ; when a man is slandered, there are two who wrong him, the slanderer and the man who listens. The slanderer acts wrongly because he speaks ill of the absent ; the listener because he believes the tale before he has ascertained its truth for himself.

Διάθεσις.

(A disposition ; state ; condition.) The state of one's physical health.

Δι' αἵματος, οὐ διὰ μέλανος, τοὺς νόμους ὁ Δράκων ἔγραψεν.—*Demades.*

Dracon wrote his law in blood, not in ink.†

Διαιρούμενα εἰς τὰ μέρη τὰ αὐτὰ μείζονα φαίνεται.—*Aristotle.*

(The parts appear greater than the whole.) When we examine a thing in its details, it appears larger than when considered as a composite whole.

Διαστολή.

(Expansion.) The dilation of the lungs.

---

* The replies of the Delphic oracle were couched in terms that might bear a double meaning. This method had obvious advantages in the event of the oracle's advice proving bad. For example, during the invasion of Xerxes, the Athenians were told to trust to their wooden walls. This was interpreted by the majority as a command to trust to a sea-battle, but some remembered the old wooden palisade round the Acropolis. They paid for their opinion with their lives when the Persians occupied Athens.

† The severity of the laws of Dracon, the Athenian lawgiver of the seventh century B.C., has become proverbial. They were drawn up on the principle that all crimes were equally culpable and deserved the severest penalties.

Διὰ τί πάντες ὅσοι περιττοὶ γεγόνασιν
ἄνδρες ἢ κατὰ φιλοσοφίαν ἢ πολιτικὴν,
ἢ ποίησιν, ἢ τέχνας, φαίνονται με-
λαγχολικοὶ ὄντες.—Aristotle.

(All who have excelled either as philosophers, or statesmen, or poets, or
artists, seem to have a touch of madness in them.)
Great wits are sure to madness near
allied
And thin partitions do their bounds
divide.—Dryden.

Διαφέρομεν δὲ καὶ ταῖς τῶν πολεμικῶν
μελέταις τῶν ἐναντίων τοῖσδε. Τήν τε
γὰρ πόλιν κοινὴν παρέχομεν καὶ οὐκ
ἔστιν ὅτε ξενηλασίαις ἀπείργομέν τινα
ἢ μαθήματος ἢ θεάματος, ὃ μὴ κρυφθὲν
ἄν τις τῶν πολεμίων ἰδὼν ὠφεληθείη,
πιστεύοντες οὐ ταῖς παρασκευαῖς τὸ
πλέον καὶ ἀπάταις ἢ τῷ ἀφ' ἡμῶν
αὐτῶν ἐς τὰ ἔργα εὐψύχῳ.
                        —Thucydides.

We feel superior to our enemies in the
art of war for these reasons. We
throw open our city to all, and we
never drive any stranger away to prevent him learning or seeing anything;
we conceal nothing, even though the
knowledge of it may aid our foes.
For we do not trust to preparations
and crafty devices so much as to our
natural courage in the hours of danger.*

Δίδου μοι τὴν σήμερον, καὶ λάμβανε τὴν
αὔριον.

(Give me to-day, and you may take to-
morrow.) Let us eat, drink, and be
merry, for to-morrow we die; sufficient unto the day is the evil thereof.

Δίκαια δράσας συμμάχους ἕξεις θεούς.
                        — Menander.

If you act justly you will have Heaven
as your ally.

Δίκαιόν ἐστι καὶ τὸ τοῦ λύκου εἴπειν

(It is just to hear even what the wolf
has to say for himself.) Give the
devil his due.

Διόπερ ῥᾷστον ἁπάντων ἐστὶν αὐτὸν
ἐξαπατῆσαι· ὃ γὰρ βούλεται, τοῦθ'
ἕκαστος καὶ οἴεται, τὰ δὲ πράγματα
πολλάκις οὐχ οὕτω πέφυκεν.
                        —Demosthenes.

Nothing is so easy as to deceive one's
self; for each man readily believes
what he wishes to be true, even
though the truth is far otherwise.

Δὶς κράμβη θάνατος.

(Cabbage, twice over, is death.) Too
much of a good thing; crambe
repetita.

Δὶς πρὸς τὸν αὐτὸν αἰσχρὸν προσκρούειν
λίθον.

(It is shameful to stumble twice against
the same stone.) Experience teaches;
the scalded cat fears cold water.

Δόγμα.

A dogma; opinion; tenet.

Δόσις δ' ὀλίγη τε, φίλη τε.—Homer.

A gift of little value, but still precious.

Δὸς ποῦ στῶ καὶ τὸν κόσμον κινήσω.
                        —Archimedes.

Give me standing-room and I will move
the world.†

Δός τι, καὶ λάβοις τι.—Prodicus.

Give something to gain something; you
must spend to earn.

Δουλεύειν πάθεσι χαλεπώτερον ἢ τυράν-
νοις.—Pythagoras.

It is more grievous to be a slave to
one's passions than to be ruled by a
despot.

Δούλους εἶναι τοὺς φαύλους ἅπαντας.
                        —Plutarch.

(He said) that all bad men are slaves.

* The panegyric on Athens in the fifth century B.C. is true, to some extent, of the England
of to-day.
† Archimedes discovered the mechanical value of the lever, and this was his proud way of
boasting of the fact.

Δράσαντι γάρ τοι καὶ παθεῖν ὀφείλεται.
— *Æschylus.*

Truly the evil-doer must suffer for his sins.

Δρυὸς πεσούσης πᾶς ἀνὴρ ξυλεύεται.
— *Menander.*

When an oak has fallen every man becomes a woodcutter.

Δύ' ἡμέραι γυναικὸς εἰσὶν ἥδισται,
ὅταν γαμῇ τις κἀκφέρῃ τεθνηκυῖαν.
— *Hipponax.*

There are two days in a woman's life that a man finds pleasant; the day he weds her, and the day he goes to her funeral.

Δύναται γὰρ ἴσον τῷ δρᾶν τὸ νοεῖν.
— *Aris'ophanes.*

To think evil is very much the same as doing it.

Δύσκολόν ἐστι καὶ τὸ ἐπὶ σχοινίου περιπατεῖν.

(Walking on a tight-rope is risky work.) It is hard to turn back upon a narrow bridge.

Δυστυχῶν κρύπτε, ἵνα μὴ τοὺς ἐχθροὺς εὐφράνῃς.—*Periander.*

Hide your misfortunes, lest your enemies rejoice.

Δῶρα πείθειν καὶ θεοὺς λόγος.
— *Euripides.*

The proverb says that "Gifts appease the gods."

Ἐὰν δ' ἔχωμεν χρήμαθ' ἕξομεν φίλους.
— *Menander.*

If we have money we are sure to have friends.

Ἐὰν ᾖς φιλομαθὴς, ἔσῃ πολυμαθής.
— *Isocrates.*

If you are fond of learning you will soon be full of learning.

Ἐὰν πάντες οἱ νόμοι ἀναιρεθῶσιν, ὁμοίως βιώσομεν.—*Aristippus.*

If all the laws were to be annulled, it would not make much difference in our manners of life.

Ἑαυτοὺς ἐμφανίζουσιν.

They show themselves in their true character.

Ἐγγύα· πάρα δ' ἄτη.—*Thales.*

(Give a pledge and you will soon have troubles.) He goes a-sorrowing who goes a-borrowing.

Ἐγκράτεια κρηπὶς εὐσεβείας.
— *Clitarchus.*

Temperance is the foundation of piety.

Ἐγὼ γὰρ εἰμὶ τῶν ἐμῶν ἐμὸς μόνος.
— *Apollodorus Carystius.*

I am myself the only friend on whom I can rely.

Ἐγὼ δέ γ' ἀντείποιμ' ἄν, ὡς, δὶς παῖδες οἱ γέροντες.—*Aristophanes.*

(I would make reply that old men are twice boys.) Old age is second childhood.

Ἐγὼ δὲ νομίζω τὸ μὲν μηδενὸς δεῖσθαι θεῖον εἶναι, τὸ δὲ ὡς ἐλαχίστων ἐγγυτάτον τοῦ θείου.—*Socrates.*

To want nothing I consider divine, and the man whose wants are fewest approachest most nearly to the gods.

Ἐγὼ μὲν εὖτ' ἂν τοὺς κακοὺς ὁρῶ βροτῶν πίπτοντας, εἶναι φημὶ δαιμόνων γένος.
— *Euripides.*

Whenever I see the wicked fall into adversity I declare that the gods do exist.

Ἐγὼ νομίζω τὸν μὲν εὖ παθόντα δεῖν μεμνῆσθαι πάντα τὸν χρόνον, τὸν δὲ ποιήσαντα εὐθὺς ἐπιλελῆσθαι.
— *Demosthenes.*

The man who has received a benefit ought always to remember it, but he who has granted it ought to forget the fact at once.

Ἐγώ σοι ἐντέλλομαι καὶ παρακαλῶ μηδὲν Ἀθηναίοις μνησικακεῖν.—*Phocion.*

I command and implore you not to feel revengeful towards the Athenians.*

* Phocion, the famous Athenian general and statesman, became in his old age unpopular, and was condemned to death. Patriotic to the last, he made this final request to his son. Phocion was one of the political opponents of Demosthenes. The great orator called the blunt man of action the "pruner of my periods."

Ἐδίδαξά σε κυβιστᾶν, καὶ σὺ βυθίσαι με θέλεις.

(I taught you to dive, and now you wish to drown me.) Do a kindness and you make an enemy.

Ἐθέλω ὑμᾶς συντῆξαι καὶ συμφῦσαι εἰς τὸ αὐτό, ὥστε δύο ὄντας ἕνα γεγονέναι. —*Plato.*

I wish you to become so much of one mind, so closely allied, so that, though you are two, you may become one.

Εἰ βούλει ἀγαθὸς εἶναι, πρῶτον πίστευσον ὅτι κακὸς εἶ.—*Epictetus.*

If you wish to be good, first consider that you are wicked.

Εἰ γάρ κεν καὶ σμικρὸν ἐπὶ σμικρῷ καταθεῖο,
καὶ θάμα τοῦτ' ἔρδοις, τάχα κεν μέγα καὶ τὸ γένοιτο.—*Hesiod.*

(If to a little you still a little add, by adding thus continually you will soon possess a large heap.) Many littles make a mickle.

Εἰ γάρ τι καλὸν ἔργον πεποίηκα, τοῦτο μνημεῖον ἐστίν· εἰ δὲ μηδὲν, οὐδ' οἱ πάντες ἀνδριάντες.
—*Agesilaus, King of Sparta.*

If I have done any noble action, that is a sufficient memorial; if I have done nothing noble, all the statues in the world will not preserve my memory.*

Εἰ δὲ θεὸν ἀνήρ τις ἔλπεται λαθέμεν ἔρδων, ἁμαρτάνει.—*Pindar.*

That man deceives himself who thinks his evil deeds escape the eyes of God.

Εἰ δείν' ἔδρασας, δείνα καὶ παθεῖν σε δεῖ.
—*Sophocles.*

If thou doest evil, thou must suffer evil also.

Εἰ δὲ πεπόνθατε δεινὰ δι' ὑμετέρην κακότητα
μὴ τι θεοῖς τούτων μοῖραν ἐπεμφέρετε.
—*Solon.*

If you suffer ills through your own folly, do not blame heaven for your sufferings.

Εἰκών.

(An icon.) An image or representation.

Εἰ μὲν γὰρ πλουτῇς πόλλοι φίλοι, ἢν δὲ πένηαι
παῦροι, κ' οὐκέθ' ὁμῶς αὐτὸς ἀνὴρ ἀγαθός.
—*Theognis.*

If you are rich you will have abundance of friends; if poor, you will lose both your friends and any good reputation you have possessed.

Εἰ μὲν οὖν καὶ ἄλλο τι ἐστὶ θεῶν δώρημα ἀνθρώποις, εὔλογον καὶ τὴν εὐδαιμονίαν θεόσδοτον εἶναι, καὶ μάλιστα τῶν ἀνθρωπίνων ὅσῳ βέλτιστον.—*Aristotle.*

If, then, there is any gift from the gods to men, it is surely reasonable to suppose that happiness is a divine gift, since it is the best of all human possessions.

Εἴπερ γάρ τε καὶ αὐτίκ' Ὀλύμπιος οὐκ ἐτέλεσσεν,
ἔκ τε καὶ ὀψὲ τελεῖ, σύν τε μεγάλῳ ἀπέτισαν,
σὺν σφῇσιν κεφαλῇσι γυναιξί τε καὶ τεκέεσσιν.—*Homer.*

Even though Olympian Jove does not avenge at once, he will do so, though he tarry long; and with their own lives and the lives of their children the wicked pay a heavy penalty for their sins.

Εἷς ἀνὴρ, οὐδεὶς ἀνήρ.

(One man, no man.) Two heads are better than one.

Εἷς αὔριον τὰ σπουδαῖα.

Business to-morrow.†

Εἷς οἰωνὸς ἄριστος, ἀμύνεσθαι περὶ πάτρης.
—*Homer.*

The best omen for a man is to fight for his country.‡

* The reply of Agesilaus, the Spartan King, according to Plutarch, to those who suggested that a memorial should be erected to his honour.
† The saying of Archias, the Spartan commander, whose procrastination brought about his death. The Spartans had occupied Thebes, and Pelopidas, with other Theban patriots, formed a plan to recover the city and kill the invaders. A letter warned Archias of the conspiracy, but being engaged in the delights of the table, he put the letter aside, saying," Business to-morrow."
‡ The reply of Hector, the Trojan hero, when told that the omens were unfavourable for fighting.

Εἰς τὸ πῦρ ἐκ τοῦ κάπνου.—*Lucian.*

(Out of the smoke into the fire.)   Out of the frying-pan into the fire.

Εἰ σῶμα δοῦλον, ἀλλ᾽ ὁ νοῦς ἐλεύθερος.
                              —*Sophocles.*

Though my body is enslaved, still my thoughts are free.

᾽Εκ θαμινῆς ῥαθάμιγγος, ὅπως λόγος αἰὲν ἰοίσας,
χἀ λίθος ἐς βρωχμὸν κοιλαίνεται.—*Bion.*

By frequent dropping, as the proverb says, the stone is hollowed away at last.

᾽Εκ θεῶν γὰρ μαχαναὶ πᾶσαι βροτέαις ἀρεταῖς
καὶ σοφοὶ καὶ χερσὶ βιαταὶ περίγλωσσοί τ᾽ ἔφυν.—*Pindar.*

From heaven comes all that makes for human excellence ; from the gods come wise men, and men of mighty hand and eloquent speech.

᾽Εκ μελέτης πλείους ἢ φυσέως ἀγαθοί.
                              —*Critias.*

It is education rather than nature that makes men good

᾽Εκ παντὸς ξύλου κίων ἂν γένηται.

(Any wood will do to make a sign-post.) Any blockhead is good enough to be shot at.

᾽Εκ τοῦ βίου κράτιστόν ἐστιν ἐξελθεῖν ὡς συμποσίου, μήτε διψῶντα μήτε μεθύοντα.—*Aristotle.*

It is best to quit life just as we leave a banquet, neither thirsty nor drunken.

᾽Εκ τοῦ ὁρᾷν γίγνεται τὸ ἐρᾷν.

(From seeing comes loving.)
      Tell me where is fancy bred,
      Or in the heart, or in the head ?
      'Tis engendered in the eyes.
                              —*Shakespeare.*

᾽Εκ τοῦ φοβεροῦ κατ᾽ ὀλίγον ὑπονοστεῖ πρὸς τὸ εὐκαταφρόνητον.—*Longinus.*

In a short time we travel from the awe-inspiring to the absurd.*

Ἐκ τῶν ἀέλπτων ἡ χάρις μείζων βροτοῖς φανεῖσα μᾶλλον, ἢ τὸ προσδοκώμενον.
                              —*Euripides.*

Men derive a keener joy from unexpected blessings than from those they have looked for.

᾽Εκ τῶν γὰρ αἰσχρῶν λημμάτων τοὺς πλείονας
ἀτωμένους ἴδοις ἂν ἢ σεσωσμένους.
                              —*Sophocles.*

More are ruined than made by ill-gotten gains

᾽Εκχύμωσις.

Extravasation of blood under the skin.

῾Εκὼν γὰρ οὐδεὶς δουλίῳ χρῆται ζυγῷ.
                              —*Æschylus.*

No one voluntarily wears the yoke of slavery.

᾽Ελαφρόν ὅστις πημάτων ἔξω πόδα ἔχει, παραινεῖν νουθετεῖν τε τὸν κακῶς πράσσοντα. -*Æschylus*

A light task it is for him who is free from troubles himself, to school and exhort one who is in misfortune's grasp.

᾽Ελέησόν με.

Pity me.

᾽Ελπίδες ἀνθρώπων, ἐλαφραὶ θεαί.
                              — *Diotimus.*

Man's hopes are spirits with fast-fleeting wings.

᾽Ελπίδες ἐν ζωοῖσιν᾽ ἀνέλπιστοι δὲ θανόντες.—*Theocritus.*

While there is life there is hope, but the dead can hope no more.

᾽Ελπὶς καὶ σὺ Τύχη, μέγα χαίρετε᾽ τὸν λίμεν᾽ εὗρον.
οὐδὲν ἐμοὶ χ᾽ ὑμῖν, παίζετε τοὺς μετ᾽ ἐμέ.

Fortune and Hope, farewell ! I've found the port :
You've done with me—Go now, with others sport.—*Merivale.*†

---

* See French section : *Du sublime au ridicule.*
† A Latin version of these lines from the Greek Anthology was used by Le Sage at the end of " Gil Blas." See *Inveni portum.*

Ἐμὲ μὲν γὰρ οὐδὲν ἂν βλάψειεν οὔτε
Μέλητος οὔτε Ἄνυτος· οὐδὲ γὰρ ἂν
δύναιτο· οὐ γὰρ οἴομαι θεμιτὸν εἶναι
ἀμείνονι ἀνδρὶ ὑπὸ χείρονος βλάπτεσθαι.
　　　　　　　　　—Socrates.

Neither Meletus nor Anytus can injure
me. Indeed they have not the power
to do so; for I imagine that it is impossible for the better man to be injured by the worse.*

Ἐμοὶ γὰρ ὁ πατὴρ οὐδὲν ἀπολείψει.
　　　　　　　　　—Alexander the Great.

My father will leave me nothing to do.†

Ἐμοὶ δὲ μόνοις πρόπινε τοῖς ὄμμασι.
　　　　　　　　　—Philostratus.

Drink to me only with thine eyes.

Ἐμοῦ θανόντος γαῖα μιχθήτω πυρί·
οὐδὲν μέλει μοι· τἀμὰ γὰρ καλῶς ἔχει.

When I am dead, let fire consume the
world: I care not so long as I
prosper.‡

Ἐμποδίζει τὸν λόγον ὁ φόβος.—Demades.

Fear curbs the tongue.

Ἔμφυτος πᾶσιν ἀνθρώποις ὁ τῆς ἐλευθερίας πόθος.
　　　　　　　　—Dionysius of Halicarnassus.

The love of liberty is innate in all mankind.

Ἐν ἀμούσοις καὶ κόρυδος φθέγγεται.

(Among the unmusical the sparrow is
reckoned a fine singer.) The fowl
is a fine bird when the peacock is
not nigh.

Ἐν ἀνδρῶν, ἐν θεῶν γένος.—Pindar.

(The race of men and gods is one.)
God made man after his own image.

Ἐν γῇ πένεσθαι κρεῖττον ἢ πλουτοῦντα
πλεῖν.—Menander.

Better be a pauper on the land than a
Crœsus on the sea.

Ἐν δ᾽ ἔπεσ᾽ ὡς ὅτε κῦμα θοῇ ἐν νηῒ πέσῃσι
λάβρον ὑπαὶ νεφέων ἀνεμοτρεφές· ἡ δέ
τε πᾶσα
ἄχνῃ ὑπεκρύφθη, ἀνέμοιο δὲ δεινὸς ἀήτης
ἱστίῳ ἐμβρέμεται, τρομέουσι δέ τε φρένα
ναῦται,
δειδιότες· τυτθὸν γὰρ ὑπὲκ θανάτοιο
φέρονται.—Homer.

He bursts upon them all:
Bursts as a wave that from the cloud
impends,
And swell'd with tempests on the ship
descends;
White are the decks with foam; the
winds aloud
Howl o'er the masts, and sing through
every shroud;
Pale, trembling, tired, the sailors freeze
with fears!
And instant death on every wave
appears.—Pope. §

Ἐν ἐλπίσιν χρὴ τοὺς σοφοὺς ἔχειν βίον.
　　　　　　　　　—Euripides.

The wise ought to possess their lives in
hope.

Ἔνεστι κἂν μύρμηκι κἂν σέρφῳ χολή.

(Even the ant and worm have got a
temper.) The worm will turn if you
tread on it.

Ἐν θαλάττῃ ζητεῖς ὕδωρ.

(You are looking for water in the sea.)
Who so blind as he that will not see?

---

* Part of the speech of Socrates given in Plato's "Apology of Socrates." Anytus and Meletus
had accused Socrates of "corrupting the youth" by his unorthodox teachings, and succeeded
in getting the Athenians to condemn him to death.
† A saying of Alexander preserved by Plutarch. Philip's conquests of the Greeks aroused
the ambition of his son, the future conqueror of Asia.
‡ Lines from an unknown Greek writer quoted by Suetonius. The historian narrates that
when the first line was repeated to Nero, the Emperor said, "Yes, and when I am alive." The
words contain the same idea as Madame de Pompadour's *Après moi le déluge.*
§ The simile describes the onset of the Trojan Hector upon the Greeks.

᾽Ενθ᾽ ῞Υπνῳ ξύμβλητο, κασιγνήτῳ Θανά·
τοιο.—*Homer.*

There he met with Sleep, Death's twin
    brother.
    How wonderful is Death,
    Death and his brother Sleep.
                —*Shelley.*

᾽Εν μύρτου, κλαδὶ τὸ ξίφος φορήσω
ὥσπερ ῾Αρμόδιος καὶ ᾽Αριστογείτων,
  ὅτε τὸν τύραννον κτανέτην
ἰσονόμους τ᾽ ᾽Αθήνας ἐποιησάτην.
             —*Callistratus.*

I'll wreathe my sword in myrtle bough,
The sword that laid the tyrant low,
When patriots, burning to be free,
To Athens gave equality.*

῎Εννους τὰ καιὰ τοῖς πάλαι τεκμαίρεται.
         — *Sophocles.*

A wise man anticipates what the future
  will bring from observing the experiences of the past.

᾽Εν νύκτι βουλή τοῖς σοφοῖσι γίγνεται.
         —*Menander.*

(The night brings counsel to the wise.)
Take counsel of your pillow.

᾽Εν οἴνῳ ἀλήθεια.

In wine there is truth ; *In vino veritas.*

᾽Εν ὀλβίῳ ὄλβια πάντα.—*Theocritus.*

All things go well with the lucky man.

᾽Εν ὄρφνῃ δραπέτης μέγα σθένει.
         —*Euripides.*

Cowards are wondrous brave in the
  darkness.

῾Ενὸς φιλία ξυνετοῦ κρέσσων ἀξυνέτων
ἀπάντων.—*Democritus.*

The friendship of one wise man is better
  than the friendship of a world of
  fools.

᾽Εν πενθοῦσι γελᾶν.

To laugh among mourners ; to laugh at
  a funeral.

᾽Εν πιθήκοις ὄντα δεῖ εἶναι πίθηκον.
         —*Apollodorus.*

(When in apes' company one must
  play the ape.) One must howl with
  the wolves.

᾽Εν τῷ φρονεῖν μηδὲν ἥδιστος βίος.
         —*Sophocles.*

Sweetest is the life that is untroubled
  with thought.

᾽Εξ ἄμμου σχοινίον πλέκειν.

(To make ropes of sand.) Your labour
  is in vain.

῎Εξω δρόμου φέρεσθαι.

(To be carried out of the course.) To
  wander from the point.

῎Εξω τοῦ πράγματος.

(Beside the question.) An argument
  not to the point.

῎Εοικεν ἡ κολακεία γραπτῇ πανοπλίᾳ·
διὸ τέρψιν μὲν ἔχει, χρείαν δὲ μηδεμίαν
παρέχεται.—*Demophilus.*

Flattery is like armour in a picture ; for
  it is pretty in appearance, but is
  absolutely useless.

῎Εοικεν ὁ βίος θεάτρῳ, διὸ πολλάκις χείρι-
στοι τὸν κάλλιστον ἐν᾽αὐτῷ κατέχουσι
τόπον.—*Aristonymus.*

Life is like a theatre ; for the greatest
  knaves often sit in the best seats.

᾽Επάμεροι· τί δέ τις ; τί δ᾽ οὔ τις ;
σκιᾶς ὄναρ ἄνθρωπος.—*Pindar.*

Creatures of a day are we ; for what is
  Man ? Naught but a phantom that
  quickly fades away.

᾽Επεὰν ἡμίονοι τέκωσι.

(When mules have foals.) When two
  Sundays come in a week ; never.

῎Επεα πτερόεντα.—*Homer.*

Winged words.

---

* The first stanza of the famous song that commemorated the attempt of Harmodius and
Aristogeiton to slay Hippias and Hipparchus, sons of Peisistratus, who succeeded their father
as tyrants of Athens. The attempt was practically a failure, and the motives of the two revolu ·
tionists were not the lofty ones assigned to them ; but their action appealed to the imagination
of the Athenians, who regarded the two conspirators as martyrs in the cause of liberty.

Ἔπεισιν ἑκάστῳ ποικίλον ἐξ ἀδήλου τὸ μέλλον.—*Solon.*

Ἐπὶ γήραος οὐδῷ.—*Homer.*

Ἐπιγλωττίς.

Ἐπὶ δυοῖν ὁρμεῖν.

Ἐπὶ ξυροῦ ἵσταται ἀκμῆς.

Ἐπὶ σαυτῷ τὴν σελήνην καθελεῖς.

Ἐποποιΐα.

Ἔργα δὲ Κυπρογενοῦς νῦν μοι φίλα καὶ Διονύσου
καὶ Μουσέων, ἃ τίθησ' ἀνδράσιν εὐφρο-
σύνας.—*Solon.*

Ἔργον δὲ παντὸς ἤν τις ἄρχηται καλῶς,
καὶ τὰς τελευτὰς εἰκὸς ἔσθ' οὕτως ἔχειν.
—*Sophocles.*

Ἔργον δ' οὐδὲν ὄνειδος, ἀεργίη δέ τ' ὄνειδος.—*Hesiod.*

Ἔργον εὑρεῖν συγγενῆ
πένητός ἐστιν. Οὐδεὶς γὰρ ὁμολογεῖ
αὑτῷ προσήκειν τὸν βοηθείας τινὸς
δεόμενον. Αἰτεῖσθαι γὰρ ἅμα τι προσδοκᾷ.
—*Menander.*

Ἔρδοι τις, ἣν ἕκαστος εἰδείη τεχνήν.
—*Aristophanes.*

Ἐρημία μεγάλη 'στὶν ἡ Μεγαλήπολις.

Ἔρως.

Ἔρως, ὃς ἐν μαλακαῖς παρειαῖς νεάνιδος
ἐννυχεύεις.—*Sophocles.*

Ἔρως σοφιστοῦ γίγνεται διδάσκαλος
σκαιοῦ πολὺ κρείττων πρὸς τὸν ἀνθρώπων
βίον.—*Anaxandrides.*

Ἔσται δὴ τοῦτ' ἄμαρ, ὁπανίκα νεβρὸν ἐν εὐνᾷ
Καρχαρόδων σίνεσθαι ἰδὼν λύκος οὐκ
ἐθελήσει.—*Theocritus.*

Ἐς Τροίαν πειρώμενοι ἦλθον Ἀχαιοί.
—*Theocritus.*

Ἐτεὸν δὲ οὐδὲν ἴδμεν· ἐν βυθῷ γὰρ ἡ
ἀληθεία.—*Diogenes Laertius.*

Futurity carries for every man many various and uncertain events in its bosom.

On the threshold of old age.

(The epiglottis.) A cartilaginous plate that covers the windpipe during the act of swallowing.

(To have two anchors to one's ship.) To be prepared for emergencies.

(It stands upon the razor's edge.) The affair is in a critical state.

(You are bringing the moon on yourself.) You are preparing a rod for your own back.

Epic poetry; the composition of an epic.

Wine, Wit, and Beauty still their charms bestow, Light all the shades of life, and cheer us as we go.

If anyone begins well his task, it is likely that the end, too, will be good.

It is idleness, not labour, that disgraces.

A poor man's relatives are hard to find, for no one will confess that a needy man is one of his kindred, since he might be asked to give something.

(Let each man practise the craft he understands.) The cobbler should stick to his last.

Megalopolis (the Great City) is a great desert; a great city is a great solitude.*

(Eros.) The god of love; Cupid.

Love, who keepest vigil on the soft cheek of a maiden.

Love is a far better teacher in the school of life than any clumsy sophist.

The day will come when the savage wolf shall see the lamb in his lair, and not wish to harm it.†

(By trying, the Greeks reached Troy.) Who perseveres succeeds at last.

We know nothing certain; for truth is hidden in the bottom of a well.

---

* See note on *Magna civitas, magna solitudo* in Latin section.
† The 24th Idyl of Theocritus contains several passages that are not unlike Chapter XI. of Isaiah. Virgil also uses similar language in the " Eclogues," and some imaginative critics have thought that Virgil may have had access to the writings of the Hebrew prophet.

L

Εὐγένεια ϗαὶ ἀρετή.

Gentle birth and virtue.

Εὐδαιμονίω; χάριν τὰ λοιπὰ πάντες πάντα πράττομεν.—Aristotle.

The desire for happiness is the incentive that moves us in all our undertakings.

Εὐδαιμονία χρᾶσις ἀρετᾶς ἐν εὐτυχίᾳ. —Archytas.

Happiness is the exercise of virtue by one who is in prosperous circumstances.

Εὐδαίμων ὁ μηδὲν ὀφείλων.

(Happy the man who has no debts.) Out of debt, out of danger.

Εὕδοντι κύρτος αἱρεῖ.

(The net of the sleeper catches fish.) Blessings come when least expected.

Εὐ 'ανασία.

(Euthanasia.)   An easy, happy death.

Εὕ κα, εὕρηκα.

(Eureka.)   I have found it.*

Εὖ τὸ σῶμα ἔχειν καὶ τὴν ψυχήν. —Cleobulus.

Keep a healthy mind in a healthy body. Mens sana in corpore sano.

Εὐτυχία πολύφιλος.

(Prosperity is never friendless.)   The rich guest is always a welcome guest.

Εὐτυχῶν μὲν μέτριος ἴσθι, ἀτυχῶν δὲ φρόνιμος.—Periander.

Be moderate in your prosperity, and prudent in adversity.

Εὔχεσθαι· πάντες δὲ θεῶν χατέουσ' ἄνθρωποι.—Homer.

(Pray; since all men stand in need of Heaven's aid.)
More things are wrought by prayer than this world dreams of.
—Tennyson.

Ἔχει τε γὰρ ὄλβιος οὐ μείονα φθόνον. —Pindar.

The lucky man is always greatly envied.

Ἐχθαίρω δὲ γυναῖκα περίδρομον. —Theognis.

I hate the woman who is ever gadding about.

Ἐχθρὸς γάρ μοι κεῖνος ὁμῶς 'Αΐδαο πύλῃσιν
ὅς χ' ἕτερον μὲν κεύθει ἐνὶ φρεσίν, ἄλλο δὲ βάζει.—Homer.

Who dares think one thing, and another tell,
My heart detests him as the gates of hell.

Ἐχθρῶν ἄδωρα δῶρα κοὐκ ὀνήσιμα. —Sophocles.

The gifts of an enemy are no gifts; they bring no profit.

Ἕως κόρακες λευκοὶ γένωνται.

(Until the crows turn white.)   Until two Sundays come in one week; never.

Ζεῖ χύτρα, ζῇ φιλία.

(While the pot boils friendship flourishes.)   An empty purse frightens away friends.

Ζεῦ βασιλεῦ, τὰ μὲν ἐσθλὰ καὶ εὐξαμένοις καὶ ἀνεύκτοις
ἄμμι δίδου, τὰ δὲ δεινὰ καὶ εὐξαμένοις ἀπερύκου.

O king Zeus, grant us good things whether we pray for them or not, and keep from us hurtful things even though we pray for them.†

Ζεὺς γὰρ μεγάλης γλώσσης κόμπους ὑπερεχθαίρει.—Sophocles.

God utterly abhors the boasts of a proud tongue.

Ζεὺς πάντων αὐτὸς φάρμακα μοῦνος ἔχει. —Simonides of Ceos.

Jove alone has a remedy for all evils.

* The exclamation of Archimedes when a sure way whereby to test the genuineness of the gold in the crown of his patron Hiero, the Syracusan King, suddenly occurred to him.
† A prayer quoted with approval by Plato in his dialogue Alcibiades

Ζῆλος γυναικὸς πάντα πυρπολεῖ δόμον.
— *Menander.*

A jealous woman sets every house on fire.

Ζηλωτὸς, ὅστις ηὐτύχησεν εἰς τέκνα.
— *Euripides.*

That man is to be envied who is fortunate in his children.

Ζῆν αἰσχρὸν αἰσχρῶς τοῖς καλῶς πεφυκόσιν.— *Sophocles.*

(To live basely shames those who have been nobly born.)   *Noblesse oblige.*

Ζώη καὶ ψυχή.

My life and soul ; my dearest love.

Ζώη μοῦ.

My life ; my darling.

Ζωῆς πονηρᾶς θάνατος αἱρετώτερος.
— *Æschylus.*

Death is better than an evil life.

Ζῶμεν ἀλογίστως, προσδοκῶντες μὴ θανεῖν.
— *Menander.*

Carelessly we live, thinking death will never come.

Ἡ αἰδὼς ἄνθος ἐπισπείρει.

(Modesty gives rise to grace.)   Modesty is essential to true beauty.

Ἡ ἅμαξα τὸν βοῦν.

(The waggon draws the ox.)   Putting the cart before the horse.

Ἥβη.

(Hebe.)   The goddess of youth.

Ἡ γὰρ ἔρωτι πολλάκις τὰ μὴ καλὰ καλὰ πέφανται.— *Theocritus.*

What is not really beautiful, often seems so to the eyes of love.

Ἡ γὰρ σιωπὴ τοῖς σοφοῖς ἐστ' ἀπόκρισις.
— *Menander.*

(Silence is a sufficient answer to the wise.)   Silence gives consent.

Ἡγεμονία.

(Hegemony.)   The lead, the chief command ; the sovereignty of one state over smaller states.

Ἡ γλῶσσ' ὀμώμοχ', ἡ δὲ φρὴν ἀνώμοτος.
— *Euripides.*

My tongue has sworn, but not my mind.*

Ἡδέως μὲν ἔχε πρὸς ἅπαντας, χρῶ δὲ τοῖς βελτίστοις.— *Isocrates.*

Be gracious to all men, but choose the best to be your friends.

Ἤδη γὰρ φράσδει πάνθ' ἅλιον ἄμμι δεδύκειν.— *Theocritus.*

Thinkest thou that all my suns are set ? †

Ἡ δημοκρατία ἡ τελευταία τυραννὶς ἐστίν.
— *Aristotle.*

Democracy is the severest form of despotism.

Ἥδιον οὐδὲν ἔρωτος.

Love is the sweetest thing in life.

Ἥδιστον ἄκουσμα ἔπαινος.— *Xenophon.*

No sound is sweeter than the sound of praise.

Ἡδονὴ μᾶλλον ἐν ἠρεμίᾳ ἐστὶν ἢ ἐν κινήσει· μεταβολὴ δὲ πάντων γλυκὺ διὰ πονηρίαν τινα.— *Aristotle.*

Pleasure really exists in rest rather than motion ; and the saying that change in everything is sweet is the outcome of wrong principles.

Ἡδονὴν φεύγε· αὕτη γὰρ λύπην τίκτει.
— *Solon.*

Shun pleasure ; for pleasure is the mother of repentance.

Ἡδὺ γὰρ τὸ φῶς βλέπειν.— *Euripides.*

Ah, sweet it is to behold the light of day.

Ἡδύ γε φίλου λόγος ἐστὶ τοῖς λυπουμένοις.— *Menander.*

The voice of a friend sounds sweet in the ears of a mourner.

Ἡδὺ δούλευμα.

(A sweet servitude.)   A happy bondage ; the golden chains of love.

---

* See Latin section, " Juravi linguâ."
† Philip V. of Macedon quoted this line when the insults of the Thessalians provoked him to attack them, 182 B.C.

Ἡ εὐδαιμονία ἐνέργειά τίς ἐστι.
—Aristotle.

Happiness consists in the active employment of the faculties.

*Ἡ ἥκιστα, ἢ ἥδιστα.—Æsop.

Speak very little, or very pleasantly.*

*Ἡ θηρίον, ἢ θεός.—Aristotle.

(Man is) either a god or a brute.

Ἦθος προκρίνειν χρημάτων γαμοῦντα δεῖ.
—Menander.

Choose a wife for her character rather than for her dowry.

Ἦθους δὲ βάσανός ἐστιν ἀνθρώποις χρόνος.
—Menander.

Time is the touchstone that proves the character of men.

Ἧλιξ ἥλικα τέρπει.

(Like pleases like.)   Birds of a feather.

Ἡ μεγάλα χάρις δώρῳ σὺν ὀλίγῳ· πάντα
δὲ τίματα τὰ πὰρ φίλων.—Theocritus.

Much kind feeling accompanies a small gift ; and what a friend has given we count of value.

Ἡ μεσότης ἐν πᾶσιν ἀσφαλέστερον.
—Menander.

(The middle course is always the safest.)
Medio tutissimus ibis.

Ἠνίδε σιγῇ μὲν πόντος, σιγῶντι δ' ἀῆται·
ἁ δ' ἐμὰ οὐ σιγῇ στέρνων ἔντοσθεν ἀνία.
—Theocritus.

The sea is still, the winds in silence rest,
Yet speaks the voice of grief within my breast.

*Ἡ πῖθι ἢ ἄπιθι.

(Either drink or depart.)   The water drinker is out of place at a drinking-bout.

Ἡ σοῦ χείρ, Κύριε, δεδόξασται ἐν ἰσχύι.

(Thy hand, O Lord, hath been glorified in strength.)   Motto of the Order of the Redeemer, Greece.

Ἥσω γὰρ καὶ ἐγώ, τὰ δέ κεν Διὶ πάντα
μελήσει.—Homer.

I hurl the spear, but Jove directs the blow.—Lord Derby.
A man's heart deviseth his way, but the Lord directeth his steps.
—Solomon, Book of Proverbs.

*Ἡ τὰν ἢ ἐπὶ τάν.

(Either with this or upon it.)   With your shield or upon it.†

Ἡ τέχνη μιμεῖται τὴν φύσιν.—Aristotle.

Art takes Nature as its model.

Ἡ τέχνη τέλειος, ἡνίκ' ἂν φύσις εἶναι
δοκῇ.—Longinus.

Art has reached its highest pitch when it seems to be nature.

Ἥ τ' ὀλίγη μὲν πρῶτα κορύσσεται, αὐτὰρ
ἔπειτα
οὐρανῷ ἐστήριξε κάρη, καὶ ἐπὶ χθονὶ βαίνει.

With humble crest at first, anon her head,
While yet she treads the earth, affronts the skies.—Lord Derby.‡

Ἡ τῶν κολάκων εὔνοια φεύγει τὰς ἀτυχίας.
—Socrates.

The kindness of flatterers disappears when misfortune comes.

Ἡ τῶν ὄντως ὄντων κτῆσις διὰ ῥᾳστώνης
οὐ περιγίγνεται.—Demophilus.

A thing worth having is never obtained without hard work.

Ἡ φιλία ἐν μόνοις τοῖς σπουδαίοις ἐστι.
—Diogenes Laertius.

Friendship exists among the good alone.

Ἡ φιλοχρημοσύνη μήτηρ κακότητος ἁπάσης.—Phocylides.

The love of money is the parent of all wickedness.

---

* The motto for a courtier.
† The words of a Spartan mother to her son when he was setting out to battle. The loss of his shield was considered a proof of cowardice in the soldier among the ancients. Epaminondas inquired anxiously for his shield when mortally wounded at Mantinea. Horace describes his inglorious flight from Philippi, "when he left his little shield behind."
‡ The description of the growth of Rumour, which is here personified. Virgil imitated the passage, Parva metu primum mox sese attollit in auras.

Θάνατον εἰσορῶ πέλας,
Ἱερέα θανόντων.—*Euripides.*

I see Death, the high-priest of the dead, standing near.

Θάνατος ἀπροφάσιστος.—*Euripides.*

Death admits of no excuses; there is no arguing with death.

Θανάτῳ πάντες ὀφειλόμεθα.
                    —*Simonides of Ceos.*

Death is a debt we all must pay.

Θάρσει μοι, θάρσει, τέκνον,
ἔτι μέγας οὐρανῷ
Ζεὺς, ὃς ἐφορᾷ πάντα καὶ κρατύνει.
                    —*Sophocles.*

Take courage, take courage, I pray you, daughter; Zeus, the mighty king, still rules in heaven, and sees and directs all things.

Θέλω τύχης σταλαγμὸν, ἢ φρενῶν πίθον.
                    —*Menander.*

(Better a drop of fortune than a barrel of wisdom.) Better be lucky than wise.

Θεοὶ δέ τε πάντα ἴσασιν.—*Homer.*

The gods are omniscient.

Θεὸς ἐκ μηχανῆς.—*Lucian.*

A god from the machine.*

Θεοῦ δὲ πληγὴν οὐχ ὑπερπηδᾷ βροτός.
                    —*Sophocles.*

None can escape the avenging arm of God.

Θεῷ δουλεύειν οὐκ ἐλευθερίας μόνον, ἀλλὰ καὶ βασιλείας ἄμεινον.—*Philo Judæus.*

The service of God is better than freedom, yea, better than the rule of a kingdom.

Θεῶν δ' ἀέκητι τέτυκτο
ἀθανάτων· τὸ καὶ οὔ τι πολὺν χρόνον
ἔμπεδον ἦεν.

Against the will of heaven The work was done, and thence not long endured.—*Lord Derby.*

Θεῶν ἐν γούνασι κεῖται.—*Homer.*

(The issue lies on the knees of the gods.) It is in the hands of God.

Θανατοῖσι μὴ φῦναι φέριστον,
μηδ' ἀελίου προσιδεῖν φέγγος·
ὄλβιος δ' οὐδεὶς βροτῶν πάντα χρόνον.
                    —*Bacchylides.*

It were better for a man never to be born, nor ever behold the light of the sun, for no mortal is happy throughout his life.

Θυμοῦ κράτει.

Rule the temper.

Θυσία μεγίστη τῷ θεῷ τὸ εὐσεβεῖν
                    —*Menander.*

A righteous life is the best sacrifice that man can pay to Heaven.

Ἰδίας νόμιζε τῶν φίλων τὰς συμφόρας
                    —*Menander.*

(Consider the sorrows of thy friends to be thine own.) "Bear ye one another's burdens, and so fulfil the law of Christ."

Ἴδιον ἀνθρώπου φιλεῖν καὶ τοὺς πταίοντας.
                    —*Marcus Aurelius.*

It is a man's duty to love even those who injure him.

Ἰκμὰς φροντίδος.

(The sap of the mind.) The power of active intellectual work.

Ἰλιὰς κακῶν.

(An Iliad of woes.) A train of disasters; a peck of trouble.

Ἱππαλεκτρύων.—*Aristophanes.*

A cock-horse.

Ἵππος με φέρει, βασιλεύς με τρέφει.

My horse carries me, but the king supports me.†

Ἰστοὶ γυναικῶν ἔργα κοὐκ ἐκκλησίαι.
                    —*Menander.*

(Women's proper place is the loom, not the public meeting.) Women should attend to their homes, and leave platforms alone.

---

* See note on *Deus ex machinâ* in Latin Section.

† This proverbial expression is said to have originated with one Corræus. He was serving as a soldier of the Macedonian king, and, being requested by his mother to apply for his discharge, made the above reply.

'Ιστορια φιλοσοφία ἐστὶν ἐκ παραδειγμάτων.—*Dionysius of Halicarnassus.*

History is philosophy teaching by examples.*

'Ισχύειν τῇ ψυχῇ αἱροῦ μᾶλλον ἢ τῷ σώματι.—*Pythagoras.*

Choose to have a vigorous mind rather than a vigorous body.

'Ισχυρὸν ὄχλος ἐστὶν, οὐκ ἔχει δὲ νοῦν.
—*Menander.*

The mob is strong, but it has no sense.

'Ιχθῦς εἰς 'Ελλήσποντον.

(Carrying fish to the Hellespont.) Coals to Newcastle.

'Ιχθὺς ἐκ τῆς κεφαλῆς ὄζειν ἄρχεται.

(Fish begins to stink at the head) Bad kings have bad subjects.

'Ιὼ βρότεια πράγματ'· εὐτυχοῦντα μὲν σκιά τις ἂν τρέψειεν· εἰ δὲ δυστυχοῖ, βολαῖς ὑγρώσσων σπόγγος ὤλεσεν γραφήν.
—*Æschylus.*

Alas for human life! in prosperity 'tis but a sketch, and when misfortune comes, the wet sponge with a touch blots out the drawing.

Κἀγὼ νὴ Δία εἰ Παρμενίων ἤμην.
—*Alexander the Great.*

And so would I, if I were Parmenio.†

Καδμεία νίκη.

(A Cadmæan victory.) A victory that has cost too much to win. A Pyrrhic victory.

Καὶ γὰρ ἀνὴρ πενίῃ δεδμημένος οὔτε τι εἰπεῖν
οὔθ' ἔρξαι δύναται, γλῶσσα δέ οἱ δέδεται.—*Theognis.*

A man whom poverty holds in its grasp, may not speak nor act as he pleases, but his tongue is tied.

Καὶ ἔστιν ὁ πόλεμος οὐχ ὅπλων τὸ πλέον, ἀλλὰ δαπάνης, δι' ἣν τὰ ὅπλα ὠφελεῖ, ἄλλως τε καὶ ἠπειρώταις πρὸς θαλασσίους.—*Thucydides.*

War is not so much a matter of weapons as of money, for money furnishes the material for war. And this is specially true when a land power is fighting those whose strength is on the sea.

Καὶ κεραμεὺς κεραμεῖ κοτέει καὶ τέκτονι τέκτων.—*Hesiod.*

(Potter hates potter, and smith hates smith.) Two of a trade never agree.

αἱ μείζον ὅστις ἀντὶ τῆς αὑτοῦ πάτρας φίλον νομίζει, τοῦτον οὐδαμοῦ λέγω.
—*Sophocles.*

If any makes a friend of more account than his fatherland, that man hath no place in my regard.—*Jebb.*

Καὶ μὴν τό γε νικῆσαι τοὺς πολεμίους καλοκἀγαθίᾳ καὶ τοῖς δικαίοις, οὐκ ἐλάττω, μείζω δὲ παρέχεται χρείαν τῶν ἐν τοῖς ὅπλοις κατορθωμάτων. Οἷς μὲν γὰρ δι' ἀνάγκην, οἷς δὲ κατὰ προαίρεσιν, εἰκουσιν οἱ λειφθέντες.—*Polybius.*

If we conquer our enemies by honest dealings and just treatment, our success is greater and more permanent than if we defeated them in war. In the latter case they yield to us under compulsion, in the former, their submission is voluntary.

Καὶ πτωχὸς πτωχῷ φθονέει.—*Hesiod.*

(Beggar envies beggar.) 'Tis one beggar's woe to see another by the door go.

Καιρὸν γνῶθι.—*Pittacus.*

(Know your opportunity.) Strike while the iron is hot.

Καιρὸς βραχὺ μέτρον ἔχει.

(Opportunity brooks but little delay.) Time and tide wait for no man.

---

* This saying is paraphrased from Thucydides.
+ Parmenio, one of Alexander's generals, had advised his master to accept a bribe: " I would do so if I were Alexander." The above was the king's reply.

Καιρῷ λατρεύειν, μηδ' ἀντιπνέειν ἀνεμοῖσι.
                                    —*Phocylides.*

(Serve the opportunity, strive not
  against the favourable breeze.)
There is a tide in the affairs of men,
Which, taken at the flood, leads on to
  fortune.—*Shakespeare.*

Καὶ σὺ, τέκνον.

Thou, too, my son.*

Καὶ τὰ λειπόμενα (κ.τ.λ.).

And the rest ; et cetera.

Καὶ τοῖς ἀγαθοῖς γέ που τῶν νέων ἐν
  πολέμῳ ἢ ἄλλοθί που γέρα δοτέον καὶ
  ἆθλα.—*Plato.*

To those young men who, either in
  war or in other circumstances, have
  deserved commendation, prizes should
  be given.

Καὶ τὸ πένεσθαι οὐχ ὁμολογεῖν τινι
  αἰσχρόν, ἀλλὰ μὴ διαφεύγειν ἔργῳ
  αἴσχιον.—*Thucydides.*

To be ashamed of one's poverty is
  shameful, but it is still more disgraceful not to labour to be rid of it.

Κακοὶ γὰρ εὖ πράσσοντες οὐκ ἀνάσχετοι.
                                    —*Æschylus.*

A prosperous knave is grievous to endure.

Κακοῖς βοηθῶν μισθὸν ἀγαθὸν οὐ λήψῃ·
  ἀλλ' ἀρκέσει σοι, μὴ τι τῶν κακῶν
  πάσχειν.—*Babrius.*

If you aid the wicked you will get no return ; but it will be enough if you are
  not made to suffer for your kindness.

Κακοῖς ὁμιλῶν, αὐτὸς ἐκβήσῃ κακός.
                                    —*Menander.*

(If you associate with knaves, you will
  become knavish yourself.) Who
  sleeps with dogs gets up with fleas.

Κακοῦ κόρακος κακὸν ᾠόν.

(Bad crow lays a bad egg.) Like father,
  like son.

Κάλλος καλὸν ἐστι τὸ παιδικὸν ἀλλ'
  ὀλίγον ζῇ.—*Theocritus.*

Lovely is the bloom of youth, but it
  quickly fades away.

Καλὸν μὲν ἐστὶν ἡ τυραννὶς χωρίον, οὐκ
  ἔχει δὲ ἀπόβασιν.—*Solon.*

Absolute monarchy is a fair field, but
  is has no outlet.

Καλῶς ἀκούειν μᾶλλον ἢ πλουτεῖν θέλε.
                                    —*Menander.*

(Choose a good name before riches.)
Good name in man and woman, dear
  my lord,
Is the immediate jewel of their souls.
                                    —*Shakespeare.*

Καλῶς πένεσθαι μᾶλλον ἢ πλουτεῖν κακῶς.
                                    —*Antiphanes.*

Honourable poverty is better than dishonourable wealth.

Κατακρύπτει δ' οὐ κόνις
  συγγόνων κεδνὰν χάριν.—*Pindar.*

          The bright actions of the just
Survive unburied in the kindred dust.
                                    —*Wheelwright.*

Κατὰ σταγόνα.

Drop by drop ; a little at a time.

Κατ' ἐξοχήν.

(Pre-eminently.)   *Par excellence.*

Κάτθαν' ὁμῶς ὅ τ' ἀεργὸς ἀνὴρ ὅ τε πολλὰ
  ἐοργώς.—*Homer.*

Death comes equally to the energetic
  and the idle man.

Κατόπιν ἑορτῆς ἥκεις.

(You are come after the feast.) You
  come too late in the day.

Κλύοντες οὐκ ἤκουον.—*Æschylus.*

Ears had they, and heard not.

Κοιναὶ γὰρ ἔρχοντ' ἐλπίδες
  πολυπόνων ἀνδρῶν.—*Pindar.*

The hopes that are cherished by ever-
  toiling men, are a bond that unites
  them all.

Κοινὰ πάθη πάντων· ὁ βίος τρόχος, ἄστα-
  τος ὄλβος.—*Phocylides.*

Misfortunes come to all alike ; life is a
  wheel, and happiness abides not.

* Julius Cæsar's dying words to Brutus, as reported by Plutarch. The words are more
familiar in the Latin form, *Et tu, Brute !*

Κοινὰ τὰ φίλων. | Friends have their goods in common.

Κοινωνικὸν ζῷον ὁ ἄνθρωπος.—*Aristotle?* | Man is a social animal.

Κολοιὸς ποτὶ κολοιόν. | (Jackdaw with jackdaw.) Birds of a feather flock together.

Κόσμος. | (Order; harmony.) The universe.

Κούφη γῇ τοῦτον καλύπτοι. | May the earth lie light upon him.*

Κουφότατον πρᾶγμα λόγος. | (A word is a very light thing.) Words are but wind, but blows unkind.

Κρεῖσσον γὰρ εἰσάπαξ θανεῖν,
ἢ τὰς ἅπασας ἡμέρας πάσχειν κακῶς.
          —*Æschylus.* | Far better is it to die once for all, than spend one's life in endless misery.

Κρεῖσσον τῆς εὐγενίας τὸ καλῶς πράσσειν.
          —*Euripides.* | (Noble acts are better than noble birth.) 'Tis only noble to be good.
          —*Tennyson.*

Κρεῖττον γάρ ἐστιν ἄρξασθαι ὀψὲ τὰ δέοντα πράττειν, ἢ μηδέποτε.
          —*Dionysius of Halicarnassus.* | (It is better to begin late to do our duty than never to do it.) It is never too late to mend.

Κρεῖττον γάρ που σμικρὸν εὖ ἢ πολὺ μὴ ἱκανῶς περᾶναι.—*Socrates.* | Better to do a little well, than a great deal badly.

Κρεῖττον ἕνα φίλον ἔχειν πολλοῦ ἄξιον ἢ πολλοὺς μηδενὸς ἀξίους.
          —*Anacharsis.* | It is better to have one good friend than a multitude of worthless ones.

Κρείττων ἡ πρόνοια τῆς μεταμελείας.
          —*Dionysius of Halicarnassus.* | It is better to be wise before than after the event.

Κρέσσων γὰρ οἰκτιρμῶν φθόνος.—*Pindar.* | Better be envied than pitied.

Κρῆτες ἀεὶ ψεῦσται. | All Cretans are liars.

Κρίνει φίλους ὁ καιρὸς ὡς χρυσὸν τὸ πῦρ.
          —*Menander.* | As gold is tried in the furnace, so friends are tried by adversity.

Κριὸς τροφεῖα ἀπέτισε. | (The crow has paid for his keep.) His owner has reared a bird to peck out his eyes; he has warmed a viper in his bosom.

Κτῆμα ἐς ἀεί. | A possession for all time.

Κτήματα καὶ χρήματα. | Property in kind and in money.

Κτῆμά τε ἐς ἀεὶ μᾶλλον ἢ ἀγώνισμα ἐς τὸ παραχρῆμα ἀκούειν ξύγκειται.
          —*Thucydides.* | I have composed my history to be a possession for all time, not a mere literary achievement to win temporary renown.

Κῦδος. | Glory : fame.

Κυμινοπρίστης. | (A splitter of cummin.) A skin-flint.

Κωφὸν γὰρ βέλος ἀνδρὸς ἀνάλκιδος οὐτιδανοῖο.—*Homer.* | Harmless is the shaft of the unwarlike coward.

Λαγὼς καθεύδων. | (A sleeping hare.) One who is never caught napping; a difficult man to tackle.

Λάθε βιώσας.—*Epicurus.* | (Seek to live obscurely.) Far from court, far from danger.

---

* A common inscription on tombstones. Compare Latin, *Sit tibi terra levis.*

Λαμπάδια ἔχοντες διαδώσουσιν ἀλλήλοις.
—*Plato.*

(Those who have lamps will pass them to others.) Those who possess knowledge will interpret to their fellows.

Λάῳ μὴ πίστευε, πολύτροπός ἐστιν ὅμιλος.
—*Phocylides.*

Trust not the people ; ever fickle is the crowd.

Λήθη.

(Lethe.) Forgetfulness ; oblivion.*

Λίθος κυλινδόμενος τὸ φῦκος οὐ ποιεῖ.

A rolling stone gathers no moss.

Λιμὸς γάρ τοι πάμπαν ἀεργῷ σύμφορος ἀνδρί.—*Hesiod.*

Hunger is the constant companion of the idle man.

Λιμῷ γὰρ οὐδὲν ἐστὶν ἀντειπεῖν ἔπος.
—*Menander.*

(There is no arguing with hunger.) Hunger pierceth stone walls.

Λόγος γὰρ τοὔργον οὐ νικᾷ ποτέ.
—*Euripides.*

Action always effects more than words.

Λοιδορεῖσθαι δ' οὐ πρέπει ἄνδρας ποιητὰς, ὥσπερ ἀρτοπώλιδας.
—*Aristophanes.*

Poets should not wrangle like hawker dames.

Λύπης δὲ πάσης γίνετ' ἰατρὸς χρόνος.
—*Diphilus.*

Time is a physician that heals every grief.

Λύχνου ἀρθέντος, γυνὴ πᾶσα ἡ αὐτή.

(When the light is removed every woman is the same.) In the dark all cats are grey.

Μακάριος ὃς οὐσίαν καὶ νοῦν ἔχει· χρῆται γὰρ εἰς ἃ δεῖ καλῶς.—*Democritus.*

Happy is the man who has both money and sense ; for he knows how to use his wealth aright.

Μακραὶ τυράννων χεῖρες.

(Kings have long arms.) Who sups with the devil must have a long spoon.

Μάντις δ' ἄριστος ὅστις εἰκάζει καλῶς.
—*Euripides.*

The best guesser is the best prophet.

Μάντις κακῶν.

A prophet of evils.

Μέγα βιβλίον, μέγα κακόν.

A great book is a great evil.†

Μέγαλα βλάπτουσι τοὺς ἀξυνέτους οἱ ἐπαινέοντες.—*Democritus.*

Those who praise the foolish injure them.

Μεγάλην παράκαιρος ἡδονὴ τίκτει βλάβην· ἐξ ἡδονῆς γὰρ φύεται τὸ δυστυχεῖν.
—*Menander.*

Pleasure when sought at the wrong time produces much evil ; for misfortune is often the child of pleasure.

Μεγάλη πόλις μεγάλη ἐρημία.

A great city is a great solitude.‡

Μεγάλων ἀπολισθαίνειν ὅμως εὐγενὲς ἁμάρτημα.

In great attempts even to fail is glorious.

Μέγα χαῖρε, θεοὶ δέ τοι ὄλβια δοῖεν.
—*Homer.*

Farewell, and heaven bless thee.

Μείζω κακὰ ἢ ὥστε ἀνακλαίειν.
—*Herodotus.*

Sufferings that awaken thoughts too deep for tears.

Μελέτη τὸ πᾶν.—*Periander.*

(Practice is everything.) Nothing is impossible to a willing mind.

Μέμνησο ἀπιστεῖν.

(Remember to distrust.) If you trust before you try, You may repent before you die.

* One of the seven rivers which, according to mythology, flow round the lower world.
† This familiar expression is an adaptation of a line from Callimachus. See Τὸ μέγα βιβλίον.
‡ See note on Ἐρημία μεγάλη.

Μεταβολὴ πάντων γλυκύ.—*Euripides.*
Μετὰ λύπης γὰρ ἡ μάθησις.—*Aristotle.*
Μετὰ τὸν πόλεμον ἡ συμμαχία.

Μέτρον ἄριστον.—*Cleobulus.*

Μέτρῳ ὕδωρ πίνοντες, ἀμέτρως μάζαν
ἔδοντες.

Μὴ γένοιτο.
Μηδέ μοι ἄκλαυστος θάνατος μόλοι, ἀλλὰ
φίλοισι
καλλείποιμι θανὼν ἄλγεα καὶ στοναχάς.
—*Solon.*

Μηδὲν ἄγαν.—*Solon.*
Μηδέποτε μηδὲν αἰσχρὸν ποιήσας ἔλπιζε
λήσειν· καὶ γὰρ ἂν τοὺς ἄλλους λάθῃς,
σαυτῷ γε συνειδήσεις.—*Isocrates.*

Μὴ εἰς τὴν αὔριον ἀναβάλλου· ἡ γὰρ
αὔριον οὐδέ ποτε λαμβάνει τέλος.
—*St. Chrysostom.*

Μὴ κακὰ κερδαίνειν· κακὰ κέρδεα ἶσ'
ἄτῃσιν.—*Hesiod.*
Μὴ κίνει Καμαρίναν.

Μὴ κινεῖν κακὸν εὖ κείμενον.

Μὴ κρίνετε ἵνα μὴ κρίθητε.
Μῆλα κακοὶ φθείρουσι νομῆες.—*Homer.*
Μὴ μοι γένοιθ' ἃ βούλομ' ἀλλ' ἃ συμφέρει.
—*Menander.*

Μῆνὶν ἄειδε, θεά, Πηληιάδεω Ἀχιλῆος
οὐλομένην, ἥ μυρί' Ἀχαιοῖς ἄλγε' ἔθηκε.
—*Homer.*

Μὴ παιδὶ μάχαιραν.

Μὴ πᾶσι πίστευε.—*Pittacus.*
Μήποτέ τοι κακὸν ἄνδρα φίλον ποιεῖσθαι
ἑταῖρον,
ἀλλ' αἰεὶ φεύγειν ὥστε κακὸν λιμένα.
—*Theognis.*

Μὴ πῦρ ἐπὶ πῦρ.
Μήτε μοὶ μέλι, μήτε μέλιττα.

Μήτηρ τῆς ἐνδείας ἡ ἀεργία.

Change is sweet in everything.
There is no learning without trouble.
(Getting allies when the war is over.)
Shutting the stable door when the
horse is stolen.

Moderation is best ; the middle course
is safest.

(Drinking water by measure, and eating
cake without.) Penny wise and
pound foolish.

God forbid.
(Let me not die unwept, but let my death
cause grief and sorrow to my friends.)
I desire to die a dry death, but am not
so very desirous to have a dry funeral.
—*Jeremy Taylor.*

Nothing in excess.
Never hope to do a shameful action
and escape detection ; for if you
deceive other men, your own con-
science will still accuse you.

Defer not till the morrow ; for the morrow
never brings accomplishment.

Seek not evil gains ; ill-gotten gains
are equal to a loss.
(Do not disturb Kamarina.) Let sleep-
ing dogs lie.

(Do not raise up an old grievance.) Do
not stir up the mud.

Judge not, that ye be not judged.
Bad shepherds destroy the sheep.
May Heaven send me not what I wish,
but what will be for my good.

Of Peleus' son, Achilles, sing, O Muse,
The vengeance deep and deadly ; whence
to Greece
Unnumbered ills arose.—*Lord Derby.**

(Put not a sword in the hands of a
child.) *Ne puero gladium.*

Do not trust everybody.
Never choose a base fellow to be your
friend, but shun such an one as a
sailor avoids an unsafe anchorage.

Add not fuel to the flame.
(No bees, no honey.) No gains without
pains.

Idleness is the mother of want.

---

* The opening lines of Homer's " Iliad."

Μὴ ὑπὲρ τὸν πόδα τὸ ὑπόδημα.—*Lucian.*

(Let not the shoe be too large for the foot.) Cut your coat according to your cloth.

Μὴ φῦναι τὸν ἅπαντα νι-
κᾷ λόγον· τὸ δ' ἐπεὶ φανῇ
βῆναι κεῖθεν ὅθέν περ ἥκει
πολὺ δεύτερον ὡς τάχιστα.—*Sophocles.*

Not to be born is, beyond all question, best ; but, when a man hath once beheld the light of day, this is next best, that speedily he should return to that place whence he came.

Μία γὰρ ἐστὶ πρὸς τύχην ἀσφάλεια, τὸ μὴ τοσαυτακὶς αὐτὴν πειρᾶσαι.
—*Diocles Carystius.*

There is one way of making sure against the tricks of Fortune ; do not tempt her often.

Μία γὰρ χελιδὼν ἔαρ οὐ ποιεῖ, οὐδὲ μία ἡμέρα· οὕτω δὲ οὐδὲ μακάριον καὶ εὐδαίμονα μία ἡμέρα οὐδ' ὀλίγος χρόνος.
—*Aristotle.*

One swallow does not make a spring, nor one day ; so neither one day nor a brief space of time makes a man happy and prosperous.

Μία λόχνη οὐ τρέφει δύο ἐριθάκους.

One cherry tree sufficeth not two jays.

Μιᾶς γὰρ χειρὸς ἀσθενὴς μάχη.
—*Euripides.*

(Weak is the fight that one hand wages.) Many hands make labour light.

Μία χελιδὼν ἔαρ οὐ ποιεῖ.

One swallow does not make a spring.

Μικρὰ πρόφασίς ἐστι τοῦ πρᾶξαι κακῶς.

(A slight excuse is enough to do wrong.) It is an easy thing to find a staff to beat a dog.

Μικρὸν ἀπὸ τοῦ ἡλίου μετάστηθι.
—*Diogenes.*

Stand a little out of the sunshine.*

Μικρὸν κακὸν, μέγα ἀγαθόν.

(A little evil is a great good.) Nothing so bad that it might not be worse.

Μισῶ γε μέντοι χὦταν ἐν κακοῖσί τις ἁλοὺς ἔπειτα τοῦτο καλλύνειν θέλῃ.
—*Sophocles.*

But verily this, too, is hateful,—when one who hath been caught in wickedness then seeks to make the crime a glory.—*Jebb.*

Μισῶ δωρέαν, ᾗ τις ἀναγκάζει ἀγρυπνεῖν.
—*Anacreon.*

I hate a gift that gives me sleepless nights.†

Μισῶ μνήμονα συμπότην.—*Plutarch.*

I hate the man who reveals what has been told over the cups.

Μισῶ σοφιστὴν ὅστις οὐκ αὐτῷ σοφός.
—*Euripides.*

I hate the man who is wise in the affairs of others, and foolish in his own.

Μόνοις οὐ γίγνεται
θεοῖσι γῆρας οὐδὲ κατθανεῖν ποτε,
τὰ δ' ἄλλα συγχεῖ πάνθ' ὁ παγκρατὴς χρόνος.
φθίνει μὲν ἰσχὺς γῆς, φθίνει δὲ σώματος,
θνήσκει δὲ πίστις, βλαστάνει δ' ἀπιστία.
—*Sophocles.*

To the gods alone comes never old age or death, but all else is confounded by all-mastering time. The strength of the earth dies, and the strength of the body ; faith dies, and distrust is born.

Μόνον ἄργυρον βλέπουσι.—*Anacreon.*

Men have eyes for nothing but money.

Μόνος θεῶν γὰρ Θάνατος οὐ δώρων ἐρᾷ.
—*Æschylus.*

Death is the only god that gifts cannot appease.

Μόνος ὁ σοφὸς ἐλεύθερος, καὶ πᾶς ἄφρων δοῦλος.—*Chrysippus?*

The wise alone are free, and every fool is a slave.

---

* The reply of the cynic Diogenes to Alexander the Great when the latter asked how he could serve him. Nevertheless, Alexander declared, " If I were not Alexander, I would be Diogenes."

† The reply of the poet to Polycrates, the despot of Samos, who desired to present him with a talent of gold.

Μοχθεῖν ἀνάγκη τοὺς θέλοντας εὐτυχεῖν.
—*Menander.*

(Those who wish to be prosperous must needs endure toil.)   No gains without pains.

Νεκρὸν ἰατρεύειν καὶ γέροντα νουθετεῖν ταὐτόν ἐστι.

(Reforming old men is like healing a corpse.)   Habits become second nature; you cannot teach an old dog new tricks.

Νεκρὸς οὐ δάκνει.

(A dead man bites not.)   Dead men tell no tales.

Νέκταρ.

(Nectar.)   The drink of the gods; any very pleasant drink.

Νέμεσις.

(Nemesis.)   Retribution; the personification of the righteous anger of Heaven against the proud and insolent.

Νέοις τὸ σιγᾶν κρεῖττόν ἐστι τοῦ λαλεῖν.

(Silence is better than speech for the young.)   Children should be seen and not heard.

Νέος ἔμπειρος οὐκ ἐστί· πλῆθος γὰρ χρόνου ποιήσει τὴν ἐμπειρίαν.
—*Aristotle.*

Youth lacks experience; length of years alone can give this.

Νήπιοι, οὐδ᾽ ἴσασιν ὅσῳ πλέον ἥμισυ παντός.—*Hesiod.*

(Fools not to know that half exceeds the whole.)   A little safely obtained is better than much acquired with danger.

Νήπιος ὃς τὰ ἕτοιμα λιπὼν, ἀνέτοιμα διώκει.—*Hesiod.*

(A fool is he who leaves a certainty to pursue the uncertain.)   A bird in the hand is worth two in the bush.

Νικᾷ δὲ καὶ σίδηρον καὶ πῦρ καλή τις οὖσα.—*Anacreon.*

(A beautiful woman conquers both fire and sword.)   Beauty is invincible.

Νίκη δ᾽ ἐπαμείβεται ἄνδρας.—*Homer.*

Victory comes now to this man, now to that.

Νόμον φοβηθεὶς μὴ ταραχθήσῃ νόμῳ.
—*Menander.*

Respect the law, lest it cause thee trouble.

Ξενίων δέ τε θύμος ἄριστος.

Welcome is the best cheer.

Ξίφος τιτρώσκει σῶμα, τὸν δὲ νοῦν λόγος.
—*Menander.*

(A sword wounds the body, but a sharp word wounds the mind.)   The tongue's not steel, yet it cuts.

Ξίφους πληγὴ κουφοτέρα γλώσσης· τὸ μὲν γὰρ σῶμα, ἡ δὲ τὴν ψυχὴν τιτρώσκει.—*Pythagoras.*

The sword inflicts a less grievous blow than the tongue; the former wounds the body, but the latter hurts the soul.

Ξύλον ἀγκύλον οὐδέποτ᾽ ὀρθον.

(A crooked log can never be straightened.)   Just as the twig is bent the tree's inclined.—*Pope.*

Ξὺν τῷ δικαίῳ γὰρ μέγ᾽ ἔξεστι φρονεῖν.
—*Sophocles.*

We may be bold when justice fights for us.

Ξυρεῖν ἐπιχειρεῖ λέοντα.

(He is trying to shave a lion.)   He has a wolf by the tail.

'Ο ἀγαθὸς φίλαυτός ἐστι· καὶ γὰρ αὐτὸς ὀνήσεται τὰ καλὰ πράττων καὶ τοὺς ἄλλους ὠφελήσει.—*Aristotle.*

The good man is a friend to himself; for by doing right, he will benefit himself and be a help to others.

'Ο ἀδικῶν οὐ βούλεται, εἶναι θεὸν ἵνα μὴ τὸ διδόναι δίκην· ὁ δὲ ἀδικούμενος βούλεται εἶναι θεὸν, ἵν' ἐπικουρίας ὧν πέπονθε τύχῃ.—*Hierocles.*

The man who wrongs another hopes there is no God, fearing that he will have to pay the penalty of his sin; but he who is wronged hopes that God does exist, in order that he may be compensated for his sufferings.

'Ο ἄνθρωπος εὐεργετικὸς πέφυκεν.
—*Marcus Aurelius.*

Man is naturally inclined to beneficence.

'Ο βίος βραχὺς, ἡ δὲ τέχνη μακρή.
—*Hippocrates.*

(Life is short, art is long.) *Ars longa, vita brevis.*

'Ο γὰρ ἄνθρωπος, φυτὸν οὐκ ἔγγειον οὐδὲ ἀκίνητον, ἀλλ' οὐράνιόν ἐστιν, ὥσπερ ἐκ ῥίζης τὸ σῶμα τῆς κεφαλῆς ὀρθὸν ἱστώσης, πρὸς τὸν οὐρανὸν ἀνεστραμμένον.—*Plutarch.*

Man is a plant, not bound to the earth, nor immovable, but belonging to heaven, which, raising its head erect from the stem, looks upward to the skies.

'Ο γὰρ διαιτητὴς τὸ ἐπιεικὲς ὁρᾷ, ὁ δὲ δικαστὴς τὸν νόμον.—*Aristotle.*

The arbitrator considers what is equitable, the judge what is legal.

'Ο δ' αὖ θάνατος κίχε καὶ τὸν φυγόμαχον.
—*Simonides of Ceos.*

Death catches even the coward as he flies.

'Ο δὴ χαρίεις καὶ ἐλευθέριος οὕτως ἕξει, οἷον νόμος ὢν ἑαυτῷ.—*Aristotle.*

In such wise the man of a frank and pleasing character will habitually act, being, so to speak, a law unto himself.

'Ο δ' ὄλβος οὐ βέβαιος, ἀλλ' ἐφήμερος.
—*Euripides.*

Happiness abideth not, enduring but for a day.

'Ο ἐλαχίστων δεόμενος ἔγγιστα θεῶν.
—*Socrates.*

He who has the smallest wants approaches the gods most nearly.

'Ο ἐλέφας τὴν μυῖαν οὐκ ἀλεγίζει.

The elephant does not take notice of the fly.

'Ο ἔχων ὦτα ἀκούειν, ἀκουέτω.

He that hath ears to hear, let him hear.

Οἱ ἀξύνετοι δυστυχέοντες σωφρονέουσι.
—*Democritus.*

(Fools learn wisdom from misfortune.) Experience is the mistress of fools.

Οἱ αὐτοὶ περὶ τῶν αὐτῶν τοῖς αὐτοῖς τὰ αὐτά.

(The same persons saying the same things to the same persons about the same things.) Wearisome iteration.

Οἱ γὰρ κακοί, κακίους ἐπαινούμενοι.
Philostratus.

Praise makes knaves more knavish.

Οἱ γὰρ Κύπριν φεύγοντες ἀνθρώπων ἄγαν νοσοῦσ' ὁμοίως τοῖς ἄγαν θηρωμένοις.
—*Euripides.*

Those who shun love altogether are as foolish as those who pursue it too sedulously.

Οἱ γὰρ πνέοντες μεγάλα, τοὺς κρείσσους λόγους
πικρῶς φέρουσι τῶν ἐλασσόνων ὕπο.
—*Euripides.*

Conceited folk are indignant when they are beaten in argument by their inferiors.

Οἱ γὰρ πολλοὶ μᾶλλον ὀρέγονται τοῦ κέρδους, ἢ τῆς τιμῆς.—*Aristotle.*

The mob strives for gain rather than honour.

Οἱ διψῶντες σιωπῇ πίνουσι.

(Thirsty folk drink in silence.) Beware of still water and of a dog that does not bark.

Οἵη περ φύλλων γενεή, τοίη δὲ καὶ ἀνδρῶν·
φύλλα τὰ μὲν τ' ἄνεμος χαμάδις χέει,
ἄλλα δέ θ' ὕλη
τηλεθόωσα φύει, ἔαρος δ' ἐπιγίγνεται ὥρη·
ὣς ἀνδρῶν γενεή, ἡ μὲν φύει, ἡ δ'
ἀπολήγει.—*Homer.*

The race of man is as the race of leaves :
Of leaves, one generation by the wind
Is scattered on the earth ; another soon
In spring's luxuriant verdure bursts to
light—
So with our race ; these flourish, those
decay.—*Lord Derby.*

Οἱ θεοὶ οὐδὲν πρότερον ποιοῦσιν ἢ τῶν
πονηρῶν ἀνθρώπων τὴν διανοίαν παρά-
γουσι.—*Lycurgus.*

(In dealing with the wicked, the gods
first deprive them of their senses.)
Whom the gods wish to destroy, they
first drive mad.

Οἴκοι λέοντες ἐν μάχῃ δ' ἀλωπέκες.
                           —*Aristophanes.*

(Lions at home, foxes in the fight.)
Brave when there is no danger nigh.

Οἱ μὲν γὰρ ἀρχαῖοι τὴν ἀρχὴν ἥμισυ τοῦ
παντὸς εἶναι φάσκοντες, μεγίστην
παρήνουν ποιεῖσθαι σπουδὴν ἐν ἑκάστοις
ὑπὲρ τοῦ καλῶς ἄρξασθαι.—*Polybius.*

When the men of old time declared
that the beginning was half the work,
they meant that we ought to use our
best endeavours to make a good beginning in whatever we undertook.

Οἰνοβαρὲς, κυνὸς ὄμματ' ἔχων, κραδίην
δ' ἐλάφοιο.—*Homer.*

Thou sot, with eye of dog, and heart
of deer !—*Lord Derby.*

Οἶνος Ἀφροδίτης γάλα.—*Aristophanes.*

Wine is the milk of love.

Οἶνος γὰρ ἀνθρώποις δίοπτρον.—*Alcæus.*

Wine is the mirror that reveals the
nature of a man.

Οἶνος καὶ παῖδες ἀληθεῖς.

Wine and children speak the truth.

Οἶνός τοι χαρίεντι μέγας πέλει ἵππος
ἀοιδῷ.

Truly wine is a great help to the tune-
ful bard.

Οἶνος, ὦ φίλε παῖ, λέγεται, καὶ ἀλάθεα.
                           —*Theocritus.*

(Wine, dear lad, and truth, the proverb
says.) *In vino veritas.*

Οἴνου κατίοντος ἐπιπλέουσιν ἔπη.
                           —*Herodotus.*

(When the wine is in the words flow
out.)   Wine loosens the tongue.

Οἶος ὁ βίος, τοῖος ὁ λόγος.

(As the life is, so will be the language.)
The tongue of a fool carves a piece of
his heart to all that sit near him.

Οἱ πλεῖστοι ἄνθρωποι κακοί.—*Bias.*

Most men are knaves.

Οἱ πολλοί.

The multitude : King Demos.

Οἱ πόνοι τίκτουσι τὴν εὐδοξίαν.
                           —*Euripides.*

Labour is the mother of fame.

Ὁ κοινὸς ἰατρός σε θεραπεύσει Χρόνος.
                           —*Philippides.*

Time, the physician of all our ills, will
heal thee.

Ὁ κόσμος οὗτος μία πόλις ἐστί.
                           —*Epictetus.*

This world of ours is one city.

Ὁ κόσμος σκηνή, ὁ βίος πάροδος· ἦλθες,
ἴδες, ἀπῆλθες.—*Democritus.*

(The world is a stage, and life a piece
of acting : you come, you see, and in
a moment you are gone.) All the
world's a stage.—*Shakespeare.*

Ὀλβίσαι δὲ χρὴ
βίον τελευτήσαντ' ἐν εὐεστοῖ φίλη.
                           —*Æschylus.*

We must not consider a man truly
happy, unless prosperity endures
with him to the end of his life.

Ὀλιγοχρόνιον γίγνεται, ὥσπερ ὄναρ
Ἥβη τιμήεσσα.—*Mimnermus.*

A few short years youth holds imperious
sway,
Then, like a dream, grows dim, and
fades away.

Ὁ λύκος τὴν τρίχα, οὐ τὴν γνώμην ἀλλάττει.

The wolf changes his coat, but not his nature.

Ὁ μηδὲν ἀδικῶν οὐδενὸς δεῖται νόμου.
— Antiphanes.

(The just man requires no law.) The righteous are a law unto themselves.

Ὄμμα γὰρ δόμων νομίζω δεσπότου παρουσίαν.
— Æschylus.

I consider the presence of the master to be the eye of the house.

Ὅμοιον ὁμοίῳ φίλον.

(Like loves like.) Birds of a feather flock together.

Ὁμοιότης τῆς φιλότητος μήτηρ.

(Likeness is the mother of love.) Like will to like.

Ὄναρ ἐκ Διός ἐστιν.— Homer.

Dreams are sent by God.

Ὄναρ καὶ ὕπαρ.

Sleeping and waking; always.

Ὃν οἱ θεοὶ φιλοῦσιν, ἀποθνήσκει νέος.
— Menander.

Whom the gods love die young.

Ὀνοματοποιία.

(Onomatopœa.) The formation of words in imitation of the sounds they indicate, e.g. buzz.

Ὄνον γένεσθαι κρεῖττον, ἢ τοὺς χείρονας ὁρᾶν ἑαυτοῦ ζῶντας ἐπιφανέστερον.
— Menander.

It is better to be born an ass, than to see one's inferiors enjoying higher positions than we hold ourselves.

Ὄνος ἐν πιθήκοις.

(An ass among apes.) A butt for others' jokes.

Ὄνος λύρας.

(An ass at the lyre.) A sow to a fiddle; a bull in a china-shop.

Ὄνος τ' ὄνῳ κάλλιστον.

(An ass thinks an ass a pretty fellow.) No mother ever had an ugly child.

Ὄνου οὐρὰ τηλίαν οὐ ποιεῖ.

(The tail of an ass does not make a sieve.) You can't make a silk purse out of a sow's ear.

Ὄνου πόκας ζητεῖς.

(You seek wool from an ass.) Ye seek hot water under cauld ice.

Ὄνῳ τις ἔλεγε μῦθον· ὁ δὲ τὰ ὦτα ἐκίνει.

(A man told a story to an ass; and the ass wagged its ears.) Cast not pearls before swine.*

Ὁ ὅρκῳ παρακρουόμενος τὸν μὲν ἐχθρὸν ὁμολογεῖ δεδιέναι, τοῦ δὲ θεοῦ καταφρονεῖν.— Plutarch.

He who takes an oath to deceive another, confesses that he fears his enemy, but despises God.

Ὁ πᾶς πρέπει ἐννέπειν τὰ δίκαια χρόνος.
— Sophocles.

Every moment is the right moment to say what is just.

Ὅπη γὰρ ἂν ἐπιθυμῇ καὶ ὁποῖός τις ὢν τὴν ψυχήν, ταύτῃ σχεδὸν ἑκάστοτε καὶ τοιοῦτος γίγνεται ἅπας ἡμῶν ὡς τὸ πολύ.— Plato.

(What each of us most aspires to, and what we are in the depths of our mind, that, for the most part, each of us becomes.) My nature is subdued to what it works in.— Shakespeare.

Ὁποῖα ἡ δέσποινα τοῖαι καὶ θεραπαινίδες.

Like mistress, like maid.

Ὅπου γὰρ μὴ νόμοι ἄρχουσιν, οὐκ ἔστι πολιτεία. Δεῖ γὰρ τὸν μὲν νόμον ἄρχειν πάντων.— Aristotle.

There is no real state where the laws are not supreme. Law ought to be above all else.

---

* A proverbial pleasantry used to hint that someone was very slow-witted.

᾿Όπου γυναῖκές εἰσι, πάντ᾽ ἐκεῖ κακά.
— *Menander.*

Where women are, there dwelleth every kind of ill.

῎Ορα τέλος μακροῦ βίου.

(Regard the end of a long life.) Respect your end.—*Shakespeare.*

᾿Οργὴ φιλούντων ὀλίγον ἰσχύει χρόνον.
—*Menander.*

(The anger of lovers is soon appeased.) Lovers' quarrels are the renewal of love.

῞Ορκους ἐγὼ γυναικὸς εἰς ὕδωρ γράφω.
— *Sophocles.*

(A woman's vows I write in water.) Frailty, thy name is Woman!
—*Shakespeare.*

῎Ορος ὄρει οὐ μίγνυται.

(Mountain does not mingle with mountain.) Friends may meet, but mountains never greet. Pride loves no man, and is beloved of no man.

᾿Ορῶ γὰρ ἡμᾶς οὐδὲν ὄντας ἄλλο πλὴν
εἴδωλ᾽ ὅσοιπερ ζῶμεν ἢ κουφὴν σκιάν.
— *Sophocles.*

(I see that we mortals who live upon the earth, are nothing but breathing ghosts and fleeting shadows.) "Man, that is born of a woman, hath but a short time to live, and is full of misery."

᾿Ορῶ γὰρ τῶν ἀνθρώπων οὐδένα ἀναμάρτητον διατελοῦντα.—*Xenophon.*

(I know no man who never errs.) To err is human, to forgive divine.
—*Pope.*

῝Ος ἂν ᾖ πρὸς ἀρετὴν καλῶς γεγονώς τοῦτον προσήκει γενναῖον λέγεσθαι, κἂν μηδεὶς ἐπίστηται τοὺς γονέας αὐτοῦ μηδὲ τοὺς προγόνους.
—*Dion Chrysostom.*

Whoever is naturally disposed to live virtuously, that man we ought to call noble, even if no one knows who are his parents or his ancestors.

῝Ος δ᾽ ἂν ἄνευ μανίας Μουσῶν ἐπὶ ποιητικὰς θύρας ἀφίκηται, πεισθεὶς ὡς ἄρα ἐκ τέχνης ἱκανὸς ποιητὴς ἐσόμενος, ἀτελὴς αὐτός.—*Plato.*

Whoever comes to the shrine of the poetic Muses without a spice of madness in him, being persuaded that Art is sufficient to make a poet, will accomplish nothing.

῝Ος δ᾽ ἂν πλεῖστ᾽ ἔχῃ, σοφώτατος.
—*Euripides.*

(The richest is counted the wisest.) Rich men's spots are covered with money.

῾Ο Σιμωνίδης τὴν μὲν ζωγραφίαν ποίησιν σιωπῶσαν προσαγορεύει, τὴν δὲ ποίησιν ζωγραφίαν λαλοῦσαν.—*Plutarch.*

Simonides says that painting is silent poetry, and poetry is speaking painting.

῾Ο σοφὸς ἐν αὑτῷ περιφέρει τὴν οὐσίαν.
— *Menander.*

(The wise man carries all his wealth within himself.) Better wise than wealthy.

῞Ος τε πολὺ γλυκίων μέλιτος καταλει βομένοιο.—*Homer.*

(Sweeter it is by far than flowing honey.) Sweet is revenge, especially to women.—*Byron.*

῞Οστις ἂν βροτῶν
κακὸς πεφύκῃ, ζημιοῦσιν οἱ θεοί.
—*Euripides.*

The gods will punish the man whose heart is full of sin.

῞Οστις γὰρ αὐτὸς ἢ φρονεῖν μόνος δοκεῖ, ἢ γλῶσσαν, ἣν οὐκ ἄλλος ἢ ψυχὴν ἔχειν, οὗτοι διαπτυχθέντες ὤφθησαν κενοί
— *Sophocles.*

For if any man thinks that he alone is wise,—that in speech or in mind he hath no peer,— such a soul, when laid open, is ever found empty.—
Jebb.

Ὅταν ἀγαθὸν πράσσῃς, θεοὺς, μὴ σαυτὸν,
αἰτιῶ.—*Bias.*

When you do a good action, give the credit, not to yourself, but to God.

Ὅταν γὰρ ἐξ ἁπάντων συνεισφέρηται,
ἑκάστῳ κοῦφον γίνεται τὸ ἐπίταγμα.
                              —*Dion Chrysostom.*

When all pay their share, the burden to each is light.

Ὅταν δ' ὁ δαίμων ἀνδρὶ πορσύνῃ κακά
τὸν νοῦν ἔβλαψε πρῶτον, ᾧ βουλεύεται.

When God wishes to bring evil on a man, he first makes him mad.*

Ὅταν πίω τὸν οἶνον,
εὕδουσιν αἱ μέριμναι.
τί πόνων, τί γόων μοι,
τί μοι μέλει μεριμνῶν ;
θανεῖν με δεῖ, κἂν μὴ θέλω·—*Anacreon.*

Whene'er my thoughts in wine I steep,
All carking cares are lulled to sleep ;
Of toil or sorrow what reck I,
Since, willy-nilly, all must die.

Ὅταν σπεύδῃ τις αὐτὸς, χὡ θεὸς συνάπτεται.—*Æschylus.*

Whenever a man deliberately chooses the downward course, God helps him on.

Ὅ τ' ἐχθρὸς ἡμῖν ἐς τοσόν δ' ἐχθαρτέος,
ὡς καὶ φιλήσων αὖθις.—-*Sophocles.*

We ought to set limits to our hatred of our enemies, remembering that in the future we may be their friends.

Ὅτι δύναται ὁ θεὸς ἐκ τῶν λίθων τούτων
ἐγεῖραι τέκνα τῷ Ἀβραάμ.

(God can raise to Abraham children of stones.)   Motto of the Paviours' Company.

Ὅτου δ' ἀπορρεῖ μνῆστις εὖ πεπονθότος,
οὐκ ἂν γένοιτ' ἔθ' οὗτος εὐγενὴς ἀνήρ.
                              —*Sophocles.*

He who forgets a kindness done to him, could never be a truly noble man.

Οὐ ἀεικὲς ἀμυνομένῳ περὶ πάτρης τεθνάμεν.—*Homer.*

A glorious death is his
Who for his country falls.
                              —*Lord Derby.*

Οὐ γὰρ ἄν ποτε τρέφειν δύναιτ' ἂν μία
λόχμη κλέπτας δύω.—*Aristophanes.*

(One coppice could never support two thieves.)   One cherry-tree sufficeth not two jays.

Οὐ γάρ ἐστι πικρῶς ἐξετάσαι τί πέπρακται
τοῖς ἀλλοῖς, ἂν μὴ παρ' ὑμῶν αὐτῶν
πρῶτον ὑπάρξῃ τὰ δέοντα.
                              —*Demosthenes.*

You ought not to be a severe critic of others' actions, unless you have first done your own duty.

Οὐ γὰρ θανεῖν ἔχθιστον, ἀλλ' ὅταν θανεῖν
χρῄζων τις εἶτα μηδὲ τοῦτ' ἔχῃ λαβεῖν.
                              —*Sophocles.*

Death is not the worst evil, but, when we wish to die, not to have the power to do so.

Οὐ γὰρ πάσχοντες εὖ ἀλλὰ δρῶντες
κτώμεθα τοὺς φίλους.—*Thucydides.*

Not by receiving benefits, but by rendering them do we gain the friendship of other men.

Οὐ γὰρ πώ τις ἑὸν γόνον ἀνέγνω.
                              —*Homer.*

(No one has ever known his own parent.) It is a wise child that knows its own father.

Οὐ γάρ τ' αἶψα θεῶν τρέπεται νόος αἰὲν
ἐόντων.—*Homer.*

Not easily changed is the mind of the eternal gods.

Οὐ γὰρ τὰ ὀνόματα πίστις τῶν πραγμάτων
ἐστί, τὰ δὲ πράγματα καὶ τῶν ὀνομάτων.—*Dion Chrysostom.*

Names are not the pledge for things, but things for names.

---

* Lines from an unknown poet quoted by the Scholiast on the *Antigone* of Sophocles. The sentiment is expressed by the orator Lycurgus, see ὃι Θεοὶ οὐδὲν, who also quotes another version of the above lines.   They seem to be the origin of the familiar *Quem Deus* (or *Jupiter*) *vult perdere, prius dementat.*

M

Οὐ γὰρ τὸν τρόπον, ἀλλὰ τὸν τόπον μόνον μετήλλαξεν.—Æschines.

A man does not change his mode of life when he changes his abode.*

Οὐδὲ Ἡρακλῆς πρὸς δύο.

(Even Hercules could not struggle against two.) Two to one is odds enough.

Οὐ δεῖ λέγειν γὰρ μακάριον τὸν χρήματα ἔχοντα πλεῖστα, τὸν δὲ μὴ λυπούμενον. —Apollodorus.

Do not call him happy who has the most wealth, but him who has the fewest troubles.

Οὐδεὶς ἀνθρώπων ἀδικῶν τίσιν οὐκ ἀποτείσει.—Herodotus.

The evil-doer has always to suffer for his wickedness.

Οὐδεὶς γὰρ ὃν φοβεῖται φιλεῖ. —Aristotle.

(No one loves the man whom he fears.) "Perfect love casteth out fear."

Οὐδεὶς γὰρ οὕτως οὐδὲ μάρτυς ἐστὶ φοβερὸς, οὔτε κατήγορος δεινὸς ὡς ἡ σύνεσις ἡ ἐγκατοικοῦσα ταῖς ἑκάστων ψυχαῖς.—Polybius.

(There is no more dreadful witness, no more terrible accuser, than the conscience that dwells in the hearts of each of us.) Thus conscience does make cowards of us all. —Shakespeare.

Οὐδεὶς διχὰ ἀπωλείας καὶ ζημίας κακός ἐστι.—Epictetus.

No wicked man is free from loss and punishment.

Οὐδεὶς, Κύρν', ἄτης καὶ κέρδεος αἴτιος αὐτὸς, ἀλλὰ θεοὶ τούτων δώτορες ἀμφοτέρων. —Theognis.

No man, friend, is the author of his own grief or happiness, but the gods impart to all both good and evil fortunes.

Οὐδὲν γὰρ ἀνθρώποισιν οἷον ἄργυρος κακὸν νόμισμ' ἔβλαστε· τοῦτο καὶ πόλεις πορθεῖ, τόδ' ἄνδρας ἐξανίστησιν δόμων· τόδ' ἐκδιδάσκει καὶ παραλλάσσει φρένας χρηστὰς πρὸς αἰσχρὰ πράγμαθ' ἵστασθαι βροτῶν.—Sophocles.

No evil so great as money ever was current among mankind. This lays waste cities, this drives men from their homes, this trains and perverts honest souls so that they essay deeds of shame.

Οὐδεὶς ἐν ἀνθρώποισι μένει χρῆμ' ἔμπεδον αἰεί· οἵηπερ φύλλων γενεὴ, τοίη δὲ καὶ ἀνδρῶν. —Simonides of Amorgos.

(Nothing that belongs to man abides for any time, for like the leaves of the tree, so man fades speedily away.) "He cometh up and is cut down like a flower."

Οὐδέν ἐστι θήριον γυναικὸς ἀμαχώτερον. —Aristophanes.

It is harder to conquer a woman than to subdue any wild beast.

Οὐδὲν μάτην ἡ φύσις ποιεῖ.—Aristotle.

(Nature creates nothing in vain.) Every created thing has its own proper function.

Οὐδὲν οὕτω πιαίνει τὸν ἵππον ὡς βασιλέως ὀφθαλμός.

(Nothing fattens the horse so well as the master's eye.) The master's eye makes the horse fat.

Οὐδὲν πρᾶγμα.

It is no matter; it is of no consequence.

Οὐδὲν πρὸς ἔπος.

Not to the point; nothing to do with the case.

Οὐδὲν σιωπῆς ἔστι χρησιμώτερον. —Menander.

(There is nought more beneficial than silence.) Silence seldom doth harm.

---

* The same sentiment is expressed by Horace. *Cælum non animum mutant.* See Latin section.

Οὐ δὴ που κακόν τι λέγων ἐμαυτὸν
λέληθα ;—Phocion.

Have I inadvertently said something wrong ? *

Οὐ δίκαιον τὴν τῶν ἀνθρώπων πονηρίαν
ἐπὶ τὰ πράγματα μεταφέρειν.
　　　　　　　　—Isocrates.

It is not right that the evil which men bring upon themselves should be imputed to circumstances.

Οὐ δοκεῖν ἄριστος ἀλλ᾽ εἶναι.
　　　　　　　　—Æschylus.

Not to seem, but to be the noblest.

Οὐ δύναται Θέτιδός τε καὶ Γαλατείας ἐρᾶν.

(You cannot love Thetis and Galatea at the same time.) You must be off with the old love before you are on with the new.

Οὐ δύναται πόλις κρυβῆναι ἐπάνω ὄρους
κειμένη.

A city that is set upon a hill cannot be hid.

Οὐκ ἀγαθὸν πολυκοιρανίη· εἷς κοίρανος
ἔστω
εἷς βασιλεύς.— Homer.

　　　　　　　　Ill fares the State
Where many masters rule ; let one be lord,
One king supreme.— Lord Derby.

Οὐκ ᾽Αθηναῖος οὐδ᾽ ῞Ελλην ἀλλὰ κόσμιος.
　　　　　　　　—Socrates.

I am a citizen, not of Athens, nor of Greece, but of the whole world.
The world is my parish.
　　　　　　　　—John Wesley.

Οὐκ αἰεὶ θέρος ἐσσεῖται· ποιεῖσθε καλιάς.
　　　　　　　　—Hesiod.

(It will not always be summer ; harvest while you may.) Make hay while the sun shines.

Οὐκ αἰσχρὸν οὐδὲν τῶν ἀναγκαίων βροτοῖς.
　　　　　　　　—Euripides.

Nothing that is compulsory should be regarded as shameful.

Οὐκ ἂν γένοιτο χωρὶς ἐσθλὰ καὶ κακὰ,
ἀλλ᾽ ἐστί τις σύγκρασις, ὥστ᾽ ἔχειν
καλῶς.—Euripides.

There could be no good without evil, but both are intermingled, so that all may be well.

Οὐκ ἀνδρὸς ὅρκοι πίστις ἀλλ᾽ ὅρκων ἀνήρ.
　　　　　　　　—Æschylus.

(Men credit gain for oaths, not oaths for them.) The word of an honest man is as good as his bond.

Οὐκ ἔθανες, Πρώτη, μετέβης δ᾽ ἐς
ἀμείνονα χῶρον.

Thou art not dead, my Prote, thou art flown unto a land much fairer than our own.†

Οὐκ εἰσὶν οἱ παμπλούσιοι ἀγαθοί.—Plato.

(The very rich are not good.) No saint was ever a millionaire.

Οὐκ ἔνι δ᾽ αὐτὸν ἀργοῦντα οὐδὲ τοῖς
φίλοις ἐπιτάττειν ὑπὲρ αὐτοῦ τι ποιεῖν,
μὴ τί γε δὴ τοῖς θεοῖς.—Demosthenes.

The man who makes no effort for himself, ought not to seek the help of either friends or the gods.

Οὐκ ἔστι θνητῶν ὅστις ἔστ᾽ ἐλεύθερος·
ἢ χρημάτων γὰρ δοῦλός ἐστιν ἢ τύχης,
ἢ πλῆθος αὐτὸν πόλεος ἢ νόμων γραφαὶ
εἴργουσι χρῆσθαι μὴ κατὰ γνώμην τρόποις.
　　　　　　　　—Euripides.

No mortal man is truly free : he is a slave either to money or fortune ; or else the populace of his city or the laws prevent him from doing as he pleases.

Οὐκ ἔστι κρεῖττον τοῦ σιωπᾶν οὐδὲ ἕν.
　　　　　　　　—Amphis.

(Nothing, nothing is more valuable than silence.) Speech is silvern, silence is golden.

* Phocion's criticisms were so unpalatable to the Athenian Assembly that, when on one occasion he was applauded, he affected to be surprised, and put the above question to a friend sitting near.
† The first line of a poem from the Greek Anthology. The sentiment is Christian rather than pagan.

Οὐκ ἔστι λύπης ἄλλο φάρμακον βροτοῖς,
ὡς ἀνδρὸς ἐσθλοῦ καὶ φίλου παραίνεσις.
　　　　　　　　　　—Euripides.

The best remedy for grief is the counsel of a kind and honest friend.

Οὐκ ἔστιν ἐν κακοῖσιν εὐγένεια,
παρ' ἀγαθοῖσι δ' ἀνδρῶν.—Euripides.

(True nobility does not exist in the base, but only in the virtuous.)
　　Howe'er it be, it seems to me
　　'Tis only noble to be good.
　　　　　　　　　　—Tennyson.

Οὐκ ἔστιν ὅστις πάντ' ἀνὴρ εὐδαιμονεῖ.
　　　　　　　　　　—Euripides.

No man has unalloyed happiness.

Οὐκ ἔστιν οὐδὲν μητρὸς ἥδιον τέκνοις·
ἐρᾶτε μητρός, παῖδες, ὡς οὐκ ἔστ' ἔρως
τοιοῦτος ἄλλος, οἷος ἡδίων ἐρᾶν.
　　　　　　　　　　—Euripides.

Children have no greater blessing than their mother; children, love your mother, for no love is so strong, so sweet, as that between a mother and a child.

Οὐκ ἔστιν οὕτω μῶρος ὃς θανεῖν ἐρᾷ.
　　　　　　　　　　—Sophocles.

No man is so foolish as to be enamoured of death.

Οὐκέτι πιστὰ γυναιξίν.—Homer.

No longer are women trustworthy.

Οὐκ οἴεται θεοὺς εἶναι ὁ ἄθεος, ὁ δὲ δεισι-
δαίμων οὐ βούλεται, πιστεύει δ' ἄκων·
ἀποθανεῖν γὰρ φοβεῖται· καί τοί γε,
ὥσπερ ὁ Τάνταλος ὑπεκδῦναι τὸν λίθον
ἐπαιωρούμενον, οὕτω καὶ οὗτος τὸν
φόβον, ὡς οὐχ ἧττον ὑπ' αὐτοῦ πιεζό-
μενος, ἀγαπήσειεν ἄν.—Plutarch.

The unbeliever thinks the gods do not exist, but the man who is afraid of the gods wishes they did not exist, and believes in them against his will, for he fears to die; and as Tantalus longs to escape the stone suspended over his head, so such a man is eager to escape this fear which weighs as heavily upon him.

Οὔκουν γέλως ἥδιστος εἰς ἐχθροὺς γελᾶν;
　　　　　　　　　　—Sophocles.

Is it not the sweetest laughter when we laugh at our foes?

Οὐκ ὠνοῦμαι μυρίων δραχμῶν μεταμέ-
λειαν.

I do not buy repentance for ten thousand drachmæ.*

Οὐ λέγειν δεινός, ἀλλὰ σιγᾶν ἀδύνατος.
　　　　　　　　　　—Epicharmus.

Not a clever speaker, but incapable of keeping silence.

Οὐ λόγῳ, ἀλλ' ἔργῳ.

(Not in theory but in practice.) Deeds, not words.

Οὐ μὰν γάρ τι πού ἐστιν ὀϊζυρώτερον
ἀνδρὸς
πάντων, ὅσσα τε γαῖαν ἔπι πνείει τε
καὶ ἔρπει.—Homer.

Of all the creatures that breathe and move upon the earth, none is more sorrowful than man.

Οὐ μὲν γάρ τι γυναικὸς ἀνὴρ ληΐζετ'
ἄμεινον
τῆς ἀγαθῆς· τῆς δ' αὖτε κακῆς οὐ ῥίγιον
ἄλλο.—Hesiod.

Nought better can a man obtain than a good wife; no greater curse than a bad one.

Οὐ μόνον ἄρ', ὡς ἔοικεν, ὁ γέρων δὶς παῖς
γίγνοιτ' ἄν, ἀλλὰ καὶ ὁ μεθυσθείς.
　　　　　　　　　　—Plato.

Not only, as it seems, is the old man, but also the drunkard, twice a child.

Οὐ παντὸς ἀνδρὸς εἰς Κόρινθον ἐσθ' ὁ
πλοῦς.

It is not every man that can go to Corinth.†

---

* The reply of Demosthenes to Lais, the courtesan, who asked exorbitant sums from those who sought her favours.

† The luxury of the wealthy commercial city of Corinth was proverbial in ancient times, and it was the home of some of the most notorious courtesans. See οὐκ ὠνοῦμαι μυρίων.

Οὔποτε ποιήσεις τὸν καρκίνον ὀρθὰ
βαδίζειν.—*Aristophanes.*

(You will never make a crab to walk
straight.) That which is bred in the
bone will never be out of the flesh.

Οὐ πρὸς ἰατροῦ σοφοῦ
θρηνεῖν ἐπῳδὰς πρὸς τυμῶντι πήματι.
　　　　　　—*Sophocles.*

It is not the skilful surgeon's part to
sing charms over a wound that needs
the knife.

Οὐ τὸ ζῆν περὶ πλείστου ποιητέον, ἀλλὰ
τὸ εὖ ζῆν.—*Plato.*

We ought not to reckon mere life, but
life spent virtuously, to be the highest
good.

Οὗτός ἐστι γαλεώτης γέρων.
　　　　　　—*Menander.*

A cute old fox this !

Οὕτως ἀπὸ τῆς τῶν ἀρχαίων μεγαλο-
φυΐας εἰς τὰς τῶν ζηλούντων ἐκείνους
ψυχὰς, ὡς ἀπὸ ἱερῶν στομίων, ἀποῤ-
ῥοιαί τινες φέρονται, ὑφ᾽ ὧν ἐπιπνεό-
μενοι, καὶ οἱ μὴ λίαν φοιβαστικοὶ, τῷ
ἑτέρων συνενθουσιῶσι μεγέθει.
　　　　　　—*Longinus.*

Thus, from the sublime spirit of the
ancients there flow into the minds of
those who imitate them certain eman-
ations, like clouds of vapour from the
cleft rocks in holy shrines ; and these
inspire even the most ungifted with
the enthusiasm and greatness of
others.

Οὕτως ἄρα ὑποληπτέον περὶ τοῦ δικαίου
ἀνδρός, ἐάν τ᾽ ἐν πενίᾳ γίγνηται ἐάν τ᾽
ἐν νόσοις ἤ τινι ἄλλῳ τῶν δοκούντων
κακῶν, ὡς τούτῳ ταῦτα εἰς ἀγαθόν τι
τελευτήσει ζῶντι ἢ καὶ ἀποθανόντι.
Οὐ γὰρ δὴ ὑπό γε θεῶν ποτὲ ἀμελεῖται,
ὃς ἂν προθυμεῖσθαι ἐθέλῃ δίκαιος γίνε-
σθαι καὶ ἐπιτηδεύων ἀρετὴν εἰς ὅσον
δυνατὸν ἀνθρώπῳ ὁμοιοῦσθαι θεῷ.
　　　　　　—*Plato.*

We must hold this opinion of the just
man, that, if he fall into poverty or
disease, or any other of these seeming
evils, all these things work together
for good to him, either during his
life, or after death. For that man is
never neglected by the gods whoso-
ever exerts himself to the utmost to
become just, and, by practising virtue,
tries to approach, as nearly as a man
may, to the likeness of God.

Οὕτως, οὐ πάντεσσι θεὸς χαρίεντα δίδω-
σιν.
ἀνδράσιν. —*Homer.*

Not on every man does God bestow
His good gifts.

Οὕτως ὑπὸ λόγων μᾶλλον, ἢ πράξεων
πονηρῶν, ἀνιάσθαι πεφύκασιν οἱ πολλοί·
χαλεπώτερον γὰρ ὕβριν, ἢ βλάβην
φέρουσι.—*Plutarch.*

It is man's nature to resent evil words
more than evil deeds ; for it is more
easy to submit to injury than insult.

Οὕτω χρὴ ποιεῖν, ὅπως ἕκαστός τις
ἑαυτῷ ξυνείσεται τῆς νίκης αἰτιώτατος
ὤν.—*Xenophon.*

We ought to exert ourselves in such
a way that each may feel that he
has gained the victory by his own
exertions.

Οὐχ εὕδει Διὸς
ὀφθαλμός· ἐγγὺς δ᾽ ἔστι καὶ παρὼν πόνῳ.

(The eye of God closes not in sleep,
but is near at hand whatever work
we engage in.) Behold, he that keep-
eth Israel shall neither slumber nor
sleep — *Psalms* cxxi. 4.*

Οὐ χρὴ παννύχιον εὕδειν βουληφόρον
ἄνδρα.—*Homer.*

(No counsellor must sleep the whole
night through.) Uneasy lies the head
that wears the crown.

Ὁ φεύγων μύλον ἄλφιτα φεύγει.

(Who shirks the mill has no meal.) No
mill, no meal ; no gains without
pains.

---

* The Greek quotation is a fragment from an unknown poet, preserved by Stobæus.

Ὁ φίλος ἕτερος ἐγώ.—*Aristotle.*

(A friend is a second self.) *Alter ego.*

Ὄχλος ἀσταθμητότατον πρᾶγμα τῶν ἁπάντων καὶ ἀσυνετώτατον.
—*Demosthenes.*

The mob is the most unreliable and senseless thing in the world.

Ὁ χοῖρος ἥδεται κόπροις καὶ βορβόρῳ.
—*Clement of Alexandria.*

(In dung and filth the swine revel.) " He that is filthy will be filthy still."

Ὀψὲ θεῶν ἀλέουσι μύλοι, ἀλέουσι δὲ λεπτά.—*Sextus Empiricus.*

Though the mills of God grind slowly, yet they grind exceeding small.
—*Longfellow.*

Ὀψιμαθῆ ἢ ἀμαθῆ.—*Cleobulus.*

(Better learn late than never.) It is never too late to mend.

Παθήματα μαθήματα.—*Æsop.*

(Sufferings are lessons.) Bought wit is best, but may cost too much.

Παθὼν δέ τε νήπιος ἔγνω.—*Hesiod.*

(Even a fool is taught by experience.) The burnt child dreads the fire.

Παλαιὰ καινοῖς δακρύοις οὐ χρὴ στένειν.
—*Euripides.*

(It is useless to weep anew over old griefs.) It is no use crying over spilt milk.

Πάλιν χρόνῳ τἀρχαῖα καινὰ γίνεται.
—*Nicostratus.*

(Old things become new in course of time.) There is nothing new under the sun.

Πᾶν γὰρ τὸ πολὺ πολέμιον τῇ φύσει.
—*Hippocrates.*

All things in excess are contrary to nature.

Πὰν ὁ μέγας τέθνηκε.—*Plutarch.*

The great god Pan is dead.

Πάντα γὰρ μίαν ἱκνεῖται δασπλῆτα Χάρυβδιν,
αἱ μεγάλαι ἀρεταὶ καὶ ὁ πλοῦτος.

Whate'er of virtue or of power,
Or good, or great we vainly call,
Each moment eager to devour,
One vast Charybdis yawns for all.
—*Merivale.*

Πάντα γυναῖκες ἴσαντι.—*Theocritus.*

Women know everything about everything.

Πάντα ἐν τῷ βασιλικῶς ἔνεστι.

Everything is contained in the words " like a king." *

Πάντα κινῆσαι πετρόν.

To leave no stone unturned.

Πάντα μὲν καθαρὰ τοῖς καθαροῖς.
—*St. Paul.*

To the pure all things are pure.

Πάντα ὑπόληψις.

Everything is a matter of opinion.

Παντὶ μέσῳ τὸ κράτος θεὸς ὤπασεν.
—*Æschylus.*

God always favours those that take the middle course.

Πᾶν τὸ σκληρὸν χαλεπῶς μαλάττεται.
—*Plutarch.*

(Everything once hardened is difficult to mould.) Youths and white paper take any impression.

Πάντων δὲ μάλιστ' αἰσχύνεο σαυτόν.

Respect thyself, let that be thy first care.†

* The reply of Porus, the Indian prince, to Alexander the Great. Alexander, during his invasion of Asia, having defeated and captured Porus, asked his prisoner how he wished to be treated. " Like a king," replied the captive, " Πάντα ἐν τῷ βασιλικῶς ἔνεστι." The reply appealed to Alexander so much that he restored to Porus his territory and kingly power.
† A quotation from the " Golden Verses " of Pythagoras.

Πάντων χρημάτων μέτρον ἄνθρωπος.
　　　　　　—Protagoras.

Man is the measure of the universe.

Πάνυ καλῶς.

No, thank you.

Παραμυθίαν φέρει τὸ κοινωνοὺς εἶναι τῶν
συμφορῶν.—Dion Chrysostom.

Misfortunes are rendered less keen when
others share them with us.

Πᾶς γοῦν ποιητὴς γίγνεται, κἂν ἄμουσος
ᾖ τὸ πρίν, οὗ ἂν Ἔρως ἄψηται.
　　　　　　— Plato.

When Love claps him on the shoulder,
even the man with no ear for poetic
harmonies becomes poetical.

Πᾶς ἐστὶ νόμος εὕρημα μὲν καὶ δῶρον
θεῶν.—Demosthenes.

All laws are an invention and gift of
Heaven.

Πᾶσι θανεῖν μερόπεσσι ὀφείλεται, οὐδέ
τις ἐστίν
αὔριον εἰ ζήσει, θνητὸς ἐπιστάμενος.
　　　　　　—Palladas.

Death is a debt all mankind must pay,
nor can any be sure that he will be
alive to-morrow.

Πᾶσιν εὐφρονοῦσι συμμαχεῖ τύχη.

Fortune is the ally of every prudent
man.*

Πάταξον μὲν, ἄκουσον δέ.

Strike, but hear me ! †

Πατρὶς γάρ ἐστι πᾶσ’, ἵν’ ἂν τις εὖ.
　　　　　　Aristophanes.

Our country is the country in which we
fare the best.

Παύροις γὰρ ἀνδρῶν ἐστὶ συγγενὲς τόδε,
φίλον τὸν εὐτυχοῦντ’ ἄνευ φθόνου σέβειν.
　　　　　　—Æschylus.

Few men have the natural inclination
to respect a friend when he prospers,
without envying him.

Παχεῖα γαστὴρ λεπτὸν οὐ τίκτει νόον.

(A full stomach breeds an empty mind.)
Plain living and high thinking.

Πειθαρχία γάρ ἐστι τῆς εὐπραξίας
μήτηρ γονῆς σωτῆρος· ὧδ’ ἔχει λόγος.
　　　　　　—Æschylus.

Obedience is the mother of prosperity,
a child that brings salvation ; so says
the proverb.

Πειθὼ μὲν γὰρ ὄνειαρ, ἔρις δ’ ἔριν ἀντι-
φυτεύει. —Phocylides.

Persuasion is a great blessing, but strife
ever breeds strife.

Πείρᾳ θὴν πάντα τελεῖται.—Theocritus.

Trying will do anything in this world.

Πείσας λάβε, μὴ βιασάμενος.—Bias.

Win by persuasion, not by force.

Πένητος ἀνδρὸς οὐδὲν εὐτυχέστερον·
τὴν γὰρ ἐπὶ τὸ χεῖρον μεταβολὴν οὐ
προσδοκᾷ.—Diphilus.

None is more fortunate than the poor
man ; for he alone does not fear that
his condition may change for the
worse.

Πενθεῖν δὲ μετρίως τοὺς προσήκοντας
φίλους·
οὐ γὰρ τεθνᾶσιν, αλλὰ τὴν αὐτὴν ὁδόν,
ἣν πᾶσιν ἐλθεῖν ἔστ’ ἀναγκαίως ἔχον,
προεληλύθασιν. Εἶτα χἠμεῖς ὕστερον
εἰς ταὐτὸ καταγωγεῖον αὐτοῖς ἥξομεν,
κοινῇ τὸν ἄλλον συνδιατρίψοντες χρόνον.
　　　　　　—Antiphanes.

We ought to bewail with moderation
the loss of friends; for they are
not dead, but have gone before along
the same road which we must all
traverse. Hereafter we shall all come
to the same abiding-place, and shall
spend the future in their company.

Πενία γὰρ ἐστὶν ἡ τρόπων διδάσκαλος.
　　　　　　—Antiphanes.

(Poverty is the teacher of manners.)
Poverty sharpens the wits.

---

* An adaptation of a line of Euripides.
† The famous reply of the Athenian Themistocles to Eurybiades, the Spartan commander,
when the latter was hotly resisting the proposal of the Athenians to meet the fleet of Xerxes
near Salamis, 480 B.C., instead of retiring to the Isthmus of Corinth. Plutarch relates that the
Spartan, enraged at the boldness of Themistocles, threatened to strike him. Herodotus gives
a different account, making Adeimantus the Corinthian, not Eurybiades, the opposer of the
Athenian's plans.

Πέρας μὲν γὰρ ἅπασιν ἀνθρώποις ἐστὶ τοῦ
βίου θάνατος, κἂν ἐν οἰκίσκῳ τις αὐτὸν
καθείρξας τηρῇ· δεῖ δὲ τοὺς ἀγαθοὺς
ἄνδρας ἐγχειρεῖν μὲν ἅπασιν ἀεὶ τοῖς
καλοῖς, τὴν ἀγαθὴν προβαλλομένους
ἐλπίδα, φέρειν δ' ὅ τι ἂν ὁ θεὸς διδῷ
γενναίως.—*Demosthenes.*

Death is the end of all men's lives,
even if a man is ever on his guard,
and hides himself in some obscure
corner. Brave men, therefore, should
always boldly engage in honourable
deeds, and, using hope as their shield
of defence, should endure with a stout
heart whatever lot God sends them.

Πῆμα κακὸς γείτων, ὅσσοντ' ἀγαθὸς μέγ'
ὄνειαρ.—*Hesiod.*

A good neighbour is a blessing, as a
bad one is a curse.

Πῖνε καὶ εὐφραίνου.—*Palladas.*

Drink and be merry.

Πίνωμεν ἁβρὰ γελῶντες.—*Anacreon.*

Drink, and let the merry laugh go
round.

Πίστει χρήματ' ὄλεσσα ἀπιστίῃ δ'ἐσάωσα.
—*Theognis.*

(By trusting I lost my money, by mis-
trusting I saved it.)
If you trust before you try,
You may repent before you die.

Πλάνη βίον τίθησι σωφρονέστερον.

Travel sharpens the wits.

Πλεόνων δέ τοι ἔργον ἄμεινον.—*Homer.*

Many hands make labour light.

Πλήρωμα νόμου ἡ ἀγάπη.—*St. Paul.*

Love is the fulfilling of the law.

Πλοῦτος ἄνευ ἀρετᾶς οὐκ ἀσινὴς πάροικος·
ἁ δὲ κρᾶσις εὐδαιμονίας ἔχει τὸ ἄκρον.
—*Sappho.*

Wealth without virtue, is a dangerous
guest :
Who holds them mingled, is supremely
blest.—*Merivale.*

Πλοῦτος δὲ πολλῶν ἐπικάλυμμ' ἐστὶν
κακῶν.—*Menander.*

Wealth is a cloak that covers a multitude of sins.

Πλοῦτος ὁ τῆς ψυχῆς πλοῦτος μόνος
ἐστὶν ἀληθής.—*Lucian.*

A well-stored mind is the only true
riches.

Πολιὰ χρόνου μήνυσις, οὐ φρονήσεως.
—*Menander.*

Grey hairs are a proof of age, but not of
wisdom.

Πόλις γὰρ οὐκ ἔσθ' ἥτις ἀνδρὸς ἔσθ'
ἑνός.—*Sophocles.*

That is no real city where the power is
vested in one man.

Πολλαῖσι πληγαῖς στερεὰ δρῦς δαμάζεται.

Little strokes fell great oaks.

Πολλάκι καὶ κηπωρὸς ἀνὴρ μάλα καίριον
εἶπεν.

(Often even a boor speaks to the purpose.)   A fool may give a wise man
counsel.

Πολλάκι καὶ ξύμπασα πόλις κακοῦ ἀνδρός
ἀπηύρα.—*Hesiod.*

(Often a whole city suffers for the sins
of one man.)   One ill weed mars a
whole pot of pottage.   One rotten
sheep ruins the whole flock

Πολλάκις δοκεῖ τὸ φυλάξαι τἀγαθὰ τοῦ
κτήσασθαι χαλεπώτερον εἶναι.
—*Demosthenes.*

It often seems more difficult to maintain
than to gain an advantage.

Πολλάκις ἐθαύμασα, πῶς ἑαυτὸν μὲν
ἕκαστος μᾶλλον πάντων φιλεῖ, τὴν δὲ
ἑαυτοῦ περὶ αὐτοῦ ὑπόληψιν ἐν ἐλάτ-
τονι λόγῳ τίθεται ἢ τὴν τῶν ἄλλων.
—*Marcus Aurelius.*

It has often surprised me that, while
each man loves himself more than
anyone else, he sets less value on his
own estimate of himself than on the
opinion of others.

Πολλὰ μεταξὺ πέλει κύλικος καὶ χείλεος
ἄκρου.—*Aristotle.*

There's many a slip 'twixt the cup and
the lip.

Πολλὰς ἂν εὕροις μηχανὰς· γύνη γὰρ εἶ.
—*Euripides.*

Many schemes you may devise, for you
are a woman.

Πολλὰ τὰ δεινὰ κοὐδὲν ἀνθρώπου δεινό-
τερον πέλει.—*Sophocles.*

Πολλὰ ψεύδονται ἀοιδοί.—*Aristotle.*

Πόλλ' ἔχει σιωπὴ καλά.—*Menander.*

Πόλλ' οἶδ' ἀλώπηξ, ἀλλ' ἐχῖνος ἓν μέγα.

Πολλοὶ δὲ πολλοὺς ηὔξησαν ἤδη καὶ
ἰδιώτας καὶ πόλεις, ὑφ' ὧν αὐξηθέντων
τὰ μέγιστα κακὰ ἔπαθον.—*Xenophon.*

Πολλοὶ μαθηταὶ κρείττονες διδασκάλων.

Πολλοὶ στρατηγοὶ Καρίαν ἀπώλεσαν.

Πολλὸς γὰρ ἡμῖν εἰς τεθνάναι χρόνος·
ζῶμεν δ' ἀριθμῷ
παῦρα κακῶς ἔτεα.—*Simonides of Ceos.*

Πολλοὺς ὁ πόλεμος δι' ὀλίγους ἀπώλεσεν.
—*Menander.*

Πολλῶν ἡ γλῶττα προτρέχει τῆς δια-
νοίας.—*Isocrates.*

Πολλῶν ἰατρῶν εἴσοδός μ' ἀπώλεσεν.
—*Menander.*

Πολλῶν ὁ λιμὸς γίγνεται διδάσκαλος.

Πολλῷ τοι πλέονας λιμοῦ κόρος ὤλεσεν
ἄνδρας.—*Theognis.*

Πολλῷ τὸ φρονεῖν εὐδαιμονίας πρῶτον
ὑπάρχει.—*Sophocles.*

Πομφόλυξ ὁ ἄνθρωπος.

Πονηρὰ κέρδη τὰς μὲν ἡδονὰς ἔχει
μικράς, ἔπειτα δ' ὕστερον λύπας μακράς.
—*Antiphanes.*

Πόντιων δὲ κυμάτων ἀνήριθμον γέλασμα.
—*Æschylus.*

Ποσὶ καὶ χερσίν.

Ποῦ στῶ.

Πράττε μεγάλα, μὴ ὑπισχνούμενος μεγάλα.—*Pythagoras.*

Πρὶν ἂν ἀμφοῖν μῦθον ἀκούσῃς οὐκ ἂν
δικάσαις.

Προλεγόμενα.

Προμηθεὺς ἐστὶ μετὰ τὰ πράγματα.

The world is full of wonders, but nothing is more wonderful than man.

Poets are responsible for many fictions.

Silence is often advantageous.

(The fox knows many tricks, but the hedgehog knows one good one.) The fox knows many tricks, but more he that catches him.

Many men have raised individuals and states to eminence, and afterwards have suffered the greatest wrongs from those they have aided.

Many scholars are wiser than those who teach them.

(Many generals lost Caria.) Too many cooks spoil the broth.

Long, long and dreary is the night
That waits us in the silent grave :
Few, and of rapid flight,
The years from Death we save.—
Merivale.

(War destroys many for the benefit of the few.) *Quicquid delirant reges.*

The tongue often runs more swiftly than the mind.

Too many doctors are my undoing.

(Hunger teaches us many lessons.) Necessity is the mother of invention.

(Satiety kills far more than famine.) Gluttony kills more than the sword.

Wisdom is the most important part of happiness.

Man is a bubble.

Ill-gotten gains give a little pleasure for the moment, but afterwards cause lasting woe.

Ye waves
That o'er th' interminable ocean wreathe Your crispèd smiles.—*Potter.*

(With feet and hands.) With might and main.

(Where I may stand.) A basis to work from ; leverage ground.

Do great actions, but make no great promises.

(Hear both sides before you judge.) There are two sides to every question.

Preliminary statements ; prefatory re-marks.

He is wise after the event.

Πρὸ πάντων γὰρ δεῖ τοὺς πατέρας τῷ
μηδὲν ἁμαρτάνειν, ἀλλὰ πάντα, ἃ δεῖ,
πράττειν, ἐναργὲς ἑαυτοὺς παράδειγμα
τοῖς τέκνοις παρέχειν, ἵνα πρὸς τὸν
τούτων βίον ὥσπερ κάτοπτρον ἀποβλέ-
ποντες ἀποτρέπωνται τῶν αἰσχρῶν
ἔργων καὶ λόγων.—*Plutarch.*

It is the chief duty of parents to set a
bright example to their children by
eschewing wrongdoing, and doing
what is right. For then, their children, looking at the life of their parents
as into a mirror, will themselves shun
evil both in word and deed.

Πρὸς τῷ λαβεῖν γὰρ ὢν ὁ νοῦς τἄλλ'
οὐχ ὁρᾷ.—*Diphilus.*

The man whose mind is fixed on gain
has eyes for nothing else.

Πρὸς τῶν ἐχόντων τὸν νόμον τίθης.
—*Euripides.*

You are making the law in the interests
of the rich.

Πρὸ τῆς νίκης τὸ ἐγκώμιον ᾄδεις.

(You are singing the triumph-song
before the victory.) Don't halloa until
you are out of the wood.

Πρῶτον ἀγαθὸν ἀναμαρτία, δεύτερον δὲ
αἰσχύνη.—*Demades.*

Innocence is the first virtue, modesty
the second.

Πτωχοῦ πήρα οὐ πίμπλαται.

A beggar's purse is bottomless.

Πῦρ μαχαίρᾳ μὴ σκαλεύειν.—*Pythagoras.*

(Don't poke the fire with a sword.) Let
an angry man be.

Ῥᾶγες ὀμφακίζουσι μάλα.—*Æsop.*

The grapes are sour.

Ῥεῖα θεοὶ κλέπτουσιν ἀνθρώπων νόον.
—*Simonides of Ceos.*

The gods easily beguile the minds of
men.

Ῥεχθὲν δέ τε νήπιος ἔγνω.—*Homer.*

(Even a fool learns by experience.) The
burnt child dreads the fire. Experience is the mistress of fools.

Ῥηΐδιον δὲ θεοῖσι, τοὶ οὐρανὸν εὐρὺν
ἔχουσι
ἢ μὲν κυδῆναι θνητὸν βροτὸν, ἠδὲ κακ-
ῶσαι.—*Homer.*

An easy task it is for gods that rule the
wide heaven, either to exalt or humble
a mortal man.

Ῥίψας λόγον τις οὐκ ἀναιρεῖται πάλιν.
—*Menander.*

A word once uttered can never be recalled.

Ῥοδοδάκτυλος ἠώς.—*Homer.*

Rosy-fingered morn.

Σεισάχθεια.

The shaking off of burdens.*

Σιγᾶν τὴν ἀλήθειαν, χρυσόν ἐστι θάπτειν.
—*Pythagoras.*

He buries gold who hides the truth

Σιγή ποτ' ἐστὶν αἱρετωτέρα λόγου.

(Silence is sometimes better than
talking.) Speech is silvern, silence is
golden.

Σκηνὴ πᾶς ὁ βίος, καὶ παίγνιον· ἢ μάθε
παίζειν,
τὴν σπουδὴν μεταθεὶς, ἢ φέρε τὰς ὀδύνας.
—*Palladas.*

Our life's a stage, a comedy; either
learn to play and take it lightly, or
bear its troubles patiently.

Σκιομαχία.

(Fighting with shadows.) Making
mountains out of mole-hills.

---

* A famous decree of Solon, the Athenian lawgiver, was so called. He relieved the hopeless condition of the poorer Athenian citizens by enacting that no one might recover money lent
on the security of the person of the borrower. Inability to pay such loans had reduced many
of the Athenians to a condition of serfdom.

Σολοικισμός.

(A solecism.)   Bad grammar ; incorrect diction.*

Σοφὴν δὲ μισῶ· μὴ γὰρ ἐν γ' ἐμοῖς δόμοις
εἴη φρονοῦσα πλεῖον ἢ γυναῖκα χρῆν.
—*Euripides.*

I hate a clever woman ; may there be in my house no woman who knows more than a woman ought to know.

Σοφίᾳ γὰρ ἐκ τοῦ κλεινὸν ἔπος πέφανται,
τὸ κακὸν δοκεῖν ποτ' ἐσθλὸν
τῷδ' ἔμμεν ὅτῳ φρένας
θεὸς ἄγει προς ἄταν.—*Sophocles.*

For with wisdom hath someone given forth the famous saying, that evil seems good, soon or late, to him whose mind the god draws to mischief.

Σοφοῖς ἐστὶ πρὸς σοφοὺς ἐπιτήδεια.

There exists a tie of kindred between all wise people.

Σοφοῖς ὁμιλῶν καὐτὸς ἐκβήσῃ σοφός.
—*Menander.*

By associating with wise people you will become wise yourself.

Σπάρτην ἔλαχες ταύτην κόσμει.

You have obtained Sparta ; be a credit to it.

Σπεῦδε βραδέως.

Hasten slowly.†

Στέντορι εἰσαμένη μεγαλήτορι χαλκεο-
φώνῳ,
ὃς τόσον αὐδήσασχ' ὅσον ἄλλοι πεντή-
κοντα.—*Homer.*

In form of Stentor of the brazen voice, Whose shout was as the shout of fifty men.—*Lord Derby.*‡

Στέργει γὰρ οὐδεὶς ἄγγελον κακῶν ἐπῶν.
—*Sophocles.*

No man loves the bearer of ill tidings.

Στῆθος δὲ πλήξας κραδίην ἠνίπαπε μύθῳ
τέτλαθι δή, κραδίη· καὶ κύντερον ἄλλο
ποτ' ἔτλης.—*Homer.*

Smiting his breast he spake aloud, " Patience, stout heart, thou hast endured even worse ills than this."

Στιγμὴ χρόνου πᾶς ὁ βίος ἐστί. Ζῆν καὶ
οὐ παραζῆν προσήκει.—*Plutarch.*

The whole of life is but a moment of time. It is our duty, therefore, to use, not to misuse it.

Στρεπταὶ μέν τε φρένες ἐσθλῶν.
—*Homer.*

The noblest minds readily hearken to persuasion.

Στῦλοι γὰρ οἴκων εἰσὶ παῖδες ἄρσενες.
—*Euripides.*

Male children are the pillars of a house.

Σύγγονον
βροτοῖσι τὸν πεσόντα λακτίσαι πλέον.
—*Æschylus.*

'Tis still the way of men to spurn the fallen.

Σῦκα φίλ' ὀρνίθεσσι φυτεύειν δ' οὐκ
ἐθέλουσι.

(Birds love figs, but they will not plant them.)   No mill, no meal ; no gains without pains.

Συκίνη μάχαιρα.

(A sword of fig wood.)   A feeble, unconvincing argument.

Συνειδὸς ἀγαθοῦ φιλεῖ παῤῥησιάζεσθαι.
—*Pausanias.*

A good conscience is wont to speak out openly and fearlessly.

Συνελόντι δὲ εἰπεῖν, πάντα τὰ μὲν τοῦ
σώματος ποταμός· τὰ δὲ τῆς ψυχῆς
ὄνειρος καὶ τύφος· ὁ δὲ βίος, πόλεμος
καὶ ξένου ἐπιδημία· ἡ ὑστεροφημία δὲ,
λήθη.—*Marcus Aurelius.*

In a word, all the attributes of the body are as a river, all of the mind as a dream and a vapour ; life is a war, and a sojourn in a strange land, and fame after death is mere oblivion.

---

* This word is said to have originated from the people of Soli, a Cilician colony of Athens, whose dialect was a very corrupt form of Attic.
† More familiar in the Latin form, *Festina lente.*   A favourite motto of Augustus Cæsar.
‡ Hence the expression, " a stentorian voice."

Συνετῶν ἐστὶν ἀνδρῶν
πρὶν γενέσθαι τὰ δυσχερῆ,
προνοῆσαι ὅπως μὴ γένηται.
ἀνδρείων δὲ, γενόμει α εὖ θέσθαι.
—*Pittacus.*

Συντριβῇ προηγεῖται ὕβρις.

Συστολή.

Σχολῇ που, τὸ κατὰ τὴν παροιμίαν λεγόμενον, ὅ γε τοιοῦτος ἂν ποτε ἕλοι πόλιν.
—*Plato.*

The wise with prudent thought provide
Against misfortune's coming tide.
The valiant, when the surge beats high,
Undaunted brave its tyranny.
—*Merivale.*

Pride goeth before a fall.

(A contraction.) A spasm of the heart.

It will be a long time, as the proverb
says, before such a man takes a town
by storm.

Τὰ γὰρ ἆθλα τοῦ πολέμου τοῖς ἀγαθοῖς
ἀνδράσιν ἐστὶν ἐλευθερία καὶ ἀρετή.
—*Lycurgus.*

Τὰ δάνεια δούλους τοὺς ἐλευθέρους ποιεῖ.
—*Menander.*

Τὰ δειλὰ κέρδη πημονὰς ἐργάζεται.
—*Sophocles.*

Τὰ ἐλάχιστα ληπτέον τῶν κακῶν.
—*Aristotle.*

Ταῖς ἀτυχίαις μήποτ' ἐπίχαιρε τῶν πέλας,
—*Menander.*

Τὰ καλὰ δύσκολα.

Τὰ μὲν
δίκαι' ἐπαινεῖ, τοῦ δὲ κερδαίνειν ἔχου.
—*Sophocles.*

Τὰ νεῦρα τῶν πραγμάτων.
—*Demosthenes.*

Τὰ πεπραγμέν' αὐτὰ βοᾷ.—*Demosthenes.*

Τὰ πολλὰ τοῦ πολέμου, γνώμῃ καὶ χρημάτων περιουσίᾳ κρατοῦνται.
—*Thucydides.*

Τὰς γὰρ ἐκ
Θεῶν ἀνάγκας, θνητὸν ὄντα δεῖ φέρειν.
—*Euripides.*

Τὰ σῦκα σῦκα, τὴν σκάφην σκάφην λέγειν.

Ταχὺς γὰρ Ἅιδης ῥᾷστος ἀνδρὶ δυστυχεῖ.
—*Euripides.*

Τεθνάμεναι γὰρ καλὸν ἐνὶ προμάχοισι
πεσόντα
ἄνδρ' ἀγαθὸν περὶ ᾗ πατρίδι μαρνάμενον.
—*Tyrtæus.*

Τέλος ὁρᾶν μακροῦ βίου.

Τέτταρας δακτύλους θανάτου οἱ πλέοντες
ἀπέχουσιν.—*Anacharsis.*

Τέχνη δ' ἀνάγκης ἀσθενεστέρα μακρῷ.
—*Æschylus.*

Τῇ γνώμῃ ὑπηρετεῖν ἐθιστέον τὸ σῶμα.
—*Xenophon.*

To brave men the prizes that war offers
are liberty and fame.

Debt makes slaves of free men.

Gains dishonourably acquired cause
sorrow.

When we must choose between evils,
we ought to choose the least.

Never exult over your neighbour's misfortunes.

(Beautiful things harass.)   No rose
without a thorn.

Praise just dealing, but let the making
of money be your chief care.

(The sinews of affairs.)   The sinews of
war.

The facts speak for themselves.

Success in war depends chiefly on
prudent counsel and abundance of
money.

A mortal man must needs endure the
ills that Heaven sends.

(To call figs figs, and a tub a tub.)   To
call a spade a spade.

For him whose life is misery a speedy
death is best.

It is a noble thing for a brave man to
die facing the foe, when he is fighting
for his own dear native land.

To see the end of a long life.

Sailors have only four inches between
them and death.

Art is far weaker than necessity.

The body ought to be trained to obey
the mind.

Τὴν δὲ μάλιστα γαμεῖν, ἥτις σέθεν ἔγγυθι
ναίει. — *Hesiod.*

(When you take a wife, choose a neighbour rather than one who lives far
away.) Know the character of the
woman you are about to marry.

Τὴν παρεοῦσαν ἄμελγε, τὶ τὸν φεύγοντα
διώκεις ;—*Theocritus.*

(Milk the cow that is nigh you ; why
pursue the one that runs away ?) A
bird in the hand is worth two in the
bush.

Τὴν πλατεῖάν σοι μόνῳ ταύτην πεποίηκεν
ὁ βασιλεύς ;—*Philemon.*

(Did the king make the street for you
alone ?) You walk as if the street
belonged to you.

Τῆς λανθανούσης μουσικῆς οὐδεὶς λόγος.

(No praise is given to music that is not
heard.) You must cry your own
wares if you wish others to praise
them.

Τῆς σῆς λατρείας τὴν ἐμὴν δυσπραξίαν
σαφῶς ἐπίστασ᾽, οὐκ ἂν ἀλλάξαιμ᾽ ἐγώ.
—*Æschylus.*

Be well assured I would not exchange
my misery for your servitude.*

Τι γὰρ ἂν μεῖζον τοῦδ᾽ ἐπὶ θνατοῖς
πάθος ἐξεύροις,
ἢ τέκνα θανόντ᾽ ἐσίδεσθαι.—*Euripides.*

What greater woe canst thou find
among mortals than when parents see
their children dead ?

Τὶ δὲ καί ἐστιν ὅλως τὸ ἀείμνηστον ;
ὅλον κενόν.—*Marcus Aurelius.*

But what is eternal fame ? Nothing but
vanity.

Τίθεται δέ γε τοὺς νόμους ἑκάστη ἡ ἀρχὴ
πρὸς τὸ αὐτῇ ξυμφέρον, δημοκρία μὲν
δημοκρατικούς, τυραννὶς δὲ τυραννι-
κούς.—*Plato.*

Every form of government passes laws
to give advantage to those who
govern. A popular government
makes laws to benefit the people ; a
despotic government legislates in the
interests of despotism.

Τίκτει τὸ κόρος ὕβριν.—*Theognis.*

Satiety breeds insolence.

Τί σε δεῖ λίθον μυρίζειν ;

(Why should you anoint a stone ?)
Why waste your labour ?

Τίς οὖν ἄρξει τοῦ ἄρχοντος.—*Plutarch.*

(Who will rule the ruler ?) *Quis custodiet ipsos custodes ?*

Τί τυφλῷ καὶ κατόπτρῳ.

(What use is a mirror to a blind man ?)
All colours are the same to a blind
man.

Τὸ αἰσχρόν.

The dishonourable ; baseness.

Τὸ γὰρ δολῶσαι πρὸς γυναικὸς ἦν σαφῶς.
—*Æschylus.*

To use deceit was surely the woman's
part.

Τὸ γὰρ
περισσὰ πράσσειν οὐκ ἔχει νοῦν οὐδένα.
—*Sophocles.*

To be over-busy is a witless task.

Τὸ γὰρ φοβεῖσθαι τὸν θάνατον λῆρος
πολύς·
πᾶσιν γὰρ ἡμῖν τοῦτ᾽ ὀφείλεται παθεῖν.
—*Aristophanes.*

Great folly is it to be afraid of death,
since all of us alike must pay that
debt.

Τὸ γὰρ ψευδὲς ὄνειδος οὐ περαιτέρω τῆς
ἀκοῆς ἀφικνεῖται.—*Æschines.*

When a man is accused falsely, the
reproach does not go farther than his
ears.

---

* The words of Prometheus, whose service to mankind had caused Zeus to punish him, to
Hermes (Mercury), the messenger of the gods.

Τό γε λοιδορῆσαι θεοῖς, ἐχθρὰ σοφία.
—*Pindar.*

To revile the gods is a sorry kind of cleverness.

Τὸ δὲ ναυτικὸν τέχνης ἐστίν, ὥσπερ καὶ
ἄλλο τι, καὶ οὐκ ἐνδέχεται, ὅταν τύχῃ,
ἐκ παρέργου μελετᾶσθαι, ἀλλὰ μᾶλλον
μηδὲν ἐκείνῳ πάρεργον ἄλλο γίγνεσθαι.
—*Thucydides.*

Skill in naval affairs, as in other crafts, is the result of scientific training. It is impossible to acquire this skill unless the matter be treated as of the first importance, and all other pursuits are considered to be secondary to it.

Τὸ δὲ παθεῖν εὖ, πρῶτον ἄθλων·
εὖ δ' ἀκούειν, δευτέρα μοῖ-
ρ· ἀμφοτέροισι δ' ἀνὴρ
ὃς ἂν ἐγκύρσῃ καὶ ἕλῃ,
στέφανον ὕψιστον δέδεκται.—*Pindar.*

Prosperity is the best prize a man can gain, and reputation is the next best lot; but the man who wins and enjoys both these boons, has received the highest crown of all.

Τὸ δ' εὖ νικάτω.—*Æschylus.*

May the right prevail.

Τὸ δ' εὐτυχεῖν.
τοδ' ἐν βροτοῖς θεός τε καὶ θεοῦ πλέον.
—*Æschylus.*

Success is counted a god by men, and they honour it far more.

Τὸ δὲ φυᾷ, κράτιστον ἅπαν,
πολλοὶ δὲ διδακταῖς
ἀνθρώπων ἀρεταῖς κλέος
ὤρουσαν ἐλέσθαι.—*Pindar.*

Natural ability is by far the best, but many men have succeeded in winning high renown by skill that is the fruit of teaching.

Τὸ ἐν τῇ καρδίᾳ τοῦ νήφοντος ἐπὶ τῆς
γλώττης ἐστὶ τοῦ μεθύοντος.
—*Plutarch.*

(What is in the heart of the sober man is on the lips of the drunkard.) Drunkenness reveals what soberness conceals. When the wine is in the wit is out.

Τὸ ζῆν ἐστιν ὥσπερ οἱ κύβοι·
οὐ ταῦτ' ἀεὶ πίπτουσιν, οὐδὲ τῷ βίῳ
ταὐτὸν διαμένει σχῆμα, μεταβολὰς δ'
ἔχει.—*Alexis.*

Life is like the dice that, falling, still show a different face. So life, though it remains the same, is always presenting different aspects.

Τοῖς ἄφροσιν, ὥσπερ τοῖς παιδίοις, μικρὰ
πρόφασις εἰς τὸ κλαίειν ἱκανή.
—*Socrates.*

Fools, like children, want but small excuse to make them weep.

Τοῖς βασιλεῦσι δεῖ ὡς ἥκιστα ἢ ὡς ἥδιστα
ὁμιλεῖν.—*Æsop.*

A man should either not converse with kings, or, if he does, say nothing except what pleases them.

Τοῖς θανοῦσι πλοῦτος οὐδὲν ὠφελεῖ.
—*Æschylus.*

Gold is useless to the dead.

Τοῦσιν εὖ φρονοῦσι συμμαχεῖ τύχη.

Fortune is ever the ally of the prudent.

Τοῖς μίκκοις μίκκα διδοῦσι θεοί.
—*Callimachus.*

To little men the gods send little things.

Τοῖς πᾶσι κοινόν ἐστι τοὐξαμαρτάνειν·
ἐπεὶ δ' ἁμάρτῃ, κεῖνος οὐκέτ' ἔστ' ἀνὴρ
ἄβουλος οὐδ' ἄνολβος, ὅστις ἐς κακὸν
πεσὼν ἀκεῖται μηδ' ἀκίνητος πέλει.
—*Sophocles.*

All men are liable to err; but prudent and happy is that man who, when he has erred, seeks a remedy for the evil into which he has fallen, and does not persist in his mistake.

Τοῖς σίτου ἀποροῦσι σπουδάζονται οἱ
ὄροβοι.

(Chick-peas are welcomed by those who lack corn.) To the hungry every bitter thing is sweet.

Τοῖς τοι δικαίοις χὡ βραχὺς νικᾷ μέγαν.
—*Sophocles.*

(In a righteous cause the weak overcomes the strong.) Thrice is he armed who has his quarrel just.
—*Shakespeare.*

Τὸ κακόν.

Τὸ καλόν.

Τὸ κηδεῦσαι καθ' ἑαυτὸν
ἀριστεύει μακρῷ.—*Æschylus.*

Τολμήεις μοι θυμός, ἐπεὶ κακὰ πολλὰ
πέπονθα.—*Homer.*

Τὸ μέγα βιβλίον ἴσον τῷ μεγάλῳ κακῷ.
—*Callimachus.*

Τὸ μὲν ἀληθὲς πικρόν ἐστι καὶ ἀηδὲς τοῖς
ἀνοήτοις· τὸ δὲ ψεῦδος γλυκὺ καὶ
προσηνές.—*Dion Chrysostom.*

Τὸ μὲν τελευτῆσαι, πάντων ἡ πεπρωμένη
κατέκρινε, τὸ δὲ καλῶς ἀποθανεῖν ἴδιον
τοῖς σπουδαίοις.—*Isocrates.*

Τὸ μὴ πιστεύειν τοῖς πονηροῖς σωφρονέστερον τοῦ προπιστεύσαντας κατηγορεῖν.
—*Dionysius of Halicarnassus.*

Τὸ μήτ' ἀλγεῖν κατὰ σῶμα μήτε ταράτ-
τεσθαι κατὰ ψυχήν.—*Epicurus.*

Τὸν γὰρ κάκιστον πλοῦτος εἰς πρώτους
ἄγει.—*Euripides.*

Τὸν δὲ ἀποιχόμενον μνήμῃ τιμᾶτε, μὴ
δάκρυσιν.—*Dion Chrysostom.*

Τὸν δῆμον αἰεὶ προσποιοῦ,
ὑπογλυκαίνων ῥηματίοις μαγειρικοῖς·
τὰ δ' ἄλλα σοι πρόσεστι δημαγωγικὰ,
φωνὴ μιαρά, γέγονας κακὸς, ἀγοραῖος εἶ.
—*Aristophanes.*

Τὸ νικᾶν αὐτὸν αὐτὸν πασῶν νικῶν πρώτη
τε καὶ ἀρίστη, τὸ δὲ ἡττᾶσθαι αὐτὸν
ὑφ' ἑαυτοῦ πάντων αἴσχιστόν τε ἅμα
καὶ κάκιστον.—*Plato.*

Τὸν Κολοφῶνα ἐπέθηκεν.

Τὸν ξύοντα ἀντιξύειν.

Τὸν οἴκοι θησαυρὸν διαβάλλειν.

Evil ; baseness.

(The beautiful.) Ideal beauty, either physical or moral.

To marry in one's own station is by far the wisest way.

Stout of heart am I, since many are the evils I have undergone.

A great book is like to a great misfortune.

Foolish men find the truth bitter and unpleasant, while they think falsehood is sweet and palatable.

To die is the destined lot of all, but to die nobly is the peculiar privilege of the good.

It is wiser not to trust knaves than, having trusted them, to revile them.

(Neither to suffer in body nor to be troubled in mind.) The ideal of happiness.

(Riches raise the worst knave to the highest rank.) Poverty is the only crime.

Honour the dead by keeping their memory green, and not by weeping over their end.

Always curry favour with the people by saying sweet, palatable things to them ; as to the other qualities necessary for a demagogue, you possess them ; I mean you have a vilely raucous voice, your character is bad, and you are a lounger and a chatterbox.*

To conquer oneself is the best and noblest victory ; to be vanquished by one's own nature is the worst and most ignoble defeat.

(He has put the Colophon to it.) He has settled the matter ; it needs no further argument.†

(Scratch him who scratches thee.) One good turn deserves another.

(To speak ill of one's own home.) That bird is not honest which defiles its own nest.

---

* Advice to a would-be demagogue. Aristophanes never wearied of attacking the political adventurers of his day.
† The origin of this proverbial expression is not certain. Colophon was one of the twelve Ionian cities of Asia Minor which had formed a federation. It is supposed that Colophon had a casting vote in the deliberations of this league. Another theory is that the famous cavalry of Colophon were so invincible that their appearance in battle gave the victory to the side on which they fought. Colophon was one of the cities that claimed to be the birthplace of Homer.

Tόν τε γὰρ μέλλοντα καλῶς ἄρχειν, ἀρχθῆναί φασι δεῖν πρῶτον.
—*Aristotle.*

It is a common saying that he who would govern must learn to obey.

Tὸν τελευτηκότα μὴ κακολόγει, ἀλλὰ μακάριζε.

Do not revile the dead, but call them blessed.*

Tὸν φίλον κακῶς μὴ λέγε, μηδ' εὖ τὸν ἐχθρόν.—*Pittacus.*

Do not revile a friend, nor eulogise an enemy.

Tὸ ξυγγενές τοι δεινὸν ἤ θ' ὁμιλία.
—*Æschylus.*

The tie of kinship and of long acquaintance is wondrous strong.

Tὸ ὅλον.

The whole; the universe.

Tὸ πρέπον.

(The right.) Rectitude; honesty.

Tὸ σπάνιον τίμιον.—*Socrates.*

What is rare is always valued.

Tότε γὰρ χρή, κᾶν ἄδηλον ᾖ τὸ μέλλον, αἱρεῖσθαι κινδυνεύειν, ὅταν τὸ τὴν ἡσύχιαν ἄγειν φανερῶς χεῖρον ᾖ.
—*Aristides the Rhetorician.*

As soon as it is obvious that it is dishonourable for us to maintain peace, we ought to choose the risk of war, even if the result is doubtful.

Tοῦ ἀριστεύειν ἔνεκα.

(In order to excel.) The motto of Lord Henniker.

Tοῦ βίου καθάπερ ἀγάλματος πάντα τὰ μέρη καλὰ εἶναι δεῖ.—*Socrates.*

A man's life, like a statue, ought to be beautiful in all its parts.

Tοῦ γὰρ καὶ γένος ἐσμέν.

For we are also his offspring.†

Tοῦ ζῆν γὰρ οὐδεὶς ὡς ὁ γηράσκων ἐρᾷ.
—*Sophocles.*

None are so much enamoured of life as those who are growing old.

Tοῦ καὶ ἀπὸ γλώσσης μέλιτος γλυκίων ῥέεν αὐδή.—*Homer.*

And from his tongue flowed words sweeter than honey.

Tοὺς γὰρ θανόντας οὐχ ὁρῶ λυπουμένους.
—*Sophocles.*

Methinks the dead know nought of sorrow.

Tοῦτ' ἔσθ', ὃ θνητῶν εὖ πόλεις οἰκουμένας δόμους τ' ἀπόλλυσ', οἱ καλοὶ λίαν λόγοι, οὐ γάρ τι τοῖσιν ὡσὶ τερπνὰ δεῖ λέγειν, ἀλλ' ἐξ ὅτου τις εὐκλεὴς γενήσεται.
—*Euripides.*

Flattering speeches destroy the cities and families of mankind. We ought not to say such things as are merely pleasing to the ears, but what will make a man live more nobly.

Tοῦτο γὰρ πρὸς τὰ ἄλλα ζῷα τοῖς ἀνθρώποις ἴδιον τὸ μόνον ἀγαθοῦ καὶ κακοῦ καὶ δικαίου καὶ ἀδίκου, καὶ τῶν ἄλλων αἴσθησιν ἔχειν.—*Aristotle.*

This is the quality peculiar to man, wherein he differs from other animals, that he alone is endowed with perception to distinguish right from wrong, justice from injustice.

Tοῦτο κᾶν παῖς γνοίη.

(Even a child would know this.) Every schoolboy knows this.

Tοῦτό τοι τἀνδρεῖον, ἡ προμηθία.
—*Euripides.*

(The truest courage is discretion.) Discretion is the better part of valour.

Tούτῳ νίκα.

In this sign conquer.‡

Tρόπος δίκαιος κτῆμα τιμιώτατον.
—*Antiphanes.*

A righteous disposition is the most precious possession.

Tροφαὶ δ' αἱ παιδευόμεναι μέγα φέρουσιν εἰς ἀρετάν.—*Euripides.*

A careful education contributes much to the making of a virtuous life.

---

* A saying attributed to Chilo, one of the Seven Sages of Greece.
† St. Paul quotes these words in his speech to the Athenians (Acts xvii.) as from "certain of your poets." The words are found in a poem of Aratus, who wrote at the beginning of the third century B.C. He lived at Soli, in Cilicia, so that it was specially appropriate for Paul of Tarsus to quote from his works.
‡ See note in Latin section on *In hoc signo.*

Τρόχος ἅρματος γὰρ οἷα
βίοτος τρέχει κυλισθείς.—*Anacreon.*

Τύραννος τυράννῳ συγκατεργάζεται.
—*Herodotus.*

Τῷ δ' ἀφανεῖ πᾶς ἕπεται δόλος.

Τῷ θεῷ δόξα.

Τῶν ἁλῶν συγκατεδηδοκέναι μέδιμνον.

Τῶν εὐτυχούντων πάντες εἰσὶ συγγενεῖς.
—*Menander.*

Τῶν ἡδέων τὰ σπανιώτατα γιγνόμενα
μάλιστα τέρπει.—*Epictetus.*

Τῶν πόνων πωλοῦσιν ἡμῖν τἀγαθὰ οἱ θεοί.
—*Epicharmus.*

Τῷ νῦν μήποτε καὶ σὺ γυναικί περ ἤπιος
εἶναι·
μὴ οἱ μῦθον ἅπαντα πιφαυσκέμεν, ὅν κ'
εὖ εἰδῇς,
ἀλλὰ τὸ μὲν φάσθαι, τὸ δὲ καὶ κεκρυμ-
μένον εἶναι.—*Homer.*

Τῶν ὤτων ἔχω τὸν λύκον, οὔτ' ἔχειν, οὔτ'
ἀφεῖναι δύναμαι.

Life is like a chariot-wheel that ever rolls along.

(One despot aids another.) A fellow feeling makes us wondrous kind.

(A snare ever lurks in the dark.) To be forewarned is to be forearmed.

Glory to God.

(To have eaten a bushel of salt together.) To be old friends.

All desire to be the relations of prosperous folk.

The pleasures that come most rarely delight us most.

It is by our work that we purchase all good things from the gods.

Never tell your wife all you know, however much you may love her ; but tell her a part, and a part conceal from her.

(I have a wolf by the ears, I can neither hold him nor let go.) I have caught a Tartar.

Ὑγιαίνειν μὲν ἄριστον ἀνδρὶ θνατῷ·
δεύτερον δὲ, φυὰν καλὸν γενέσθαι·
τὸ τρίτον δὲ πλουτεῖν ἀδόλως·
καὶ τὸ τέταρτον ἡβᾷν μετὰ τῶν φίλων.
—*Simonides of Ceos.*

Ὑγίεια.

Ὑγίεια, πρεσβίστα μακάρων.—*Ariphron.*

Ὕδραν τέμνεις.

Ὑπεροχῆς γὰρ ἐπιθυμεῖ ἡ νεότης.
—*Aristotle.*

Ὑπὲρ σεαυτοῦ μὴ φράσῃς ἐγκώμιον.
—*Menander.*

Ὕπν' ὀδύνας ἀδαής, Ὕπνε δ' ἀλγέων,
εὐαὲς ἡμῖν ἔλθοις,
εὐαίων εὐαίων, ὦναξ.—*Sophocles.*

Ὕπνος δὲ πάσης ἐστὶν ὑγίεια νόσου.
—*Menander.*

Ὕπνος τὰ μικρὰ τοῦ θανάτου μυστήρια.
—*Mnesimachus.*

The first of mortal joys is health ;
Next beauty ; and the third is wealth.
The fourth, all youth's delights to prove
With those we love.—*Merivale.*

(Hygeia.) The goddess of health.

Health, the greatest of all we count as blessings.

(You are wounding a Hydra.) You are making bad worse.*

Youth always longs for pre-eminence.

(Do not utter your own praises.) Self-praise is no recommendation.

Sleep, stranger to anguish, painless sleep, come, at our prayer, with gentle breath, come with benison, O King.—*Jebb.*

(Sleep is a healing balm for every ill.) Tired Nature's sweet restorer, balmy sleep !—*Young.*

Sleep the lesser mysteries of death.

---

* One of the labours of Hercules was to slay the Hydra, the many-headed water-snake. As fast as the hero cut off one of the heads of the monster, two heads grew in its place.

'Υπὸ παντὶ λίθῳ σκόρπιος εὕδει.

'Υπόπτερος δ' ὁ πλοῦτος.—*Sophocles.*

Ὓς ποτ' 'Αθηναίαν ἔριν ἤρισε.
— *Theocritus.*

Ὕστερον πρότερον.

(Beneath every stone a scorpion sleeps.)
A hidden danger threatens us.*

Wealth has wings.

(A sow once strove to rival Athene.)
Fools rush in where angels fear to
tread.

(The last put first.) Putting the cart
before the horse.

Φάγωμεν καὶ πίωμεν· αὔριον γὰρ ἀπο-
θνήσκομεν.

Φαίδρυνον σεαυτὸν ἁπλότητι καὶ αἰδοῖ καὶ
τῇ πρὸς τὸ ἀνὰ μέσον ἀρετῆς καὶ
κακίας, ἀδιαφορίᾳ· φίλησον τὸ ἀνθρώ-
πινον γένος· ἀκολούθησον θεῷ.
—*Marcus Aurelius.*

Φάρμακον νηπενθές.

Φαῦλος γὰρ κριτὴς καλοῦ πράγματος
ὄχλος.—*Demophilus.*

Φαύλου ἀνδρὸς, καθάπερ κυνὸς κακοῦ,
μᾶλλον δεῖ τὴν σιγὴν ἢ τὴν φωνὴν
εὐλαβεῖσθαι.—*Demophilus.*

Φείδεο τῶν κτεάνων.—*Lucian.*

Φέρειν τε χρὴ τά τε δαιμόνια ἀναγκαίως
τά τε ἀπὸ τῶν πολεμίων ἀνδρείως.
— *Thucydides.*

Φεῦ· τοῦ θανόντος ὡς ταχεῖά τις βροτοῖς
χάρις διαρρεῖ.—*Sophocles.*

Φήμη γε μέντοι δημόθρους μέγα σθένει.
—*Æschylus.*

Φήμη δ' οὔτις πάμπαν ἀπόλλυται, ἥντινα
πολλοὶ
λαοὶ φημίζουσι, θεὸς νύ τις ἐστὶ καὶ αὐτή.
—*Hesiod.*

Φημὶ πολυχρονίην μελέτην ἔμμεναι, φίλε·
καὶ δὴ
ταύτην ἀνθρώποισι τελευτῶσαν φύσιν
εἶναι.—*Hesiod.*

Φησὶν σιωπῶν.—*Euripides.*

Φθείρουσιν ἤθη χρήσθ' ὁμιλίαι κακοί.
—*Menander.*

Φθονέεσθαι κρέσσον ἐστὶν ἢ οἰκτείρεσθαι.
— *Herodotus.*

Φθονεραὶ θνατῶν φρένας ἀμφικρέμανται
ἐλπίδες.—*Pindar.*

Let us eat and drink, for to-morrow we
die.

Cultivate simple tastes, a modest demeanour, and contempt of any compromise between virtue and vice;
love your fellow creatures, and obey
the commands of God.

(A drug that kills sorrow.) The ne-
penthe of the gods. The anodyne
of the heart.

The mob is a bad judge of real merit.

The silence of a treacherous man, like
that of a dog, is more to be feared
than his words.

Be a thrifty steward of thy goods.

The sufferings that fate inflicts on us
should be borne with patience, what
enemies inflict, with manly courage.

Alas! how quickly is reputation of the
dead forgotten by mankind.

Strong is the power of the people's
voice.

No rumour, which folk have once spread,
ever dies; but it becomes, as it were,
one of the immortal gods.

Long exercise, my friend, inures the
mind;
And what we once disliked we pleasing
find.

His silence gives consent.

Evil communications corrupt good
manners.

It is better to be envied than pitied.

Envious hopes still hover round the
minds of men.

* Aristophanes puts a humorous variation of this proverb in the mouth of the chorus of his
play, the *Thesmophoriazusæ* : " Beneath every stone we must look lest there be lurking there
—an orator."

Φιλαργυρία μὲν νόσημα μικροποιὸν, φιλη-
δονία δ' ἀγεννέστατον.—*Longinus.*

The love of money is a disease that makes us petty in all our actions, and the love of pleasure utterly degrades us.

Φιλέει γὰρ ὁ θεὸς τὰ ὑπερέχοντα πάντα
κολούειν.—*Herodotus.*

(God is wont to humble overweening pride.) "He hath put down the mighty from their seat, and hath exalted the humble and meek."

Φιλεῖ δ' ἑαυτοῦ μᾶλλον οὐδεὶς οὐδένα.

(No one loves another more than himself.)   Charity begins at home.

Φιλεῖ δὲ τῷ κάμνοντι συσπεύδειν θεός.
                                    —*Æschylus.*

God loves to aid a man in sore distress.

Φίλον ὕπνου θέλγητρον.—*Euripides.*

The blessed, healing spell of sleep.

Φιλοσοφία ὄρεξις τῆς θείας σοφίας.
                                    — *Plato.*

Philosophy is a striving after heavenly wisdom.

Φιλόφιλον δεῖ εἶναι τὸν ἀγαθὸν ἄνδρα καὶ
φιλόπατριν.—*Polybius.*

The good man should love his friends and love his country.

Φιλῶ τέκν', ἀλλὰ πατρίδ' ἐμὴν μᾶλλον
φιλῶ.—*Plutarch.*

I love my children, but I love my country more.

Φρέατα ἀντλούμενα βελτίω γίνεται.

Drawn wells have sweetest water.

Φύεται μὲν ἐκ τῶν τυχόντων πολλάκις τὰ
μέγιστα τῶν πραγμάτων.—*Polybius.*

The most important events are often the results of accidents.

Φύσει σοφὸς μὲν οὐδείς.—*Aristotle.*

None are wise by natural instinct.

Χαῖρε.

Happiness to you!   Welcome!   Farewell!

Χαίρων πορεύου.

Go in peace; may luck attend you.

Χαλεπὰ τὰ καλά ἐστιν ὅπῃ ἔχει μαθεῖν.

Whatever is good to know is difficult to learn.*

Χαλεπὸν μέν ἐστιν πρὸς γαστέρα λέγειν
ὦτα οὐκ ἔχουσαν.—*Plutarch.*

(It is difficult to argue with the belly, as it has no ears.)   Hunger listens to no reason.

Χαλεπὸν τὸ μὴ φιλῆσαι·
χαλεπὸν δὲ καὶ φιλῆσαι·
χαλεπώτερον δὲ πάντων
ἀποτυγχάνειν φιλοῦντα.—*Anacreon.*

Grievous is it not to love, and grievous, too, to love; but far more grievous is it to love and love in vain.

Χάος.

(Chaos.)   The first state of the universe; void; infinite space.

Χάρις ἀμεταμέλητος.—*Theophrastus.*

(Kindness knows no repentance.)   No one repents of a good action.

Χάρις χάριν γὰρ ἐστιν ἡ τίκτουσ' ἀεί.
                                    —*Sophocles.*

(Kindness is ever the mother of kindness.)   One good turn deserves another.

Χαρίτων μία.

(One of the Graces.)   A pretty, charming she.

Χάρων.

(Charon.)   The ferryman who conducted the dead in his boat across the Styx.

---

* An old proverb quoted by Socrates in Plato's dialogue "Cratylus" to show that there is no smooth and easy road to knowledge, as the Athenian sophists declared.

Χεὶρ χεῖρα νίπτει, δάκτυλός τε δάκτυλον.

(Hand washes hand, and finger finger.) All men live by another's aid.

Χειρῶν νόμος.

The law of might.

Χελιδὼν ἔαρ οὐ ποῖει.—*Aristotle*

One swallow does not make a spring.

Χρεία διδάσκει, κἂν βραδύς τις ᾖ, σοφόν. —*Euripides.*

(Necessity teaches wisdom even to the stupid man.) Necessity is the mother of invention.

Χρειὼ πάντ' ἐδίδαξε, τί δ' οὐ χρειώ κεν ἀνεύροι;
Χρεὼν τέλος ὁρᾶν.—*Solon.*

Need all things taught; what cannot need invent?
(We must look to the end.) The end approves the work; *respice finem.*

Χρὴ γὰρ οὐ μόνον ἑαυτὸν εἰδέναι θνητὸν ὄντα τὴν φύσιν, ἀλλὰ καὶ ὅτι θνητῷ σύγκληρός ἐστι βίῳ.—*Plutarch.*

A man ought to think not only that his own nature is mortal, but also that he shares the common lot of the human race.

Χρὴ καὶ ἐν τοῖς ἤθεσιν ὥσπερ καὶ ἐν τῇ τῶν πραγμάτων συστάσει ἀεὶ ζητεῖν ἢ τὸ ἀναγκαῖον, ἢ τὸ εἰκός.—*Aristotle.*

(Both in the treatment of character and in the composition of the narrative we must always observe what the necessity of the case requires, or what probability demands.) A writer should not put too much strain on the credulity of the reader.

Χρήματα γὰρ ψυχὴ πέλεται δειλοῖσι βροτοῖσι.—*Hesiod.*

Money is life to wretched mortals.

Χρήματα, χρήματ' ἀνήρ, πενιχρὸς δ' οὐδεὶς πέλετ' ἐσλός.—*Alcæus.*

Money, money makes a man, no poor man is ever reckoned noble.

Χρήματ' ἔχων οὐδεὶς ἔρχεται εἰς Ἀΐδεω, οὐδ' ἂν ἄποινα διδοὺς θάνατον φύγοι οὐδὲ βαρεία
νούσους οὐδὲ κακὸν γῆρας ἐπερχόμενον. —*Theocritus.*

No man can take his wealth with him to the grave, nor can he escape death by paying a ransom, nor does his hoard of money ward off disease and the approach of age.

Χρὴ μὲν σφωίτερόν γε θεὰ ἔπος εἰρύσ-σασθαι,
καὶ μάλα περ θυμῷ κεχολωμένον· ὡς γὰρ ἄμεινον.
ὅς κε θεοῖς ἐπιπείθηται, μάλα τ' ἔκλυον αὐτοῦ.—*Homer.*

I needs must yield to your goddess' commands,
Indignant though I be—for so 'tis best;
Who hears the gods, of them his prayers are heard.—*Lord Derby.*

Χρὴ σιγᾶν ἢ κρείσσονα σιγῆς λέγειν. —*Pythagoras.*

Either be silent, or speak words that are better than silence.

Χρῆσις ἀρετῆς ἐν βίῳ τελείῳ. —*Diogenes Laertius.*

The exercise of virtue in a complete and perfect life.*

Χρόνος καθαιρεῖ πάντα γηράσκων ὁμοῦ. —*Æschylus.*

Advancing time sifts and cleanses all alike.

Χρόνος ὀξὺς ὀδόντας
πάντα καταψήχει καὶ βιαιότατα. —*Simonides of Ceos.*

The gnawing teeth of Time soon devour all things, even the strongest.

Χρόνῳ τὰ πάντα κρίνεται.

Time judges everything.

Χρυσαῖ πέδαι.

(Fetters of gold.) Chains of love.

Χρυσὸς δ' ἀνοίγει πάντα κἀΐδου πύλας. —*Menander.*

A golden key will open any gate, even those of hell.

---

* A definition of happiness.

Χρυσὸς μὲν οἶδεν ἐξελέγχεσθαι πυρί,
ἡ δ' ἐν φίλοις εὔνοια καιρῷ κρίνεται.
                  —Menander.

Χωρὶς ὑγιείας ἀβίος βίος, βίος ἀβίωτος.

Gold is tested by fire, and the reality of a friend's professions is proved in a critical time.

Without health life is not life at all, but a lifeless life.

Ψεκάδες ὄμβρον γεννῶνται.

(Many drops make the rain.) Many littles make a mickle.

Ψευδηγορεῖν γὰρ οὐκ ἐπίσταται στόμα
τὸ Δῖον· ἀλλὰ πᾶν ἔπος τελεῖ.
                  —Æschylus.

God's lips know not how to lie, but he will accomplish all his promises.

Ψευδόμενος οὐδεὶς λανθάνει πολὺν χρόνον.
                  —Menander.

(No liar can long escape detection.) A liar should have a good memory.

Ψυχῇ μιᾷ ζῆν, οὐ δυοῖν, ὀφείλομεν.
                  —Euripides.

One life, not two, is our apportioned span.

Ψυχῆς πόνος γὰρ ὑπὸ λόγου κουφίζεται.
                  —Philemon.

Telling our sorrows lightens the burden of our heart.

ᾮ γῆρας, ὡς ἐπαχθὲς ἀνθρώποισιν εἶ
καὶ πανταχῇ λυπηρόν, οὐ καθ' ἓν μόνον,
ἐν ᾧ γὰρ οὐδὲν δυνάμεθ' οὐδ' ἰσχύομεν,
σὺ τηνικαῦθ' ἡμᾶς προδιδάσκεις εὖ φρονεῖν.
                  —Pherecrates.

Old age, what a grievous burden thou art to mankind, yea, a plague in everything and not in one alone, for when we have no power or vigour left, then thou teachest us to be wise.

Ὤδινεν ὄρος, Ζεὺς δ' ἐφοβεῖτο τὸ δ'
ἔτεκεν μῦν.—Athenæus.

(The mountain was in labour. Jove was frightened, and then a little mouse was born.) *Parturiunt montes, nascetur ridiculus mus.**

Ὦ θάνατε, θάνατε, νῦν μ' ἐπισκέψαι
μολών.—Sophocles.

O Death, Death, come now and cast thy eyes on me.†

Ὦ θάνατε Παιὰν, μόνος ἰατρὸς τῶν
ἀνηκέστων κακῶν.—Æschylus.

Death, the Great Healer, thou alone art the physician of unendurable sorrows.

Ὠκεῖαι χάριτες γλυκερώτεραι.

(Benefits given quickly are most welcome.) He gives twice who gives in a trice. *Bis dat qui cito dat.*

Ὦ Κρίτων, τῷ Ἀσκληπίῳ ὀφείλομεν
ἀλεκτρυόνα· ἀλλ' ἀπόδοτε καὶ μὴ
ἀμελήσητε.—Socrates.

Crito, we owe a cock to Æsculapius; by no means forget to give it.‡

Ὦ ξεῖν', ἀγγέλλειν Λακεδαιμονίοις, ὅτι
τῇδε
κείμεθα, τοῖς κείνων ῥήμασι πειθόμενοι.—Simonides of Ceos.

Stranger! to Sparta say, her faithful band
Here lie in death, remembering her command.—*Hodgson.*§

Ὦ ὀλίγον οὐχ ἱκανόν, ἀλλὰ τούτῳ γε
οὐδὲν ἱκανόν.—Epicurus.

He who doesn't find a little enough, will find nothing enough.

---

* Said of Agesilaus, King of Sparta, whose stature was not equal to his great courage.
† These words form part of the last speech of Ajax in Sophocles' tragedy of that name.
‡ The last words of Socrates as he was dying from the effects of the hemlock that he had been condemned to drink. Cocks were sacrificed as a thank-offering to the patron god of the healing art.
§ This was the famous epitaph on the gallant Spartans who were slain at the battle of Thermopylæ.

᾿Ω παῖ γένοιο πατρὸς εὐτυχέστερος,
τὰ δ' ἄλλ' ὅμοιος· καὶ γένοι' ἂν οὐ κακός.
                                    —Sophocles.

My son, mayst thou be more fortunate than thy father; in all else be
like him; then wilt thou be no base
man.*

᾿Ω πατρὶς, εἴθε πάντες οἱ ναίουσί σε
οὕτω φιλοιεν ὡς ἐγώ· καί γε ῥᾳδίως
οἰκοῖμεν ἂν σε, κοὐδὲν ἂν πάσχοις κακόν.
                                    —Euripides.

Dear land of my fathers, would that all
thy citizens loved thee as I do; then
should we possess thee more worthily,
nor would any evil thing come nigh
to hurt thee.

᾿Ω πόποι ἦ ῥά τις ἐστὶ καὶ εἰν 'Αΐδαι
   δόμοισιν
ψυχὴ καὶ εἴδωλον, ἄταρ φρένες οὐκ ἔνι
πάμπαν.—Homer.

O Heaven, there are then, in the realms
   below,
Spirits and spectres, unsubstantial all.†
                                    —Lord Derby.

ᾬς ἀπόλοιτο καὶ ἄλλος ὅτις τοιαῦτα γε
ῥέζοι.—Homer.

So let others perish whoever make a
similar attempt.‡

᾿Ως ἀρχὴ ἄνδρα δείκνυσιν.

(How office proves the man.)   Offices
are given, but not discretion.

ᾬς γὰρ ἐπεκλώσαντο θεοὶ δειλοῖσι βροτοῖσι,
ζώειν ἀχνυμένοις· αὐτοὶ δέ τ' ἀκηδέες
εἰσίν.—Homer.

Such lot have the gods given to
wretched mortals—to live in wretchedness, while they themselves are free
from sorrows.

᾿Ως δὲ κινηθὲν αὐτὸ καὶ ζῶν ἐνόησε
ἀϊδίων θεῶν γεγονὸς ἄγαλμα ὁ γεννή-
σας πατήρ, ἠγάσθη τε καὶ εὐφρανθεὶς
ἔτι δὴ μᾶλλον ὅμοιον, πρὸς τὸ παράδειγμα ἐπενόησεν ἀπεργάσασθαι.
                                    —Plato.

And when he saw that what was
created after the image of the eternal
gods had motion and life, God said
that it was good, and, pleased with
his handiwork, bethought him how
he might make it still more like the
gods, after whose image it had been
made.

᾿Ως ἡδὺ κάλλος ὅταν ἔχῃ νοῦν σώφρονα.

Beauty is truly beauty, when its comrade
is a modest mind.

᾿Ως ἡδὺ τὴν θάλατταν ἀπὸ γῆς ὁρᾶν.
                                    —Archippus.

'Tis sweet to view the sea when we
stand upon the shore.

᾿Ως ἡδὺ τὸν σωθέντα μεμνῆσθαι πόνου.
                                    —Euripides.

How sweet it is to remember dangers
when they are past and gone.

᾿Ωτα γὰρ τυγχάνει ἀνθρώποισι ἐόντα
ἀπιστότερα ὀφθαλμῶν.—Herodotus.

(Men's ears are less reliable than their
eyes.)   Believe what you see and not
what you hear; seeing is believing.

᾿Ω τρισκακοδαίμων, ὅστις ἂν πένης γαμῇ.
                                    —Menander.

Thrice wretched he who, being a poor
man, takes a wife.

᾿Ω τύχη μικρόν τι μοι κακὸν ἀντὶ τοσού-
των ἀγαθῶν ποίησον.
                        —Philip, King of Macedon.

O Fortune, do me one small ill turn to
make up for so much success.

᾿Ω φίλον ὕπνου θέλγητρον, ἐπίκουρον
νόσου
ὡς ἡδύ μοι προσῆλθες ἐν δέοντί γε.
ἆ πότνια λήθη τῶν κακῶν, ὡς εἶ σοφὴ,
καὶ τοῖσι δυστυχοῦσιν εὐκταία θεός.
                                    —Euripides.

O Sleep, thou sweet solace, and bulwark against disease; how welcome
comest thou in this time of trouble.
O blessed oblivion, how kind thou
art, a heaven-sent messenger ever
welcome to those who mourn.

* The parting words of the hero Ajax to his son before committing suicide.
† The exclamation of Achilles when he sees the ghost of Patroclus appear before him.
‡ This line was quoted by Scipio Æmilianus as his comment on the fate of his kinsman,
Tiberius Gracchus, whose attempts to introduce reforms were rewarded by assassination.

Ὦ φιλτάτη γῆ μῆτερ, ὡς σεμνὸν σφόδρ' εἶ
τοῖς νοῦν ἔχουσι κτῆμα.—*Menander.*

Dear native land, how do the good and
wise
Thy happy clime and countless blessings prize.

Ὦ φύσις, ἐν ἀνθρώποισιν ὡς μέγ' εἶ
κακὸν,
σωτήριόν τε τοῖς καλῶς κεκτημένοις.
                              —*Euripides.*

(O Nature, how powerful thou art in
mortals when bad, yet how beneficial to those who possess thee when
good.)   Our nature is very bad in
itself ; but very good to them that use
it well.—*Jeremy Taylor.*

French.

A barbe de fou on apprend à raser.	Men learn to shave on a fool's chin.
A bas le traître.	Down with the traitor.
A bâtons rompus.	By fits and starts; in a desultory manner.
Abbé.	An abbot; a priest.
A beau demandeur, beau refuseur.	A polite request must be politely refused.
A beau jeu beau retour.	One good turn deserves another.
A beau mentir qui vient de loin.	Travellers from afar can lie with impunity
Abîmé dans des réflexions.	Lost, wrapped up in thoughts.
A bis et à blanc.	By fits and starts.
A bon appétit il ne faut point de sauce.	(A good appetite needs no sauce.) Hunger is the best sauce.
A bon chat, bon rat.	(To a good cat, a good rat.) Well matched; set a thief to catch a thief.
A bon cheval point d'éperon.	Do not spur the willing horse.
A bon chien il ne vient jamais un bon os.	(A good bone does not always come to a good dog.) Merit seldom meets with its reward.
A bon commencement bonne fin.	A good beginning makes a good end.
Abondance de biens ne nuit pas.	Store is no sore.
A bon entendeur il ne faut que demi-mot.	(To one of good intelligence half a word is enough.) A word is sufficient to the wise.
A bon vin point d'enseigne.	(No sign-post is needed where good wine is sold.) Good wine needs no bush.
A brebis tondue Dieu mesure le vent.	God tempers the wind for the shorn lamb.
Abrégé.	An abridgment.
Absent le chat, les souris dansent.	When the cat's away the mice play.
A Carême-prenant chacun a besoin de sa poële.	On Shrove Tuesday everyone wants his own frying-pan.
Acariâtre.	Peevish; churlish.
A chacun son fardeau pèse.	We all our burdens bear.
A chacun son goût.	Everyone to his liking.
A chaque fou plaît sa marotte.	Every fool rides his own hobby.

A chaque jour suffit sa peine.

Sufficient unto the day is the evil thereof.

A chaque oiseau
Son nid est beau.

(Every bird thinks its own nest beautiful.) Home is home, be it ever so homely.

A chaque saint son cierge.

(To each saint his candle.) Honour to whom honour is due.

A charge de revanche.

On condition of repayment.

A chemin battu ne croît point d'herbe.

No grass grows on the highway.

Acheter des objets d'occasion.

To buy second-hand things.

A cheval.

On horseback.

A cheval donné il ne faut jamais regarder la bride.

Never look a gift horse in the mouth.

A chien endormi rien ne tombe en la gueule.

A closed mouth catcheth no flies.

A chose faite conseil pris.

Too late is advice when the mischief is done.

A cœur ouvert.

With open heart; candidly; unreservedly.

A cœur vaillant rien d'impossible.

To a valiant heart nothing is impossible.*

A confesseurs, médecins, avocats, la vérité ne cèle de ton cas.

To confessors, doctors, and lawyers, tell the truth about yourself.

A contre cœur.

Unwillingly; with one's face against.

A corps perdu.

Neck or nothing; post haste; without ballast.

A coup sûr.

With a dead certainty; sure as fate; clear as noon-day.

Acquérir méchamment et dépenser sottement.

(To acquire wickedly and spend foolishly.) Ill-gotten goods seldom prosper.

Adieu.

(I commit you to God.) Good-bye.

Adieu, France, adieu, je ne te reverrai plus.

Farewell, France, farewell, I shall never see thee more !†

Adieu la voiture, adieu la boutique.

(Good-bye to the carriage, good-bye to the shop.) The affair is over; it is finished and done with.

Adieu, plaisant pays de France !
    Ô ma patrie
    La plus chérie,
Qui as nourri ma jeune enfance !
Adieu, France ! adieu mes beaux jours.
La nef qui disjoint nos amours,
N'a eu de moi que la moitié,
Une part te reste, elle est tienne ;
Je la fie à ton amitié,
Pour que de l'autre il te souvienne.
A discrétion.

Farewell, thou pleasant land of France, my beloved country, the nurse of my infant days. Farewell to France; farewell to happiness! The ship that sunders me from thee carries away but half of my being. With thee I leave half of my soul, for it is thine ; I entrust it to thy love that there it may be a constant reminder of me to thee when I am far away.‡

At discretion ; without stint.

* The motto of Henri IV.
† The farewell of Mary Queen of Scots to France, when she left it on August 15th, 1561, to return to her kingdom of Scotland.
‡ These verses are popularly attributed, on very slight evidence, to Mary Queen of Scots.

A dix-huit ans, on adore tout de suite ;
à vingt ans, on aime ; a trente, on
désire ; à quarante, on réfléchit.
—*Paul de Kock.*

At eighteen we learn to adore a woman
in a moment ; at twenty we love her ;
we yearn for her at thirty ; but at
forty we consider whether she is worth
the trouble.

A dur âne dur aiguillon.

For a stubborn ass a sharp goad.

Affaire d'amour.

A love affair.

Affaire de cœur.

An affair of the heart.

Affaire d'honneur.

An affair of honour.

Affiche.

A placard.

A fond ; de fond en comble.

Thoroughly ; from top to bottom.

A force de parler d'amour, on devient
amoureux.—*Pascal.*

By dint of talking about love we are apt
to fall in love.

A fripon fripon et demi.

(Against a rogue set a rogue and a-
half.)   Set a thief to catch a thief.

Agacerie.

Allurement.

Agent de change.

A stockbroker.

Agiotage.

Stock-Exchange gambling.

A grands frais

At great expense.

Agrément.

Consent.

A haute voix.

Loudly ; openly.

Ah ! doit-on hériter de ceux qu'on
assassine ?
—*Crébillon.*

Ought one to inherit the goods of those
whose murderers we are ? *

A homme hardi fortune tend la main.

Fortune has a helping hand for the
daring.

A huis clos.

(With closed doors.)   Secretly ; *in
camerâ.*

Aide-de-camp.

Assistant to a General.

Aide-toi, et le ciel t'aidera.
— *La Fontaine.*

Help yourself, and Heaven will help
you.

Aidons-nous l'un et l'autre à porter nos
fardeaux.—*Voltaire.*

Let us help one another to bear the
burdens of life.

Aidons-nous mutuellement,
La charge des malheurs en sera plus
légère ;
Le bien que l'on fait à son frère,
Pour le mal que l'on souffre est un
soulagement.—*Florian.*

Yes, let each man help a brother,
     And try to make his burden light ;
Kind acts done to help another
     Will make our own dark hours seem
     bright.

Aimable.

Amicable ; courteous.

Aime-moi un peu, mais continue.

Love me little, love me long.

Aimer à lire, c'est faire un échange des
heures d'ennui que l'on doit avoir en
sa vie contre des heures délicieuses.
—*Montesquieu.*

A fondness for reading changes the in-
evitable dull hours of our life into
hours of exquisite delight.

---

* A line from the tragedy *Rhadamiste et Zénobie.* In the original the words are full of
tragic irony, but they are now generally quoted in a playful sense.   Crébillon himself was the
first to use them in this manner.   When he was seriously ill, the physician who attended him
asked the dramatist to make him a present of the unfinished tragedy *Catilina.* "*Ah ! doit-on
hériter de ceux qu'on assassine ?* " replied Crébillon.

Aimer, c'est être deux et n'être qu'un :
un homme et une femme qui se fon-
dent en un ange, c'est le ciel.
　　　　　—*V. Hugo*.

To love is to be two and yet one; a
man and a woman blended as an angel
—Heaven itself.

Aimer éperdument.

To love to distraction; to hold dear.

Aimer et savoir ne sont pas la même
chose.

To love and to be wise are two different
things.

Aimer ses aises.

To love one's comforts.

Aimez, mais d'un amour couvert
Qui ne soit jamais sans mystère.
Ce n'est pas l'amour qui vous perd,
C'est la manière de le faire.
　　　　　—*Bussy-Rabutin*.

Let love be clothed in mystery,
　There's no true love without it;
It is not love that ruins, but
　The way we go about it.

Ainsi que la vertu, le crime a ses degrés.
　　　　　—*Racine*.

As in virtue, so in crime there are
degrees.

Air distingué.

A distinguished appearance.

Air distrait.

An absent, abstracted look.

Air noble.

A distinguished, patrician air, manner,
or presence.

Aisé à dire est difficile à faire.

What is easy to say is hard to do.

Ajustez vos flûtes.

Settle your differences yourselves.

A l'abandon.

At random.

A la belle étoile.

In the open air; *al fresco;* out of
doors.

A la bonne heure.

(At the lucky moment.)　Good; well
timed.

A l'abri.

In shelter; under cover.

A la chandelle la chèvre semble
demoiselle.

All cats are gray alike in the dark.

A la cour du roi chacun pour soi.

At the king's court every man for
himself.

A la dérobée.

Stealthily.

A la faim il n'y a point de mauvais
pain

(With hunger no bread is nasty.)
Hungry dogs eat dirty puddings.

A la fin ils en vinrent aux coups.

At last they came to blows.

A la française.

After the French mode.

A la guerre comme à la guerre.

(At the wars as they do at the wars.)
Suit yourself to the company you are
in.

A la lettre.

Word for word; literally.

A l'amiable.

In a friendly way; amicably.

A l'amitié, Monsieur, il n'est rien d'impossible.—*Colin d'Harleville*.

To friendship, sir, nothing is impossible.

A la mode.

According to the fashion.

A l'amour et au feu on s'habitue.

One grows hardened to love and to fire.

A l'anglaise.

After the English fashion.

A la portée de tout le monde.

Within everyone's reach.

A la presse vont les fous.

(Fools herd together.)　Birds of a
feather.

A la queue gît le venin.

In the tail lies the sting.

A la sourdine.

A la tête de l'échelle de notre globe est placé l'homme, chef-d'œuvre de la création terrestre.

A laver la tête d'un âne on ne perd que le temps et la lessive.

A l'envi.

A l'extrémité.

A l'impossible nul n'est tenu.

A l'improviste.

Allant à tort et à travers.

Allégresse.

Aller à tâtons.

Aller en enfants perdus.

Aller en vendanges sans panier.

Aller planter ses choux.

Aller sur les brisées de quelqu'un.

Allez dire à votre maître que nous sommes ici par la volonté du peuple, et que nous n'en sortirons que par la force des baïonnettes.

Allez, vous êtes une ingrate,
Ne tombez jamais sous ma patte.
                    —*La Fontaine.*

Allons donc!

Allons, enfants de la patrie.

Allons, je puis mourir, tu m'as pleuré, tu m'aimes.—*C. Delavigne.*

A l'œil malade la lumière nuit.

A l'œuvre on connaît l'ouvrier.

A loisir.

A l'ongle on connaît le lion.

A longue corde tire qui d'autrui mort désire.

A l'origine de tous les pouvoirs, je dis de tous indistinctement, on rencontre la force.—*Guizot.*

A main armée.

A mal enfourner on fait les pains cornus.

Amant de cœur.

A ma puissance.

Silently; with bated breath.

Man is placed at the top of the ladder in this world of ours; he is the masterpiece of creation.

(To wash an ass's head is but loss of time and soap.) All your pains will not give an ass brains.

In a spirit of rivalry.

At the point of death; without resource.

The best can do no more.

Unawares.

Going at random; wide of the mark.

Cheerfulness; mirth; hilarity; vivacity.

To walk irresolutely.

To go with the forlorn hope.

To go to the vintage without a basket.

(To go and plant cabbages.) Rustication; estrangement from the world.

To be on the track of someone.

Go and tell your master that we are here by the will of the people, and we will not depart unless driven out at the point of the bayonet.*

Get you gone, you are an ungrateful wretch. Mind you never let me get hold of you.

Nonsense!

Come, children of our country.†

I can die happy now, since you wept for me, and you love me.

Light hurts sore eyes.

A workman is known by his work; a carpenter is known by his chips.

At leisure.

The lion is known by his paw.

He pulls at a long rope who desires another's death.

At the base of all authority and power, I say all, without distinction, we find that force exists.

By force of arms.

Lay your loaves straight in the oven or they will come out crooked.

(The heart's lover.) He whom one truly loves.

(According to my power.) Motto of the Earl of Stamford.

---

* The traditional reply of Mirabeau to a messenger sent by Louis XVI. to the Assembly. Fournier, however, gives a different and milder version of Mirabeau's message.
† The opening words of the Marseillaise, the words of which were written by Rouget de Lisle in 1792.

A marmite qui bout mouche ne s'attaque.

Flies will not light on a boiling pot.

Amateur.

(A lover.) One that devotes his time to some employment for other than pecuniary reasons.

A mauvais chien l'on ne peut montrer le loup.

There's no setting a cur on a wolf.

A méchant chien court lien.

To a vicious dog a short chain.

Ame damnée.

A miserable drudge.

Ame de boue.

(A soul of mud.) A contemptible person.

Amende honorable.

A sufficient and courteous apology.

A merle soûl cerises sont amères.

Cherries are sour to the glutted blackbird.

A merveille.

In a wonderful way ; remarkably done.

A mesure que l'homme s'approche des éléments de la nature, les principes de sa science s'évanouissent.
      —*Bernardin de Saint-Pierre.*

The nearer man approaches the elements of nature, the more the principles of his science fade away.

Ami de table est variable.

A boon companion is changeable.

Amitié.

Friendship.

Amitié, doux repos de l'âme,
Crépuscule charmant des cœurs,
Pourquoi, dans les yeux d'une femme
As-tu plus tendres langueurs ?
      —*Lamartine.*

Friendship, sweet resting-place of the soul, the gloaming wherein our hearts find peace. Why is it that thy most tender calm is found in a woman's eyes ?

Amour, amour, quand tu nous tiens,
On peut bien dire : Adieu prudence !
      —*La Fontaine.*

When love casts over us his spell,
To prudence we may say farewell !

Amour et seigneurie ne se tinrent jamais compagnie.

Love and lordship like no fellowship.

Amour fait moult, argent fait tout.

Love is powerful, money omnipotent.

Amour-propre.

Self-esteem.

Amour, tous les autres plaisirs
Ne valent pas tes peines.—*Charleval.*

All other pleasures are not worth love's pains.

Amour, toux, et fumée, en secret ne font demeurée.

Love, a cough, and smoke cannot be hid.

Ancienne noblesse.

(The old nobility.) French families ennobled before the Revolution of 1792.

Ancien régime.

(The former government or administration.) The rulers of the ante-Revolution period.

Ane chargé de reliques.

An ass laden with sacred relics.*

Ane piqué convient qu'il trotte.

Spur an ass and he'll consent to go.

A nouveaux seigneurs nouvelles lois.

(New lords, new laws.) New brooms sweep clean.

---

* The title of one of La Fontaine's fables, where the ass thinks that the homage paid to his load is paid to himself. Hence the words are generally applied to a person who gives himself airs when dressed in a little brief authority.

A nul ne peut être ami qui de soi-même est ennemi.

He cannot be another's friend who is his own enemy.

A outrance.

To the uttermost.

A paroles lourdes oreilles sourdes.

To hard words turn deaf ears.

A pas de géant.

With great strides.

A peindre.

Fit for a model.

Aperçu.

Glimpse ; epitome ; digest.

A père avare enfant prodigue.

A miser has a spendthrift son.

A perte de vue.

As far as the eye can reach.

A petite fontaine boit-on à son aise.

At a little spring one drinks at ease.

A petit mercier, petit panier.

A little pack suffices for a petty pedlar.

Appartement.

A suite of two or more rooms.

Apprenons à subordonner les petits intérêts aux grands, et faisons généreusement tout le bien qui tente nos cœurs : on ne peut être dupe d'aucune vertu.—*Vauvenargues.*

Learn to overrule minor interests in favour of great ones, and generously do all the good the heart prompts ; a man is never injured by acting virtuously.

Approuvez qu'il n'est rien qui blesse un noble cœur
Comme quand il peut voir qu'on le touche en l'honneur.—*Molière.*

Rest assured that there is nothing which wounds the heart of a noble man more deeply, than the thought that his honour is assailed.

Après dommage chacun est sage.

Every one is wise when the mischief is done.

Après la fête on gratte la tête.

After a feast a man thinks of the bill.

Après l'Agésilas,
    Hélas !
Après l'Attila,
    Holà !—*Boileau.*

After Agesilas, Alas ! After Attila, Great Heavens ! *

Après la mort le médecin.

(After death the doctor.) Shutting the stable when the horse has gone.

Après la pluie le beau temps.

Sunshine follows after rain.

Après le fait ne vaut souhait.

It's no use wishing when the thing is done.

Après le plaisir vient la peine ;
    Après la peine, la vertu.

After pleasure comes repentance ; after repentance, virtue.

Après lui, il faut tirer l'échelle.

(After him we must take away the ladder.) He is the worst knave of the lot.†

Après nous le déluge.

After us the deluge.‡

---

* This was Boileau's epigram on the production of *Agesilas* and *Attila*, the two tragedies written by Corneille in his declining years, in which the tragedian showed a marked falling off in dramatic power. It is said that Corneille naïvely supposed Boileau wished to praise and not to condemn these plays. The lines are often applied to a condition of affairs where the last state proves to be worse than the first.
† This saying is based on the old custom of hanging the worst criminal last, when a number were executed. When the last victim was dead, the gallows might be removed as no longer required. The proverbialism is nowadays often used in an opposite sense, *i.e.*, to say that a person or thing is "the best of the bunch."
‡ A saying attributed to Madame de Pompadour, the favourite of Louis XV., who saw that there were signs of the approach of the Revolution in the general discontent of the French people. The sentiment was not new, for it appears in a line of a Greek comic poet, Ἐμοῦ θανόντος γαῖα μιχθήτω πυρί. "When I am dead, may the earth be consumed by fire." See also note on these words in Greek section.

Après perdre, perd on bien.

After losing at first, one becomes a good loser.

A prix d'or.

(At price of gold.)   Very costly ; fetching a fancy price.

A propos.

To the point ; seasonably.

A propos de bottes.

By the way ; by the by.

A propos de rien.

Talking of nothing ; by the way.

A quelque chose malheur est bon.

It is an ill wind that blows nobody any good.

A qui chapon mange chapon lui vient.

(Capon comes to him who eats capon.) Spend and God will send.

A quinze ans, la danse est un plaisir ; à vingt-cinq, un prétexte ; à quarante, une fatigue.—*A. Ricard.*

At fifteen, dancing is a pleasure ; at twenty-five, an excuse for courting ; at forty, a weariness.

A qui veut rien n'est impossible.

Nothing is impossible to a determined will.

A quoi bon faire cela ?

What's the good of doing that ?

A quoi sert l'examen avant le mariage ? A rien. Ce n'est qu'après qu'on se connaît à fond.
Las de se composer avec un soin extrême,
Le naturel caché prend alors le dessus ;
  Le masque tombe de lui-même,
Et, malheureusement, on ne le reprend plus.—*La Chaussée.*

What use is study of a partner's character before marriage ? None at all. It is only after the wedding that knowledge comes. Weary of making strenuous pretensions, the natural character then shows itself as it is ; the mask falls off, and, unhappily, it is never again put on.

A raconter ses maux souvent on les soulage.—*Corneille.*

A man often softens his sorrows by telling them to another.

Araignée au matin, chagrin ; araignée au midi, espoir.

A spider seen in the morning foretells grief ; but seen at midday brings a message of hope.

A reculons, à rebours.

To the right about.

A rez-de-chaussée.

On the ground floor.

Argent comptant.

Ready money.

Argent comptant porte médecine.

Money down works wonderful cures.

Argent emprunté porte tristesse.

Who goes a-borrowing, goes a-sorrowing.

Argent est rond, il faut qu'il roule.

Money is round, so it must circulate.

Argot.

The jargon of the streets ; the slang talk of hucksters, &c.

Armes blanches.

Side arms ; cold steel.

A Rome comme à Rome.

At Rome do as Rome does.

Arrière-garde.

The rear-guard.

Arrière-pensée.

An after thought ; a mental reservation.

Arts d'agrément.

Accomplishments ; the " extras " of the academies for young ladies.

A rude âne rude ânier.

(For a stubborn ass a stubborn driver.) Like cures like.

A ses moments perdus.

In one's spare hours.

Assez à qui se contente.

Enough is as good as a feast.

Assez consent, qui ne mot dit

Silence gives consent.

Assez demande qui bien sert.

Who serves well may charge enough.

Assez d'histoires inventées à plaisir.

That's enough of your tales.

Assez dort qui rien ne fait.

The idler gets enough sleep.

Assez gagne qui malheur perd.

He gains enough who loses sorrow.

Assez parents, assez tourments.

Many relations are tribulations.

Assez sait qui sait vivre et se taire.

He is wise enough who can live and keep his own counsel.

Assez tôt, si bien.

Soon enough, if well enough.

Assez y a, si trop n'y a.

(There is enough, if there be not too much.) Enough is as good as a feast.

Assignat.

French paper money issued after the Revolution at the end of last century.

Assistance obligée.

Compulsory help ; poor relief.

A tard crie l'oiseau quand il est pris.

The bird cries out too late when in the trap.

A tâtons.

Experimentally ; irresolutely ; at a venture.

Atelier.

A work-shop ; studio.

A tort et à travers.

Anyhow ; confusedly.

A tort ou à raison.

Reason or none.

A tous les cœurs bien nés que la patrie est chère !—*Voltaire*.

To all true hearts how dear is their native land !

A tous oiseaux leurs nids sont beaux.

All birds fancy their own nests.

A toute outrance.

Desperately ; tremendously ; with a vengeance.

A toutes jambes.

As fast as one's legs can carry one.

A tout propos.

At every turn, ever and anon.

A tout seigneur tout honneur.

(To every lord give all due honour.) Render to Cæsar the things that are Cæsar's.

A trop acheter n'y a que revendre.

For overbuying there's no remedy but selling again.

Attaché.

An official belonging to an embassy.

Attelez les chevaux.

Put the horses to.

Attroupement

A mob ; a muster ; a congregation.

Au battre faut l'amour.

Love is not made more tender by blows.

Auberge.

An inn.

Au besoin l'on connaît l'ami.

A friend in need is a friend indeed.

Au bon droit.

With just right.

Au bout de son Latin.

(At the end of his Latin.) At the end of his mental resources.

Au bout du compte.

On the whole ; in conclusion ; in short ; taking one thing with another.

Au contraire.

On the contrary.

Au courant.

Fully acquainted with matters.

Aucun chemin de fleurs ne conduit à la gloire.—*La Fontaine*.

It is no primrose-path that leads to glory.

Aucun n'est prophète chez soi.—*La Fontaine.*

No one is a prophet in his own house.

Au dedans ce n'est qu'artifice,
Et ce n'est que fard au dehors :
Otez-leur le fard et le vice,
Vous leur ôtez l'âme et le corps.
—*Charleval.*

Deceit within, powder without,
Describes coquettes inside and out ;
For if they are of both bereft,
There's naught whatever of them left.

Au demeurant, le meilleur fils du monde.
—*Clément Marot.*

As for the rest, he was the best fellow in the world.*

Au dernier les os.

The last-comer gets the bones.

Au désespoir.

In utter despair.

Au diable tant de maîtres, dit le crapaud à la herse.

"You are too many for me ! " as the toad said to the harrow.

Au fait.

Well informed ; master of.

Au fond.

To the bottom ; thoroughly.

Au grand sérieux.

With great seriousness; entirely in earnest.

Aujourd'hui roi, demain rien.

(To-day a king, to-morrow nothing.) To-day a man, to-morrow a mouse.

Au jour le jour.

From hand to mouth.

Au lieu de me plaindre, de ce que la rose a des épines, je me félicite de ce que l'épine est surmontée de roses et de ce que le buisson porte des fleurs.
—*Joubert.*

Instead of deploring that roses have thorns, I am glad the thorny stem is capped with roses and that the tree bears bloom.

Au long aller petit fardeau pèse.

Even a light burden becomes heavy if you have to carry it far.

Au naturel.

In the natural state.

A un boiteux femme qui cloche.

(Let the cripple wed a limping wife.) Marry among your own class.

Au nouveau tout est beau.

Novelty is always lovely.

Au pays des aveugles les borgnes sont rois.

In the land of the blind, the one-eyed are kings.

Au pied de la lettre.

Literally.

Au pis-aller.

At the worst; if the worst comes to the worst.

Au plaisir fort de Dieu.

(At the all-powerful disposal of God.) Motto of the Earl of Mount Edgecumbe.

Au premier abord la chose n'est pas claire.

At first sight the matter is not clear.

Au premier coup ne tombe pas l'arbre.

The first blow does not fell the tree.

Au renard endormi rien ne tombe en la gueule.

When the fox is asleep, nothing fall into his mouth.

Au reste.

In addition to this ; besides.

Au revoir.

Adieu, until we meet again.

* These words occur in some verses addressed by Marot to Francis I., in which he asks the King for money. In this missive he describes the qualities of his valet. After attributing all the possible vices to his servant, he terminates the catalogue of his sins with the above quotation. This is now commonly applied to any good-natured man, whose other virtues are somewhat conspicuous by their absence.

Au secours! — Help! To the rescue.

Au sérieux. — Seriously ; in a serious mood.

Aussitôt dit, aussitôt fait. — No sooner said than done.

Aussi tôt meurt veau que vache. — A calf may die as soon as the cow.

Autant de têtes autant d'opinions. — So many heads, so many wits.

Autant de trous, autant de chevilles. — There is a peg for every hole.

Autant d'hommes, autant d'avis. — So many men, so many opinions.

Autant en emporte le vent. — (So much the wind carries away.) It is all idle talk.

Autant vaut bien battu que mal battu. — (One may as well be well beaten as badly beaten.) One may as well be hanged for a sheep as a lamb.

Autant vaut être mordu d'un chien que d'une chienne. — It is all the same whether it is the dog or the bitch that bites you.

Autant vaut l'homme comme il s'estime. — A man is valued by his own estimate.

Autant vaut porter de l'eau à la rivière. — You might as well carry coals to Newcastle.

Autre droit. — Another's right.

Autres temps, autres mœurs. — Other times, other customs.

Aux abois. — At death's door; *in extremis*; having one foot in the grave.

Aux aguets. — Watchful; vigilant.

Aux grands maux les grands remèdes. — Desperate diseases need desperate remedies.

Aux petits des oiseaux il donne leur pâture.—*Racine*. — God feeds the young birds.

Aux regards de Celui qui fit l'immensité L'insecte vaut un monde, ils ont autant coûté.—*Lamartine*. — In the eyes of Him who made the universe the insect is worth a world ; for it needed the same skill to create it.

A vaillant homme courte épée. — A brave arm makes a short sword long enough.

A vaincre sans péril, on triomphe sans gloire.—*Corneille*. — Conquest without danger is a barren triumph.

Avaler des couleuvres. — (To swallow snakes.) To endure many crosses ; to pocket the affront.

Avant. — Forward ; advance.

Avant-coureur. — A forerunner.

Avant-propos. — Prelude ; preface ; prologue.

Avec de bon sens, le reste vient. — (With good sense all other things come.) Good sense will conduct a man to success.

Avec le temps et la paille l'on mûrit les mêles. — Time and straw make medlars ripe.

Avec nantissement. — (With security.) A law term.

Avec votre permission. — With permission.

A vieux comptes nouvelles disputes. — (Old reckonings cause new disputes.) Short reckonings make long friends.

Avis au lecteur. — (Notice to the reader.) A word to the wise is sufficient.

Avise la fin. — (Consider the end.) *Respice finem*

Avocat, il s'agit d'un chapon Et non point d'Aristote et de sa politique.—*Racine*.

The question before the court is the fate of a fowl, and not Aristotle and his politics.*

Avoir de l'entregent.

To possess tact ; to have an aptitude for business.

Avoir du cachet.

To have a distinctive character ; to possess qualities that raise one above the common run of men or things.

Avoir du fil à retordre.

(To have some thread to unwind.) To be in a quandary ; to be placed in an embarrassing position.

Avoir du front ; avoir du toupet.

To have effrontery ; to have plenty of cheek.

Avoir du guignon.

(To be the victim of an evil eye.) To be down on one's luck.

Avoir la frousse.

To be in a state of alarm.

Avoir l'air emprunté.

To look awkward.

Avoir la langue bien pendue.

To have the gift of the gab.

Avoir l'aller pour le venir.

To have nothing but one's labour for one's pains.

Avoir le cœur haut et la fortune basse.

To have high spirit and low fortune.

Avoir le cœur sur la main ; avoir le cœur sur les lèvres.

(To have one's heart on one's hand ; to have the heart on the lips.) To be of a frank, ingenuous disposition.

Avoir le diable au corps

(Out of one's mind.) To have a bee in one's bonnet.

Avoir les coudées franches.

To have elbow-room ; to be able to act according to one's inclination.

Avoir un caprice pour une femme.

To have a passing fancy for a woman ; to be inspired with a transient passion.

Avoir une idée fixe.

(To have a fixed idea.) To be possessed of a prejudice that nothing can remove.

Avoir une mémoire de lièvre.

To have a treacherous memory.

Avoir une peur bleue.

(To be blue with fear.) To be frightened out of one's wits.

A volonté.

At will ; at pleasure.

A votre santé.

Here's to your health.

A vous le dé, Monsieur.

(It is your turn to play, sir.) It's your turn now.

A vue d'œil.

Forthwith ; speedily ; at short notice.

Ayez toujours plusieurs cordes à votre arc.

Always have more than one string to your bow.

Aymez loyaulté.

(Love loyalty.) Motto of the Marquis of Winchester.†

* The words of Dandin in the *Plaideurs* have become proverbial as an illustration of people who will not stick to the point under discussion. See also note on *Passons au déluge*.
† John Paulet, Marquis of Winchester, during the Civil War in the reign of Charles I., withstood the attacks of the Parliamentary soldiers upon his house for nearly two years. To commemorate his loyalty to the King, he ordered these words to be written on every window of the house. His descendants have adopted them as their motto.

Badaud.	(A lounger.) A regular Parisian.
Badauderie.	Silliness; foolery.
Badinage.	Playful discourse.
Bagatelle.	A trifle.
Baisser le pavillon.	To strike the colours.
Baissez les stores.	Draw the blinds down.
Bal champêtre.	A country ball.
Baliverne.	Humbug; nonsense.
Ballon d'essai.	(A trial balloon.) A device to see which way the wind blows; a ruse to discover the bent of popular feeling.
Balourdise.	Stupidity; want of skill.
Bal par souscriptions.	A subscription ball.
Bande noire.	The black gang; a bad lot.
Barbouillage.	Scrawl; rigmarole.
Bas bleu.	A blue stocking; a learned woman.
Baste pour cela.	Well, so be it; mum for that.
Bastille.	A castle or stronghold in Paris, where state prisoners were confined until the end of last century.
Bâtir des châteaux en Espagne.	To build castles in the air.*
Bâton.	A stick; a staff.
Bâton porte paix.	(A stick is a good peacemaker.) If you wish for peace, prepare for war.
Battre en brèche.	To destroy the arguments or character of another.
Battre la campagne.	(To scour the country.) To go on a fool's errand; to reckon without one's host.
Battre la générale.	(To beat to arms.) A warning voice; to give the signal of danger, or distress.
Battre le chien devant le lion.	(To beat the dog before the lion.) A plan not likely to make the dog courageous.
Battue.	A massacre of game.
Bavarde.	A foolish gossiping woman.
Beaucoup de mémoire et peu de jugement.	(A good memory, but little sense.) A good memory is no proof of cleverness.
Beau idéal.	A perfect model.
Beau monde.	The world of fashion; the upper ten.
Beauté du diable.	(Beauty of the devil.) The transient beauty that depends on youth and health alone.

---

* The origin of this expression is doubtful. It may have arisen from the fact that in early times French Knights were wont to serve under the banner of the Spanish Kings, and were rewarded with grants of land for their services. *Bâtir des châteaux en Albanie,* "To build castles in England," is another phrase that bears the same meaning.

Beauté et folie sont souvent en com- | Beauty and folly go often together.
pagnie.

Beauté sans bonté ne vaut rien. | Beauty without goodness is nothing worth.

Beaux esprits. | Men of wit and humour.

Beaux yeux de sa cassette. | (The pretty eyes of her cash-box.) Her money is her chief attraction.

Bel esprit. | (A pretty wit.) A brilliant mind.

Belle, bonne, riche, et sage, | Pretty, good, rich, sensible—that's a
Est une femme en quatre étages. | woman four storeys high.

Belle chose est tôt ravie. | Beauty is fleeting.

Belle fille et méchante robe trouvent | A pretty girl and a tattered gown always
toujours qui les accroche. | meet something to catch them.

Belle hôtesse un mal pour la bourse. | A pretty hostess makes the hotel bill heavy.

Belles-lettres. | Refined literature.

Belle tournure. | Symmetry; shapeliness.

Bénéficiaire. | A person obtaining a benefit; beneficiary.

Besoin fait vieille trotter. | (Need makes the old woman trot.) Needs must when the devil drives.

Bête. | A beast; a stupid person.

Bête noire. | (Wild boar.) One especially disliked; a pet abomination.

Bêtise. | Gross folly; nonsense.

Bévue. | A blunder; a false step.

Bien-aimé. | Well-loved.

Bien attaqué, bien défendu. | (Well matched.) Set a thief to catch a thief.

Bien conduire sa barque. | (To steer one's boat well.) To manage one's affairs well.

Bien dire fait rire ; bien faire fait taire. | They will be hushed by a good deed who laugh at a wise speech.

Bien écrire, c'est tout à la fois bien | To write well is to think well, feel and
penser, bien sentir et bien rendre ; | express well, and to have at the same
c'est avoir en même temps de l'esprit, | time wit, soul, and taste.
de l'âme et du goût.—*Buffon.*

Bien entendu. | (Well understood.) To be sure ; of course.

Bien est larron qui larron dérobe. | He is a thorough thief who robs a thief.

Bien nourri et mal appris. | (Well fed but ill taught.) Strong in the arm and weak in the head.

Bien perdu, bien connu. | (Once lost, then prized.) We never know the worth of water till the well is dry.

Bienséance. | Good manners; decorum.

Bijou. | A jewel ; a treasure.

Bijouterie. | Jewellery.

Billet à la Châtre.	The letter to la Châtre.*
Billet doux.	A love-letter.
Billets d'état.	Government paper ; bank notes.
Bise.	A north-east wind ; a fresh breeze.
Bizarre.	Odd ; quaint.
Blague.	A boastful tale ; an incredible story.
Blâmer un jeune homme d'être amoureux, c'est reprocher à quelqu'un d'être malade.—*Duclos.*	To blame a youth for being love-sick is like reproaching a man because he has bad health.
Blasé.	Surfeited; cloyed.
Bois ont oreilles et champs ont œillets.	(Woods have ears and fields have eyes.) The very walls have ears.
Bon avocat, mauvais voisin.	A good lawyer is a bad neighbour.
Bon bourgeois.	A substantial citizen ; a comfortable tradesman.
Bon chien chasse de race.	(A good dog hunts from natural instinct.) Good natures instinctively choose the right course.
Bon compagnon, mauvais mari.	A merry comrade makes a bad husband.
Bon diable.	A jolly good fellow.
Bon droit a besoin d'aide.	Even a good cause needs help.
Bon gré, mal gré.	Whether you like it or not ; willy-nilly.
Bon guet chasse malaventure.	Good watching drives away mischance.
Bonheur.	Good luck.
Bonhomie.	Good nature ; easy temper ; credulity.
Bon jour, bonne œuvre.	The better the day, the better the deed.
Bonjour lunettes, adieu fillettes.	Good morrow spectacles, farewell lasses.
Bon marché tire l'argent hors de la bourse.	A bargain draws the money out of the purse.
Bon mot.	A pun, a witty expression.
Bonne.	A nurse-maid.
Bonne bête.	A good-natured stupid creature.
Bonne-bouche.	A luscious morsel ; a toothsome tit-bit.
Bonne épée, point querelleur.	A good sword never picks a quarrel.
Bonne et belle assez.	Good and handsome enough.
Bonne foi.	Good faith ; plain dealing.
Bonne journée fait qui de fol se délivre.	It is a good day's work to get rid of a fool.
Bonne la maille qui sauve le denier.	(It is a good halfpenny that saves a penny.) A penny saved is a penny gained.
Bonne ou mauvaise santé Fait notre philosophie.—*Chaulieu.*	Our philosophy depends on our state of health.

* This expression has become proverbial, to illustrate the fickleness of women. The Marquis de la Châtre, being compelled to go away from his mistress Ninon, caused her to write a letter to him in which she promised fidelity. But when another suitor appeared on the scene, she exclaimed, " That fine *billet à la Châtre !*" and promptly forgot her former lover.

Bonne renommée vaut mieux que ceinture dorée.
: A good name is better than riches.

Bonnet de nuit.
: A nightcap.

Bonnet rouge.
: (The red cap.) The cap of liberty.

Bonne vie, bonne fin.
: A good life makes a good end.

Bon pays, mauvais chemin.
: (A good country, a bad road.) The worse for the rider, the better for the bider.

Bon poète, mauvais homme.
: (A good poet, a bad man.) The better workman, the worse husband.

Bons mots n'épargnent nuls.
: (Jesters spare no one.) Better lose your friend than waste your jest.

Bons nageurs sont à la fin noyés.
: (Even good swimmers are drowned at last.) A pitcher goes once too often to the well.

Bon ton.
: The height of fashion.

Bon vivant.
: A good liver ; a jolly companion.

Bon voyage.
: A pleasant journey.

Bordereau.
: A note ; memorandum.

Borné dans sa nature, infini dans ses vœux
L'homme est un dieu tombé qui se souvient des dieux.—*Lamartine.*
: Limited in his nature, unbounded in his aspirations, Man is a fallen God who is ever mindful of his divine origin.

Bouche à feu.
: A field piece.

Bouche serrée, mouche n'y entre.
: Keep your mouth shut and you will swallow no flies.

Bouillabaisse.
: Fish soup.

Boule-Miche.
: The familiar name used for the Boulevard St. Michel, an important thoroughfare running throughout the old Latin Quarter of Paris.

Bourgeois.
: A citizen.

Bourgeoisie.
: The body of citizens ; burgesses ; the shop-keeping class.

Bourse.
: The Stock Exchange.

Boutade.
: (A whim ; a freak.) A cock-and-bull story ; a wild goose-chase.

Boute-en-train.
: The leader of the fun ; the life and soul of the company.

Boutez en avant.
: Push forward.

Branler dans la manche.
: (To be loose in the handle.) To be threatened in one's fortune or reputation ; to be in a parlous case.

Brebis comptées, le loup les mange.
: Worry about your sheep and the wolf will worry them.

Brebis qui bêle perd sa goulée.
: While the sheep is bleating it is losing a mouthful.

Brebis rogneuse
Fait l'autre tigneuse.
: One rotten sheep will mar a whole flock.

Bref.
: In short.

Brevet.	Patent; license.
Breveté.	Patented.
Brigue.	Indirect means; intrigue; cabal.
Briller par son absence.	To be conspicuous by his absence.
Brimade.	The tricks that students play upon new-comers; horse-play.
Brisons là !	That's enough of it !
Brochure.	A pamphlet.
Brouhaha.	An uproar.
Brouillerie.	(Falling out.) State of variance; enmity.
Bruit ; rumeur.	Rumour.
Brûler la chandelle par les deux bouts.	To burn the candle at both ends.
Brûler le pavé.	To rush along.
Brûler n'est pas répondre. *— Camille Desmoulins.*	Burning is no answer.*
Brûler ses vaisseaux.	(To burn one's boats.) To risk all on the attempt ; neck or nothing.
Brusque.	Abrupt ; blunt.
Brusquerie.	Rudeness.
Bureau *(pl.* bureaux).	A (public) office.
Bureaucratie.	(Bureaucracy.) The undue influence of the permanent officials in the administration.
Bureau de conciliation.	(The conciliation committee.) A committee for settling disputes.
Bureau de la guerre.	The War Office.
Cadastre.	A register of the survey of lands.
Cahotage.	Jolting ; chaos.
Ça ira.	That will go on all right.†
Calomniez, calomniez ; il en restera toujours quelque chose. *—Beaumarchais.*	Slander and keep on slandering ; some of the mud will stick.
Camaraderie.	Good fellowship.
Camisade.	A night attack.
Canaille.	The rabble.
Canard.	A false story.
Cap-à-pie.	From head to foot.‡
Car c'est double plaisir de tromper le trompeur.*—La Fontaine.*	To trick the trickster is doubly a pleasure.
Caresser sa marotte.	To ride one's hobby-horse.

* The reply to Robespierre, who threatened to destroy the newspaper in which Desmoulins deprecated the policy of the indiscriminate butchery of those who were opposed to the "sea-green incorruptible."

† A phrase used by Benjamin Franklin, which became popular by its constant use in songs written during the Revolution.

‡ This expression is consecrated by ancient usage, but it is now French as she is spoken out of France.   The correct French phrase is *de pied en cap.*

Car je connais votre cœur équivoque :
Respect le cabre, amour ne l'adoucit ;
Et ressemblez à l'œuf cuit dans sa coque:
Plus on l'échauffe, et plus il se durcit.
                    —*J. B. Rousseau.*

Your fickle heart love cannot quell,
And e'en respect 'gainst it is foiled ;
'Tis like the egg cooked in its shell,
Which hardens all the more it's boiled.

Carte.

A card, a bill of fare.

Carte blanche.

A blank sheet of paper ; full powers.

Carte de visite.

A small photographic portrait.

Carte du pays.

A rough sketch ; a bird's-eye view.

Cartel.

(A challenge.)   An agreement between belligerent states for an exchange of prisoners, &c.

Car tel est notre plaisir.

(For such is our pleasure.)   The justification of despotic acts.

Casser une croûte.

(To break a crust.)   To partake of a light, hasty meal.

Catalogue raisonné.

A catalogue with illustrations or notices.

Cause célèbre.

(A celebrated case.)   A trial which has become the talk of the town.

Causeries.

Familiar talk ; chat.

Ce garçon ne vaut pas le pain qu'il mange.

That boy is not worth his salt.

Cela arrive comme marée en Carême.

(That comes like fish in Lent.)   In the nick of time.

Cela fait dresser les cheveux.

That makes one's hair stand on end.

Cela fera du bruit dans Landerneau.

(That will make an uproar in Landerneau.)   There will be a row about that.*

Cela heurte le sens commun.

That is opposed to common sense.

Cela me donne la chair de poule.

That makes my flesh creep.

Cela n'est pas de mon bail.

(That is no affair of mine.)   I am not responsible for that.

Cela saute aux yeux.

That tells its own tale.

Cela sert à faire bouillir la marmite.

That helps to make the pot boil.

Cela tombe bien.

That is lucky.

Cela va sans dire.

That goes without saying ; it is obvious.

Cela viendra.

(That will come one day.)   All in good time.

Celui a bon gage du chat qui en tient la peau.

He holds a good pledge of the cat who has her skin.

Celui est homme de bien qui est homme de biens.

(A good man is a man of goods.)   Money makes the man.

Celui-là cherche toujours midi à quatorze heures.

That fellow is always too late.

---

* As to the origin of this proverbialism, it was a custom in Landerneau, a small town in Brittany, for the townsfolk to make matters a little unpleasant for widows who were about to marry again.   It was Alexandre Duval, however, who made the fortune of the phrase in his comedy, *Les Héritiers*.   The scene of this play, produced in 1796, is laid in Landerneau, and the above saying is constantly introduced.   The humour of the situation consists in the exaggerated opinion that those dwelling in a small town have of the importance of their little scandals.

Celui-là gouverne bien mal le miel, qui n'en goûte, et ses doigts n'en lèche.

(He is a bad manager who tastes not the honey nor licks his fingers.) It is a poor cook that cannot lick his own fingers.

Celui-là peut prendre, qui goûte un plaisir aussi délicat à recevoir que son ami en sent à lui donner.
—*La Bruyère.*

He is a fortunate man who feels as much pleasure in receiving a boon as his friend feels in granting it.

Celui peut hardiment nager à qui l'on soutient le menton.

A man may swim boldly who is held up by the chin.

Celui qui à tâché de vivre de manière à n'avoir pas besoin de songer à la mort, la voit venir sans effroi.
—*Montesquieu.*

He who has tried to live in such a way that he does not think it necessary to think of death, sees it approach without alarm.

Celui qui a trouvé un bon gendre a gagné un fils ; mais celui qui en a rencontré un mauvais, a perdu une fille.

He who has got a good son in-law, has found a son, but he who has got a bad one, has lost a daughter.

Celui qui est sur les épaules d'un géant voit plus loin que celui qui le porte.

He who rides on the giant's shoulders sees further than the giant himself.

Celui qui met un frein à la fureur des flots
Sait aussi des méchants arrêter les complots.—*Racine.*

He who can still the raging sea
Can also check knaves' villainy.

Celui qui ne dit rien consent.

Silence gives consent.

Celui qui reçoit ses amis et ne donne aucun soin personnel au repas qui leur est destiné n'est pas digne d'avoir des amis.—*Brillat-Savarin.*

The host who gives no personal heed to the dinner to which he invites his friends, is not worthy of having friends.

Celui qui veut, celui-là peut.

(He who has the will, has the power.) Where there's a will, there's a way.

Ce mariage est sur le tapis.

That wedding is talked of.

Ce monde-ci n'est qu'une œuvre comique
Où chacun fait ses rôles différents.
Là, sur la scène, en habit dramatique,
Brillent prélats, ministres, conquérants.
Pour nous, vil peuple, assis aux derniers rangs,
Troupe futile et des grands rebutée,
Par nous d'en bas la pièce est écoutée.
Mais nous payons, utiles spectateurs ;
Et, quand la farce est mal représentée,
Pour notre argent nous sifflons les acteurs.—*J. B. Rousseau.*

This world is merely a comedy, where each man plays a different part. There, on the stage, in theatrical garb, shine prelates, ministers, conquerors. As for us, base groundlings seated in back seats, scorned by the great ones of the earth, we listen to the play from a humble place. But we are useful to the spectacle, for we pay for it, and, when the farce is acted ill, we get a return for our money by hissing the players.

Ce monde est plein de fous.

The world is full of fools.

Ce ne sont pas les plus belles qui font les grandes passions.

The greatest beauties do not inspire the deepest love.

Ce n'est jamais l'opinion des autres qui nous déplaît, mais la volonté qu'ils ont quelquefois de nous y soumettre lorsque nous ne le voulons pas.
—*Joubert.*

It is never the opinion of others which displeases us, but their desire at times to force their opinions on us, when we do not wish to accept them.

Ce n'est ni la Providence ni la vie qui nous trompent ; c'est nous qui nous trompons sur les desseins de l'une et sur le but de l'autre.—*Jouffroy.*

Ce n'est pas assez de faire entendre ce qu'on dit, il faut encore le faire voir ; il faut que la mémoire, l'intelligence et l'imagination s'en accommodent également.—*Joubert.*

Ce n'est pas aux regards, ni aux façons ; mais c'est au changement de la voix en s'adressant à un homme, que nous avons toujours deviné le plus sûrement, l'apparition de l'amour chez une femme.—*L. Dépret.*

Ce n'est pas dans des cages, fussent-elles dorées, qu'il faut élever les aigles.—*Victor Hugo.*

Ce n'est pas être bien aise que de rire.
　　　　　　　—*St. Évremond.*

Ce n'est pas être sage
D'être plus sage qu'il ne faut.
　　　　　　　—*Quinault.*

Ce n'est pas la mer à boire.

Ce n'est pas le souverain, c'est la loi, Sire, qui doit régner sur les peuples. Vous n'en êtes que le ministre et le premier dépositaire. —*Massillon.*

Ce n'est pas pour vous que le four chauffe.

Ce n'est pas tout que des choux, il faut encore de la graisse.

Ce n'est point assez d'avoir un front qui pense, un œil qui voit : il faut encore avoir une main qui parle.
　　　　　　　—*A. Houssaye.*

Ce n'est point en courant et la brune et la blonde,
Qu'on peut rencontrer le bonheur ;
Il faut, pour être heureux, avoir en ce bas monde,
Bon estomac et mauvais cœur.
　　　　　　　—*Deville.*

Ce n'est qu'un centon.

Ce n'est tout l'avantage de courir bien tost, mais bien de courir de bonne heure.—*Rabelais.*

Cent ans de chagrin ne payent pas un sou de dettes.

Neither Providence nor life deceives us, but we deceive ourselves as to the designs of the one, and as to the goal of the other.

It is not enough to make people hear what you say—you must make them understand it ; memory, intelligence, and imagination must be equally called into play.

It is not by the way she looks or acts, but by a change in her voice when she speaks to a man, that one can most surely divine when love has sprung up in a woman's heart.

It is not in cages, gild them as ye may, that eagles should be reared.

A laugh is not always a proof that the mind is at ease.

To be wiser than is necessary is not wisdom at all.

(It is not the sea to be drunk.) It is not a mountain to remove ; it is not an impossibility.

It is not the king, Sire, but the law which ought to rule nations. You are only the administrator and chief depositary of the law.

(The oven is not warmed for you.) There is nothing for you.

Cabbage will not make soup without fat.

It is not enough for an artist to have a mind that thinks, and an eye that sees, but he must also have an eloquent hand.

Upon the choice of dark or fair,
Of happiness rests not the question ;
You'll find it come if you've the pair :
A heart that's bad and good digestion.

(That is a mere cento.) It is only patchwork ; a medley of other people's work.

The race is not to him who runs the fastest, but to him who starts soonest.

A hundred years' fret will not pay a penny of debt.

Cent ans n'est guère, mais jamais c'est beaucoup.

A hundred years is not much, but Never is a long day.

Ce que fait la louve plaît au loup.

The wolf is proud of his litter.

Ce que femme veut Dieu le veut.

(What a woman wishes God wishes.) A wilful woman must have her way.

Ce que le poulain prend en jeunesse Il le continue en vieillesse.

(The habits that the colt learns are seen in the old horse.) What is bred in the bone comes out in the flesh.

Ce que le sobre tient au cœur est sur la langue du buveur.

(What the sober man hides in his heart is on the tongue of the drunkard.) When the wine is in, the wit is out.

Ce que plaît, Est à demi fait.

(A thing that pleases is half done.) Well-made goods will sell themselves.

Ce qui allége le labeur, ce qui sanctifie le travail, ce qui rend l'homme fort, bon, sage, patient, bienveillant, juste, à la fois humble et grand, digne de l'intelligence, digne de la liberté, c'est d'avoir devant soi la perpétuelle vision d'un monde meilleur rayonnant à travers les ténèbres de cette vie.
—*Victor Hugo.*

What lightens labour, sanctifies toil and makes a man good and strong, wise and patient, just and benevolent, both lowly and great, as well as worthy of intelligence and freedom, is the perpetual vision before him of a better world beaming through life's shadows.

Ce qui caractérise les vrais penseurs, c'est un mélange de mystère et de clarté.—*Victor Hugo.*

True thinkers are characterised by a blending of clearness and mystery.

Ce qui est différé n'est pas perdu.

That which is merely deferred is not lost.

Ce qui fait que la plupart des femmes sont peu sensibles à l'amitié, c'est qu'elle est fade quand on a senti l'amour.—*La Rochefoucauld.*

Most women are indifferent to friendship, as friendship is tame to those who have experienced love.

Ce qui fait que les amants et les maîtresses ne s'ennuient point d'être ensemble, c'est qu'ils parlent toujours d'eux-mêmes.—*La Rochefoucauld.*

Lovers and their mistresses never become bored in one another's society, because they are always talking about themselves.

Ce qui fait que peu de personnes sont agréables dans la conversation, c'est que chacun songe plus à ce qu'il a dessein de dire qu'à ce que les autres disent, et que l'on n'écoute guère quand on a bien envie de parler.
—*La Rochefoucauld.*

Few are agreeable in conversation, because each thinks more of what he intends to say than of what others are saying, and listens no more when he himself has a chance to speak.

Ce qui flatte le plus une femme, c'est de voir amoureux d'elle seule, un homme dont beaucoup d'autres femmes sont amoureuses.
—*Rochebrune.*

A woman is most flattered when her lover is a man many other women dote on.

Ce qu'il y a de plus grand, ce qu'il y a de divin dans l'homme, c'est la pitié et le pardon.—*A. Dumas, fils.*

The divine and grandest sentiments in man are pity and forgiveness.

Ce qui manque aux orateurs en profondeur ils vous la donnent en longueur.
—*Montesquieu.*

What orators lack in depth, they make up in length.

Ce qui m'a toujours beaucoup nui, c'est que j'ai toujours méprisé ceux que je n'estimais pas.—*Montesquieu.*

I have always done myself much harm by despising those people for whom I have no respect.

Ce qui nuit à l'un duit à l'autre.

One man's meat is another's poison.

Ce qui rend la jeunesse si belle et qui fait qu'on la regrette quand elle est passée, c'est cette double illusion qui recule l'horizon de la vie et qui la dore. — *Jouffroy.*

What makes youth so fair, and so dearly regretted when past, is its double illusion which makes the horizon of life seem far away, and at the same time gilds it.

Ce qui vient par la flûte, s'en va par le tambour.

(What comes by the flute, goes with the drum). Soon earned, soon spent ; lightly come, lightly go.

Ce qu'œil ne voit, au cœur ne deult.

What the eye sees not, the heart grieves not for.

Ce qu'on a bien aimé l'on ne peut le haïr.—*Corneille.*

We cannot learn to hate that which we have once deeply loved.

Ce qu'on apprend au berceau dure jusqu'au tombeau.

What is learned in the cradle remains with us to the grave.

Ce qu'on fait maintenant, on le dit ; et la cause en est bien excusable : on fait si peu de chose.—*Alfred de Musset.*

Whatever we do nowadays we talk about ; but there is much excuse : for we do so very little.

Certaines gens trouvent à redire à tout propos.

Some people find fault on every occasion.

Certaines personnes sont nées coiffées.

Some are born with silver spoons in their mouths.

　　　　　　Certes, ce sentiment
Qui m'envahit, terrible et jaloux, c'est vraiment
De l'amour, il en a toute la fureur triste !
De l'amour—et pourtant il n'est pas égoïste !
Ah, que pour ton bonheur je donnerais le mien,
Quand même tu devrais n'en savoir jamais rien,
S'il se pouvait parfois, que de loin, j'entendisse
Rire un peu le bonheur né de mon sacrifice.—*Edm. Rostand.*

Yes, this feeling that possesses me, terrible and jealous as it is, is truly love ; it has all love's passion, all its sadness.   Still, it is not selfish, for to give thee happiness, I would gladly renounce my own, though thou mightst never know what I had sacrificed ; yes, I would renounce it, if only I might sometimes hear the distant sound of thy exulting in the bliss my loss had gained for thee.*

Ces deux tableaux font pendant.

Those two pictures match.

Ces fabricants sont hors de pair.

Those manufacturers are unrivalled.

Ces gens-là font leurs orges en pillant les autres.

(They reap themselves by pillaging others.) They feather their own nest at the expense of other people.

　　　　Ce sont là jeux de prince :
On respecte un moulin, on vole une province.—*Andrieux.*

Such are the playful ways of princes ; they leave a mill alone, while they steal a whole province.

Ce sont les Cadets de Gascogne
De Carbon de Castel-Jaloux,
Bretteurs et menteurs sans vergogne
Ce sont les Cadets.—*Edm. Rostand.*

These are the Cadets of Gascony, of Carbon of Castel-Jaloux, braggarts and shameless brawlers all, these are the Cadets of Gascony.

* See note on passage *Je vous aime ; j'étouffe,* etc., in this section.

Ce sont les pires bourdes que les vraies. | Truths are the hardest jests.

Cessez de vous en prendre aux autres de vos propres fautes.
—*J. J. Rousseau.*

Cease to blame others for your own faults.

C'est à dire. | That is to say; namely.

C'est ainsi qu'en partant je vous fais mes adieux.—*Quinault.*

In this way I bid you a last farewell.*

C'est à peu près le même. | It's about the same thing.

C'est autant de gagné. | That is so much to the good.

C'est bien le cas de le dire. | You may indeed say so.

C'est bonnet blanc et blanc bonnet. | (It is white cap and cap white.) There are six of the one and half a dozen of the other.

C'est clair comme deux et deux font quatre. | (It is as clear as that two and two make four.) It is as plain as a pike-staff.

C'est dans les grands dangers qu'on voit les grands courages.—*Regnard.* | It is in great dangers that great courage is seen.

C'est décoiffer St. Pierre pour coiffer St. Paul. | (Stripping St. Peter's shrine to adorn St. Paul's.) Robbing Peter to pay Paul.

C'est de l'argent en barre. | It is as good as ready money.

C'est de l'eau bénite de cour. | Those are empty promises.

C'est de l'hébreu pour lui. | That's Greek to him.

C'est de l'homme que la femme apprend ce qu'il faut voir, et de la femme que l'homme apprend ce qu'il faut faire.
—*J. J. Rousseau.*

Man teaches woman what she ought to see, and woman teaches man what he ought to do.

C'est donc une révolte ?—*Louis XVI.* | Is it a revolt then ? †

C'est du blé en grenier. | (Wheat in one's granary.) It brings grist to the mill.

C'est du Nord aujourd'hui que nous vient la lumière.—*Voltaire.* | To-day it is from the North that the light of culture comes to us.‡

C'est égal. | No matter; it is all one.

C'est en amour surtout que les absents ont tort.—*Fournier.* | In love especially the absent are in the wrong.

C'est en fait de lui. | All is over with him.

C'est être médiocrement habile que de faire des dupes. | It takes only average cunning to make dupes.

C'est Foi dans la langue du ciel, Amour dans la langue des hommes.
—*Victor Hugo.*

" Faith," in the language of heaven, is " Love," in the language of men.

* In Quinault's *Thésée* the enchantress Medea, having failed to win the love of Theseus, the son of the King of Athens, uses her magical arts to take vengeance upon those who have scorned her. Failing in these attempts, she is about to depart, but, before making her exit, she calls down avenging spirits upon the palace and city of the Athenians, and, with the words *c'est ainsi que*, etc., vanishes. The line is often quoted as a proverbial illustration of revengeful fury. It was quoted with grim humour on the occasion of the death of Louis XV. On the day that the King died an announcement of a fresh addition to the already heavy taxes was posted outside the palace of Versailles. During the night someone wrote this line of Quinault beneath the official notice of the new tax.

† The exclamation of the king when he heard of the attack on the Bastille. *Non, sire, c'est une révolution.* " No, Your Majesty, it is a revolution," replied the Duc de Liancourt.

‡ These words occur in a letter written to Catherine II.

C'est folie de bayer contre un four.

Only a fool would face an oven in a grinning match.

C'est folie de faire son médecin son héritier.

He is a fool who makes his doctor his heir.

C'est folie de faire un maillet de son poing.

A man makes a mallet of his fist only once.

C'est la cour du roi Pétaud.

(It is the court of King Pétaud.) A house wherein all wish to rule: a meeting where all present wish to speak at once.

C'est la mouche du coche.

He's like the fly on the coach wheel.

C'est la pelle qui se moque du fourgon.

It's the pot calling the kettle black.

C'est là que le bât le blesse.

That's the spot where the shoe pinches.

C'est la raison
Et non pas l'habit, qui fait l'homme.
　　　　　—*Lebrun.*

It is the mind and not the garb that makes the man.

C'est la tête de Méduse.

(It is the head of Medusa.) It is paralysing in its effect; it is an astounding event.

C'est le bonheur de vivre
Qui fait la gloire de mourir.
　　　　　—*Victor Hugo.*

The happiness of life makes the glory of death.

C'est le commencement de la fin.

It is the beginning of the end.*

C'est le fils de la poule blanche.

He was born with a silver spoon in his mouth.

C'est le jouir et non le posséder qui rend heureux.—*Montaigne.*

Happiness is in the enjoyment, not in the possession.

C'est le mot de l'énigme.

It is the (key-)word of the riddle.

C'est le refrain de la ballade.

The old story over again.

C'est le secret de Polichinelle.

(That is a secret of Punchinello.) A secret that everyone knows.

C'est le ton qui fait la musique.

It is the tone that makes the music.

C'est l'imagination qui gouverne le genre humain.—*Napoleon 1.*

Mankind is governed by its imagination.

C'est magnifique, mais ce n'est pas la guerre.

It is magnificent, but it is not war.†

C'est ma plaisanterie qui m'a tué.
　　　　　Camille Desmoulins.

My joke has killed me.‡

C'est notre bonheur apparent qui nous fait le plus d'ennemis.
　　　　　—*Alex. Dumas, fils.*

It is our apparent happiness which gains for us most enemies.

C'est par le caractère, et non par l'esprit, que l'on fait fortune.—*Voltaire.*

Men make fortune by their mettle, not their wits.

---

* Talleyrand is said to have made this remark during the Hundred Days, but he was probably not the author of it. It was, however, his habit never to deny that he was the originator of any good *mot* that others attributed to him.

† The comment made by one of the French Generals on the charge of the Light Brigade at Balaclava.

‡ So Desmoulins, who had been one of the authors of the Revolution, exclaimed when he was sent to the guillotine with Danton, 1794. He had once laughed at the solemn demeanour of St. Just, and regarded his condemnation as the work of the man whom the jest had turned into an enemy.

C'est peu que de courir, il faut partir à point.

It is not enough to run; one must start in time.

C'est plus qu'un crime, c'est une bêtise.

It is worse than a crime, it is a blunder.*

C'est posséder les biens que savoir s'en passer.—*Regnard.*

To know how to do without a thing is to possess it.

C'est pour l'achever de peindre.

(This is to finish his picture.) This is to complete his character.

C'est quand l'enfant est baptisé qu'il arrive des parrains.

(When the child is christened the godfathers arrive.) When the need is greatest the help comes.

C'est se mépriser soi-même, que de n'oser paroître ce qu'on est. L'art de se contrefaire et de se cacher, n'est souvent que l'aveu tacite de nos vices.
　　　　　　　　　　—*Massillon.*

Not to dare to appear as one really is, is to despise oneself. The art of concealing and counterfeiting is often only a tacit acknowledgment of our vices.

C'est son affaire.

(It is his business.) Leave that to him.

C'est son cheval de bataille.

(That is his war-horse.) That is his strong point.

C'est sur le tapis.

It is talked of.

C'est toujours la plus mauvaise roue qui crie.

The worst wheel always creaks the loudest.

C'est toujours une femme de quarante ans qui trouvera vieille une femme de trente.—*Gerfaut.*

It is always the woman of forty who calls a woman of thirty old.

C'est trop aimer quand on en meurt.

It is overdoing the thing to die of love.

C'est un avare, il tondrait sur un œuf.

(He is a miser, he would shave an egg if he could.) He is a skin-flint.

C'est un balai neuf, il fait balai neuf.

New brooms sweep clean.

C'est un barbare aimable.—*Thiers.*

He is a barbarian, but an amiable one.†

C'est un bon enfant, mais il n'a pas inventé la poudre.

He is a good fellow, but he won't set the Thames on fire.

C'est un bon parti.

She is a good match.

C'est un chevalier d'industrie.

He is an adventurer.

C'est une autre paire de manches.

(That is a very different pair of sleeves.) Quite another pair of shoes. That's quite another thing.

C'est une bonne fourchette.

He is a good trencher-man.

C'est une bonne lieue au bas mot.

It's at the very least three miles off.

C'est une chose admirable, que tous les grands hommes ont toujours du caprice, quelque petit grain de folie mêlé à leur science.—*Molière.*

It is pleasant to see the greatest men have always had some whim—some little chaff of folly amongst their golden grain of knowledge.

C'est une fort mauvaise tête.

He is a sad dog.

C'est une grande folie de vouloir être sage tout seul.—*La Rochefoucauld.*

(It is very foolish to try to be wise alone.) Two heads are better than one.

C'est une grande habilité que de savoir cacher son habilité.
　　　　　　　—*La Rochefoucauld.*

It is the greatest cleverness to know how to conceal one's cleverness.

* This is said to have been Talleyrand's comment on the execution of the Duc d'Enghein. It is also quoted in the form, *C'est pire qu'un crime, c'est une faute.*
† This was the French statesman's mistaken estimate of the character of Bismarck.

C'est une grande misère que de n'avoir pas assez d'esprit pour bien parler, ni assez de jugement pour se taire.
—*La Bruyère.*

It is wretched not to have enough wit to speak well, nor enough sense to keep silent.

C'est une plaisante chose que la pensée dépende absolument de l'estomac, et que, malgré cela, les meilleurs estomacs ne soient pas les meilleurs penseurs.—*Voltaire.*

It is amusing to reflect that the mind utterly depends on the stomach, and that, nevertheless, the best digestion does not belong to the greatest thinkers.

C'est une tempête dans un verre d'eau.

(It is a tempest in a drinking-glass.) A storm in a tea-cup.*

C'est une terrible affaire que de s'obliger d'aimer par contrat.
—*Bussy-Rabutin.*

It is a dangerous business to bind a man down to love a woman by a marriage contract.

C'est une vraie aubaine.

It is quite a god-send.

C'est un faible roseau que la prospérité.
—*D'Anchères.*

Prosperity is a weak reed.

C'est un fin matois.

He's a knowing card.

C'est un grand signe de médiocrité, de louer toujours modérément.
—*Vauvenargues.*

To be niggard in one's praise of others is a sure proof of mediocrity in oneself.

C'est un heureux dégagement
Que de quitter les sots qu'on trouve
    dans les villes,
Pour aller jouir doucement
De l'aimable entretien des campagnes
    fertiles ;
On y trouve, il est vrai, des sots, petits
    et grands ;
Mais le monde est plus rare aux champs.
—*De Cailly.*

What bliss it is to leave behind
    The crop of fools the city yields,
And far from these town-bores to find
    Sweet pleasures in the peaceful fields ;
For though one finds fools great and
        small
    Dwelling near a village steeple,
'Tis better there, for, after all,
    You do not find so many people.

C'est un homme qui ne sait pas vivre.

He is an ill-mannered man.

C'est un métier que de faire un livre comme de faire une pendule. Il faut plus que de l'esprit pour être auteur.
—*La Bruyère.*

The writing of books is as much a trade as the making of watches. Something more than mere ability is necessary in order to be an author.

C'est un opéra très couru.

This opera is very popular.

C'est un pauvre vaisseau.

(He is a poor ship.)   A feeble fellow who cannot manage his own affairs.

C'est un pesant fardeau d'avoir un grand mérite.—*Regnard.*

A great reputation is a heavy burden to carry.

C'est un poëme plein de verve.

It is a spirited poem.

C'est un prêté pour un rendu.

(That is something lent for something given back.)   That's a Roland for his Oliver.

C'est un sot à vingt-quatre carats.

(He is a fool of twenty-four carats.) An unalloyed, absolute fool.

C'est un sot en trois lettres.

He is an absolute fool.

C'est un sot personnage que celui d'un roi exilé et vagabond.—*Napoleon I.*

An exiled and vagabond king is a contemptible person.

C'est un vieux routier—défiez-vous-en !

He is an old bud—beware of him !

* The Grand Duke Paul of Russia thus described a popular rising in Geneva.

C'est un vrai homme de bien.
He is a very honest man.

C'est un zéro en chiffres.
(He is nought in the accounts.) He is a mere nobody.

C'est votre affaire.
That's your business.

Cet âge est sans pitié.—*La Fontaine*.
This age (childhood) is pitiless.

Cet animal est très méchant :
Quand on l'attaque, il se défend.
This animal is very wicked : when it is attacked it defends itself.*

Cet enfant tient de son père.
That child takes after his father.

Cet habit a bonne façon.
This coat is well made.

Cet oracle est plus sûr que celui de Calchas.—*Racine*.
This prophecy is surer than that of Calchas.†

Cette demoiselle a la vue basse.
That young lady is short-sighted.

Cette histoire est vieille comme les rues.
That tale is as old as Adam.

Cette propriété sera mise aux enchères.
That estate will be sold by auction.

Cette vie est le berceau de l'autre.
—*Joubert*.
This life is the cradle in which we are prepared for the life to come.

Ceux qui parlent beaucoup, ne disent jamais rien.
(People that talk much never say anything.) Great talkers seldom say anything worth hearing.

Ceux qui se moquent des penchants sérieux aiment sérieusement les bagatelles.—*Vauvenargues*.
People who sneer at those who give importance to their hobbies are wont themselves to give importance to trifles.

Ceux qui s'indigèrent ou qui s'enivrent ne savent ni boire ni manger.
—*Brillat-Savarin*.
Those who get indigestion or become intoxicated do not understand the art of eating and drinking.

Ceux qui sont à vendre ne valent pas la peine d'être achetés.—*L. Andrieux*.
Men who are eager to sell themselves are not worth buying.

Ceux qui sont incapables de commettre de grands crimes n'en soupçonnent pas facilement les autres.
—*La Rochefoucauld*.
Those who are incapable of committing great crimes themselves do not readily suspect others of them.

Ceux qui veulent qu'on ne parle pas mal d'eux n'ont qu'une seule ressource, qui est de bien faire.—*Fénelon*.
Those who do not want to be spoken ill of have only to be righteous in their actions.

Chacun a sa manie (*or* sa marotte).
Everyone has his hobby.

Chacun à son goût.
Every man to his taste.

Chacun à son métier ;
Les vaches seront bien gardées.
—*Florian*.
If every man will attend to his own business, the cows will be well looked after.

Chacun a un fou dans sa manche.
Every one has a fool under his cap.

Chacun avec son pareil.
Like will to like.

Chacun cherche son semblable.
Each one seeks his like ; like draws to like.

---

* Words from a comic song which have become proverbial. They are a skit on the account of a traveller, who naively remarked that certain wild animals were so savage that they attacked the person who attempted to kill them.
† The confident boast of Achilles in the tragedy *Iphigénie*. Achilles promises Clytemnestra to rescue her daughter from the death to which her father, Agamemnon, obedient to the commands of the seer Calchas, has condemned her. The words are often quoted to indicate a sense of absolute conviction that some event will take place.

Chacun chez soi et tous chez Victor Hugo.

Every man in his own house and all with Victor Hugo.*

Chacun dit du bien de son cœur, et personne n'en ose dire de son esprit. —*La Rochefoucauld.*

Everybody praises his heart, but none ventures to boast of his mental gifts.

Chacun doit balayer devant sa porte.

Each man should sweep before his own door.

Chacun ira au moulin avec son propre sac.

(Everyone must go to the mill with his own sack.) Let every tub stand on its own bottom.

Chacun joue au roi dépouillé.

All men jeer at a fallen king.

Chacun n'est pas aise qui danse.

A man may dance and not for joy.

Chacun paie son écot.

Each one pays his own score.

Chacun porte sa croix.

Everyone bears his cross; none knows the weight of another's burden.

Chacun pour soi et Dieu pour tous.

Every man for himself and God for us all.

Chacun se fait fouetter à sa guise.

Every one takes a whipping in his own way.

Chacun sent le mieux où le soulier le blesse.

Every one knows best where the shoe pinches him.

Chacun tire l'eau à son moulin.

Every man wishes to bring grist to his own mill.

Chacun vaut son prix.

Every man has his value.

Chamade.

A parley.

Champ clos.

(Closed field.)   The lists.

Champs-Elysées.

(Elysian fields.)   A well-known district in Paris.

Changer de note.

To turn over a new leaf.

Changer son cheval borgne pour un aveugle.

(To exchange a one-eyed horse for a blind one.) To change for the worse.

Chansons à boire.

Drinking-songs.

Chapeau bas !

Hats off!

Chapelle ardente.

(A burning chapel; so-called from the great number of wax lights.) The place where a dead body lies in state.

Chaque âge a ses défauts : les jeunes gens sont fougueux et insatiables dans leurs plaisirs ; les vieux sont incorrigibles dans leur avarice.—*Fénelon.*

Each period of life has its failings. Youth is fiery and insatiable in its pleasures; age is incorrigible in its avarice.

Chaque chose a son temps.

To everything there is a season.

Chaque demain apporte son pain.

(The morrow brings its own bread. Sufficient unto the day.

Chaque instant de la vie est un pas vers la mort.—*Corneille.*

Each moment of life is a step towards death.

* Towards the end of his days Victor Hugo proposed to build a large mansion into which he intended to receive all his relatives ; but he insisted on the above principle that all the inmates should be able to withdraw to their own apartments when they, as he often did, felt the need of solitude.

Chaque médaille a son revers.

There are two sides to every medal.

Chaque oiseau trouve son nid beau.

(Every bird thinks its own nest handsome.)   No place like home.

Chaque pays chaque mode; (*or*, à sa guise).

So many countries so many customs.

Chaque potier vante son pot.

Every workman praises his own work.

Charbonnier est maître chez soi.

(A charcoal-burner is master in his own house.)   Every man's house is his castle.*

Chargé d'affaires.

One entrusted with state affairs at a foreign court.

Charité bien ordonnée commence par soi-même.

Charity begins at home.

Charlatan.

A quack; mountebank; humbug.

Chasse-cousin.

(Chase away cousin.)   Anything fitted to drive away poor relations and other importunate persons; bad wine.

Chasser le bouc émissaire.

To drive out the scapegoat.

Chassez le naturel, il revient au galop.
     —*Destouches.*

Though you drive away natural impulses, back they will come at full speed.

Château qui parle, femme qui écoute, sont prêts à se rendre.

(A castle which parleys and a woman who listens are both ready to surrender.)   He who hesitates is lost.

Châteaux en Espagne.

Castles in the air; fanciful plans.

Chat échaudé craint l'eau froide.

A scalded cat dreads cold water.   A burnt child dreads the fire.

Chat en poche.

(To buy a pig in a poke.)   To make a blind bargain.

Chef de cuisine.

The head or the chief cook.

Chef de police.

The chief of the police.

Chef-d'œuvre.

A master-piece.

Chemin faisant.

By the way; in passing.

Chercher à connaître
N'est souvent qu'apprendre à douter.
     —*Mme. Deshoulières.*

Seeking to learn is often only learning to doubt.

Chercher midi à quatorze heures.

(To look for mid-day at fourteen o'clock.)   To go on a wild goose chase; to create needless troubles.†

Chercher une aiguille dans une botte de foin.

To look for a needle in a haystack.

Cherchez la femme.

(Look for the woman.)   A woman is generally at the bottom of every scandal.‡

* The well-known story of Francis I. and the charcoal-burner is the origin of this saying. The king took shelter in the hut of a charcoal-burner, who, with the words quoted above, took the head of the table, and set before the king the head of a boar, which had been poached from the royal preserves.   At last the king's retinue arrived, and the owner of the hut discovered to his terror the identity of his guest.

† In the 15th century watches in France used to have twenty-four hours marked on their dials, the time being reckoned as in Italy at the present time.

‡ The phrase is generally attributed to Fouché, but its origin is uncertain.

Chère amie.	A dear friend ; a mistress.
Cherté foisonne.	Dearness causes a glut.
Cheval de bataille.	(A war-horse.) The main argument.
Chevalier d'industrie.	(A knight of industry.) One who lives by fraud ; a swindler ; a sharper.
Chevalier sans peur et sans reproche.	A knight without fear and without reproach.*
Cheval rogneux n'a cure qu'on l'étrille.	A galled horse shrinks from the curry-comb.
Chez elle un beau désordre est un effet de l'art.—*Boileau.*	There a charming disorder is the effect of art.†
Chez soi comme en prison, Vieillir, de jour en jour plus triste ; C'est l'histoire de l'égoïste Et celle du colimaçon.—*Arnault.*	To grow sadder from day to day, while enclosed in a prison of one's own—that is the life history of a selfish man and of a snail.
Chic.	Stylish : smart.
Chien hargneux a toujours l'oreille déchirée.	Snarling curs have always torn ears.
Chien qui aboie ne mord pas.	A snarling cur does not bite.
Chien sur son fumier est hardi.	Every cock crows on his own dunghill.
Chose perdue, chose connue.	When you lose anything, everybody knows you had it.
Chose qui plaît est à demi vendue.	Pleasing ware is half sold.
Choses promises sont choses dues.	What you promise you should perform.
Chose trop vue n'est chère tenue.	Familiarity breeds contempt.
Ci-devant.	Formerly.

Ci-gît Cléon, ce président avare,
Qui vendit la justice à chaque citoyen,
    Croyant qu'une chose si rare
    Ne doit pas se donner pour rien.
            —*François (de Neufchâteau).*
	Cleon, the greedy magistrate,
	Sold justice at a heavy rate,
	Holding a thing so rare to see
	Should never be imparted free.

Ci-gît ma femme : oh ! qu'elle est bien Pour son repos et pour le mien. —*J. du Lorens.*	Beneath this stone my wife doth lie, She now has rest,—and so have I.
Ci-gît Piron, qui ne fut rien, Pas même académicien.—*Alexis Piron.*	Here lies Piron, who was nothing, not even a member of the Academy.‡
Clair-semé.	Thinly sown ; scattered here and there.
Claqueur.	One paid to applaud a performance.
Clientèle religieuse.	The religious clique ; the clerical party.
Clique.	A set, or party.
Coiffeur.	A hairdresser.
Coiffure.	An ornamental head-dress.

---

* The description of the heroic Bayard.

+ So Boileau describes the rules for the composition of an ode, in which style of poetic composition, though sometimes apparently free from the bonds of laws of metre, as Horace said of Pindar, the disorder is the result of the art that conceals art. This phrase is commonly applied to affected simplicity, either in literary composition, speech, or dress, etc.

‡ With this epitaph on himself, Piron, the playwright, sneered at the French Academy. The sneer is in rather dubious taste, as he had endeavoured to become an Academician, but was refused admission by Louis XV., whose mistress, Madame de Pompadour, the poet had offended.

Combien celui qui doute est malheureux ! C'est comme un roulis et comme un tangage auquel son esprit ballotté se trouve en proie. Le bateau s'élève, puis il retombe, et, de droite à gauche, de bas en haut, le passager malade est balancé, toute son énergie vaincue, et, à chaque fois, il croit qu'il va mourir. Il n'y a qu'un remède, aux envahissements de l'imagination il faut opposer le réel.—*Paul Bourget.*

What an unhappy wretch is the man who doubts ! His troubled mind is, so to speak, tossed about on a ship, rolling and pitching in the sea. The ship rises, then falls, and the sick voyager is buffeted from side to side, now up, now down; all his strength is gone, and every moment he expects to die. There is only one remedy for this condition of doubt : we must defeat these insidious attacks that proceed from the imagination by turning our thoughts to the realities of life.

Combien tout ce qu'on dit est loin de ce qu'on pense.—*Racine.*

What a difference there is between what we say and what we think.

Comédiens, c'est un mauvais temps,
La Tragédie est par les champs.

Actors, it is a bad time for us, now that tragedy is being acted outside.*

Comité de Salut Public.

The Committee of Public Safety.†

Comme c'est le caractère des grands esprits de faire entendre en peu de paroles beaucoup de choses, les petits esprits, au contraire, ont le don de beaucoup parler et de ne rien dire.
                    —*La Rochefoucauld.*

As it is the stamp of great wits to put much in few words, so it is that of petty minds to speak much and say nothing worth listening to.

Comme deux gouttes d'eau.

As like as two peas.

Comme il faut.

In good taste.

Comme je trouve.

(As I find.) Motto of the Marquis of Ormonde.

Comme on fait son lit on se couche.

As a man makes his bed so he must lie on it.

Commis.

A clerk (in business).

Commissaire, commissaire,
Colin bat sa ménagère ;
C'est un beau jour pour l'amour.
                    —*Béranger.*

Commissioner, commissioner, Colin is thrashing his wife ; O 'tis a glorious day for love.‡

Commissaire de police.

A commissioner of police.

Commissionaire.

(A person commissioned.) A messenger; hotel employé.

Commis voyageur.

A commercial traveller.

Compagnon de voyage.

A fellow traveller.

Comparaisons sont odieuses.

Comparisons are odious.

Compte rendu.

(Account rendered.) An account ; a report.

Comptoir.

A counting-house.

Concierge.

A door-keeper.

---

* Words from a popular song composed during the Reign of Terror.
† The governing body that was responsible for so much of the bloodshed during the Revolution.
‡ A parody of the idea that *Amantium iræ amoris integratio est,* "The quarrels of lovers are love's renewal."

Conciergerie

A door-keeper's lodge ; a noted prison in Paris.

Concours universel.

Open competitive examination.

Condition de l'homme : inconstance, ennui, inquiétude.—*Pascal.*

Changeableness, weariness, restlessness, are the conditions of human life

Confrère.

A colleague.

Congé.

Discharge ; leave.

Congé d'élire.

Leave to elect.*

Connaisseur.

A critical judge.

Connaissez-vous ces têtes d'épis qui sont vides et qui ne se dressent que plus superbes sur le sillon ? Le jour de la moisson venu, elles retombent et ne sont plus qu'une paille légère et stérile. C'est l'image de beaucoup de livres.— *Ch. de Mazade.*

Mark the heads of corn which are empty, yet stand up only the more proudly in the field ! On harvest day, they fall and are but light and valueless straw. This is the simile that describes many of our books.

Connaissez-vous un feu qui prend toutes les formes que le souffle lui donne, qui s'irrite, qui s'affaiblit, selon que l'impression de l'air est plus vive ou plus modérée ? il se sépare, il se réunit, il s'abaisse, il s'élève ; mais le souffle puissant qui le conduit ne l'agite que pour l'animer, et jamais pour l'éteindre. L'amour est ce souffle ; nos âmes sont ce feu.
—*Bernis.*

There is a flame which assumes all the shapes breath gives it, is heightened or enfeebled as the air impresses it. It breaks up, re-unites, sinks, and rises again ; but the mighty blast only blows to enliven, and never to quench the flame. Love is the breath ; our hearts the flame.

Connais-toi toi-même.

Know thyself. Γνῶθι σαυτόν.

Conseil de famille.

A family council.

Conseil de prud'hommes.

(A council of wise men ; men with special knowledge.) A mixed council of master tradesmen and workmen, for the consideration of disputes between masters and men.

Conseiller d'état.

Privy councillor.

Conseil tenu par les rats.

(The council held by the rats.) An assembly of people where there is much talking but no practical result.†

Contentement passe richesse.

Contentment is better than riches.

Conter fleurettes.

To say pretty things ; to pay compliments.

Contour.

The outline of a figure.

Contre coignée serrure ne peut.

A hatchet is a key for any lock.

Contre fortune bon cœur.

(A good heart against fortune.) Set a stout heart to a stey brae. *Nil desperandum.*

* Theoretically, the Dean and the Chapter have *congé d'élire* a new bishop when a bishopric becomes vacant. This privilege is, however, nugatory, as the appointment is always made by the Crown.
† In the fable of La Fontaine, which bears this name, the rats are unanimous that it would be an excellent thing for them if the cat had a bell round his neck, but no one will undertake to bell the cat.

Contretemps.

A mischance.

Convier quelqu'un, c'est se charger de son bonheur pendant tout le temps qu'il est sous notre toit.
—*Brillat Savarin*.

When you invite a man to partake of your hospitality, you make yourself responsible for his happiness all the time that he is under your roof.

Coras lui dit : " La pièce est de mon cru " ;
Le Clerc répond : " Elle est mienne et non vôtre."
Mais, aussitôt que l'ouvrage eut paru,
Plus n'ont voulu l'avoir fait l'un ni l'autre.—*Jean Racine*.

Two authors claimed the play
Before the stage had shown it ;
But when the play came out,
Neither was found to own it.

Cordon.
Cordon bleu.

A surrounding girdle of troops, &c.
(A blue ribbon.) A good cook ; an eminent person in any walk of life.*

Cordon militaire.

A military line. A guard drawn up round a place to prevent approach to it.

Cordon sanitaire.

A sanitary line ; a boundary drawn around an infected spot.

Corps d'armée.
Corps diplomatique.
Corps dramatique.
Cortège.
Corvée.
Coterie.
Coucher à la belle étoile.
Couci-couci.
Coudre la peau du renard à celle du lion.

An army corps.
The diplomatic body.
A dramatic body ; a company of players.
A procession.
Forced labour.
A set of acquaintances ; a society.
Sleep in the open air.
No great catch ; so-so.
(To sew the fox's skin to the lion's.) To supplement strength and boldness with cunning.

Couleur de rose.

Rose colour ; of flattering, or pleasing appearance.

Coup.
Coup de boutoir.

A stroke ; a trick.
(A blow from the wild-boar's snout.) A brusque attack in an argument which silences all dispute.

Coup de grâce.
Coup de main.
Coup de maître.

A finishing stroke.
An armed surprise.
A master-stroke ; with consummate skill.

Coup de pied.
Coup de plume.
Coup de soleil.
Coup d'essai.
Coup d'état.

A kick.
A literary attack ; a satire.
A sunstroke.
A first essay; attempt.
A stroke of policy or of violence in state affairs.

Coup de théâtre.

An unexpected event ; a surprise.

Strictly, this expression signifies a female cook, as a medal suspended by a blue ribbon used to be given to those French women who passed a certain examination in the culinary art.

Coup d'œil.	A quick glance of the eye ; a twinkling.
Coupé.	The front covered outside part of the "diligence," or stage coach.
Courage sans peur.	Courage without fear.
Courbe ton front, fier Sicambre. —*St. Remi.*	Bow thy head, proud Sicambrian.*
Cour des miracles.	(A court of miracles.) Courts, alleys, etc., in old Paris, where mountebanks and beggars dwelt.
Court plaisir, long repentir.	(Short pleasures, long repentance.) The evening's amusement should bear the morning's reflection.
Coûte que coûte.	Let it cost what it may.
Coûte que coûte je ferai mon devoir.	At any cost I will do my duty.
Craignez la honte.	Fear shame.
Craignez tout d'un auteur en courroux.	Fear everything from a writer in a rage.
Crédit Foncier.	(Agricultural Bank.) An institution that advances money to farmers, &c.
Crême de la crême. La crême ; le dessus du panier.	Pink of perfection ; " The glass of fashion and the mould of form."
Crever de rire.	To split one's sides with laughing.
Crier famine sur un tas de blé.	To moan : " I am starving ! " on a heap of corn.
Crier haro sur le baudet.	(To cry shame on the ass.) To voice a feeling of popular indignation.†
Critique.	Criticism ; a piece of criticism.
Croire tout découvert est une erreur profonde, C'est prendre l'horizon pour les bornes du monde.—*Lemierre.*	It is a profound error to believe everything has been discovered ; it is mistaking the horizon for the boundary of the world.
Croquer le marmot.	To dance attendance on another.
Cruauté, envie, mensonge sont des rétrécissements de l'âme ; amour, charité, vérité, sont des élargissements de l'âme. Les premières nous diminuent ; les secondes nous augmentent. —*Ph. Chasles.*	Envy, falsehood and cruelty are outcomes of the soul's ebb; love, truth, and charity, those of its flood. The former dwarf us, the latter add to our moral stature.
Cuisine.	The kitchen ; method of cooking.
Cul-de-sac.	The bottom of the bag ; a blind alley.
Curé.	The incumbent of a church living.
D'accord.	In harmony ; agreed.
Dame de comptoir.	A counter-woman ; bar-woman.
Dame d'honneur.	A lady of honour.
Dames de la halle.	Market women.

* The words he addressed to Clovis when the latter presented himself for baptism, having abjured paganism. The actual form of these words is much disputed.
† Haro was an old Norman expression, which signified an appeal for an immediate judicial trial without further dispute. *Crier haro sur le baudet* is one of the many phrases from the fables of La Fontaine which have become proverbial in the French language.

Dames quêteuses.

Ladies who collect for charitable purposes.*

Dans cette affaire je vous donne carte blanche.

You can act as you please in that affair.

Danser sur un volcan.

(To dance on a volcano.) To be in a dangerous position without being conscious of the fact.

Dans l'adversité de nos meilleurs amis nous trouvons quelque chose que ne nous déplaît pas.—*La Rochefoucauld.*

In the misfortunes of our best friends we find a certain gratification.

Dans la jeunesse, c'est par les sens que l'on arrive au cœur; dans l'âge mûr, c'est par le cœur que l'on arrive au sens.—*R. de la Bretonne.*

In youth, the road to the heart is through the senses; in manhood, the road to the senses is through the heart.

Dans la jeunesse, nous vivons pour aimer; dans un âge plus avancé, nous aimons pour vivre.—*St.-Evremond.*

In youth we only live for loving; later, we have to love or it would not be life.

Dans l'amour, si l'inconstance donne des plaisirs, la constance seule donne le bonheur.—*L'Abbé Trublet.*

In love, inconstancy may give pleasure, but constancy alone gives happiness.

Dans la nuit tous chats sont gris.

(All cats are alike grey at night.) Joan's as fair as my lady in the dark.

Dans la postérité, perspective inconnue, Le poëte grandit et le roi diminue.
—*Théophile Gautier.*

In time to come, at near or distant date, The king grows less, the poet still more great.

Dans l'art d'interesser consiste l'art d'écrire.—*Delille.*

The art of writing is the art of interesting.

Dans la vie, comme à la promenade, une femme doit s'appuyer sur un homme un peu plus grand qu'elle.
—*Alphonse Karr.*

Through life, as when taking a walk, a woman should be supported by a man greater than herself.

Dans le monde vous avez trois sortes d'amis : vos amis qui vous aiment, vos amis qui ne se souviennent pas de vous, et vos amis qui vous haïssent.—*Chamfort.*

In society there are three kinds of friends : those who love you, those who hate you, and those who do not think of you at all.

Dans les grandes choses, les hommes se montrent comme il leur convient de se montrer; dans les petites, ils se montrent comme ils sont.
—*Chamfort.*

In great emergencies men show themselves as they should be; in minor matters, as they are.

Dans un bal les hommes sont le sexe timide, le sexe décent, comme ils y sont le sexe faible, car ils sont toujours les premiers fatigués.
—*Alphonse Karr.*

In the ballroom men are the bashful and quiet sex, and the weaker, too, for they are always the first to be wearied.

De bon augure.

Propitious.

De bon commencement bonne fin.

A good beginning makes a good ending.

Débonnaire.

(Debonair ; gracious.) Motto of Earl Lindsay.

* It is not an uncommon practice for ladies in France to collect the offertory in church on special occasions, when a sermon on behalf of some charity has been preached.

De bonne grâce.

With a good grace.

De bon vouloir servir le roy.

(To serve the King with right good will.) Motto of the Earl Grey.

Débris.

Fragments remaining ; ruins.

Début.

The first appearance.

Débutant.

One who makes a début.

Décoiffer St. Pierre pour coiffer St. Paul.

Rob Peter to pay Paul.

De court plaisir, long repentir.

Short pleasure, long lament.

De deux maux il faut choisir le moindre.

Of two evils one should choose the least.

De deux regardeurs il y en a toujours un qui devient joueur.

Of two lookers-on one is sure to take a hand in the game.

De femme folle ne fit
Jamais homme son profit.

(From a silly wife no man ever gained anything.) A man must ask a wife's leave to thrive.

Défiez-vous des belles paroles des gens qui se vantent d'être vertueux. Jugez-en par leurs actions, et non pas par leurs discours.—*Fénelon.*

Beware the fair speech of those who boast of being virtuous. Judge them by their actions, not their words.

De fol juge brève sentence.

(A foolish judge passes a hasty sentence.) A fool's bolt is soon shot.

De forte coûture forte déchirure.

The stronger the seam the worse the tear.

Dégagé.

Free ; untrammelled.

De gaieté de cœur.

From lightness of heart.

De grande montée, grande chute.

The higher the climb the farther it is to fall.

De haute lutte.

By a violent struggle.

De haut en bas.

(From top to bottom.) In a haughty, supercilious manner.

Dehors.

Outside.

De la Fortune on vante les appas ;
  Méfions-nous de la traîtresse ;
Non-seulement la dame n'y voit pas,
  Mais elle aveugle encor tous ceux
    qu'elle caresse.—*Albéric Deville.*

Some say that Fortune's ways are kind ;
  Still she's a traitress ; shun her wiles !
Not only is the goddess blind,
  But blinds the men on whom she smiles.

De la main à la bouche se perd souvent la soupe.

There's many a slip 'twixt the cup and the lip.

De l'audace, encore de l'audace, toujours de l'audace.—*Danton.*

Boldness, and again boldness, and always boldness.*

De l'eau bénite de cour.

Shallow promises.

De loin, c'est quelque chose, et de près, ce n'est rien.—*La Fontaine.*

(From afar it is something, but nothing when close at hand.) Distance lends enchantment to the view.

De mal en pis.

From bad to worse.

Demander de la laine à un âne.

To look for wool on an ass.

---

* This saying, which has become proverbial, was the keynote of the success that attended the French armies in their conflicts with the many external foes of the young Republic.

Demi-monde.

(The half-world.) People of easy virtue.

Demi-solde.

Half-pay.

Demodé.

Out of fashion ; behind the times.

Dénoûment.

The end of a plot.

De oui et non vient toute question.

All disputes arise out of Yes and No.

De par le roi.

By authority.

De par le roi défense à Dieu
De faire des miracles en ce lieu.

'Tis forbidden to God, by Royal command,
To perform any miracles on this land.*

Dépends le pendard et il te pendra.

Save a rogue from the rope, and he will hang you with it.

De petit vient-on au grand.

(From little we come to great.) Many littles make a mickle. We must creep before we walk.

De peu de drap courte cape.

Of little cloth you can only make a short cloak.

De pied en cap.

From head to foot.

Dernier cri.

(The latest cry.) The latest fashionable fad.

Dernier ressort.

A last resource.

Dés du juge de Rabelais.

The dice of Rabelais' judge.†

Déshabillé.

Undressed.

Désir de Dieu et désir de l'homme sont deux.

God's will and man's will are two different things.

Des preuves à l'appui.

Proofs in corroboration.

Dès que les femmes sont à nous, nous ne sommes plus à elles.—*Montaigne.*

As soon as women yield to our domination, we are no longer their slaves.

Des taupes dans chez nous, et des lynx chez autrui.—*Esternod.*

We are moles at home and lynxes abroad.

Détour.

A circuitous march.

De tout ce que nous possédons les femmes sont seules qui prennent plaisir d'être possédées.—*Malherbe.*

Of all our possessions, our wives are the only ones that are glad to own us as their masters.

De toutes les démoralisations la plus grande est celle qui est renfermée dans le respect accordé aux richesses.
        —*S. Guinand d'Epery.*

The greatest demoralisation lies in the respect shown for mere riches.

De toutes les ruines du monde, la ruine de l'homme est assurément la plus triste à contempler.—*Th. Gautier.*

Of all the ruins the world can show, that of a man is surely the saddest to contemplate.

De toute taille bon chien.

There are good dogs of all sizes.

---

* When Louis XV. ordered the cemetery of St. Médard to be closed, because the Jansenists were gaining power on the strength of the miracles reported to be performed there, an unknown person wrote this couplet on the gates.
† This familiar phrase refers to the anecdote in which Rabelais satirises the way that justice was administered in his time. Bridoie is a worthy judge, who, fearing to trust his own decisions, settles all cases brought before him by the aid of a dice-box. This plan works admirably, although the litigants are ignorant of the secret. But there comes a day when one of Bridoie's sentences is disputed. He is horrified, but at last finds that it is he, not the dice, that is to blame. According to the importance of the case, he was wont to use big or little dice, and on this occasion he had used the wrong set.

De tout s'avise à qui pain faut.

A man who wants bread is willing to do anything.

De tout temps les petits ont pâti des sottises des grands.—*La Fontaine.*

In every age the petty have paid for the follies of the great.

De trop.

(Too much.) In the way; one too many; something too much.

Deux chiens ne s'accordent point à un os.

(Two dogs never agree about one bone.) Two of a trade seldom agree.

Deux hommes se rencontrent bien, mais jamais deux montagnes.

Two men may meet, but two mountains never greet.

Deux têtes sous le même bonnet.

(Two heads under the same cap.) Two of the same opinion; "Two souls with but a single thought."

Deux yeux voient plus clair qu'un.

(Two eyes see more clearly than one.) Two heads are better than one.

Devant si je puis.

(Foremost if I can.) Motto of the Mainwaring family and others.*

Devenir amoureux n'est pas le difficile, c'est de savoir dire qu'on l'est.
—*Alfred de Musset.*

It is not hard to catch the infection of love, but it is hard to diagnose the complaint.

Devenir d'évêque meunier.

(To become a miller after being a bishop.) To come down in the world.

De vive voix.

Orally: by word of mouth; *vivâ voce.*

Devoir.

Duty.

Dieu aide à trois sortes de personnes: aux fous, aux enfants, et aux ivrognes.

There is a special providence for the mad, the young, and drunkards.

Dieu avec nous.

(God with us.) Motto of Earl Berkeley.

Dieu défend le droit.

God defends the right.

Dieu donne le froid selon le drap.

(God sends the cold according to the cloth.) He tempers the wind to the shorn lamb.

Dieu est le poëte, les hommes ne sont que les acteurs. Ces grandes pièces qui se jouent sur la terre ont été composées dans le ciel.
—*Jean Louis Balzac.*

God is the playwright and men His actors. The great dramas played upon earth were composed in Heaven.

Dieu et mon droit.

God and my right.†

Dieu le veuille.

God grant it.

Dieu n'a créé les femmes que pour apprivoiser les hommes.—*Voltaire.*

God created women to mollify men.

Dieu n'a pas donné aux grands hommes le génie comme un parfum léger qui s'évapore dès qu'on secoue le flacon qui le contient, mais comme un viatique généreux qui soutient l'homme pendant un long voyage.
—*Saint Marc Girardin.*

Heaven does not give great men genius as a volatile perfume which flies when the vase is shaken, but as a bountiful viaticum which sustains man on a long journey.

* Ranulph de Mesnilwaren, who accompanied William the Conqueror, was one of the first of the Normans to leap upon the English shore. These words were uttered by him as he did so, and they have been adopted as the motto of his descendants.
† The motto of the English sovereigns. The words were the countersign chosen by Richard I. before the battle of Gisors, 1198, where he defeated the French.

Dieu pour la Tranchée, qui contre ?

(If God be for the Trenches, who shall be against them ?) Motto of Earl Clancarty.

Dieu sait qui est bon pélerin.

God knows who is the true worshipper.

Dieu vous garde.

God keep you.

Diligence passe science.

(Diligence is better than knowledge.) Diligence is the mother of good fortune.

Dîners à la carte.

Dinners according to the bill of fare.

Diseur de bons mots.

A joker.

Diseur de bons mots, mauvais caractère.—*Pascal.*

The sayer of " good things " has a bad disposition.

Dis-moi ce que tu manges, je te dirai ce que tu es.—*Brillat Savarin.*

Tell me what you eat, and I will tell you what manner of man you are.

Dis-moi qui tu hantes, et je te dirai qui tu es.

Tell me with whom you consort, and I will tell you who you are.

Distingué.

Of aristocratic appearance.

Distrait.

Absent-minded.

Dites du bien des bonnes choses : on trouve toujours assez de gens pour louer les mauvaises.
                    —*Charles Narrey.*

Speak well of the good—there will always be enough to praise things evil.

Dites-moi, s'il vous plaît.

Tell me, if you please.

Dites-vous cela pour rire ou pour le bon ?

Do you say that in earnest or in jest ?

Dit qu'il a pour les vers le secret de Racine :
Jamais secret ne fut, à coup sûr, mieux gardé !—*L'Abbé Arnaud.*

He boasts that he possesses the secret of Racine's poetic skill ; if so, no secret has been better kept.

Divertissement.

Entertainment.

Dix lignes d'un orateur ou d'un écrivain vraiment philosophe le soutiendront sur le courant des âges ; elles placeront leur auteur au nombre de ces grands esprits qui représentent non un temps, non un peuple, mais l'humanité même. Il sera l'égal de ceux qui ont si peu d'égaux.
                    —*S. de Sacy.*

Ten lines of a really philosophic writer or orator will uphold him on the stream of time ; they will raise their author among the great souls representing not an age, not a people, but humanity itself. He will be the equal of those who have so few equals.

Doctrinaire.

A theorist.

Donner dans le piège.

To fall into the trap.

Donner prise sur soi.

To lay one's self open.

Donner tête baissée.

Headstrong ; to go farther and fare worse.

Donner un œuf pour avoir un bœuf.

(To give an egg to have an ox.) A sprat to catch a herring.

Donnez-moi l'enseignement pendant un siècle, et je serai maître de l'état.
                    —*Napoleon I.*

Let me teach for a generation, and I will become ruler of the state.

Dorer la pilule.

(To gild the pill.)   To refuse a request in so polite a manner as to spare the feelings of the asker.

Dos à dos.

Back to back.

Dossier.	(A packet of papers.) The official record of a person's behaviour.*
Double entente.	(A double meaning.) Words used to convey an obvious and a second meaning at the same time.
Douce parole n'écorche pas langue.	Soft words don't scotch the tongue.
Douceur.	Sweetness; a gift.
Doux yeux.	Soft glances; ogling.
Dragonnades.	(Dragoonings.) Persuasion by force.
Droit d'aubaine.	The right of confiscation.†
Droit des gens.	The law of nations; international law.
Droit et avant.	(Just and forward.) Motto of Viscount Sydney.
Droit et loyal.	(Just and loyal.) Motto of Dudley, Earl of Leicester.
Drôle.	Droll; funny.
Drôle de corps.	A droll fellow; a punster.
Du choc des esprits jaillissent les étincelles.	When great wits meet, then sparks do fly.
Du côté de la barbe est la toute-puissance.—*Molière.*	All the power is with the sex that wears the beard.
Du cuir d'un vieux mari on en achète un jeune.	With an old husband's goods one buys a young one.
Du dire au fait il y a grand trait.	Between the word and the deed is a long way to go.
Du fort au faible.	(From the strong to the weak.) One with another.
D'un dévot souvent au chrétien véritable La distance est deux fois plus longue, à mon avis, Que du pôle antarctique au détroit de Davis.—*Boileau.*	From the truly devout to the devotee I rate the distance greater than from the Antarctic Pole to Davis Straits.
D'une mouche il fait un éléphant.	(He makes an elephant out of a mouse.) He makes mountains of mole-hills.
D'une pierre faire deux coups.	To kill two birds with one stone.
D'une vache perdue c'est quelque chose de recouvrer la queue.	When a cow is lost it is something to recover its tail.
D'un sac à charbon ne saurait sortir de blanche farine.	Fair words cannot come out of a foul mouth.
Du poisson le chat très bien mangerait, Mais des pattes ne baignerait.	(The cat would fain eat fish, but will not wet his feet to catch them.) Nothing venture, nothing have.
Du sublime au ridicule il n'y a qu'un pas.—*Napoleon I.*	From the sublime to the ridiculous is only a step.‡

* This term has become familiar owing to the frequent use of it in the Affaire Dreyfus. It signifies all the documents that have a bearing on the case. Generally speaking, a *dossier* means the record of anybody to whom an official license has been given, as, for example, to the *femmes inscrites*

† An old law that endured until the last century, whereby the personal property of a foreigner, dying in France, fell into the hands of the king.

‡ These familiar words were often used by Napoleon in reference to the utter failure of his invasion of Russia in 1812. The same sentiment is expressed by Longinus in *On the Sublime.* See Ἐκ τοῦ φοβεροῦ, *et seq.*

Echappé belle. — A narrow escape.

Echelon. — (An army in form like the steps of a staircase.) Marching in detached groups.

Eclaircissement. — A clear explanation.

Eclat. — Splendour ; brilliancy.

Eclat de rire. — A burst of laughter ; a guffaw.

Ecole militaire. — A military school.

Ecorcher l'anguille par la queue. — (To begin to skin the eel at the tail.) To begin at the wrong end.

Ecorcher les oreilles. — To jar upon the nerves.

Ecrasez l'infâme ! — (Crush the infamous !) Down with the discredited system.*

Egalité. — Equality.

Elan. — Vigour ; impetuosity.

Elève. — A pupil.

Elève le corbeau, il te crèvera les yeux. — Warm a viper in your bosom and he will sting you.

Elite. — The best society.

Elle a fait des siennes. — That's an old trick of hers.

Elle a jeté son bonnet par-dessus les moulins. — (She has thrown her cap over the mill.) She has thrown propriety to the winds.

Elle a les yeux à fleur de tête. — She has staring eyes.

Elle a très bonne mine. — She looks very well.

Elle est continuellement dans le monde. — She goes out a great deal into society.

Elle est douée de beaucoup de sang-froid. — She is endowed with great self-possession.

Elle est en butte aux médisances des autres. — She is exposed to scandal.

Elle l'a achevé tant bien que mal. — She finished it as best she could.

Elle l'a fait par mégarde. — She did not do it on purpose.

Elle m'a compris à demi-mot. — A hint was sufficient for her.

Elle m'a pris à partie. — She took me to task.

Elle mène son mari à la lisière. — (She has her husband in leading-strings.) She leads him by the nose.

Elle ne laisse pas de le flatter. — She continually flatters him.

Elle n'est pas l'époque de la grande épée.—*Chateaubriand.* — (It is no longer the era of the powerful sword.) The days of chivalry are gone.

Elle ne veut pas coiffer Sainte Catherine. — She does not want to be an old maid.†

Elle paie de mine. — She has a good appearance.

Elle prend tout pour argent comptant. — She believes anything.

Elles se ressemblaient comme deux gouttes d'eau. — They were as like as two peas in a pod.

* The watchword of Voltaire, Diderot, and their companions, who prepared the way for the Great Revolution, 1792.

† St. Catherine, the virgin martyr, is the patroness of unmarried women. Hence those who have reached an age when it is improbable that they will marry, are said to have " put a head-dress on St. Catherine," *i.e.*, to make an offering to her as their patron saint.

Elle trouvera à qui parler. — She will find her match.

Elle voit tout en noir. — She looks on the black side.

Elle voulait me tenir tête. — She wanted to oppose me.

Eloge. — Eulogium.

Eloignement. — Estrangement.

Embarras de richesse. — (Embarrassment of riches.) Encumbrance of wealth.*

Embonpoint. — Stoutness of body.

Embouchure. — The mouth of a river.

Emeute. — Insurrection ; riot.

Eminemment. — Eminently ; so as to be the very ideal.

Employé. — A person employed by another.

Empressement. — Eagerness ; earnestness.

En ami. — As a friend.

En amour, aujourd'hui vaut mieux que demain ; le bonheur que l'on diffère est toujours du bonheur perdu. —*A. Ricard.* — In love, to-day is better than to-morrow ; happiness deferred is always lost.

En amour, ceux qui feignent d'être amoureux réussissent beaucoup mieux que ceux qui le sont véritablement. —*Ninon de Lenclos.* — In love-making, feigning lovers succeed much better than the really devoted.

En amour, comme en toutes choses, l'expérience est un médecin qui n'arrive qu'après la maladie. —*Mme. de la Tour.* — In love, as in all other matters, experience is a doctor who comes too late.

En amour il est vrai que le *moi* domine. Mais aussi en amour le *moi* se dédouble ; par conséquent il se détruit. —*Ph. Chasles.* — The *Ego* indeed predominates in love-making, but as both sides use it, one annuls the other.

En amour, les vieux fous sont plus fous que les jeunes.—*La Rochefoucauld.* — In love, old fools are worse fools than young fools.

En amour, pour être téméraire avec succès, il faut l'être à propos. —*Ninon de Lenclos.* — In love, to be bold and successful, you must be bold at the right moment.

En amour, quand deux yeux se rencontrent ils se tutoient.—*Alphonse Karr.* — In love-making, no sooner do eyes meet than they are on intimate terms.

En amour querelle vaut mieux qu'éloge. —*Marivaux.* — Lovers' quarrels help love on more than eulogy.

En attendant. — In the meantime.

En avant ! — Forward ! advance.

En avez-vous à lui ? — Are you angry with him ?

En bloc. — In the lump.

En bon train. — In a fair way ; on the road to success.

En connaissance de cause. — With full knowledge of the subject.

En dernier ressort. — As a last expedient.

En Dieu est ma fiance. — In God do I trust.

En Dieu est mon espérance. — (In God is my hope.) Motto of the Gerard family.

* These words were used as the title of a play, written by the Abbé d'Allainval in 1753.

Q

Endurer la soif auprès d'une fontaine.

(To put up with thirst near a fountain.) Why starve in a cook-shop ?

En effet.

In effect ; just so.

En fait de prêt, le sort me traite
Avec grande inhumanité :
Je perds l'affection de ceux à qui je prête,
Si je ne perds l'argent que je leur ai prêté.—*De Cailly.*

Whenever I lend, Fate treats me most unkindly ; I lose either the friendship of the man to whom I have lent, or else the money that I have lent him.

En famille.

(As among one's family.)   Unceremoniously.

Enfant gâté

A spoiled child.

Enfants et fols sont devins.

Children and fools are true prophets.

Enfants perdus.

(Lost children.)   A forlorn hope.

Enfant terrible.

(A terrible child.)   One that is apt to do or say something exceedingly ill-timed and embarrassing.

Enfant trouvé.

A foundling.

Enfermer le loup dans la bergerie.

To shut up the wolf in the sheepfold.

Enfin.

At last ; finally.

Enfin, je m'en lave les mains.

Well, I shall wash my hands of it.

Enfin les renards se trouvent chez le pelletier.

(At last the fox comes to the skinner.) Thieves come to the gallows at last.

Enfin Malherbe vint.—*Boileau.*

And then Malherbe came.*

Enfin, vous n'êtes jamais de trop.

Anyhow, you are never in the way.

En flûte.

Armed with guns only on the upper deck.

En forgeant on devient forgeron.

Working in the smithy makes the smith.

En foule.

In a crowd.

En grande tenue.

In full dress.

En grande toilette.

Full-dressed ; in full fig.

En grand fardeau n'est pas l'acquêt.

Large stocks are not the most profitable.

En habiles gens.

Like able men.

En la maison du ménétrier chacun est danseur.

In the fiddler's house all are dancers.

En la rose je fleurie.

(I flourish in the rose.)   Motto of the Duke of Richmond.

En masse.

In a body.

En me voyant il m'a battu froid.

As soon as he saw me he gave me the cold shoulder.

Ennemi ne s'endort.

An enemy never sleeps.

Ennui.

Weariness ; spleen.

En passant.

In passing.

En peinture, l'étude patiente et consciencieuse de la nature, il n'y a que cela !—*Bastien Lepage.*

The patient and conscientious study of Nature is, in painting, the all in all.

---

* These words occur in *l'Art Poétique.* Boileau describes the uncouth style of early French poetry, "and then Malherbe came," who put the art of writing poetry on a proper basis. Hence the words are commonly applied to any person who comes as a *deus ex machinâ* to bring order to what was before a chaos.

En petit champ croît bien bon blé.

Large ears of corn may grow in little fields.

En petites boîtes met-on les bons onguents.

Good things are done up in small parcels.

En plein jour.

In broad daylight.

En rapport.

In touch ; well-versed in a subject.

En règle.

According to rule.

En revanche.

In return ; in retaliation.

En route.

On the way.

Ensemble.

Together ; the general effect.

En suivant la vérité.

In following the truth.

En sûreté dort qui n'a que perdre.

He sleeps sound who has nothing to lose.

Entente cordiale.

Friendly feeling ; complete understanding.

En toutes compagnies il y a plus de fous que de sages, et la plus grande partie surmonte toujours la meilleure.
　　　　　　　　—*Rabelais*.

In all gatherings of men there are more dolts than wise-heads, and the majority always overrules the wise minority

Entr'acte.

Between the acts.

Entre bouche et cuillier
Vient souvent grand encombrier.

There is many a slip
'Twixt the cup and the lip.

Entre chien et loup.

(Between dog and wolf.) The time of day when it is impossible to distinguish a dog from a wolf; twilight.

Entre deux feux.

Between two fires.

Entre deux selles le cul à terre.

Between two stools one falls to the ground.

Entre deux vins.

Half drunk.

Entrée.

Freedom of access ; a course of dishes.

Entre gens de même nature
L'amitié se fait et dure.

Between folk of like nature friendships grow and will endure.

Entre la poire et le fromage.

(Between the pear and the cheese.) Over the walnuts and wine.

Entre le marteau et l'enclume.

Between hammer and anvil ; between the devil and the deep sea.

Entre le ministre qui gouverne l'Etat et l'artisan qui contribue à sa prospérité par le travail de ses mains, il n'y a qu'une différence, c'est que la fonction de l'un est plus importante que celle de l'autre ; mais, à les bien remplir, le mérite moral est le même.
　　　　　　　　—*Jouffroy*.

Between the Prime Minister and the workman who contributes to the prosperity of the state by his manual toil, there is but one difference : the former's function is more important than the other's, but the moral value of the right fulfilment of these functions is the same.

Entre les deux alternatives : Ou pas de maître ou un mauvais maître, le choix pour un homme sensé ne saurait être douteux : il répondra : " Pas de maître."—*Jules Simon*.

Between the alternatives of no teacher or a bad one, the sensible man does not hesitate : he replies at once "No teacher."

Entremets.

Dainty side dishes.

Entre nos ennemis les plus à craindre sont souvent les plus petits.
—*La Fontaine.*

The enemies most to be dreaded are often the paltriest.

Entre nous.

Between ourselves; in confidence.

Entrepôt.

A warehouse.

Entrepreneur.

A contractor; the chief director of an undertaking.

Entre promettre et donner doit-on marier sa fille.

Between promises and gifts a man should get his daughter wed.

En un clin d'œil.

In the twinkling of an eye.

En vérité.

In truth.

En vieillissant on devient plus fou et plus sage.—*La Rochefoucauld.*

(As we grow old we become more foolish and more wise.) Our good and bad qualities are intensified by age.

Envie passe avarice.

Envy is stronger than avarice.

Envoyez-le promener.

Pack him off.

En y arrivant il a trouvé visage de bois.

When he got there he found the door shut.

Epergne.

An ornamental stand for the centre of a table.

Erreur n'est pas compte.

A mistake is no reckoning.

Espérance en Dieu.

(Hope in God.) Motto of the Duke of Northumberland and others.

Espionnage.

System of spies.

Esprit de corps.

Corporate feeling.

Esquisse.

A sketch.

Est assez riche qui ne doit rien.

Out of debt is riches enough.

Estrade.

A raised stand.

Etat d'âme.

State of feeling.

Etat-major.

A number of officers forming the general's council.

Et la garde qui veille aux barrières du Louvre
N'en défend pas nos rois.—*Malherbe.*

The soldiers who stand on guard at the gates of the Louvre cannot defend our kings from death.

Et l'avare Achéron ne lâche point sa proie.—*Racine.*

But greedy Acheron ne'er lets go his prey.

Et le combat cessa faute de combattants.—*Corneille.*

And the combat ceased through lack of combatants.

Etouderie.

Giddiness; imprudence.

Etre au bout de son rôle (*or* rouleau)

To be at one's wits' end.

Etre aux abois.

To be in great distress; at the last gasp.

Etre bête est une qualité de plus en plus rare. Autrefois on était bête, aujourd'hui on n'est que sot.
—*A. Houssaye.*

Stupidity is a quality that is becoming more rare every day. Formerly we called people stupid, to-day we call them fools.

Etre comme l'oiseau sur la branche.

(To be like the bird on the bough.) A rolling stone gathers no moss.

Etre confit dans la dévotion.

To be hypocritically devout; unco guid.

Etre cousu d'or.

(To be embroidered with gold.) Rich beyond the dreams of avarice.

Etre dans le mouvement

(To be in the movement.)   To be in the swim ; abreast with the times ; up-to-date.

Etre de rop.

To be one too many; an unwelcome visitor.

Etre discrète et femme tout ensemble,
Ce sont deux points que jamais on n'assemble ;
Et la moins femme, en ce sexe indiscret,
Garderait mieux son honneur qu'un secret.—*La Chaussée.*

Discretion and woman are two things which never go together ; so indiscreet is the sex, that the weakest woman can guard her honour better than a secret.

Etre en goguettes.

To be in one's cups ; to be slightly intoxicated.*

Etre gris.

To be slightly drunk ; half-seas over.

Etre pauvre sans être libre, c'est le pire état où l'homme puisse tomber.
—*J.-J. Rousseau.*

To be poor without being free is the direst condition into which a man can fall.

Etre sans gêne.

To be free and easy.

Etre sur des charbons ardents.

(To stand on hot coals.)   To be in a great flutter of excitement.

Etre sur la sellette.

(To be on the judgment-stool.)   To be on one's trial; to be in a painful position.

Etre toujours par monts et par vaux.

To be always on the move.

Etre un sot fieffé.

To be a complete fool.

Et rose, elle a vécu ce que vivent les roses,
L'espace d'un matin.—*Malherbe.*

A rose herself, she lived no longer than the roses—the space of a morning.†

Etui.

A case for instruments.

Et voilà justement comme on écrit l'histoire.—*Voltaire.*

And that is the way that history is written.

Evêque d'or, crosse de bois ; crosse d'or, évêque de bois.

For a golden-hearted bishop, wooden crozier; for a wooden-headed bishop, golden crozier.

Exigeant.

Troublesome.

Exposé.

An exposition ; a concise statement ; a revelation.

Façade.

Front of a building.

Facilité de parler :
C'est impuissance de se taire.
—*J.-B. Rousseau.*

Readiness of speech is often inability to hold the tongue.

Façon de parler.

Manner of speaking.

Faire bonne mine.

To put a good face on a thing.

Faire bonne mine à mauvais jeu.

(When you are losing, wear a winning face.)   To put a good face on a bad business.

---

* Goguette was the name given to those popular societies which assembled in taverns for the purpose of holding a free-and-easy singing entertainment.   These singing clubs were very common in Paris in the middle of the present century.

† Lines written on the death of a young girl.   It is said that Malherbe wrote *Et Rosette a vécu*, which was altered to *Et rose, elle*, through an admirable blunder on the part of the printer

Faire claquer son fouet.	(To crack his own whip.) To take merit to oneself.
Faire comme le singe, tirer les marrons du feu avec la patte du chat.	Like the monkey, to get the chestnuts out of the fire with the cat's paw.
Faire contre fortune bon cœur.	To put a good face on the matter.
Faire de la prose sans le savoir. —*Molière.*	(To speak prose without knowing it.) To be clever unconsciously.*
Faire de l'esprit.	To show off one's wit.
Faire des contes à dormir debout.	(To tell stories while asleep standing.) To tell old women's tales.
Faire des économies de bouts de chandelle.	To be penny wise and pound foolish.
Faire du cuir d'autrui large courroie.	A man cuts broad thongs from another man's leather.
Faire d'une mouche un éléphant.	(To make an elephant of a fly.) To make a mountain of a molehill.
Faire d'une pierre deux coups.	To kill two birds with one stone.
Faire jouer une mine.	To spring a mine.
Faire la culbute.	(To be overthrown.) To lose one's fortune or reputation.
Faire la mouche du coche.	(To play the part of the fly and the coach.) To take the credit for what someone else has done.†
Faire la noce.	To revel in luxury ; to enjoy a merry time.
Faire la rodomont.	To act the braggart.‡
Faire la sourde oreille.	To turn a deaf ear.
Faire l'école buissonnière.	To play the truant.
Faire le diable à quatre.	To thunder at the top of one's voice ; to fume and fret.
Faire le pied de grue.	(To stand on one leg like a crane.) To dance attendance on another.
Faire mon devoir.	(To do my duty.) Motto of Earl Roden.
Faire patte de velours.	(To show a velvet paw.) To sham Abraham ; to caress treacherously.
Faire ripaille ; faire bombance.	To fare sumptuously.
Faire sans dire.	To act unostentatiously.
Faire ses choux gras.	(To make one's cabbages fat.) To bask in the sunshine.
Faire triste figure.	To have a sad expression ; to pull a long face.
Faire un coq-à-l'âne.	To tell a long, incoherent tale.§

* The remark of the Bourgeois Gentilhomme, who found, to his astonishment, that he had been talking in prose all his life.
† This expression is based on La Fontaine's fable of *Le Coche et la Mouche*, where the tale is narrated of the fly who buzzed around the horses' ears, and thought that made them go more quickly.
‡ See note in Italian section on *Rodomontata.*
§ The same phrase is applied to a person who changes the subject by asking some inane question such as *As-tu vu la lune ?* "Have you seen the moon ?"

Faire une trouée. | To convince others of the truth of a statement, concerning which they have been sceptical; to establish a theory.

Faire un impair. | To make a blunder in conversation; to say something which might have been expressed differently.

Faire un trou à la lune. | To be unable to meet one's pecuniar liabilities; to become bankrupt.

Faire un trou pour en boucher un autre. | To make one hole to stop another.

Faire venir l'eau à la bouche. | To make one's mouth water.

Faire venir l'eau au moulin. | To bring grist to the mill.

Faire voile à tout vent. | To set up his sail to every wind.

Fais ce que dois, advienne que pourra. | Do your duty, come what may.

Fais-moi la barbe et je te ferai le toupet. | Scratch my back and I will scratch yours.

Faisons généreusement, et sans compter, tout le bien qui tente nos cœurs; on ne peut être dupe d'aucune vertu. —*Vauvenargues.* | Do all the good your heart suggests generously and without calculation; no virtue ever deceives.

Fait accompli. | A thing accomplished; an accomplished fact.

Faites des perruques. | Stick to your wigs.*

Faites taire ces sans-culottes. —*Abbé Maury.* | Silence these sans-culottes.†

Faites votre devoir et laissez faire aux dieux.—*Scudéri.* | Do your duty and leave the rest to God.

Fascine; fagot. | A fagot.

Faubourg. | An outskirt of a town; a suburb.

Faut d'la vertu, pas trop n'en faut, L'excès en tout est un défaut.—*Monvel.* | Virtue is necessary, but not too much of it. Excess in everything is a defect.

Faute de mieux il se contente de pain. | For want of something better he put up with bread.

Fauteuil. | An arm-chair.

Faux pas. | A false step; a mistake.

Femme, argent, et vin, ont leur bien et leur venin. | In women, money, and wine, lurks both profit and poison.

Femme bonne est oiseau de cage. | A good wife is always a home-bird.

Femme (*sole*) célibataire; vieille fille. | A spinster; an unmarried woman.

Femme de chambre. | Chambermaid.

Femme et melon à peine les connaît-on. | A woman and a melon are hard to select.

Femme (*couverte*) mariée. | A married woman.

Femme qui beaucoup se mire peu file. | The more women look in the mirror the less they look to their house.

---

* The reply of Voltaire to a hairdresser, who, having written a tragedy, dedicated it "to his dear confrère Voltaire."

† Maury took a prominent part as a supporter of the Royalist side during the early days of the Revolution. In one of his speeches in the Assembly he was interrupted by the shouts of the *sans-culottes* thronging in the gallery of the House, and uttered this exclamation. The *sans-culottes*, the rabble of the Revolution, were so-called because they had ceased to wear the tight breeches (culottes), but were garbed in loose trousers.

Femme qui va de place en place, parle de tous, et tous d'elle.

A woman who gads from place to place, gossips about all folk, and all folk about her.

Femme rit quand elle peut, et pleure quand elle veut.

Women laugh when they can and weep when they will.

Femme sotte se cognoit à la cotte.

You may know a foolish woman by her finery.

Ferme modèle (*ornée*).

A model farm.

Fête.

A festival.

Fête champêtre.

An open-air entertainment; a rural merry-making.

Feu de joie.

A firing of guns in token of joy; a bonfire.

Feuilleton.

(A small leaf or fly sheet.) The name given to the novels appearing in French newspapers.

Feu, toux, amour, et argent, Ne se cachent longuement.

Fire, a cough, love, and gold, cannot long be hid.

Fidélité est de Dieu.

(Fidelity is of God.) Motto of Viscount Powerscourt.

Fi de manteau quand il fait beau.

A waterproof is a clog on a sunny day.

Fi du plaisir que la crainte peut corrompre.—*La Fontaine*.

Out on the pleasure which fear can spoil!

Fier comme Artaban.

(Proud as Artabanes.) As proud as Lucifer.*

Fille de chambre.

A chambermaid; a lady's maid.

Fille de joie.

A wench of easy virtue.

Fille d'honneur

A lady of honour.

Fille oisive, à mal pensive.

An idle girl is hatching mischief.

Fille trop vue, et robe trop vêtue, n'est chère tenue.

A maid often seen, and a dress often worn, are never valued.

Fils aînés de l'antiquité, les Français Romains par le génie, sont Grecs par le caractère.—*Chateaubriand*.

The French are the eldest sons of antiquity; they have the intelligence of the Romans, and the disposition of the Greeks.

Fils de Saint Louis, montez au ciel.

Son of St. Louis, ascend to heaven.†

Fin contre fin.

Set cunning against cunning; diamond cut diamond.

Fin contre fin n'est pas bon pour faire doublure.

Fine against fine makes but a thin coat.

Fin de siècle.

(End of century.) Extremely modern; up-to-date.

Flâneur.

A lounger.

Fleur de lis.

(Blossom of the lily.) The arms of the French monarchy.

---

* Artabanes was the name of many of the old Persian kings. The saying originated from the romance *Cléopâtre* of La Calprenède.

† The Abbé Edgeworth is said to have spoken these words to Louis XVI. when the king was about to be guillotined. The Abbé, however, declared afterwards that he had no recollection of saying anything of the kind, and his emotion at the time was so great that the incident is very improbable.

Flux de bouche ; flux de paroles. — A flow of words ; garrulity.

Flux de mots. — To spin a long yarn.

Foi est tout. — (Faith is everything.) Faith works wonders.

Folle est la brebis qui au loup se confesse. — A silly sheep indeed is that which makes the wolf her confessor.

Folles amours font les gens bêtes. — Passionate love makes fools of men.
    —*Villon.*

Fondre en larmes. — To cry one's eyes out.

Force majeure. — (Superior force.) The right of the stronger.

Force n'a pas droit. — Might does not make right.

Fortune de la guerre. — The fortune of war.

Fortune du pot. — Pot-luck.

Fou qui se tait passe pour sage. — Silence makes the fool seem wise.

Foy pour devoir. — (Faith for duty.) Motto of the Duke of Somerset.

Fracas. — A disturbance ; a noisy quarrel.

Fraternité ou la mort. — Fraternity or death.*

Froides mains, chaud amour. — A cold hand and warm heart.

Frondeur. — A declaimer against the existing administration.

Fumée, pluie, et femme sans raison, chassent l'homme de sa maison. — Smoke, floods, and a senseless spouse, drive a man out of his house.

Gabelle. — The salt tax.

Gage d'amour. — A love pledge.

Gageure est la preuve des sots. — A wager is a fool's argument.

Gaieté de cœur. — Flow of spirits ; liveliness.

Galoper ventre-à-terre. — To ride furiously.

Gamin. — A street arab.

Garçon. — A youth ; a waiter ; a bachelor.

Garde à vous ! — (Attention !) Word of command.

Garde du corps. — Life-guardsman ; a body-guard.

Garde le roy. — Defend the King.†

Garde mobile. — The French militia.

Garder une poire pour la soif. — (To keep a pear until one is thirsty.) To save up for a rainy day.

Garde ta foi. — Keep thy faith.

Gardez bien. — Take care.

Gardez la foi. — Keep faith.

Gardez-vous bien de confondre le nom sacré de l'honneur avec ce préjugé féroce qui met toutes les vertus à la pointe d'une épée, et n'est propre qu'à faire de braves scélérats. — Beware of confounding the sacred name of honour with that savage idea which sets all the virtues at the point of a duellist's sword. Such a notion is suitable to none but bold cut-throats.
    —*J.-J. Rousseau.*

* The declared policy of the instigators of the Great Revolution.
† Colonel John Lane, who, with his father, brother, and sister, concealed Charles II. when he was fleeing after the battle of Worcester, took these words as the motto of his family.

Gare !	Look out !
Gare à lui, c'est un mauvais plaisant.	Take care, he likes practical jokes.
Gasconnade.	Boasting, bragging.
Gâteau et mauvaise coutume se doivent rompre.	Piecrust and a bad custom are made to be broken.
Gâter une chandelle pour trouver une épingle.	(To burn out a candle in search of a pin.) To throw good money after bad.
Gâte-sauce.	(A spoil-sauce.) A bad cook.
Gauche.	Clumsy; awkward.
Gaucherie.	Clumsiness; awkwardness.
Gavroche.	A street-arab.*
Gendarmerie.	The armed police force.
Gendarmes.	Men-at-arms; police.
Genre d'écrire.	Style of writing.†
Gens de condition.	People of rank.
Gens d'église.	Churchmen.
Gens de guerre.	Military men.
Gens de lettres.	Literary men.
Gens de même famille.	Birds of a feather.
Gens de peu.	Men of a low order; unimportant men.
Gentilhomme.	A gentleman.
Gibier de potence.	A gaol bird.
Glacis.	A slope; earthwork.
Glissez, mortels, n'appuyez pas.—*Roy.*	Glide on, mortals, press not hard.‡
Glissez sur ce sujet.	Pass that matter over.
Gobemouches.	Bumpkins.
Gommeux.	A fop ; man about town ; dude.
Gosse.	A babe ; child.§
Goût.	Taste.
Gourmand.	A glutton.
Goutte à goutte.	Drop by drop.
Goutte à goutte la mer s'égoutte.	Drop by drop the sea is drained.
Goutte à goutte la pierre se creuse.	Drop by drop wears away the stone.
Gracieux accueil vaut la chère la plus délicate.	Welcome is the best cheer.
Graisser le marteau.	To give the porter a tip.
Grand besoin a de fol qui de soi-même le fait.	He must have much need of a fool who makes one of himself.
Grand bien ne vient pas en peu d'heures.	A fortune is not made in a few hours.

---

* This name of one of the characters in Victor Hugo's *Les Misérables* is commonly used to signify the poor loafers of the streets of Paris.

† In painting, the term *genre* is applied to pictures which have as their subject some incident of ordinary life : all pictures, therefore, which do not represent landscape, sacred, mythological, or historical subjects, may be roughly classed as *genre*.

‡ Part of an inscription written below a painting of a skating scene. It is often quoted in the sense of a warning against undue curiosity.

§ This word belongs to the *argot* of the streets. Yvette Guilbert's pathetic song *Ma Gosse*, and M. Decourcelle's *Les Deux Gosses*—the "Two Little Vagabonds" of Mr. G. R. Sims—has made it familiar to many English people.

Grand bien vous fasse !

Much good may it do you .

Grand diseur n'est pas grand faiseur.

Great talkers are no great doers.

Grande chère petit testament.

(A fat kitchen has little to leave.)   A gourmand seldom amasses wealth.

Grande dispute vérité rebute.

Truth holds back from a quarrel.

Grande parure.

Full dress.

Grandes promesses et peu d'effets.

Great promises and little deeds ; great cry and little wool.

Grand et bon.

Great and good.

Grand parleur grand menteur.

A great talker, a great liar.

Grands oiseaux de coutume sont privés de leurs plumes.

It's the finest bird that is soonest plucked.

Grands vanteurs, petits faiseurs.

(Great boasters, little doers.)   Great boast, little roast.

Grasse panse, maigre cervelle.

A fat belly, a lean brain.

Grippe.

Influenza.

Grisette.

(A gray-gown.)   A young work-woman.

Grosse tête, peu de sens.

Great head and little sense.

Grossir un néant en montagne.

(To make mountains out of nothing.) Making mountains out of mole-hills.

Guerre à mort.

War till death.

Guerre à outrance.

War to the knife.

Guerre aux châteaux, paix aux chaumières.

War to the mansions, peace to the cottages.*

Guêt-à-pens.

Ambush.

Guinguette.

A rustic hostelry ; tea-garden ; country villa.†

Habillé comme un moulin à vent.

Dressed like a windmill ; dressed in vulgar fashion.

Habitué.

An habitual frequenter of a place.

Hardi gagneur, hardi mangeur.

Quick at meat, quick at work.

Hardiment heurte à la porte qui bonne nouvelle y apporte.

He knocks loudly who brings good news.

Haricot.

The kidney bean ; a kind of ragout.

Hauteur.

Haughtiness ; pride.

Haut goût.

High flavour.

Haut ton.

High tone ; elegance.

Hectare.

2·47 English acres of land.

Heureux au jeu, malheureux en amour.

Lucky in gambling, unlucky in love.

Heureux commencement est la moitié de l'œuvre.

Well begun is half done.

Heureux les peuples qui n'ont pas d'histoire.

Happy are the nations who have no history.

* The watchword of the Revolution of 1793.
† Guinguette is the name given to the tea-gardens outside the walls of Paris, whither the Parisian goes to spend a happy day.

Heureux qui n'alla pas après les richesses ! Plus heureux qui les refusa, quand elles allèrent à lui.—*Fléchier*.

Happy they who do not run after riches ! but happier they who reject them when they come to them !

Heureux qui peut vivre de ses rentes.

Happy is he who has a competency.

Homme chiche jamais riche.

A stingy man is never rich.

Homme d'épée.

A military man.

Homme de robe.

A gownsman.

Homme d'esprit.

A man of talent, or of wit.

Homme d'état.

A statesman.

Homme matineux, sain, allègre, et soigneux.

The early riser is healthy, cheerful, and industrious.

Honi soit qui mal y pense.

Evil to him who evil thinks.*

Honnête pauvreté est clair semée.

The honest poor are few and far between.

Honnêtes gens.

Honest people.

Honneur fleurit sur la fosse

Honour blossoms on the grave.

Hors de combat.

Disabled ; out of condition to fight.

Hors de cour.

(Out of court.) Non-suited in a trial.

Hors de propos.

(Out of place.) Not to the purpose.

Hospice d'allaitement.

A Foundling Hospital.

Hôtel des Invalides.

Hospital for old and disabled soldiers.†

Hôtel de ville.

A town hall.

Hôtel Dieu.

A house of God ; an hospital.

Hurler à la lune.

(To howl at the moon.) To utter vain threats against a powerful person.

Idée fixe.

A fixed idea.

Il a affaire à forte partie.

He has a rough customer to deal with.

Il a battu les buissons et un autre a pris les oisillons.

One beat the bushes and another caught the birds.

Il a beau parler on ne l'écoute pas.

He talks in vain, no one listens.

Il a beau se lever matin qui a le renom de dormir la grasse matinée.

If you have the name of a sluggard, it is no use rising betimes.

Il a beau se taire de l'écot qui ne paie rien.

He would do well to say nothing about the score who pays nothing.

Il a des moyens.

He's a clever fellow.

Il a donné sa parole.

He gave his word.

Il a épousé une bonne femme de ménage.

His wife is a good manager.

Il a éventé la mèche.

He got wind of it.

Il a fait main basse sur tout.

He pounced on everything.

Il a fallu battre en retraite.

They were obliged to retreat.

Il aime bien d'avoir les coudées franches.

He likes to be perfectly free.

Il a l'air de ne pas y toucher.

He looks as if butter would not melt in his mouth ; he shams innocence.

---

* The motto of the Order of the Garter. The story that Edward III. uttered the words when he picked up the garter of the Countess of Salisbury has very little evidence to support it.
† This famous institution was founded by Louis XIV. in 1669.

Il a la mer à boire.

(He has the sea to drink.)　He has an impossible task.

Il a le diable au corps.

The devil is in him.

Il a les yeux cernés.

He looks dark round the eyes.

Il a le vin mauvais.

He is quarrelsome in his cups.

Il a l'œil au guêt.

He is on the look out.

Il a mangé son blé en herbe.

He has eaten his corn in the ear.

Il a mangé son pain blanc le premier.

(He has eaten his white bread first.) His best days are passed.

Il a mis son bonnet de travers aujourd'hui.

He got out of bed the wrong side this morning.

Il a mis tous ses œufs dans un panier.

He has put all his eggs into one basket.

Il a montré beaucoup d'humeur.

He showed a good deal of temper.

Il a prêché d'abondance.

He preached extempore.

Il a pris mes paroles à contre sens.

He took what I said in the wrong light.

Il a pris ses jambes à son cou.

He made off.

Il a pris son courage à deux mains.

He screwed his courage to the sticking point.

Il a recommencé de plus belle.

He began again worse than ever.

Il a remué ciel et terre pour y parvenir.

He moved heaven and earth to succeed.

Il a semé des fleurs sur un terrain aride.

(He has planted flowers on a barren soil.)　He has written on a dry subject in an ornate style.

Il avait son discours sur le bout du doigt.

He knew his speech by heart.

Il brode très-bien.

He can tell a good tale.

Il broie du noir.

He is in a brown study.

Il chasse de race.

He's a chip of the old block.

Il conduit bien sa barque.

(He manages his boat well.)　He can paddle his own canoe; he understands the art of success.

Il coûte peu à amasser beaucoup de richesse, et beaucoup à en amasser peu.

(It takes little trouble to amass great wealth, but much to amass a little.) The first hundred pounds is the hardest to save.

Il débite ses propos à tout bout de champ.

He is always thrusting his remarks forward.

Il dépense beaucoup en menus plaisirs.

He spends a great deal in trifles.

Il écorche le français.

He murders French.

Il écrit à bâtons rompus.

He writes by fits and starts.

Il en a été quitte pour la peur.

He escaped scot-free with nothing worse than a fright.

Il en a fait une bonne affaire.

That was good business for him.

Il en est de la neige comme du cœur de la femme ; à peine souillée, elle devient tout de suite de la fange.
　　　　—*G. de Cherville.*

Woman's heart is like the snow : once sullied, it becomes mud.

Il en est d'un homme qui aime, comme d'un moineau pris à la glu ; plus il se débat, plus il s'embarrasse.

A man in love is like a sparrow caught with bird-lime ; the more he strives, the more he is entangled.

Il en fait ses choux gras.

(He makes his cabbages fat by it.)   He feathers his nest by it.

Il en fait toujours faire à sa guise.

He always wants to go his own road.

Il en rabattra de sa première demande.

He will take something less than he asked.

Il en sait long.

He's a knowing card.

Il est aisé d'être femme quand on est insensible.—*Madame de Staël.*

It is easy for a woman to be womanly when she has no feeling.

Il est au bout de son latin.

He is at his wits'-end.

Il est aussi absurde de prétendre qu'il est impossible de toujours aimer la même femme, qu'il peut l'être de dire qu'un artiste célèbre a besoin de plusieurs violons pour exécuter un morceau de musique.—*Balzac.*

To assert that it is impossible to love one woman for ever, is as absurd as to say that a virtuoso needs several violins to execute a piece of music.

Il est aussi facile de se tromper soi-même sans s'en apercevoir, qu'il est difficile de tromper les autres sans qu'ils s'en aperçoivent.
                    —*La Rochefoucauld.*

It is as easy to deceive ourselves unconsciously, as it is difficult to deceive others successfully,

Il est avec le ciel des accommodements.

It is possible to make compromises with Heaven.*

Il est bas percé.

He is in low water ; his funds are low.

Il est beau de triompher de soi.
                    —*T. Corneille.*

'Tis a noble triumph to triumph over self.

Il est beau qu'un mortel jusques aux cieux s'élève,
   Il est beau même d'en tomber.
                    —*Quinault.*

It is grand in a man to aspire to the highest, even though he falls.

Il est bien aisé d'aller à pied quand on tient son cheval par la bride.

It is pleasant walking when you lead a horse by the bridle.

Il est bien fou qui s'oublie.

He is an arrant fool who forgets himself.

Il est bien plus aisé d'accuser un sexe que d'excuser l'autre.—*Montaigne.*

It is easier to accuse one sex than to excuse the other.

Il est bon d'avoir des amis partout.

It is a good thing to have friends everywhere.

Il est bon de faire de nécessité vertu.

It is wise to make a virtue of necessity.

Il est bon de frotter et limer notre cervelle contre celle d'autrui.
                    —*Montaigne.*

Contact with other wits brightens one's own.

Il est bon de parler, et meilleur de se taire.

(It is good to speak, but it is better to be silent.)   Speech is silvern, silence is golden.

Il est bon d'être habile, mais non pas de le paraître.

'Tis a good thing to be clever, but it is well to disguise the fact.

Il est comme le chien du jardinier.

He is like the dog in the manger.

Il est comme un coq en pâte.

(He is living like a cock that is being fattened.)   He is living in clover.

Il est comme une poule mouillée.

He is a perfect stupid.

Il est coutumier du fait.

He is an old hand at it.

* An adaptation of one of Molière's lines.

Il est dangereux de trop faire voir à l'homme combien il est égal aux bêtes sans lui montrer sa grandeur. Il est encore dangereux de lui trop faire voir sa grandeur sans sa bassesse. Il est encore plus dangereux de lui laisser ignorer l'un et l'autre, mais il est très avantageux de lui représenter l'un et l'autre.—*Pascal.*

It is dangerous to make man see how like he is to animals without keeping his greatness in view. It is dangerous, also, to show him his greatness and not his baseness; and still more to leave him ignorant of both. But it is most profitable to picture to him one and the other.

Il est dit habile, qui fraude ami et pille.

He who cheats and robs a friend is called a clever fellow.

Il est du naturel du chat, il retombe toujours sur ses pieds.

Like a cat, he always falls on his feet.

Il est du véritable amour comme de l'apparition des esprits; tout le monde en parle, mais peu de gens en ont vu.
　　　　—*La Rochefoucauld.*

True love has something in common with apparitions of ghosts. Everybody discusses them, but few have seen them.

Il est faux qu'on ait fait fortune lorsqu'on ne sait pas en jouir ?
　　　　—*Vauvenargues.*

Men who are said to have made their fortune, have not done so if they do not know how to enjoy it.

Il est juste que le prêtre vive de l'autel.

(It is fair that the priest should live by the altar.) The labourer is worthy of his hire.

Il est marqué à l'A.

(He stands A1.) He is a splendid fellow.

Il est mort criblé de dettes.

He was over head and ears in debt when he died.

Il est né coiffé.

(He was born with a caul.) Born lucky.

Il est né dimanche, il aime besogne faite.

He was born on a Sunday, he likes a job where there is nothing to do.

Il est parti prenant la clef des champs.

He made off.

Il est peu de distance de la roche Tarpéienne au Capitole.

(It is not far from the Tarpeian rock to the Capitol.) It is a short step from the throne to the scaffold.*

Il est plus aisé de se tirer de la rive que du fond.

(It is easier to get away from the bank than the bottom of the stream.) Leave the fire when it begins to scorch.

Il est plus aisé d'être sage pour les autres, que pour soi-même.
　　　　—*La Rochefoucauld.*

It is easier to be wise about other people's business than about our own.

Il est plus facile à une femme de défendre sa vertu contre les hommes que sa réputation contre les femmes.
　　　　—*Rochebrune.*

A woman may more easily defend herself from men, than her reputation from women.

Il est plus honteux de se défier de ses amis, que d'en être trompé.
　　　　—*La Rochefoucauld.*

It is more shameful to distrust our friends than to be deceived by them.

Il est plus nécessaire d'étudier les hommes que les livres.
　　　　—*La Rochefoucauld.*

Men, not books, are the proper subject for study.

---

* A line from Jouy's *La Vestale.* Mirabeau quoted the words in a speech delivered in 1790.

Il est rendu.

He is quite done up.

Il est revenu de ses erreurs.

(He has given up his errors.) He has turned over a new leaf.

Il est sain de se lever de bonne heure.

Early rising is healthy.

Il est si beau de mourir jeune.
—*André Chénier.*

It is so beautiful to die young.

Il est sujet à caution.

You must discount what he says.

Il est toujours par monts et par vaux.

(He is always going over mountains and valleys.) He is always on the move; he is ever on the wing.

Il est tout prêché qui n'a cure de bien faire.

It is useless to preach to a man who does not care to do well.

Il est très comme il faut.

He is a perfect gentleman.

Il est très maniéré.

He is very stiff.

Il est trop tard de fermer l'écurie quand les chevaux sont pris.

When the horses are stolen, it is useless to lock the stable-door.

Il est venu à point nommé.

He came in the nick of time.

Il était en train de sortir

He was just going out.

Il était grippé.

He had caught cold.

Il fait beau temps.

It is fine (weather).

Il fait bien mauvais au bois quand les loups se mangent l'un l'autre.

'Tis very hard times in the wood when wolf eats wolf.

Il fait bon battre l'orgueilleux quand il est seul.

It is good to beat a proud man when he is alone.

Il fait celui qui n'entend pas.

He plays the deaf man.

Il fait cher vivre dans la capitale.

Living is expensive in the metropolis.

Il fait déjà le barbon.

(He already plays the gray-beard.) He has an old head on young shoulders.

Il fait flèche de tout bois.

(He makes an arrow of all wood.) He turns everything to account.

Il fait toujours bon tenir son cheval par la bride.

Don't leave hold of the bridle if you wish to be sure of the horse.

Il fallait me tenir à quatre pour ne pas rire.

I did my best not to laugh.

Il fallait un calculateur, ce fut un danseur qui l'obtint.—*Beaumarchais.*

A man " good at figures " was wanted, and a dancing-master obtained the post.

Il faudra bien en passer par là.

We must put up with it.

Il faudra se soumettre ou se démettre.
—*Gambetta.*

(He must needs submit or demit.) He must give way or resign.*

Il faut amadouer la poule pour avoir les poussins.

To get chicks, coax the hen.

Il faut attendre le boiteux.

(It is necessary to wait for the lame man.) Wait for the truth.

Il faut, autant qu'on peut, obliger tou le monde :
On a souvent besoin d'un plus petit que soi.—*La Fontaine.*

It is best to act kindly to everybody, for there's no hand so small that it may not help.

---

* This was Gambetta's declaration when the elections of 1877 went against Marshal Mac Mahon.

Il faut avoir pitié des morts.
         —Victor Hugo.

We ought to have pity on the dead.

Il faut battre le fer tandis qu'il est chaud.

Strike while the iron is hot.

Il faut bien laisser le jeu quand il est beau.

Leave off playing when the game is at its best.

Il faut briguer la faveur de ceux à qui l'on veut du bien, plutôt que de ceux de qui l'on espère du bien.
         —La Bruyère.

Seek the favour of those to whom you wish happiness, rather than of those from whom you hope to gain an advantage.

Il faut casser la noix pour manger le noyau.

To eat the kernel you must break the shell.

Il faut croire au mariage comme à l'immortalité de l'âme.—*Balzac.*

Marriage must be believed in, as you do in the soul's immortality.

Il faut découdre l'amitié, mais il faut déchirer l'amour.
         —Richelieu (le Duc-Maréchal).

You may unpick the seam of friendship, but you must tear love's bond asunder.

Il faut de l'argent pour commencer le jeu.

(You must have money to commence the game.) You must have money to make it.

Il faut des années de repentir pour effacer une faute aux yeux de l'homme : une seule larme suffit à Dieu.

Years of repentance are necessary in order to blot out a sin in the eyes of men, but one tear of repentance suffices with God.

Il faut être enclume ou marteau.

(One must be either anvil or hammer.) You must endure if you can't hit back.

Il faut faire ce qu'on fait.

Whatever you do, do it with all your might.

Il faut gratter les gens par où il leur démange.

Scratch people in the right place.

Il faut hasarder un petit poisson pour prendre un grand.

(Venture a small fish to catch a great one.) A sprat to catch a herring.

Il faut hurler avec les loups.

(One must howl with the wolves.) When you are at Rome, do as Rome does.

Il faut laisser l'enfant morveux plutôt que lui arracher le nez.

Better leave the child's nose dirty than wring it off.

Il faut laver son linge sale en famille.
         —Napoleon I.

Dirty linen ought to be washed in private.

Il faut le faire bon gré mal gré.

You are bound to do it, willy-nilly.

Il faut louer la mer et se tenir en terre.

Praise the sea, but keep on land.

Il faut passer par la porte ou par la fenêtre.

One must leave a room by door or window.

Il faut perdre un véron pour pêcher un saumon.

(A minnow's well lost to catch a salmon.) Set a sprat to catch a herring.

Il faut prêcher d'exemple.

Example is better than precept.

Il faut prendre la balle au bond.

Take time by the forelock.

Il faut prendre le bénéfice avec les charges.

(The benefice must be taken with its liabilities.) You must take the rough with the smooth.

R

Il faut que la vérité soit charitable, c'est-à-dire qu'elle soit dite pour le bien de celui qui est repris. La vérité doit être douce. Elle est assez forte pour n'avoir pas besoin d'être dure. C'est l'huile du Samaritain sur les plaies du malade, et non pas le vinaigre, c'est le miel et non le fiel.
—*Saint François de Sales.*

Truth must be charitable; that is, it must be spoken for the good of him who is blamed. Truth must be gentle. It is strong enough not to require to be hard. It must be the Samaritan's oil on the wounds of the sick, and not vinegar. It is honey and not gall.

Il faut que les actions de valeur reçoivent leur perfection des mains de la sagesse et de la justice : à moins de cela elles sont des diamants, si vous voulez, mais des diamants sans être taillés.—*Mascaron.*

Valiant deeds must receive their perfection from the hands of wisdom and justice ; otherwise, they may be diamonds, but uncut ones.

Il faut que tout le monde vive.

Everybody must live somehow.

Il faut qu'une porte soit ouverte ou fermée.

A door must be open or shut.

Il faut reculer pour mieux sauter.

A step back makes the better leap.

Il faut se défier d'un ennemi réconcilié.

Beware of a friend who has once been your enemy.

Il faut se dire beaucoup d'amis et s'en croire peu.

Assert that you have many friends, but believe you have few.

Il faut souvent plus de courage pour faire simplement son devoir, que pour affronter le feu de l'ennemi.

Frequently it requires more courage simply to do our duty, than to face the fire of an enemy.

Il faut tendre voile selon le vent.

Set your sail as the wind blows.

Il faut tondre les brebis et non les écorcher.

Shear the sheep, but don't flay them.

Il faut tourner la langue sept fois dans la bouche avant de parler.

Turn your tongue seven times before speaking.

Il faut vouloir ce qu'on ne peut empêcher.

What can't be cured must be endured.

Il fit un vent à écorner un bœuf.

The wind was enough to shave your eyebrows.

Il gelait à pierre fendre.

It froze very hard.

Il jette feu et flamme.

He frets and fumes.

Il l'a battu à bras raccourci.

He beat him with all his might and main.

Il l'a échappé belle.

He had a narrow escape.

Il lit au front de ceux qu'un vain luxe environne,
Que la fortune vend ce qu'on croit qu'elle donne.
Approche-t-il du but ? quitte-t-il ce séjour ?
Rien ne trouble sa fin : c'est le soir d'un beau jour.—*La Fontaine.*

The wise, on the brows 'neath the hollow gilt crown,
Reads what fortune sells what the rich man thinks given ;
Naught troubles his end, for the life he lays down
Was a beautiful day, and death is its even.

Il lui a mis martel en tête.

He tormented him to death.

Il lui obéit au doigt et à l'œil.

He is at his beck and call.

Il m'a battu froid.

He gave me the cold shoulder.

Il m'a coupé l'herbe sous le pied.

He cut the ground from under my feet.

Il m'a débité tout cela à brûle-pourpoint.	All that he told me point-blank.
Il m'a donné une poignée de main.	He shook hands with me.
Il m'a mis au pied du mur.	He got me into a corner.
Il m'a poussé à bout.	He exasperated me.
Il m'a pris au dépourvu.	He took me unawares.
Il m'a ri au nez.	He laughed in my face.
Il me faut coucher sur la dure.	My lodging is on the cold, cold ground.
Il ment comme un arracheur de dents.	He lies like a quack dentist.
Il me traita de Turc à Maure.	He used me abominably.
Il met sa faucille dans la moisson d'autrui.	(He puts his sickle into another man's harvest.) He wishes to reap where he has not sown.
Il n'a pas inventé la poudre.	(He did not discover gunpowder.) He is not a genius, nor likely to do anything remarkable.
Il n'a pas soufflé mot de notre entrevue.	He did not say a single word about our interview.
Il n'appartient qu'à ceux qui n'espèrent jamais être cités, de ne citer personne. — *Naudé.*	Only those who never hope to be quoted themselves, abstain from quoting others.
Il n'appartient qu'aux grands hommes d'avoir de grands défauts. — *La Rochefoucauld.*	(Only great men have great defects.) Men have the defects of their qualities.
Il n'a que faire de poësie.	Poetry is not his forte.
Il n'aura jamais bon marché qui ne le demande pas.	He that does not ask will never get a bargain.
Il ne choisit pas qui emprunte.	He who goes a-borrowing does not care who the lender is.
Il ne faudrait pas lui annoncer cette nouvelle de but en blanc.	It would not do to tell this news abruptly.
Il ne faut jamais défier un fou.	Never bid defiance to a fool.
Il ne faut jamais dépasser la mesure.	Never o'erstep the bounds.
Il ne faut pas badiner avec le feu.	It won't do to play with fire.
Il ne faut pas chômer les fêtes avant qu'elles ne soient venues.	(Do not keep your holidays before they arrive.) Count not your chickens before they are hatched.
Il ne faut pas clocher devant les boiteux.	Do not limp before cripples.
Il ne faut pas enseigner les poissons à nager.	(Don't teach fish to swim.) Don't teach your grandmother to suck eggs.
Il ne faut pas faire d'un diable deux.	(Do not make out the ghost was two.) Don't make a bad business worse.
Il ne faut pas jeter des pierres dans le jardin de ton voisin.	You must not throw stones into your neighbour's garden.
Il ne faut pas laisser de semer pour crainte des pigeons.	Don't let pigeons frighten you from sowing.
Il ne faut pas lier les ânes avec les chevaux.	Asses must not be harnessed with horses.

Il ne faut pas mettre le doigt entre l'arbre et l'écorce.

(One ought not to put a finger between the trunk and the bark.) Do not interfere between husband and wife.

Il ne faut pas nous fâcher des choses passées.—*Napoleon I.*

It is no use troubling about past events.

Il ne faut pas parler de corde dans la maison d'un pendu.

(You should not talk of the halter in the house of a man that was hanged.) There is no limping before cripples.

Il ne faut pas parler latin devant les cordeliers.

Don't talk Latin before the learned.

Il ne faut pas regarder de si près dans ces affaires.

In such matters you must not be so particular.

Il ne faut pas remplir ses devoirs comme par manière d'acquit.

Duty must not be done as a mere matter of form.

Il ne faut pas se moquer des chiens qu'on ne soit hors du village.

Don't halloa till you are out of the wood.

Il ne faut pas vendre la peau de l'ours avant de l'avoir mis par terre.

You should not sell the bearskin till you have killed the bear.

Il ne faut qu'une brebis galeuse pour gâter tout le troupeau.

One tainted sheep will mar the flock.

Il ne faut qu'un faux pas pour casser la bouteille.

(One false step will break the bottle.) Virtue once lost can never be regained.

Il n'en peut mais.

He can't do anything in the matter.

Il n'en pouvait plus de fatigue et de soif.

He was worn out with fatigue and thirst.

Il n'entend jamais raillerie.

He can never take a joke.

Il ne peut plus y tenir.

He can hold out no longer.

Il ne restait plus que le nid.

The bird had flown.

Il ne s'agit pas de tout cela.

That's not the question at all.

Il ne s'agit peut-être, pour s'emparer de ces êtres si subtils, si souples et si pénétrants, que de savoir manier la louange et chatouiller l'amour-propre. La flatterie est le joug qui courbe si bas ces têtes ardentes et légères. Malheur à l'homme qui veut porter la franchise dans l'amour !
—*G. Sand.*

To captivate beings so subtle, supple and penetrative as women, clever praise and artful pandering to conceit may suffice. Flattery is the yoke with which to make their light and ardent heads submissive. Woe to the man who tries to be frank in love-making.

Il ne sait sur quel pied danser.

(He knew not on which foot to dance.) He's at his wit's end.

Il n'est chasse que de vieux chiens.

There is no good hunting but with old hounds.

Il n'est cheval qui n'ait sa tare.

There is no horse without a fault.

Il n'est d'heureux que qui croit l'être.

The only happy man is he who thinks himself happy.

Il n'est pas aussi diable qu'il est noir.

He is not so black as he is painted.

Il n'est pas bon d'avoir tout le néces-saire.—*Pascal.*

It is not a good thing to have all that we require.

Il n'est pas bon d'être trop libre.
—*Pascal.*

It is not a good thing to possess too much freedom.

Il n'est pas de pire sourd que celui qui ne veut écouter.

Who so deaf as he that will not hear ?

Il n'est pas échappé qui traîne son licou.

The horse that draws his halter is not quite escaped.

Il n'est pas nécessaire de tenir les choses pour en raisonner.
—*Beaumarchais.*

It is not necessary to have a thorough grasp of a subject in order to discourse upon it.

Il n'est pire eau que l'eau qui dort.

Still waters run deep.

Il n'est point de belles prisons ni de laides amours.

Never was a prison fair, nor a lady-love foul.

Il n'est rien d'inutile aux personnes de sens.—*La Fontaine.*

(There is nothing useless to people of sense.)   A clever man finds some use for everything.

Il n'est rien moins qu'un avare.

He is anything but a miser.

Il n'est rien si bien fait où l'on ne trouve à redire.

There is nothing so well done but may be carped at.

Il n'est rien tel que d'avoir la clef des champs.

There's nothing like living at Liberty Hall.

Il n'est secret que de rien dire.

The only way to keep a secret is to say nothing.

Il n'est si bon charretier qui ne verse.

Accidents will occur in the best-regulated families.

Il n'est si grand dépit que de pauvre orgueilleux.

There is no spite like that of a poor man proud.

Il n'est si homme de bien qu'il mette à l'examen des loix toutes ses actions et pensées, qui ne soit pendable dix fois en sa vie.—*Montaigne.*

There is no man so good who, if all his actions and thoughts were put to the test of the laws, would not deserve hanging ten times in his life.

Il n'est si petite chapelle qui n'ait son saint.

There is no chapel so small but has its saint.

Il n'est si poltron sur la terre, qui ne puisse trouver un plus poltron que soi.
—*La Fontaine.*

No man is so great a coward that he may not find another even more cowardly than himself.

Il n'est si riche festin, où il n'y ait quelqu'un qui mal dîne.

There never was so rich a banquet but some one dined ill at it.

Il nous a donné le change.

(He has put us on the wrong scent.) He has deceived us.

Il nous a faussé compagnie.

He has given us the slip.

Il n'y a au monde que deux manières de s'élever, ou par sa propre industrie, ou par l'imbécillité des autres.
—*La Bruyère.*

A man rises in the social scale in two ways; either by his own works, or by the stupidity of others.

Il n'y a cheval si bien ferré qui ne glisse.

(There is no horse so well shod but he may slip.)   Accidents will happen in the best-regulated families.

Il n'y a cheval si bon qui ne bronche.

However good a horse may be, it sometimes stumbles.

Il n'y a de nouveau que ce qui est oublié.
—*Mlle. Bertin.*

There is nothing new but what has been forgotten.

Il n'y a pas à s'y tromper, cela saute aux yeux.

There is positively no mistaking that.

Il n'y a pas de gens plus affairés que ceux qui ne font rien.

Idlers are always busy.

Il n'y a pas de grand homme pour son valet-de-chambre.
—*Madame de Cornuel.*

No man is a hero to his valet.*

Il n'y a pas de miroir au monde qui ait jamais dit à une femme qu'elle était laide.

There never was a looking-glass that reflected an ugly woman.

Il n'y a pas de petit chez soi.

There's no place like home.

Il n'y a pas de plus forte chaîne pour lier une femme que celle de se savoir aimée.
—*Mme. de Motteville.*

There is no stronger tie upon a woman than the knowledge she is beloved.

Il n'y a pas de quoi rire.

That's no laughing matter.

Il n'y a pas de sots métiers, il n'y a que de sottes gens.

There are no stupid trades, but there are stupids in them.

Il n'y a pas de vie heureuse, il y a seulement des jours heureux.
—*André Theuriet.*

There is no such thing as a happy life—there are only happy days.

Il n'y a pas là de quoi fouetter un chat.

(That is not enough to whip a cat for.) That offence is not worth talking about.

Il n'y a pas moins d'invention à bien appliquer une pensée que l'on trouve dans un livre qu'à être le premier auteur de cette pensée. On a ouï dire au Cardinal du Perron que l'application heureuse d'un vers de Virgile était digne d'un talent.—*Stendhal.*

To make good use of a thought found in a book requires almost as much cleverness as to originate it. Cardinal du Perron said that the apt quotation of a line of Virgil was worthy of the highest capacity.

Il n'y a personne qui ne soit dangereux pour quelqu'un.—*Madame de Sévigné.*

There is no man who may not be a danger to somebody.

Il n'y a pire eau que l'eau qui dort.

Still waters run deep.

Il n'y a plus de Pyrénées.—*Louis XIV.*

There are no longer any Pyrenees.†

Il n'y a point au monde un si pénible métier que celui de se faire un grand nom : la vie s'achève que l'on a à peine ébauché son ouvrage.
—*La Bruyère.*

The most arduous task in the world is to make a great name ; life ends ere the whole is spelt out.

Il n'y a point d'amour sans jalousie.

Without jealousy there is no love.

Il n'y a point de petit ennemi.

There is no such thing as a petty enemy.

Il n'y a point d'esclaves plus tourmentés que ceux de l'amour.
—*Mlle. de Lespinasse.*

No slaves so tortured as the slaves of love.

Il n'y a point de terroir si ingrat qui n'ait quelque propriété.—*La Bruyère.*

There is no ground so ungrateful as not to yield something.

Il n'y a pour l'homme que trois événements, naître, vivre et mourir : il ne se sent pas naître, il souffre à mourir, et il oublie de vivre.—*La Bruyère.*

There are three events in man's life : birth, life, and death ; he is not aware of his birth, he suffers in dying, and he forgets to live.

* This saying in some form is of great antiquity. Plutarch attributes a similar expression to Antigonus I., King of Macedonia in the third century, B.C.
† Voltaire attributes this *mot* to Louis XIV., saying that the King made the remark when the Duke of Anjou set out to occupy the Spanish throne. It has, however, been also attributed to the Spanish Ambassador to the Court of Versailles.

Il n'y a que la religion qui rende les hommes braves, patients, intrépides par conscience ; et si l'on était fidèle à la religion, l'on serait invincible.
—*Duguet.*

Religion alone makes a man brave, patient, and intrepid through conscience ; and if a man would remain faithful to religion, he would be invincible.

Il n'y a que le premier pas qui coûte.

It is only the first step that costs.*

Il n'y a que les bons marchés qui ruinent.

It is only the cheap bargains that bring us to ruin.

Il n'y a que les honteux qui perdent.

The battle is to the bold.

Il n'y a que les morts qui ne reviennent pas.—*Bertrand Barère.*

It is only the dead that never return.†

Il n'y a qu'heur et malheur en ce monde.

There is only luck or ill luck in this world.

Il n'y a qu'une chose qui revienne chaque jour dans le ménage, c'est le dîner.
—*Mme. de Flahaut.*

There is only one thing that comes round every day in married life : it is the dinner-hour.

Il n'y a rien de changé en France ; il n'y a qu'un Français de plus.
—*Charles X.*

Nothing is changed in France ; there is only one Frenchman more.‡

Il n'y a si bel acquêt que le don.

No purchase is as good as a gift.

Il n'y a si grand jour qui ne vienne pas à vêpres.

No day so long but has its evening.

Il n'y a si méchant pot qui ne trouve son couvercle.

There is no pot so mis-shapen but finds its cover.

Il n'y a si petit buisson qui n'ait son ombre.

The smallest bush casts a shadow.

Il n'y eut jamais bon marché de peaux de lions.

Lion-skins were never to be got cheaply.

Il n'y va pas par quatre chemins.

(He goes straight to the point.) He does not beat about the bush.

Il parla bien à propos.

He spoke most opportunely.

Il parle en connaissance de cause.

He knows what he is talking about

Il pêche en vain
Qui n'amorce son haim.

He fishes in vain who does not bait the hook.

Il pleut à verse.

It is pouring with rain.

Il porte lanterne à midi.

He carries a lantern in broad day.

Il prend cela pour argent comptant.

He takes that for sterling truth.

Il regarde l'affaire à un tout autre point de vue.

He considers the matter from quite a different point of view.

Il retourna trempé comme une soupe.

He came back wet through.

Il s'acharne à dire.

He will keep saying.

Il savait son discours sur le bout du doigt.

He knew his speech by heart.

* This saying is attributed to Madame du Deffand. Cardinal Polignac was enlarging on the long distance that the martyred St. Denis had walked with his head in his hands. "The distance is nothing," said Madame, "*il n'y a que le premier pas qui coûte.*"

† Barère, whose savage speeches earned for him an unenviable notoriety during the Revolution, commented thus on the folly of allowing certain English prisoners to be exchanged, as thereby they might return to take part again in active hostilities against France.

‡ Words used by the Comte d'Artois, afterwards Charles X., at the Restoration, when Louis XVIII. was proclaimed King of France, 1814.

Ils chantent, ils payeront.—*Mazarin.*
They sing, they will pay.*

Ils courent sur ses brisées.
They are treading on his heels.

Ils disputent à tout propos.
They dispute about everything.

Il se mettrait en quatre pour vous.
(He would cut himself in four for us.) He would do anything to serve us.

Il se noyerait dans une goutte d'eau.
(He would drown himself in a drop of water.) To be penny wise and pound foolish.

Il s'en prend toujours à moi.
He always blames me.

Ils en riaient sous cape.
They laughed in their sleeve at it.

Ils en sont venus aux mains.
They came to fisticuffs.

Il se recule pour mieux sauter.
He draws back in order to make a better leap.

Il sert de risée à toute la société.
He is the butt of the whole company.

Il s'est brûlé la cervelle.
He blew his brains out.

Ils étaient à couteaux tirés.
They were at daggers drawn.

Ils étaient bien certainement d'intelligence.
There is no doubt they were accomplices.

Ils étaient ruinés de fond en comble.
They were utterly impoverished.

Il se voit par expérience que les mémoires excellentes se joignent volontiers aux jugements débiles.
—*Montaigne.*
Experience teaches that excellent memories are too often joined to weak judgments.

Ils firent bonne chère.
They fared sumptuously.

Ils jettent de la poudre aux yeux.
(They are throwing dust in people's eyes.) They are deceiving everybody.

Ils l'ont fait à mon insu.
They did it unbeknown to me.

Ils marchent bon train.
They are getting on fast.

Ils ne se sentaient pas de satisfaction.
They were overjoyed.

Ils n'ont rien appris, ni rien oublié.
They have learned nothing, and forgotten nothing.†

Ils nous ont donné le change.
They gave us the slip.

Ils paient argent comptant.
They pay ready money.

Ils s'accordent comme chien et chat.
They agree like dog and cat.

Ils se croient profonds, et ne sont que creux.—*Jean d'Alembert.*
They think themselves profound, when they are merely hollow.‡

Ils se firent force compliments.
They complimented each other highly.

Ils se ressemblent comme deux gouttes d'eau.
They are as like as two peas.

Ils se sont brouillés.
They have quarrelled with each other.

Ils se sont mangé le blanc des yeux.
(They have eaten the white of each other's eyes.) They are mortal foes.

Ils se voient de loin en loin.
They see each other from time to time.

Ils sont à bout de leurs forces.
They are at their wits' end.

* When Mazarin imposed extra taxes, the French people opposed him merely by singing derisive songs, which were named on this account *mazarinades.*
† This criticism on the Bourbons and their followers is commonly attributed to Talleyrand.
‡ A description of the pseudo-philosophers of every age.

Il suffit quelquefois d'être grossier pour n'être pas trompé par un habile homme.—*La Rochefoucauld.*

Sometimes bluntness is enough to baffle a sharper.

Ils vont se faire la courte échelle.

They mean to give one another a turn.

Il tient table ouverte toujours.

He always keeps open house.

Il tondrait un œuf.

He would skin a flint.

Il travaille à bâtons rompus.

He works by fits and starts.

Il tue la poule aux œufs d'or.

He is killing the hen that lays the golden eggs.

Il vaut mieux être fou avec tous que sage tout seul.

Better be mad with the crowd than wise by yourself.

Il vaut mieux être marteau qu'enclume.

It is better to be the hammer than the anvil.

Il vaut mieux être oiseau de campagne qu'oiseau de cage.

Better be a bird in the field than a bird in a cage.

Il vaut mieux faire envie que pitié.

Better be envied than pitied.

Il vaut mieux plier que rompre.

Better to bend than break.

Il vaut mieux s'exposer à l'ingratitude que de manquer aux misérables.
—*La Bruyère.*

Better risk ingratitude than turn your face from the poor and wretched.

Il veut avoir le drap et l'argent.

He wants to eat his cake and have it too.

Il veut toujours s'en faire accroire.

He is always putting himself forward.

Il vit au jour le jour.

He lives from hand to mouth.

Il vous dira au juste ce que cela coûtera.

He will tell you exactly what it will cost.

Il y a dans la politique comme dans la religion, une espèce de pénitence plus glorieuse que l'innocence même, qui répare avantageusement un peu de fragilité par des vertus extraordinaires, et par une ferveur continuelle.
—*Fléchier.*

There is in politics, as well as in religion, a kind of penitence more glorious than innocence itself; this amply atones for a little frailty by extraordinary virtues and continual fervour.

Il y a de certaines choses dont la médiocrité est insupportable, la poésie, la musique, la peinture, le discours public.—*La Bruyère.*

In music and poetry, in painting and oratory, mediocrity is unendurable.

Il y a des âmes ainsi façonnées que la souffrance les paralyse et les empêche d'agir.—*Paul Bourget.*

There are some minds so constituted that suffering paralyses them and prevents them from performing their functions.

Il y a des gens à qui la vertu sied presque aussi mal que le vice.
—*Bouhours.*

There are some folk on whom virtue sits as awkwardly as vice.

Il y a des gens qui n'auraient jamais été amoureux, s'ils n'avaient jamais entendu parler de l'amour.
—*La Rochefoucauld.*

There are some people who would have never fallen in love, if they had never heard love talked about.

Il y a des gens qui n'ont de morale qu'en pièce ; c'est une étoffe dont ils ne se font jamais d'habit.—*Joubert.*

There are some people who never have more than a mere groundwork of morality ; it is with them a piece of cloth which they never convert into a garment for daily wear.

Il y a des gens qui ressemblent aux vaudevilles, qu'on ne chante qu'un certain temps.—*La Rochefoucauld.*

There are some people who are like comic songs, on every one's lips to-day and forgotten to-morrow.

Il y a des hochets pour tous les âges.

Every age has its hobby.

Il y a des reproches qui louent. —*La Rochefoucauld.*

There are some kind of reproaches which are equal to flattery.

Il y a du mérite sans élévation, mais il n'y a point d'élévation sans quelque mérite.—*La Rochefoucauld.*

Merit exists without high position, but no one can reach high position without some merit.

Il y a du plaisir à rencontrer les yeux de celui à qui on vient de donner. —*La Bruyère.*

It is a pleasure to meet the eyes of one to whom we have just given aid.

Il y a en Angleterre soixante sectes différentes, et une seule sauce.

In England there are sixty different religious sects, and but one sauce.*

Il y a encore de quoi glaner.

(There is still something to be gleaned.) The subject is not quite threshed out.

Il y a fagots et fagots.

(There are faggots and faggots.) What looks alike is not always the same.

Il y a plus de fous acheteurs que de fous vendeurs.

There are more fools among buyers than among sellers.

Il y a plus de gens qui veulent être aimés que de gens qui veulent aimer eux-mêmes.—*Chamfort.*

More wish to be loved by others than to love others themselves.

Il y a quelque anguille sous roche.

(There's a snake under the stone.) There's something brewing.

Il y a remède à tout fors à la mort.

There is a cure for everything but death.

Il y a toujours des vents brûlants qui passent sur l'âme de l'homme et la dessèchent. La prière est la rosée qui la rafraîchit.—*Lamennais.*

There are always burning winds to pass over the soul of man and dry it up. Prayer is the dew which refreshes it.

Il y a un cochon qui sommeille au fond de tout cœur humain. —*Sarcey.*

There is something swinish at the bottom of all human hearts.

Il y a une femme à l'origine de toutes les grandes choses.—*Lamartine.*

There is a woman at the origin of all great events.

Il y a une résignation qui ressemble à l'indifférence comme la mort ressemble au sommeil.—*Victor Hugo.*

There is a kind of resignation resembling indifference as death resembles sleep.

Il y avait une fois un hérisson philosophe, armé de pointes et de piquants comme ceux de son espèce. . . . Un jour, ce grand penseur se dit : A quoi bon cette agglomération de petites baïonnettes improductives qui se dressent sur mon dos à la moindre alerte ? Cet appareil de guerre est vraiment désobligeant pour mes voisins. . . . Supprimons-le. Il le supprima, l'imbécile ! Il arriva une fouine, qui, le trouvant gras et sans défense, le croqua comme un œuf !—*Labiche.*

There was once a philosophical hedgehog, covered with spines like the rest of his species. One day this deep thinker said to himself, " What is the good of all this collection of unproductive bayonets, which bristle on my back at every alarm ? This warlike preparation must be annoying to my neighbours. I will get rid of them." And he did so, the idiot ! For a weasel came along, and finding him defenceless, gobbled him up like an egg.

* The opinion of the Marquis Caraccioli. who acted as Neapolitan ambassador in London during part of the last century.

Il y va de la corde. — That is a hanging matter.

Il y va de la vie. — Life is at stake.

Impossible ! Ne me dites jamais ce bête de mot !—*Mirabeau*. — Impossible! Never use such an absurd word as that to me.*

Ingres a dit, " Le dessin est la probité de la peinture.'' Il eut pu ajouter que la couleur en est l'ennoblissement.—*Alfred Stevens*. — Ingres has said : ''Drawing is the probity of painting.'' He might have added that colour is its crowning virtue.

Insouciance. — Coolness ; unconcern.

J'accepte mais à charge de revanche. — I will accept on condition that I pay you back at another time.

Jacquerie. — A revolt of the French peasants in 1358.

J'ai abattu tout l'ouvrage. — I despatched all the work.

J'ai bonne cause. — (I have good reason.) Motto of the Marquis of Bath.

J'ai cédé à mon corps défendant. — I gave way against my will.

J'ai des chants pour toutes ses gloires, Des larmes pour tous ses malheurs.
            —*Delavigne*. — I have songs for all her (France) glories, and tears for all her griefs.

J'ai dû faire le pied de grue toute la journée. — I had to wait about all day.

J'ai eu mal au cœur pendant la traversée. — I was sick when crossing.

J'ai eu toujours pour principe de ne faire jamais par autrui, ce que je pouvais faire par moi-même.—*Montesquieu*. — I made it a rule of life never to do by the aid of others what I could do by myself.

J'ai failli attendre.—*Louis XIV*. — I was almost kept waiting.†

J'ai fait dix mécontents et un ingrat.
            —*Louis XIV*. — I have made ten men discontented and one ungrateful.‡

J'ai maille à partir avec vous. — I have a bone to pick with you.

J'aime mieux un raisin pour moi que deux figues pour toi. — One of my grapes is sweeter than any two of your figs.

J'aime mieux un vice commode Q'une fatigante vertu.—*Molière*. — I prefer a comfortable vice to a virtue that bores.

J'ai passé une nuit blanche. — I passed a sleepless night.

J'ai pitié de celui qui fier de son système, Me dit : " Depuis trente ans ma doctrine est la même, Je suis ce que je fus, j'aime ce que j'aimais.'' L'homme absurde est celui qui ne change jamais.—*Barthélemy*. — I pity the man who, proud of his system, says, '' My ideas have not changed for thirty years ; I am what I was ; I love what I loved.'' The ridiculous man is he who never changes.

J'ai sauté l'escalier quatre à quatre. — I bolted upstairs.

J'ai toujours vu que, pour réussir dans le monde, il fallait avoir l'air fou et être sage.—*Montesquieu*. — I have always observed that success in the world is won by the wise man who looks like a fool.

---

* The utterance of this sentiment has been attributed to several eminent people. Lytton put a similar remark into the mouth of Richelieu, " In the bright lexicon of youth there is no such word as 'fail.' "
† A complaint uttered by the King when one of his courtiers was unpunctual.
‡ A saying of Louis XIV. when he granted an appointment to a petitioner.

J'ai vécu.—*Sieyès*.

I lived.*

Jamais bon chien n'aboie à faux.

A good dog never barks without cause.

Jamais en arrière.

Never behind.

Jamais grand nez n'a gâté joli visage.

A big nose never spoiled a pretty face.

Jamais honteux n'eut belle amie.

Faint heart never won fair lady.

Jamais les mots ne manquent aux idées ; ce sont les idées qui manquent aux mots. Dès que l'idée en est venue à son dernier degré de perfection, le mot éclôt, se présente et la revêt.
—*Joubert*.

Words are never lacking to ideas, but ideas are wanting to words. As soon as an idea is perfectly ripe, the proper word buds forth, blooms and clothes the idea in the most fitting form of expression.

Jamais les peines de la vie
Ne me coûteront de soupirs ;
Avec l'amour je les change en plaisirs ;
Avec le vin je les oublie.—*Sedaine*.

Though griefs fill my life with alloy,
They cost me nor sigh nor regret,
For love changes all into joy,
And wine shows me how to forget.

Jamais l'esprit aimable et vaste qui s'intéresse à toute chose, qui est curieux de toute découverte, qui a du goût pour tout ce qui est intellectuel, n'aura le temps d'acquérir une supériorité quelconque dans un art ou dans une science déterminé.—*G. Lachaud*.

Never will the mind that takes a wide and kindly interest in everything, and is curious about all discoveries, and has also a taste for all that is intellectual, find time to acquire superiority in an art or science.

Jamais l'innocence et le mystère n'habitèrent longtemps ensemble.

Never did innocence and mystery long together dwell.

Jamais on fit bon potage avec de l'eau seule.

You can never make good broth with nothing but water.

J'appelle un chat un chat, et Rolet un fripon.—*Boileau*.

I call a cat a cat, and Rolet a scoundrel.†

Jardin des plantes.

A botanical garden.

J'aurais dû mourir à Waterloo.
—*Napoleon I*.

I ought to have died at Waterloo.‡

J'avais cru plus difficile de mourir.
—*Louis XIV*.

I had thought it more difficult to die.

Jean s'en alla comme il était venu.
—*La Fontaine*.

John departed as he came.§

Je cherche un passage que je ne saura i trouver.—*Bassompierre*.

I am looking for a passage which I cannot find.

Je cognois tout, fors que moy-même.
— *Villon*.

I understand everything—except myself.

Je crois à l'autorité comme moyen, à la liberté comme moyen, à la charité comme but.—*Ozanam*.

I believe in authority as a means, and in freedom as a means, but in charity as the end and goal of our aims.

Je crois encore les citations chose utile, chose ingénieuse, chose excellente lorsqu'on n'en abuse pas, et qu'on les fait à propos.—*Fournier*.

Quotations are useful, ingenious, and excellent, when not overdone, and aptly applied.

* The reply made by Sieyès to one who asked him how he had fared during the Reign of Terror.
† This well-known line from the Satires of Boileau has become a proverb in France, in the same sense as the English "I call a spade a spade." Rolet was an attorney who fully deserved the title of *fripon*.
‡ This remark was made to Dr. O'Meara when the Emperor was at St. Helena.
§ Louis-Philippe is said to have applied this quotation to himself when he left Paris to go into exile.

Je hais les hommes,
Les uns, parce qu'ils sont méchants et
malfaisants,
Et les autres pour être aux méchants
complaisants.—*Molière.*

I hate all men, some because they are
wicked and evil-doers, others because
they permit the wicked to do the
evil.

Je l'accompagnerai malgré lui.

I will go with him in spite of his un-
willingness.

Je l'ai pris à condition.

I had it on approval.

Je l'ai vu, dis-je, vu, des mes propres
yeux vu,
Ce qu'on appelle vu.—*Molière.*

I have seen it, I tell you, seen it with my
own eyes, seen it, which is what people
call seeing a thing.*

Je languis nuit et jour, et mon mal est
extrême,
Depuis qu'à vos rigueurs vos beaux yeux
m'ont soumis,
Si vous traitez ainsi, belle Iris, qui vous
aime,
Hélas! que pourriez-vous faire à vos
ennemis?—*Molière.*

Night and day I languish, and deep is
my sorrow since your bright eyes
brought grief to me. Fair Iris, if thus
you treat one who loves you, how
would you act towards your foes?

Je le reconnais bien là!

That's just like him!

Je le renvoie toujours affligé, et jamais
désespéré.—*Madame de Maintenon.*

I always send him away despondent,
but never in despair.†

Je lui donnerais des points.

I am more than a match for him.

Je lui en veux pour sa négligence.

I owe him one for his neglect.

Je maintiendrai.

(I will maintain.) Motto of the Royal
family of Holland.

Je marche, suivez-moi.

I lead on, follow me! ‡

J'embrasse mon rival, mais c'est pour
l'étouffer.—*Racine.*

I embrace my rival, but I do so to
choke him.

Je me mettrais au feu pour lui.

I would go through fire and water for
him.

Je m'en lave les mains.

I wash my hands of the matter.

Je m'en vay chercher un grand Peut-
estre.

I am going to seek a great Perhaps.§

Je méprise ces insectes et ces follicu-
laires ne mordant que pour vivre.
—*Voltaire.*

I despise these insects, these scribblers,
who bite merely to gain their bread.

Je mettrais plutôt toute l'Europe
d'accord que deux femmes.
—*Louis XIV.*

I could sooner reconcile all Europe than
two women.

J'en ai bien vu d'autres.

I have gone through worse than that.

Je n'aime ni n'estime la tristesse, quoique le monde ait entrepris de l'honorer
de faveur particulière. Ils en habillent
la sagesse, la vertu, la conscience.
Sot et vilain ornement.—*Montaigne.*

I neither like nor value gloominess,
albeit the world honours it with special favour. Men clothe wisdom,
virtue, and the moral sense in this
dress of gloom, but it is a ridiculous
and hideous garb.

---

* The words of Orgon in *Tartuffe,* when he explains how he has had ocular evidence that
Tartuffe is an impostor. They are often quoted for their intensity of expression, when it is
desired to express an absolute conviction that some extraordinary event has really happened.
† The method whereby Madame de Maintenon professed to maintain her ascendancy over
Louis XIV.
‡ The words of Louis Napoleon to his followers before the *coup d'état* of December 2nd,
1851.
§ Rabelais is said to have made this remark when on his deathbed.

Je n'ai mérité
Ni cet excès d'honneur ni cette indig-
nité.—*Racine.*

I have merited neither this excess of
honour nor of insult.*

Je n'ai pas besoin de vous conduire,
vous connaissez les êtres.

I need not show you the way, you know
how the land lies.

Je n'ai pas un sou vaillant.

I have not a penny to my name.

J'en aurais levé la main.

I could have sworn to it.

Je n'avais ni sou ni maille.

I was quite cleared out.

Je ne cherche qu'ung.

(I seek but one.)   God only do I seek.
Motto of the Marquis of North-
ampton.

Je ne dois qu'à moi seul toute ma renommée. – *Corneille.*

I owe my renown to myself alone

Je n'en vois pas la nécessité.

I do not perceive the necessity.†

Je ne peux pas en revenir.

I can't get over my surprise.

Je ne peux pas être au four et au
moulin.

I cannot be in two places at one time.

Je ne sais quoi.

(I know not what.)   Any subtle quality
that, though palpable to the senses,
it is impossible to define.

Je ne suis qu'au printemps, je veux voir
la moisson.—*André Chénier.*

I am only in the springtime now, and I
wish to behold the harvest.

Je n'étais pas bien dans mon assiette.

I did not feel quite at ease.

Je ne veux pas qu'il en soit quitte à si
bon compte.

He shan't get off so easily as that.

Je ne vis plus : j'assiste à la vie.
                        – *Lamartine.*

I no longer live.   I am merely a spectator of life.‡

Je n'oublierai jamais.

(I will never forget.)   Motto of the
Marquis of Bristol.

J'en suis fâché, mais mon siège est fait.
                    —*Abbé Vertot.*

I am sorry, but my siege is finished.§

J'en suis fâché pour les textes.
                —*Royer Collard.*

So much the worse for the texts.‖

Je pense.

(I think.)   Motto of Earl of Wemyss.

Je pense, donc j'existe.—*Descartes.*

I think, therefore I exist.

Je peux parler en connaissance de cause.

I can speak from experience of it.

Je prends mon bien où je le trouve.
                    —*Molière.*

I take my goods where I find them.¶

---

* The lines are from Racine's tragedy *Britannicus*.   The Emperor Nero having become
enamoured of Junia, the promised bride of Britannicus, offers her marriage, but is scornfully
repulsed.   Madame de Staël applied these lines to herself when the French Government exiled
her after the publication of her book, *L'Allemagne.*

† "I must live," said a writer of political squibs, excusing himself to the Comte d'Argental,
censor of the press to Louis XV.   The above was d'Argental's caustic reply.

‡ The remark of the aged Lamartine when he found himself poor and neglected at the end
of his distinguished career.

§ The reply to one who offered to supply him with fresh facts concerning the siege of
Rhodes, when Vertot had already published his book on the subject.

‖ When he was told that the Port Royal theologians differed from him on a doctrinal
question, and that the texts were on their side, Royer-Collard replied, " Then I am sorry for
the texts."

¶ The reply of Molière to those who accused him of plagiarism.   Another account says that
Molière's words were *Je reprends*, meaning that it was others who plagiarised his works.
Cyrano de Bergerac appears to have suggested to Molière the idea of the famous scene in
Les Fourberies de Scapin.

Je prévois du malheur pour beaucoup de maris.—*Corneille.*

I foresee troubles ahead for many married men.

Je puis faire des nobles quand je veux, et même de très grands seigneurs; Dieu seul peut faire un homme comme celui que nous allons perdre.
—*Francis I.*

I can make nobles and great lords when I please; but God alone can make such a man as this whom we are about to lose.*

Je sais à mon pot comment les autres bouillent.

I can judge by my own pot how the others boil.

Je saurai en tirer parti.

I shall be able to turn it to account.

Je suis bête et tu une autre bête, Marie-toi avec moi, Antoinette.

I'm a fool and you're another, so let us marry, Antoinette.

Je suis convaincu que les plus grands révolutionnaires, dans l'ordre des idées, ceux qui ont le plus épouvanté les hommes, ceux qui ont fait répandre le plus de sang et de larmes, ont été des enfants aux premières questions desquels on n'a pas répondu ce qu'il fallait répondre.—*Alex. Dumas, fils.*

I am convinced that the greatest revolutionists as far as ideas are concerned, who most have terrified mankind and caused most tears and bloodshed, were, when children, those whose questions were not properly answered.

Je suis dans ses petits papiers.

I am in his good books.

Je suis oiseau, voyez mes ailes.

I am a bird, behold my wings.   I am a mouse, hurrah for rats.†

Je suis souris, vivent les rats.

Je suis roi, c'est mon métier.

I am a king, that is my trade.‡

Jet d'eau.

A fountain , a water-spout.

Jeter des pierres dans le jardin de quelqu'un.

(To throw stones into another's garden.) To make insinuations.

Jeter le froc aux orties.

To throw off the cowl.

Jeter le manche après la cognée.

To throw the helve after the hatchet.

Jeter son argent par les fenêtres.

(To pitch one's money out of the window.)   To be extravagant.

Jeu de hasard.

Game of chance.

Jeu de mots.

A play upon words.

Jeu d'esprit.

A witticism.

Jeu de théâtre.

Stage-trick, or attitude.

Jeune on conserve pour la vieillesse; vieux on épargne pour la mort.
— *La Bruyère.*

A young man saves up for his old age, when he is old he hoards up for death.

Jeune, on est riche de tout l'avenir qu'on rêve; vieux, on est pauvre de tout le passé qu'on regrette.
—*Rochepèdre.*

Youth is made rich by its dreams of the future ; age is made poor by its regrets for the past.

Jeunesse dorée.

The gilded youth.§

---

* Francis I. made this remark at the death-bed of Leonardo da Vinci, reproving the courtiers who seemed to think that the King did too much honour to the painter.   Doubts, however, have been cast upon the authenticity of the words, and the whole incident may be apocryphal.

† These lines, from different parts of La Fontaine's fable of the "Bat and the two weasels," are commonly applied to people of the type of the Vicar of Bray, who can adapt their views to circumstances.   The bat in the fable manages to live amicably with the two weasels, though one hates rats, and the other birds, by the aid of his form, half bird, half mouse.

‡ A saying attributed to Victor Emmanuel.

§ This name was first given, in 1794, to the young men of wealth who were attached to the revolutionary party.

Jeux de mains jeu de vilains. — Horse play is the rough's play.

Je vais lui dire son fait. — I shall give him a piece of my mind.

Je vais lui faire une farce. — I am going to play him a trick.

Je vais rejoindre votre père. — I am going to be re-united to your father.*
　　　　—Marie Antoinette.

Je veux de bonne guerre. — (I wish fair play.) Motto of Lord Wenlock.

Je veux que le dimanche chaque paysan ait sa poule au pot. — I wish every peasant to have a fowl in his pot on a Sunday.†

Je viendrai mais contre cœur. — I will come, but against my wish.

Je vis d'espoir. — I live in hope.

Je voudrais bien voir la grimace qu'il fait à cette heure sur l'échafaud. — I should like to see the grimace that he is making now upon the scaffold.‡
　　　　—Louis XIII.

Je vous aime ; j'étouffe,
Je t'aime, je suis fou, je n'en peux plus, c'est trop ;
Ton nom est dans mon cœur comme dans un grelot,
Et comme tout le temps, Roxane, je frissonne,
Tout le temps le grelot s'agite, et le nom sonne ;
De toi, je me souviens de tout, j'ai tout aimé.—*Edm. Rostand.*

I love thee, I love thee! My passion stifles, maddens, overwhelms me. Thy name is like a bell that rings in my heart, and as I am always trembling in the fever of my love for thee, Roxane, my heart is always ringing with the sound of thy name. In all things I remember thee, since thou art the possessor of all my love.§

Je vous demande bien pardon. Il n'y a pas de quoi. — I really beg your pardon. Don't mention it.

Je vous déplairai souvent, mais je ne vous tromperai jamais.—*Dumouriez.* — I shall often displease your Majesty, but I shall never deceive you.

Je vous donne carte blanche. — I give you full power to do as you please.

Je vous le donne en trois. — I give you three guesses to find it out.

Je vous paierai au fur et à mesure de votre ouvrage. — I'll pay you as you go on.

Je vous sais gré de me l'avoir dit. — I am much obliged to you for telling me.

Joie et courage
Font beau visage. — Joy and courage make a handsome face.

Joli. — Pretty, attractive.

Jouer sa vie. — To risk one's life.

Jour de fête. — A fête day.

Journal des débats. — The journal of the (Parliamentary) debates.

---

* The parting words of Marie Antoinette to her children, when she was on her way to the scaffold, 1793.
† The pious wish of Henri IV., who understood that empty stomachs breed revolutions.
‡ The brutal saying of Louis XIII. when he heard that M. le Grand was being executed.
§ This quotation from M. Rostand's *Cyrano de Bergerac* forms part of the scene where Cyrano, conscious of his own lack of good looks, quixotically woos Roxane in the character of his rival Christian. The real Cyrano de Bergerac, poet and swashbuckler, has earned immortality by the coining of a single phrase. In his play *Le Pédant joué* occurs the *Que diable allait-il faire dans cette galère*, or rather a slight variation of it, which Molière borrowed for the most amusing scene in the *Fourberies de Scapin.*

Juste-milieu.

(The exact middle.) The golden mean ; the middle course is the safest.

J'y perdais mon latin.

I could make neither head nor tail of it.

J'y suis, j'y reste.

Here I am, here I stay.*

J'y suis pour mon coût.

I paid dearly for it.

La bataille se fit en rase campagne.

The battle was fought in the open country.

L'abattu veut toujours lutter.

It is the beaten man who clamours for more fighting.

La beauté est une éloquence muette.

Beauty is eloquent even when silent.

La beauté sans grâce est un hameçon sans appât.—*Ninon de Lenclos.*

Without grace beauty is an unbaited hook.

La beauté sans vertu est une fleur sans parfum.

Beauty without virtue is a flower without perfume.

La belle cage ne nourrit pas l'oiseau.

Gold on the cage won't feed the bird.

La belle plume fait le bel oiseau.

Fine feathers make fine birds.

La blessure est pour vous, la douleur est pour moi.—*Charles IX.*

The wound is yours, but the pain is mine.†

La bonne fortune, et la mauvaise, sont nécessaires à l'homme pour le rendre habile.

Good and bad fortune are necessary to a man in order to develop his character.

La bonté, c'est le fond des natures augustes,
D'une seule vertu Dieu fait le cœur des justes,
Comme d'un seul saphir la coupole du ciel.—*V. Hugo.*

Kindness is the basis of noble natures ; of this single virtue God makes the just man's heart, as with one hollowed sapphire He made the heavenly dome.

La bouche obéit mal, lorsque le cœur murmure.—*Voltaire.*

The lips are slow to obey the brain when the heart is mutinous.

La brebis sur la montagne est plus haute que le taureau dans la plaine.

The sheep on the mountain is higher than the bull on the plain.

L'absence
Est un prétexte à l'inconstance
Plutôt qu'un remède à l'amour.
　　　　—*La Fare.*

Absence is an excuse for inconstancy rather than a cure for love.

La cage et le mariage
Ne font sentir les maux que quand on est dedans.—*Mlle. de Scudéri.*

Outside marriage and prison none know the miseries felt within them.

La caque sent toujours le hareng.

The cask always smells of the herring.

La carrière des armes.

The career of arms.

La carrière ouverte aux talents.
　　　　—*Napoleon I.*

(The career open to talent.) The prizes to those who can win them ; the spoils to the victors.

---

* The reply of Marshal MacMahon to those who urged him to abandon the Malakoff Tower after it had been captured by the French troops.
† Charles IX., King of France, is said to have spoken thus when he visited Admiral de Coligny, who had been wounded by the hired assassin of the Guises Two days afterwards, August 24th, 1572, the massacre of the Huguenots took place, and Coligny himself was slain. How far Charles IX. was an active instigator of the crime of St. Bartholomew's Day is a disputed point.

L'accomplissement du devoir est le véritable but de la vie et le véritable bien.—*Jouffroy.*

The fulfilment of duty is the true end of life and the true welfare.

La charte sera désormais une vérité.
—*Louis-Philippe.*

Henceforth the charter will be a reality.*

Lâcheté.

Cowardice ; laxity.

La cinquième roue au chariot ne fait qu'empêcher.

(A fifth wheel in the waggon hinders rather than helps.) Too much of anything is good for nothing.

La civilisation, c'est Pandore la bien nommée, brillante, souriante, tournant les têtes, enivrant les cœurs ; mais que de maux cuisants elle traîne après elle, cette ravissante statue pétrie dans la boue!—*Alb. Reville.*

Civilisation is Pandora the aptly-named, brilliant and smiling, turning all heads and intoxicating all hearts ; but what afflicting woes she brings along with her—this delightful statue modelled out of mud !

La clémence des princes n'est souvent qu'une politique pour gagner l'affection des peuples.—*La Rochefoucauld.*

The clemency of princes is often nothing but a politic measure to gain the affection of their subjects.

La clémence est la plus belle marque, Qui fasse à l'univers connaître un vrai monarque.—*Corneille.*

Clemency is the infallible sign, whereby the world knows the true king.

La cœur d'une femme aimante est un sanctuaire d'or où règne souvent une idole d'argile.—*P. Limayrac.*

A loving woman's heart is a golden shrine where often a clay idol is enthroned.

La colère suffit, et vaut un Apollon.
—*Boileau.*

(Anger suffices, and is worth an Apollon.) Indignation makes even the stupid man eloquent.†

La conscience fournit une preuve de l'immortalité de notre âme Chaque homme a au milieu de cœur un tribunal où il commence par se juger soi-même, en attendant que l'Arbitre souverain confirme la sentence.
—*Chateaubriand.*

Conscience gives a proof of the soul's immortality. In every man's heart is a court where he judges himself before the Sovereign Arbitrator confirms the sentence.

La considération pour les femmes est la mesure des progrès d'une nation dans la vie sociale.—*Grégoire.*

Respect for woman is the test of national progress in social life.

La constance est la chimère de l'amour.
—*Vauvenargues.*

Constancy is a fiction of love.

La conviction est la conscience de l'esprit.—*Chamfort.*

Conviction is the mind's conscience.

La coquetterie est le désir de plaire sans le besoin d'aimer.—*Rochepèdre.*

Coquetry is the wish to please in one who feels no need of love.

La coquetterie est un mensonge continuel qui rend une femme aussi méprisable et plus dangereuse qu'une courtisane qui ne ment jamais.
—*Ph. de Varennes.*

Coquetry is a continuous lie, making a woman as contemptible and dangerous as an Aspasia who never deceives.

---

* The declaration of Louis-Philippe to the French people when he was called to the throne after the dethronement of Charles X., whose policy of reaction was the cause of the second downfall of the Bourbon régime.
† A paraphrase of Juvenal's *Facit indignatio versum.*

La cour en conseillers foisonne :
Est-il besoin d'exécuter ?
L'on ne rencontre plus personne.
　　　　　　　—*La Fontaine.*

The court swarms with counsellors, but there are none to execute their advice.

La critique est aisée et l'art est difficile.
　　　　　　　—*Destouches.*

Criticism is easy and art is difficult.

La curiosité a perdu plus de jeunes filles que l'amour.—*Mme. de Pinzieux.*

Curiosity has destroyed more women than love.

La découverte d'un mets nouveau fait plus pour le bonheur du genre humain que la découverte d'une étoile.
　　　　　　　—*Brillat-Savarin.*

The discovery of a new dish confers more happiness on the human race than the discovery of a star.

La démocratie instituée excitait nos ambitions sans les satisfaire ; la philosophie proclamée allumait nos curiosités sans les contenter.—*H. Taine.*

The introduction of democratic ideals excited our ambitions without satisfying them ; the declaration of the principles of philosophy inflamed our curiosity without appeasing it.

La destinée des nations dépend de la manière dont elles se nourrissent.
　　　　　　　—*Brillat-Savarin.*

The future of nations depends on how they are fed.

La dignité de la femme est d'être ignorée, sa gloire est dans l'estime de son mari, ses plaisirs sont dans le bonheur de sa famille.—*J. J. Rousseau.*

Woman's dignity consists in her being ignored, her glory in being esteemed by her husband, her pleasures in the happiness of her family.

La docte antiquité fut toujours vénérable,
Je ne la trouve pas cependant adorable.
　　　　　　　—*Boileau.*

I have always respected the learning of antiquity, but I am not one of its worshippers.

La douceur de la gloire est si grande, qu'à quelque chose qu'on l'attache, même à la mort, on l'aime.—*Pascal.*

So great is the sweetness of glory that it is adored no matter what it entails, even though it involves death itself.

La douleur est un siècle, et la mort un moment.—*Gresset.*

Pain is a century, Death but a moment.

La douleur qui se tait n'en est que plus funeste.—*Racine.*

Silent sorrow is only the more fatal.

L'adresse surmonte la force.

Skill is better than strength.

La droiture est une pureté de motif et d'intention qui donne la forme et la perfection à la vertu, et qui attache l'âme au bien pour le bien même.
　　　　　　　—*Fléchier.*

Uprightness is a purity of motive and intention which gives to virtue beauty and perfection, and makes the soul cling to goodness for the sake of goodness itself.

L'adversité fait l'homme, et le bonheur les monstres.

Adversity makes a man, but prosperity makes monsters.

La faiblesse est le seul défaut qu'on ne saurait corriger.—*La Rochefoucauld.*

Weakness of mind is the only defect that can never be corrected.

La faim chasse le loup du bois.

Hunger breaks through stone walls.

La faim épouse la soif.

(It is hunger marrying thirst.) A penniless man marrying a dowerless maid.

La tantaisie de diffamation dévore les esprits provinciaux.—*G. Sand.*

Country-bred wits are consumed by a passion for scandal.

La farine du diable s'en va moitié en son.

The devil's corn runs half to chaff.

La faute en est aux dieux, qui la firent si bête.—*Gresset.*

The fault is the gods', who made her so ugly.*

* A skit on a line of an old poem, *La faute en est aux dieux, qui la firent si belle.* " The gods are to blame who made her so fair."

La faute est grande comme celui qui la commet.

La femme à la maison et la jambe rompue.

La femme ambitionne pour unique génie, de se savoir délicieuse à l'homme amoureux, ou nécessaire à l'inquiet, au faible et à l'ennuyé.
—*L. Dépret.*

La femme a un sourire pour toutes les joies, une larme pour toutes les douleurs, une consolation pour toutes les misères, une excuse pour toutes les fautes, une prière pour toutes les infortunes, un encouragement pour toutes les espérances.—*Sainte-Foix.*

La femme, c'est le cœur de l'homme.
—*P. Leroux.*

La femme, chez les sauvages, est une bête de somme ; en Orient, un meuble ; en Europe, un enfant gâté.
—*De Meilhan.*

La femme est un diable très-perfectionné.—*V. Hugo.*

La femme est une créature transitoire entre l'homme et l'ange.—*Balzac.*

La femme excuse jusqu'aux mauvaises actions que sa beauté fait commettre.
—*Lesage.*

La femme ne peut être savante impunément qu'à la charge de cacher ce qu'elle sait avec plus d'attention que l'autre sexe n'en met à le montrer.
—*J. de Maistre.*

La femme ne peut être supérieure que comme femme ; mais dès qu'elle veut émuler l'homme, ce n'est qu'un singe.
—*J. de Maistre.*

La fenêtre donne sur la cour intérieure.

La feuille tombe à terre, ainsi tombe la beauté.

L'affaire se traita de gré à gré.

La fin couronne l'œuvre.

La flatterie est une fausse monnaie qui n'a cours que par notre vanité.
—*La Rochefoucauld.*

La fleur des pois.

La fleur des troupes.

The higher the man, the baser his crime.

(A wife and a broken leg are best kept at home.)
The wife that expects to have a good name
Is always at home, as if she were lame.

Woman longs for the single gift of being delightful to the man who loves her, or necessary to the anxious, the weak and the wearied.

Woman has a smile for every joy, a tear for every grief, consolation for all misery, excuses for all faults, a prayer for misfortune, and encouragement for all hopes.

Woman is the very heart of man.

Among savages woman is a beast of burden ; among Orientals, a piece of furniture ; among Europeans, a spoilt child.

Woman is a highly-perfected demon.

Woman is the connecting link between man and the angels.

Women are ready to find excuse for those misdeeds which their own beauty has provoked.

Woman may not be learned with impunity, unless she conceals her knowledge with as much care as the other sex takes to display its own.

Woman cannot be superior except as a woman ; for, as soon as she tries to emulate man, she becomes merely an ape.

The window looks on to the inner courtyard.

As the leaf falls to the ground, so beauty fades away.

They settled the matter by themselves.

All's well that ends well.

Flattery is a false coinage, which our vanity puts into circulation.

The very pink of fashion ; a beau of the first water.

Choice troops ; picked soldiers.

La fortune est toujours pour les grands bataillons.—*Madame de Sévigné*.

Fortune is always on the side of the big battalions.*

La fortune la plus amie vous donne le croc-en-jambe.

The biggest piece of luck is oft a stumbling-block.

La fortune ne paraît jamais si aveugle qu'à ceux à qui elle ne fait pas de bien. *La Rochefoucauld*.

Fortune never appears so blind as to those to whom she has granted no benefit.

La fortune ne peut nous ôter que ce qu'elle nous a donné.

Fortune can only deprive us of what she has given us.

La fortune peut se jouer de la sagesse des gens vertueux, mais il ne lui appartient pas de faire fléchir leur courage.—*Vauvenargues*.

Fortune may sport with the wisdom of virtuous men, but it is not in her power to bend their courage.

La fourbe n'est le jeu que des petites âmes,
Et c'est la proprement le partage des femmes.—*Corneille*.

Deceit is the game that only small minds play at, and it is thus properly the quality innate in women.

La France est une monarchie absolue tempérée par des chansons.

France is an absolute monarchy tempered by songs.†

La France est un soldat.
　　　　　　　—*Chateaubriand*.

(France is a soldier.) The fate of France depends upon its army.

La France jamais ne périt tout entière.
　　　　　　—*Casimir Delavigne*.

France is never utterly ruined.

La France marche à la tête de la civilisation.—*Guizot*.

France advances at the head of civilization.

La galanterie de l'esprit est de dire des choses flatteuses d'une manière agréable.—*La Rochefoucauld*.

The gallantry of (the man of) wit is the ability to say flattering things in an agreeable manner.

La Garde meurt et ne se rend pas.

The Guards die, but do not surrender.‡

L'âge d'or était l'âge où l'or ne régnait pas.—*L. de Marnezia*.

The golden age was the period when gold had no power.

La générosité n'est que la pitié des âmes nobles.—*Chamfort*.

Generosity is but the pity that is felt by noble minds.

La gloire est le but où j'aspire;
On n'y va point par le bonheur.
L'alcyon, quand l'Océan gronde,
Craint que les vents ne troublent l'onde
Où se berce son doux sommeil.
Mais pour l'aiglon, fils des orages,
Ce n'est qu'à travers les nuages
Qu'il prend son vol vers le soleil!
　　　　　　　　V. Hugo.

The road to glory is not through happiness. The halcyon, when the ocean thunders, fears the winds will vex the waves that rock it in soft slumber; but the eagle, son of the tempest, rushes through the clouds as it soars upwards towards the sun.

La gloire et la présomption n'attirent que la haine et l'indignation.
　　　　　　　—*Destouches*.

Vanity and presumption can only attract hatred and indignation.

---

* This saying is sometimes wrongly attributed to Napoleon, but, in point of act, he denied the truth of it, saying that " Fortune was on the side of the last reserve."

† The author of this saying is not known. It has been the model for many similar sayings, *e.g.*, " The Indian Government is a despotism of despatch-boxes, tempered by the loss of the keys."

‡ Tradition says this magnificent reply was made by Cambronne, the commander of the Old Guard at Waterloo, when called upon to surrender. The words, however, are said to be apocryphal, for Cambronne used to blush when asked if he had used them.

La gloire n'est jamais où la vertu n'est pas.—*Le Franc de Pompignan.*

There is no glory where there is no virtue.

La gloire ne va, en nos temps compliqués, où les connaissances humaines se morcellent parce qu'elles sont étendues, la gloire ne va qu'aux hommes spéciaux.— *G. Lachaud.*

In our complex times, when human knowledge splits up because it is made to extend too far, great reputations come only to specialists.

La gloire s'achète par les travaux accomplis, les périls affrontés, surtout les iniquités subies.—*Ph. Chasles.*

Glory is won by work accomplished, by dangers dared, and, above all, by sufferings undergone.

La gourmandise a tué plus de gens que l'épée.

Gluttony has killed more than the sword.

La grammaire, qui sait régenter jusqu'aux rois,
Et les fait, la main haute, obéir à ses lois. — *Molière.*

Grammar rules even royal speeches
And kings obey whate'er it teaches.

La grande affaire, et la seule chose, c'est de vivre heureux.—*Voltaire.*

The great and only serious business of life is to live happily.

La grande auréole ne rayonne que sur le front des morts.—*Ph. Chasles.*

The aureole of Glory shines only round the head of the dead.

La grande nation.

(The great nation.)   France.*

La grande pensée.

The splendid idea.†

La grande sagesse de l'homme consiste à connaître ses folies.

The great wisdom of man consists in knowing his follies.

La grandeur a besoin d'être quittée pour être sentie.—*Pascal.*

One must stand away from greatness in order to appreciate it.

La grandeur de l'homme est grande en ce qu'il se connaît misérable.   Un arbre ne se connaît pas misérable.
—*Pascal.*

The greatness of man consists in the fact that he knows he is miserable. A tree, on the other hand, knows not its misery.

La gravité est un mystère du corps, inventé pour cacher les défauts de l'esprit.—*La Rochefoucauld.*

Solemnity is a mystery of the body, invented to hide the defects of the mind.

La Grèce, si féconde en fameux personnages
Que l'on vante tant parmi nous,
Ne put jamais trouver chez elle que sept sages :
Jugez du nombre de ses fous !
—*Grécourt.*

The Greeks, so rich in famous names,
Whose deeds we glorify to-day,
Could ne'er find but Seven Wise Men,
Lord, what a crowd of fools had they !

La guerre fait les larrons, et la paix les amène au gibet.

War makes thieves, and peace brings them to the gallows.

L'aigle d'une maison n'est qu'un sot dans une autre.—*Gresset.*

The eagle in one house is a goose elsewhere.

L'aigle ne chasse point aux mouches.

The eagle does not hunt flies.

L'aimable siècle où l'homme dit à l'homme,
" Soyons frères, ou je t'assomme ! "
—*Le Brun.*

Those glorious days when man said to man,
" Be my brother, or I will slay thee."‡

* A phrase that was constantly on the lips of Napoleon I.
† The idea of universal domination, which was ever present in the mind of Frenchmen during the supremacy of Napoleon I.
‡ A skit on *Fraternité ou la mort,* the cry of the moving spirits of the Great Revolution.

Laisser à désirer.

Laisser-aller.

Laissez dire les sots : le savoir a son prix.—*La Fontaine.*

Laissez-faire.

Laissez-nous faire.

La jalousie, c'est l'art de se faire encore plus de mal à soi qu'aux autres.
—*A. Dumas, fils.*

Laissons faire le temps. L'enfant est de l'opinion de sa mère, l'homme sera de l'opinion de son père.
—*General Hugo.*

La jalousie est la sœur de l'amour : Comme le diable est le frère des anges.
—*Boufflers.*

La jeunesse revient de loin.

La jeunesse vit d'espérance, la vieillesse de souvenir.

La joie de faire du bien est tout autre-ment douce et touchante que la joie de le recevoir. C'est un plaisir qui ne s'use point ; plus on le goûte, plus on se rend digne de le goûter.
—*Massillon.*

La journée sera dure, mais elle se pas-sera.—*Damiens.*

La lâcheté des honnêtes gens fait le triomphe des coquins.—*Voltaire.*

La lame use le fourreau.

La langue lui a fourché.

La langue va où la dent fait mal.

La libéralité consiste moins à donner beaucoup qu'à donner à propos.
—*La Bruyère.*

La liberté de la presse est le seul droit dont tous les autres dépendent.
—*Mme. de Staël.*

L'allégorie habite un palais diaphane.
—*Lemierre.*

La logique du cœur est absurde.
—*Mademoiselle Lespinasse.*

La loi dit ce que le roi veut.

La loi souvent permet ce que défend l'honneur.—*B. J. Saurin.*

To leave room for improvement.

To let matters go on as they will.

Let fools say what they will : knowledge has its value.

(Let things go their own way.)   A policy of non-interference.

Let us alone.

Jealousy is the art of injuring ourselves more than we injure others.

Let time work it out.   The child is of its mother's belief ; the man will be of its father's.

Jealousy is the sister of love, as Lucifer was a brother of the angels.

(Youth returns from afar.)   Youth astray comes home at last.

Youth lives on its hopes, Age on its memories.

The joy of being the doer of a good action awakens in us an emotion quite different in its sweetness from that of being the recipient of kindness.   It is a pleasure which never cloys ; the more one indulges in it, the more worthy one is of the delight it affords.

The day of trial will be severe, but it will come to an end.

The triumph of rogues springs from the cowardice of the honest.

The blade wears out the sheath.

He made a slip of the tongue.

(The tongue touches the aching tooth.) The foot knows where the shoe pinches.

Liberality consists less in giving liberally than in giving at the right moment.

The freedom of the Press is the right upon which all other rights depend.

(Allegory dwells in a transparent palace.) An allegory (to be effective) should not be obscure.

Argument, when the heart is involved, is absurd.

The law says what the king pleases.

The law often allows us to do what honour forbids.

La lune de miel est courte ; mais la lune d'or est la lumière qui ne s'éteint pas. Ne fût-ce qu'un jour, le premier jour de mon mariage, je veux aimer et croire ! Sans cela, le mariage est une honte et un martyre.—*G. Sand.*

The honeymoon is brief, but the moon of the golden wedding has an undying lustre. May we all believe and love on one day at least—our wedding-day ! Otherwise, wedlock would be shame and martyrdom.

La maison est misérable et méchante, Où la poule plus haut que le coq chante.

That house doth every day more wretched grow, Where the hen louder than the cock doth crow.

La maladie sans maladie ; hypocondrie.

Disease without disease; hypochondria.

La marquise n'aura pas beau temps pour son voyage.—*Louis XV.*

The marchioness will have bad weather for her journey.*

La mauvaise garde paît souvent le loup.

The bad shepherd often feeds the wolf.

L'ambition prend aux petits âmes plus facilement qu'aux grandes, comme le feu prend plus aisément aux chaumières qu'aux palais.—*Chamfort.*

Ambition overcomes petty spirits more easily than great ones, as fire catches a thatched cottage sooner than a stone palace.

L'âme accoutumée à être émue par de grandes passions qui l'agitent vivement, n'est plus touchée de ces impressions foibles et légères qu'elle reçoit dans la retraite. De-là vient l'attachement qu'on a à cette vie, quoique difficile et tumultueuse.
—*Fléchier.*

The soul accustomed to strong passions is not affected by the light, feeble impressions of solitude. Hence the attachment we feel for an active life, however difficult and tumultuous it may be.

La médecine expectante.

At the eleventh hour.

L'âme du poëte, âme d'ombre et d'amour, Est une fleur des nuits qui s'ouvre après le jour Et s'épanouit aux étoiles !
—*Victor Hugo.*

The poet's soul is the soul of darkness and of love; it is a flower which unfolds its petals when the day has fled, and bares its beauties to the stars.

L'âme est comme la moelle des jeunes arbres ; elle veut être soutenue et dirigée dès qu'ils naissent ; mais nous devons, comme fait la nature, attendre un certain degré de force et de maturité pour en tirer des fruits.
—*G. Sand.*

The soul is as the pith of young trees ; it may be upheld and directed from birth ; but man, as nature does, should await the proper degree of strength and maturity to gather the fruit.

La mère est ici-bas le seul Dieu sans athée.—*E. Legouvé.*

The mother is the only god on earth for whom there are no atheists.

L'amitié est de tous les attachements le plus digne de l'homme. C'est l'âme de son ami qu'on aime, et pour aimer son ami il faut en avoir une.—*Buffon.*

Friendship is the most worthy of human ties. A man loves his friend's soul, and to do that he must have a soul himself.

L'amitié véritable est un pacte en vertu duquel on doit tenir sans cesse sa fortune, sa vie même, à la libre disposition de celui à qui l'on s'est uni.
—*Auger.*

True friendship is a compact founded on virtue ; and it requires that one must always hold one's fortune, and even life itself, at the absolute disposal of him to whom one is united.

---

* Louis XV. is reported to have made this remark when the funeral procession of Madame de Pompadour set out during a downpour of rain.

La mode est un tyran dont rien ne nous délivre,
Le sage n'est jamais le premier à la suivre,
  Ni le dernier à la garder.—*Pavillon.*

Fashion is a tyrant we must endure ; the wise man is not the first to follow its laws nor the last to obey them.

La modestie est au mérite ce que les ombres aux figures dans un tableau ; elle lui donne de la force et du relief.
  —*La Bruyère.*

Modesty is to merit what the shadows are to the figures in a picture, emphasising and making it stand out the more.

La moitié des humains rit aux dépens de l'autre.—*Destouches.*

Half of the human race laughs at the expense of the other half.

La monnaie de M. Turenne.

Turenne's small change.*

La montagne est passée, nous irons mieux.—*Frederick the Great.*

We have crossed the mountain, we shall go better now.†

La moquerie n'est souvent que la pauvreté de l'esprit.—*La Bruyère.*

Sneering is often merely the outcome of a lack of intelligence.

La mort est plus aisée à supporter sans y penser, que la pensée de la mort sans péril.—*Pascal.*

Death is easier to endure when it arrives before it has been contemplated, than the thought of death even when no danger is at hand.

La mort sans phrase.

Death without phrases.‡

L'amour a des dédommagements que l'amitié n'a pas.—*Montaigne.*

Love has consolations unknown to friendship.

L'amour apprend aux ânes à danser.

Love teaches even asses to dance.

L'amour, c'est la bataille des sexes. Les deux adversaires savent bien ce qu'ils veulent et tous les moyens sont bons.—*A. Dumas, fils.*

Love is the war of the sexes. Both sides know their aim and all is fair to attain it.

L'amour, c'est le plus fier des despots : il faut être tout ou rien.—*Stendhal.*

Love is the haughtiest of despots, he will have all or nothing.

L'amour décroît quand il cesse de croître.—*Chateaubriand.*

When love stops growing, it decreases.

L'amour de la justice n'est en la plupart des hommes, que la crainte de souffrir l'injustice.—*La Rochefoucauld.*

Love of justice among the majority of mankind is nothing but the fear of enduring injustice.

L'amour d'une belle est un sable mouvant
Où l'on ne peut bâtir que châteaux en Espagne.—*Quitard.*

Love of a beautiful woman is a quicksand on which castles-in-Spain are built.

L'amour est le désir d'achever le bonheur d'autrui au moyen de notre propre bonheur.—*Ph. Chasles.*

Love is the longing to achieve another's happiness by means of our own.

L'amour est l'égoïsme à deux.
  —*De la Salle.*

Love is the selfishness of two persons.

L'amour est le plus matinal de nos sentiments.—*Fontenelle.*

Love is the earliest of our feelings.

---

* Madame de Cornuel's comment on the inferior generals who had succeeded the great Turenne in the command of the army.
† The last words of Frederick the Great, King of Prussia.
‡ The traditional form in which Sieyès gave his vote for the execution of Louis XVI. *Sans phrase* ("without phrases"), is probably an addition made by those who reported the words, contrasting this laconic sentence with the florid phrases of the other deputies, but the words have become historical in the form quoted.

L'amour est le roi des jeunes gens et le tyran des vieillards.—*Louis XII.*

Love is the young man's king and the old man's tyrant.

L'amour est le roman du cœur Et le plaisir en est l'histoire. —*Osselin.*

Love is the heart's novel and pleasure is its history.

L'amour est l'étoffe de la nature que l'imagination a brodée.—*Voltaire.*

Love is the groundwork which imagination has embroidered.

L'amour est un de ces maux qu'on ne peut cacher ; un mot, un regard indiscret, le silence même le découvre. —*Abeilard.*

Love is an ill none can conceal ; a look, a word, or even silence reveals it.

L'amour est une chose frivole, et cependant c'est la seule arme avec laquelle on puisse frapper les âmes fortes. —*Stendhal.*

Love is a trifling thing, and yet is the only weapon that can wound stout hearts.

L'amour est une passion qui vient souvent sans savoir comment, et qui s'en va aussi de même.

Love is a passion which often comes we know not how, and leaves us in the same way.

L'amour est une pure rosée qui descend du ciel dans notre cœur, quand il plaît à Dieu.—*Arsène Houssaye.*

Love is a pure dew which drops from heaven into our heart, when God wills.

L'amour est un grand maître, Il fait le lourdaud gentil être.

Love does wonders in his school, He makes a wise man of the fool.

L'amour est un oiseau qui chante au cœur des femmes.—*Alphonse Karr.*

Love is a bird that sings in the heart of woman.

L'amour est un plaisir qui nous tourmente, mais ce tourment fait plaisir. —*Scribe.*

Love is a pleasure that teases, but this teasing is pleasing.

L'amour est un traître qui nous égratigne lors même qu'on ne cherche qu'à jouer avec lui.—*Ninon de Lenclôs.*

Love is a traitor who scratches us even when we want only to play with him.

L'amour étant un sentiment profondément sensuel, il faut que la possession soit possible et même prochaine pour que l'amour naisse. On aime d'ordinaire la femme que les circonstances mettent fréquemment sur votre route, et l'on ne s'attache pas à celle qui passe sans qu'on sache si elle reviendra. On adore l'une, on oublie l'autre sans calcul, sans raisonnement, parce que l'instinct vous pousse vers celle près de laquelle le désir a chance de se satisfaire.—*G. Lachaud.*

Love being a deeply sensual feeling, possession of its object must be possible and even approximate to give birth to love. The woman is usually loved whom circumstances throw frequently in our way, and not the acquaintance whose return is doubtful. We adore the one and forget the other without reasoning, because instinct impels us towards her who offers some chance of conquest.

L'amour et la fumée ne peuvent se cacher.

Love and smoke cannot be concealed.

L'amour il est le désir pour l'inconnu étendu à la folie.—*Petiet.*

Love is the yearning for the unknown carried to madness.

L'amour ne meurt jamais de besoin, mais souvent d'indigestion. *Ninon de Lenclos.*

Love never dies of want, but often of indigestion.

L'amour, pour les mortels, est le souverain bien.—*Louis Ferrier.*

Love is mortals' crowning blessing.

L'amour-propre est flatté des hommages, l'orgueil s'en passe, la vanité les publie.—*Meilhan.*

Self-esteem is flattered by homage; pride dispenses with it; vanity boasts of it.

L'amour-propre est le plus grand de tous les flatteurs.

Self-love is the greatest of all flatterers.

L'amour-propre est un ballon gonflé de vent dont il sort des tempêtes quand on y fait une piqure.—*Voltaire.*

Conceit is a balloon out of which the gas rushes in a tempest when you give it the least prick.

L'amour-propre est un instrument utile, mais dangereux; souvent il blesse la main qui s'en sert, et fait rarement du bien sans mal.—*Rousseau.*

Conceit is a useful but dangerous instrument: often it wounds the holder's hand, and it seldom does any unalloyed good.

L'amour-propre offensée ne pardonne jamais.—*Vigée.*

Offended vanity never forgives.

L'amour qui naît subitement est le plus long à guérir.—*La Bruyère.*

Love that springs into being in a moment takes the longest time to cure.

L'amour sans désirs est une chimère; il n'existe pas dans la nature.
Ninon de Lenclos.

Platonic love is a delusion; it does not exist in nature.

L'amour sans l'estime ne peut aller bien loin, ni s'élever bien haut; c'est un ange qui n'a qu'une aile.
—*Alex. Dumas, fils.*

Without respect, love cannot go far or rise high: it is an angel with but one wing.

L'amour sincère et pur c'est un feu d'aloès qui brûle sans fumée.
—*Quitard.*

Pure, sincere love is a fire of aloes-wood which burns without smoke.

La musique, comme la religion, prête sans conditions toutes les vertus morales aux cœurs qu'elle visite, ces cœurs fussent-ils même les moins dignes de les recevoir.—*Montégut.*

Music, like religion, unconditionally brings in its train all the moral virtues to the heart it enters, even though that heart is not in the least worthy to receive such guests.

La musique est l'interprète le plus pur et le plus pathétique de la poésie, de l'amour, de la douleur.—*Legouvé.*

The purest and most sympathetic interpreter of poetry, love, and grief, is music.

La naissance n'est rien où la vertu n'est pas.—*Molière.*

(Birth is nothing where virtue does not have a place.) 'Tis only noble to be good.

La nation boutiquière.

(The nation of shop-keepers.) England.*

La nature! la nature! Il faut la chasser ou lui obéir. Rien ne prévaut contre le vrai.—*Diderot.*

Nature must be eluded or obeyed. Nothing can prevail against the true.

L'âne de la montagne porte le vin et boit de l'eau.

The ass carries wine but drinks water.

La négation de l'Infini mène droit au Nihilisme. Tout devient "une conception de l'esprit." Avec le nihilisme pas de discussion possible. En somme, aucune voie n'est ouverte pour la pensée par une philosophie qui fait tout aboutir au monosyllabe Non. A Non, il n'y a qu'une réponse: Oui.—*Victor Hugo.*

Denial of the Infinite Being leads straight to Nihilism: all creation becomes merely "a conception of the mind." Discussion is not possible with Nihilism, for no way is opened to the mind by a philosophy which meets every opinion with a "Nay." To "Nay" there is but one reply—"Yea!"

* A saying commonly attributed to Napoleon I. He was not the first to use it, however, although he quoted the expression in one of his speeches.

L'ange du martyre est le plus beau des anges
Qui portent les âmes au ciel !
—*Victor Hugo.*

The angel of martyrdom is the fairest of all the angels which transport souls into heaven.

L'Anglais a les préjugés de l'orgueil, et les Français ceux de la vanité.
—*J. J. Rousseau.*

Pride is the defect of the English, vanity the defect of the French.

Langue de miel et cœur de fiel.

A honeyed tongue and a heart of gall.

L'animal le plus fier qu'enfante la nature
Dans un autre animal respecte sa figure.
—*Boileau.*

(The proudest animal that nature produces respects his own form in another.) Man is the only animal that preys on his own kind.

La nuit donne conseil.

(To take counsel of one's pillow.) To sleep on an idea.

La nuit était si sombre qu'il fallait marcher à tâtons.

The night was so dark that we had to grope our way.

Là où Dieu veut, il pleut.

When God wills all winds bring rain.

Là où sont les poussins la poule a les yeux.

The hen's eyes are with her chickens.

La parfaite raison fuit tout extrémité,
Et veut que l'on soit sage avec sobriété.
—*Molière.*

Absolute good sense avoids all extremes, and requires that we should be temperate even in our wisdom.

La parole a été donnée à l'homme pour déguiser sa pensée —*Talleyrand.*

Words have been given to man for the purpose of concealing his thoughts.

La parole a été donnée à l'homme pour expliquer ses pensées ; et, tout ainsi que les pensées sont les portraits des choses, de même nos paroles sont-elles les portraits de nos pensées.
—*Molière.*

Speech has been given to man to explain his thoughts ; and just as our thoughts are the pictures of things, so our words are the pictures of our thoughts.

La patience est amère, mais son fruit est doux.—*J. J. Rousseau.*

(Patience is bitter, but its fruit is sweet.) "Sweet are the uses of adversity."

La patience est l'art d'espérer.
—*Vauvenargues.*

Patience is the art of hoping.

La patrie de la pensée.
—*Madame de Staël.*

(The fatherland of thought.) Germany.

La peau est plus proche que la chemise.

(The skin is nearer than the shirt.) Charity begins at home.

La peine est déjà loin quand le bonheur commence.—*Dorat.*

We leave sorrow far behind us, as soon as happiness returns.

La pelle qui se moque du fourgon.

The pot calling the kettle black.

La petite aumône est la bonne.

The little alms are the best alms.

La petite vérole est la bataille de Waterloo des femmes. Le lendemain elles connaissent ceux qui les aiment véritablement.—*Balzac.*

Disfigurement is woman's Waterloo ; next day she knows who really loves her.

La peur est grand inventeur.

Fear is a great inventor.

La philosophie n'aura jamais d'influence que sur les classes lettrées, et la religion est nécessaire pour le peuple.
—*V. Cousin.*

Philosophy will never have influence save over the learned classes, whilst religion is necessary for the masses.

La philosophie, qui nous promet de nous rendre heureux, nous trompe.

Philosophy, which promises to make us happy, deceives us.

La plupart des hommes emploient la première partie de leur vie à rendre l'autre misérable. — *La Bruyère.*

Most men employ half their life in piling up misery for the other part.

La plus belle pièce de ménage est une bonne femme.

The finest piece of furniture is a good wife.

La plus courte folie est toujours la meilleure. — *La Giraudière.*

The shortest folly is always the best.

La plus expresse marque de la sagesse, c'est une enjouissance constante.
　　　　　　　　　— *Montaigne.*

Constant cheerfulness is the surest sign of a wise mind.

La plus grande finesse est de n'en avoir point.

The greatest cunning is to have none at all.

La plus perdue de toutes les journées est celle où l'on n'a pas ri. — *Chamfort.*

That day is the most utterly wasted in which one has not laughed.

La plus subtile de toutes les finesses est de savoir bien feindre de tomber dans les pièges qu'on nous tend, et l'on n'est jamais si aisément trompé que quand on songe à tromper les autres.
　　　　　　　— *La Rochefoucauld.*

The subtlest cunning lies in pretending to fall into traps laid for us by others, for none are so easily entrapped as those who prepare pitfalls for their neighbours.

La plus sûre règle qu'on ne puisse donner, c'est écouter beaucoup, parler peu et ne rien dire dont on puisse avoir sujet de se repentir.
　　　　　　　— *La Rochefoucauld.*

The surest rule (to excel in conversation) is to listen much, speak little, and say nothing that you may be sorry for.

La poésie aura un jour à compter avec la science. La grande poésie de ce siècle, c'est la science, avec son épanouissement merveilleux de découvertes, sa conquête de la matière, les ailes qu'elle donne à l'homme pour décupler son activité. — *Zola.*

Poetry will have to reckon with science some day. The great poetry of our age is science, with its marvellous blossoming forth of discoveries, its conquest of matter, and the wings it gives man to augment his activities.

La poésie est l'étoile
Qui mène à Dieu rois et pasteurs.
　　　　　　　— *Victor Hugo.*

Poetry is the star which guides kings and shepherds unto God.

La Poésie, métier jaloux, veut que l'ouvrier se montre créateur, dans l'invention du *motif* comme dans l'exécution ; et la Nature, qui a pour le poète des sévérités adorables, se refuse absolument à lui donner les sujets tout faits ! — *Banville.*

Poetry, a jealous craft, requires the worker to be a creator as well in invention of the motive as in its execution ; and Nature, who is a gracious but stern mistress to the poet, utterly refuses him ready-made subjects.

La politique est un tripot dans lequel les spectateurs sont exposés à payer autant que les joueurs. — *Nisard.*

Politics are a gaming-hell, in which lookers-on are exposed to paying as much as the players.

La politique ! . . . Frapper sur des utopies à coups d'utopies, c'est amusant. Regarde ces grands enfants se poursuivant toujours sans se rencontrer jamais, par les corridors de ce château de la parole, sonore et vide. Quand l'un est en haut, l'autre appelle en bas, et monte à son tour pour parler d'en haut. . . . C'est amusant, car cela ne finit pas. — *Gavarni.*

Politics ! to knock the heads of Utopias together is amusing. Look at those great children who run after one another without overtaking through the echoing, empty passages of the Temple of Talk. When one is above floors, the other calls below, and runs up in his turn to be called to. An amusing game, for it never ends.

La popularité c'est la gloire en grands sous.—*Victor Hugo.*

Popularity is glory coined into coppers.

La porte ouverte tente le saint.

(The open door tempts the saint.) Opportunity makes the thief.

La poule ne doit pas chanter devant le coq.

The hen ought not to cackle when the cock is by.

L'appétit vient en mangeant.

(Appetite comes in the eating.) Use makes all things sweet.

La première larme d'amour qu'on fait verser paraît un diamant, la seconde une perle, et la troisième une larme.
—*Poincelot.*

The first tear shed in love appears a diamond, the second a pearl, the third merely a tear.

La prière est un cri d'espérance.
—*Alfred de Musset.*

Prayer is a cry of hope.

La prière rend l'affliction moins douloureuse et la joie plus pure : elle mêle à l'une je ne sais quoi de fortifiant et de doux, et à l'autre un parfum céleste.
—*Lamennais.*

Prayer makes affliction less painful, and gladness more pure; with one it mingles an indescribable sweetness, and with the other a heavenly perfume.

La propre volonté ne se satisferait jamais quand elle aurait tout ce qu'elle souhaite ; mais on est satisfait dès l'instant qu'on y renonce.
—*Pascal.*

One's own desires are never satisfied when they have all they wish; but they are satisfied as soon as the wish is renounced.

La propriété c'est le vol.—*Proudhon.*

Property is theft.*

La propriété exclusive est un vol dans la nature.—*Brissot.*

Exclusive property is a theft in nature.

La prospérité fait peu d'amis.
—*Vauvenargues.*

Prosperity makes few friends.

La pudeur est la plus proche parente de la vertu.—*Mme. de Coulanges.*

Shame is virtue's next of kin.

La puissance du génie peut se manifester dans la création de l'idée ou dans la perfection qu'il ajoute à la forme, au métier, à la langue de son temps.—*P. Scudo.*

The power of genius may be manifested in the creation of an idea, or in the perfection it adds to the manners, crafts, and speech of the time in which it exists.

La raillerie est un discours en faveur de son esprit contre son bon naturel.
—*Montesquieu.*

Sarcasm is a plea in favour of the wit against one's natural goodness.

La raison du plus fort est toujours la meilleure.—*La Fontaine.*

(The reasoning of the strongest is always the best.) Might is stronger than Right.†

La raison n'est pas ce qui règle l'amour.
—*Molière.*

Reason plays no part in the bestowing of love.

L'arbre de la liberté ne croît qu'arrosé par le sang des tyrans.
—*Bertrand Barère.*

The tree of liberty only grows when it is watered by the blood of tyrants.‡

L'arbre et l'écorce.

(The tree and the bark.) The man and wife.

---

* This maxim has become the basis of the doctrines taught by Karl Marx and other Socialist writers. Capital, in their opinion, represents the surplus value of the labour of the workers over and above the wages they receive.

† Compare the saying of his contemporary, Madame de Sévigné, *La fortune est toujours, etc.*

‡ The amiable Barère made this remark in a speech, delivered in 1792, in the Convention.

L'arbre n'est point jugé sur ses fleurs
  et son fruit ;
    On le juge sur son écorce.
                        —*Sedaine.*

L'arbre ne tombe pas du premier coup.

La recherche de la paternité est inter-
  dite.

La reconnaissance est la mémoire du
  cœur.

La république, c'est le gouvernement qui
  nous divise le moins.—*Thiers.*

La résistance d'une femme n'est pas
  toujours une preuve de sa vertu, elle
  l'est plus souvent de son expérience.
                —*Ninon de Lenclos.*

La ressource de ceux qui n'imaginent
  pas est de conter.—*Vauvenargues.*

L'argent est un bon serviteur, et un
  méchant maître.

La rouillé use plus que le travail.

L'art de s'en aller est un art que le Pari-
  sien seul connaît, cependant il fait
  quelque fois des visites un peu bien
  longues—parce que, au moment de
  prendre congé, il se préoccupe du mal
  qu'on dira de lui, en songeant au mal
  qu'il a dit des autres.—*Chas. Narrey.*

L'art de vaincre est celui de mépriser
  la mort.—*De Sivry.*

L'artiste est arrivé au sommet de l'art
  quand il a excité la pitié, l'amour et
  l'admiration par la représentation
  fidèle de la vie, de la beauté, de la
  douleur et de la vertu.
                —*Emeric David.*

L'art par excellence, celui qui surpasse
  tous les autres parce qu'il est incom-
  parablement le plus expressif, c'est la
  poésie, le type de la perfection de
  tous les arts, l'art qui comprend tous
  les autres, auquel tous aspirent,
  auquel nul ne peut atteindre.
                —*V. Cousin.*

La satire ment sur les gens de lettres
  pendant leur vie, et l'éloge ment
  après leur mort.—*Voltaire.*

La sauce vaut mieux que le poisson.

(Nowadays we do not judge trees by
  their flowers and fruit, but by their
  bark.) Outward show, not character,
  is regarded as the criterion of merit.

The tree is not felled by the first blow.

Inquiry into paternity is forbidden.*

Gratitude is the heart's memory.†

The republic is the form of government
  which divides us least.

Woman's coyness is not always a proof
  of her virtue ; it is more often a proof
  of her experience.

The narration of anecdotes is the resource
  of those who have no imagination.

Money is a good servant, and a bad
  master.

Rust wears more than use.

The art of ending a visit is known only to
  a Parisian, although he sometimes pro-
  tracts a call beyond the proper limits,
  because, at going, he worries about the
  bad things which will be spoken of
  him, judging by the scandals he has
  just been spreading concerning others.

Conquering is the art of despising death.

The artist arrives at the summit of his
  art when he has roused pity, love, and
  admiration by the faithful representation of life, beauty, pain and virtue.

The art above all others, from its being
  incomparably the most expressive, is
  poetry—the type of perfection of all
  the arts, the one comprising the
  others, the one all the others yearn for
  and never can attain.

During life Satire lies about literary
  men, and after death Eulogy does
  the same.

The sauce is better than the fish.‡

---

* Article 340 of the Code Napoléon. French law gives immunity to the father of an illegitimate child.
† The reply written by the deaf mute, Massieu, when asked to define gratitude.
‡ Joseph Scaliger applied this saying to some of Casaubon's classical commentaries, meaning that the commentary was more worthy of praise than the work itself.

La saveur des pensées détachées dépend d'une expression concise ; ce sont des grains de sucre ou de sel qu'il faut savoir fondre dans une goutte d'eau.
—*J. Petit-Senn.*

La science et la philosophie doivent suffire un jour à l'humanité.
—*Vacherot.*

La sentinelle cria : " Qui vive ? "

La société est partagée en deux classes : les tondeurs et les tondus. Il faut toujours être avec les premiers contre les seconds.—*Talleyrand.*

La société qui fait tant de mal ressemble à ce serpent des Indes dont la demeure est la feuille d'une plante qui guèrit sa morsure ; elle présente presque toujours le remède à côté de la souffrance qu'elle a causée.
—*Alfred de Musset.*

La solitude est à l'esprit ce que la diète est au corps.—*Vauvenargues.*

La spiritualité de l'âme est un fait, un fait positif, un fait aussi éclatant que la lumière du soleil. On cherche encore et on cherchera peut-être toujours ce que c'est que la matière ; mais quant à l'esprit, nous le connaissons, car nous en avons en nous le type, savoir le moi pensant, sentant et voulant.—*Saïsset.*

L'assassinat d'une nation est impossible. Le droit, c'est l'astre ; il s'éclipse, mais il reparaît. La Hongrie le prouve, Venise le prouve, la Pologne le prouve.—*V. Hugo.*

L'Assommoir.

La table est le seul endroit où l'on ne s'ennuie pas pendant la première heure—*Brillat-Savarin.*

La terre est au soleil ce que l'homme est à l'ange ;
L'un est fait de splendeur, l'autre est pétri de fange.—*V. Hugo.*

La terre ne saurait être éclairée de deux soleils, ni une seule âme de deux lumières d'amour.

La tête montée.

L'athéisme est le dernier mot du théisme.
—*H. Heine.*

The flavour of quotations depends on terse expression ; they are grains of salt or sugar which one must know how to mix in a drop of water.

The human race will have, some day, to be contented with what science and philosophy offers.

The sentry cried, " Who goes there ? "

Society is split up into two classes: the shearers and the shorn. We must always side with the former against the latter.

Society, in causing evil, resembles that Indian serpent whose nest is in the plant which is the antidote for the reptile's venom : it almost always affords a remedy for the suffering it has given.

Solitude is to the mind what diet is to the body.

The spirituality of the soul is a positive fact as clearly bright as sunlight. Search has been and search will be always made probably into the subject of Matter ; but we know what Mind is, from having in us the example, the sentient pulsating *ego* within us.

A nation cannot be murdered. Right is a star which, eclipsed, will shine again. Bear witness, Hungary, Venice, Poland !

(The bludgeon.) A low tavern.*

The dining-room is the only place where a man is not bored before the first hour is over.

As the earth to the sun, so is man to the angel, for as the one is made of clay, the other is made of splendour.

The earth cannot receive light from two suns, nor can a single heart be warmed by two flames of love.

Excited ; hot-headed.

Atheism is the last word of theism.

---

* This is the title of a well-known novel by Zola, from which the English play " Drink" has been adapted. Assommoir is the name of a low-class drinking-shop in Belleville, the Whitechapel of Paris. Hence the name is given to any tavern where bad liquor is sold.

La vanité n'a pas de plus grand ennemi que la vanité.

Vanity has no greater foe than vanity.

L'avare et le cochon ne sont bons qu'après leur mort.

The miser and the pig are useless until they are dead.

L'avarice rompt le sac.

Avarice bursts the bag.

L'avenir des enfants est l'ouvrage des mères.—*Napoleon I.*

The future generation is woman's work.

La vérité entre si naturellement dans l'esprit, que quand on l'apprend pour la première fois, il semble qu'on ne fasse que s'en souvenir.
　　　　　　　—*Fontenelle.*

Truth comes into the mind so naturally, that when we hear it for the first time it seems to be merely a reminiscence of what we have known before.

La vérité est cachée au fond du puits.

Truth lies hidden at the bottom of the well.

La vérité est comme la rosée du ciel ; pour la conserver pure, il faut la recueillir dans un vase pur.

Truth is like the dew of Heaven ; to preserve its purity it must be gathered in a clean vessel.

La vérité est toujours précieuse.
　　　　　　　—*Voltaire.*

Truth is always valuable.

Laver la tête.

To bring to book.

La vertu, d'un cœur noble est la marque certaine.—*Boileau.*

Virtue is the certain token of a noble heart.

La vertu est la seule noblesse.

(Virtue is the only nobility.)　Motto of the Earl of Guildford.

La vertu est le premier titre de noblesse.
　　　　　　　—*Molière.*

Virtue is the best title of true nobility.

Lavez, peignez chien, toutefois n'est chien qu'chien.

(Though you wash and comb a dog, it's still a dog.)　Cut off a dog's tail, and he will be a dog still.

La vie est brève,
Un peu d'amour,
Un peu de rêve,
Et puis, Bonjour.

Life is short, a little love, a little dreaming, and then, Good-day.

La vie est vaine,
Un peu d'espoir,
Un peu de haine,
Et puis, Bonsoir.—*Alfred de Musset.*

Life is vain, a little hope, a little hate, and then, Good-night.

La vie est comme une fiancée hypocrite qui trahit toutes ses promesses et ne laisse à son amant d'autre consolation que le droit de la mépriser.
　　　　　　　—*Alfred Mercier.*

Life is like a deceitful woman who breaks all her pledges to her lover, and leaves him no other consolation than the right to despise her.

La vie est facile pour les hiboux, les espaces ne les invitent pas ; mais l'aigle veut monter au soleil : dût-il retomber l'œil consumé, l'aile brisée, et livrer pour jouet à l'écume des mers sa morne dépouille . . . . un instant du moins la splendeur de l'empyrée aura étanché les soifs ardentes de sa prunelle, et ses regards auront vidé d'un seul trait la coupe des célestes clartés.—*Cherbuliez.*

Life is easy for owls, whom the expanse of the heavens does not tempt to soar ; but the eagle seeks the sun, even though it may fall with scorched eye and broken pinion into the sea to be the sport of the billows ; at least for a moment the splendour of the empyræan quenched its ardent glances, and it has drained the cup of celestial glory.

T

La vie est une fleur, l'amour en est le miel.—*Victor Hugo.*

Life is a flower, and its honey is love.

La vie est une garde ; il faut la monter proprement et la descendre sans tache. —*Charlet.*

Life is a sentry beat ; you must mount guard in a proper manner, and be relieved without blame.

La vie est un sommeil. Les vieillards sont ceux dont le sommeil a été le plus long ; ils ne commencent à se réveiller que quand il faut mourir.—*La Bruyère.*

Life is a sleep. Old men are those who have slept the longest time ; when they wake up, they find it is time to die.

La vie humaine est semblable à un chemin dont l'issue est un précipice affreux : on nous en avertit dès le premier pas, mais la loi est prononcée, il faut avancer toujours. On voudrait retourner en arrière, plus de moyen ; tout est tombé, tout est évanoui, tout échappé.—*Bossuet.*

Human life is like a road with a dreadful precipice at the end of it. At the first step we are warned of this, yet the law says we must proceed. When we want to turn back we cannot, all the road behind us has fallen in and become an abyss.

La vieillesse n'a rien de beau que la vertu.—*Amyot.*

The only lovely thing about old age is virtue.

La vie moderne comporte si peu le drame sanglant, les rudes sauvageries du meurtre et de la passion, que les scènes tragiques auxquelles une famille a pu assister semblent bien vite, aux personnes mêmes de cette famille, un cauchemar dont il est impossible de douter et auquel on ne croit pourtant pas entièrement.—*Paul Bourget.*

Modern life is so little in harmony with bloodshed, the savage acts of murder and passion, that, when a family is forced to witness a tragedy, each individual regards the occurrence as a kind of nightmare. They are compelled to acknowledge that the apparition exists, but they cannot entirely realise it.

La vie ne semble souvent qu'un long naufrage dont les débris sont l'amitié, la gloire et l'amour. Les rives du temps qui s'est écoulé pendant que nous avons vécu en sont couvertes. —*Mme. de Staël.*

Life often seems but a shipwreck, whose fragments are friendship, glory and love. The shores of time that we pass during our life are covered with these derelicts.

La vie privée d'un citoyen doit être murée.—*Talleyrand.*

The private life of a citizen ought to have a wall built around it.

L'eau en vient à la bouche.

That makes one's mouth water.

Le beau monde.

The fashionable world.

Le beau soulier blesse souvent le pied.

A handsome shoe oft pinches the foot.

Le bedeau de la paroisse est toujours de l'avis de monsieur le curé.

The beadle always agrees with the rector.

Le bœuf par la corne et l'homme par la parole.

Hold an ox by his horns, a man by his word.

Le bon de l'histoire.

The cream of the story.

Le bonheur des méchants comme un torrent s'écoule.—*Racine.*

The prosperity of the evildoer rushes away like a torrent.

Le bonheur semble fait pour être partagé.—*Racine.*

Happiness seems made to be shared.

Le bon sang ne peut mentir.

Good blood cannot tell a lie.

Le bon sens est une qualité du caractère plus encore que de l'esprit. —*Vauvenargues.*

Common sense is rather a trait of the temperament than of the mind.

Le bon temps viendra.

There is a good time coming.

Le bon veneur ne prend
La bête qui se rend.

A good sportsman does not take the beast that makes no fight.

Le bossu ne voit pas sa bosse, mais il voit celle de son confrère.

The hunchback does not see his own hump, but he sees his brother's.

Le bourgeois gentilhomme.

The cit turned nobleman.*

Le bruit des armes l'empeschoit d'entendre la voix des loix.—*Montaigne.*

The din of arms prevents us from hearing the voice of the laws.

Le bruit pend l'homme.

(Reputation hangs a man.)　Give a dog a bad name and you may as well hang him.

Le bureau et la fabrique sont de plainpied.

The office and the factory are on the same floor.

Le capitaine devait au tiers et au quart.

The captain was over head and ears in debt.

Le célibataire riche, qui dîne en ville tous les jours, est ce que l'on appelle un homme répandu; le même, pauvre, est un pique-assiette.
　　　　　—*Chas. Narrey.*

The rich bachelor who dines out daily is called a welcome guest; the poor one, a sponger.

Le cerf était aux abois.

The stag was at bay.

Le chant du cygne.

(The swan-song.)　A funeral dirge.

L'écharpe blanche.

(The white scarf.)　The insignia of the Legitimists.

Le chef d'œuvre de Dieu est la figure humaine.　Le regard d'une femme a plus de charme que le bel horizon de paysage ou de mer, et plus d'attrait qu'un rayon de soleil.
　　　　　—*Alfred Stevens.*

Heaven's masterpiece is the human form.　The glance of a woman has more charm than a lovely stretch of sea or landscape, and more attraction than a sunbeam.

Le ciel me prive d'une épouse qui ne m'a jamais donné d'autre chagrin que celui de sa mort.

Heaven has deprived me of a wife who never caused me any grief save by her death.†

Le cœur a ses raisons que la raison ne connaît point.—*Pascal.*

The heart has its reasons, whereof reason knows nothing.

Le cœur d'une femme galante est comme une rose dont chaque amant emporte une feuille; il ne reste que l'épine au mari.—*Sophie Arnould.*

The heart of a flirt is a rose from which each lover bears away a leaf; the thorns fall to the husband's share.

Le cœur est comme ces sortes d'arbres qui ne donnent leur baume pour les blessures des hommes que lorsque le fer les a blessés eux-mêmes.
　　　　　—*Chateaubriand.*

The heart is like the balsam which gives no balm for men's wounds until cut and bruised itself.

Le cœur mène où il va.

The heart leads us whither it lists.

Le cœur n'a pas de rides.
　　　　　—*Mme. de Sévigné.*

The heart never becomes wrinkled.

Le cœur ne veut douloir ce que l'œil ne peut voir.

What the eye doth not see the heart doth not crave for.

---

* The name of one of Molière's most famous comedies.
† The remark of Louis XIV. on the death of his wife.

Le cœur qui n'aima point fut le premier athée.—*Alfred Mercier.*

The heart that never loved was the first atheist.

Le cœur sent rarement ce que la bouche exprime.—*Campistron.*

The heart rarely feels what the lips utter.

Le commun caractère est de n'en point avoir.—*L. Andrieux.*

The most common character is not to possess one at all.

Le congrès ne marche pas, il danse.

The congress does not advance, it dances.*

Le coup de pied de l'âne.

(The donkey's kick.) "The most unkindest cut of all."†

Le courage est souvent un effet de la peur.—*Corneille.*

Courage is often an effect of fear.

L'écoutant fait le médisant.

If it were not for listeners, there would be no slanderers.

Le coût en ôte le goût.

The cost takes away the taste.

Le crime fait la honte, et non pas l'échafaud.—*Th. Corneille.*

The crime causes the shame and not the scaffold.‡

Le cygne noir.

The pink of perfection.

Le demi-monde.

(The half-world.) The fringe of Society.§

Le désir rend beau ce qui est laid.

(Love makes the ugly seem fair.) Luve hae nae lack, be the dame e'er sae black.

Le devoir, c'est ce qu'on exige des autres.—*Dumas, fils.*

Duty is what we expect others to practise.

Le diable boiteux.

The devil on two sticks.

Le dîner est cuit à point.

The dinner is done to a T.

Le droit du plus fort.

(The right of the strongest.) Might is right.

Le droit qu'un esprit vaste et ferme en ses desseins
A sur l'esprit grossier des vulgaires humains.—*Voltaire.*

The right that a mind ambitious and firm in its designs, has over the gross minds of ordinary men.‖

Le fabricateur souverain
Nous créa besaciers tous de même manière,
Tant ceux du temps passé que du temps d'aujourd'hui :
Il fit pour nos défauts la poche de derrière,
Et celle de devant pour les défauts d'autrui.—*La Fontaine.*

The Creator has made us all indifferently, both men of former times and those of to-day, to carry a wallet. That which contains our own sins hangs behind us, but that wherein are the sins of others is ever placed before us.

Le feu le plus couvert est le plus ardent.

Hidden fires are always the hottest.

---

* The comment of the Prince de Ligne on the Congress held in Vienna in 1814.
† The words are from La Fontaine's fable of the sick lion, whom all the other beasts insult ; then, as the last straw, the ass comes to kick the king of beasts.
‡ Charlotte Corday quoted these words of her ancestor, Thomas Corneille, in a letter written on the eve of her execution.
§ The title given by Dumas fils to one of his novels.
‖ Voltaire, in his tragedy, *Mahomet*, puts these words into the mouth of the prophet who thus defends his right to power. An amusing story is told of the actor Lekain in connection with these lines. One day he was caught trespassing in the shooting preserves of a wealthy nobleman, but when the gamekeeper demanded by what right he was there, the tragedian rolled out this reply in his best theatrical manner. So overwhelmed was the poor gamekeeper with these sonorous words that he allowed the actor to continue his poaching undisturbed.

Le fils d'un coquin enrichi peut être un honnête homme, son gendre, jamais.
—*Charles Narrey.*

The son of an enriched rogue may be an honest man, but the man who marries the rogue's daughter must be a knave.

Le fou cherche son malheur.

The fool hunts for misfortune.

Le fou demande beaucoup, mais plus fol est celui qui donne.

The fool asketh much, but he is more foolish that giveth to him.

Le frère est ami de nature,
Mais son amitié n'est pas sûre.
—*Baudoin.*

A brother is a friend that nature gives us, but his friendship is not reliable.

Le fruit du travail est le plus doux plaisir.—*Vauvenargues.*

The sweetest fruit is that of labour.

Le génie a besoin du public.—Sans doute. Comme la foudre a besoin de conducteur. Souvent aussi le conducteur fait défaut. L'avenir le donnera.
—*Ph. Chasles.*

Genius requires a public to appeal to. No doubt, just as the lightning requires a conductor. Often the conductor fails to do its work; the future will make good the omission.

Le génie, en somme, consiste probablement à exprimer les choses banales d'une façon originale, et à fixer la vie courante dans une forme définitive.
—*Richepin.*

Genius, in short, probably consists in expressing commonplaces in an original manner, and in giving concrete shape to the evanescent things of life.

Le génie est la raison sublime.
—*A. Chénier.*

Genius is reason in its loftiest form.

Le génie n'a pas de sexe.
—*Madame de Staël.*

Genius is sexless.

Le génie n'est autre chose qu'une grande aptitude à la patience.—*Buffon.*

Genius is nothing but a great aptitude for being patient.

Le génie, quelle que soit sa force innée, ne crée pas à lui tout seul la langue dont il a besoin pour se révéler.
—*P. Scudo.*

Whatever be the inborn power of Genius, it cannot create the needful language to reveal itself.

Le goût n'est rien ; nous avons l'habitude
De rédiger au long, de point en point,
Ce qu'on pensa ; mais nous ne pensons point.—*Voltaire.*

Taste goes for nothing with us (pedantic writers) ; our habit is to write, with much verbosity and circumstance, the thoughts of other people; as for ourselves, we never think.

Le gouvernement américain fut fait à l'instar du gouvernement Anglais.

The American government was modelled on the English.

Le grand homme vaincu peut perdre en un instant
Sa gloire, son empire, et son trône éclatant,
        Et sa couronne qu'on renie,
Tout, jusqu'à ce prestige à sa grandeur mêlé
Qui faisait voir son front dans un ciel étoilé ;
        Il garde toujours son génie !
—*Victor Hugo.*

The great man vanquished may lose in a moment his glory, empire, glittering throne, and crown—even the aureole of fame which makes his face to shine as a star of heaven—but his genius he retains as an everlasting possession.

Le grand œuvre.

The great work ; the philosopher's stone.

Le grand poison du cœur, c'est le silence.
—*Paul Bourget.*

The most injurious poison to the heart is silence.

Le hasard est un sobriquet de la Providence.—*Chamfort.*

Chance is a nickname that we give to Providence.

Le Jésuitisme est un épée, dont la poignée est à Rome, et la pointe partout.—*Dupin.*

Jesuitism is a sword. Its hilt is in Rome, its point everywhere.

Le jeune homme est recherché pour ce qu'il sait, la jeune fille pour ce qu'elle ignore.—*Charles Narrey.*

The young man is sought after for what he knows ; the young lady for what she does not know.

Le jeu ne vaut pas la chandelle.

The game is not worth the candle.*

Le jour n'est pas plus pur que le fond de mon cœur.—*Racine.*

The light of day is not more pure than the inmost recesses of my heart.

Le jour viendra.

(The day will come.)   Motto of the Earl of Durham.

Le juste milieu.

The golden mean.†

L'éloquence est au sublime ce que le tout est à sa partie.—*La Bruyère.*

Eloquence is to the sublime what the whole is to a part.

L'éloquence est quelque chose de plus que la science de penser et d'écrire Le génie même n'a pas toujours droit sur elle; c'est un don à part, un privilége unique.—*Villemain.*

Eloquence is more than the science of thinking and writing. Genius itself has not always a claim upon it ; it is a special boon and unique privilege granted to him who possesses it.

Le maître l'a dit.

(The master said it.)   *Ipse dixit.*

Le mal vient à cheval et s'en va à pied.

Misfortune comes on horseback and goes away on foot.

Le mariage doit combattre sans repos ni trève ce monstre qui dévore tout, l'habitude.—*Balzac.*

Wedlock should fight, without truce or rest, that all-devouring monster, Habit.

Le mariage est de toutes les choses sérieuses la chose la plus bouffonne.
    —*Beaumarchais.*

Of all serious matters marriage is the funniest.

Le masque tombe, l'homme reste,
Et le héros s'évanouit.
   - *J. B. Rousseau.*

The mask falls, the man remains,
And the hero disappears.

Le médecin est souvent plus à craindre que la maladie.

The doctor is often more to be dreaded than the disease.

Le meilleur vin a sa lie.

There are dregs in the best bottle of wine.

Le miel est doux, mais l'abeille pique.

Honey is sweet, but the bee stings.

Le miel n'est pas pour les ânes.

Honey is not for asses.

Le mieux est l'ennemi du bien.

(Better is the enemy of good.)   A present good is sometimes lost in the vain pursuit of a greater blessing. Leave well alone.

Le miroir n'est point flatteur.

The looking-glass is no flatterer.

Le moi est haïssable.—*Pascal.*

The word *I* is a hateful thing.

Le moineau en la main vaut mieux que l'oie qui vole.

(A sparrow in the hand is better than a goose on the wing.)   A bird in the hand is worth two in the bush.

---

* It was an old custom for poor folk to meet in a neighbour's house to play cards. At the end, they each subscribed something towards the expenses of the entertainment. If they were stingy, their host found that the gifts were less than the cost of the candle which he had provided.

† A favourite expression of Louis-Philippe.

Le moine répond comme l'abbé chante.
Le monde est le livre des femmes.
　　　　　　　—*J. J. Rousseau.*

The monk responds as the abbot chants.
The world is the women's book.

Le monde est une guerre ; celui qui vit aux dépens des autres est victorieux.
　　　　　　　—*Voltaire.*

The world is a war ; the victor in it is the man who lives at the expense of others.

Le monde récompense plus souvent les apparences du mérite que le mérite même.—*La Rochefoucauld.*

The world rewards the appearance of merit more often than merit itself.

Le mortier sent toujours les aulx.

(The smell of the garlic always remains in the jar.)
" You may break, you may shatter the vase if you will,
But the scent of the roses will cling to it still."

Le mot de l'énigme.

The key of the mystery.

Le motif seul fait le mérite des actions des hommes, et le désintéressement y met la perfection.—*La Bruyère.*

The merit of human actions springs from their motive ; and disinterestedness is their crowning virtue.

Le mot pour rire.

The cream of the jest.

L'Empire, c'est la paix.—*Napoleon III.*

The Empire, it is peace.*

L'Empire, c'est l'épée.

The Empire is the sword.†

L'empire des lettres.

The republic of letters.

L'empire est au phlegmatique.
　　　　　　　—*St. Just.*

It is the cool man that rules.‡

Le nez de Cléopatre, s'il eut été plus court, toute la face de la terre auroit changé.—*Pascal.*

If Cleopatra's nose had been shorter, the whole aspect of the world would have been changed.

L'enfance est le sommeil de la raison.
　　　　　　　—*J. J. Rousseau.*

Childhood is the slumber time of the intellect.

L'enfant a plutôt l'air de venir du ciel, que le vieillard tout couvert de souillures n'a l'air d'y aller.—*Gerfaut.*

The babe seems much more like one coming from heaven than an old man stained with sin seems like one going there.

L'ennemi était sur le qui vive.

The enemy was on the alert.

Le nom, les armes, la loyauté.

(My name, my arms, my loyalty.) Motto of the Newland family.§

L'entente est au diseur.

The meaning is best known to the speaker.

L'envie est au fond du cœur humain comme une vipère dans son trou.
　　　　　　　—*Balzac.*

Envy dwells in the heart's core as a viper in its hole.

---

* Louis Napoleon used these words in one of his speeches before he became Emperor of the French, little anticipating the series of wars in which France was about to be plunged, and the crowning disaster of Sedan.

+ The pun of the German *Kladderadatsch* on *L'empire, c'est la paix.* The empire meant taxes said *Punch : l'empire c'est la pay.*

‡ The motto of the colleague of Robespierre, who, however, did not manage by his own cold disposition to escape the guillotine.

§ This motto is adapted from the last words of Roger Newland, who was executed for aiding the attempt of Charles I. to escape from Carisbrooke Castle. " Deprived of my life and property, I leave to posterity my name, which none can assail ; my arms, which traitors, ignorant alike of gentility and heraldry, cannot efface ; and my loyalty, which none can impugn."

Le papier souffre tout.

You may put anything on paper.

Le pauvre homme !

The poor man ! *

Le pays du mariage a cela de particulier, que les étrangers ont envie de l'habiter, et que les naturels voudraient en être exilés.—*Dufresny.*

The peculiarity of marriage-land is that the foreigners wish to dwell in it, and the inhabitants long to be exiled from it.

Le Père Gratias.

Father Bountiful.†

Le petit caporal.

The little corporal ; Napoleon.

Le petit monde.

The lower classes.

Le peuple demandait vengeance à cor et à cri.

The people howled for vengeance.

Le peuple ne se trompe pas en croyant que l'hirondelle est la meilleure du monde ailé. Pourquoi ? elle est la plus heureuse, étant de beaucoup la plus libre.—*Michelet.*

The masses are not wrong in believing the swallow the best of birds, for it is the happiest because by far the most free.

Le philtre de l'amour, c'est l'amour même.—*Péréfixe.*

Love's philtre is love itself.

L'épigramme est un jeu d'escrime.
　　　　　　—*Lebrun.*

The art of epigram is a game of fence.

L'épine en naissant va la pointe devant.

A thorn comes forth point foremost.

L'épitaphe de l'art de la scène est NIHIL. Rien, rien, qu'un souvenir vague, la fumée d'un lustre, les lambeaux d'une affiche, les débris d'un masque, l'écho d'un applaudissement.—*Paul de Saint Victor.*

The epitaph on theatrical art is NIHIL. Nothing lingers save a vague memory—the smoke of the footlights, the tatters of a playbill, the rags of a mask, and the echo of applause.

Le plaisir de la critique nous ôte celui d'être vivement touché de très-belles choses.—*La Bruyère.*

In the pleasures of criticism we lose the delightful emotions which the admiration of beautiful things arouses.

　　　Le Plaisir est fils de l'Amour,
Mais c'est un fils ingrat qui fait mourir son père.—*Panard.*

Pleasure is the son of Love, but an ingrate who causes his father's death.

Le plancher des vaches.

(The cows' flooring.)　　The land, as opposed to the sea.

Le plus grand de tous les plaisirs est d'en donner à ce qu'on aime.
　　　　　　—*Boufflers.*

The greatest of delights is to give yourself over to your beloved.

Le plus grand miracle de l'amour est de guérir de la coquetterie.
　　　　　　—*La Rochefoucauld.*

The greatest miracle of love is that it cures one of coquetry.

Le plus grand secret pour le bonheur, c'est d'être bien avec soi. Il est bon d'y avoir une retraite agréable ; mais elle ne peut l'être si elle n'y a été préparée par les mains de la vertu.
　　　　　　—*Fontenelle.*

The great secret of happiness is to be at ease with yourself. It is well to have in oneself a pleasant refuge, but no such refuge can exist if not prepared by virtue.

---

* This familiar exclamation, that occurs in Molière's *Tartuffe*, is thought to have been suggested by Louis XIV. The phrase is applied in the play to Tartuffe, who receives much commiseration which he does not deserve. Now it is always used in an ironical sense when speaking of a person who grumbles at his misfortunes without any real cause.

† The nickname given to President Grévy by the poor of Paris in recognition of his generous disposition.

Le plus malheureux de tous les hommes est celui qui croit l'être, car le malheur dépend moins des choses qu'on souffre, que de l'impatience avec laquelle on augmente son malheur.

The most wretched of all men is he who thinks that he is so, for wretchedness depends less on what we suffer, than on the impatience whereby we increase our unhappiness.

Le plus riche n'emporte qu'un linceul.

The richest man takes only a shroud to the grave.

Le plus sage est celui qui ne pense point l'être.—*Boileau.*

The wisest man is he who does not think that he is the wisest.

Le plus sage se tait.

Wisdom keeps silent.

Le potier au potier porte envie.

Two of a trade seldom agree.

Le premier coup en vaut deux.

The first blow is half the battle.

Le premier pas engage au second.

If you put your little finger in, the whole hand goes.

Le premier pas vers la philosophie, c'est l'incrédulité.—*Diderot.*

Scepticism is the first step on the road to philosophy.

Le premier soupir de l'amour
Est le dernier de la sagesse.—*Bret.*

The first sigh of love is the last of wisdom.

Le premier venu engrène.

First come, first served.

Le Président lui donna la parole.

The Speaker gave him leave to speak.

Le public! combien faut-il de sots pour faire un public ?—*Chamfort.*

The public! how many fools are required to make a public ?

Le quart d'heure de Rabelais.

The quarter of an hour of Rabelais.*

Le radicalisme n'est que le désespoir de la logique.—*Lamartine.*

Radicalism is only the desperation of logic.

Le regard chez une jeune femme est un interprète toujours charmant qui dit avec complaisance ce que la bouche n'ose prononcer.—*Marivaux.*

A girl's gaze is an ever-delightful interpreter of her thoughts, graciously revealing what the mouth dares not utter.

Le repentir coûte bien cher.

Repentance is a costly thing.

Le repentir n'est qu'une desdicte de nostre volonté, et opposition de nos fantaisies.—*Montaigne.*

Repentance is merely a contradiction of our will and an opposition to our whims.

Le reste ne veut pas l'honneur d'être nommé.—*Corneille.*

The rest do not deserve the honour of being named.

Le riche a plus de parents qu'il ne connaît.

The rich man has more relations than he knows.

Le roi de France ne venge pas les injures du Duc d'Orléans.—*Louis XII.*

The King of France does not avenge wrongs done to the Duke of Orleans.†

Le roi est mort, vive le roi!

The king is dead, long live the king !

Le roi et l'état.

The king and the state.

Le roi le veut.

The king wills it.

Le roi règne et ne gouverne pas.
—*Thiers.*

(The king reigns and does not govern.) A description of a limited monarchy.‡

Le roi s'en avisera.

The king will consider the matter.

* This reference to an incident in Rabelais is more familiar to English readers in the form *mauvais quart d'heure.*
† Words used by Louis XII. on his accession in 1498. As Duke of Orleans he had suffered indignities, but refused to avenge them when his assumption of sovereign power gave him the opportunity to do so.
‡ Thiers is said to have coined this expression, but it is really a translation of the Latin phrase uttered by Zamoiski in the Polish Diet, *Rex regnat sed non gubernat.*

Le rouge soir et blanc matin
Font réjouir le pélerin.

(A red evening and a white morning make glad the heart of the pilgrim.)
An evening red and a morning grey Will set the traveller on his way.

Le roy et l'estat.

(The King and the State.)　Motto of the Earl of Ashburnham.

Les absents ont toujours tort.

The absent are always in the wrong.

Les adulateurs font leurs orges en pillant les autres.

Flatterers feather their nest by robbing others.

Les affaires, c'est l'argent des autres.
—*Alex. Dumas, fils.*

Business means other people's money.

Les affaires font les hommes.

Business makes men.

Le sage entend à demi mot.

The wise man understands with half a word.

Le sage ne se repent pas, il se corrige. Le peuple ne se corrige pas, il se repent. Les femmes se jettent dans la pénitence sans se corriger, et même sans se repentir. La pénitence est le dernier plaisir des femmes.
—*Lemontey.*

The wise do not repent, but correct themselves; the masses never correct but repent.　Women fly to repentance without correcting themselves, and often without repenting.　Penitence is woman's latest pleasure.

Les âmes sensibles ont plus d'existence que les autres.—*Duclos.*

Sensitive souls have more real life than others.

Les amis de l'heure présente
Ont le naturel du melon,
Il faut en essayer cinquante
Avant qu'en rencontrer un bon.
—*Claude Mermet.*

Friends are like melons, you may try fifty before you meet a good one.

Les amoureux sans fortune injurient le sort qui a décidé que toutes les grâces des plus belles seraient pour les plus riches.　Cependant, Crésus suffoque d'indignation à se voir volontiers abandonner pour des meur-de-faim.
—*L. Dépret.*

Penniless lovers curse the fate which decides that the richest carry off all the beauties. Yet Crœsus would choke with indignation were he to be jilted for a beggar.

Les amours des gens rustiques se font à coups de poing.

The love of rustic folk begins with blows and scratches.

Les anciens, monsieur, sont les anciens ; et nous sommes les gens de maintenant.—*Molière.*

(The ancients, Sir, are the ancients ; we are the people of to-day.)　Modern customs suit modern people.

Les Anglais ont l'esprit public, et nous l'honneur national.—*Chateaubriand.*

The English have public spirit, the French a jealous sense of their national honour.

Les Anglais ont plus de bon sens qu'aucune nation, et ils sont fous.
—*Metternich.*

The English have more good sense than any other nation, but even they are mad.

Les Anglais sont occupés : ils n'ont pas le temps d'être polis.
—*Montesquieu.*

The English are a busy nation : they have no time to cultivate fine manners.

Le sang qui coule est-il donc si pur ?

Is the blood that was shed so pure ?*

---

* This was the question asked by Barnave in the National Assembly when some were deploring the massacre of the colonists of St. Domingo.　When Barnave was himself condemned to be guillotined, the onlookers shouted out this brutal remark of his as he mounted the scaffold.

Les animaux se repaissent; l'homme mange; l'homme d'esprit seul sait manger.—*Brillat-Savarin.*

Animals feed; man eats, but the man of sense alone knows the right way to do it.

Le savoir-faire.

Tact.

Le savoir-vivre.

Good breeding; knowledge of the world.

Les battus payent l'amende.

(The beaten pay the fine.) The prizes to the victors.

Les beaux esprits se rencontrent.

Great wits meet.

Les belles passions cherchent les belles âmes.—*T. Corneille.*

Noble passions look for noble souls.

Les bons comptes font les bons amis.

Short reckonings make long friends.

Les bras croisés.

With folded arms; idle.

Les cavaliers couraient à bride abattue.

The horsemen rode at full speed.

Les chevaux courent les bénéfices et les ânes les attrapent.

Horses run after prizes and asses get them.

Les circonstances ne forment pas les hommes; elles les montrent: elles dévoilent, pour ainsi dire, la royauté du génie, dernière ressource des peuples éteints. Ces rois qui n'en ont pas le nom, mais qui règnent véritablement par la force du caractère et la grandeur des pensées, sont élus par les événements auxquels ils doivent commander. Sans ancêtres et sans postérité, seuls de leur race, leur mission remplie, ils disparaissent en laissant à l'avenir des ordres qu'il éxecutera fidèlement.—*F. de Lamennais.*

Circumstances do not shape men, but merely reveal them; they unveil the royalty of genius—the last resource of declining races. These uncrowned kings, who really reign by dint of their mettle and the greatness of their mind, are elected by the events they are born to control. With no ancestors and no offspring, sole of their race, they go when their task is fulfilled, and leave orders to the future which will be faithfully carried out.

Les conseillers ne sont pas les payeurs.

Those who are ready to advise you will not pay your debts.

Les consolations indiscrètes ne font qu'aigrir les violentes afflictions.
—*J. J Rousseau.*

Consolation given without tact adds to the affliction.

Les coquettes sont comme les chats qui se caressent à nous plutôt qu'ils ne nous caressent.—*Rivarol.*

Coquettes are like cats, playing on us rather than with us.

Les coquettes sont les charlatans de l'amour.—*La Rochefoucauld.*

Coquettes are love's sham-doctors.

Les corbeaux ne crèvent pas les yeux aux corbeaux.

Ravens do not peck out ravens' eyes.

Les cordonniers sont toujours les plus mal chaussés.

The shoemaker's wife and the farmer's horse are always the worst shod.

Les courtes absences animent l'amour, mais les longues le font mourir.
—*Mirabeau.*

Short absences enliven love, but long ones kill it.

Les courtisans sont des jetons,
Leur valeur dépend de leur place;
Dans la faveur, des millions,
Et des zéros dans la disgrâce.
—*Brébeuf.*

Courtiers are counters—valued by their place:
Millions, in favour—zero in disgrace.

Les cygnes ont le lac, les aigles la montagne,
   Les âmes ont l'amour !— *V. Hugo.*

As the swans have the lake and the
eagles the mountain, souls have love.

Les défauts des femmes leur ont été
donnés par la nature pour exercer les
qualités des hommes.—*Mme. Necker.*

Women's failings were given them by
Nature so as to try men's virtues.

Les délicats sont malheureux ;
Rien ne saurait les satisfaire.
            —*La Fontaine.*

The dainty are to be pitied, for nothing
will satisfy them.

Les derniers venus sont souvent les
maîtres.

The last to come is often the master.

Les doux yeux.

Soft glances.

Les eaux sont basses chez lui.

(The waters are low with him ; he is at
low water.) He is hard up.

Le secret d'ennuyer est celui de tout
dire.— *Voltaire.*

The secret of becoming a bore in company is to say everything you know.

Lèse-majesté.

(Injured majesty.) High treason.*

Les enfants tiennent de leurs parents
en général.

Children generally resemble their parents.

Les enigmes mêmes que se pose l'intelligence témoignent de sa grandeur,
car n'est-il pas vrai de dire que celui-
là sait le plus qui se fait à lui-même
le plus de questions ?

The very enigmas Intelligence puts to
itself are proof of its greatness, for is
it not true that he who knows the
most, questions himself the most ?

Le sens commun est le génie de
l'humanité.

Common sense is the genius of humanity.

Le sentiment de devoir finit par dominer tellement l'esprit, qu'il entre
dans le caractère et devient un de ses
traits principaux, justement comme
une saine nourriture, perpétuellement
reçue, peut changer la masse du sang
et devenir un des principes de notre
constitution.—*Alfred de Vigny.*

The feeling of duty finally masters the
soul and enters into one's character
and becomes its leading trait, just
as a wholesome food, perpetually
received, may change the blood and
become an element of our constitution.

Les envieux mourront mais non jamais
l'envie.—*Molière.*

The envious will die, but envy is immortal.

Les êtres sensibles ne sont pas des êtres
sensés.—*Balzac.*

Sensitive persons are not the sensible
ones.

Les extrêmes se touchent.—*Mercier.*

Extremes meet.

Les femmes aiment la témérité. Quand
on les étonne on les intéresse, et
quand on les intéresse on est bien
près de leur plaire.—*Ch. Nodier.*

Women do not like faint hearts.
When startled they become interested ; and when interested, they
are near to being pleased.

Les femmes aiment mieux qu'on froisse
leur robe que leur amour-propre.
         —*Commerson.*

Women would rather have their dress
than their conceit ruffled.

---

* The words are derived from the Latin *læsa majestas,* which was a charge commonly made
by the *delatores,* the infamous professional accusers who plied their trade under the Roman
Emperors, against suspected persons, especially against those from whose downfall these
rogues hoped to gain pecuniary advantage. Nowadays, this accusation is frequently employed
by the German Emperor against those of his subjects who, differing from his notions of government, venture to assail in speech or writing the dignity of his august person. The German
term for this crime is *majestäts beleidigung.*

Les femmes distinguées se mettent avec bon goût.

Ladies are distinguished by their good taste in dress.

Les femmes ne sont nullement condamnées à la médiocrité ; elles peuvent même prétendre au sublime, mais au sublime *féminin*. Chaque sexe doit se tenir à sa place et ne pas affecter d'autres perfections que celles qui lui appartiennent.
—*J. de Maistre.*

Women are in no wise condemned to mediocrity ; they may even aspire to the sublime—in a womanly way. Each sex should keep to its place and not seek other perfections than those that belong to it.

Les femmes ont corrompu plus de femmes que les hommes n'en ont aimé.—*Balzac.*

Women have corrupted more women than men have loved.

Les femmes ont plus de petits défauts, et les hommes plus de vices achevés.
—*Quitard.*

Women have the more petty faults and man the more finished vices.

Les femmes ont toujours quelque arrière-pensée.—*Destouches.*

Women always have some mental reservation.

Les femmes ont trop d'imagination et de sensibilité pour avoir beaucoup de logique.—*Mme. du Deffand.*

Women have too much imagination and sensitiveness to have much power of reasoning.

Les femmes sont coquettes par état.
—*J. J. Rousseau.*

Coquetry is woman's business.

Les femmes sont des poëles à dessus de marbre.—*Charles Lemesle.*

Women are stoves covered in with marble.

Les femmes sont passionnées dans tout ce qu'elles disent, et la passion fait parler beaucoup.—*Fénelon.*

Women are enthusiastic about everything they talk of, and enthusiasm makes one talk freely.

Les femmes sont souvent plus sensibles que sensées.

Women are frequently more sensitive than sensible.

Les femmes trompent quelquefois l'amant, jamais l'ami.
—*Alfred Mercier.*

A woman sometimes deceives her lover, but her friend, never.

Les femmes vont plus loin en amour que la plupart des hommes, mais les hommes l'emportent sur elles en amitié.—*La Bruyère.*

Women go further in love than most men, but men distance them in friendship.

Les finesses et les trahisons ne viennent que de manque d'habileté.
—*La Rochefoucauld.*

Trickery and treachery are the outcome of a lack of tact.

Les fous font les festins, et les sages les mangent.

Fools make feasts, and wise men eat them.

Les fous inventent les modes, et les sages les suivent.

Fools invent fashions, and wise folk follow them.

Les gens de mérite logent dans des greniers, et les sots habitent dans des hôtels.—*L'Abbé Marly.*

Men of merit dwell in garrets, and fools in mansions.

Les gens fatigués sont querelleurs.

Tired folk are quarrelsome.

Les grandes pensées viennent du cœur.
—*Vauvenargues.*

Great thoughts proceed from the heart.

Les grands bœufs ne font pas les grandes journées.

It is not the biggest oxen that do the best day's work.

Les grands diseurs ne sont pas les grands faiseurs.

Great talkers are never great doers.

Les grands hommes d'action ne construisent pas d'avance et de toutes pièces leur plan de conduite.
—*Guizot.*

Great men of action do not plan beforehand all the details of their future course of action.

Les grands hommes qui ne doivent ce titre qu'à certaines actions d'éclat, n'ont quelquefois de grand que le spectacle. C'est que, dans les occasions d'éclat l'homme est comme sur le théâtre ; il représente : mais, dans le cours ordinaire des actions de la vie, il est, pour ainsi dire, rendu à lui-même ; c'est lui qu'on voit ; il quitte le personnage, et ne montre plus que sa personne.—*Massillon.*

Great men, whose only claim to this title is based on certain famous acts in their life, are sometimes merely great in a theatrical sense. In moments of strenuous action man is, so to speak, on the stage ; he is acting a part : but in the ordinary habits of life, he is, as it were, restored to himself ; we then see the *man ;* he ceases to be an actor, and displays his real character.

Les grands mangeurs et les grands dormeurs sont incapables de rien faire de grand.—*Henri IV.*

Great eaters and great sleepers are incapable of doing anything else that is great.

Les grands ne sont grands que parceque nous sommes à genoux : relevons-nous.—*Prud'homme.*

Great men are only great because we are on our knees : let us rise to our feet.*

Les grèves font beaucoup de tort aux ouvriers.

Strikes injure the workmen.

Les gros larrons ont toujours les manches pleines de baillons.

Knowing thieves always have a gag handy.

Les gros larrons pendent les petits.

Great thieves hang the little ones.

Les heureux n'ont point d'amis, puisqu'il n'en reste point aux malheureux.
—*De Neuville.*

The fortunate have no friends, for there are none for the unfortunate.

Les hommes font les lois, les femmes font les mœurs.—*Guibert.*

Men make laws, women make manners.

Les hommes fripons en détail sont en gros de très honnêtes gens.
—*Montesquieu.*

Men who, taken singly, are rogues, are often very honest men when taken collectively.

Les hommes prêchent chacun pour son saint.

(Every man extols his own saint.) Men all have an eye to their own interest.

Les hommes rougissent moins de leurs crimes que de leurs faiblesses et de leur vanité.—*La Bruyère.*

Man blushes less for his crimes than for his frailties and his vanity.

Les hommes seraient de grands saints s'ils aimaient autant Dieu que les femmes.—*Saint-Thomas.*

Men would be saints if they loved heaven as well as they do women.

Les hommes sont la cause que les femmes ne s'aiment point.—*La Bruyère.*

Men are the cause of women hating one another.

Les hommes sont rares.

Real men are scarce.

Les hommes veulent être esclaves quelque part et puiser là de quoi dominer ailleurs.—*La Bruyère.*

Men are willing to be slaves somewhere, to derive thence the wherewithal to domineer elsewhere.

* The motto of his *Révolutions de Paris.*

Les honnêtes femmes parlent très-volontiers de l'amour platonique, mais, tout en paraissant l'estimer beaucoup, elles s'habillent de telle façon qu'il n'y a pas un seul ruban de leur toilette qui ne nous en éloigne.
—*A. Ricard.*

Virtuous women freely prate of platonic affection and seem to value it highly, yet they always dress so that not a ribbon waves us away.

Les honneurs changent les mœurs.

Honours change manners.

Les honneurs comptent.

Honours come dear.

Le silence du peuple est la leçon des rois.

The people's silence is the lesson of kings.*

Le silence est le parti le plus sûr pour celui qui se défie de soi-même.
—*La Rochefoucauld.*

When a man is doubtful about himself, silence is his safest course.

Le silence est l'esprit des sots
Et l'une des vertus du sage.
—*Bonnard.*

Silence is the wit of the foolish and a virtue in the wise.

Le silence éternel de ces espaces infinis m'effraye.—*Pascal.*

The eternal silence of the infinite inspires me with awe.

Les inventeurs ont le premier rang, à juste titre, dans la mémoire des hommes.—*Voltaire.*

Inventors hold the first rank, justly, in man's memory.

Les jours approchent où l'héroïsme sera aussi facile à l'âme de l'homme que le sourire est facile au visage de l'enfant.—*Montégut.*

The time is nigh when heroism will come as readily to the human soul as the smile does to the child's face.

Les jours se suivent et ne se ressemblent pas.

The days follow each other but are not alike.

Les jugements de la foule ne sont jamais revisés. Ils sont toujours *renversés.* C'est que la foule a plus de passions que d'idées.—*Ph. Chasles.*

The judgments of the mob are never revised but *quashed*, for the mob has more passions than ideas.

Les larmes aux yeux.

In the melting mood.

Les larrons s'entrebattent et les larcins se découvrent.

When thieves fall out honest men come to their own.

Les loups ne se mangent pas entre eux.

Wolves do not devour their own kind.

Les mariages les plus parfaits sont les moins imparfaits ; les plus pacifiques sont les moins orageux.—*La Roche.*

The most perfect marriages are those least imperfect, and the most peaceful are the least stormy.

Les mariages sont écrits dans le ciel.

Marriages are made in heaven.

Les mauvaises nouvelles ont des ailes.

Bad news travels apace.

Les maux viennent à livres, et s'en vont à onces.

Troubles come in pounds and depart in ounces.

Les médisants enfin sont une affreuse peste,
Qu'un homme de bon sens blâme, fuit, et déteste.—*Gosse.*

Slanderers are a hateful pest which wise men flee from and detest.

Les mensonges passent, la vérité reste.
—*Napoleon I.*

Lies perish, but truth abides.

* A phrase that is of disputed origin. Mirabeau quoted it in one of his speeches.

Les mortels sont égaux; ce n'est pas la naissance,
C'est la seule vertu qui fait la différence.
— *Voltaire.*

Mortals are equal; virtue, not birth, makes all the difference.

Les morts font toujours tort.

(The dead are always doing wrong.) It is easy to blame the dead, because they cannot reply.

Les murailles ont des oreilles.

Walls have ears.

Les nerfs des batailles sont les pécunes.
— *Rabelais.*

The sinews of war are money.

Les oisons veulent mener les oies paître.

(The goslings would lead the geese out to grass.) Jack would teach his granny to suck eggs.

Le sort fait les parents, le choix fait les amis.— *Delille.*

Destiny gives us parents, but we choose our own friends.

Les parfums des fleurs, c'est leur prière et l'encens qu'elles offrent au ciel.
— *Stahl (Hetzel).*

The perfume of flowers is the prayer and incense that they offer up to heaven.

Le spectre rouge.

The red spectre.*

Les pensées sont la pierre de touche de l'esprit.— *Molière.*

Thoughts are the touchstone of wit.

L'espérance est le songe d'un homme éveillé.

Hope is the dream of a waking man.

L'espérance et la crainte sont inséparables.— *La Rochefoucauld.*

(Hope and fear never can be separated.) They always go hand in hand.

Les petits cadeaux entretiennent l'amitié.

Little presents foster friendship.

Les petits ruisseaux font les grandes rivières.

The small streams make the great rivers. Many a mickle makes a muckle.

Les plaisirs de la pensée sont des remèdes contre les blessures du cœur.
— *Mme. de Staël.*

Mental recreation is the remedy for wounds of the heart.

Les plaisirs fatiguent à la longue.

Even pleasures pall.

Les plaisirs sont amers sitôt qu'on en abuse.

Pleasures become bitter as soon as they are abused.

Les plus courtes folies sont les meilleures.

The shortest follies are the best.

Le plus grands clercs ne sont pas les plus fins.— *Regnier.*

The best-educated men are not the cutest.

Les plus habiles affectent toute leur vie de blâmer les finesses, pour s'en servir en quelque grande occasion et pour quelque grand intérêt.
— *La Rochefoucauld.*

The craftiest schemers affect all their life long to censure cunning in order to make use of it on a great occasion to gain some great advantage.

Les plus rusés sont les premiers pris.

The craftiest folk are the first to be cheated.

L'espoir du plaisir vaut le plaisir luimême.— *Fabre d'Eglantine.*

The hope of pleasure is as good as pleasure itself.

---

* The title of a pamphlet by M. Romieu, published in 1851, when the political designs of Louis Napoleon were becoming apparent.

Les pots fêlés sont ceux qui durent le plus.

The cracked pot lasts longest.

Les préjugés sont les rois du vulgaire.
—*Voltaire.*

Prejudices are kings over the common herd.

Les premiers sentiments sont toujours les plus naturels.—*Louis XIV.*

Our first impulses are always the most natural.

Les premiers vont devant.

First come first served.

Les princes se servent des hommes comme le laboureur des abeilles.

Princes use men as the cottager uses bees.

Les principes reçus dans l'enfance ressemblent à ces caractères tracés sur l'écorce d'un jeune arbre, qui croissent, qui se développent avec lui, et font partie de lui-même.

The principles which we imbibe in our infancy resemble the marks on the bark of a young tree, which grow and increase with it, and become part of its being.

L'esprit de l'homme a trois clefs qui ouvrent tout : savoir, penser, rêver, tout est là.—*Victor Hugo.*

The human mind has three keys opening all locks : knowledge, reflexion, imagination—in these three things everything is contained.

L'esprit est toujours la dupe du cœur.
—*La Rochefoucauld.*

The mind is always the dupe of the heart.

L'esprit nous sert quelquefois à faire hardiment des sottises.
—*La Rochefoucauld.*

Wit sometimes helps us to carry off follies with a bold face.

L'esprit qu'on veut avoir gâte celui qu'on a.—*Gresset.*

Striving to be witty spoils what wit we have.

L'esprit révolutionnaire n'enseigne aux peuples que ses droits ; l'esprit religieux lui enseigne de plus ses devoirs.
—*X. Aubryet.*

The revolutionary spirit teaches peoples their rights alone; the religious spirit teaches them their duties, too.

Les regards sont les premiers billets-doux de l'amour.—*Ninon de Lenclos.*

Glances are love's first epistles.

Les rois ont les mains longues.

Kings have long arms.

Les sots depuis Adam sont en majorité.—*Casimir Delavigne.*

The fools have been in the majority ever since Adam's time.

Les souvenirs embellissent la vie, l'oubli seul la rend possible.
—*General Cialdini.*

Memories make life beautiful, forgetfulness alone makes it possible.

Les talents sont distribués par la nature, sans égard aux généalogies.
—*Frederic the Great.*

Talents are bestowed by nature impartially, regardless of the receiver's pedigree.

Les tonneaux vides sont ceux qui font le plus de bruit.

Empty barrels sound the loudest.

Le style c'est de l'homme.—*Buffon.*

(Style is the possession of the man.) The character of a man forms his style.*

Le style des vrais amants est limpide. Aussi, dès qu'une lettre d'amour peut faire plaisir à un tiers qui la lit, est-elle à coup sûr sortie de la tête et non du cœur.—*Balzac.*

True love writes clearly; hence, when a love-letter pleases a third party, it was written out of one's head, not from the heart.

---

* This aphorism is quoted with many variations, *e.g.*, *Le style c'est l'homme :* "Style is the man " is perhaps the most familiar form of it.

Le style est l'homme même. Le style ne peut donc ni s'enlever, ni se transporter, ni s'altérer : s'il est élevé, noble, sublime, l'auteur sera également admiré dans tous les temps ; car il n'y a que la vérité qui soit durable, et même éternelle.—*Buffon.*

The style is the man. Hence it cannot rise of itself, or change or shift. If it be noble, sublime, and elevated, the author will be admired similarly in all time ; for truth is durable, aye, eternal.

Le style n'est que l'ordre et le mouvement qu'on met dans ses pensées.
         —*Buffon.*

Style is nothing more than the order and movement in which thoughts are set.

Le suffrage universel a beau avoir des éclipses, il est l'unique mode de gouvernement : le suffrage universel, c'est la puissance, bien supérieure à la force.—*Victor Hugo.*

Though universal suffrage has many eclipses, it remains the only true mode of government : it is power, a superior thing to force.

Le superflu, chose très nécessaire.
         —*Voltaire.*

The superfluous, a very necessary thing.

Les vices de la cour ont commencé la révolution : les vices du peuple l'acheveront.—*Chamfort* (?)

The vices of the court commenced the revolution : the vices of the people will finish it.

Le talent est un don que Dieu nous a fait en secret, et que nous révélons sans le savoir.—*Montesquieu.*

Talent is a gift which Heaven has granted to men in secret, and when they possess this gift, men reveal the fact unconsciously.

L'état, c'est moi.

The State ! I am the State.*

Le temps est un grand maître, il règle bien les choses.—*Corneille.*

Time is a great master who rules things well.

Le temps fuit, et nous traîne avec soi. Le moment où je parle est déjà loin de moi.—*Boileau.*

Time flies, with us behind his car—even the moment in which I speak is already far away.

Le temps guérit les douleurs et les querelles, parcequ'on change, on n'est plus la même personne.—*Pascal.*

Time cures pain and appeases quarrels, because we change and are no longer the same.

Le temps présent est gros de l'avenir.
         —*Leibnitz.*

The present time is big with the future.

Le temps se change en peu d'heure, Tel rit le matin qui le soir pleure.

The weather changes in a very short time ; who laughs this morning may to-night weep.

Le terrain le plus vulgaire gagne un certain lustre à devenir champ de bataille. Austerlitz et Marengo sont de grands noms et de petits villages.
         —*Victor Hugo.*

The commonest ground gains some lustre by being a battlefield : Austerlitz and Marengo are little villages but bear great names.

Le tout ensemble.

The effect of the whole ; the general effect.

Le travail éloigne de nous trois grands maux, l'ennui, le vice, et le besoin.

Labour rids us of three great evils— irksomeness, vice, and need.

Le trident de Neptune est le sceptre du monde.—*Lemierre.*

(The trident of Neptune is the sceptre of the world.) The rule of the sea is the empire of the world.

---

* This saying is constantly attributed to Louis XIV. There is, however, no reliable evidence that it was ever uttered by him, and it is unlikely that the astute king, whatever his own thoughts may have been, was so impolitic as to express them so openly.

Le trop grand empressement qu'on a de s'acquitter d'une obligation est une espèce d'ingratitude.
—*La Rochefoucauld.*

To repay a favour too soon is a kind of ingratitude.

Lettre de cachet.

A warrant of arrest.

L'étude commence un honnête homme, le commerce des femmes l'achève.
—*St. Evremond.*

A gentleman begins his training by study, but female society finishes it.

Le vaisseau était à deux doigts de sa perte.

The vessel was all but lost.

Lever à six, manger à dix, souper à six, coucher à dix, font vivre l'homme dix fois dix.

To rise at six, eat at ten, sup at six, to bed at ten, makes a man live years ten times ten.

Le véritable Amphitryon est l'Amphitryon où l'on dine.—*Molière.*

The real Amphitryon is the Amphitryon with whom we dine.*

Le véritable génie de notre époque consiste dans le simple bon sens.
—*Thiers.*

The true genius of the time in which we live is plain common-sense.

Le vin donné aux ouvriers est le plus cher vendu.

Gifts to your workmen are the best outlay.

Le vrai n'est pas toujours vraisemblable.

(The truth is not always probable.) Truth is stranger than fiction.

Le vrai peut quelquefois n'être pas vraisemblable.—*Boileau.*

Truth does not always look like truth.

Le vraisemblable est le vrai pour les sots.—*Gavarni.*

What looks like the truth is truth enough for fools.

L'exactitude de citer est un talent plus rare qu'on ne pense.—*Bayle.*

Accuracy in quotation is a rarer talent than is imagined.

L'exactitude est la politesse des rois.
—*Louis XVIII.*

Punctuality is the politeness of kings.

L'expérience, c'est le nom que la plupart des hommes donnent à leurs folies et à leur chagrins.—*A. de Musset.*

Experience is the name most men give their follies and their vexations.

L'expression étant le but suprême, l'art qui s'en rapproche le plus est le premier de tout les arts.—*Victor Cousin.*

Expression being the supreme aim, the art best recalling it is the foremost of all the arts.

L'habit ne fait pas le moine.

The frock doesn't make the monk.

L'heure du berger.

(The shepherd's hour.) The lucky moment ; the opportunity which, lost, can never be regained.

L'histoire de l'amour est l'histoire du genre humain ; c'est un beau livre à faire.—*Charles Nodier.*

The history of love is that of mankind ; a splendid work to write.

L'histoire est bonne personne ; soyez en possession d'une forte idée dramatique, elle vous fournira toujours le milieu qui lui sied le mieux et le cadre qui la met le plus en relief.
—*Alex. Dumas, fils.*

History is kind to playwrights ; be possessed of a strongly dramatic idea, and history will always supply you with the most suitable scene and the surroundings to set it in the highest relief.

* A quotation from the Amphitryon, a play in which the plot, derived from the Latin comedy, turns on the familiar stage trick of mistaken identity. The words are frequently quoted in an incomplete form with a different meaning from that contained in the original play. They are used to signify the ideal of the sycophant who estimates friendship by the worldly advantages to be gained from it.

L'homme de paix est un plus grand conquérant que l'homme de guerre, et un conquérant meilleur ; celui-là qui a dans l'âme la vraie charité divine, la vraie fraternité humaine, a en même temps dans l'intelligence le vrai génie politique, et en un mot, pour qui gouverne les hommes, c'est la même chose d'être saint et d'être grand.—*Victor Hugo.*

The man of peace is a greater conqueror than the man of war, and a nobler one ; he who has in his soul real divine charity, real love of his brother man, has, at the same time, real political genius in his mind.   In a word, for the ruler of men saintliness and greatness are identical qualities.

L'homme doit se mettre au dessus des préjugés, et la femme s'y soumettre.
—*Mme. Necker.*

Men should rise above prejudices, but women should submit to them.

L'homme est de glace aux vérités ;
Il est de feu pour le mensonge.
—*La Fontaine.*

Man is ice towards truth, and fire towards falsehood.

L'homme est toujours l'enfant, et l'enfant toujours l'homme.

The man is always the child, and the child is always the man.

L'homme est un apprenti, la douleur est son maître.—*Alfred de Musset.*

Man is an apprentice, Sorrow is his master.

L'homme est un voyageur qui cherche sa patrie.   Ne marchez point la tête baissée ; il faut lever les yeux pour reconnaître sa route.—*Lamennais.*

Man is a traveller seeking his own land.   Let him not walk with downcast eyes, but keep them uplifted to the stars in order to know the right path to follow.

L'homme nécessaire.

The right man.

L'homme n'est ni ange, ni bête.
—*Pascal.*

Man is neither an angel, nor a beast.

L'homme n'est qu'un roseau, le plus faible de la nature, mais c'est un roseau pensant.   Il ne faut pas que l'univers entier s'arme pour l'écraser. Une vapeur, une goutte d'eau suffit pour le tuer.   Mais quand l'univers l'écraserait, l'homme serait encore plus noble que ce qui le tue, parce qu'il sait qu'il meurt ; et l'avantage que l'univers a sur lui, l'univers n'en sait rien.—*Pascal.*

Man is a reed, the feeblest thing in nature.   But a reed that can think. The whole universe need not fly to arms to kill him ; for a little heat or a drop of water can slay a man.   But, even then, man would be nobler than his destroyer, for he would know he died, while the whole universe would know nothing of its victory.

L'homme propose et Dieu dispose.

Man proposes and God disposes.

L'homme qui entre dans le cabinet de toilette de sa femme est un philosophe ou un imbécile.—*Balzac.*

The husband who intrudes in his wife's dressing-room is either a fool or a philosopher.

L'homme qui n'aime que soi ne hait rien tant que d'être seul avec soi.
—*Pascal.*

The man who loves himself alone, hates nothing so much as being left in solitude.

L'homme qui vit dans l'indifférence est celui qui n'a point encore vu la femme qu'il doit aimer.—*La Bruyère.*

The man who lives a calm, unruffled life, is he who has not yet seen the woman whom it is his destiny to love.

L'homme repu n'est pas le même que l'homme à jeun.—*Brillat-Savarin.*

The man replete with food is not the the same man as when fasting.

L'homme s'agite, Dieu le mène.
—*Fénelon.*

Man flutters and God guides his flight.

L'honneur est comme une île escarpée et sans bords ;
On n'y peut plus rentrer dès qu'on en est dehors.—*Boileau.*

Honour's an isle where none may land
Who once have left its rugged strand.

L'hôte et le poisson en trois jours sont poison.

In three days a fish and a guest
Are far from being at their best.

L'huissier massier.

The mace-bearer.

L'hymen vient après l'amour comme la fumée après la flamme.—*Chamfort.*

Marriage comes after love as smoke after flame.

L'hypocrisie est un hommage que le vice rend à la vertu.
　　　　—*La Rochefoucauld.*

Hypocrisy is the homage which vice pays to virtue.

L'hypocrite et le flatteur ne pardonnent point à ceux qu'ils flattent ; cela les diminue. Ils en souffrent. Voilà pourquoi le maître est abhorré du courtisan.—*Ph. Chasles.*

The hypocrite and the flatterer never forgive those they fawn upon, for it belittles them and they feel it ; hence the king is hated by the courtier.

Liaison.

An illicit connection.

L'ignorance toujours même à la servitude.—*Mme. Desbordes-Valmore.*

Ignorance always leads to servitude.

L'imagination est la folle du logis.
　　　　—*Malebranche.*

Imagination is the crazy person shut up in the habitation of the mind.

L'imagination est une libertine qui déshabille tout ce qu'elle convoite.
　　　　—*A. Ricard.*

Imagination is a libertine unveiling all it covets.

L'impossibilité de durée et de longueur dans les liaisons humaines, me ramènent sans cesse à la nécessité de l'isolement.—*Chateaubriand.*

The impossibility of continuance and duration in human relationships ever forces me to believe in the necessity of cultivating solitude.

L'impôt sur le revenu.

The income-tax.

L'indolence est toujours indocile.
　　　　—*Piron.*

Indolence will not be led or driven.

L'indulgence pour soi et la dureté pour les autres n'est qu'un seul et même vice.—*La Bruyère.*

Indulgence towards one's self and sternness towards others are one and the same vice.

L'ingratitude attire les reproches, comme la reconnaissance attire de nouveaux bienfaits.—*Madame de Sévigné.*

As ingratitude reaps reproach, so does gratitude gather in fresh benefits.

L'injustice à la fin produit l'indépendance.—*Voltaire.*

(The final fruit of injustice is independence.) Despotism leads to revolution.

L'intention de ne jamais tromper nous expose à être souvent trompés.
　　　　—*La Rochefoucauld.*

The resolve never to deceive exposes us to being often deceived.

Littérateur.

A literary man.

Livraison.

Part of a book published in series.

Livres défendus.

(Prohibited books). Books not allowed by the Roman Catholic Church to be read.

L'obstination et ardeur d'opinion est la plus sure preuve de bêtise.
　　　　—*Montaigne.*

Heat and stubbornness in opinions are sure proofs of stupidity.

Locale.

Place ; premises.

L'occasion fait le larron.

Opportunity makes the thief.

L'œil du maître engraisse le cheval.

The master's eye makes the horse fat.

Loin des yeux loin du cœur.

Out of sight out of mind.

L'oiseau ne doit pas salir son nid.

It's a dirty bird that fouls its own nest.

L'oisiveté est la mère de tous les vices.

Satan finds some mischief still for idle hands to do.

L'on confie son secret dans l'amitié, mais il échappe dans l'amour.
—*La Bruyère.*

Friendship may be trusted with a secret, but love lets it escape.

Longue demeure fait changer ami.

Long absence changes friends.

Longue langue, courte main.

Quick tongue, slow hand.

Longues paroles font les jours courts.

Long talks make days seem short.

L'orage est encore une des cruelles épreuves de l'été. Il est bien difficile d'avoir un bon caractère et d'être aimable un jour d'orage.
— *Mme. de Girardin.*

A summer shower is a cruel experience. It is hard to have a good disposition and to be pleasant on a rainy day.

L'ordre moral est régi par des lois aussi immuables que l'ordre physique. C'est ce qui cause un si grand étonnement aux révolutionnaires naïfs, ignorants et superficiels. Ils arrivent à produire un ébranlement, un bouleversement, une révolution ; et quelques années, quelques mois, quelques jours après, ces grands réformateurs s'aperçoivent que c'est exactement la même chose qu'autrefois.
—*Alex. Dumas, fils.*

Moral order is regulated by laws as immutable as those of the physical world. It is this fact which confounds the simple minds of ignorant and superficial revolutionists. These bring about an upheaval, a social earthquake, a revolution, and then, a few years, or a few months, or a few days after this event, these great reformers discover that things are in exactly the same condition they were in before.

L'ordre règne à Varsovie.

Order reigns at Warsaw.*

L'oreille est le chemin du cœur,
Et le cœur l'est du reste.
—*Mlle. de Scudéri.*

The ear is the roadway to the heart, and the heart to the rest.

L'orgueil fait faire autant de bassesses que l'intérêt. —*Duclos.*

Pride prompts as many acts of baseness as love of gain.

Lorsque l'amitié devient amour ils se mêlent comme deux fleuves dont le plus célèbre fait perdre le nom de l'autre.—*Mlle. de Scudéri.*

When friendship becomes love, they blend like two streams, of which the most famous absorbs even the name of the other.

Lorsque l'enfant paraît, le cercle de famille
Applaudit à grands cris, son doux regard qui brille
Fait briller tous les yeux,
Et les plus tristes fronts, les plus souillés peut-être
Se dérident soudain à voir l'enfant paraître
Innocent et joyeux.— *V. Hugo.*

When the child appears on the scene, the family circle loudly welcomes it ; and all eyes brighten at the sight of the child's bright eyes. The brows that are most wrinkled with care— yea, even those that perchance are stained with sin—at once are smoothed when the innocent and merry child is seen.

L'oubli est la fleur qui croît le mieux sur les tombeaux.—*G. Sand.*

Oblivion is a plant that thrives best upon graves.

* Words used by Sebastiani, the French Minister, to the Chamber, on September 16th, 1831, announcing the end of the Polish insurrection. Order had been restored by the effective method of massacre.

Loyal à mort. | (Loyal to death). Motto of the Marquis of Ely.

Loyal devoir. | Loyal duty.

Loyauté m'oblige. | Loyalty binds me.

Loyauté n'a honte. | (Loyalty knows no shame.) Motto of the Duke of Newcastle.

Lune de miel. | Honeymoon.

L'union fait la force. | (Union makes strength.) Motto of the King of the Belgians.

L'un mort dont l'autre vit. | What is one man's meat is another man's poison.

L'utilité de la vertu est si manifeste, que les méchants la pratiquent par intérêt.—*Vauvenargues.* | The value of virtue is so manifest, that knaves practise it to serve their material interests.

Madame se meurt! Madame est morte!
—*Bossuet.* | Madam is dying! Madam is dead!*

Ma foi! | (My faith.) Good gracious!

Ma foi, vous êtes bien curieux.
— *Talleyrand.* | You are really very inquisitive.†

Maille à maille on fait le haubergeon. | Link by link the chain is made.

Maintiens le droit. | Maintain the right.

Maints sont bons parce qu'ils ne peuvent nuire. | Many a one is good because he can do no harm.

Mais dans ce monde, il n'y a rien d'assuré que la mort et les impôts. | Nothing is certain in this world but death and taxes.

Mais la grande marque d'amour, c'est d'être soumis aux volontés de celle qu'on aime.—*Molière.* | The great proof of love is to obey the whims of her whom one loves.

Mais l'honneur sans argent n'est qu'une maladie.—*Racine.* | Honours without money are simply a plague.

Maison d'arrêt. | House of custody; prison.

Maison de force. | House of correction; bridewell.

Maison de santé. | Lunatic asylum.

Maison de ville. | The town hall.

Mais qu'on quitte aisément une ancienne maîtresse!
Qu'on embrasse avec peine un ancien ennemi!—*Régnier-Desmarets.* | It is as easy to part with an old sweetheart as it is hard to shake hands with an old enemy.

Mais voici bien une autre fête.
—*La Fontaine.* | But then a different sort of festival took place.‡

Maître d'hôtel. | Steward.

Malades imaginaires. | People that fancy themselves ill.

* A famous exclamation of Bossuet in the funeral sermon delivered on Henrietta of England, Duchesse d'Orléans. He is describing the effect on the minds of the people, when they hear that the Duchess is dying, and then that she is dead.
† The reply of Talleyrand to an impatient creditor, who ventured to inquire when his bill would be paid.
‡ A line from the fable of "The cat and the old rat," in which is related the ruse of the cat who pretends to be dead in order to deceive the mice. In the midst of their merrymaking, the dead cat suddenly comes to life. The line is now quoted to express an unpleasant surprise, like our English phrase, " Here's a pretty kettle of fish."

Maladie du pays.

Home-sickness.

Maladresse.

Want of tact ; awkwardness.

Mal à propos.

Ill-timed ; out of place.

Mal de mer.

Sea-sickness.

Malgré le tort.

(Despite of wrong.) Motto of Lord Houghton.

Malgré nous.

In spite of us.

Malgré soi.

In spite of one's self; against the grain.

Malgré tout le succès de l'esprit des méchants,
Je sens qu'on en revient toujours aux bons gens.—*Gresset.*

In spite of all the successes of the evil, the world always come round to the good in the end.

Malheureuse France, malheureux roi !

Unhappy France, unhappy king !

Malheur ne vient jamais seul.

Misfortunes never come alone.

Malle-poste.

The mail-coach ; the mail.

Mal soupe qui tout dîne.

He has a scanty supper who eats up all at dinner.

Manége.

The art of horsemanship.

Manger son blé en herbe.

(To eat your corn when it is only sprouting.) To burn the candle at both ends.

Manger un morceau sur le pouce.

(To eat a morsel on the thumb.) To partake of a hurried, scanty meal.

Manière d'être.

Manner; deportment.

Marchand d'oignons se connaît en ciboules.

A dealer in onions is a good judge of leeks.

Marchandise qui plaît, est à demi vendue.

Goods that please are half sold.

Marchand qui perd ne peut rire.
—*Molière.*

(The salesman who loses cannot laugh.) Do not expect the loser to laugh.

Marcher bras dessus bras dessous.

To walk arm in arm.

Mariage d'épervier : la femelle vaut mieux que le mâle.

A hawk's marriage : the hen is the better bird.

Marie ton fils quand tu voudras, mais ta fille quand tu pourras.

Marry your son when you will, and your daughter when you can.

Mari sourd et femme aveugle font toujours bon ménage.

A deaf husband and a blind wife make a happy home.

Marqué à l'A.

(Marked with an A.) Of first-class quality; it is A1.†

Mauvaise est la saison quand un loup mange l'autre.

'Tis a hard winter when one wolf eats another.

Mauvaise herbe croît toujours.

A weed always grows.

Mauvaise honte.

False shame.

Mauvaise humeur.

Peevishness.

Mauvaise plaisanterie.

An ill-timed jest.

Mauvais goût.

Bad taste.

---

* This was the heading of a newspaper article commenting on the causes of the revolution of 1830, which drove Charles X., the last of the Bourbons to reign in France, into exile.

† Money coined at Paris used to be marked A, as money coined in other towns bore other letters. The coins made in Paris were considered to be superior in quality. Hence the expression is used to denote great merit.

Mauvais quart d'heure. | (A bad quarter of an hour.) An uncomfortable time ; a disagreeable experience.

Mauvais sujet. | A rascal.

Mauvais ton. | Vulgarity.

Méchant chien, court lien. | A vicious dog must have a short chain.

Méchant ouvrier jamais ne trouvera bons outils. | A bad workman always finds fault with his tools.

Méchant poulain peut devenir bon cheval. | An ugly colt may make a good horse.

Médecin, guéris-toi toi-même. | Physician, heal thyself.

Médiocre et rampant, et l'on arrive à tout.—*Beaumarchais.* | The man with commonplace aspirations, who crawls through life, may reach any position of eminence.

Mélange. | (A mixture.) A light entertainment of a mixed character.

Mêlée. | A disorderly fight.

Même l'abeille ne peut rien sans fleurs. | Even the bee cannot make honey without flowers.

Même le Grand Napoléon ne pouvait pas dîner deux fois.—*Alphonse Karr.* | Even the great Napoleon could not dine twice in a day.

Même quand l'oiseau marche on sent qu'il a des ailes.—*Lemierre.* | (Even when a bird walks, we feel that it has wings.) The man of genius is revealed even in trivial matters.

Ménage. | Household ; housekeeping ; economy.

Ménager la chèvre et le chou. | (To save the goat and the cabbage.) To run with the hare and hold with the hounds.*

Mener à la lisière ; mener en laisse ; mener par le nez. | To lead by the nose.

Mentir, c'est l'absolu du mal ! Peu mentir n'est pas possible ; celui qui ment, ment tout le mensonge ; mentir, c'est la face même du démon ; Satan a deux noms, il s'appelle Satan et il s'appelle mensonge. —*Victor Hugo.* | Lying is the acme of evil. White lies are non-existent, for a lie is wholly a lie ; falsehood is the personification of evil ; Satan has two names : he is called Satan, and he is called the Father of Lies.

Menu. | The bill of fare.

Mère des passions, des arts et des talents, Qui, peuplant l'univers de fantômes brillants, Et d'espoir tour à tour et de crainte suivie, Ou dore ou rembrunit le tableau de la vie.—*Chênedollé.* | Imagination, mother of the arts, the passions, and talent, you people the universe with brilliant phantoms, and with hope or fear alternately gild or blacken the picture of life.

Mère pitieuse fait la fille rogneuse. | (A tender mother has a worthless daughter.) Spare the rod and spoil the child.

* This phrase is founded on the old tale of the man who had to cross a stream with a goat, a cabbage, and a wolf. As he could only take one over at a time, the puzzle was which he could safely leave together. A sack of corn, a goose, and a fox, are the man's load in the common English version, but the solution is the same.

Mérite un nom ; mais, pour être heureux, tâche,
Avant ta mort, de n'être point nommé.
—*De la Faye.*

Yes, merit fame, but, to be happy, try Not to enjoy that fame before you die.

Mésalliance.

Marriage with a person of inferior rank.

Messe rouge.

(Red Mass.)*

Messieurs les Anglais, tirez les premiers.

Gentlemen of England, fire first.†

Mets ton manteau comme vient le vent.

Arrange your cloak as the wind blows.

Mettre de l'eau dans son vin.

(To put water in his wine.) To pour oil on troubled waters.

Mettre la charrue devant les bœufs.

To put the cart before the horse.

Mettre les pieds dans le plat.

(To put one's feet in the dish.) To utter unwelcome truths.

Mettre un document au net.

To make a fair copy of a document.

Mieux seul que mal accompagné.

Better alone than in bad company.

Mieux vaut assez que trop.

Enough is better than too much.

Mieux vaut avoir ami en voie qu'or ou argent en courroie.

Better a friend upon the road than gold or silver as your load.

Mieux vaut bon repas que bel habit.

Better a good lining to your stomach than a fine coat on your back.

Mieux vaut couard que trop hardi.

Better be a coward than too rash.

Mieux vaut engin que force.

Artifice is better than force.

Mieux vaut être tête de chien que queue de lion.

Better be a dog's head than a lion's tail.

Mieux vaut glisser du pied que de la langue.

Better a slip of the foot than of the tongue.

Mieux vaut goujat debout qu'empereur enterré.—*La Fontaine.*

(Better a living beggar than a buried emperor.) A living dog is better than a dead lion.

Mieux vaut marcher devant une poule que derrière un bœuf.

Better to walk before a hen than behind an ox.

Mieux vaut perdre la laine que la brebis.

Better to lose the wool than the sheep.

Mieux vaut plier que rompre.

Better to bend than break.

Mieux vaut pour un pays être dévasté physiquement que d'être ruiné moralement.—*Beulé.*

A country had better be physically devastated than morally ruined.

Mieux vaut règle que rente.

Thrift is better than a thousand a year.

Mieux vaut tard que jamais.

Better late than never.

Mieux vaut terre gâtée que terre perdue.

Better waste than lost land.

Mieux vaut un pied que deux échasses.

One foot is better than two wooden legs.

Mieux vaut un poing de bonne vie, que plein muy de clergie.

A handful of good life is better than a bushel of learning.

Mieux vaut un "tiens" que deux "tu l'auras."

A bird in the hand is better than two in the bush.

* This is the name given, on account of the colour of the vestments worn by the officiating priest, to the celebration of the Mass which is attended by Roman Catholic judges, barristers, etc., at the annual re-opening, after the Vacation, of the Courts of Justice.
† At the battle of Fontenoy Lord Charles Hay, who was marching at the head of the English troops, called out to the French to fire first, but they gallantly refused to do so. The above is the reply that a French officer made to Lord Charles Hay's request.

Mis à la quarantaine.	(Sent into quarantine.) Sent to Coventry.
Mise en scène.	(The setting on the stage.) The manner in which a drama is put on the stage ; the scenic effects, &c.
Moi ! dis-je, et c'est assez.—*Corneille.*	I ! say I ; that one word is sufficient.
Moins vaut rage que courage.	Any day, pluck will beat running a-muck.
Monde chic.	World of taste ; fashionable people.
Mon Dieu est ma roche.	(My God is my rock.) Motto of Lord Fermoy.
Mon Dieu, pourvu que l'on choisisse pour Ambassadeur un honnête homme, le reste est de peu d'importance.—*Jules Grévy.*	Provided that you choose an honest man to be your Ambassador, the rest (of diplomacy) is of little importance.
Monsieur Dimanche.	(Mr. Dimanche.) A timid creditor.*
Montjoie St. Denys.	(Montjoy St. Denis.) The old war-cry of France.†
Montrer le bout de l'oreille.	(To show the tip of the ear.) To be the ass with the lion's skin.
Montrer le soleil avec un flambeau.	(To show the sun with a candle.) To carry coals to Newcastle.
Montrer patte blanche.	(To show a white paw.) To prove one's identity.‡
Monument de Vanité Détruit pour l'utilité ; L'an 2 de l'égalité.	Monument of vanity, destroyed for utility ; the second year of equality.§
Morceau avalé n'a plus de goût.	There is no flavour in a tit-bit when you have swallowed it.
Morgue.	A mortuary.
Morte la bête, mort le venin.	Dead men tell no tales.
Mot à mot on fait les gros livres.	Word by word big books are made.
Mot du guêt ; mot de passe.	The watchword.
Mot pour rire.	A witty saying ; a joke.
Mots d'usage.	Words in common use.
Mourir ! C'est le seul cas où il soit permis à un homme de passer devant une femme.—*Alex. Dumas, fils.*	Death is the only time when a man may allow himself to precede a woman.
Mourir pour la patrie, c'est encore du bonheur.	To die for one's country—that still remains a joy.
Mousseline de laine.	A thin woollen material.

* Dimanche is a character in Molière's *Don Juan.* Coming to collect a debt from Don Juan he is so overwhelmed by the effusive reception given him that he has not the courage to ask for his money.

† The word Montjoie was derived from the *Monte gaudii,* the old name for the halting-places on the road leading to the Abbey of St. Denis. They were called *Monte gaudii,* or Mountjoys, because the pilgrim rejoiced when he reached them, knowing that he was nearing his journey's end.

‡ The expression is taken from one of the Fables of La Fontaine. The wolf, attempting to get into the goat's house, is discomfited when asked to prove that he is what he pretends to be and to thrust his *patte blanche* under the door.

§ The famous old bell of Rouen, Georges d'Amboise, was melted down by the Revolutionists of 1793. Medals were made of the metal, and this inscription placed upon them.

Moutons de Panurge.

Sheep of Panurge.*

N'achète point l'âne d'un muletier,
Ni te marie avec la fille du tavernier.

Do not buy the muleteer's ass, nor marry the inn-keeper's daughter.

Nager entre deux eaux.

To play fast and loose.

Naïveté.

Ingenuousness ; innocence.

N'a pas fait qui commence.

Only begun is not done.

N'aurai-je pour me reposer l'éternité entière ? —*Boileau.*

Shall I not have the whole of eternity to rest in ? †

Né (*fem.* Née).

Born.

Ne battre que d'une aile.

To while away one's time.

Nécessité est mère d'invention.

Necessity is the mother of invention.

Nécessité n'a pas de loi.

Necessity has no law.

Ne compte jamais sur le présent ; mais soutiens-toi dans le sentier rude et âpre de la vertu, par la vue de l'avenir. Prépare-toi, par des mœurs pures et par l'amour de la justice, une place dans l'heureux séjour de la paix.
—*Fénelon.*

Never rely on the present ; but sustain yourself in virtue's rugged path by fixing your eyes on the future. By pure manners and love of justice, prepare for yourself a place in the blessed kingdom of Peace.

Ne crachez pas dans le puits, vous pouvez en boire l'eau.

Don't foul the well, you may have to drink from it yet.

Négligé.

Undress.

Ne jetez pas ce qui n'est pas tombé.
—*Victor Hugo.*

Never push down what was not falling.

Ne manquez jamais à votre parole.

Never break a promise.

Ne mets ton doigt en anneau trop étroit.

Don't put your finger into a ring too tight for it.

Ne pas faire à autrui ce que nous ne voudrions pas qu'on nous fît : voilà la justice. Faire pour autrui, en toute rencontre, ce que nous voudrions qu'il fît pour nous : voilà la charité.
—*Lamennais.*

Not to do unto others but what we would like others to do unto us : that is justice. To do unto others, on all occasions, what we would have others do to us ; this is charity.

Né pour la digestion.

(Born merely for the purpose of digestion.) A social drone. *Fruges consumere nati.*

Ne prends pas si facilement la mouche.

Don't be so short-tempered.

Ne prenez pas ce que je dis au pied de la lettre.

Don't take what I say literally.

Ne remettez pas à demain ce que vous pouvez faire aujourd'hui.

Do not put off till to-morrow what you can do to-day.

Ne reprends ce que n'entends.

(Don't criticise what you don't understand.) Cobbler, stick to your last.

Ne restez jamais entre deux airs.

Never stay in a draught.

Ne réveillez pas le chat qui dort.

(Do not waken the sleeping cat.) Let well alone.

---

* In the *Pantagruel* of Rabelais, the lively Panurge has a quarrel with the merchant Dindenault. In order to punish his adversary, Panurge, having bought a sheep from him, throws it into the sea, when the whole flock follow. Hence the words are used of persons who are too ready to imitate the example of other people.
† Boileau's reply to those friends who begged him to refrain from overwork.

Ne sers pas, ne sers jamais, ni les républicans, ni les royalistes, ni les farceurs généralement quelconques qui aspirent, disent-ils, à faire ton bonheur. Ils ne valent guère mieux les uns que les autres. Sers-toi d'eux, c'est légitime, car ils aspirent à se servir de toi ; mais écoute bien cette parole sensée : Ne te dévoue jamais.
—*J'. Hérisson.*

Never serve any political party, though these funny folk say they aspire to give you happiness ; they are no better one than another. Make use of them, which is fair, for they mean to make use of you ; but observe this pregnant warning : " Never surrender yourself absolutely to any party."

Ne sont pas tous chasseurs qui sonnent du cor.

All are not hunters who blow the horn.

N'est-il pas temps de plier bagage ?

Is it not time to be off ?

Ne touchez point à l'argent d'autrui, car le plus honnête homme n'y ajouta jamais rien.

Touch not another man's money, for the most honest touch never increases it.

Nettoyer les écuries d'Augias.

To cleanse the Augean stables ; to accomplish a Herculean task.

N'éveillez pas le chat qui dort.

(Do not disturb the sleeping cat.) Let sleeping dogs lie.

Ne vendez jamais la peau de l'ours avant de l'avoir mis par terre.

(Don't sell the skin before you have caught the bear.) Never count your chickens before they are hatched.

Ne vous faites pas tirer l'oreille.

Don't be so unwilling.

N'hâtez jamais, et vous arriverez à temps.—*Talleyrand.*

Never hurry, and you will arrive in the nick of time.

Niaiseries.

Follies, fooleries, absurdities.

Ni l'or ni la grandeur ne nous rendent heureux.—*La Fontaine.*

Neither money nor rank can give us happiness.

Ni l'un ni l'autre.

Neither the one nor the other.

N'importe.

No matter ; it does not signify ; never mind.

Noblesse oblige.

(Nobility obliges.) Persons who are noble ought to act nobly ; we ought to cultivate self-respect.

Nom de guerre.

Assumed name ; cognomen.

Nom de plume.

A name assumed for literary purposes.

Nonchalance.

Carelessness ; indifference.

Non, le Dieu qui m'a ait, ne m'a point fait en vain.—*Voltaire.*

Nay, the God who created me, created me not in vain.

Nonpareil.

Unequalled.

Nos actions sont comme les bouts-rimés, que chacun fait rapporter à ce qui lui plaît.—*La Rochefoucauld.*

Our actions are lines of verse to be capped—anybody may end them as he will.

Nos besoins sont nos forces.

(Our wants are our strength.) Necessity is the mother of invention.

Nos passions se dévorent les unes les autres, et ce sont souvent les petites qui mangent les grosses.—*Cherbuliez.*

Our passions devour one another, and it is often the less which devour the greatest.

Nos plaisirs les plus doux ne sont pas sans tristesse.—*Corneille.*

Our sweetest joys are with sadness mingled.

Nos vertus ne sont le plus souvent que des vices déguisés.
— *La Rochefoucauld.*

Our virtues are often only vices in disguise.*

Notre choix fait nos amitiés, mais c'est Dieu qui fait notre amour.
— *Mme. de Staël.*

We choose our friends, but love is a gift of God.

Notre-Dame.

(Our Lady.) The Church of Notre-Dame is the Cathedral of Paris.

Notre envie naturelle pour tout ce qui nous dépasse nous a fait inventer cette fiction de la Fortune. Il nous semble si dur de reconnaître le mérite des autres. Il fallait bien imaginer la Fortune, en manière de transaction, pour ménager notre orgueil blessé. La Fortune, c'est le magnétisme qu'on exerce sur les hommes et sur les choses ; on porte la Fortune en soi !
— *Rounat.*

Our natural envy for all who surpass us, led us to invent the fable of Fortune. It seemed too hard to acknowledge the merit of others, and was but too easy to create the idea of Fortune to spare our wounded pride. Fortune is really the magnetism we exercise over men and things, and its home is within us.

Notre mal s'empoisonne Du secours qu'on lui donne.

(Our disease is made worse by the remedies given to cure it.) The remedy is worse than the disease.

N'oubliez pas.

Do not forget.

Nourriture passe nature.

(Nurture passes beyond nature.) Birth is much, but good breeding is more.

Nous avons changé tout cela.—*Molière.*

(We have changed all that.) We are rid of those old-fangled notions.†

Nous avons maille à partir ensemble.

(We have a farthing to divide.) We have a bone to pick with one another.

Nous avons tous assez de force pour supporter les maux d'autrui.
La Rochefoucauld.

We are all of us strong enough to endure the misfortunes of others.

Nous battons en retraite.

We are retreating.

Nous craignons quasi toujours des maux qui perdent ce nom par le changement de nos pensées et de nos inclinations.—*Madame de Sévigné.*

We are always frightened about ills, which cease to deserve the name owing to the change of our thoughts and inclinations.

Nous croyons à propos de le quitter.

We think it proper to leave him.

Nous dansons sur un volcan.

We are dancing on a volcano.‡

Nous devons travailler à nous rendre très-dignes de quelque emploi : le reste ne nous regarde point, c'est l'affaire des autres.—*La Bruyère.*

We should work to make ourselves worthy of any position : the rest is not our look out, but depends on other people.

Nous employons aux passions l'étoffe qui nous a été donnée par le bonheur.
— *Joubert.*

We clothe our passions in the fabric woven for us by happiness.

* The motto of La Rochefoucauld's famous "Moral Maxims."
† The words of Sganarelle in *Le médecin malgré lui.* Sganarelle propounds a new theory of the position of the organs of the body, and when Géronte suggests that the heart used to be on the left side and the liver on the right, "Yes," says Sganarelle, "that used to be the case, *mais nous avons changé tout cela.*"
‡ The remark of M. de Salvandy to the Duke of Orleans at a fête given by the latter to the King of Naples shortly before the Revolution of 1830 which drove Charles X., the last of the direct Bourbon line, into exile. Like the Neapolitans, who dance on the side of Mount Vesuvius, the French Court was in a position of peril.

Nous étions parmi les gros bonnets de l'endroit.

We were amongst the swells of the place

Nous gagnerions plus de nous laisser voir tels que nous sommes que d'essayer de paraître ce que nous ne sommes pas.—*La Rochefoucauld.*

We should gain more by letting ourselves be seen as we really are than by trying to appear what we are not.

Nous l'avons forcé à mettre les pouces.

We made him give way to us.*

Nous naissons, nous vivons, bergère,
Nous mourons sans savoir comment ;
Chacun est parti du néant :
Où va-t-il ?—Dieu le sait, ma chère.
—*Voltaire.*

We are born, we live, shepherdess,
We die—than this no more is known ;
For all men come from nothingness,
And where they go—God knows alone.

Nous ne céderons ni un pouce de terrain ni une pierre de nos forteresses.
—*Jules Favre.*

We will not surrender an inch of territory or a stone of our fortresses.†

Nous n'écoutons d'instincts que ceux qui sont les nôtres,
Et ne croyons le mal que quand il est venu.—*La Fontaine.*

We only listen to our own instincts and believe in no evil till it arrives.

Nous ne savons ce que c'est que bonheur ou malheur absolu.

We do not know what is absolutely good or bad fortune.

Nous ne vivons jamais, nous attendons la vie.—*Voltaire.*

We never truly *live*, but we are always hoping to do so.

Nous oublions aisément nos fautes, lorsqu'elles ne sont sues que de nous.
—*La Rochefoucauld.*

We readily forget our failings when they are known only to ourselves.

Nous querellons les malheureux pour nous dispenser de les plaindre.
—*Vauvenargues.*

We pick quarrels with the unfortunate to avoid sympathising with them.

Nous sommes si accoutumés à nous déguiser aux autres, qu'à la fin nous nous déguisons à nous-mêmes.
La Rochefoucauld.

We are so used to disguising our real selves from others, that the disguise, in the end, deceives even us who wear it.

Nous sommes tellement prêts, que si la guerre durait dix ans, nous n'aurions pas même à acheter un bouton de guêtre.—*Marshal Lebœuf.*

We are so thoroughly prepared, that if the war were to last ten years, we should not have to buy so much as a gaiter-button.‡

Nous verrons.

We shall see.

Nous voyons bon nombre de gens tant heureux, qu'en leur mariage semble reluire quelque idée et représentation des joies de paradis.—*Rabelais.*

We see many married couples so happy that their union seems to shine with some reflection and representation of the joys of paradise.

Nul bien sans peine.

No gains without pains.

Nul n'aura bon marché s'il ne le demande.

You'll get no bargain unless for asking.

Nul n'aura de l'esprit, hors nous et nos amis.—*Molière.*

None shall have wit save us and our friends.

---

* Literally, " We made him give us his thumbs," a saying derived from the custom of the police, who make captured criminals put their fingers into a kind of handcuffs.
† This patriotic utterance of Jules Favre, after the defeat of Sedan, is often quoted. After the fall of Paris, however, his opinions necessarily underwent a change.
‡ It was this declaration of a responsible official, that the army was in a perfect state of equipment, which caused the French people to enter upon the war of 1870 "with a light heart."

Nul n'est content de sa fortune
Ni mécontent de son esprit.
—*Mme. Deshoulières.*

Nul n'est prophète dans son pays.

Nul n'est si large que celui qui n'a rien
à donner.

No one is content with his fortune, nor
discontented with his intellect.

No man is a prophet in his own country.

No one is so generous as he who has
nothing to give.

Observez cette barque conduite par deux
matelots : s'ils rament ensemble, ils
voguent doucement sur les flots agités ;
mais s'ils ne sont pas d'accord, chaque vague produit une secousse, et tel
coup d'aviron donné à contre-sens
pourrait faire chavirer leur frêle esquif.
Le bateau est le mariage, les rameurs
sont les deux époux ; ils naviguent
sur le fleuve de la vie, et ce n'est qu'en
unissant leurs efforts qu'ils adoucissent
les contrariétés du voyage.
Le duc de Lévis.

See that boat rowed by two men ; when
they keep time in rowing it goes
smoothly over the rough waters ; but
if not, each wave gives its shock and
any stroke of the oar wrongly applied
may capsize the frail skiff. Marriage
is the bark, the rowers the wedded
couple on the sea of life. Only by
pulling together can they lessen the
dangers of the voyage.

Occasions manquées.

Favourable opportunities missed.

O combien d'actions, combien d'exploits célèbres sont demeurés sans
gloire au milieu des ténèbres !
—*Corneille.*

O how many noble actions, how many
exploits have remained hidden ingloriously in obscurity !

Octroi.

A tax on articles (for sale) entering a
town.

O femmes ! vous êtes des enfants bien
extraordinaires.—*Diderot.*

O women ! You are most extraordinary
children.

Oignez vilain il vous poindra, poignez
vilain il vous oindra.

Stroke a nettle and it will sting you,
grasp it and it is soft as silk.

O l'amour d'une mère ! amour que nul
n'oublie !
Pain merveilleux, que Dieu partage et
multiplie !
Table toujours servie au paternel foyer !
Chacun en a sa part et tous l'ont tout
entier.—*Victor Hugo.*

Maternal love ! Love which is never
forgotten ; it is a miraculous bread
which God distributes and multiplies ;
it is a table ever spread in the home ;
a banquet of which each member of
the family has a share, yet each enjoys
it undivided.

O Liberté, que de crimes on commet en
ton nom !—*Madame Roland.*

O Liberty, how many crimes are committed in thy name ! *

On achète tout fors le jour et la nuit.

(Money can buy everything but night
and day.) Life cannot be bought.

On a de la fortune sans bonheur, comme
on a des femmes sans amour.
—*Rivarol.*

One may have fortune without happiness, just as one may have a wife
without love.

On affaiblit toujours tout ce qu'on
exagère.—*La Harpe.*

Exaggeration weakens everything it
touches.

On aime plus la première fois, mais on
aime mieux la seconde.—*Rochepèdre.*

The first time love is strongest, the
second time it is best.

* This is said to have been the exclamation of Madame Roland when she mounted the
scaffold and perceived that the guillotine had been erected close to a statue of Liberty.

On aime sans raison, et sans raison l'on hait.—*Regnard.*

There's no reasoning in love and hate.

On alla aux voix.

It was put to the vote.

On a peu de temps à être belle et long-temps à ne l'être pas.
— *Mme. Deshoulières.*

A woman has a few years wherein to own beauty, and many wherein she lacks it.

On apprend en faillant.

Man is taught by failures.

On a souvent besoin d'un plus petit que soi.—*La Fontaine.*

We often need the aid of one weaker than ourselves.

On a toujours une certaine supériorité morale sur ceux dont on sait la vie.
—*Alex. Dumas, fils.*

The knowledge of another's life gives one a kind of moral superiority over him.

On commence par être dupe ;
On finit par être fripon.
—*Mme. Deshoulières.*

We begin by being fools, and end in becoming knaves.

On compte les défauts de ceux qu'on attend.

When you keep a man waiting, he employs the time reckoning up your faults.

On connaît l'ami au besoin.

A friend in need is a friend indeed.

On coupe les cheveux ras aux forçats.

Convicts have their hair cropped.

On débite un grand nombre d'histoires fausses sur les femmes, mais elles ne sont qu'une faible compensation des véritables, qu'on ignore.—*Meilhan.*

Many as are the false tales recited about women, they are but a weak compensation for the true ones of which we are unaware.

On devient cuisinier, mais on naît rôtisseur.—*Brillat-Savarin.*

A cook is made, a roaster is born.

On devient innocent quand on est malheureux.—*La Fontaine.*

A man in misfortune becomes guileless.

On dit.

It is said ; a rumour.

On dit est un sot.

"Town talk" is a fool.

On dit que "ceux qui savent bien haïr savent bien aimer," comme si ces deux sentiments avaient le même principe. L'affection part du cœur, et la haine de l'amour-propre ou de l'intérêt blessé.—*Meilhan.*

The saying goes that "A good hater makes a good lover;" as if the two feelings had the same motive prin-**ciple.** Affection springs from the heart, and hate from wounded pride or disappointment.

On doit appeler un chat un chat.

(You should call a cat a cat.) Call a spade a spade.

On doit se consoler de n'avoir pas les grands talents, comme on se console de n'avoir pas les grandes places. On peut être au-dessus de l'un et de l'autre par le cœur.—*Vauvenargues.*

Man should comfort himself for not having great talent as for not having a high station. The possession of a good heart may give a nobler rank than either talents or worldly eminence can bestow.

On en a vu bien d'autres.

We are used to that sort of thing.

On entre, on crie,
Et c'est la vie !
On bâille, on sort,
Et c'est la mort !—*A. de Chancel.*

We enter and utter a cry—and that is life !
We yawn and depart—and that is death!

On est aisément dupé par ce qu'on aime.—*Molière.*

We are easily deceived by those whom we love.

On est mieux seul qu'avec un sot.

One is better alone than with a fool.

x

On est plus heureux dans la solitude que dans le monde, parce que dans la solitude, on pense aux choses, et que dans le monde, on est forcé de penser aux hommes.—*Chamfort.*

There is greater happiness in solitude than in society, for when alone we muse on things, whilst in a throng we must think about men.

On est—quand on veut— le maître de son sort.—*Louis Ferrier.*

We can be, when we wish, the masters of our fate.

On est seul dans la foule quand on souffre ou quand on aime.
                    —*Rochepèdre.*

The lover and the mourner are alike lonely in the throng.

On est souvent puni par où l'on a péché.

We are often punished in the way we have sinned.

On fait dire aux cloches tout ce qu'on veut.

The ringers make the bells say what they please.

On fait le loup plus grand qu'il n'est.

The devil is not so black as they paint him.

On fait plus souvent du bien pour pouvoir impunément faire du mal.
                    —*La Rochefoucauld.*

Men often do good in order to have impunity for their evil-doing.

On fait presque toujours les grandes choses sans savoir comment on les fait, et on est tout surpris qu'on les a faites.—*Fontenelle.*

Great deeds are nearly always accomplished without our knowing how we have done them, and their achievement fills us with surprise.

On fausse son esprit, sa conscience, sa raison, comme on gâte son estomac.
                    —*Chamfort.*

Mind, reason, and conscience may be impaired, just as digestion may be spoilt.

On ferait un bien gros livre de tous les peut-être qui se disent en un jour.

It would take a very big book to hold all the ifs and ans uttered in a day.

On frotte tant le fer qu'à la fin il s'échauffe.

Even iron may be chafed into a heat.

On lie bien le sac avant qu'il soit plein.

A sack is best tied before it is brimfull.

On meurt deux fois, je le vois bien.
Cesser d'aimer et d'être aimable,
C'est une mort insupportable ;
Cesser de vivre, ce n'est rien.
                    —*Voltaire.*

I perceive that we are to endure two kinds of death. The first, the loss of love and the loss of the power to win it, is the unendurable death. The other—the loss of life, is a mere trifle.

On n'aime que ceux auxquels on pardonne ; voilà pourquoi les démocraties aiment les médiocrités.—*Ph. Chasles.*

We have love only for those we can forgive : hence democracies like commonplace men.

On naît général comme l'on naît poète.
                    —*Marshal Saxe.*

A general, like a poet, is born and not made.

On n'a jamais bon marché de mauvaise marchandise.

(Bad merchandise is never a good bargain.) Buy cheap, buy dear.

On n'a jamais vu chèvre morte de faim.

No one ever saw a goat dead of hunger.

On n'a point pour la mort de dispense de Rome.—*Molière.*

There is no dispensation of the Church against death.

On n'a rien pour rien.

Nothing is bought for nothing.

On n'aurait guère de plaisir, si l'on ne se flattait point.

But little pleasure would a man have if he did not flatter himself.

On ne cherche point à prouver la lumière.

There is no need to prove (the existence of) light.

On ne comprend rien à son barbouillage.

There is no understanding his scrawls (rigmarole) ; one cannot make head or tail of them.

On ne connaît point le vin aux cercles.

You cannot tell good wine by the barrel.

On ne doit jamais écrire que de ce qu'on aime.—*Renan.*

One ought never to write upon a subject that one does not love.

On ne doit pas laisser bonne terre pour mauvais seigneur.

Do not give up good land because of a bad landlord.

On ne doit pas prendre au sérieux cette chose sans cohésion et sans but qui s'appelle le monde, et où l'on n'aperçoit rien qui ait un sens sérieux. Dire des riens dont le souvenir s'efface à mesure qu'on les dit, écouter des discussions oiseuses que le bon goût défend même d'approfondir, c'est faire preuve d'usage du monde, mais ce n'est rien faire du tout.
—*Georges Sand.*

Do not take seriously that aimless, incoherent thing called society, for it has no serious sense in it. To prattle trifles, forgotten as soon as uttered, to hear dull discussions into which good taste forbids one to enter—this is gaining experience of the world, but it is an idle employment.

On ne donne rien si libéralement que ses conseils.

People give nothing so liberally as their advice.

On ne fait pas de rien grasse purée.

Fat broth cannot be made of nothing.

On ne jette des pierres qu'à l'arbre chargé de fruits.

It is only the fruit-laden tree that is pelted with stones.

On ne meurt jamais trop tôt, quand on ne vit que pour soi.

Death never comes too soon, when a man lives only for himself.

On n'emporte pas la patrie à la semelle des souliers.—*Danton.*

A man does not carry his country on the sole of his shoes.*

On ne peut corriger les hommes qu'en les faisant voir tels qu'ils sont. La comédie utile et véridique n'est point un éloge menteur, un vain discours d'académie.—*Beaumarchais.*

Men can only be corrected by showing them what they really are. A play, therefore, which is truthful and useful must not be an exaggerated description of men's good qualities, nor a vain didactic lecture.

On ne peut désirer ce qu'on ne connaît pas.—*Voltaire.*

One cannot desire what one does not know.†

On ne peut être dupe de la vertu ; ceux qui l'aiment sincèrement y goûtent un secret plaisir, et souffrent à s'en détourner.—*Vauvenargues.*

Man cannot be the dupe of virtue ; for those who sincerely love it find pleasure in that love, and pain if they go astray.

On ne peut être juste si l'on n'est humain.—*Vauvenargues.*

None can be just if not humane.

On ne peut faire d'une buse un épervier.

No one can make a hawk of a buzzard.

On ne peut faire qu'en faisant.

To do, one must be doing.

On ne peut jamais aimer son prochain sans aimer Dieu.—*Bossuet.*

No man can love his neighbour without loving God.

---

* The reply of Danton to his friends who advised him to flee, when, having opposed further unnecessary bloodshed, he incurred the enmity of Robespierre.
† A translation of Ovid's *Ignoti nulla cupido.*

On ne peut pas avoir le drap et l'argent.

You cannot have your cake and eat it too.

On ne peut pas avoir toujours raison.

One can't be always right.

On ne peut pas empêcher le vent de venter.

One can't hinder the wind from blowing.

On ne peut pas être et avoir été.

You cannot enjoy the present and the past.

On ne peut pas s'aviser de tout.

One cannot think of everything.

On ne peut sonner les cloches et aller à la procession.

One cannot ring the bells and also walk in the procession.

On ne prend pas le lièvre au son du tambour.

Old birds are not caught by chaff.

On ne saurait contenter tout le monde et son père.

None can please all the world and his wife.

On ne saurait faire boire un âne s'il n'a soif.

You cannot make an ass drink when he is not thirsty.

On ne saurait tirer de l'huile d'un mur.

(You cannot squeeze oil out of a wall.) You cannot get blood from a stone.

On n'est jamais bien juste à l'égard d'un rival.

We are never very just towards a rival.

On n'est jamais si heureux, ni si malheureux, qu'on se l'imagine.

We are never so happy, nor so unhappy, as we suppose.

On n'est point l'ami d'une femme lorsqu'on peut être son amant.—*Balzac.*

No man who could be a woman's lover, is content to be her friend.

On n'est point un homme d'esprit pour avoir beaucoup d'idées, comme on n'est pas un bon général pour avoir beaucoup de soldats.

One is not a genius merely by possessing many ideas, as, in the same way, a general is not a great strategist because he has many soldiers under his command.

On ne trompe point en bien ; la fourberie ajoute la malice au mensonge.
          —*La Bruyère.*

We never use deceit when engaged in a good action; but knavery cloaks malice with lies.

On pardonne les infidélités, mais on ne les oublie pas.—*Mlle. de Lafayette.*

Infidelities may be forgiven, but never forgotten.

On parle peu quand la vanité ne fait pas parler.—*La Rochefoucauld.*

There is little spoken unless vanity prompts.

On parle trop de l'ingratitude de l'enfant. Le don de la vie peut bien être payé en rancune.—*Gerfaut.*

The ingratitude of children is often censured. But the gift of life may often justly be paid for in rancour.

On perd plus de la moitié d'un ami quand il devient amoureux.
          —*Mme de Sartory.*

More than half your friend is lost to you when he falls in love.

On perd tout le temps qu'on peut mieux employer.—*La Bruyère.*

All the time is lost that might be better employed.

On peut aisément se faire trop valoir.

It is easy to be too conceited.

On peut avoir un grand esprit et une âme vulgaire; une intelligence capable d'illuminer son siècle et une âme capable de le déshonorer : on peut être un grand homme par l'esprit et un misérable par le cœur.—*Lacordaire.*

A man may have a lofty mind and a base soul ; intelligence capable of enlightening his generation and a spirit capable of disgracing it ; his intellect may make him great, and his heart make him despicable.

On peut diviser la vie des femmes en trois époques : Dans la première elles rêvent l'amour ; dans la seconde elles le font ; dans la troisième elles le regrettent.—*Saint Prosper.*

Woman's life may be divided into three stages; in the first she dreams of love, in the second experiences it, in the last she regrets it.

On peut faire d'énormes sottises à Paris, sans que la passion soit de la partie. La vanité est cent fois plus coûteuse que tous les vices.—*Edm. About.*

In Paris one may commit great follies without feeling any impulse of passion to do so. Vanity is a hundred times more expensive than all the vices.

On peut longtemps, chez notre espèce,
Fermer la porte à la raison ;
Mais, dès qu'elle entre avec adresse,
Elle reste dans la maison,
Et bientôt elle en est maîtresse.
—*Voltaire.*

We are able to keep the door shut against reason for a long time ; but, when it has once effected an entry, it soon becomes mistress of the house.

On peut payer l'or trop cher.

Too heavy a price may be paid for wealth.

On peut savoir à un sou près ce que cela coûtera.

You can tell to a halfpenny what it will cost.

On peut souvent faire d'une pierre deux coups.

One can often kill two birds with one stone.

On pourrait s'attirer une bien mauvaise affaire.

You might get yourself into very hot water.

On pourra toujours payer d'audace.

Anyhow we can put a bold front on it.

On prend le peuple par les oreilles, comme on prend un pot par les anses.

The people should be taken by the ears as a pot is taken by the handle.

On prend souvent l'indolence pour la patience.

Indolence is often taken for patience.

On revient toujours à ses premiers amours.

We always return to our first loves.

On s'écrie qu'il ne faut au génie que deux choses : *la vie et la rêverie, le pain et le temps.* Le pain ! Dieu a dit à l'homme qu'il ne le mangerait qu'à la sueur de son visage. Pourquoi le génie serait-il dispensé de cette loi du travail, qui est la loi de Dieu ? —Mon travail, dit le génie, c'est de rêver.—Hélas ! la rêverie n'est pas une profession que la société puisse reconnaître et récompenser.
—*Saint Marc Girardin.*

It is asserted that genius requires " Life and meditation—bread and time." Bread ! God hath said : man must earn his bread by the sweat of his brow. Why should genius be set free from this heavenly law of labour ? My labour is in musing, says Genius. Alas ! musing is not a calling that society can approve and recompense.

On se croyait aimé, parce que *la personne* était aimable, avait des yeux brillants à notre approche, et se trouvait n'avoir habituellement jusque là, presque jamais parlé à nous. Et puis un jour, dans une simple reflexion échappée à *la personne* devant un visiteur, on découvre que l'on avait jamais eu, même la plus simple idée en commun.—*L. Dépret.*

A man fancies himself loved because the woman is pleasant and looks brighter at his approach, although she hardly speaks to him. But one day, a simple remark discovers that they had never a single idea in common.

On se fait à tout.

They can turn their hand to anything.

On se fait cuisinier, mais on est né rôtisseur.

A man may learn to be a cook, but he must be born a roaster.

On se fait toujours aimer, pourvu qu'on se rende aimable ; mais on ne se fait pas toujours estimer, quelque mérite qu'on ait.—*Malebranche.*

We may always become beloved if we will but be loveable ; but we cannot always be highly valued whatever our deserts may be.

On se l'arrache.

He is very popular.

On se persuade mieux, pour l'ordinaire, par les raisons qu'on a trouvées soi-même, que par celles qui sont venues dans l'esprit des autres.—*Pascal.*

Usually a man is better persuaded by the arguments he has discovered himself, than by those which are the fruit of another's mind.

On se soûle bien de manger tartes.

Eating sweets may sicken one.

On touche toujours sur le cheval qui tire.

The willing horse is whipped the most.

On traîne ses malheurs en croyant qu'on les fuit.—*Carmontelle.*

Men drag their miseries at their heels in full belief they have dropped them.

On va bien loin depuis qu'on est las.

Even when a man is tired he may still go a long way.

On vend toutes les marchandises au prix de revient.

All these goods are sold at cost price.

On veut avoir ce qu'on n'a pas,
Et ce qu'on a cesse de plaire.
                              —*Monvel.*

We are fain to love what we do not possess,
While what we have no longer pleases.

On vient de me voler.—Que je plains ton malheur !
Tous mes vers manuscrits !—Que je plains le voleur !—*Le Brun.*

" Oh ! I have been robbed ! "—" I pity your grief."
" Of all my verses ! "—" I pity the thief ! "

O patrie, O doux nom que l'exil fait comprendre.—*C. Delavigne.*

O fatherland, the sweet name which exile teaches us to understand.

Or est qui or vaut.

Gold is that which buys gold.

Orgeat.

A liquor made from barley.

O Richard, O mon roi,
L'univers t'abandonne :
Sur la terre il n'est donc que moi
Qui s'intéresse à ta personne.
                              —*Sedaine.*

O Richard, O my king, the universe abandons thee ; no one on the earth save myself cares for thy welfare.*

Oriflamme.

(The oriflamme.) The former national flag of France.†

Os à ronger.

A bone to pick.

O sexe fait pour la tendresse !
Le transport de notre jeunesse,
Le calme de notre vieillesse,
Notre bonheur dans tous les temps.
                              —*Ducis.*

O Woman, sex for love created !
The transport of our youthful prime,
To life's decline a solace mated,
Our constant gladness in all time.

Ote-toi de là que je m'y mette.

Away from there ! I want your place.

---

* This song was popular among the faithful partisans of the Bourbons. At a dinner given to some of the soldiers at Versailles on the first of October, 1789, the guests greeted Louis XVI. and Marie-Antoinette by singing this song when the ill-fated king and queen entered the room.

† The word is derived from the Latin, *Aurea-flamma,* " the flame-coloured" flag. It was the standard of the Abbey of St. Denis, the patron saint of France. This Abbey was the property of the Counts of Paris, and when they came to the throne, the banner of their family's Abbey was made the national standard.

Oublier je ne puis.	I can never forget.
Oui, alors je serai sans souci.	Yes, then I shall be free from care.*
—Frederick the Great.	
Où il est faible le fil se rompt.	A chain snaps in its weakest link.
Où il n'y a aucune délicatesse, il n'y a aucune littérature.—*Joubert.*	Without delicacy there can be no literature.
Oui, votre orgueil doit être immense ; Car, grâce à notre lâcheté, Rien n'égale votre puissance, Sinon votre fragilité. *—Alfred de Musset.*	Fair ladies, the pride that you wear Is immense, for thanks to men's fears With your empire naught can compare, Save only your frailty, my dears.
Où la foi place un mystère, la philosophie cherche une raison.—*S. de Sacy.*	Where Faith sets up a mystery, Philosophy seeks a reason.
Où la guêpe a passé le moucheron demeure.	Where the wasp got through, the fly gets caught.
Où la vertu va-t-elle se nicher ?	Where does virtue have its lodging ? †
Où peut-on être mieux qu'au sein de sa famille ?—*Marmontel.*	In what better place can a man be than in the bosom of his family ?
Où sont les neiges d'antan ?—*Villon.*	Where are the snows of yester-year ? ‡
Outrance	Excess ; extremity.
Outré.	Extravagant.
Ouvrage.	Work.
Ouvrez, c'est la fortune de France.	Open, it is the fortune of France. §
Ouvrier.	Workman.
Pain tant qu'il dure, vin à mesure.	Bread, as far as 'twill go, but wine, dole it out slow.
Panier percé.	(A leaky basket.) A spendthrift ; a man who cannot manage his own affairs.
Papeterie.	A case with writing materials.
Papier maché.	A substance made of a pulp obtained from rags.
Papillote.	Curl paper.
Par accord.	In harmony with.
Parce que les qualités de l'âge mûr excluent celles de la première jeunesse, ce n'est pas une raison pour regretter d'avoir échangé les dons brillants qui ne donnent qu'un jour contre les solides avantages de la maturité. *—Ernest Renan.*	Although the qualities of ripe age exclude those of early manhood, this is no reason to regret that one has exchanged the bloom of a day for the solid fruit of maturity.
Par-ci par-là.	Here and there.

* So Frederick spoke of his death. His favourite house at Potsdam is called Sans Souci.
† The question of Molière when he discovered unsuspected honesty in a beggar.
‡ This is the refrain of Villon's ballad, *Les Dames du temps jadis,* "The Fair Women of Former Days." After recalling to memory the famous beauties of the past, he demands *Où sont les neiges ?* etc., deploring the evanescence of all earthly delights.
§ After Crecy, Philip VI., the defeated French King, fled for refuge to the castle De l'Arboie. The warder hesitated to open the door until the king revealed his identity in the words quoted above. Another version gives the king's remark as, " *C'est l'infortuné roi de France.*" "Open, it is the unhappy king of France."

Par complaisance.	With a desire to be agreeable
Par excellence.	Eminently ; the very ideal.
Par exemple.	For example ; for instance.
Parfaitement bien.	Perfectly well.
Par faveur.	By favour.
Par hasard.	By chance.
Paris vaut bien une messe.	Paris is worth a mass.*
Par la sambleu.	Hang it ! Confound it !
Par la splendeur de la naissance de Dieu.	By the glorious birth of God.†
Par le droit du plus fort.	By right of the strongest.
Par les mêmes voies on ne va pas toujours aux mêmes fins.	By the same roads we do not always arrive at the same ends.
Parlez du loup, et vous verrez sa queue.	(Speak of the wolf and you will see his tail.) Speak of the devil, and he will appear.
Parlez peu et bien, si vous voulez qu'on vous regarde comme un homme de mérite.	Speak but little and well, if you wish people to consider you a man of merit.
Par manière d'acquit.	(By way of discharge.) Carelessly.
Par moitié.	By halves.
Parole d'honneur !	On my word of honour !
Parole jetée va partout à la volée.	A word once uttered flies everywhere.
Par parenthèse.	By way of parenthesis.
Par précaution.	By way of precaution.
Par principe.	On principle.
Par privilège.	By way of privilege.
Par quel destin faut-il, par quelle étrange loi, Qu'à tous ceux qui sont nés pour porter la couronne Ce soit l'usurpateur qui donne L'exemple des vertus que doit avoir un roi ?—*Pavillon.*	Strange work of fate past wondering, That, unto those born to the throne, 'Twas the usurper who hath shown The parts that make the perfect king.‡
Par signe de mépris.	As a token of contempt.
Part du lion.	The lion's share.
Parti.	Party ; partner.
Partie carrée.	(A square party.) A party consisting of two men and two women.§
Partir comme des frères, le mien est mien et le tien est à nous deux.	To share as brothers' do, mine is mine, and thine belongs to both of us.
Partout.	Everywhere.
Par trop débattre la vérité se perd.	In the fogs of debate truth is lost.
Par trop presser l'anguille on la perd.	Grasping an eel too tightly is the way to loose it.

---

* The words are attributed to Henri IV., who exchanged his Protestant for Catholic opinions, when he found that the majority of the French people looked askance at a Protestant king.
† An oath constantly on the lips of William the Conqueror.
‡ A eulogy of Cromwell.
§ Often used incorrectly by English writers in the sense of "a small but select party."

Par un prompt désespoir souvent on se
  marie,
Qu'on s'en repent après tout le temps de
  sa vie.—*Molière.*

In a fit of despair a man oft takes a wife,
Then repents of his rashness the rest of
  his life.

Parvenu.

A person of low origin who has risen;
  upstart.

Pas.

A step.

Pas à pas on va bien loin.

Step by step one goes a long way.

Pas de nouvelles, bonnes nouvelles.

No news is good news.

Passé.

Past; out of date.

Passe-partout.

A master-key.

Passer le Rubicon.

To cross the Rubicon.

Passer sous les Fourches Caudines.

(To pass through the Caudine Forks.)
  To be publicly humiliated.*

Pas seul.

A dance performed by one person.

Passez-moi la rhubarbe, je vous passerai
  le séné.

(Give me the rhubarb and you may take
  the senna.)   Scratch me and I'll
  scratch thee.

Passons au déluge.— *Racine.*

(Let us pass on to the Deluge.)   Come
  to the point.†

Patience et longueur de temps
Font plus que force ni que rage.
                            —*La Fontaine.*

Time and patience do more than might
  and anger.

Patois.

A dialect.

Patte de velours.

A velvet paw.

Pauvres mortels, tant de haine vous
  lasse;
Vous ne goûtez qu'un pénible sommeil.
D'un globe étroit divisez mieux l'espace;
Chacun de vous aura place au soleil.
Tous attelés au char de la puissance,
Du vrai bonheur vous quittez le chemin.
Peuples, formez une sainte alliance,
Et donnez-nous la main.—*Béranger.*

Poor mortals, so much hatred wearies
  you; broken are your slumbers; make
  a better division of the narrow earth
  you inhabit, as each of you will hold
  a captive in the sun; now drawn as
  captives, bound to the chariot of
  Power you leave behind the path of
  true happiness.   Peoples of the earth,
  form a holy alliance, and give us your
  hand.

Pauvreté est une espèce de ladrerie.

Poverty is a kind of plague.

Pauvreté n'est pas vice.

Poverty is no vice.

Pays de Cocagne.

An imaginary country, where everything
  is to be had in abundance and without labour.

Pays Latin.

(The Latin territory, district, region.)
  The students of the Pays Latin, that
  is, of the University.

Péché caché est à demi pardonné.

A sin concealed is half forgiven.

Peine forte et dure.

Severe punishment; strong and severe
  pain.

---

* The expression is derived from the disaster that the Roman army suffered when they invaded Samnium.
† The request of Dandin in the *Plaideurs* to the tedious advocate who starts his speech for the defence from the period before the creation of the world. The English pleasantry, " Cut the cackle, and come to the 'osses," would seem to be a rough equivalent of the sentiment.

Penchant.
Strong inclination for anything.

Pends-toi, brave Crillon, on a vaincu sans toi.—*Henri IV.*
Hang thyself, brave Crillon, we have conquered without you.*

Pensée.
A thought ; consideration.

Père de famille.
The father of the family ; paterfamilias.

Périssent les colonies plutôt qu'un principe.
Perish the colonies, rather than a principle.†

Perruques.
(Wigs.)　Drivelling old men.

Persiflage.
Chaff ; banter.

Personnel.
The staff of an establishment.

Personne presque ne s'avise de lui-même du mérite d'un autre.
　　　　　　　—*I a Bruyère.*
Scarcely anybody sees of his own free impulse the merit of another man.

Petit à petit l'oiseau fait son nid.
Twig by twig, the bird builds its nest.

Petit-bleu.
A letter card.‡

Petit bourgeois.
A second-rate citizen ; cit.

Petit chaudron, grandes oreilles.
Little pitchers have long ears.

Petite chose aide souvent.
Every little helps.

Petite étincelle engendre grand feu.
A tiny spark kindles a great fire.

Petite étincelle luit en ténèbres.
In dark places a little spark gives light.

Petite pluie abat grand vent.
A little rain calms a great wind.

Petites affiches.
Advertisements.

Petit homme abat grand chêne
(A small man fells a great oak.)　Little strokes fell great oaks.

Petit-maître.
A swell ; a fop.

Peu.
Little, few.

Peu à peu.
By degrees.

Peu de bien, peu de soin.
Little wealth, little care.

Peu de bien, peu de souci.
Few possessions, few cares.

Peu de chose nous console, parce que peu de chose nous afflige.—*Pascal.*
A little thing consoles us, because a little thing causes us grief.

Peu de femmes désirent coiffer Sainte Catherine.
Few women wish to die old maids.

Peu de gens savent être vieux.
　　　　　—*La Rochefoucauld.*
(Few persons know how to be old.) Youthful manners should not accompany old age.

Peu de gens savent s'amuser. Quelques-uns se disent : Je fais ceci ou cela, donc, je m'amuse.　J'ai payé tant de pièces d'or, donc, je ressens tant de plaisir.　Et ils usent leur vie sur cette meule.—*A. de Musset.*
Few know how to amuse themselves. Some say : I spent so much and had so much amusement; I did so and so, and hence was pleased.　And they wear out their life on this treadmill.

---

* Tradition says that the king wrote these words in a letter to Crillon, but the words are probably apocryphal.

† The declaration of Barnave, a member of the Assembly, when, in 1791, it was suggested that the French colonies would not submit to the principles of complete equality which the Revolution affirmed.

‡ This is the name given to the little blue folding-slips of paper, which are used for sending messages, to be transmitted by pneumatic tubes, in Paris. One of these *petit-bleu* has figured prominently in the Dreyfus case.

Peu d'hommes ont été admirés par leurs domestiques.—*Montaigne.*

Few men have been admired by their own servants.*

Peu et paix c'est don de Dieu.

A little and peace with it is the gift of God.

Peuples, formez une sainte alliance, Et donnez-nous la main. —*Béranger.*

Nations, form a holy alliance, and give us your hand.

Peu s'en est fallu qu'il ne soit tombé.

He very nearly fell.

Peut-on affliger ce que l'on aime ?

Can we cause grief to that which we love ?

Pièce de circonstance.

(A composition to suit the occasion.) A work written to celebrate a particular event.

Pièce de résistance.

The principal dish.

Pièces à conviction.

(Things that aid the conviction.) Clothes &c., that are produced at a trial to incriminate a prisoner.

Pièces de position.

Heavy guns.

Pied poudreux.

A vagabond.

Pierre qui roule n'amasse point de mousse.

A rolling stone gathers no moss.

Pioupiou.

(A private soldier.) A French "Tommy Atkins."

Piquant.

Pointed ; pungent.

Piquer des deux.

To put spurs to one's horse.

Piquer une tête.

To tumble head-first into the water ; to take a header.

Pis aller.

The last resort.

Place aux dames.

(Make) way for the ladies.

Plaqué ; doublé (*ormolu*).

Ormolu ; brass with the appearance of gold.

Pleins pouvoirs.

Full powers.

Pleurer à chaudes larmes.

(To shed hot tears.) To weep unrestrainedly.

Pleurer des larmes de sang.

(To shed tears of blood.) To suffer the agonies of remorse or disappointment.

Plus ça change, plus c'est la même chose.

The more it changes, the more it is the same thing.

Plus d'honneur que d'honneurs.

(More honour than honours.) More glory than gain.

Plus fait douceur que violence. —*La Fontaine.*

Gentleness counts more victories than violence.

Plus inconstant que l'onde et le nuage, La temps s'enfuit, pourquoi le regretter?

More quickly changing than the waves and clouds, Time flies, so why regret it ?

Plus le péril est grand, plus doux en est le fruit.—*Corneille.*

The greater the peril, the sweeter the gain.

* See note on *Il n'y a pas de grand homme.*

Plus l'homme de génie se rapproche de Dieu, plus il a charge d'âmes.
—*A. Houssaye.*

The more divine a man of genius becomes, of the more souls he is the guide.

Plus on est de fous, plus on rit.

The greater the fool, the louder his laugh.

Plus on se hâte, moins on avance.

The more haste, the less speed.

Plus près est la chair que la chemise.

(My flesh is nearer to me than my shirt.) I love my friends well, but myself better.

Plus royaliste que le roi.

A greater royalist than the king himself.

Plus sages que les sages.

More wise than the wise.

Plutôt mourir que changer.

Sooner die than change.

Plutôt souffrir que mourir, C'est la devise des hommes.
—*La Fontaine.*

" Better to suffer than to die "—that is the guiding motto of mankind.

Point d'appui.

Point of support ; prop.

Point d'argent, point de Suisse.
—*Racine.*

(No money, no Swiss.) No work without pay.*

Point de nouvelles, bonnes nouvelles.

No news is good news.

Point de roses sans épines.

No rose without a thorn.

Polisson.

A rascal ; a blackguard.

Port de relâche.

A port which ships can put into.

Pose.

Position ; attitude.

Possession vaut titre.

Possession is nine points of the law.

Poste restante.

(Post left.) Place at the Post Office where letters may be addressed to be left till called for.

Pot au feu.

(Vegetable broth.) The staple food of the French peasantry.

Pour avoir du goût, il faut avoir de l'âme.—*Vauvenargues.*

To have taste one must have an imaginative soul.

Pour bien instruire, il ne faut pas dire tout ce qu'on sait, mais seulement ce qui convient à ceux qu'on instruit.
—*La Harpe.*

To teach well we need not say all that we know, but only what is useful for the pupil to hear.

Pour comble de bonheur.

As the height of happiness.

Pour connaître un homme, if faut avoir mangé un muid de sel avec lui.

To know a man, you must have eaten a bushel of salt with him.

Pour couper court.

To cut matters short.

Pour encourager les autres.—*Voltaire.*

To encourage the others.†

Pour faire rire.

To move laughter.

Pour féconder le sillon où germe l'avenir des peuples libres, il n'est pas nécessaire de verser le sang, il suffit de répandre les idées.
—*Victor Hugo.*

To fecundate the field whence will spring the future of free peoples, it is not necessary to spill blood thereon, for sowing ideas will be sufficient.

---

* The Swiss were the soldier-mercenaries of the Middle Ages.
† A sarcastic comment on the motives that induced the English to shoot Admiral Byng when he was accused of cowardice and neglect of duty.

Pour fuir la vulgarité, on tombait dans le factice.—*Renan.*

In avoiding vulgarity one falls into artificiality.

Pour l'amour du grec.—*Molière.*

For the love of Greek.*

Pour la populace ce n'est jamais par envie d'attaquer qu'elle se soulève, mais par impatience de souffrir.
—*Sully.*

The people never revolt for the mere love of it, but because they cannot endure their suffering.

Pour le peuple, mieux valait s'abaisser devant un maréchal de France qui a reçu de l'éducation, que devant un manant de grippe-sou paré de son écharpe tricolore.—*Marat.*

The lower classes had better bow to a field-marshal who has been educated fitly, than to a money-grubbing clown in a mayor's chain-of-office.

(Pour les étrangers) le voyageur n'est qu'un sac d'écus qu'il s'agit de désenfler le plus vite possible.
—*Victor Hugo.*

The tourist (among foreigners) is merely a moneybag that must be lightened as soon as possible.

Pour le succès il ne faut pas de talent, mais de l'à-propos. Habileté d'aujourd'hui, d'hier et d'avant-hier, soutenue, vigilante, indéfatigable—voilà le succès.—*Ph. Chasles.*

To succeed, talent is not so much needed as timeliness. Sustained, vigilant, and indefatigable dexterity—this is success.

Pour néant demande conseil qui ne le veut croire.

It is no use asking advice if you will not follow it.

Pour paraître honnête homme, en un mot, il faut l'être ;
Et jamais, quoi qu'il fasse, un mortel ici-bas,
Ne peut aux yeux du monde être ce qu'il n'est pas.—*Boileau.*

In a word, in order to appear a man of honour, one must be one in reality. Whatever he does, no mortal man on the earth can appear to the eyes of others different from what he really is.

Pour passer le temps.

To pass away the time.

Pour prendre congé (P.P.C.).

To take leave.

Pour que la goutte d'eau sorte de la poussière,
Et redevienne perle en sa splendeur première,
Il suffit, c'est ainsi que tout remonte au jour,
D'un rayon de soleil ou d'un rayon d'amour !—*Victor Hugo.*

To restore the drop of water in the mire to its primitive pearl-like splendour, it suffices to apply the remedy which brings all things from darkness to light, a sunbeam or a ray of love.

" Pourquoi avez-vous si mal parlé de cet homme ? " demandai-je un jour à Henri Heine. " Parce que je l'avais mal jugé." " Pourquoi l'avez-vous mal jugé ? " " Parce que *je l'enviais.*" L'envie est une infériorité qui s'avoue.
—*Ph. Chasles.*

" Why did you speak so ill of that man ? " I asked Henri Heine one day. " Because I misjudged him." "Why did you misjudge him ? " "Because I envied him." Envy is a confession of inferiority.

Pourquoi pleurez-vous ? M'avez-vous cru immortel ?—*Louis XIV.*

Why do you weep ? Did you think me to be immortal ? †

---

* In the famous comedy, the *Femmes savantes*, Philaminte, one of these learned ladies, hearing that Vadius knows Greek, is so enchanted by finding so learned a man, that she kisses him, saying that it is "for love of Greek" that she does so.
† So the dying king said to some pages whom he saw weeping near his bed.

Pourrait-il d'un feu qui dévore
Eprouver deux fois les effets ?
Les cendres s'échauffent encore,
Mais ne se rallument jamais.
—*L. Andrieux.*

Is it possible to experience a second time the force of love's devouring flame ? The ashes may renew their warmth, but the fire is never kindled again.

Pour rire.

(To laugh at.) Ludicrous ; absurd.

Pour s'établir dans le monde, on fait tout ce que l'on peut pour y paraître établi.—*La Rochefoucauld.*

To gain a position in the world, one must do one's best to appear as if it has been already gained.

Pour toujours.

For ever.

Pour une femme, les romans qu'elle fait sont plus amusants que ceux qu'elle lit.—*T. Gautier.*

A woman's own adventures are more entertaining than any she can read.

Pour un Orphée qui fut chercher sa femme en enfer, combien de veufs, hélas ! qui n'iraient pas même en paradis s'ils pensaient y retrouver la leur.— *J. Petit-Senn.*

For one Orpheus who followed his wife to Hades, how many widowers, alas ! would not even go to Paradise if there they expected to find theirs.

Pour un plaisir mille douleurs.

One pleasure may cost a thousand pains.

Pour vivre longtemps, il faut être vieux de bonne heure.

In order to live long, one must be old (in habits) early.

Pour y parvenir.

To accomplish the object.

Pouvez-vous traduire à livre ouvert ?

Can you translate at sight ?

Précis.

A summary ; an epitome.

Prend-moi tel que je suis.

(Take me as I am.) Motto of the Marquis of Ely.

Prendre des vessies pour des lanternes.

To think the moon is made of green cheese.

Prendre fait et cause pour quelqu'un.

To take anybody's side.

Prendre la balle au bond.

To catch the ball as it bounds ; to seize an opportunity.

Prendre la clef des champs.

(To take the key of the fields.) To take French leave.

Prendre la lune avec les dents.

(To seize the moon with one's teeth.) To try to do the impossible.

Prendre la mouche.

(To catch the fly.) To make a fuss about nothing.

Prendre l'occasion aux cheveux.

Take time by the forelock.

Prendre ne dois à la chandelle,
Ni or, ni toile, et moins pucelle.

Choose neither jewels, linen, nor wife by candle-light.

Prendre ses jambes à son cou.

To run away as fast as one's legs will go.

Prendre un billet de parterre.

(To take a ticket for the pit.) To tumble ; to come down in the world.

Prendre une condition.

To take service.

Prends le premier conseil d'une femme et non le second.

Follow a woman's first advice, not her second.

Prenez de l'amour ce qu'un homme sobre prend de vin, mais ne devenez pas un ivrogne.—*Alfred de Musset.*

Sip love as a sober man takes wine, and never become besotted with it.

Prenez des informations là-dessus.
Make enquiries about it.

Prenez garde.
Take care.

Près de l'église, loin de Dieu.
The nearer the church, the farther from God.

Prestige.
Magic spell ; position ; influence.

Prêt d'accomplir.
(Ready to accomplish.) Motto of the Earl of Shrewsbury.

Prêt pour mon pays.
Ready for my country.

Prie-Dieu.
A praying-chair ; a pew.

Pris sur le fait.
Caught in the act.

Procès verbal.
(Official report.) A summary of the charge and evidence against an accused person.

Projet.
A plan or project.

Prolétaire.
A person of the lower orders.

Promettre c'est donner, espérer c'est jouir.—*Delille.*
Promising is giving, hoping is enjoying.

Promettre et tenir sont deux.
Promises and performance are two very different things.

Promettre monts et merveilles.
(To make professions of future actions.) Promises ending in smoke.

Propos de soir le vent emporte.
(The wind carries away lovers' promises.) At lovers' perjuries they say Jove laughs.

Propriété littéraire.
Literary property ; copyright.

Protégé.
One protected or patronized.

Provision faite en saison
Fait du bien à la maison.
(Provision made in season, brings a blessing to the house.) A stitch in time saves nine.

Pythagore, Epicure, Socrate, Platon, sont des flambeaux ; le Christ, c'est le jour.—*Victor Hugo.*
Pythagoras, Epicurus, Socrates, Plato, these are the torches of the world ; Christ is the light of day.

Quai d'Orsay.
The street in which the French Foreign Office is situated ; the French office for Foreign Affairs.

Quand Auguste avait bu, la Pologne était ivre.—*Voltaire.*
When Augustus had drunk, Poland was drunken.*

Quand celui qui écoute n'entend rien, et celui qui parle n'entend plus, c'est métaphysique.—*Voltaire.*
When the man who listens understands nothing, and the man who talks understands as little, then they are discussing metaphysics.

Quand il n'y a point de vent chacun sait naviguer.
Every man is a pilot when the sea is calm.

Quand il tomberait des hallebardes, je viendrais.
I will come though it rain cats and dogs.

---

* This line is a slight variation of a verse written by Frederick II. of Prussia. It is merely another way of expressing the statement that subjects model their ways on those of the king who rules them.

Quand je pense qu'il y a des hommes assez hardis pour regarder une femme en face, pour l'aborder, pour lui serrer la main et pour lui dire sans mourir de frayeur : Voulez-vous m'épouser ? Je ne puis m'empêcher d'admirer jusqu'-où va l'audace humaine.—*Stendhal.*

When I think there are men bold enough to look a woman in the eyes, take her hand, and tell her they love her, without being daunted, I cannot help admiring the extent to which human audacity will go.

Quand la porte est basse il faut se baisser.

One must stoop when the door is low.

Quand l'arbre est tombé tout le monde court aux branches.

When the tree is down everybody runs with his hatchet.

Quand l'aveugle porte la bannière, mal pour ceux qui marchent derrière.

When the blind man carries the banner, woe to his followers.

Quand le bonheur vous guide, on doit suivre ses pas.—*Destouches.*

When happiness shows the way, we ought to follow it.

Quand le diable dit ses patenôtres il veut te tromper.

When Satan quotes Scripture, he most means to deceive.

Quand le fer est chaud, il le faut battre.

Strike while the iron is hot.

Quand le Français dort le diable le berce.

When the Frenchman sleeps the devil rocks him.

Quand les biens viennent les corps faillent.

As wealth increases, health decreases.

Quand les femmes ont passé trente ans la première chose qu'elles oublient c'est leur âge ; lorsqu'elles sont arrivées à quarante, elles en perdent entièrement le souvenir.
      —*Ninon de Lenclos.*

When women pass thirty they first forget their age; when forty, they forget that they ever remembered it.

Quand les vices nous quittent, nous nous flattons de la créance que c'est nous qui les quittons.
      —*La Rochefoucauld.*

When our vices leave us, we flatter ourselves with the notion that we are leaving them.

Quand on a besoin des hommes, il faut bien s'ajuster à eux.—*Molière.*

When we need men's help we must conduct ourselves so as to please them.

Quand on a des filles on est toujours berger.

He who has daughters is always a shepherd.

Quand on court après l'esprit, on attrape la sottise.—*Montesquieu.*

In the race after wit, folly is caught.

Quand on écrit avec facilité, on croit toujours avoir plus de talent qu'on n'en a. Pour bien écrire, il faut une facilité naturelle et une difficulté acquise.—*Joubert.*

The fluent writer accredits himself with more talent than he really possesses. To write well, one must have an innate facility and an acquired difficulty in composition.

Quand on est bien il faut s'y tenir.

When you are well off, there is no need to move.

Quand on n'a pas ce que l'on aime, il faut aimer ce que l'on a.

When one has not what he likes, he must like what he has.

Quand on ne trouve pas son repos en soi-même, il est inutile de le chercher ailleurs.

When one does not find repose in oneself, it is vain to seek it elsewhere.

Quand on parle du loup, on en voit la queue.

(Talk of the wolf and you see his tail.) Talk of the devil, he's sure to appear.

Quand on se fait entendre on parle toujours bien,
Et tous vos beaux dictons ne servent
pas de rien.—*Molière.*

Quand on voit la chose on la croit.

Quand quelque chose nous défaut,
On sait alors ce qu'elle vaut.

Quand sur une personne on prétend se
régler
C'est par les beaux côtés qu'il lui faut
ressembler.—*Molière.*

Quand tous péchés sont vieux l'avarice
est encore jeune.

Quand tout le monde a tort, tout le
monde a raison.—*La Chaussée.*

Quand un ami a un grand succès, on
l'aime un peu moins, mais on se vante
plus souvent de son amitié.
                          —*Chas. Narrey.*

Quand un chien se noie, chacun lui
offre à boire.

Quand une chose peut être de deux
manières, elle est presque toujours de
la manière qui paraît la moins naturelle.—*François Arago.*

Quand une fois on a trouvé le moyen
de prendre la multitude par l'appât
de la liberté, elle suit en aveugle,
pourvu qu'elle en entende seulement
le nom.—*Bossuet.*

Quand une lecture vous élève l'esprit,
et qu'elle vous inspire des sentiments
nobles et courageux, ne cherchez pas
une autre règle pour juger de l'ou-
rage : il est bon, et fait de main
d'ouvrier.—*La Bruyère.*

Quand vient la gloire s'en va la mémoire.

Quand vos yeux en naissant s'ouvraient à
la lumière
Chacun vous souriait, mon fils, et vous
pleuriez.
Vivez si bien, qu'un jour à votre dernière heure
Chacun verse des pleurs et qu'on vous
voie sourire.—*Marquise de Créquy.*

Que ceux qui lisent soient moraux,
ceux qui écrivent le deviendront par
la force des choses. Si la foule se
presse autour des étalages à scandale, l'explosion d'immoralité fera
des blessés. S'il y a vide, elle sera
sans danger.—*Pierre Véron.*

The speech held the hearers because
understood,
Whilst all your fine nonsense for nothing
was good.

Seeing is believing.

When a thing is lost to us, we know
how much 'twas worth.

When we claim to model our acts on
another's, we ought to imitate the
good side of his character.

When all other sins grow old avarice is
still young.

(When everybody is wrong, everybody
is right.) When all are sinners, the
single sinner escapes punishment.

When a friend is successful he is loved
somewhat less, but his friendship is
more often boasted of.

When a dog is drowning, every one
offers him a drink.

When a thing may be done in two ways,
it is almost always done in the apparently least natural.

When once the multitude are led by one
who knows how to use liberty as a
lure, they blindly follow at the mere
sound of that word.

When a passage in a book elevates
the mind and inspires noble and
courageous feelings, look for no other
standard whereby to judge the work :
it is good and wrought by a master
hand.

When glory comes memory departs.

When your eyes at your birth did open
to the world, you wept, my child,
while those who saw you smiled. May
you live so well that, at your last
moments, all may weep and you may
smile.

If readers be moral, writers become so
by the force of circumstances. If the
mob will flock up to scandalous shows,
the explosion of immorality will hurt
them. Establish a vacuum round
them, and there will cease to be any
danger.

Y

Que diable allait-il faire dans cette galère ?

(What the devil did he go to do in that galley?) Why on earth did he go to that place ? *

Que faire ?

What is to be done ?

Que la terre est petite à qui la voit des cieux !—*Delille.*

How small is the earth to him who looks from Heaven.

Quelle imprévoyance de vivre toujours au jour le jour.

How imprudent always to live from hand to mouth.

Quelque chose.

A trifle ; something.

Quelque heureusement doués que nous soyons, nous ne devons en tirer vanité.
                        —*Boniface.*

However richly we may be endowed, we ought not to be vain on that account.

Quelques crimes toujours précèdent les grands crimes.—*Racine.*

(Great crimes are always preceded by lesser ones.) *Nemo repente fuit turpissimus.*

Que lui importe cela ?

What's that to him ?

Que nous habitions ici ou à côté, nous sommes, non les citoyens d'un pays ou d'un monde, mais, en vérité, les citoyens du Ciel.
            —*Camille Flammarion.*

Whether we dwell here or there, we are not citizens of this country or this world, but citizens of Heaven.

Qu'est-ce que le Tiers État ? Tout. Qu'a-t-il ? Rien. Que veut-il ? Y devenir quelque chose.

What is the Third Estate ? Everything. What does it possess ? Nothing. What does it desire ? To become something.†

Que ta chemise ne sache ta guise.

Don't let your cap know what thoughts it covers.

Que vous faut-il ?

What do you require ?

Qui a bon cœur a toujours le temps à propos.—*Gaucher de Châtillon.*

Every moment is the right moment for the man who has a stout heart.

Qui a bonne femme, est bien allié.

He who has a good wife, has a good ally.

Qui a bonne tête ne manque pas de chapeaux.

A good head need not go hatless.

Qui a bu boira.

(He who has drunk will drink again.) Ever drunk, ever dry.

Qui a des filles est toujours berger.

He who has daughters must always be a shepherd.

Qui à deux maîtres servira
À un de ceux il mentira.

He who would two masters serve, is false to one or the other.

Qui a froid souffle le feu.

(Let the one who is cold blow the fire.) Who has most need should the most work.

Qui a honte de manger a honte de vivre.

He who is ashamed to eat is ashamed to live.

Qui aime bien, châtie bien.

(He loves well who chastises well.) Spare the rod and spoil the child.

---

* This familiar saying is found in Molière's *Fourberies de Scapin.* The miser Géronte is told that his son has been carried off in a Turkish galley. Unwilling to offer a ransom, he constantly repeats this question.
† This was the title of a famous pamphlet by Sieyès, which had an important part in helping the Revolution. The title itself is thought to have been not the work of Sieyès but of Chamfort.

Qui aime bien, tard oublie.

Qui aime trop le petit succès renonce à la grande gloire. —*Ph. Chasles.*

Qui a la bourse pleine prêche au pauvre.

Qui a tête de cire ne doit pas s'approcher du feu.

Qui attend les souliers d'un mort risque d'aller pieds nus.

Qui bien mange, et qui bien dort,
Ne doit encore craindre la mort.

Qui casse les verres les paye.

Qui cesse d'être ami ne l'a jamais été.

Qui chapon mange chapon lui vient.

Qui commence et ne parfait, sa peine perd.

Qui compte sans son hôte, compte deux fois.

Quiconque refuse d'être loué par les autres, se loue lui-même.—*Mascaron.*

Quiconque veut trouver quelques bons mots n'a qu'à dire beaucoup de sottises.—*J. J. Rousseau.*

Qui court deux lièvres, n'en prendra aucun.

Qui donner peut, il a maint bon voisin.

Qui dort, dîne.

Qui doute ne se trompe point.

Qui écoute aux portes, entend plus qu'il ne désire.

Qui en dit du mal, veut l'acheter.

Qui épargne, gagne.

Qui épargne le vice, fait tort à la vertu.

Qui est avec les loups, il lui faut hurler.

Qui est-ce qui attachera le grelot ?

Qui est content est riche.

Qui est malade au mois de Mai,
Tout l'an demeure sain et gai.

Qui est malade de folie,
Ne s'en guérit toute sa vie.

Qui est sur la mer, il ne fait pas des vents ce qu'il veut.

A true lover is slow in forgetting.

When a man covets petty successes, he has given up hopes of glory.

Full purse preaches to the penniless.

A head of wax must not go near the fire.

He who waits for a dead man's shoes is like to go barefoot.

He who eats well and sleeps well need not think his end is near.

Who breaks, pays.

(He who has ceased to be my friend, was never my friend.) True friendship never dies.

Live high, and high living will come to you.

It is labour lost to begin and not complete.

He who reckons without his host, will have to reckon a second time.

Whoso refuses others' praise, praises himself.

Chatter a lot of nonsense and you'll find a few clever phrases amongst it.

(He that hunts two hares will catch neither.) Two many irons in the fire.

(He who is able to give has many a kind neighbour.) The rich never lack friends.

He who sleeps, dines.

Doubt, and you'll not be deceived.

(He who listens at doors hears more than he likes.) Listeners never hear any good of themselves.

He who decries a thing, wants to buy it.

A penny saved is a penny gained.

He who spares vice wrongs virtue.

(You must howl with the wolves.) When you are at Rome, do as the Romans do.

(Who will bell the cat ?) Who will take the post of danger ?

The contented man is always rich enough.

He who is sick in the month of May The rest of the year is well and gay.

He who is sick with folly, is sick and sorry all his life.

A man at sea cannot direct the winds.

Qui femme a, noise a.

Who hath a wife hath always strife.

Qui femme vieille ou laide prend,
Donne à entendre qu'il aime argent.

Who doth an ugly maiden woo,
'Tis plain that he loves money too.

Qui fuit, peut revenir aussi,
Qui meurt, il n'en est pas ainsi.
—*Scarron*.

(He who runs away may return again,
  but he who is killed cannot do so.)
For he who fights and runs away
May live to fight another day;
But he who is in battle slain
Can never rise and fight again.—*Ray*

Qui gagne, joue bien.

It's always the clever player who wins.

Qui loin se va marier
Ou est trompé, ou veut tromper.

He who goes far from home to seek a
  wife, is either deceived or a deceiver.

Qui m'aime, aime mon chien.

Love me, love my dog.

Qui m'aime me suive.—*Francis I.*

Let him who loves me follow me ! *

Qui mal cherche, mal trouve.

He who seeks for evil, never fails to
  find it.

Qui menace, a peur.

A bully is always a coward.

Qui monte la mule, la ferre.

He who rides the mule must shoe her.

Qu'importe !

What does it matter !

Qui naît le dimanche, jamais ne meurt
de peste.

A child born on Sunday never dies of
  the plague.

Qui n'a, ne peut.

Empty pockets cannot give.

Qui n'a pas argent en bourse, ait miel
en bouche.

He who has no money in his purse must
  have a honeyed tongue.

Qui n' a pas l'esprit de son âge,
De son âge a tout le malheur !
—*Voltaire*.

The man whose inclinations are not
  suited to his age, feels the full burden
  of his years.

Qui n'a point de sens à trente ans, n'en
aura jamais.

(He who has no sense at thirty, will
  never have any.) A fool at forty is
  a fool indeed.

Qui naquit chat, court après les souris.

(Who is born a cat will run after mice.)
  Nature will out.

Qui n'a qu'un œil, bien le garde.

A man with only one eye must take
  good care of it.

Qui n'a rien, ne craint rien.

(He who owns nothing, has nothing to
  fear.) The beggar is not afraid of
  the thief.

Qui n'a santé, n'a rien.

Without health, the rest is nothing.

Qui ne châtie culot, ne châtie culasse.

He who corrects not youth controls
  not age.

Qui ne craint point la mort ne craint
point les menaces.—*Corneille*.

The man who dreads not death cannot be daunted by threats.

Qui ne dit rien consent.

Silence gives consent.

Qui ne fait rien, fait mal.

He who does nothing, does amiss.

Qui ne gagne, perd.

He who does not win, loses.

Qui n'entend qu'une cloche n'entend
qu'un son.

(Who hears only one bell, hears only
  one sound.) One story is good till
  another is told.

Qui ne parle, n'erre.

Silence makes no mistakes.

* The battle-cry of Francis I. at Marignano, where the French army defeated the Milanese in the year 1515.

Qui ne peut mordre, ne doit pas montrer les dents.

He who can't bite should not show his teeth.

Qui ne prend quand il peut,
Il n'aura quand il veut.

He that will not when he may,
When he will shall have nay.

Qui ne regarde pas en avant, se trouve en arrière.

He who looks not ahead finds himself behind.

Qui ne retire de sa vache que la queue, ne perd pas tout.

He who gets back only the tail of his cow does not lose all.

Qui ne risque rien n'a rien.

Nothing venture nothing gain.

Qui ne sait bien parler de son métier, il ne le sait pas.

A good workman does not defame his craft.

Qui ne se lasse pas, lasse l'adversité.

He who does not grow tired, tires out his ill-luck at last.

Qui ne sort que de jour, n'a que faire de lanterne.

He who goes abroad by day has no need of a lantern.

Qui ne souffre pas seul, ne souffre pas tant.

Sufferings are lessened when you share them with others.

Qui nous délivrera des Grecs et des Romains ?—*Berchoux.*

(Who will deliver us from the Greeks and Romans ?) Who will set us free from the tyranny of the ancient classical models in literature ?

Qui pardonne aisément invite à l'offenser.—*Corneille.*

He who pardons too readily invites fresh insult.

Qui parle, sème ; qui écoute, recueille.

Who speaks, sows ; who listens, reaps.

Qui partout va, partout prend.

He who goes everywhere gleans everywhere.

Qui passe un jour d'hiver, il passe un de ses ennemis mortels.

Get over a winter's day, and you " get over " a mortal enemy.

Qui paye, a bien le droit de donner son avis.

He who pays, has the right to advise.

Qui paye tôt, emprunte quand il veut.

The ready payer can borrow anywhere.

Qui pense ?

(Who thinks ?) Motto of the Earl of Howth.

Qui perd, pèche.

He who loses sins.

Qui peut ce qui lui plaît, commande alors qu'il prie.—*Corneille.*

He who can realize his wishes can command what he prays for.

Qui plaisir fait plaisir requiert.

One good turn asketh another.

Qui plus qu'il n'a vaillant dépend, il fait la corde à quoi se pend.

He that spends more than he is worth makes a rope to hang himself with.

Qui plus sait, plus se tait.

The more a man knows, the less he talks.

Qui pourrait vivre sans espoir ?

If hope were dead, who could live ?

Qui premier vient au moulin, premier doit mouldre.

(Whoso first cometh to the mill, first grist.) First come, first served.

Qui prend une femme pour sa dot, à la liberté tourne le dos.

Who takes a wife for a dower, surrenders his power.

Qui prête à l'ami, perd au double.

Lend your friend money and you will lose friend and money.

Qui prouve trop, ne prouve rien.

Who proves too much proves nothing.

Qui que tu sois, voici ton maître ;
Il l'est, le fut, ou le doit être.
—*Voltaire.*

Qui répond, paie.

Qui reste dans la vallée ne passera jamais la montagne.

Qui s'arrête à chaque pierre, n'arrive jamais.

Qui saurait les aventures, ne serait jamais pauvre.

Qui se couche avec des chiens se lève avec les puces.

Qui se détourne, évite le danger.

Qui se fâche, a tort.

Qui se fait brebis le loup le mange.

Qui se hâte en cheminant,
Se fourvoye bien souvent.

Qui se marie à la hâte, se repent à loisir.

Qui sème des chardons, recueille des épines.

Qui se ressemble s'assemble.

Qui sert bien son pays n'a pas besoin d'aïeux.—*Voltaire.*

Qui se sent galeux, se gratte.

Qui s'excuse, s'accuse.

Qui tard se couche, et se lève matin,
Il pourrait bientôt voir sa fin.

Qui terre a, guerre a.

Qui tient la poële par la queue, il la tourne là où il veut.

Qui tient le fil, tient le peloton.

Qui tôt donne, deux fois donne.

Qui tourmente les autres, ne dort pas bien.

Qui trébuche et ne tombe pas, avance son chemin.

Qui trop change, empire.

Qui trop embrasse mal étreint.

Qui un punit, cent menace.

Qui va chercher de la laine, revient tondu.

Qui va et retourne, fait bon voyage.

Qui veut apprendre à prier, aille souvent sur la mer.

(Whoe'er you are, your master see. He is, or was, or he will be.) Love the conqueror.

Who answers for another, pays.

He that lingers in the valley will never get over the hill.

He who stops at every stone never gets to his journey's end.

Could we foretell the future, we should never be poor.

He that sleeps with dogs gets up with fleas.

He who turns aside avoids danger.

He who loses his temper is in the wrong.

He that makes himself a sheep shall be eaten by the wolves.

Who hastens too much on his way
Doth often find himself astray.

Marry in haste and repent at leisure.

He who sows thistles must reap thorns.

Birds of a feather flock together.

He who serves his country well needs no ancestors.

If the cap fits, wear it.

He who excuses himself accuses himself.

He who goes late to bed, and is up betimes, is likely soon to die.

He who owns land is ever at war.

He who holds the handle of the frying-pan turns it as he pleases.

He who holds the thread holds the ball.

(He who gives quickly, gives twice.)
Bis dat, qui cito dat.

He who breaks another's rest, his slumbers ne'er are the best.

He that stumbles and falls not is still getting on.

Ever changing, never gaining.

(He who grasps too much holds little.)
Avarice overreaches itself.

In punishing one, a hundred are threatened.

He who goes a-shearing may come back shorn.

Who goes and returns makes a good enough journey.

If a man would learn to pray, let him go often to sea.

Qui veut être riche en un an, au bout de six mois est pendu.	He who wants to be rich in a year will get hanged in six months.
Qui veut faire une porte d'or, il y met tous les jours un clou.	He who wishes to make a golden door must drive a nail in every day.
Qui veut la fin veut les moyens.	Where there's a will, there's a way.
Qui veut noyer son chien l'accuse de la rage.	Give a dog a bad name and hang him.
Qui veut plaire à tout le monde, doit se lever de bonne heure.	He must rise betimes who would please everybody.
Qui veut prendre un oiseau il ne faut pas l'effaroucher.	He who would catch a bird, must not frighten it.
Qui veut voyager loin, ménage sa monture.	He who wishes to travel far, takes care of his horse.
Qui vient, est beau ; qui apporte, est encore plus beau.	The empty-handed is welcome, but far more is he who brings a present.
Qui vit à compte, vit à honte.	Who lives on credit lives disgraced.
Qui vit content de rien possède toute chose.—*Boileau.*	He who lives contented possesses everything.
Qui vit longtemps, sait ce qu'est douleur.	He who lives long knows what pain is.
Qui vive ?	Who goes there ? (On the *qui vive, i.e.* on the alert.)*
Qui vivra, verra.	Who lives will see.
Qui voit une épingle et ne la prend vient un temps qu'il s'en repent.	If you see a pin and let it lie, You may yet want it before you die.
Quoi, donc, les rois meurent-ils ?	What, do kings die ?
Quoique fol tarde, jour ne tarde.	Though the fool lingers, the day does not wait.
Qu'on me donne six lignes de la main du plus honnête homme, j'y trouverai de quoi le faire pendre. *— Cardinal Richelieu.*	Show me six lines written by the most honest man in the world, and I will find enough in them to hang him.†
Racine passera comme le café.	Racine will go out of fashion as coffee will.‡
Raconteur.	A narrator.
Ragoût.	A highly seasoned dish.
Raison d'être.	Reason for existence.
Raison froide.	(Cold reasoning.) Indifference.
Raisonné, catalogue raisonné.	Explanatory catalogue.
Raisonner sur l'amour, c'est perdre la raison !—*Boufflers.*	If you bring reason to bear on love, you lose your reason.
Ramollissement.	Softening of the brain.

* The cry of French sentinels when on guard was, until the sixteenth century, *Qui va là,* " Who goes there ? " It is said that the expression *Qui vive* has nothing to do with *vivre,* " To live," but is derived from the Italian *Chi viva,* which is itself a corruption of *Chi vi, va,* " Who goes there ? "

† A saying popularly attributed to Richelieu, although M. Fournier declares it to be most unlikely that the Cardinal ever expressed such an opinion, since it was foreign to his character to be guilty of petty conduct worthy only of an executioner.

‡ A saying that has been wrongly attributed to Madame de Sévigné.

Ranz des vaches.

(Ranks or rows of the cows.) Swiss melodies played as cow-calls — so called because the cows on hearing the air come up to the player in rows.

Rapprochement.

The act of bringing together : reconciliation.

Rarement à courir le monde
On devient plus homme de bien.
—*Régnier-Desmarets*.

Rarely does a man gain any advantage by constantly moving from land to land.

Réchauffé.

(Warmed up.) Cauld kail het again.

Recherché.

Elegant ; attractive.

Réclame.

A puff ; log-rolling.

Reconnaissance.

A survey of the position.

Recueil choisi.

A choice collection.

Rédacteur (en chef).

Editor (of a newspaper).

Régime.

Government ; mode of living.

Remercier.

To return thanks.

Remettez-vous.

Compose yourself.

Renaissance.

Regeneration ; revival.*

Renard qui dort la matinée
N'a pas la bouche emplumée.

(The fox that sleeps in the morning never feathers his mouth.) The early bird catches the worm.

Rencontre.

An encounter.

Rendezvous.

A place fixed for a meeting.

Rendre l'âme.

To give up the ghost.

Rendre pois pour fève.

(To give a pea for a bean.) To give tit for tat.

Rentes.

The funds ; Government stocks.

Répondre en Normand.

To give an evasive answer.

Réponse sans réplique.

(A reply that admits of no rejoinder.) A conclusive answer.

Résumé.

An abstract or epitome.

Réunion.

A reunion ; a social gathering.

Revanche.

Revenge.

Réveil.

The beat of the drum at daybreak.

Revenons à nos moutons.

(Let us return to our sheep.) Let us return to our subject.†

Rien de plus éloquent que l'argent comptant.

(Nothing speaks so well as cash down.) Money is a great persuader.

Rien n'abâtardit les esprits comme le spectacle perpétuel du médiocre.
—*F. Frank*.

Nothing so dulls the wit as the perpetual view of commonplaces.

Rien n'aiguise l'esprit comme les études théologiques.—*Talleyrand*.

Nothing so sharpens the wit as theological study.

Rien n'a qui assez n'a.

He has nothing who has not enough.

---

* The word is generally used in reference to the revival of learning and art in the early part of the sixteenth century.
† These words occur originally in an old French farce, *L'Avocat Pathelin*, where a lawyer, inclined to wander from the point, is recalled to the subject before the Court.

Rien ne m'est seur que la chose incertaine.—*Villon*.

Nothing is so sure to me as uncertainty.

Rien n'empêche tant d'être naturel que l'envie de le paraître.
—*La Rochefoucauld*.

Nothing so much prevents one being natural as the seeking so to appear.

Rien ne pèse tant qu'un secret :
Le porter loin est difficile aux dames ;
Et je sais même sur ce fait
Bon nombre d'hommes qui sont femmes.
—*La Fontaine*.

Nothing is so heavy to carry as a secret : it is difficult for women to keep it long ; and I know even in this matter a good number of men who are women.

Rien ne ressemble mieux à un honnête homme qu'un fripon.

Nothing more closely resembles an honest man than a knave.

Rien n'est aussi divers que la beauté des femmes, si ce n'est l'impression qu'elle produit sur nous.—*Edm. About*.

Nothing is more varied than feminine beauty, unless it be the impression it produces upon us.

Rien n'est beau que le vrai.—*Boileau*.

Nothing is beautiful but truth.

Rien n'est inutile dans une œuvre sortie d'une tête bien faite.—*De Vigny*.

There is nothing useless in a work that issues from a well-constituted brain.

Rien n'est si utile que la réputation, et rien ne donne la réputation si sûrement que le mérite.—*Vauvenargues*.

Nothing is so useful as reputation, and nothing wins it so surely as merit.

Rien ne vaut poulain s'il ne rompt son lien.

A colt is worthless if it does not break its halter.

Rien ne vieillit plus vite qu'un bienfait.

Nothing grows old more quickly than a kindness.

Rira bien, qui rira le dernier.

He laughs best who laughs last.

Rire dans sa barbe.

(To laugh in one's beard.) To ridicule secretly.

Rire jaune.

To laugh on the wrong side of one's mouth.

Rire sans propos est propre aux fous.

Ill-timed laughter is the mark of fools.

Rire sous cape.

To laugh in one's sleeve.

"Rodrigue, as-tu du cœur ?" "Tout autre que mon père l'éprouverait sur l'heure."—*Corneille*.

"Hast thou courage, Rodrigue ?" "Anyone but my father would test it at once."*

Rôle.

A character in a play.

Rôle d'équipage.

A list of the crew ; muster-roll.

Rome n'a pas été faite en un jour.

Rome was not built in a day.

Rome n'est plus dans Rome.

(Rome is no longer in Rome.) The place is not itself; everybody is out of town.†

Rompez les rangs !

Break off !

Ronger son frein.

(To gnaw the bit.) To fret inwardly.

Roué.

A rake ; a profligate.‡

---

* The question of Diègue, in *Le Cid*, to his son Rodrigue, appealing for vengeance against his foes. The question and reply are often quoted with playful application.

† A proverbial saying adapted from a line of Corneille's *Sertorius*, in which the hero declares that for him, forced to live as an exile in Spain, *Rome est toute où je suis*, "Rome is where I am," *i.e.*, that is the old saying that, "Every land is a fatherland to a brave man," *Omne solum forti patria est*.

‡ The friends of the Duke of Orleans, Regent of France, were such profligates that it was commonly said they deserved to be broken on the wheel (*roue*). This is the popular account of the origin of this expression.

Ruse contre ruse.

Diamond cut diamond.

Ruse de guerre.

A stratagem.

S'abstenir pour jouir, c'est la philosophie du sage, c'est l'épicuréisme de la raison.—*J. J. Rousseau.*

To enjoy by abstention is the sage's philosophy and the epicureanism of reason.

Sain et sauf.

Safe and sound.

Saint ne peut, si Dieu ne veut.

Saint cannot do what God will not do.

Saint Nicolas, mon bon patron,
Donnez-moi quelquechose du bon,
Plein mes bas, plein mes souliers,
Saint Nicolas bien obligé.

Saint Nicholas, my kind patron, give me something good,
Fill my stockings, fill my shoes, Saint Nicolas, grant my prayer.*

Salle.

A hall.

Salle à manger.

A dining room.

Salle des Pas Perdus.

Hall of the lost footsteps.†

S'amuser à la moutarde.

(To play with the mustard.)   To stand trifling.

Sang-froid.

Cold blood ; indifference ; apathy.

Sans changer.

Without changing.

Sans culottes.

Ragged men ; the lower classes of the French Revolution.

Sans-culottides.

The holidays of the Sans-culottes.‡

Sans Dieu, rien.

Nothing without God.

Sans dot !

Without a dowry ! §

Sans doute.

Without doubt.

Sans façon.

Without ceremony.

Sans la femme, l'homme a dû faire des grandes choses.—*Roqueplan.*

Were it not for woman, man would have done greater deeds.

Sans pain et sans vin, l'amour n'est rien ; quand la pauvreté entre par la porte, l'amour s'envole par la fenêtre.

Without bread and without wine, love is nothing ; when poverty enters the door, love flies out of the window.

Sans souci.

Free from care ; free and easy.

Sans tâche.

Without stain.

Santé.

Health.

Sapristi !

By Jove ! How provoking !

Sauter de la poële sur la braise.

Out of the frying pan into the fire.

Saute-ruisseau.

(A leap-gutter.)   The office-boy of lawyers, etc., who is employed to carry messages.

Sauve qui peut.

Save themselves who can.

* French children repeat this verse when they hang up their stockings before going to sleep. St. Nicholas is the patron saint of children and sailors. He has his festival on the 6th of December, but this custom of hanging up the stockings is now associated with Christmas, when the good Santa Claus (St. Nicholas) brings the children gifts.

† This is the name given to the large hall in the Palais de Justice of Paris. It is so called because it is always thronged with barristers and their clients, &c., who constantly cross and recross one another's steps as they walk about.

‡ Days when the Revolutionists abstained from bloodshed were so called.

§ A remark constantly repeated by Harpagon, the chief character in Molière's *l'Avare.* The miser cannot resist the attractions of the old suitor for his daughter's hand, who offers to marry her without a dowry. To all objections the father has but one reply, *Sans dot !*

Savant.

A learned man.

Savoir.

Knowledge.

Savoir dissimuler est le savoir des rois.
— *Richelieu.*

Dissimulation is the art of kings.

Savoir faire.

Ability ; skill ; wits.

Savoir par cœur n'est pas savoir : c'est tenir ce qu'on a donné en garde à sa mémoire.—*Montaigne.*

To know a thing by heart is not real knowledge ; that is only ability to lay one's hand on a thing which we have placed in the storehouse of the mind.

Savoir vivre.

Good breeding ; refined manners.

Scrutin d'arrondissement.

Municipal ballot.*

Scrutin de liste.

(Voting by ballot.) The voting for the Departmental representatives.

Séance.

Session ; sitting.

Secret de deux, secret de Dieu ; secret de trois, secret de tout.

The secret of two is God's secret, the secret of three is everybody's secret.

Secret de la comédie.

Everybody's secret.

Se jeter dans l'eau de peur de la pluie.

(To jump into the pond to get out of the rain.) From Scylla to Charybdis.

Selon le saint l'encens.

The grander the saint, the sweeter the incense.

Selon les règles.

According to rule.

Selon le vent la voile.

(Set your sail as the wind blows.)

Selon que vous serez puissant ou misérable,
Les jugements de cour vous rendront noir ou blanc.

According as you are powerful or wretched, the judgments of the Court will paint you black or white.

S'embarquer sans biscuit.

(To embark without provisions.) To begin an undertaking without the means of carrying it out.

Sème le jour de S. François,
Ton grain aura de poids.

(Sow your wheat on St. Francis' day, if you wish to have a heavy crop.) Sow on the 4th of October.

Se mettre en quatre.

(To cut oneself in four.) To do anything to oblige another.

Sens dessus dessous.

Topsy-turvy, upside down.

Serait-il sage de croire qu'un mouvement qui vient de si loin pourra être suspendu par les efforts d'une génération ? Pense-t-on qu'après avoir vaincu les rois, détruit la féodalité, la démocratie reculera devant les bourgeois et les riches ?—*Tocqueville.*

Is it wise to believe that a movement (the tendency to Democracy traced to the beginning of society) coming from so far back, can be stayed by the effort of one generation ? Can anyone believe that after overcoming kings and destroying feudalism, Democracy will retreat before the onslaught of the tradesman and capitalist classes ?

Se rompre le cou.

To break one's neck.

Ses folies sautent aux yeux.

His foibles are palpable.

Ses ouvrages font loi.

His works are quite classics.

* *Scrutin de liste* and *Scrutin d'arrondissement* are two different modes of voting. In the former case the voter indicates the names of all the candidates he wishes to elect to represent the Department collectively ; in the latter case the members are voted for individually.

Ses rides sur son front ont gravé ses exploits,
Et nous disent encore ce qu'il fut autrefois.—*Corneille.*

'Twas his exploits that furrowed thus his brow,
And what he did of yore they tell us now.

Se tirer d'affaire.

To save one's bacon.

Se trouver à la hauteur de la situation.

To rise to the occasion.

Si ce n'est toi, c'est donc ton frère.
                    — *La Fontaine.*

If it is not you, it must be your brother.*

Si Dieu n'existait pas, il faudrait l'inventer.—*Voltaire.*

If God did not exist, it would be necessary to invent him.†

Si Dieu veult.

(If God so wills it.) Motto of the Preston family.

Siècle.

An age.

Siècle d'or.

The golden age (of Louis XIV.).

Siècles des ténèbres.

The dark ages.

Si je n'y suis pas, qu'il plaise à Dieu de m'y rétablir ; si j'y suis, qu'il plaise à Dieu de m'y maintenir.
                    —*Jeanne d'Arc.*

If I am not in a state of grace before God, I pray God that it may be vouchsafed to me ; if I am, I pray God that I may be preserved in it.‡

Si je puis.

If I can.§

Si je savais quelque chose qui me fût utile et qui fût préjudiciable à ma famille, je le rejetterais de mon esprit. Si je savais quelque chose qui fût utile à ma famille et qui ne le fût pas à ma patrie, je chercherais à l'oublier. Si je savais quelque chose utile à ma patrie et qui fût préjudiciable à l'Europe et au genre humain, je le regarderais comme un crime.
                    — *Montesquieu.*

If I knew some scheme which was advantageous to myself but hurtful to my kindred, I would banish it from my mind. If I knew some scheme which was advantageous to my kindred but hurtful to my country, I would try to forget it. If I knew what was of advantage to my country, but hurtful to Europe and the human race, I should regard it as a crime.

Si je tenais toutes les vérités dans ma main, je me donnerais bien de garde de l'ouvrir aux hommes.
                    —*Fontenelle.*

If I held all truths in my hand, I should be very careful how I delivered them to mankind.||

Si jeunesse savait ! si vieillesse pouvait !

If youth had knowledge ! if age had the power !

Si la bonne foi était bannie du reste du monde, il fallait qu'on la trouvât dans la bouche des rois.

If good faith were to be banished from the rest of the world, it must still be found in the mouth of kings.¶

* A saying from the fable of the *Wolf and the Lamb.* The wolf, being unable to show that the lamb has dirtied the water in the river, is determined to find an excuse for a quarrel by some means.
† Voltaire justified this expression of his opinion by erecting a church to the Deity (*Erexit Deo Voltaire*) in Ferney at his own charges.
‡ The reply of Jeanne d'Arc to her judges, when asked if she was in a state of grace.
§ This is the motto of the Colquhoun family. An ancestor of this family, being asked by the king to retake Dumbarton Castle, replied : *Si je puis.*
|| The opinion that truths may sometimes be dangerous, if too freely imparted to untrained minds, is common both to philosophers and theologians.
¶ After the Black Prince had won the battle of Poictiers, 1356, John II., King of France, was brought as a prisoner to England. Permitted to return to France for a time, in order to arrange terms of peace, he was implored by his friends not to return to England. Like the Roman Regulus, true to a promise made even to a foe, he made this reply to the suggestions of his friends.

Si l'âme est immatérielle, elle peut sur-vivre au corps; et si elle lui survit, la Providence est justifiée. Quand je n'aurais d'autre preuve de l'immatéria-lité de l'âme que le triomphe du méchant et l'oppression du juste en ce monde, cela seul m'empêcherait d'en douter.—*J. J. Rousseau.*

If the soul be immaterial, it may sur-vive the body, and then Providence is justified. The triumph of the evil-doer and oppression of the just man in this world alone prevents me doubting that the soul is spiritual in its nature, even if I had no other proof of it.

Si l'amour donne de l'esprit aux bêtes, c'est sans doute celui qu'il ôte aux gens d'esprit.—*Alphonse Karr.*

If Cupid gives wit to the stupid, it must be what he deprives wise men of.

Si l'amour porte des ailes
N'est-ce pas pour voltiger ?
—*Beaumarchais.*

(If Love wears wings, is it not that he may fly ?) Cupid has wings and quickly flies away.

Si l'amour résiste rarement à l'absence, ce n'est pas seulement par l'oubli. C'est que, de loin, les imperfections disparaissent, et que lorsque l'on voit ensuite sa maîtresse telle qu'elle est, et non telle qu'on se la figurait, on se dit : " Comment, ce n'est que cela ? " Et l'on passe.—*La Bruyère.*

If love rarely survives absence, it is not only through forgetfulness, but because imperfections vanish when observed from afar. When, how-ever, the idol is seen as she is and not as fancied, one says : Is this all ? and passes by.

Si l'amour vit d'espoir, il périt avec lui ; C'est un feu qui s'éteint faute de nour-riture.—*Corneille.*

If hope feeds love, when hope is gone love must expire, and lacking fuel, it dies, an extinguished fire.

Si la pauvreté est la mère des crimes, le défaut d'esprit en est le père.
—*La Bruyère.*

If the mother of crime be Poverty, the father is deficiency of intellect.

Si la vie et la mort de Socrate sont d'un sage, la vie et la mort de Jésus sont d'un dieu.—*J. J. Rousseau.*

If the life and death of Socrates are those of a sage, the life and death of Jesus Christ are those of a God.

Si le ciel tombait il y aurait bien des alouettes prises.

If the sky were to fall we should catch plenty of larks.

Si le diable étoit or, il deviendroit monnoie.—*Angot.*

If the devil were made of gold, he would turn into money.

Si le monde n'attachoit les hommes que par le bonheur de leur condition présente, comme il ne fait point d'heureux, il ne feroit point d'adora-teurs : l'avenir qu'il nous montre tou-jours, est sa grande ressource et sa séduction la plus inévitable ; il nous lie par ses espérances, ne pouvant nous satisfaire par ses dons ; et l'er-reur de ses promesses nous endort toujours sur le néant de tous ses bienfaits.—*Massillon.*

If the world gained the affection of men for no other reason than the happiness of their present condition, it would have few worshippers, since it makes no men happy. It is the future which is the great and in-vincible attraction which the world offers. Not being able to satisfy us with its present gifts, the world binds us to itself by the hopes of the future which it holds out ; and the deceitful fancies that its promises arouse, dull our perceptions to the nothingness of all its gifts.

Si le peuple manque de pain, qu'il mange de la brioche.

If the people have no bread, let them eat cake.*

* This was the naïve reply of Marie Antoinette when she was told that the people were starving for want of bread.

Si les cornets vous manquent, ralliez-vous à mon panache blanc ; vous le trouverez toujours au chemin de l'honneur et de la victoire.—*Henri IV*.

If the ensigns fail you, rally round my white plume ; you will always find it in the path of honour and victory.*

Si les époux se connaissaient avant de s'aimer, la plupart ne se mariaient pas.—*Chamfort*.

If men and women knew one another before falling in love, there would be few marriages.

Si les hommes font les lois, les femmes font les mœurs.

If men make laws, women make customs.

Si les hommes n'entendent rien au cœur des femmes, les femmes n'entendent rien à l'honneur des hommes.
—*Dumas, fils*.

If we men never understand the feminine heart, women understand nothing about the honour of men.

S'il est des jours amers, il en est de si doux !
Hélas ! quel miel jamais n'a laissé de dégoûts ?
Quelle mer n'a point de tempête ?
—*André Chénier*.

If there are days of bitterness, there are also days as sweet. What honey is there that never cloys ? What sea is there that never knows a storm ?

S'il est un fruit qui se puisse manger crû, c'est la beauté.
—*Alphonse Karr*.

Beauty is a fruit to be served up " without trimmings."

S'il est vrai, il peut être.

If true, it may be so.

S'il était légitime et nécessaire de prendre ses modèles dans sa nature, il fallait savoir atteindre ce qui ne passe pas à travers ce qui passe.
—*Prévost-Paradol*.

Granting it be needful and lawful to choose models in nature, the painter must know how to seize on what never happens through what is happening.

S'il fait beau, prends ton manteau ; s'il pleut, prends-le si tu veux.

If the weather is fine, take your cloak from the shelf ; if the weather is wet, do what pleases yourself.

Si l'homme savait bien ce que c'est que la vie, il ne la donnerait pas si facilement.—*Mme. Roland*.

If man knew rightly what life is, he would not so easily throw it away.

Silhouette.

A small portrait in profile.

S'il ne tient qu'à jurer, la vache est à nous.

If it only depends on swearing, the cow is ours.

S'il n'y avait point de jugement dernier, voilà ce que l'on pourrait appeler le scandale de la Providence, la patience des pauvres outragés par la dureté et l'insensibilité des riches.
—*Bourdaloue*.

Were there to be no Last Judgment, the scandal of Providence would be the patience of the poor under the outrages of the rich man's harshness and insensibility.

Si nous n'avions point de défauts, nous ne prendrions tant de plaisir à en remarquer dans les autres.
—*La Rochefoucauld*.

If we had not any faults ourselves, we should not take so much delight in noticing those of other people.

Si nous payons la musique, nous voulons aussi danser.

If we pay the piper we will join in the dance.

Si nous résistons à nos passions, c'est plus par leur faiblesse que par notre force.—*La Rochefoucauld*.

When we withstand our passions, it is because they are weak, and not because we are strong.

* The exhortation of Henry of Navarre to his troops at Ivry, 1590.

Sire, je vais combattre les ennemis de Votre Majesté, et je la laisse au milieu des miens.—*Marshal Villars.*

Sire, I am going to fight your Majesty's enemies, and I leave you in the midst of mine.*

Si tu as la tête de beurre, ne te fais pas boulanger.

If your head is made of butter, don't be a baker.

Si votre ramage se rapproche à votre plumage
Vous êtes le phénix des hôtes de ces bois.—*La Fontaine.*

If your singing matches your feathers, you are the finest fellow of all the dwellers in these woods.

Si vous êtes assez simple pour tenir à la reconnaissance de quelqu'un, donnez-lui un peu et promettez-lui beaucoup.—*Charles Narrey.*

If simple enough to wish for gratitude, give a little and promise much.

Si vous êtes dans la détresse,
Mes chers amis, cachez-le bien ;
Car l'homme est bon, et s'intéresse
A ceux qui n'ont besoin de rien.
　　　　　—*Pons de Verdun.*

If you are wise, be silent when
In penury and sorrow,
The world will gladly lend to men
Who have no need to borrow.

Si vous lui donnez un pied, il vous en prendra quatre.

Give him an inch and he'll take an ell.

Si vous observez avec soin qui sont les gens qui ne peuvent louer, qui blâment toujours, qui ne sont contents de personne, vous reconnaîtrez que ce sont ceux mêmes dont personne n'est content.—*La Bruyère.*

Carefully observe those who never praise but blame always, and are contented with nobody, and you will see that they are the people with whom nobody is contented.

Si vous vouliez avoir du succès avec les femmes, flattez leur amour-propre : ça sera toujours apprécié.
　　　　　—*Mme. de Rieux.*

Flatter woman's conceit if you would win her ; she will always value that.

Sobriquet.

A nickname.

Sociétés anonymes.

Joint-stock companies.

Soi-disant.

Self-styled ; would-be ; pretended.

Soi-même.

One's self.

Soirée.

An evening party.

Sois juste et tu seras heureux.
　　　　　—*J. J. Rousseau.*

Be just and you will be happy.

Soit. Ainsi soit-il.

So be it. Amen.

Solidarité.

(A union of interest between individuals.) Joint liability.

Soliveau de la fable.

(The log in the fable.) A stupid but harmless ruler.†

Son cheval a la tête trop grosse, il ne peut sortir de l'écurie.

He rides too high a horse, it cannot get out of the stable.

Son esprit n'est pas de bon aloi.

His wit is something musty.

Songes sont mensonges.

Dreams are lies. Don't trust dreams.

---

* When about to take command of the army in the field, Villars took leave of Louis XIV. with these words. The Court of Versailles was full of backbiters, and then, as always, the absent were ever in the wrong.

† The origin of this proverbialism is the old fable of the frogs, who asked Jupiter for a king. At first he sent them a log, but they foolishly asked for a more active monarch. So the angry god sent them a water-snake (a crane in La Fontaine's version), who swallowed up all his subjects.

Songez que du haut de ces pyramides, quarante siècles vous contemplent.
—*Napoleon I.*

Reflect that from the top of these pyramids forty centuries behold you.*

Sonnez le boute-selle.

Sound the boot and saddle.

Sortie.

A sally.

Soubrette.

A female attendant.

Souffler le chaud et le froid.

To blow hot and cold.

Souffrir est la première chose qu'il doit apprendre, et celle qu'il aura le plus grand besoin de savoir.
—*J. J. Rousseau.*

Endurance is the first lesson a child should learn, and it is the one that he will have most need to know.

Souhaiter une bonne fête.

To wish many happy returns of the day.

Soupçon.

A little of anything; a suspicion; a taste.

Soupçon est d'amitié poison.

Suspicion is the poison of friendship.

Soupe aux poireaux.

Soup made of leeks.

Sourire du bout des lèvres.

(To smile with one's lips.)   To wear a forced smile.

Souris qui n'a qu'un trou est bientôt prise.

The mouse that has but one hole is soon taken.

Sous ce tombeau pour toujours dort
Paul, qui toujours contait merveilles.
Louange à Dieu, repos au mort,
Et paix sur terre à nos oreilles.
— *La Fontaine.*

Forever sleeps beneath these stones
Paul, whose horrific tales caused fears.
Praise be to God! rest to his bones,
And peace on earth unto our ears.

Sous tous les rapports.

In all respects; under all circumstances.

Souvenez-vous que les bons comptes font les bons amis.

Remember, short reckonings make long friends.

Souvenir.

A keepsake.

Souvent à mauvais chien tombe un bon os en gueule.

Into the mouth of a bad dog falls many a good bone.

Souvent d'un grand dessein un mot nous fait juger.—*Racine.*

One word will often enable us to judge a great design.

Souvent femme varie,
Bien fol est qui s'y fie.

Woman often changes, and foolish is the man who trusts her.†

Souvent le mieux est l'ennemi du bien.

(Better is often the enemy of good.) It's often best to leave well alone.

Soyez ferme.

Be staunch.

Soyez plutôt maçon, si c'est votre talent;
Ouvrier estimé dans un art nécessaire,
Qu'écrivain du commun et poète vulgaire.—*Boileau.*

Choose to be mason, if that is what you can do best: it is better to be a workman in a necessary craft, than a common-place writer and an inferior poet.

---

* These words formed part of the speech that Napoleon delivered to his soldiers when he invaded Egypt.   A good story is told in connection with this well-known saying.   When the English army were occupying Egypt in 1882, an officer is said to have repeated these words in a message that he signalled from one of the pyramids to Lord Wolseley.   The general, however, so far from appreciating the quotation, replied, " Come down, and don't make a fool of yourself."

† Lines said to have been scratched by Francis I. on a window of the castle of Chambord. They are an obvious reminiscence of Virgil's *Varium et mutabile semper femina.* Louis XIV. had the window removed in deference to the wish of Mlle. de la Vallière, who resented the imputation made against her sex.

Soyons amis, Cinna, c'est moi qui t'en convie.—*Corneille.*

Let us be friends, Cinna; I myself ask you.*

Spirituel.

Possessing wit; witty.

Suite.

Remaining part; attendants; a series.

Suivez de l'œil l'aigle au plus haut des airs, traversant toute l'étendue de l'horizon; il vole et ses ailes semblent immobiles: on croirait que les airs le portent. C'est l'emblème de l'orateur et du poëte dans le genre sublime. —*La Harpe.*

Watch the eagle cleave the skies, crossing the whole spread of the horizon; he flies, yet the wings seem so little to move that the air appears to buoy him up. This is the emblem of the sublime poet and orator.

Suivez la raison.

Follow reason.

Suivez la rivière et vous gagnerez la mer.

All rivers lead to the sea.

Sujet.

A subject.

Sûrement va qui n'a rien.

He goes safely who has nothing to lose.

Sur espérance.

(Upon hope.) Motto of Lord Moncrieff.

Sur le tapis.

On the carpet; under consideration.

Surtout, point de zèle.—*Talleyrand.*

Above all, avoid zeal.†

Tableau.

Picture; striking representation.

Table d'hôte.

The ordinary (dinner).

Tâche sans tache.

A work without a stain.

Tâchez de ne pas nous faire faux bond.

Try not to disappoint us.

Taisez-vous.

Be quiet.

Tant bien que mal il en sut sortir.

Somehow or other he got through it.

Tant de gens, tant de guises.

So many countries, so many customs.

Tant mieux.

So much the better.

Tant pis.

So much the worse.

Tant soit peu.

Never so little.

Tant va la cruche à l'eau qu'à la fin elle se brise.

The pitcher which goes often to the well gets broken at last.

Tapis.

A carpet.

Tard donner, c'est refuser.

Slow in giving is next to refusing.

Tel a du pain qui n'a plus de dents.

Bread comes to some who have no teeth left.

Tel bat les buissons
Qui n'a pas les oisillons.

One beats the bush, and another catches the birds.

Tel brille au second rang qui s'éclipse au premier.—*Voltaire.*

Often a man who is eclipsed in the first rank, shines in the second.

Tel croit se chauffer qui se brûle.

He burnt his fingers though only meaning to warm them.

Tel en pâtit qui n'en peut mais.

Many a one suffers for what he can't help.

Tel est notre bon plaisir.

Such is our good pleasure.‡

* The magnificent words of Augustus in *Cinna,* where the Emperor, having discovered a plot against his life, magnanimously forgives the ringleader of the conspiracy.
† Talleyrand's advice to his subordinates.
‡ The formula with which the French kings signified their assent to a new law. Similarly in England the Royal assent is expressed by the words *La Reine le veult,* "The Queen wishes it."

Tel est très-susceptible qui taquine les autres.

Very touchy persons often tease others.

Telle qui dans son habit de grisette, a l'air princesse . . . en costume de princesse, reprend, avec usure, l'air grisette.—*L. Dépret.*

The woman who looks a princess in a peasant's dress, resumes the low-born aspect with usury when she dons the costume of a princess.

Tel maître, tel valet.

Like master, like man.

Tel menace, qui a peur.

He who threatens is always afraid.

Tel porte le bâton dont à son regret le bat on.

You gather a rod for your own back.

Tel qui rit vendredi dimanche pleurera.
                         —*Racine.*

(He who laughs on Friday will weep on Sunday.) Mirth and sorrow are near neighbours.

Tel qui se dit un ami sûr
Est en tout point semblable à l'ombre,
Qui paraît quand le ciel est pur,
Et disparaît quand il est sombre.
                         —*Gobet.*

The man who calls himself "a trusty friend," is very like the tiny cloud which appears when the sky is clear, and vanishes when the sky is lowering.

Tel vend, qui ne livre pas.

(Some sell who cannot deliver.) Cut your coat according to your cloth.

Tenez bon!

Hold!

Tenez bonne table et soignez les femmes.
                         —*Napoleon I.*

Keep a good table, and flatter the ladies.*

Tenir le loup par les oreilles.

To hold the wolf by the ears.

Tes destins sont d'un homme, et tes vœux sont d'un dieu.—*Voltaire.*

Thy destinies are those of a man, and thy aspirations those of a god.

Tête-à-tête.

Face to face; conversation.

Tête de fou ne blanchit jamais.

A fool's head never whitens.

Tiens à la vérité.

Keep the truth.

Tiens ta foi.

Keep thy faith.

Tiers-état.

(The third estate.) The people of France as distinguished from the nobility and the higher clergy. The commons.

Timbre-poste.

Postage stamp.

Tirage au sort.

(Drawing lots.) Impanelling a jury.

Tiré à quatre épingles.

Neat as a pin.

Tirer à la courte paille.

To draw lots.

Tirer le diable par la queue.

(To pull the devil by the tail.) To go to the dogs.

Tirer les marrons du feu avec la patte du chat.

To take the chestnuts out of the fire with the cat's paw.†

Tirez le rideau, la farce est jouée.
                         —*Rabelais.*

Draw the curtain, the farce is over.‡

Tocsin.

An alarm bell.

---

* This was the Emperor's advice to the Abbé Pradt, whom he sent as a special envoy to conciliate the people of Poland.
† This familiar proverbialism is taken from one of La Fontaine's fables. It is commonly applied to those persons who use others as tools to serve their private ends.
‡ "I am going to seek a great Perhaps. *tirez le rideau, la force est jouée,*" are said to have been the last words of the dying Rabelais.

Toi, tu la contemplais, n'osant approcher
   d'elle,
Car le baril de poudre a peur de l'étincelle.—*Victor Hugo.*

Tomber des nues.

Ton.

Ton oncle, dis-tu, l'assassin,
M'a guéri d'une maladie :
La preuve qu'il ne fut jamais mon méde-
   cin,
   C'est que je suis encore en vie.
                  —*Boileau.*

Tope là donc !

Toujours amoureux, jamais marié.

Toujours à toi.

Toujours pêche qui en prend un.

Toujours perdrix !

Toujours prêt.

Tour de force.

Tour d'expression.

Tous ceux qui connaissent leur esprit ne
   connaissent pas leur cœur.
            —*La Rochefoucauld.*

Tous les biens, nous les devons, ou à la
   fortune, ou à la naissance : celui-là
   nous ne le devons qu'à nous-mêmes.
                 —*Massillon.*

Tous les efforts de la violence ne peuvent affaiblir la vérité, et ne servent
   qu'à la relever davantage. Toutes
   les lumières de la vérité ne peuvent
   rien pour arrêter la violence, et ne
   font que l'irriter encore plus. Qu'on
   ne prétende pas de là néanmoins que
   les choses soient égales, car il y a cette
   extrême différence, que la violence n'a
   qu'un cours borné par l'ordre de Dieu,
   qui en conduit les effets à la gloire de
   la vérité qu'elle attaque ; au lieu que
   la vérité subsiste éternellement, et
   triomphe enfin de ses ennemis, parce
   qu'elle est éternelle et puissante
   comme Dieu même.—*Pascal.*

Tous les égards sont dus à ceux avec
   qui nous vivons, et nous ne devons
   rien aux autres que la vérité.—*Mothe.*

Tous les genres sont bons, hors le genre
   ennuyeux.—*Voltaire.*

Although you gazed you did not dare
   approach the maid,
For powder near a spark must ever be
   afraid.

Unexpected ; without parallel.

Tone ; taste ; fashion

Your uncle, that murderous brute,
Cured me of an illness, you say :
That he was my doctor this fact will
   refute,
That I am still living to-day.

Agreed !

Always in love, never married.

Ever thine.

He fishes on who catches one.

(Always partridge.) Always the same
   old tale ! *

Always ready.

A feat of strength.

A peculiar mode of expression.

Those who read their mind aright do
   not know their heart.

We owe all boons to fortune or to birth
   (except a friend). That is the only
   possession we can regard as gained by
   our own merits.

All the efforts of violence cannot en-
   feeble truth ; they only exalt it the
   more. All the light of truth can do
   nothing to stay violence, but only
   irritates it the more. Nevertheless,
   let none maintain that this makes
   things even, because there is this absolute difference between them : the
   course of violence is bounded by God's
   order, who makes its onslaught re-
   dound to the glory of the truth assailed, to the end that truth shall
   exist eternally and finally triumph
   over its enemies. For truth is eternal
   and mighty as God himself.

Every respect is due to the living : to
   the others we owe nothing but the
   truth.

All kinds (of literature) are good, except
   the kind that bores you.

---

* The exclamation of the confessor of the French King, Henri IV., when that lively monarch
illustrated the maxim that variety is the secret of happiness by ordering every course at dinner
to consist of partridge.

Tous les hommes sont fous, il faut pour n'en point voir S'enfermer dans sa chambre et briser son miroir.—*Marquis de Sade.*

All men are fools, and if you do not want to see one, you must shut yourself up in your bedroom and—break the mirror.

Tous nos goûts sont des réminiscences. —*Lamartine.*

All our tastes are reminiscences.

Tout-à-fait.

Quite ; entirely.

Tout à l'heure.

Just now.

Tout au contraire.

On the contrary ; quite the reverse.

Tout au monde est mêlé d'amertume et de charmes, La guerre a ses douceurs, l'hymen a ses alarmes.—*La Fontaine.*

All things in life are a mingling of bitterness and joy ; war has its delights, and marriage its alarms.

Tout bois n'est pas bon à faire flèche.

Every sort of wood is not suited for making arrows.

Tout ce qui branle ne tombe pas.

A house may stand though shaky.

Tout ce qui brille n'est pas or.

All that glitters is not gold.

Tout ce qu'il y a d'hommes sont presque toujours emportés à croire non par la preuve, mais par l'agrément.—*Pascal.*

All men have, almost always, been persuaded by compromise rather than conviction.

Tout ce qu'on dit de trop est fade et rebutant.—*Boileau.*

All that is superfluously spoken is mawkish and repulsive.

Tout chemin va à Rome.

(Every road leads to Rome.)   By hook or by crook.

Tout chien qui aboie ne mord pas.

(Every dog that barks does not bite.) Barking dogs seldom bite.

Tout chien sur son fumier est hardi.

(Every dog is valiant on his own dunghill.)   Every cock crows loudest on his own dunghill.

Tout comprendre, c'est tout pardonner.

To understand everything is to forgive everything.

Tout de même.

All the same.

Tout d'un coup.

At one stroke ; suddenly.

Toute chair n'est pas venaison.

All meat is not venison.

Toute chose qui est bonne à prendre est bonne à rendre.

What is worth taking is worth returning.

Toute eau éteint feu.

Any water puts out fire.

Toute femme porte en elle une arme mystérieuse, inconnue, que la nature a caché au plus profond de son âme, *l'instinct*, cet instinct vierge, incorruptible, sauvage, qui fait qu'elle n'a besoin, ni d'apprendre, ni de raisonner, ni de savoir ; qui fait plier la forte volonté de l'homme, domine sa raison souveraine, et fait pâlir nos petits flambeaux scientifiques.—*A. de Musset.*

Hidden in woman's soul is a mysterious weapon, Instinct, virgin, wild, incorruptible, which saves her from any need to learn, know, or reason ; it bends man's strong will, overrules his sovereign reason, and makes our paltry lights of knowledge pale before it.

Toute la suite des hommes, pendant le cours de tant de siècles, doit être considérée comme un même homme qui subsiste toujours et qui apprend continuellement.—*Pascal.*

The whole line of mankind, throughout the course of so many ages. ought to be considered as one man who always exists and continually learns.

Tout enfant qui n'aura pas éprouvé de grandes craintes n'aura pas de grandes vertus ; les puissances de son âme n'auront pas été remuées. Ce sont les grandes craintes de la honte qui rendent l'éducation publique préférable à la domestique, parce que la multitude des témoins rend le blâme terrible, et que la censure publique est la seule qui glace d'effroi les belles âmes.—*Joubert.*

Children who have never known great fears will have no great virtues ; the powers of their mind will not have been stirred. The great fears of open disgrace make public education preferable to private schooling, because the number of the bystanders makes rebuke feared, and it is public censure alone which intimidates fine natures.

Toutes grandes vertus conviennent aux grands hommes.—*Racine.*

All great virtues befit great men.

Toutes les clefs ne pendent pas à une ceinture.

(All keys hang not from one girdle.) One head does not contain all the knowledge in the world.

Toutes têtes ne sont pas coffres à raison.

All heads are not knowledge-boxes.

Tout est perdu fors l honneur.

All is lost save honour. *

Tout est pour le mieux dans le meilleur des mondes possibles.—*Voltaire.*

Everything is for the best in the best of possible worlds.†

Tout est pris.

All is taken ; every avenue preoccupied.

Tout est tentation à qui la craint.

Everything tempts the man who fears temptation.

Toutes vérités ne sont pas bonnes à dire.

All truths are not good to be told.

Tout faiseur de journaux doit tribut au Malin.—*La Fontaine.*

All journalists owe tribute to the Father of Lies.

Tout fait ventre, pourvu qu'il entre.

All's fish that comes into my net.

Tout finit par des chansons.
                    —*Beaumarchais.*

All ends with songs.‡

            Tout flatteur
Vit aux dépens de celui qui l'écoute.
            —*La Fontaine.*

All flatterers live on their hearers.

Tout homme de courage est homme de parole.—*Corneille.*

Every courageous man is a man of his word.

Tout homme est formé par son siècle.
            —*Voltaire.*

Every man is shaped by the times he lives in.

Tout homme qui à quarante ans n'est pas misanthrope n'a jamais aimé les hommes.—*Chamfort.*

Every man who is not a misanthrope at forty years of age has never loved mankind.

Tout le malheur des hommes vient d'une seule chose, qui est de ne pas savoir demeurer en repos dans une chambre.
            —*Pascal.*

All man's misery springs from his inability to rest with tranquillity in one room alone.

Tout le monde ne gagne pas à être connu.

Everyone does not improve on acquaintance.

* Thus Francis I. is said to have written to his mother, when announcing the disastrous defeat at Pavia. The letter is still extant, and it there appears that the King wrote : " I have lost all save my honour and my life," a far less heroic expression.
† This optimistic declaration was not Voltaire's personal opinion, but a satirical summing up of the optimism of some of his contemporaries, Leibnitz and others.
‡ The line from the *Marriage of Figaro* is often quoted as a typical illustration of the French character, which turns even the most serious subjects to ridicule.

Tout le monde se plaint de sa mémoire, et personne ne se plaint de son jugement.—*La Rochefoucauld.*

Everybody complains of their bad memory, but never of their bad sense.

Tout le monde veut du bien à cette personne.

Everyone wishes her well.

Tout lui sourit.

Everything goes well with him.

Tout ou rien.

All or nothing.

Tout paraît jaune à qui a la jaunisse.

All things are yellow to the jaundiced eye.

Tout par amour, rien par force.

(All by love, nought by force.) Gentleness wins more than violence.

Tout par raison.

Everything guided by reason.*

Tout passe, tout casse, tout lasse.

All is fleeting, all is brittle, all is wearisome.

Tout passe vite, tout a passé, tout passera. On vit peu, et l'on est beaucoup plus longtemps mort que vivant. Vos yeux de chair ne voient pas ce qui est. Aspects, formes, mirages sont fugitifs et passagers ; ce qui demeure, ce qui vit, ce qui régit le monde, c'est l'invisible. Ne vivez point par les sens : vivez par l'esprit.
　　　　—*Camille Flammarion.*

All flies by, all has flown, and all will fly. Short is life and man lies dead longer than he lived. Our earthly eyes do not see what really exists. Aspect, form—these are mere fugitive mirages; what remains and rules the world is the Unseen. Let not the senses but the intelligence be the guide of your life.

Tout se passa en un clin d'œil.

The whole thing took place in a flash of lightning.

Tout soldat français porte dans sa giberne le bâton de maréchal de France.
　　　　—*Napoleon I.*

Every French soldier carries in his knapsack a marshal's bâton.

Tout va à qui n'a pas besoin.

Everything comes to the man who does not need it.

Tout va bien.

All is well.

Tout vient à point à qui sait attendre.

All things come to him who knows how to wait.

Traduire à livre ouvert.

To translate at sight.

Traiter de haut en bas.

To laugh to scorn.

Travailler en plein air.

To work out of doors.

Travaillez jour et nuit à acquérir de l'expérience, elle vous servira tôt ou tard à voir les fautes—des autres.
　　　　—*Chas. Narrey.*

Work night and day to acquire experience ; it will enable you sooner or later to see the faults of—others.

Tremblez, tyrans, vous êtes immortels !
　　　　—*Delille.*

Tremble, tyrants, you are immortal !

Trève de plaisanteries.

A truce to joking.

Tricherie revient à son maître.

Knavery comes home at last.

Triste.

Sad ; melancholy.

Tristesse.

Sadness ; depression.

Trois frères, trois châteaux.

Three brothers, three castles.

Trop achète le miel qui le lèche sur les épines.

He pays too dear a price for honey who licks it off thorns.

Trop de zèle gâte tout.

Too much zeal spoils everything.

* A favourite saying of Cardinal Richelieu.

Trop tranchant ne coupe pas, trop pointu ne perce pas.

(Too sharp an edge does not cut, too fine a point does not pierce.) The cunning man over-reaches himself.

Trouvaille.

A god-send.

Tue-la.

Kill her.*

Un amant, dont l'ardeur est extrême, Aime jusqu'aux défauts des personnes qu'il aime.—*Molière.*

A lover, whose ardour is very great, loves even the faults of those whom he adores.

Un amant qui ne peut dépenser qu'en soupirs
　　N'est plus payé qu'en espérance.
　　　　　　—*De Méré.*

A lover who only expends sighs is paid in hopes alone.

Un aveugle mène l'autre en la fosse.

When the blind leads the blind, both fall into the ditch.

Un badinage qui fait sourire une femme honnête souvent effarouche une prude: mais quand un danger réel force l'une à fuir, l'autre n'hésite pas s'avancer.
　　　　　　—*Laténa.*

The jest that makes a good woman smile would alarm a prude; but when real danger forces the former to flee, the other does not hesitate to advance.

Un baiser, mais à tout prendre, qu'est-ce ?
Un serment fait d'un peu plus près, une promesse
Plus précise, un aveu qui veut se confirmer,
Un point rose qu'on met sur l'i du verbe aimer.—*Edm. Rostand.*

A kiss—well, what is a kiss ? 'Tis an avowal uttered at closer quarters, a promise ratified, a confession that is eager to confirm itself, a rose point on the i of the word *(aimer)* " I love you."

Un bon avis vaut un œil dans la main.

Good advice is as good as an eye in the hand.

Un bon bailleur en fait bailler deux.

One gaper makes another.

Un bon esprit cultivé est, pour ainsi dire, composé de tous les esprits des siècles précédents.—*Fontenelle.*

A cultivated mind is, so to speak, the storehouse of all the wisdom of previous generations.

Un bon marché n'est pas toujours bon marché.

A bargain is not always a cheap purchase.

Un bon renard ne mange pas les poules de son voisin.

A cunning fox does not eat his neighbour's fowls.

Un bon repas doit commencer par la faim.

Hunger should be the first course to a good dinner.

Un cerveau ne vaut guère sans langue.

A brain is worth little without a tongue.

Un chien regarde bien un évêque.

A cat may look at a king.

Un citoyen, obscur, sans biens, qui fait de sa vertu tout son appui, est au-dessus du conquérant du monde.
　　　　　　—*Pascal.*

An obscure, penniless man, who has no support but his virtue, is above the conqueror of the world.

Un clou pousse l'autre.

One nail drives out another.

Une belle action est celle qui a de la bonté, et qui demande de la force pour la faire.—*Montesquieu.*

A fine action is one which has kindness for its motive, and requires vigour for its performance.

* The famous saying in *L'Homme-Femme*, of Dumas fils, has become a typical example of the feeling of an outraged husband towards a wife who has proved unfaithful.

Une belle femme qui a les qualités d'un honnête homme est ce qu'il y a au monde de plus délicieux ; l'on trouve en elle tout le mérite des deux sexes.
—*La Bruyère.*

Une bonne à tout faire.

Une bonne pensée, de quelque endroit qu'elle parte, vaudra beaucoup mieux qu'une sottise de son cru, n'en déplaise à ceux qui se vantent de trouver tout chez eux et de ne tenir rien de personne.—*Lamothe le Vayer.*

Une des premières vertus sociales est de tolérer dans les autres ce qu'on doit s'interdire à soi-même.—*Duclos.*

Une extrême justice est souvent une injure.—*Racine.*

Une femme, c'est le premier domicile de l'homme.—*Diderot.*

Une femme qui écrit a deux torts, elle augmente le nombre des livres et diminue le nombre des femmes.
—*Alphonse Karr.*

Une femme sensée ne devrait jamais prendre d'amant sans le consentement de son cœur, ni de mari sans le consentement de sa raison.
—*Ninon de Lenclos.*

Une fleur ne fait pas une guirlande.

Une fois n'est pas coutume.

Une grande rivière est un mauvais voisin.

Une heure vient de sonner.

Une hirondelle ne fait pas le printemps.

Une horloge entretenir,
Jeunes dames à gré servir,
Vieille maison reparer,
Est toujours recommencer.

Une lettre à cheval.

Une nation de singes à larynx de perroquets.—*Sieyès.*

　　　　　Un endroit écarté,
Où d'être homme d'honneur on ait la liberté.—*Molière.*

Une science requiert tout son homme.

Une tromperie en attire une autre.

A handsome woman with an honourable man's qualities is the most delightful thing in the world : she has all the merit of both sexes.

A general servant.

A good thought from any quarter is better than a silly idea of one's own, in spite of those who boast that they manufacture their own ideas and borrow from nobody else.

One of the foremost social virtues is toleration in others of what we should prohibit in ourselves.

Law, when too strictly applied, is often injustice.

A wife gives a man his first home.

The literary woman commits two faults : she adds to the number of books and lessens the number of women.

A sensible woman never should fall in love without her heart's consent, nor marry without that of her reason.

One swallow does not make a summer.

One act does not make a habit ; one swallow does not make a summer ; no rule without an exception.

(A large river is a dangerous neighbour.) A great lord is a bad neighbour.

One o'clock has just struck.

One swallow does not make a spring.

To see a clock's kept wound with care, To please young maidens who are fair, To keep old houses in repair, One is always recommencing.

An imperious letter.

A nation of apes with the throats of parrots.*

A spot withdrawn from the world, where one may be a man of honour if one pleases.†

To master one art you must give yourself wholly to it.

One lie makes many.

---

* This comment on the French nation appeared in a letter written to Mirabeau.
† The words of Alceste, the Misanthrope, the hero of the famous comedy of that name, when, disgusted with the ways of the world, he goes into voluntary banishment.

Une vérité que l'on ne comprend pas devient une erreur.—*Desbarolles.*

A truth beyond comprehension becomes an error.

Un fou avise bien un sage.

A wise man may sometimes take a lesson from a fool.

Un fou fait toujours commencement.

A fool is always beginning.

Un homme averti en vaut deux.

To be forewarned is to be forearmed.

Un homme bien monté est toujours orgueilleux.

A man on a handsome horse is always proud.

Un homme criblé de dettes.

A man over head and ears in debt.

Un homme de cinquante ans est plus redoutable à cet âge qu'à tout autre. C'est à cette époque de la vie qu'il use d'une expérience chèrement acquise et de la fortune qu'il doit avoir. —*Balzac.*

At fifty a man is more to be dreaded than at any other age. Then he employs a dearly bought experience and the fortune he probably possesses to make conquests.

Un homme est le fils de ses œuvres.

A man is the child of his own works.

Un homme est plus fidèle au secret d'autrui qu'au sien propre : une femme, au contraire, garde mieux son secret que celui d'autrui.—*La Bruyère.*

A man keeps another's secret better than his own ; a woman, on the contrary, keeps her own secret better than that of another.

Un homme mort n'a ni parents ni amis.

A dead man has neither relations nor friends.

Un homme nul homme.

A man by himself is no man.

Un homme sage est au-dessus de toutes les injures qu'on lui peut dire, et la grande réponse qu'on doit faire aux outrages, c'est la modération et la patience.—*Molière.*

A wise man is superior to every insult that one may offer him ; and restraint and endurance are the dignified reply that we ought to make to such attacks.

Un je ne sais quoi qui n'a plus de nom dans aucune langue.—*Bossuet.*

An indescribable something which has no name in any language.*

Un livre a toujours été pour moi un conseil, un consolateur éloquent et calme, dont je ne voulais pas épuiser vite les ressources, et que je gardais pour les grandes occasions. —*G. Sand.*

A book has always been for me a counsellor, an eloquent and soothing consoler, whose aid I am not fain to exhaust at once, but which I keep for great events.

Un livre est un ami qui ne trompe jamais. —*Guilbert de Pixérécourt.*

A book is a friend that never deceives us.

Un mal attire l'autre.

One mischief falls upon the neck of another.

Un malheur ne vient jamais seul.

Misfortunes seldom come alone.

Un mari est un emplâtre qui guérit tous les maux des filles.—*Molière.*

A husband is a panacea for all the woes of maidenhood.

Un marteau d'argent rompt une porte de fer.

(A silver hammer breaks down an iron door.) A silver key will open any gate.

Un mauvais accommodement vaut mieux qu'un bon procès.

Better be worsted in a compromise, than successful in a lawsuit.

---

* So Bossuet, in his famous funeral oration over Henrietta of England, the Duchess d'Orléans, speaks of the condition of the human body after death. *Je ne sais quoi*, as an expression for something impossible to define, has become almost a part of our own language.

Un menteur est toujours prodigue de serments.—*Corneille.*

A liar is always full of vows and protestations.

Un ministre du commerce a dit ce beau mot : " Si la Parisienne n'existait pas, il faudrait l'inventer." En effet, le budget d'une Parisienne ne passerait pas aussi vite au Corps législatif que le budget de la France. Elle se moque du nécessaire pourvu qu'elle ait le superflu. Elle a ses jours d'économie. Elle prend une voiture à l'heure pour aller acheter une demi-livre de crevettes.—*Arsène Houssaye.*

A Secretary of the Board of Trade said wittily : " If there were no Parisian ladies, they would have to be invented." Indeed their budget would not pass the House as quickly as the National one. The Parisian lady laughs at the necessities of life if she has the superfluities, and on her saving days, hires a cab by the hour to buy a dish of prawns.

Un peu d'absence fait grand bien.

(A little absence does great good.) Absence makes the heart grow fonder.

Un peu d'aide fait grand bien.

A little help when needed most is the greatest boon.

Un peu de fiel gâte beaucoup de miel.

A drop of gall spoils a pound of honey.

Un pince sans rire.

A dry joker.

Un poète manqué.

A would-be poet.

Un regard de Louis enfantait des Corneilles.—*Delille.*

One glance from Louis produced Corneilles.

Un Robespierre à cheval.
—*Madame de Staël.*

(A Robespierre on horseback.) A military revolutionist.*

Un sac percé ne peut tenir le grain.

A torn sack holds no corn.

Un saint homme de chat.
—*La Fontaine.*

(A very pious fellow of a cat.) A treacherous fellow.†

Un sot à triple ètage.

An egregious blockhead.

Un sot trouve toujours un plus sot qui l'admire.

A fool always finds a greater fool to admire him.

Un style serré.

Concise style.

Un tel écrit beaucoup ; mais, résultat funèbre !
Plus il devient connu, moins il devient célèbre.—*Jules Viard.*

Since Mr. Blank writes many books
His name is widely known ;
Alas ! the more he publishes
The less his fame has grown.

Un tiens vaut deux tu l'auras.

A bird in the hand is worth two in the bush.

Un traducteur est un musicien barbare qui veut absolument jouer sur la flûte un air qui a été écrit pour le violon.
—*Gerfaut.*

A translator is a barbarous musician who persists in playing on the flute a composition written for the violin.

Un vaurien qui bat le pavé.

A vagabond loafing about.

Un ver se recoquille quand on marche dessus.

Even a worm will turn when you tread on it.

Vache de loin a lait assez.

A cow in another county gives plenty of milk.

Valet de chambre.

An attendant ; footman.

* This was Madame de Staël's estimate of Napoleon when he first began to appear as a star on the political horizon.
† A proverbial expression taken from the fable of La Fontaine, *The Cat, the Weasel, and the Little Rabbit,* where the cat, pretending to be a saint, gobbles up his unsuspecting visitors.

Valet devant, maître derrière,
En pont, en planche, en rivière.

The servant in front and the master behind, on a bridge, a plank, or a river.

Va-t'en voir s'ils viennent.

Don't you wish you may get it.

Vedettes.

Sentinels on horseback.

Venez au fait.

Come to the point.

Venir de Pontoise.

(To come from Pontoise.) To have a confused, puzzled manner.*

Vent au visage rend un homme sage

(A head wind makes a man wise.) In hard times a man learns wisdom.

Ventre affamé n'a point d'oreilles.

An empty belly has no ears.

Ventre à terre.

With whip and spur · helter-skelter.

Ventre plein conseille bien.

A man well fed has a prudent head.

Vérité.

Truth.

Vérité en deçà des Pyrénées, erreur au delà.—*Pascal.*

(Truth on this side of the Pyrenees, is error on that.) Every nation has its own standard of justice and morality.

Vérité sans peur.

Truth without fear.

Vers de société.

(Society verses.) Poetry dealing lightly with trifling subjects.

Verser des larmes de crocodile.

To shed crocodile tears.

Verve.

Animation ; spirit.

Viande d'ami est bientôt prête.

A friend's meat is soon ready.

Vieil en sa terre, et jeune en étrangère,
Mentent tous deux d'une même manière.

An old man in his own land, and a young man abroad, both lie in the same fashion.

Vieille avec deniers est mieux
Que jeune fille avec cheveux.

An old woman with money is fairer than a young maid with nothing but her hair for a dowry.

Vieux amis et comptes nouveaux.

Long friendships and short reckonings.

Vieux bœuf fait sillon droit.

An old ox makes a straight furrow.

Vieux garçon.

Old bachelor.

Vilain enrichi ne connaît ni parent ni ami.

A lout enriched forgets his relations and friends.

Ville qui parlemente est moitié rendue.

The town which parleys is half-surrendered.

Vin d'honneur.

(Wine of honour.) Cup of welcome ; wine drunk in honour of a welcome guest.

Vingt années de vie sont pour nous une bien sévère leçon.— *Mme. de Staël.*

Twenty years' life is a very severe lesson for us.

Vin versé n'est pas avalé.

There's many a slip 'twixt the cup and the lip.

Vis-à-vis.

Opposite ; face to face.

Vive la bagatelle !

Success to trifling ! Trifles for ever !

Vive le roi !

Long live the king.

---

* During the 18th century the French Parliament was twice expelled to Pontoise, as the members had incurred the displeasure of the king. At Pontoise they were out of touch with current affairs, and, on their return to the capital, gave uncertain replies to questions that were put to them. This is said to be the origin of this proverbial expression.

Vivre au jour la journée.
To live from hand to mouth.

Vivre comme un coq en pâte.
To live in clover.

Vivre content de peu, c'est être vraiment riche.—*Gaudin*.
To live content with little is to possess true riches.

Vogue la galère.
(Row on the galley.)   Here goes, come what may.*

Voilà qu'il broie du noir.
Look at him in a brown study.

Voilà tout.
That is all.

Voilà une autre chose.
That's quite a different matter.

Voir le dessous des cartes.
To be in the secret.

Voir rouge.
(To see red.)   To be in a mad, un-governable rage.

Voir tout couleur de rose ; voir tout en rose.
To regard everything favourably ; to look always on the sunny side.

Voiture.
A carriage.

Voulez-vous donc qu'on vous fasse des révolutions à l'eau-rose ?
—*Chamfort*.
Do you wish revolutions to be made with rose-water ? †

Voulez-vous faire une partie de boules ?
Will you have a game of bowls ?

Voulez-vous que je vous indique une bonne manière de vous singulariser ? Quand tout le monde attaque une femme, défendez-la.—*Chas. Narrey*.
To become prominent, defend the woman whom everybody attacks.

Vouloir, c'est pouvoir.
Will is power.

Vouloir prendre la lune avec les dents.
(To wish to take the moon in one's teeth.)   To attempt the impossible.

Vouloir rompre l'anguille au genou.
To try to break an eel on one's knee.

Vous allez voir comment on meurt pour vingt-cinq francs.—*Antoine Baudin*.
You are going to see how a man dies for twenty-five francs a day.

Vous apprendrez, maroufle, à rire à nos dépens.—*Molière*.
I will teach you, scoundrel, to laugh at our expense.

Vous avez bon caractère.
You are good-tempered.

Vous avez fait là un pas de clerc.
You have made a silly blunder.

Vous avez fait, monsieur, trois fautes d'orthographe.—*De Favras*.
You have made three orthographical blunders.‡

Vous avez mis le doigt dessus.
You have hit the nail on the head.

Vous caressez ce chien parce qu'il est petit ;
S'il devenait trop grand, il n'aurait rien d'aimable.
    Un petit amour divertit ;
    S'il devient très-grand, il accable.
—*Fontenelle*.
A dog is fondled when small, but, grown up, he would not be so delightful ; thus, a flirtation amuses, but, become real love, it overpowers.

Vous êtes orfèvre, Monsieur Josse.
—*Molière*.
(You are a goldsmith, Mr. Josse.)   Your advice merely cries your own wares. §

Vous faites la sourde oreille.
You are deaf to the voice of the charmer.

* These words are the refrain of a popular old ballad.
† A reply to Marmontel, who deprecated the outrages of the Revolutionists.
‡ The remark made by De Favras when the clerk of the court read out to him the sentence of death.
§ The reply to a goldsmith, who recommended a present of jewels as a cure for melancholy.

Vous l'avez voulu, vous l'avez voulu, George Dandin.—*Molière.*

(You have wished it, you have wished it, George Dandin.) You are paying the price of your own folly.*

Vous leur fîtes, Seigneur,
En les croquant, beaucoup d'honneur.
—*La Fontaine.*

You did them too much honour, my lord, when you devoured them.†

Vous m'aimez, vous êtes roi, et je pars.
—*Marie Mancini.*

You love me, you are king, and I depart.‡

Vous ne me garderez pas rancune pour cela.

You won't bear me malice on that account.

Vous ne me jetterez pas ainsi de la poudre aux yeux.

(You won't throw dust in my eyes in that way.) You cannot cajole me.

Vous ne pourrez être impunément le mari d'une très jolie femme que si vous avez assez de jeunesse, assez de fortune et assez de générosité pour lui donner tout ce que les autres lui offrent.—*Charles Narrey.*

A beauty's husband should have enough youth, money, and generosity, to offer her all which others are ready to offer her.

Vous n'êtes pas dans mes petits papiers.

You are not in my good books now.

Vous n'y êtes pas.

(You are not there.) You have not hit the right nail upon the head.

Vous parlez devant un homme à qui tout Naples est connu.—*Molière.*

(You are talking before a man to whom all Naples is known.) You cannot deceive me.

Vous prêtez continuellement à rire.

You are always making yourself ridiculous.

Vous sortez du sujet, revenez à vos moutons.

You are wandering from the subject ; come back to the point.

Vous verrez que vous vous en mordrez les doigts.

You will find you will be sorry for it.

Vous vous adressez mal.

You mistake your man.

Vous vous moquez de moi.

You are laughing at me.

Vous vous prêtez-là à quelque chose d'équivoque.

You are engaged in doubtful business.

Vous y perdrez vos pas.

You will lose your labour.

Vraie noblesse nul ne blesse.

True nobility can suffer no hurt.

Vraisemblance.

Likelihood ; probability.

Wagons-lits.

Sleeping-cars.

---

* The lament of the man who has married above his station, and learns to repent it.
† The remark of the fox, who is a type of the sycophant, to the lion who regrets that he has sometimes eaten the shepherd as well as the sheep.
‡ Louis XIV. in his youth had an affection for Marie Mancini, Mazarin's niece. When she was sent away from the Court she is said to have spoken thus to the disconsolate king. M. Fournier, however, shows that it is more than improbable that this remark was ever made, as the rupture between the monarch and the lady occurred months before she left the Court circle.

German.

Abgeordneter.

A deputy ; a parliamentary representative.

Absichtlich.

On purpose.

Ach, die Welt ist Sterbenden so süss.
—Schiller.

Ah, the world is so sweet to the dying !

Ach ! so ist der Menschen Geschlecht : wir sehnen und hoffen, Und das ersehnte Glück wird uns errungen zur Last. *— Th. Körner.*

Ah ! such is the race of men : we long and hope, and then the longed-for happiness, when obtained, proves burdensome.

Acht Tage.

(Eight days.) A week.

Ach ! warum, ihr Götter, ist unendlich Alles, alles, endlich unser Glück nur ?
—Goethe.

Ah, why, ye gods, is everything eternal, while our happiness alone abideth not ?

Ach, wie glücklich sind die Todten.
—Schiller.

Ah ! how happy are the dead.

Adam muss eine Eva haben, die er zeiht, was er gethan.

Adam must have an Eve, in order that he may blame her for what he has done.

Adler brüten keine Tauben.

(Eagles do not give birth to doves.) Brave men breed no cowards.

Aengstlich zu sinnen und zu denken, was man hätte thun können, ist das Uebelste, was man thun kann.
—Lichtenberg.

Anxiously to reflect and ponder on what one could have done, is the very worst thing one can do.

Affen bleiben Affen, wenn man sie auch in Sammet kleidet.

Apes are still apes, though you clothe them in velvet.

Alle anderen Dinge müssen ; der Mensch ist das Wesen, welches will.—*Schiller.*

All other creatures act under compulsion ; but Man is the only being that has the power of free-will.

Alle Beschränkung beglückt. Je enger unser Gesichts-, Wirkungs- und Berührungskreis, desto glücklicher sind wir : je weiter, desto öfter fühlen wir uns geängstigt.—*Schopenhauer.*

All limitation gives happiness. The narrower our circle of vision, action, and contact, the happier we are ; the more extended it is, the more we feel our anxieties increase.

Alle Frachten lichten, sagte der Schiffer, da warf er seine Frau über Bord.

All freight lightens the ship, said the skipper, as he pitched his wife overboard.

Alle Länder gute Menschen tragen
—Lessing.

Every land produces good men.

Alle Menschen, gleichgeboren,
Sind ein adliges Geschlecht.
—*H. Heine.*

All men now are free and equal,
All are noble from their birth.
—*J. E. Wallis.*

Alle Menschen müssen sterben !

All men must die.

Alle Menschen sind Lügner.

All men are liars.

Alle Menschen werden Brüder,
Wo dein sanfter Flügel weilt.
—*Schiller.*

All men are brethren wherever thy (Joy)
gentle wings do rest.

Aller Ausgang ist ein Gottesurtel.
—*Schiller.*

The issue of all things is of God's or-
daining.

Allerheiligen.

All Saints' Day.

Alles freuet sich und hoffet,
Wenn der Frühling sich erneut.
—*Schiller.*

All is full of hope and joy, when the
Spring returns.

Alles Grosse muss im Tod bestehen.

All greatness must suffer death.

Alles in der Welt lässt sich ertragen,
Nur nicht eine Reihe von schönen
Tagen.—*Goethe.*

Everything in the world is endurable,
save only a succession of fine days.

Alles was geschieht, vom Grössten bis
zum Kleinsten, geschieht nothwen-
dig.—*Schopenhauer.*

Everything that happens, from the
greatest to the least, happens of
necessity.*

Alles zu seiner Zeit.

Everything in its proper time.

Allwissend bin ich nicht ; doch viel ist
mir bewusst.—*Goethe.*

I do not know everything ; still, many
things I understand.

Allzuviel ist nicht genug.

Too much of anything is good for nothing.

Als Adam grub und Eva spann,
Wer war denn da ein Edelmann ?

When Adam delved and Eve span,
Where was then the gentleman ?

Alte Bäume lassen sich nicht biegen.

(Old trees cannot be bent.) As the
twig grows, the tree's inclined.

Alte Liebe rostet nicht.

True love does not rust with age.

Alte Wunden bluten leicht.

Old wounds readily bleed anew.

Am Abend wird man klug
Für den vergangnen Tag ;
Doch nimmer klug genug
Für den, der kommen mag.—*Rückert.*

In the evening one becomes wise as to
the day that is past ; but we never
learn wisdom for that which may
come upon us.

Am Baume des Schweigens hängt
seine Frucht, der Friede.

From the tree of Silence hangs its fruit,
Tranquillity.†

Am Ende.

After all ; in a word.

Amerika, du hast es besser.—*Goethe.*

(America, thou art more fortunate.)
America is more fortunately situated
than the States of Europe.

Am Herzen liegen.

To be near one's heart ; to be much
beloved.

Am Rhein, am Rhein, da wachsen
unsre Reben.—*M. Claudius.*

By the Rhine, by the Rhine, there
thrive our vines.

---

* The recognition of this fact, and the wisdom of shunning the pursuit of pleasure, may be
taken as a summary of Schopenhauer's philosophy of life.
† This saying is quoted by Schopenhauer in his *Parerga et Paralipomena.* He says that it
is an Arabic proverb. The same remark applies to the proverb *Was dein Feind nicht wissen
soll,* &c., which is also to be found in this section.

Am Tage.	By day ; in the daytime.
Am Tode sein.	To be on the point of death ; at the last gasp.
Amt ohne Geld macht Diebe.	Office without pay is the breeder of thieves.
Am Werke erkennt man den Meister.	The craftsman is known by his work.
An armer Leute Bart lernt der Junge scheeren.	On the chins of the poor the barber learns to shave.
An der Armut will jeder den Schuh wischen.	Every one is ready to wipe his boots on poverty.
Andere nach sich selbst abmessen.	To judge other people by oneself.
Andere Saiten aufziehen.	To change one's tune ; to turn over a new leaf.

Anfangs wollt ich fast verzagen,
　Und ich glaubt, ich trüg es nie ;
Und ich hab es doch getragen—
　Aber fragt mich nur nicht : wie ?—
　　　　　H. Heine.

At first I fancied in despair
　I ne'er should learn my fate to bear,
Yet I have learned to bear it now—
　But oh ! you must not ask me how !
　　　　　—*J. E. Wallis.*

Arbeit ist des Blutes Balsam,
Arbeit ist der Tugend Quell.—*Herder.*

Work's the balsam of the blood
Work's the source of every good.

Arbeit ist des Bürgers Zierde,
　Segen ist der Mühe Preis :
Ehrt den König seine Würde,
　Ehret uns der Hände Fleiss.
　　　　　—*Schiller.*

To freedom labour is renown
　Who works—gives blessings and commands :
Kings glory in the orb and crown—
　Be ours the glory of our hands.
　　　　　—*Lytton.*

Arbeit macht das Leben süss,
　Macht es nie zur Last,
Der nur hat Bekümerniss,
　Der die Arbeit hasst.
　　　　　—*G. W. Burmann.*

It is work that makes the life sweet and never makes it wearisome. He only has deep sorrow who hates work.

Armut schändet nicht.	Poverty is no shame.
Armut und Hunger haben viel gelehrte Jünger.	Poverty and hunger have many apt pupils.
Art lässt nicht von Art.	What is bred in the bone comes not out of the flesh.
Aschermittwoch.	Ash Wednesday.
Auch das Schöne muss sterben.　—*Schiller.*	Even the beautiful must die.
Auch der beste Gaul stolpert einmal.	Even the best horse will stumble once.
Auch ich war in Arkadien geboren.　— *Schiller.*	(I also was born in Arcadia.)　I am an idealist.*
Auf den Abend soll man den Tag loben.	(One may praise the day when evening comes.)　Don't halloa until you are out of the wood.
Auf den Bergen ist Freiheit.—*Schiller.*	Freedom dwells upon the mountains.

* Goethe used an adaptation of this phrase, *Auch ich in Arkadien,* " I, too, have been in Arcadia," as the motto for his " Travels in Italy." In the Latin form, *Et ego in Arcadia,* these words appear upon the monument erected in Rome by Chateaubriand in honour of Poussin, the great painter having used them as the title of one of his pictures. In the foreground of this picture, representing a dance of shepherdesses, Poussin introduced a tombstone, with the words inscribed, *Et moi aussi, je vécus en Arcadie.* " I, too, once lived in Arcadie."

Auf den Busch schlagen.	To beat about the bush.
Auf den Hund kommen.	To go to the dogs.
Auf frischer That ertappt.	(Caught in the act.) *In flagrante delicto.*
Aufgeschoben ist nicht aufgehoben.	Deferred is not denied.
Auf Regen folget Sonnenschein.	The sunshine follows after rain.
Auf's eheste.	At the earliest moment; as soon as possible.
Auf seinem Miste ist der Hahn ein Herr.	On his own dunghill the cock is a lord.
Auf's Gerathewohl.	At random.
Auf Wiedersehen.	(Till we meet again.) *Au revoir.*
Aus dem Regen in die Traufe kommen.	(To get out of the rain and stand under the spout.) From Scylla to Charybdis.
Aus den Augen, aus dem Sinn.	Out of sight, out of mind.
Aus der Hand in den Mund leben.	To live from hand to mouth.
Aus der Mode.	Old-fashioned.
Aus derselben Ackerkrume Wächst das Unkraut wie die Blume; Und das Unkraut macht sich breit. —*Fr. Bodenstedt.*	From the same clod of earth grows both weed and flower—and the weed gives itself airs.
Aus des Esels Wadel wird kein Sieb.	(You can't make a sieve from a donkey's tail.) You can't make a silk purse out of a sow's ear.
Aus nichts wird nichts.	Nothing comes from nothing.
Autorität, nicht Majorität.	Authority, not majority!
Bahnhof.	Railway station.
Bedenke das Ende.	(Look to the end.) *Respice finem.*
Begonnen ist halb gewonnen.	Well begun is half done.
Beim Anbruch des Tages.	At daybreak.
Beim wunderbaren Gott! Das Weib ist schön.—*Schiller.*	By the wonderful God! How fair woman is!
Bei Nacht sind alle Katzen grau.	In the dark all cats are grey.
Beinahe bringt keine Mücke um.	Almost never killed a fly.
Beleidigst du einen Mönch, so klappen alle Kuttenzipfel bis nach Rom.	Insult a single monk, and you will put all the cowls into a flutter as far as Rome.
Bellende Hunde beissen nicht.	Yelping curs do not bite.
Benutzt den Augenblick.	(Make use of the present moment.) *Carpe diem.*
Berühre nicht alte Wunden.	Do not disturb old sores.
Beschlafen Sie es.	Sleep upon it; look before you leap.
Besser ein halb Ei als eitel Schale.	(Half an egg is better than empty shells.) Half a loaf is better than no bread.
Besser ein lebender Hund als ein todter Löwe.	A living dog is better than a dead lion.

A A

Besser frei in der Fremde als Knecht daheim.	Better to be a freeman abroad than a slave at home.
Besser ist besser.	Better is better.
Besser spät als nie.	Better late than never.
Besser Unrecht leiden als Unrecht thun.	It is better to suffer wrong than to do wrong.
Besser was als gar nichts.	Half a loaf is better than no bread.
Bewahre Gott!	Heaven forbid!
Bierhaus.	Alehouse.
Bitte.	Please.
Bittre Pillen vergoldet man.	Bitter pills are gilded.
Blaustrumpf.	A blue-stocking.
Blöder Hund wird selten fett.	(A timid dog seldom becomes fat.) Faint heart never won fair lady.
Blödes Herz buhlt keine schöne Frau.	Faint heart never won fair lady.
Blut ist dicker als Wasser.	Blood is thicker than water.
Blut und Eisen.	Blood and iron.
Borgen macht Sorgen.	He who goes a-borrowing, goes a-sorrowing.
Böse Geschwätze verderben gute Sitten.	Evil communications corrupt good manners.
Böser Brunnen, da man Wassen muss eintragen.	It is a bad well into which water must be poured.
Böser Vogel, böses Ei.	A bad bird lays a bad egg.
Böses Werk muss untergehen, Rache folgt der Frevelthat.—*Schiller*.	Evil deeds must end in ruin; vengeance follows hard on crime.
Böse Waare muss man aufschwatzen.	Bad wares need crying up to sell them.
Brief.	Letter.
Briefmarke.	Postage stamp.
Briefträger.	Postman; letter-carrier.
Dampf boot.	Steamboat.
Darunter und darüber.	Topsy-turvy.
Das Alter macht nicht kindlich, wie man spricht Es findet uns nur noch als wahre Kinder.—*Goethe*.	It is not old age that makes us childlike, as people declare, but it merely reveals that we are still nothing but children.
Das alte romantische Land.—*Wieland*.	The old land of romance.
Das arme Herz, hienieden Von manchem Sturm bewegt, Erlangt den wahren Frieden, Nur wo es nicht mehr schlägt.—*Salis*.	The heart of man by griefs oppressed, In Life's storms stricken sore, Can never hope to gain true rest Until it throbs no more.
Das beste Glück, des Lebens schönste Kraft, Ermattet endlich.—*Goethe*.	The greatest happiness, the fairest joys of life, at last fade away.
Das Beste ist gut genug.—*Goethe*.	The best is good enough.
Das Beste kauft man am wohlfeilesten.	(The best is the cheapest thing to buy.) A useless thing is dear at any price.

Das Beste, was wir von der Geschicte haben, ist der Enthusiasmus, den sie erregt.—*Goethe*.

The greatest gain that we derive from the study of history, is the enthusiasm that it arouses in us.

Das eben ist der Fluch der bösen That, Das sie fortzeugend immer Böses muss gebären.—*Schiller*.

That is still the curse of the evil action, that for the future it must always continue to breed evil.

Das Edle zu erkennen ist Gewinnst, Der nimmer uns entrissen werden kann. —*Goethe*.

The appreciation of noble things is a possession of which we can never be deprived.

Das Ei will klüger sein als die Henne.

(The egg will be wiser than the hen.) Don't try to teach your granny to suck eggs.

Das Erste und Letzte was vom Genie gefordert wird, ist Wahrheitsliebe. —*Goethe*.

Devotion to truth is the first and last thing that we demand of genius.

Das Ewig-Weibliche.—*Goethe*.

The eternal feminine.

Das fragt sich.

That remains to be seen.

Das geht nicht.

That will never do.

Das geht über meine Begriffe.

That is beyond my powers; the subject is too difficult for me.

Das Genie bleibt sich immer selbst das grösste Geheimniss.—*Schiller*.

Genius always remains most inexplicable to itself.

Das Glück giebt Vielen zu viel, aber Keinem genug.

Fortune gives too much to many people, but no one is ever satisfied with her gifts.

Das Glück ist dem Kühnen hold.

Fortune favours the brave.

Das glücklichste Wort es wird verhöhnt Wenn der Hörer ein Schiefohr ist. —*Goethe*.

The happiest speech is depreciated, when the listener's ears are at fault.

Das hat viel auf sich.

That is a weighty matter.

Das heisst.

That is to say.

Das Herz und nicht die Meinung ehrt den Mann.—*Schiller*.

It is his own heart and not the opinions of others that honour a man.

Das Huhn legt gern ins Nest, worin schon Eier sind.

The hen lays in the nest where there are eggs already.

Das irdische Glück.

Earthly happiness.

Das ist für die Katze.

(That is for the cat.) A worthless trifle.

Das ist gesprochen, wie ein Mann! —*Schiller*.

That is spoken like a man.

Das ist Recht.

That is right.

Das ists ja, was den Menschen zieret, Und dazu ward ihm der Verstand, Dass er im innern Herzen spüret, Was er erschafft mit seiner Hand. —*Schiller*.

And this is mankind's greatest pride, And hence the gift to understand, That man within his heart can guide All that he fashions with his hand.

Das klassiche Land der Schulen und Kasernen—Preussen.

Prussia, the classic land of schools and barracks.

Das kleinste Haar wirft seinen Schatten. —*Goethe*.

The smallest hair casts a shadow.

Das Leben ist das einzge Gut des Schlechten.—*Schiller*.

Life is the only blessing that wickedness possesses.

Das Leben ist der Güter höchstes nicht,
Der Uebel grösstes aber ist die Schuld.
—*Schiller.*

Life is not the highest good, but the consciousness of sin is life's greatest evil.

Das Leben ist die Liebe.—*Goethe.*

Life is Love.

Das Leben ist doch schön.—*Schiller.*

Life is still so fair.

Das Leben kann allerdings angesehen werden als ein Traum, und der Tod als das Erwachen.—*Schopenhauer.*

Life may be considered altogether as a dream, and Death as the awakening from sleep.

Das Naturell der Frauen
Ist so nah mit Kunst verwandt.
—*Goethe.*

Nature in women is so near akin to art.

Das Neue daran ist nicht gut, und das Gute daran ist nicht neu.

The new in it is not good, and the good in it is not new.

Das Postamt.

Post-office.

Das Publikum, das ist ein Mann,
Der alles weiss und gar nichts kann.

The public is a person who knows everything, and can do nothing.

Das schlechteste Rad am Wagen knarrt am meisten.

It is the worst wheel in the cart that creaks the loudest.

Das schöne Geschlecht.

The fair sex.

Das thut nichts.

It doesn't matter ; don't trouble about that !

Das Universum ist ein Gedanke Gottes.
— *Schiller.*

The universe is a thought of God.

Das Vaterland.

The Fatherland (Germany).

Das versteht sich von selbst.

That is self-evident ; it goes without saying.

Das Weib wollte die Natur zu ihrem Meisterstücke machen.—*Lessing.*

It was Nature's purpose to make Woman the masterpiece of creation.

Das Wenige verschwindet leicht dem Blick,
Der vorwärts sieht, wie viel noch übrig bleibt.—*Goethe.*

The little (that has been done) soon fades from the sight of the man who sees how much before him still remains to be done.

Das Werk lobt den Meister.

The work proves the craftsman.

Das Wunder ist des Glaubens liebstes Kind.—*Goethe.*

Miracle is the dearest child of Faith.

Dawider behüte uns Gott.

Heaven forbid !

Delicatessen.

Dainties.

Dem Himmel sei Dank.

To Heaven be the praise !

Dem lieben Gotte weich nicht aus,
Findst du ihn auf dem Weg.—*Schiller.*

Do not turn aside from God, shouldst thou meet him by the way.

Dem Menschen ist ein Mensch noch immer lieber als ein Engel.—*Lessing.*

A man is always dearer than an angel to a man.

Dem Mutigen ist das Glück hold.

Fortune favours the brave.

Dem Wandersman gehört die Welt
In allen ihren Weiten.—*F. Rückert.*

To the wanderer the wide, wide world belongs.

Dem Zuschauer ist keine Arbeit zu viel.

No work is very hard to the man who merely looks on.

Den alten Hund ist schwer bellen lehren.

It is a hard task to teach old dogs to bark.

Den Baum muss man biegen, wenn er jung ist.

(You must bend the tree while it still is young.) As the twig is bent, the tree's inclined.

Den Freund erkennt man in der Not.

(In trouble a friend is known.) A friend in need.

Den Gelehrten ist gut predigen.

A word to the wise is enough.

Den Himmel überlassen wir
Den Engeln und den Spatzen.
— *H. Heine.*

We leave Heaven to the angels and the spirits.

Denke nur niemand, dass man auf ihn als den Heiland gewartet habe.
—*Goethe.*

Let no man think that the world has been waiting for him as its deliverer.

Den Nagel auf den Kopf treffen.

To hit the nail on the head.

Denn alle Schuld rächt sich auf Erden.
—*Goethe.*

All guilt is avenged upon earth.

Denn, geht es zu des Bösen Haus,
Das Weib hat tausend Schritt voraus.
—*Goethe.*

For, when we go to the devil's house, woman leads the way a thousand paces ahead.

Den todten Löwen kann jeder Hase an der Mähne zupfen.

Every hare may pull at the dead lion's mane.

Den Ton angeben.

To set the tune ; to set the fashion.

Der Abend rot, der Morgen grau
Bringt das schönste Tagesblau.

Evening red, morning grey,
Are sure signs of a sunny day.

Der Adler fängt nicht Fliegen.

The eagle does not catch flies.

Der Apfel fällt nicht weit vom Stamm.

The apple does not fall far from the tree-trunk.) The son takes after his father.

Der Arme isst, wenn er was hat, der Reiche, wenn er will.

The poor man eats when he can, the rich man when he wills.

Der Ausgang giebt den Thaten ihre Titel.—*Goethe.*

The issue gives the title to the work.

Der Bart macht den Mann.

(The beard makes the man.) Wisdom comes with age.

Der Bauch ist ein böser Rathgeber.

The stomach is an evil counsellor.

Der beste Prediger ist die Zeit.

Time is the best preacher.

Der Bettelsack wird nie voll.

(There is no filling a beggar's purse.) Beggars are never satisfied.

Der brave Mann denkt an sich selbst zuletzt.—*Schiller.*

The gallant man thinks of himself last.

Der edle Mensch ist nur ein Bild von Gott.—*Tieck.*

The noble man is but an image of God.

Der Eichwald brauset, die Wolken ziehn ;
Das Mägdlein wandelt an Ufers Grün,
Es bricht sich die Welle mit Macht, mit Macht,
Und sie singt hinaus in die finstre Nacht,
Das Auge von Weinen getrübet.
—*Schiller.*

The wind roars through the oak trees, the clouds scud across the sky ; the maiden wanders by the green strand. The waves beat loudly against the shore, while she sings out into the dark night, and her eyes are full of tears.

Der Eine schlägt auf den Busch, der Andere kriegt den Vogel.

One man beats the bush, while another catches the bird.

Der Erde Gott, das Geld.—*Schiller.*

Gold is the god of the earth.

Der Erde Paradies und Hölle
Liegt in dem Worte Weib.—*Seume*
Der ewige Jude.

Earth, Heaven, and Hell, are all comprised in the one word—Woman.
The everlasting Jew; the wandering Jew.

Der Feige droht nur, wo er sicher ist.
—*Goethe.*
Der Freihandel.
Der Freiheit eine Gasse!
    Der Freunde Eifer ist's, der mich
Zu Grunde richtet, nicht der Hass der
Feinde.—*Schiller.*
Der Fuchs ändert den Pelz, und behält
den Schalk.
Der Fürst ist der erste Diener seines
Staates.—*Frederick the Great.*

The coward does not threaten save when he is in no danger.
Free trade.
Liberty has only one road.
('Tis my friend's zeal, not my enemy's hate, that overthrows me.) Save me from my friends.
The fox may change his skin, but he is still a fox.
(The king is the first servant of his country.) The king is subject to the laws, and is the chief administrator of them.

Der Glaube ist nicht der Anfang,
sondern das Ende alles Wissens.
—*Goethe.*
Der Glaube ist wie die Liebe: er lässt
sich nicht erzwingen.—*Schopenhauer.*

Faith is not the beginning but the end of all knowledge.
Faith and Love have one thing in common: neither of them can be created by compulsion.

Der Glückliche glaubt nicht, dass noch
Wunder geschehen; denn nur im
Elend erkennt man Gottes Hand und
Finger, der gute Menschen zum
Guten leitet.—*Goethe.*
Der Gott, der Eisen wachsen liess,
Der wollte keine Knechte.—*Arndt.*

The happy have no faith in the existence of miracles; for it is only in sorrow that we recognise the hand and finger of God, which leads good men to goodness.
(God, who placed iron in the earth, wished none to be slaves.) None should be slaves while they may hold a sword.

Der Hahn im Korbe sein.

(To be the cock in the basket.) To be the most important person in the company.

Der Hass ist parteiisch, aber die Liebe
ist es noch mehr.—*Goethe.*
Der hat die Macht, an den die Menge
glaubt —*Frederick II.*
Der hat nie das Glück gekostet,
Der die Frucht des Himmels nicht
Raubend an des Höllenflusses
Schauervollem Rande bricht.
—*Schiller.*

Hate is unjust, but love is even more so.
That man has the power whom the people believe in.
Ah! never he has rapture known,
Who has not, where the waves are driven
Upon the fearful shores of Hell,
Pluck'd fruits that taste of Heaven.
—*Lytton.*

Der Herr ruft kein Geschöpfe aus dem
Nichts zum Elend hervor.—*Gessner.*
Der Historiker ist ein rückwärts ge-
kehrter Prophet.—*F. von Schlegel.*
Der Horcher an der Wand hört seine
eigne Schand.

The Lord brought none of his creatures out of nothing into existence to make them miserable.
The historian is a prophet whose eyes are turned to the past.
The listener never hears any good of himself.

Der Hunger ist der beste Koch.

Hunger is the best sauce.

Der ist der glücklichste Mensch, der das Ende seines Lebens mit dem Anfang in Verbindung setzen kann.
                                        —*Goethe.*

He is the happiest man who can join in close union the beginning with the end of his life.

Der Junge kann sterben, der Alte muss sterben.

The young may die, but the old must die.

Der Kaiser.

The Emperor.

Der katholische Priester ist von dem Augenblick, wo er Priester ist, ein einregimentierter Offizier des Papstes.
                                        —*Bismarck.*

The Catholic priest, from the moment in which he becomes a member of the priesthood, is a commissioned officer of the Pope.

Der kreisende Berg hat ein Maus geboren.

(The mountain is in labor and brings forth a mouse.)   Much cry and little wool.   *Parturiunt montes.*

Der Krieg ernährt den Krieg.
                                        —*Schiller.*

War fosters war.

Der Krieg ist lustig den unerfahrnen.

War is a fine thing to those who have not experienced it.

Der Kummer, der nach Hülfe und Trost verlangt, ist nicht der höchste.
                                        —*W. von Humboldt.*

The grief which yearns for help and comfort is not the deepest.

Der Liberalismus gerät immer weiter, als seine Träger wollen.—*Bismarck.*

Liberal policy has always a tendency to extend its aims according to the will of those who direct it.

Der Mensch denkt, Gott lenkt.

Man proposes, God disposes.

Der Mensch ist frei wie der Vogel im Käfig; er kann sich innerhalb gewissen Grenzen bewegen. —*Lavater.*

Man is free like the bird in a cage; he can move himself within certain limits.

Der Mensch ist, was er isst.

(Man is what he eats.)   A man's nature is formed by the food he eats.

Der Mensch kann, was er soll; und wenn er sagt, er kann nicht, so will er nicht.—*Fichte.*

A man can do what is his duty; and when he says " I cannot," he means, " I will not."

Der Mensch liebt nur einmal.

Man loves but once.

Der Mensch mag sich wenden, wohin er will, er mag unternehmen, was es auch sei, stets wird er auf jenen Weg wieder zurückkehren, den ihm Natur einmal vorgezeichnet hat.—*Goethe.*

Man may go whither he will; he may undertake what he pleases; still he will come back to that path which Nature has appointed for him.

Der Mohr hat seine Arbeit gethan, der Mohr kann gehen.—*Schiller.*

The Moor has done his work, the Moor may go.

Der Mutter schenk' ich,
Die Tochter denk' ich.—*Goethe.*

The mother gets my presents, but the daughter has my thoughts.

Der Pfennig macht den Thaler.

(A penny makes the thaler.)   Many pennies make a pound; a penny saved is a penny gained.

Der preussiche Schulmeister hat die Schlacht bei Sadowa gewonnen.
                                        — *Moltke.*

The Prussian schoolmaster won the battle of Sadowa.*

* Moltke was not the first to make use of this saying, but quoted it from a speech delivered by Dr. Peschel. The words are, however, commonly attributed to the great strategist.

Der Schmerz ist die Geburt der höheren Naturen.—*A. Tiedge.*
(Grief is the birth of the higher nature.) Sorrow refines a noble mind.

Der Schuster hat die schlechtesten Schuhe.
The shoemaker has always the worst shoes.

Der Sinkende greift selbst nach einem Strohhalm.
A drowning man snatches at a straw.

Der Stärkste hat Recht.
Right is on the side of the strongest.

Der Stil ist die Physiognomie des Geistes.—*Schopenhauer.*
(Style is the mind's physiognomy.) *Le style c'est de l'homme.*

Der Teufel ist ein Egoist.—*Goethe.*
The devil is all for himself.

Der Teufel ist nie so schwarz, als man ihn malt.
The devil is never so black as he is painted.

Der Thor läuft den Genüssen des Lebens nach und sieht sich betrogen : der Weise vermeidet die Uebel.
    —*Schopenhauer.*
The fool pursues the pleasures of life, and finds himself deceived : the wise man avoids its evils.

Der Tod, das ist die kühle Nacht
Das Leben ist der schwüle Tag.
    —*H. Heine.*
Death is the cooling night, and Life the sultry day.

Der Umgang mit Frauen ist das Element guter Sitten.—*Goethe.*
The society of the fair sex is the school of good manners.

Der Unendliche hat in den Himmel seinen Namen in glühenden Sternen gesäet, aber auf die Erde hat er seinem Namen in sanften Blumen gesäet.—*Jean Paul Richter.*
The Eternal God has written his name in shining stars upon the heavens ; upon the earth he has written it in tender flowers.

Der Volksgeist Preussens ist durch und durch monarchisch.—*Bismarck.*
The temperament of the Prussian people is entirely favourable to a monarchical government.

Der Wahn ist kurz, die Reu ist lang.
    —*Schiller.*
Short is the intoxication (of love), but the repentance is long.

Der Wald hat Ohren.
The wood has ears.

Den Wald vor lauter Bäumen nicht sehen.—*Wieland.*
Not to see the wood because of the trees.

Der Weg des Verderbens.
The road to ruin.

Der Weg zur Hölle ist mit guten Vorsätzen gepflastert.
The way to hell is paved with good intentions.

Der Wein erfindet nichts.
(Wine invents nothing.) *In vino veritas.*

Der Wermuth des Gewissens verbittert sogar den Schmerz.
    —*Jean Paul Richter.*
The wormwood of conscience adds bitterness even to sorrow.

Der Zufriedene hat immer genug.
The contented man has always enough.

Des einen Glück ist des andern Unglück.
(One man's happiness is the misery of another.) What is meat to one, is poison to the other.

Des Lebens Mai blüht einmal und nicht wieder.—*Schiller.*
The May of life blooms once, and never blooms again.

Des Lebens Mühe
Lehrt uns allein des Lebens Güter schätzen.—*Goethe.*
The toils of life alone teach us to value the blessings of life.

Des Menschen Engel ist die Zeit.
　　　　—Schiller.

Time is the angel of men.

Des Menschen Wille, das ist sein Glück.
　　　　—Schiller.

(The will of man is the arbiter of his fortune.)
I am the master of my fate.
I am the captain of my soul.*—Henley.*

Des Volkes Stimme ist Gottes Stimme.

(The voice of the people is the voice of God.) *Vox populi, vox Dei.*

Deutsch.

German.

Deutschland.

Germany.

Deutschland, Deutschland über alles
Über alles in der Welt.*—H. Hoffmann.*

Germany, Germany, over all throughout the world.

Deutschland, ein geographischer Begriff.

Germany is a geographical expression.*

Dichtung und Wahrheit.

Poetry and truth.†

Die Abwesenden haben immer unrecht.

(The absent are always blamed.) *Les absents ont toujours tort.*

Die Baukunst ist eine erstarrte Musik.
　　　　— Goethe.

Architecture is frozen music.

Die edelste That hat doch nur einen zeitweiligen Einfluss; das geniale Werk hingegen lebt und wirkt, wohlthätig und erhebend, durch alle Zeiten. Von den Thaten bleibt nur das Andenken, welches immer schwächer, entstellter und gleichgültiger wird, allmählich sogar erlöschen muss, wenn nicht die Geschichte es aufnimmt und es nun im petrificirten Zustande der Nachwelt überliefert. Die Werke hingegen sind selbst unsterblich, und können, zumal die schriftlichen, alle Zeiten durchleben.*—Schopenhauer.*

The noblest action has always only a temporary influence; a work of genius, on the contrary, exists and moves, beneficent and inspiring, throughout the ages. Of actions only the memory abides, and this becomes continually more and more vague, changed, and indifferent, and is bound to be gradually effaced, unless history takes it up, and petrifying it, hands it on to posterity. Works, however, are of themselves immortal, and, especially if they are written, may survive for all time.

Die Ehre ist, objektiv, die Meinung Anderer von unserm Werth, und subjektiv, unsere Furcht vor dieser Meinung.*—Schopenhauer.*

Honour is, objectively, the opinion others hold of our worth, and, subjectively, the fear which this opinion inspires in us.

Die ersten Entschliessungen sind nicht immer die klügsten, aber gewöhnlich die redlichsten.*—Lessing.*

One's first resolves are not always the best, but they are generally the most honest.

Die Extreme berühren sich.

Extremes meet.

Die Freuden, die man übertreibt,
Verwandeln sich in Schmerzen.
　　　　—Bertuch.

The pleasures in which we indulge too much become pains.

Die Froheit ist wie ein Sonnenglanz des Lebens.*— W. von Humboldt.*

Mirth is, so to speak, the sunbeam of life.

Die Gegenwart ist eine mächtige Göttin.*— Goethe.*

The present is a mighty divinity.

Die Gewohnheit ist eine zweite Natur.

Habit is second nature.

---

* In these terms Metternich described the disunited condition of Germany in the year 1849. Two years before he had made a similar remark with regard to Italy.
† This is the title of one of Goethe's best-known books.

Die goldne Zeit, wohin ist sie geflohen ?
—*Goethe.*

The golden age, whither has it flown ?

Die Hand im Spiele haben.

To have a hand in the game.

Die Hausfreunde heissen meistens mit Recht so, indem sie mehr die Freunde des Hauses, als des Herrn, also den Katzen ähnlicher, als den Hunden sind.—*Schopenhauer.*

"Friends of the house" are generally rightly so-called, for they are more friends of the house than friends of its master. They resemble the cats rather than the dogs.

Die Hölle selbst hat ihre Rechte ?
—*Goethe.*

Has even Hell its rights ?

Die Irrthümer des Menschen machen ihn eigentlich liebenswürdig.
—*Goethe.*

It is a man's failings that make him truly lovable.

Die Kunst geht nach Brod.—*Luther.*

(Art comes after bread.) Art is long, but man must live.

Die Kunst ist Himmelsgabe.
—*Schiller.*

Art is a gift of Heaven.

Die Kunst ist lang
Und kurz ist unser Leben.—*Goethe.*

(Art is long, and our life is short.) *Ars longa vita brevis.*

Die Kunst ist zwar nicht das Brod, aber der Wein des Lebens.
—*Jean Paul Richter.*

Art is not the bread, but the wine of life.

Die Leute, die niemals Zeit haben, thun am wenigsten.—*Lichtenberg.*

People who never have any time are those who do least.

Die Liebe ist der Liebe Preis.
—*Schiller.*

Love is love's reward.

Die Liebe macht zum Goldpalast die Hütte.—*Hölty.*

Love transforms the humble cottage into a golden palace.

Die Liebe überwindet alles.

(Love conquers all.) *Omnia vincit amor.*

Die meisten Menschen sind so subjektiv, dass im Grunde nichts Interesse für sie hat, als ganz allein sie selbst.
—*Schopenhauer.*

Most men are so subjective that at the bottom nothing has any interest for them except their own selves alone.

Die Menschen glauben gern an das, was sie wünschen.

Men readily believe what they wish to be true.

Die Menschen gleichen darin den Kindern, dass sie unartig werden, wenn man sie verzieht ; daher man gegen keinen zu nachgiebig und liebreich seyn darf.—*Schopenhauer.*

Men are like children in that they become ill-mannered when they are spoiled ; therefore we ought not to be too yielding and amiable to anyone.

Die Natur ist das einzige Buch, das auf allen Blättern grossen Inhalt bietet.—*Goethe.*

Nature is the only book that presents words of deep significance on all its pages.

Die Natur weiss allein, was sie will.
—*Goethe.*

Nature alone knows what her purpose is.

Die Pferde hinter den Wagen spannen.

To put the cart before the horse.

Die Politik ist keine Wissenschaft, wie viele der Herren Professoren sich einbilden, sondern eine Kunst.
—*Bismarck.*

Politics are not a science, as many professors declare, but merely an art.

Die Probe eines Genusses ist seine Erinnerung.—*Jean Paul Richter.*

The test of pleasure is the memory that it leaves behind.

Die Rechnung ohne den Wirt machen.	To reckon without one's host.
Die Regierung.	The administration ; the government.
Die Religion muss dem Volke erhalten werden.—*Emperor William I.*	Religion must be preserved for the good of the nation.
Die Religion selbst ist in der Natur des Menschen eingepflanzt. ——*W. von Humboldt.*	Religion has its roots in man's own nature.
Die Saiten zu hoch spannen.	To take too high a tone.
Die Schönen Tage in Aranjuez Sind nun zu Ende.—*Schiller.*	The happy days in Aranjuez are past and gone.
Die Schönheit ist ein guter Empfehlungsbrief.	Beauty is a good letter of introduction.
Dieser Monat ist ein Kuss, den der Himmel giebt der Erde. ——*F. von Logau.*	This month (May) is a kiss that heaven gives to the earth.
Die Sonne geht in meinem Staat nicht unter.—*Schiller.*	The sun never sets on my empire.*
Die Sonne wirds bringen an den Tag, was unterm Schnee verborgen.	What snow conceals, the sun reveals.
Die süssesten Trauben hängen am höchsten.	The sweetest grapes hang on the top of the tree.
Die Todten reiten schnell!—*Bürger.*	The dead ride quickly.†
Die Uhr schlägt keinem Glücklichen. ——*Schiller.*	(The clock does not strike for any happy people.) The happy man does not notice the flight of time.
Die Wacht am Rhein.	(The watch on the Rhine.) The title of the German national song.‡
Die Wände haben Ohren.	Walls have ears.
Die Weisheit ist nur in der Wahrheit. ——*Goethe.*	There is no wisdom, save in truth.
Die Weltgeschichte ist das Weltgericht. ——*Schiller.*	History is the world's criticism of the past.
Die Welt ist dumm, die Welt ist blind, Wird täglich abgeschmachter. ——*H. Heine.*	The world is stupid, the world is blind, and grows more tedious every day.
Die Zeit ist kurz, die Kunst ist lang. ——*Goethe.*	(Time is short, but art is long.) *Ars longa, vita brevis.*
Doch der den Augenblick ergreift, Das ist der rechte Mann.—*Goethe.*	He who seizes the opportune moment is the right man.
Donner und Blitz.	Thunder and lightning.
Doppel-gänger.	A second self ; *alter ego.*
Doppelt giebt, wer gleich giebt.	(He gives twice who gives in a trice.) *Bis dat qui cito dat.*

* Schiller puts these words into the mouth of Philip II. of Spain in "Don Carlos." The idea, according to Büchmann, is an old one, for Herodotus narrates that Xerxes, the Persian king, made a somewhat similar remark concerning his own projected conquests.

† In Bürger's famous poem *Lenore*, the heroine, distracted owing to her lover's not returning from the war, denies the existence of a Divine Providence. But at midnight her lover rides up to her door, and asks her to ride back with him to the army. Throughout the night they gallop at a furious pace, and whenever Lenore asks the reason for such haste, her lover replies—*Die Todten reiten schnell !* Finally, the form of the man changes into that of a skeleton, and the earth opens to swallow up both the rider and the maid.

‡ This song was written by Schneckenburger in 1840.

Dreikönigstag.
Duldet mutig, Millionen!
Duldet für die bessre Welt!
Droben überm Sternenzelt
Wird ein grosser Gott belohnen.
—*Schiller.*

(Three kings' day.) Twelfth Night.
Endure patiently, ye millions! Endure for the better world to come. Yonder above the canopy of the stars Almighty God will reward you.

Durch Schaden wird man klug.

Experience is the mistress of fools.

Durch Todesnacht bricht ewges Morgenrot! —*Körner.*

Through the night of death shines the brightness of the eternal morning.

Du sprichst ein grosses Wort gelassen aus.—*Goethe.*

Calmly dost thou utter a momentous saying.

Edel ist, der edel thut.

Handsome is that handsome does.

Ehret die Frauen! sie flechten und weben
Himmlische Rosen ins irdische Leben.
— *Schiller.*

Honour women! They entwine and weave the roses of heaven into the life we live on earth.

Ehre, wem Ehre gebührt.

Give honour to whom honour is due.

Ehrlich währt am längsten.

Honesty is the best policy in the end.

Eile mit weile.

(Hasten slowly.) More haste, less speed. *Festina lente.*

Eilen thut nicht gut.

The more haste, the less speed.

Ein Appell an die Furcht findet in deutschen Herzen niemals ein Echo.
—*Bismarck.*

An appeal to fear never finds an echo in the hearts of Germans.

Ein Augenblick gelebt im Paradies,
Wird nicht zu teuer mit dem Tod gebüsst.—*Schiller.*

For a moment lived in Paradise, death is not too dear a price to pay.

Ein Dienst ist des andern werth.

One good turn deserves another.

Ein Doctor und ein Bauer wissen mehr als ein Doctor allein.

(A doctor and a fool know more than a doctor alone.) Two heads are better than one.

Ein edler Mensch zieht edle Menschen an.—*Goethe.*

A noble man attracts a noble man.

Eine Hand wäscht die andere.

(One hand washes the other hand.) Every man lives by the help of another.

Ein Ei ist dem andern gleich.

(One egg is like another.) As like as two peas.

Ein einziger dankbarer Gedanke gen Himmel ist das vollkommenste Gebet.
—*Lessing.*

A single thought of thankfulness to Heaven is the most acceptable prayer we can make.

Einem auf die Finger klopfen.

(To rap one on the knuckles.) To clip his wings.

Einem das Fell über die Ohren ziehen.

(To pull the skin over one's ears.) To fleece a man artfully.

Eine Nadel im Heu suchen.

To look for a needle in a bundle of hay.

Einen Mohren weiss waschen.

(To wash a blackamoor.) To waste one's toil.

Eine schöne Menschenseele finden ist Gewinn.—*Herder.*

To discover a beautiful human soul is a great gain

Eine Schwalbe macht keinen Sommer.
One swallow does not make a summer.

Ein Esel bleibt ein Esel.
(A fool remains a fool.) There is no cure for an empty head.

Eines Mannes Rede ist keine Rede.
(One man's tale is no man's tale.) One tale is good until another is told.

Ein fauler Apfel steckt hundert gesunde an.
(One bad apple spoils a hundred.) One rotten sheep mars the whole flock.

Ein faules Ei verdirbt den ganzen Brei.
One bad egg spoils the whole pudding.

Ein feste Burg ist unser Gott.
                              —*Luther.*
Our God is a strong tower of defence.

Ein Frauenhaar zieht mehr als ein Glockenseil.
A single hair of a woman draws more than a bell-rope.

Ein Freund ist ein Wesen, das uns ganz trägt mit unsern Fehlern und Mängeln allen.—*George Forster.*
A friend is a person who cheerfully bears with all our failings and weaknesses.

Ein gekränktes Herz erholt sich schwer.
                              —*Goethe.*
It is difficult to heal a wounded heart.

Ein Gelehrter hat keine lange Weile.
                       —*Jean Paul Richter.*
A scholar never suffers from boredom.

Ein guter Mensch in seinem dunkeln Drange
Ist sich des rechten Weges wohl bewusst.—*Goethe.*
A good man, amid all the dark wrestlings of his mind, is ever conscious of the right path to follow.

Ein guter Name ist ein reiches Erbtheil.
A good name is a rich inheritance.

Ein guter Name ist mehr werth als Reichthum.
A good name is better than riches.

Ein guter Name ist unschätzbar.
A good name is beyond price.

Ein Herz und ein Sinn.
(One heart and one mind.) Close friends.

Ein Kaiserwort
Soll man nicht drehn noch deuteln!
                              —*Bürger.*
An Emperor's word must not change or be lightly kept.

Ein Keil treibt den andern.
One nail drives in another.

Ein Leben wie in Paradies
Gewährt uns Vater Rhein!
                       —*Chr. Hölty.*
A life, like that in Paradise, our father Rhine bestows upon us.

Ein Mann, ein Wort.
(A man, a word.) An honest man's word is his bond.

Ein schlechtes Pferd, das sein Futter nicht verdient.
It is a poor horse that does not earn its keep.

Ein Schuh is nicht Jedem gerecht.
The same shoe will not fit every foot.

Ein Thor findt allemal noch einen grössern Thoren.
One fool can always find another who is a still greater fool.

Ein tiefer Sinn wohnt in den alten Bräuchen.—*Schiller.*
There is a deep meaning hidden in old customs.

Ein unbedeutender Mensch.
A man of no account; a worthless fellow.

Ein Unglück kommt niemals allein.
A misfortune never comes alone.

Ein unnütz Leben ist ein früher Tod.
                              —*Goethe.*
A wasted life is premature death.

Ein Vogel in der Schüssel ist besser als hundert in der Luft.

(One bird on the dish is worth a hundred flying.) A bird in the hand is worth two in the bush.

Ein Weib verschweigt nur, was sie nicht weiss.

A woman only keeps one secret—what she does not know herself.

Eisenbahn.

(Iron way.) Railroad.

Eisen und Blut.

Iron and blood.*

Ende gut, alles gut.

All's well that ends well.

Entbehren sollst du ! sollst entbehren.
—*Goethe.*

Thou shalt, thou must refrain ! †

Erfahrung ist die beste Lehrmeisterin.

Experience is the best schoolmaster.

Er hat aller Schande den Kopf abgebissen.

He is lost to all sense of shame.

Er hat Bohnen in den Ohren.

(He has beans in his ears.) None so deaf as those who will not hear.

Er hat Haare auf den Zähnen.

(He has hairs on his teeth.) He is a sharp customer.

Erinnerung.

Recollection ; memory.

Er ist sein Vater, wie er leibt und lebt.

He is the very image of his father.

Erlaubt ist, was gefällt.—*Goethe.*

What a person likes to do, that he thinks 'tis right to do.

Er misst alle anderen nach seiner Elle aus.

He measures others by his own measure.

Ernst ist das Leben, heiter ist die Kunst.—*Schiller.*

Life is earnest, Art is joyful.

Eröffnung des Reichstages.

The opening of Parliament.

Erst besinn's, dann beginn's.

Look first before you leap.

Erste wägen und dann wagen.

(First weigh, then go ahead.) Consider first the chances of success, but, when you have adopted a plan of action, at once pursue it.‡

Ertragen muss man was der Himmel sendet.

What Heaven sends we must endure.

Es bildet ein Talent sich in der Stille, Sich ein Charakter in dem Strom der Welt.—*Goethe.*

Talent is formed in calm solitude ; Character amid the busy stream of life.

Es bleibt dabei.

Agreed !

Es erben sich Gesetz' und Rechte Wie eine ew'ge Krankheit fort.
—*Goethe.*

Laws and rights are handed down like perennial hereditary disease.

Es fällt keine Eiche von einem Streiche.

You can't fell an oak with a single stroke.

Es geschicht dir eben recht.

You have got your deserts ; it serves you right.

Es gibt.

There is ; there are.

* Bismarck used these words in a speech delivered by him in September, 1862. It is usual to speak of the great statesman as the " man of blood and iron." The expression *Eisen und Blut* seems to have been suggested by a phrase in one of Arndt's poems.
† In these words is said to be contained the moral of Goethe's " Faust," that life must be a constant renunciation and a shunning of all unholy pleasures.
‡ This was the favourite maxim of Moltke.

Es gibt drei Aristokratien : die der Geburt und des Ranges ; die Geld-aristokratie ; die geistige Aristo-kratie. Letztere ist eigentlich die vornehmste.—*Schopenhauer.*

There are three aristocracies ; **the first** of birth and rank ; the second of wealth ; the third of intellect. The last is really the most honoured.*

Es gibt ja nichts Reineres und Wär-meres als unsere erste Freundschaft, unsere erste Liebe, unser erstes Streben nach Wahrheiten, unser erstes Gefühl für die Natur.
—*Jean Paul Richter.*

There is nothing more pure and warm than our first friendship, our first love, our first striving after truth, our first appreciation of the works of Nature.

Es irrt der Mensch so lang' er strebt.
—*Goethe.*

So long as a man strives, he makes mistakes.

Es ist besser, das geringste Ding von der Welt, als eine halbe Stunde für gering halten.—*Goethe.*

It is better to be engaged in the most unimportant matter, than to think half an hour of no importance.

Es ist doch den Mädchen wie angeboren, dass sie allein gefallen wollen, was nur Augen hat.—*Gleim.*

It is, so to speak, an inborn quality of girls, to wish to please everything that has a pair of eyes.

Es ist ein böser Vogel, der sein eigen Nest beschmutzt.

It is a sorry bird that fouls its own nest.

Es ist eine der grössten Himmelsgaben, So ein lieb Ding im Arm zu haben.
—*Goethe.*

It is one of Heaven's greatest gifts to hold so loved a thing in one's arms.

Es ist ein gross Ergötzen Sich in den Geist der Zeiten zu versetzen, Zu schauen, wie vor uns ein weiser Mann gedacht.—*Goethe.*

It is a great pleasure to return to the spirit of former days, and to see what a wise man has thought before us.

Es ist nicht alles Gold, was glänzt.

All is not gold that glitters.

Es ist Schade.

That is a pity.

Es lebe der König.

Long live the King.

Es lebt, ein Gott zu strafen und zu rächen. – *Schiller.*

God lives, who will punish and avenge.

Es schlafen nicht alle welche die Augen zu haben.

(Everyone with closed eyes is not asleep.) Appearances are deceptive.

Es sind nicht alle Jäger, die das Horn gut blasen.

All are not huntsmen who can blow the huntsman's horn.

Es stirbt als Knabe, wen die Götter lieben.—*E. Geibel.*

Whom the gods love die young.

Es waren mir böhmische Dörfer.

(It was Bohemian to me.) It was all Greek to me.

Es wird kein blöder Hund fett.

A timid dog never grows fat.

Es wird kein Hahn darnach krähen.

(No cock will crow over that.) No one will care twopence about it.

Eulen nach Athen tragen.

(To take owls to Athens.) To pour water into the Thames.

Ewigkeit.

Eternity.

* Schopenhauer illustrates the last part of this remark by recounting an incident connected with the friendship of Frederick the Great and Voltaire. Frederick's Court Chamberlain remonstrated with his master for admitting Voltaire to his own table, though men of high rank had perforce to sit at another. *Les âmes privilégiées rangent à l'égal des rois,* " Privileged persons rank equal with kings," was the reply of Frederick to this remonstrance.

Fasten.

The season of Lent.

Faulheit ist der Schlüssel zur Armuth.

Idleness is the key to Poverty's door.

Feiertage.

Holidays.

Feindlich ist die Welt
Und falsch gesinnt! Es liebt ein jeder
nur
Sich selbst.—*Schiller.*

Hostile is the world, and treacherous!
Each man loves nothing but himself.

Fette Küche, magere Erbschaft.

A fat kitchen leaves few legacies.

Fliegende Blätter.

Fly-leaves; pamphlets.

Folge meinem Worte, nicht meinen
Thaten.

Imitate my words, and not my actions.

Fort von hier.

Be off with you! Begone!

Frau.

Mrs.; wife; lady.

Fräulein.

Miss; young lady.

Frei geht das Unglück durch die ganze
Welt.—*Schiller.*

Misery travels free throughout all the
earth.

Freiheit ist bei der Macht allein.
—*Schiller.*

Freedom cannot exist save when united
with might.

Freiheit ist nur in dem Reich der
Traüme,
Und das Schöne blüht nur im Gesang.
—*Schiller.*

Freedom exists only in the realm of
dreams, and Beauty blooms not save
in song.

Freiheit „liebt das Tier der Wüste,
Frei im Äther herrscht der Gott.
—*Schiller.*

The wild beast in the desert loves its
freedom, and free is God who ruleth
in the heavens.

Freimarke.

Postage-stamps.

Fremdes Pferd und eigene Sporen haben
bald den Wind verloren.

The horse of a stranger and your own
spurs go more quickly than the
wind.

Freuet euch des Lebens,
Weil noch das Lämpchen glüht
Pflücket die Rose, eh' sie verblüht.

Rejoice in life, while still the light
burns bright; pluck the roses while
they are in bloom.*

Freunde in der Noth wären selten?—
Im Gegentheil! Kaum hat man mit
Einem Freundschaft gemacht; so ist
er auch schon in der Noth und will
geld geleihen haben.
—*Schopenhauer.*

Friends in need are rare?—On the contrary! No sooner have we contracted
a new friendship, than we find that
we have a friend in need, and ready
to borrow money from us.

Friede.

Peace.

Friedensheim.

Home of Peace.

Frisch auf!

Cheer up.

Frisch gewagt ist halb gewonnen.

A bold attack is half the battle.

Früh zu Bett und früh wieder auf
Macht gesund und reich in Kauf.

Early to bed and early to rise
Makes a man healthy, wealthy, and
wise.

Für den Tod ist kein Kraut gewach-
sen.

There is no cure for death.

Für einen Kammerdiener giebt es
keinen Held.—*Hegel.*

No man is a hero to his own valet.

* The first lines of a well-known song, familiar to English people under the name " Life let
us cherish."

Für Gerechte giebt es keine Gesetze.	(There are no laws for the good.) The righteous man is a law to himself.
Für Gott und Ihr.	All for God and her.*
Fürsten haben lange Hände.	Kings have long arms.
Gebranntes Kind scheut das Feuer.	The burnt child dreads the fire.
Gebraucht die Zeit, sie geht so schnell von hinnen.—*Goethe.*	Make use of the time, for it flies away so fast.
Gedanken sind zollfrei.	Thoughts are free.
Geduld! Geduld! wenn's Herz auch bricht!—*Bürger.*	Patience! Patience! e'en though thy heart is breaking!
Gefährte munter kürzet die Meilen.	(Cheerful companions shorten the miles.) A cheerful companion is as good as a coach.
Geflügelte Worte.	Winged words.
Geld ist der Mann.	It is money that makes the man.
Geld regiert die Welt.	Money rules the world.
Gelegenheit macht Diebe.	It is opportunity that makes the thief.
Gesagt, gethan.	No sooner said than done.
Geschäftiger Müssiggang.	(Busy idleness.) Very busy doing nothing.
Gesundheit ist besser als Reichthum.	Health is better than riches.
Gewarnter Mann ist halb gerettet.	(A forewarned man is half saved.) Forewarned is forearmed.
Gewohnheit ist ein' andere Natur.	Habit is second nature.
Glänzende Elend.—*Goethe.*	(Glittering sorrows.) Sorrows that outward splendour cannot hide.
Gleiche Brüder, gleiche Kappen.	Birds of a feather flock together.
Gleichheit ist immer das festeste Band der Liebe.—*Lessing.*	Similarity of temperament is always the surest bond of love.
Gleich und gleich gesellt sich gern.	Birds of a feather flock together.
Glück auf den Weg.	Good luck on the way ; may good fortune attend you.
Glück auf! Glück zu!	Good luck!
Glückliche Kinder geben glückliche Menschen.—*G. Forster.*	Happy children become happy men.
Glück und Weiber haben die Narren lieb.	Fortune and women favour fools.
Goldene Berge versprechen.	To make great promises.
Goldene Mitte.	The golden mean.
Goldener Hammer bricht eisernes Thor.	(A golden hammer breaks an iron door.) A golden key will open any door.
Gottes Mühlen mahlen langsam, mahlen aber trefflich klein.	The mills of God grind slowly, but they grind exceeding small.
Gottes Wort bleibt ewig.	God's word lasts for ever.
Gott ist überall.	God is over all.

* In the Thirty Years' War, Christian, Duke of Brunswick, supported the cause of the Elector. As he had done this for love of the Electress Elizabeth, rather than from any other motive, he caused this device to be inscribed on his standard.

Gott macht gesund, und der Doktor kriegt das Geld.

God effects the cure, but the doctor gets the money.

Gott mit uns!

(God with us.) Motto of the Kings of Prussia.

Gott sei Dank!

God be thanked! Heaven be praised!

Grau, teurer Freund, ist alle Theorie, Und grün des Lebens goldner Baum. —*Goethe*.

Gray, my dear friend, is every theory, and green the golden tree of life.

Grosse Diebe hängen die kleinen.

Great thieves hang the little ones.

Grosse Leidenschaften sind Krankheiten ohne Hoffnung.—*Goethe*.

Great passions are maladies, the cure of which is hopeless.

Grosse Seelen dulden still.—*Schiller*.

Great souls suffer silently.

Güte bricht einem kein Bein.

Kindness breaks no bones.

Gute Freunde, getreue Nachbarn. —*Luther*.

Good friends, trusty neighbours.

Guten Abend.

Good evening.

Guten Morgen.

Good morning.

Guten Willen muss man für die That nehmen.

You must take the will for the deed.

Guter Anfang ist die halbe Arbeit.

A good beginning is half the work.

Guter Rath kommt über Nacht.

(Good counsel comes overnight.) In the night there is counsel.

Gutes und Böses kommt unerwartet dem Menschen.

Both good and evil come to man when he does not expect them.

Gute Tage können wir nicht ertragen. —*Luther*.

It is prosperity that we cannot endure.

Gute Ware verkauft sich selbst.

Good bargains sell themselves.

Gut Gewissen ist ein sanftes Ruhekissen.

A good conscience is a soft pillow.

Hals über Kopf.

(Heels over head.) Headlong.

Hänge nicht alles auf einen Nagel.

(Do not hang all on one nail.) Don't put all your eggs into one basket.

Hast du Geld, so setz dich nieder; Hast du keins, so pack dich wieder.

Have you money, come and stay. Have you nothing, go away.

Hauptstadt.

Chief town.

Hausfrau.

Lady of the house; housewife.

Heimweh.

Home-sickness; nostalgia.

Heirathen in Eile Bereut man mit Weile.

Marry in haste, repent at leisure.

Herr.

Mr.

Herzchen.

Little heart! Darling!

Heute mir, Morgen dir.

My turn to-day, yours to-morrow.

Heute rot, Morgen tot.

To-day red, to-morrow dead.

Hier liegt der Hund begraben.

(Here lies the dog buried.) There's the sore point.

Hilf dir, und der Himmel wird dir helfen!

(Help thyself and heaven will help thee.) Heaven helps those who help themselves.

Himmel!
Hin ist hin.

Heavens!
(Gone is gone.)   It is no use to cry over spilt milk.

Hinter der Thür Abschied nehmen.

To take French leave.

Hoch lebe der Kaiser!

Long live the Emperor.

Hochmut kommt vor dem Fall.

Pride goes before a fall.

Hof.

Court.

Höflichkeit ist Klugheit; folglich ist Unhöflichkeit Dummheit.
　　　　　　　—*Schopenhauer.*

Politeness is prudence; therefore impoliteness is folly.

Hof-prediger.

Court-chaplain.

Hoher Sinn liegt oft im kind 'schem Spiel.—*Schiller.*

Deep meaning often lies in children's play.

Hunde, die viel bellen beissen nicht.

(Dogs that bark the loudest are slowest to bite.)   Boasters seldom accomplish much.

Hundert graue Pferde machen nicht einen einzigen Schimmel.—*Goethe.*

A hundred grey horses do not make a single white one.

Hut ab!

Hats off!

Ich bin der Geist, der stets verneint.
　　　　　　　—*Goethe.*

I am the spirit that ever denies.*

Ich bin es müde, über Sklaven zu herrschen.—*Frederick II.*

I am weary of ruling over slaves.

Ich bin gewohnt in der Münze wiederzuzahlen, in welcher man mich bezahlt.—*Bismarck.*

It is my wont to pay back people in the same coin with which they have paid me.

Ich danke Ihnen.

I thank you.

Ich dien.

I serve.†

Ich habe genossen das irdische Glück; Ich habe gelebt und geliebet.
　　　　　　　—*Schiller.*

I have experienced the joy that earth bestows; I have lived and loved.

Ich habe keine Zeit, müde zu sein.
　　　　　　　—*Emperor William I.*

I have no time to be tired.‡

Ich hatt einen Cameraden,
Einen bessern find'st du nicht.
Die Trommel schlug zum Streite,
Er ging an meiner Seite
In gleichem Schritt und Tritt.
　　　　　　　—*Uhland.*

I had a comrade, a better none could find.   When the drum called us to arms, we marched along together, step by step and side by side.§

Ich sag'es dir; ein Kerl, der spekuliert,
Ist wie ein Tier, auf dürrer Heide
Von einem bösen Geist im Kreis herum geführt,
Und rings umher liegt schöne grüne Weide.—*Goethe.*

I tell you this: a fellow who speculates is like a beast that roams upon a barren heath, urged to wander in a circle by some evil spirit, while all around fair green pastures lie.

---

* This is the reply of Mephistopheles when pressed by Faust to reveal his name.
† The motto of the Prince of Wales.   It was first assumed by the Black Prince after Crecy, 1346, where John, King of Bohemia, whose motto it had been, was killed in battle.
‡ The aged Emperor made this reply, during his last illness, to those who inquired whether he felt tired.
§ The first stanza of *Der gute Kamerad*, "the good comrade," one of the best-known German popular songs.

Ich weiss nicht, was soll es bedeuten,
Dass ich so traurig bin ;
Ein Mährchen aus alten Zeiten,
Das kommt mir nicht aus dem Sinn.
— *H. Heine.*

My heart is heavy. I know not what it may portend ; a story told from ancient times keeps running through my mind.*

Im Alter versteht man besser die Unglücksfälle zu verhüten ; in der Jugend, sie zu ertragen.
—*Schopenhauer.*

In old age we understand better how to avert troubles ; in youth, how to endure them.

Im Deutschen lügt man, wenn man höflich ist.—*Goethe.*

To pay compliments in German, you must tell lies.

Im Gegentheil.

On the contrary ; from the opposite point of view.

Im härtesten Winter.

In the depth of winter.

Im Hause der Gehenkten soll man nicht vom Stricke reden.

One must not talk of a rope in the house of the man who was hanged.

Immer schlimmer.

From bad to worse.

Immer wird, nie ist.

(Ever coming, never coming.) What is always going to happen, never happens.

In der einen Hand Brot, in der anderen einen Stein.

In one hand, bread ; in the other a stone.

In der freien Luft.

In the open air.

In der Klemme sein.

To be in a tight place ; not to know which way to turn.

In der Kunst ist das beste gut genug.
—*Goethe.*

In Art the best is good enough.

Indessen das Gras wächst, verhungert der Gaul.

While the grass is growing, the horse perishes with hunger.

In einen sauren Apfel beissen.

(To put one's teeth into a sour apple.) Here goes ! In for a penny, in for a pound.

Irren ist menschlich.

To err is human.

Ist die Welt erst tugendhaft, dann wird sie von selbst frei.—*G. Forster.*

When the world is once virtuous, then will it have won its own freedom.

Ist dir wohl, so bleibe.

(If you are well off, remain so.) Never quit certainty for hope.

Ists Gottes Werk, so wirds bestehn ;
Ists Menschenwerk, wirds untergehn.

If it is God's work, it will abide ; if it is man's, it will fall.†

Je älter der Geck, je schlimmer.

(The older the fool is, the more foolish he grows.) No fool like an old fool.

Jedem dünket sein' Eul' ein Falk

(The owl seems a falcon to his owner.) All think their own geese are swans.

Jeder Arbeiter ist seines Lohnes wert

The labourer is worthy of his hire.

Jeder fege vor seiner Thür.

Let each man sweep before his own doorstep.

---

* The opening words of Heine's *Lorelei*.
† These lines are inscribed on the Luther monument at Wittenburg. They are merely an adaptation of the words of Gamaliel to the Jews. See Acts v. 38.

Jeder für sich, Gott für alle.

Each man for himself, and God for us all.

Jeder ist Herr in seinem Hause.

Every man is master in his own house.

Jeder ist seines Glückes Schmied.

Every man is the master of his own fortune.

Jeder ist sich selbst der Nächste.

(Every man is nearest to himself.) Charity begins at home.

Jeder ist werth, dass man ihn aufmerksam betrachte; wenn auch nicht Jeder, dass man mit ihm rede.
—Schopenhauer.

Every man is worth studying carefully; but every man is not worth talking to.

Jeder liebt sein Land, seine Sitten, seine Sprache, sein Weib, seine Kinder, nicht weil sie die besten auf der Welt, sondern weil sie die bewährten Seinigen sind, und er in ihnen sich und seine Mühe selbst liebt.
—Herder.

Every man loves his own country, manners, language, wife, and children, not because they are the best in the world, but because they are peculiarly his own, and, loving them, he loves himself, and the toil he has undergone for them.

Jedermann ist Herr bei sich.

(Every man is a lord in his own house.) A man's house is his castle.

Jeder muss ein Paar Narrenschuhe verschleissen verschleisst er nicht mehr.

Every man must wear out one pair of fool's shoes, if he does not wear out more.

Jeder Vogel hat sein Nest lieb.

(Every bird loves its own nest.) *A chaque oiseau son nid est beau.*

Jede Strasse führt an's End der Welt.

(Every road leads to the end of the world.) All roads go to Jericho.

Jedes Weib will lieber schön als fromm sein.

Every woman prefers prettiness to saintliness.

Jede Unthat
Trägt ihren eignen Rache-Engel schon.
—Schiller.

Every evil deed brings with it its own angel of vengeance.

Jedoch das Allerschlimmste
Das haben sie nicht gewusst;
Das Schlimmste und das Dümmste
Das trug ich geheim in der Brust.
—H. Heine.

But the worst of all my failings
They have not even guessed;
For my worst, my greatest sin is——
Kept secret in my breast.

Je früher reif, je früher faul.

Early ripe, early rotten.

Je näher dem Bein, je süsser das Fleisch.

The nearer the bone, the sweeter the flesh.

Je näher der Kirche, je weiter von Gott.

The nearer to church, the farther from God.

Johannistag.

Midsummer day.

Junkerschaft.

The young nobility; squirearchy.

Kalte Hände, warme Liebe.

Cold hands, and a loving heart.

Kampf ums Dasein.

The struggle for existence.

Keiner kann über sich sehn.
—Schopenhauer.

(No man can see beyond himself.) No man can appreciate the virtues and merits of another, if he has not, at least, the germs of those virtues within himself.

Keine Rosen ohne Dornen. — No rose without a thorn.

Kein Geld, keine Freunde mehr. — No money, no friends.

Kein Rauch ohne Feuer. — No smoke without fire.

Kein Talent, doch ein Charakter. — No talent, but still a character.
—*H. Heine.*

Kein Unglück allein. — Misfortunes never come alone.

Kellner. — Waiter.

Kennst du das Land, wo die Citronen blühn, Im dunkeln Laub die Gold-Orangen glühn, Ein sanfter Wind vom blauen Himmel weht, Die Myrte still und hoch der Lorbeer steht? Kennst du es wohl? Dahin! Dahin! Möcht' ich mit dir, O mein Geliebter, ziehn.—*Goethe.* — Knowest thou the land where the lemon trees bloom, where the golden oranges gleam through the dark foliage; a gentle breeze blows from the blue heavens, the myrtle is motionless, and the laurel raises its head? Dost thou know it? Thither, O thither, my darling, my loved one, with thee would I fly.*

Kinder und Narren sprechen die Wahrheit. — Children and fools speak the truth.

Kladderadatsch. — Slap-bang! †

König und Kaiser. — King and Emperor.

Krieg. — War.

Kulturkampf. — Culture-struggle.‡

Kunst. — Art.

Kunst ist die rechte Hand der Natur. —*Schiller.* — Art is the right hand of Nature.

Kurze Rechnung, lange Freundschaft. — Short reckonings make long friendships.

Kurz ist der Schmerz, und ewig ist die Freude.—*Schiller.* — Brief is the pain, and eternal is the joy.

Kurz und gut. — Short and to the point.

Landsturm. — (General levy of the people.) All men capable of bearing arms that are not included in the line, the reserve, or the landwehr.

Landwehr. — Militia.

Langsam. — Slowly.

Lassen Sie es gut sein. — Never mind.

Lass uns, geliebter Bruder, nicht vergessen, Dass von sich selbst der Mensch nicht scheiden kann.—*Goethe.* — Let us never forget, dear brother, that man can never separate himself from his own nature.

Leben Sie wohl! — Farewell.

Leben und leben lassen.—*Schiller.* — To live and to let live.

---

* The opening lines of Mignon's song in *Wilhelm Meister.* It is often quoted as a description of the charm of Italy.
† The name of a well-known comic paper.
‡ See note on *Nach Canossa gehen wir nicht.*

Lebe, wie du, wenn du stirbst, Wünschen wirst, gelebt zu haben. —*Gellert.*
Live in such a way as, when you come to die, you will wish to have lived.

Leere Tonnen geben grossen Schall.
Empty barrels give the loudest sound.

Leg deinen Reichthum nicht all' auf ein Schiff.
(Don't put all your wealth into one boat.) Put not all your eggs into one basket.

Lehrjahre.
(Instruction years.) Apprenticeship.

Leichter ist Vergeben als Vergessen.
It is more easy to forgive an injury than to forget it.

Leitartikel.
Leading article.

Lerne leiden, ohne zu klagen.
Learn to suffer without complaining.*

Lerne schweigen, O Freund! Dem Silber gleichet die Rede; Aber zur rechten Zeit schweigen, ist lauteres Gold.—*Herder.*
Learn to keep silence, friend! Speech is like silver, but to be silent at the proper season is like pure gold.

Liebchen.
Beloved! Darling!

Liebe ist blind, und macht blind.
Love is blind, and makes its victims blind.

Liebe kann viel, Geld kann Alles.
Love is powerful, money omnipotent.

Liebe kennt der allein, der ohne Hoffnung liebt.—*Schiller.*
That man alone knows what love is, who loves when hope is gone.

Liebe ohne Gegenliebe ist wie eine Frage ohne Antwort.
Love which is not returned is like a question without an answer.

Lieber biegen als brechen.
Better to bend than break.

Liebeszorn ist neuer Liebeszunder.
(Lovers' quarrels are the tinder of love.) The quarrels of lovers are the renewal of love.

Liebe wintert nicht.—*Tieck.*
Love knows no winter.

Lied.
A song.

Lieder ohne Worte.
Songs without words.

Lied von der Glocke.
The Lay of the Bell.

List gegen List.
(Set cunning against cunning.) Set a thief to catch a thief.

List geht über Gewalt.
Cunning overcomes strength.

Luft-Schlösser bauen.
To build castles in the air.

Lustspiel.
A comedy.

Macht geht vor Recht.
Might takes precedence of Right.†

Mädchen.
Girl; maid.

Mährchen.
Fabulous tale.

Majestäts beleidigung.
Defaming the king; *lèse majesté.*

* The advice of the late Emperor, Frederick the Noble, to his son, the present Emperor of Germany.

† It is generally supposed that Bismarck was the coiner of this phrase, and that it was acknowledged by him to be the key-note of his policy. As a matter of fact, he repudiated it altogether. In a speech made in the Prussian Lower House on the 13th of March, 1863, he advocated very drastic measures. One of his political opponents, Count Von Schwerin, followed in the debate, and declared that the policy advocated by Bismarck might be summed up in the words *Macht geht vor Recht.*

Man hat immer Zeit genug, wenn man sie gut anwenden will.— *Goethe.*	We have always time enough, if we will make good use of it.
Man kann die Erfahrung nicht früh genug machen, wie entbehrlich man in der Welt ist.—*Goethe.*	This is a lesson we cannot learn too soon, that the world can go on easily without us.
Man kann Gold zu teuer kaufen.	One can buy gold too dear.
Man kauft die Katze nicht im Sack.	(No one buys cats when they are in a sack.) Do not buy a pig in a poke.
Man lebt nur einmal in der Welt. —*Goethe.*	Man lives only once in the world.
Man liebt an dem Mädchen, was es ist, und an dem Jünglung, was er ankündigt.—*Goethe.*	We love girls for what they are ; we love lads for what they seem likely to become.
Man mag wollen oder nicht.	Whether one likes it or not; willy-nilly.
Man muss das Eisen schmieden, wenn es warm ist.	You must strike the iron while it is hot.
Man muss Heu machen während die Sonne scheint.	Make hay while the sun shines.
Man sagt.	(They say.) Report says ; *on dit.*
Man soll den Tag nicht vor dem Abend loben.	We ought not to praise the day before the evening comes.
Man spricht selten von der Tugend, die man hat ; aber desto öfter von der, die uns fehlt.—*Lessing.*	We seldom speak of the good qualities that we possess; but far more often of those we lack.
Man spricht vergebens viel, um zu versagen ; Der Andre hört allein nur das Nein. —*Goethe.*	It is a vain employment to use many words in order to refuse ; the other person, in spite of all your talk, only hears your " No."
Man wird nie betrogen, man betrügt sich selbst.—*Goethe.*	We are never deceived, but we deceive ourselves.
Mässig.	Moderate.
Mehr Licht !	More light.*
Mein Herr.	Sir (in addressing one).
Mein Herz gleicht ganz dem Meere, Hat Sturm und Ebb und Flut, Und manche schöne Perle In seiner Tiefe ruht. —*H. Heine.*	My heart is like the restless sea, Has storm, and ebb, and flow, And many shining pearls lie hid In secret depths below.
Mit den Wölfen, muss man heulen.	(You must howl with the wolves.) When in Rome, you must do as Rome does.
Mit der Dummheit kämpfen Götter selbst vergebens.—*Schiller.*	With stupidity the gods themselves contend in vain.
Mit der Mutter soll beginnen, Wer die Tochter will gewinnen.	With the mother first begin, If you would the daughter win.
Mit der Thür in das Haus fallen.	(To fall into the house with the door.) To blurt out a tale.
Mit der Zeit pflückt man Rosen.	(In time we gather roses.) Everything comes to him who waits.

* The last words of Goethe. He died peacefully on March 22nd, 1832, in his eighty-third year.

Mit Gewalt.	By force; by compulsion.
Mit gleicher Münze zahlen.	To pay back in the same coin; to give tit for tat.
Mit Haut und Haaren.	(With skin and hair.) Tooth and nail; thoroughly.
Mit lauter Stimme.	At the top of one's voice.
Mittelweg ein sichrer Steg.	(The middle way is the safe way.) *Medio tutissimus ibis.*
Mitten im Sommer.	In the height of summer.
Mit umgehender Post.	By return of post.
Morgen, morgen, nur nicht heute, Sprechen alle trägen Leute.	All foolish people are wont to say, " To-morrow, to-morrow, not to-day ! "
Morgenstunde hat Gold im Munde.	(The morning hour has gold in its mouth.) Early to bed and early to rise, makes a man healthy, wealthy, and wise.
Mündlich.	By word of mouth.
Münze.	Coin.
Musik ist Poesie der Luft. *—Jean Paul Richter.*	Music is the poetry of the air.
Nach Canossa gehen wir nicht *—Bismarck.*	We are not going to Canossa.*
Nach meinem Bedünken.	In my opinion ; according to my view of the case.
Nachricht.	News.
Nach und nach.	Gradually; by degrees.
Nehmt die gute Stimmung wahr, Denn sie kommt so selten.—*Goethe.*	(Seize the right mood, for it comes so seldom.) Do not let the moment of inspiration pass disregarded.
Neue Allgemeine Deutsche Bibliothek.	New Universal German Library.
Neue Besen kehren gut.	New brooms sweep clean.
Neuere Poeten thun viel Wasser in die Tinte.—*Goethe.*	The poets of to-day put a great deal of water in their ink.
Neujahrstag.	New Year's Day.
Nicht alles an einen Nagel hängen.	(Not to hang all on one nail.) To have two strings to one's bow.
Nicht Alles, was glänzt, ist Gold.	All is not gold that glitters.
Nicht Glückseligkeit ist der Zweck unsers Daseins, sondern Glückwürdigkeit.—*Fichte.*	Not to attain happiness, but to be worthy of it, is the purpose of our existence.
Nichts andres bleibt uns übrig.	(Nothing else remains over for us.) We have no alternative.

* This saying, which has become proverbial, was uttered by Bismarck in a speech delivered by him in the Reichstag in the year 1872.   At that time the Kulturkampf, the famous struggle against the claims of the Clerical Party, was going on, and the relations between the German government and the Vatican were strained.   The Iron Chancellor expressed his unyielding attitude towards the Pope in these words.   The reference is to the abject submission that the Emperor Henry IV. made to Gregory VII.—the Pope who resuscitated the power and reputation of the Papacy—at Canossa, in North Italy, in the year 1077.

Nichts halb zu thun ist edler Geister Art.—*Wieland.*

High-souled men are wont to do nothing by halves.

Nichts mit Hast als Flöhe fangen.

Naught in a hurry save the catching of fleas.

Nichts thun lehrt Übel thun.

(Idleness the teacher of wickedness.) Satan still finds work for idle hands to do.

Nicht Stimmenmehrheit ist des Rechtes Probe.—*Schiller.*

It does not prove a thing to be right because the majority say it is so.

Nichts von Bedeutung.

Nothing of importance; a mere trifle.

Nichtswürdig ist die Nation, die nicht Ihr Alles freudig setzt an ihre Ehre.
　　　　　　　　　—*Schiller.*

Worthless is the nation which is not ready to risk everything for its honour.

Nichts zuviel.

Nothing in excess.

Niemand ist mehr Sklave, als der sich für frei hält, ohne es zu sein.
　　　　　　　　　—*Goethe.*

He is most truly a slave, who thinks himself free without being so.

Niemand kann den Schleier wegziehen, den die Vorsehung gewiss mit tiefer Weisheit über das Jenseits gezogen hat.—*W. von Humboldt.*

No one is able to remove the veil with which Providence, in its infinite wisdom, has concealed the next world from our eyes.

Niemand wird in seinem Lande als Prophet geehrt.

No man is ever a prophet in his own country.

Niemand wird tiefer traurig, als wer zu viel lächelt.—*Jean Paul Richter.*

Nobody is so utterly sad as he who laughs too much.

Nimm die Zögernden zum Rath, nicht zum Werkzeng deiner That.

(Deliberate slowly, execute promptly.) Strike while the iron is hot.

Not kennt kein Gebot.

(Necessity knows no law.) Needs must when the devil drives.

Not lehrt beten.

Necessity teaches one to pray.

Not lehrt Künste.

Necessity is the mother of the arts.

Nur der Irrthum ist das Leben Und das Wissen ist der Tod.
　　　　　　　　　—*Schiller.*

Life is but error, and it is death that brings knowledge.

Nur die Tugend ist ein Kampf, durch die man Fehler besiegt.
　　　　　　　　　—*Schleiermacher.*

Virtue is merely a struggle wherein we overcome our weaknesses.

Oberhaus und Unterhaus.

(Upper House and Lower House.) Houses of Lords and Commons.

O dass sie ewig grünen bliebe, Die schöne Zeit der jungen Liebe.
　　　　　　　　　—*Schiller.*

O that they might remain for ever vernal, those happy days of youthful love.

Offenherzig gesagt.

Speaking frankly; to be candid.

Ohne Abschied weggehen.

To take French leave.

Ohne Hast, aber ohne Rast.—*Goethe.*

Without haste, but without rest.*

Ohne Kampf und Entbehrung ist kein Menschenleben.—*W. von Humboldt.*

The life of no man is free from struggle and suffering.

Ostern.

Easter.

* His description of the steady onward march of the sun.

Ost, Süd, West,
Daheim ist's am best!

East or West
Home is best.

" O was müssen wir der Kirche Gottes
    halber leiden! " rief der Abt, als
    ihm das gebratene Huhn die Finger
    versengt.

" Ah!   How we have to suffer for the
    Church," exclaimed the abbot, when
    the roast chicken burnt his fingers.

O weh mir armen Korydon.—*Bürger.*

O woe is me, poor Corydon.

O, wunderschön ist Gottes Erde,
Und wert, darauf vergnügt zu sein.
                            —*Hölty.*

O wondrous fair is God's earth; 'tis
    meet that we should rejoice therein.

Pantoffel-regiment.

Petticoat government.

Pfaffen und Weiber vergessen nie.

Priests and women never forget.

Pfennig ist Pfennig's Bruder.

(Penny is the penny's brother.) Money
    makes money.

Pflücke Rosen, weil sie blühn,
Morgen ist nicht heut.—*Gleim.*

Gather the roses while the bloom is
    still on them; for to-morrow is not
    to-day.

Posthaus.

Post-office.

Prophete rechts, Prophete links,
Das Weltkind in der Mitten.—*Goethe.*

A prophet on the right, a prophet on
    the left, and the world-child in the
    middle.

Prosit.

Good luck!   Here's to your health!

Prosit Neujahr!

A happy New Year (to you)!

Rache trägt keine Frucht.—*Schiller.*

Revenge brings no fruit.

Raphael wäre ein grosser Maler gewor-
    den, selbst wenn er ohne Hände auf
    die Welt gekommen wäre.—*Lessing.*

Raphael would have been a great
    painter, even if he had come into
    the world without hands.

Rathhaus.

Town hall.

Raum ist in der kleinsten Hütte
Für ein glücklich liebend Paar.
                        — *Schiller.*

In the tiniest cottage there is room
    enough for a happy, loving pair.

Real-schulen.

(" Real " schools.)   Secondary schools
    giving a general practical education.

Reden ist Silber, Schweigen ist Gold.

Speech is silvern, silence is golden.

Rede wenig, rede wahr.

Speak little, but speak the truth.

Reich ist genug, wer sich genügen lässt.

Who allows himself to be contented, is
    rich enough.

Reichsanzeiger.

Official gazette;   the organ of the
    government.

Reichskanzler.

Imperial Chancellor.

Reichsrath.

Council of the Empire.

Reichstag.

The Imperial Diet.

Reichsverfassung.

Constitution of the Empire.

Rinderpest.

Cattle plague.

Rom ward nicht in einem Tage ge-
baut.

Rome was not built in a day.

Rosen auf den Weg gestreut. Und des Harms vergessen!—*Hölty*.	Scatter roses on the path, and forget your sorrows.
Rückwärts, rückwärts, Don Rodrigo! Rückwärts, rückwärts, stolzer Cid! —*Herder*.	Back, back, Don Rodrigo! Back, back, haughty Cid!
Ruhe ist die erste Bürgerpflicht.	Tranquillity is the first duty of citizens.
Sauerkraut.	Pickled cabbage.
Scherz bei Seite.	Seriously; joking apart.
Schlafende Hunde soll man nicht wecken.	Let sleeping dogs lie.
Schlafen Sie wohl!	(Sleep well.) Good-night!
Schloss.	Castle; royal palace.
Schnaps.	A dram; a glass of spirits.
Schnellzug.	Express train.
Schönen Dank.	Best thanks.
Schöne Worte machen den Kohl nicht fett.	Fine words butter no parsnips.
Schönheit ist ein offener Empfehlungsbrief, der die Herzen zum voraus für uns gewinnt.—*Schopenhauer*.	Beauty is an open letter of recommendation, which gains for us the hearts of others beforehand.
Schön war ich auch, und das war mein Verderben.—*Goethe*.	I, too, was beautiful, and that was my ruin.
Seine Gedanken beisammen haben.	To have one's wits about one.
Sein Sie so gut.	If you please.
Selbst gethan ist wohl gethan.	(Self-done is well done.) The master's eye makes the horse fat.
Selbst ist der Mann.	(Self is the man.) If you want a thing done well, do it yourself.
Seltener Vogel.	(A rare bird.) An uncommon thing; *rara avis*.
Setzen wir Deutschland, so zu sagen, in den Sattel! Reiten wird es schon können.—*Bismarck*.	Put Germany, so to speak, in the saddle; you will find that she can ride.*
Setzt einen Frosch auf goldenen Stuhl, Er hüpft doch wieder in den Pfuhl.	Set a frog on a golden stool, He soon jumps back into the pool.
Sich das Leben nehmen.	To commit suicide.
Sich die Hörner ablaufen.	To sow one's wild oats.
Sich um des Kaisers Bart streiten.	(To quarrel about the Emperor's beard.) To quarrel about a trifle.
Sieht doch wohl die Katze den Kaiser an.	Even a cat may look at a king.
Sie ist die erste nicht.	(She is not the first.) Other women have been betrayed.†

---

* Bismarck said this in a speech delivered by him in 1869. How well Germany could ride was proved in the following year.

† This is one of the cynical sayings of Mephistopheles in Goethe's *Faust*. Goethe did not originate it, but it is an old German proverbialism.

Sie loben ewig das Geringe,
Weil sie das Gute nie gekannt.
                        —*Gellert.*

They (incapable critics) always praise
the trivial, because they have never
known the good.

Sitzung des Abgeordnetenhauses.

Sitting of the delegates.

So ?

Really ? Indeed ?

So geht es in der Welt.

That's the way of the world.

Sogleich.

Presently.

So gut man kann.

To the best of one's ability; as well as
one can.

So schnell als möglich.

As quickly as possible.

So schwer es demnach ist, den Ruhm
zu erlangen, so leicht ist es, ihn zu
behalten.—*Schopenhauer.*

It is as difficult to win a reputation, as
it is easy to maintain it.

So viel ich weiss.

To the best of my knowledge.

So wahr ich lebe.

As sure as I'm alive.

So weit als das Gesicht reicht.

As far as the eye can see.

So, wie man sich bettet, muss man
liegen.

As you make your bed, so you must lie
upon it.

Spanien, das Land des Weins und der
Gesänge.—*Goethe.*

Spain, the land of wine and song.

Sparen bringt Haben.

(Saving produces wealth.)   A penny
saved is a penny gained.

Spare nicht auf morgen was du heute
thun kannst.

Do not put off till the morrow what you
can do to-day.

Spätestens.

At the very latest.

Sprechen ist silber,
Schweigen ist gold.

Speech is silvern, silence is golden.

Sprechen sie Deutsch ?

Do you speak German ?

Steuer.

Tax ; rate.

Stille Wasser gründen tief.

Still waters run deep.

Strasse.

Street.

Stückweise.

By fits and starts.

Sturm und Drang.

Storm and stress.

Sünder und böse Geister scheuen das
Licht.—*Schiller.*

Sinners and evil spirits avoid the light.

Tadeln können zwar die Thoren
Aber klüger handeln nicht.—*Langbein.*

Fools can easily criticise, when they
cannot do better themselves.

Tag wird es auf die dickste Nacht.
                        —*Schiller.*

After the darkest night there comes the
day.

Tausch ist kein Raub.

Exchange is no robbery.

Treue Liebe bis zum Grabe
Schwör ich dir mit Herz und Hand :
Was ich bin und was ich habe,
Dank ich dir, mein Vaterland !
Nicht in Worten nur und Liedern
Ist mein Herz zum Dank bereit ;
Mit der That will ich's erwiedern
Dir in Noth, in Kampf und Streit.
        —*Hoffmann von Fallersleben*

Love unchanging to the grave
Swear I now with heart and hand .
What I am and what I have,
Springs from thee, my Fatherland.
Not in song alone or word
Doth my grateful soul o'erflow ;
But in deed I draw my sword
Thee to shield from dreaded foe.
        —*Elizabeth M. Sewell*

Trink Halle.

A refreshment-room.

Tropfen höhlen den Stein aus.

Continual droppings wear away the stone.

Turnverein.

Gymnastic society.

Über allen Gipfeln ist Ruh'.—*Goethe*.

Beyond all the peaks is rest.*

Übung macht den Meister.

(Practice makes the craftsman.) Practice makes perfect.

Ulk.

Fun ; frolic.

Um das Unglück voll zu machen.

To complete the misfortune ; the last straw.

Um ein Haar.

Within a hair's breadth ; a near shave.

Undank ist der Welt Lohn.

Ingratitude is the world's payment.

Und Marmorbilder stehn und sehn mich an :
Was hat man dir, mein armes Kind, gethan ?—*Goethe*.

And marble statues stand and gaze at me :
" Say, my poor child, what have they done to thee ? " †

Unglück ist nichts wie Unverstand, und nicht so wohl durch Tugend als durch Verstand wird man furchtbar und glücklich.—*Jean Paul Richter*.

There is no greater misfortune than ignorance, and it is not so much through virtue as through knowledge that one becomes respected and successful.

Universität.

University.

Unkraut wuchert immer.

A weed always grows.

Unkraut vergeht nicht.

Ill weeds grow apace.

Unrecht Gut gedeiht nicht.

Ill-gotten gains go apace.

Unser Gefühl für Natur gleicht der Empfindung des Kranken für die Gesundheit.—*Schiller*.

The emotion, which the consideration of Nature arouses within us, is like that which the thought of health awakens in a sick man.

Unter den Blinden ist der Einäugige König.

In the land of the blind the one-eyed is king.

Unter den Linden.

(Under the limes.)   Name given to the principal street in Berlin from the rows of limes in it.

Unterdessen.

In the meantime.

Unter vier Augen.

Between ourselves.

Vaterland.

Fatherland.

Verächtlich ist eine Frau, die Langweile haben kann, wenn sie Kinder hat.—*Jean Paul Richter*.

A woman is to be despised, who, having children to care for, can ever feel bored.

Verbunden werden auch die Schwachen mächtig.

(Even the weak, when united, become powerful.)   Union is strength.

* These words were written by Goethe on the window of a country inn in the Thuringian Forest.   They appear also as the first words of his song *Ein Gleiches*.
† Part of Mignon's song in *Wilhelm Meister*.   See *Kennst du das Land* for the first stanza.   Macaulay declared that he knew no two lines in the whole range of literature which he would rather have written than these.

Vernunft und Wissenschaft, Des Menschen allerhöchste Kraft.
　　　　　　—Goethe.

Reason and knowledge are by far the highest strength of man!

Versammlung.

Meeting.

Vertrau' auf Gott.

Put your trust in God.

Verweile doch! Du bist so schön.
　　　　　　—Goethe.

Stay! thou art so fair.*

Viele Händ' machen bald ein End.

Many hands make labour light.

Viele Kinder, viele Segen.

Many children are so many blessings.

Viele kleine Bäche machen zuletzt einen Strom.

(Many little rivulets make a river at last.) Every little helps.

Viele Köche verderben den Brei.

Too many cooks spoil the broth.

Viele Köpfe, viele Sinne.

So many men, so many minds.

Vieles wünscht sich der Mensch, und doch bedarf er nur wenig.—*Goethe.*

Man's aspirations are great, but his needs are few.

Viel Geschrei und wenig Wolle.

Great cry, and little wool.

Vögel von gleicher Feder fliegen zusammen.

Birds of a feather flock together.

Volkslied.

Folk-song; popular ballad.

Vom Pferde auf den Esel kommen.

(From horse to ass.) To go from bad to worse.

Von der Hand in den Mund leben.

To live from hand to mouth.

Von einem Funken, kommt ein grosses Feuer.

A spark kindles a great fire.

Vor einem Achtung hegen.

To have a great respect for one.

Vor Leiden kann nur Gott dich wahren Unmuth magst du dir selber sparen.
　　　　　　— Geibel.

God alone can deliver you from sorrow, but from dejection you can deliver yourself.

Vorrath schadet nimmer.

Store is no sore.

Vorsicht schadet nicht.

Safe bind, safe find.

Vorwärts!

Forward! †

Waffenstillstand.

Armistice.

Wähle von zwei Uebeln das Kleinste.

Choose the lesser of two evils.

Wahrheit ist der Zeit Tochter.

(Truth is the daughter of Time.) Time brings everything to light.

Wälzender Stein wird nicht moosig.

A rolling stone gathers no moss.

Wanderjahre.

(Wandering years.) Travels in which a journeyman went from place to place after his *Lehrjahre,* his year of apprenticeship, in order to gain further experience.

Wappen.

Arms; coat of arms.

Was dein Feind nicht wissen soll, das sage deinem Freunde nicht.

What you would not have your enemy know, tell not to your friend.

---

* Faust makes a compact with Mephistopheles to give himself up to the Evil One, as soon as he shall see anything so desirable as to force this request from his lips. How he falls when tempted is a familiar story.

† This was the motto and also the nickname of Marshal Blücher. The leading journal of the German Socialists at the present time bears this title.

Was die Augen nicht sehen, bekümmert das Herz nicht.	What the eye does not see, the heart does not grieve for.
Was die Augen sehen, glaubt das Herz.	(The heart believes what the eyes see.) Seeing is believing.
Was die Schickung schickt, ertrage! Wer ausharret wird gekrönt.—*Herder*.	Endure the lot that destiny sends! Whosoever perseveres will receive a crown at last.
Was du ererbt von deinen Vätern hast, Erwirb es, um es zu besitzen.—*Goethe*.	What thou hast inherited from thy fathers, be sure thou earn it, so that it may become thine own.
Was du liebst, das lebst du.—*Fichte*.	(What thou lovest, that thou livest.) A man forms his life according to the standard of what he considers gives happiness.
Was ein Weib will, muss geschehen.	A wilful woman must have her way.
Was giebt es?	What is the matter?
Was glänzt, ist für den Augenblick geboren.—*Goethe*.	The thing that glitters is created only for the moment.
Was Gott thut, das ist wohlgethan. —*S. Rodigast*.	What God does, is done well.
Was Hänschen nicht lernt, lernt Hans nimmermehr.	(What little Hans does not learn, Hans will never know.) You cannot bend a tree when it is old.
Was ist das Leben ohne Liebesglanz! —*Schiller*.	What is life without the light of love!
Was ist der Mensch? Halb Tier, halb Engel.—*J. L. Evers*.	What is man? Half beast, half angel.
Was Jeder thun soll, thut Keiner.	What is Everyone's business is Nobody's work.
Was man nicht kann meiden, soll man willig leiden.	What cannot be cured, must needs be endured.
Was man nicht nützt, ist eine schwere Last.—*Goethe*.	The possession we do not make use of becomes a troublesome burden.
Was man nicht versteht, besitzt man nicht.—*Goethe*.	What a man does not comprehend, that he does not possess.
Was sein muss, das geschehe.	(Let what must be, happen.) One cannot fight against fate.
Wasser in's Meer tragen.	(To carry water to the sea.) Coals to Newcastle.
Was uns alle bändigt, das Gemeine. —*Goethe*.	The bond that unites us all — the commonplace.
Was vernünftig ist, das ist wirklich; und was wirklich ist, das ist vernünftig.—*Hegel*.	(Whatever is reasonable is true, and whatever is true is reasonable.) Whatever is, is right.—*Pope*.
Was verschmerzte nicht der Mensch? —*Schiller*.	What sorrow cannot a man learn to endure?
Was vom Herzen kommt, das geht zum Herzen.	What comes from the heart, goes to the heart.
Was von mir ein Esel spricht Das acht' ich nicht.—*Gleim*.	What a fool says of me, that I heed not.
Weder gehauen noch gestochen.	Neither fish nor flesh.

Weder Sinn noch Verstand.

Weihnachten.

Wein und Weiber machen alle Welt zu Narren.

Weisheit ist nicht, wie ihr denkt
Eine Kunst, die zu erlernen;
Weisheit kommt doch aus den Sternen.
Sie ist's, die der Himmel schenkt.
— *Paul Flemming.*

Welch Glück geliebt zu werden;
Und lieben, Götter, welch ein Glück!
— *Goethe.*

Wenig und oft macht zuletz viel.

Wenn alle Stricke reissen.

Wenn deine Schrift dem Kenner nicht gefällt
So ist es schon ein böses Zeichen:
Doch wenn sie gar des Narren Lob erhält
So ist es Zeit, sie auszustreichen.
— *S. Gessner.*

Wenn der Leib in Staub zerfallen
Lebt der grosse Name noch.
— *Schiller.*

Wenn die Katze fort ist, tanzen die Mäuse.

Wenn die Könige bau'n, haben die Kärrner zu thun.— *Schiller.*

Wenn ich dich lieb habe, was geht's dich an?— *Goethe.*

Wenn jemand eine Reise thut
So kann er was verzählen.— *Claudius.*

Wenn man alt ist, muss man mehr thun, als da man jung war.— *Goethe.*

Wenn Wein eingeht, geht Witz aus.

Wenn wir Andern Ehre geben,
Müssen wir uns selbst entadeln.
— *Goethe.*

Wenn wir schön sind, sind wir ungeputzt am schönsten.— *Lessing.*

Wer andern eine Grube gräbt, fällt selbst hinein.

Wer A sagt, muss auch B sagen.

Wer bringt, ist willkommen.

Wer dem Pöbel dient, hat einen schlechten Herrn.

Wer dem Publicum dient, ist ein armes Thier;
Er quält sich ab, niemand bedankt sich dafür.— *Goethe.*

Neither rhyme nor reason.

Christmas.

Wine and women make fools of all world.

Wisdom is not, as you suppose, an art that can be learnt. Wisdom cometh from the heavens, and is God's own gift to men.

What happiness to be beloved; and O, what bliss, ye gods, to love!

Little and often make a heap at last.

If the worst comes to the worst.

When your writings fail to please the critics, that is certainly a bad omen; but when they win the praise of a fool, it is high time to blot them out.

When the life of a great man has fallen to the dust, his name still lives on.

When the cat is away, the mice will play.

When kings go a building, then waggoners have something to do.

If I love you, what is that to you?

When any man has gone on his travels, he has a story to tell.

When we are old, we must do more than when we were young.

When the wine is in, the wit is out.

When we pay honour to others, we are bound to depreciate ourselves.

(If we are beautiful, we are most beautiful without adornment.) Beauty unadorned, adorned the most.

Who digs a trench for another, tumbles in himself.

He that says A must also say B.

He who brings something in his hand is a welcome guest.

The people's servant has a bad master.

The man who is the servant of the public is a creature to be pitied; he wears himself out, and nobody says "Thank you" for his pains.

C C

Wer dem Spiele zusieht, kann's am besten.

Lookers-on see most of the game.

Wer den Besten seiner Zeit genug Gethan, der hat gelebt für alle Zeiten.
—*Schiller*.

The man who has gained the approval of the best of his time, has lived for all times.

Wer den Dichter will verstehen Muss in Dichters Lande gehen.—*Goethe*.

He who will understand the poet, must visit the poet's country.

Wer den Kern essen will, muss die Nuss kracken.

He who would eat the kernel must crack the nut.

Wer den kleinsten Theil eines Geheimnisses hingibt, hat den andern nicht mehr in der Gewalt.
—*Jean Paul Richter*.

The man who reveals the smallest tittle of a secret, can no longer be said to possess the rest of it.

Wer den Sieg behält, der hat Recht.

The victor is always in the right.

Wer der Bösen schont, schadet den Frommen.

He who spares the wicked injures the good.

Wer die Leiter hinauf will, muss bei der untersten Sprosse anfangen.

If you wish to mount the ladder, you must begin at the lowest rung.

Wer ein Kalb stiehlt, stiehlt eine Kuh.

(He who steals a calf, steals a cow.) He who stole the egg to-day will steal a cow to-morrow.

Wer für sich selbst nicht sorget, kann für andere nicht sorgen.

He who bewails not his own sorrows, cannot bewail another's.

Wer gar zu viel bedenkt wird wenig leisten.—*Schiller*.

The man who ponders too much will accomplish little.

Wer hängen soll, ersäuft nicht.

The man born to be hanged is never drowned.

Wer hoch steigt, fällt tief.

He who stands the highest, has the farthest to fall.

Wer im Alter will jung sein, der muss in der Jugend alt sein.

He who would be youthful in old age, must in his youth be old.

Wer im Glashause sitzt, muss andere nicht mit Steinen werfen.

He who lives in a glass house should not throw stones.

"Wer ist ein unbrauchbarer Mann?" Der nicht befehlen und auch nicht gehorchen kann.—*Goethe*.

"Who is a useless man?" He who can neither command nor obey.

Wer kann was Dummes, wer was Kluges denken,
Das nicht die Vorwelt schon gedacht.
—*Goethe*.

Who can think of anything, whether stupid or smart, that former ages have not already thought of?

Wer langsam geht, kommt auch.

(He who goes slowly, also arrives.) Slow and steady wins the race.

Wer nicht arbeitet, soll auch nicht essen.

He who will not work shall not eat.

Wer nicht liebt, der lebt im öden Winter.—*Gessner*.

He who loves nothing, lives a dark and wintry life.

Wer nicht liebt Wein, Weib, und Gesang,
Der bleibt ein Narr sein Lebenlang.

Who loves not wine, women, and song, Remains a fool his whole life long.*

* These lines have been attributed to Martin Luther, but it is more than doubtful whether he was the author of them.

Wer nichts wagt, gewinnt nichts.

Nothing venture, nothing gain.

Wer nie sein Brot mit Thränen ass
Wer nie die kummervollen Nächte
Auf seinem Bette weinend sass,
Der kennt euch nicht, ihr himmlischen
Mächte.—*Goethe.*

Who ne'er his bread in sorrow ate,
Who ne'er the mournful midnight hours
Weeping upon his bed has sate,
He knows you not, ye Heavenly Powers.—*Longfellow.*

Wer oft schiesst, trifft endlich.

Who shoots often, hits at last.

Wer Ohren hat, soll hören ;
Wer Geld hat, soll's verzehren.—*Goethe.*

Who has ears, let him hear ; who has money, let him spend it.

Wer Pech angreift, besudelt sich.

You cannot play with pitch without being defiled.

Wer Recht fordert, soll auch Recht pflegen.

He who asks justice for himself, must also grant it to others.

Wer redet was er will, muss hören was er nicht will.

He who says what he pleases, must hear what does not please him.

Wer schlägt meinen Hund, der liebt mich nicht.

(Who beats my dog, he loves me not.)
Love me, love my dog.

Wer schlechte Botschaft bringt, kommt früh genug.

He who brings ill news, comes soon enough.

Wer sich der Einsamkeit ergiebt,
Ach ! der ist bald allein.—*Goethe.*

The man who gives himself to solitude, alas ! soon finds himself alone.

Wer sich für den allerklügsten hält,
muss stets die allerdummsten Streiche
machen.—*Tieck.*

The man who regards himself as pre-eminently wise, is always sure to make the most ridiculous blunder.

Wer sich nicht nach der Decke streckt
Dem bleiben die Füsse unbedeckt.
—*Goethe.*

(He who stretches himself beyond the sheet,
Leaves nothing with which to cover his feet.)
Cut your coat according to the cloth.

Wer sich selber kitzelt, lacht wenn er will.

He who tickles himself, laughs when he will.

Wer über gewisse Dinge den Verstand
nicht verlieret, der hat keinen zu ver-
lieren.—*Lessing.*

The man who does not lose his senses in certain matters, has none to lose.

Wer verachtet, der will kaufen.

He who decries the goods, is sure to buy them.

Wer viel anfängt, endet wenig.

He who commences much, finishes little.

Wer von Hoffnung lebt, der stirbt am Fasten.

Who lives on hopes, dies of hunger.

Wer zuerst kommt, mahlt zuerst.

First come, first served.

Wer zuletzt lacht, lacht am besten.

He laughs best, who laughs last.

Wer zum ersten Male liebt,
Sei's auch glücklos, ist ein Gott.
— *H. Heine.*

The man who is in love for the first time, even if his love is unrequited, is a godlike being.

Wer zu viel unternimmt, ist selten glücklich.

(He who undertakes too much, is seldom successful.) Don't have too many irons in the fire.

Wider den Strom schwimmen ist schwer.

(It is hard to swim against the stream.)
Do not kick against the pricks.

Wie der Herr, so der Diener.	Like master, like servant.
Wie der Herr, so der Knecht.	Like master, like man.
Wie Einer ist, so ist sein Gott. 　　　　　　—*Goethe.*	(As a man is, so is his God.) Every man derives his conception of God from his own nature.
Wie fruchtbar is der kleinste Kreis, Wenn man ihn wohl zu pflegen weiss! 　　　　　　— *Goethe.*	How fertile is the smallest field of action, if we know how to tend it well.
Wie geht's ?	How goes it ; how do you do ?
Wie gesäet so geschnitten.	As you sow, so you reap.
Wie gewöhnlich.	In the customary way.
Wie gewonnen, so zerronnen.	(As earned, so spent.) Lightly come, lightly go.
Wie Hund und Katze zusammenleben.	(To live as dog and cat together.) To live a cat-and-dog life.
Wie man sich bettet so schläft man.	As you make your bed, so you must lie on it.
Wie viel Uhr ist es ?	What is the time ?
Wille ist des Werks Seele.	(Will is the soul of work.) Where there's a will, there's a way.
Williges Pferd soll man nicht treiben.	Do not spur the willing horse.
Willst du dich selber erkennen, so sieh, wie die Andern es treiben ; Willst du die Andern verstehn, blick'in dein eigenes Herz!—*Schiller.*	Wouldst thou know thyself, mark how others behave; wouldst thou understand others, look into thine own heart.
Willst du immer weiter schweifen ? Sieh, das Gute liegt so nah. Lerne nur das Glück ergreifen, Denn das Glück ist immer da. 　　　　　　—*Goethe.*	Wilt thou always wander farther ? See the good doth dwell so near. Learn this one lesson, to pluck the flower of happiness, for it is ever by thy side.
Wir Deutsche fürchten Gott, aber sonst niemand.—*Bismarck.*	We Germans fear God, but no one else.
Wir müssen das Eisen schmieden, solang es warm ist.	We must strike the iron while it is hot.
Wir schwimmen in dem Strom der Zeit Auf Welle Welle fort ; Das Meer der Allvergessenheit Ist unser letzter Ort.—*Herder.*	By Time's broad stream borne swiftly on From wave to wave we're cast ; The Ocean of Oblivion Receives us all at last.
Wir sind gewohnt, dass die Menschen verhöhnen was sie nicht verstehn. 　　　　　　—*Goethe.*	We generally see that men scoff at the things which they do not understand.
Wissen ist leichter als thun.	Theory is easier than practice.
Wissenschaft ist Macht.	Knowledge is power.
Wo das Herz reden darf, braucht es keiner Vorbereitung.—*Lessing.*	When the heart dares to speak, no preparation is needed.
Wo der liebe Gott eine Kirche baut, da baut der Teufel eine Kapelle.	Where God builds a church, there the Devil builds a chapel.
Wohlfeil.	Cheap.
Wohlgeboren.	Well-born ; people of good birth
Wohlgethan überlebt den Tod.	A good deed survives death.

Wohlhabend sein.	To be well off, prosperous.
Wohlthaten, still und rein gegeben, Sind Todte, die im Grabe leben, Sind Blumen, die im Sturm bestehn, Sind Sternlein, die nicht untergehn. —*Claudius.*	Good deeds, that are done silently and for a good motive, are the dead that live even in the grave; they are flowers that withstand the storm; they are stars that know no setting.
Wo keine Eifersucht, da ist keine Liebe.	No love without jealousy.
Wollte Gott!	Would to God.
Wollt ihr immer leben? —*Frederick the Great.*	Do you wish to live for ever?*
Wozu das?	What is the use of that?
Zartem Ohre halbes Wort.	(Half a word is enough for a quick ear.) *Verbum sat sapienti.*
Zeit, Ebbe und Flut, warten auf Niemand.	Time and tide wait for no man.
Zeit ist Geld.	Time is money.
Zeitung.	Journal; gazette; newspaper.
Zollfrei.	Free of customs.
Zollhaus.	Custom house.
Zollverein.	Customs-union.
Zorn thut nicht mit Rath.	Anger and counsel have nothing in common.
Zu dienen.	At your service.
Zufriedenheit geht über alles.	Contentment is the best possession.
Zufriedenheit geht über Reichthum.	Contentment is better than riches.
Zu Nacht sind alle Katzen grau.	In the dark all cats are grey.
Zur rechten Zeit.	In the nick of time.
Zu Sanct-Nimmerstag.	When two Sundays come in a week; at the Greek Calends.
Zu spät ist es, am Ende sparen.	It is late to spare when the cupboard's bare.
Zu tief ins Glas schauen.	(To look too deeply into the glass.) To imbibe too freely.
Zu viel kann man wohl trinken, Doch nie trinkt man genug.—*Lessing.*	Though one may well drink too much, but one can never drink enough.
Zu wiederholten Malen.	Time after time; repeatedly.
Zwang erbittert die Schwärmer immer, aber bekehrt sie nie.—*Schiller.*	Opposition irritates an enthusiast, but it never converts him.
Zwar der Tapfere nennt sich Herr der Länder Durch sein Eisen, durch sein Blut. —*Arndt.*	The brave man calls himself lord of the land through his iron, through his blood.†
Zwei Fliegen mit einem Schlage treffen.	To kill two birds with one stone.

* Frederick put this question to some of his soldiers, when on one occasion they hesitated to attack the enemy.
† These lines are supposed to have suggested Bismarck's well-known saying *Eisen und Blut.*

Zwei Seelen und ein Gedanke,
Zwei Herzen und ein Schlag!—*Halm*.
Zwischen Amboss und Hammer.

Zwischen Thür und Angel stecken.

Two souls with but a single thought,
Two hearts that beat as one.
(Between anvil and hammer.) Between
the devil and the deep sea.
(To be between the door and the hinge.)
To be on the horns of a dilemma.

Italian.

A Ballata.	In ballad style.
A Battuta.	In strict time.
Abbacchiato.	Mournful, sad.
Abbandonarsi.	To lose oneself in the music.
Abbassamento di mano.	The downward stroke of the hand in marking time.
Abbassamento di voce.	Lowering of the voice.
Abbassare.	To lower, to drop, to diminish.
Abbellare.	To embellish, to beautify.
Abbimo pur fiorini che troveremo cugini.	If we possess florins, we shall find cousins.
Abbondanza genera fastidio.	Abundance creates daintiness.
Abbreviatura.	An abbreviation.
A bene placito.	(At pleasure.) At the discretion of the performer.
A buon cavallo non occorre dirgli trotta.	To a good horse you need not say "trot."
A buon intenditor poche parole.	(To a good listener few words.) A word is enough to the wise.
A cader va chi troppo alto sale.	(Who climbs too high may fear a fall.) Climb not too high lest the fall be greater.
A can che lecchi cenere non gli fidar farina.	A dog that licks ashes trust not with meal.
A cane scottato l'acqua fredda pare calda.	(The scalded dog thinks cold water hot.) A burnt child dreads the fire.
A cattiva vacca, Dio da corte corna.	To a curst cow, God gives short horns.
A causa persa, parole assai.	(What is done cannot be undone.) Advice comes too late when a thing is done.
A cavallo donato non si guarda in bocca.	Look not a gift horse in the mouth.
Accade ogni giorno nelle città divise, che gli uomini non si curano di impedire il ben' publico, per sbattere la riputazione degli avversari. —*Guicciardini.*	It happens daily in cities where dissensions are rampant, that men do not care if they are hindering the public welfare, so long as they can injure the reputations of their opponents.
Accelerando (*Accel.*)	Gradually faster ; with increasing quickness.
Accelerato	Accelerated.

Accentuare.	To accentuate.
Acciaccatura.	A small quaver written with a stroke running through its stem, to be played rapidly before the large note it precedes.
Accidenti.	Accidentals.
Accigliamento.	Grief.
Acclamazione.	Applause.
Accomodare.	To bring instruments into tune ; to raise them to the same pitch.
Accomodare le bisaccie nella strada.	(To shift the pack-saddles on the road.) To make a sudden change in one's design.
Accomodato.	Adjusted.
Accompagnamento ad libitum.	An accompaniment to be played or omitted at the will of the performer.
Accompagnamento obbligato.	An accompaniment that cannot be omitted.
Accompagnato.	Accompanied.
Accompagnatore.	An accompanist.
Accompagnatrice.	A female accompanist.
Accoppiato.	In connected style.
Accordamento.	In tune.
Accordando.	Tuning.
Accordanza.	In tune.
Accordare.	To tune.
Accordato.	Tuned.
Accordatore.	A tuner of instruments.
Accordo.	A musical chord.
Accordo consono.	A concord.
Accordo dissono.	A discord.
Accrescendo.	More loudly.
Accrescimento.	Increase of sound.
Accresciuto.	With increased loudness.
A cembalo.	For the pianoforte.
A che giova.	What's the good of it ; *cui bono ?*
A chi consiglia non duole il capo.	Counsel is easier than help.
A chi dici il tuo segreto, doni la tua libertà.	You surrender your liberty to him to whom you tell your secrets.
A chi fa male, mai mancano scuse.	Who does evil, is never short of excuse.
A chi ha testa, non manca capello.	A good head need never go short of a hat.
A chi la riesce bene, è tenuto per savio.	He who succeeds, is held to be wise.
A chi non si lascia consigliare, non si può ajutare.	There is no help for him who will not be advised.
A chi, per tempo passar, legge, niuna cosa puote esser lunga.—*Boccaccio.*	To the man who reads in order to amuse himself, nothing can be tedious.
A chi piace il bere, parla sempre di vino.	He who is fond of drinking, talks always of wine.

A chi vuole, non è cosa difficile.
To him who wills, nothing is difficult.

A chi vuole, non mancano modi.
Where there's a will, there is always a way.

A cinque.
In five parts, a quintet.

Acqua cheta rovina i ponti.
(A silent stream destroys the bridges.) Still waters run deep.

Acqua, fumo, e mala femmina, cacciano la gente di casa.
Water, smoke, and a bad wife, drive men out of the house.

Acqua lontana non spegne fuoco vicino.
Distant water does not quench a neighbouring fire.

Acquista buona fama e mettiti a dormire.
A good reputation makes a soft pillow.

Acustica.
Acoustics.

Adagietto.
Rather slow.

Adagio (*Adg⁰·*)
Slowly.

Adagio a ma' passi.
Go slowly over dangerous ground.

Adagio assai.
Very slow.

Adagio cantabile.
Slow and in a singing manner.

Adagio di molto.
Exceedingly slow.

Adagio patetico.
Slow and in a pathetic manner.

Adagio pesante
Slow and well-marked.

Adagio sostenuto.
Slow and sustained.

Adagissimo.
Extremely slow.

Ad arbor che cade, ognun grida—dagli, dagli.
When a tree is falling, all exclaim "Down with it, down with it!"

Ad arca aperta il giusto pecca.
(With an open chest by him, the just man sins.) Opportunity makes the thief.

Addolcendo.
Softening style.

Addolorato.
Afflicted, grieved.

　　　　　　　Ad estirpar que' semi
Di libertà, che in cuor d'ogni uomo ha posto
Natura, oltre i molti anni, arte e maneggio
Vuolsi adoprar, non poco : il sangue sparso
Non gli estingue, li preme ; e assai più feri
Rigermoglian talor dal sangue.
　　　　　　　　　　—*Alfieri*.

　　　　　　　To eradicate
Those seeds of liberty by nature placed
In every human breast, no little art,
And management, besides a length of time,
Are requisite : these seeds may be suppress'd,
By spilling human blood, but not extinguish'd.
And oftentimes from blood they shoot again
With fresh luxuriance.—*C. Lloyd*.

Adiratamente.
In an angry style ; passionately.

Adirato.
Enraged.

Ad ogni cosa è rimedio fuora ch'alla morte.
(For everything there's a remedy except death.) There's a salve for every sore.

Ad ogni santo la sua torcia.
(To every saint his own candle.) Render unto Cæsar the things that are Cæsar's.

Ad ogni santo vien la sua festa.
Every saint has his own festival.

Ad ogni uccello, suo nido è bello. | (Every bird loves its own nest.) There is no place like home. *A chaque oiseau son nid est beau.*

Ad ognuno par più grave la croce sua. | To every man his own cross appears the heaviest.

Ad ora, ad ora, vola tutto il tempo. | Hour by hour, time quickly flies.

Adornamente. | In an ornate manner.

Adornamento. | An adornment.

A due corde. | For two strings.

A due cori. | For two choirs.

A due stromenti. | For two instruments.

A due voci. | For two voices.

Ad un colpo non cade a terra l'albero. | A tree is not felled by one blow.

Affabile. | In affable style.

Affabilmente. | Affably.

Affannato. | In a sorrowful manner.

Affannosamente. | Mournfully.

Affermo bene di nuovo questo essere verissimo, secondo che per tutte l'istorie si vede, che gli uomini possono secondare la fortuna, e non opporsegli, possono tessere gli orditi, e non romperli.—*Machiavelli.* | Once more I declare this to be most true, and every page of history confirms my words, that men can assist Fortune, but they cannot resist her; they may weave her webs, but they cannot break them.

Affettuosamente. | Tenderly.

Affettuoso (*Affet⁰·*) | Softly, affectingly, pathetically.

Afflitto. | (Afflicted.) In a sad manner.

Affogarsi in un bicchier d'acqua. | (To drown oneself in a glass of water.) To make mountains out of mole-hills.

Affrettando. | Hurrying the time.

Affrettare. | To accelerate the time.

Affrettato. | In a hurried manner.

Affrettoso. | Hasty; impetuous.

Agevole. | In an agile manner.

Agevolmente. | In an easy style.

Aggio. | (Exchange, discount.) The difference in value between one sort of money and another, and especially (on the Continent) between notes and coin.

Aggiungere legna al fuoco | To add fuel to the flames.

Aggiustamente. | In strict time.

Agilmente. | Lightly.

Agitamente. | An agitated manner.

Agitato (*Agit⁰·*) | With agitation.

Agitazione. | Agitation.

Ahi quanto cauti gli uomini esser denno Presso a color, che non veggon pur l'opra Ma per entro i pensier miran col senno.   —*Dante.* | Ah! what caution must men use With those who look not at the deed alone, But spy into the thoughts with subtle skill.—*Cary.*

Ai mali estremi, mali rimedi.	For severe ills, severe remedies.
Ai ricchi non mancano parenti.	(The rich have never relations to seek.) Land was never lost for want of an heir.
Ajutati, che Dio l'ajuti.	Heaven helps those who help themselves. *Aide-toi, le ciel t'aidera.*
Al bisogno si conoscono gli amici.	(In the hour of trouble we prove our friends.) A friend in need is a friend indeed.
Al bugiardo non si crede la verità.	No credence is given the liar, even when he speaks the truth.
Al buon vino non bisogna frasca.	Good wine needs no bush.
Al confessor, medico, ed avvocato, non si de' tener il vero celato.	Hide nothing from thy confessor, physician, or lawyer.
Al fine.	To the end.
Al finir del giuoco, si vede chi ha guadagnato.	At the end of the game one may see who hath won.
Al fin la pace È necessaria al vinto, Utile al vincitor.—*Metastasio*	Peace is a necessity for the vanquished, and an advantage to the victor.
Al fresco.	In the fresh, or open, air.
Al giovenile Bollor tutto par lieve.—*Alfieri.*	To the fire of youth all tasks seem light.
Alla barba dei pazzi, il barbier impara a radere.	A barber learns to shave on a fool's chin.
Alla breve.	In the time of one breve to a bar.
Alla buona derrata, pensaci su.	When fine wares are nigh, then stop and buy.
Alla buon' ora.	At last; well done you. *A la bonne heure.*
Alla caccia.	In hunting style; after the manner of the chase.
Alla cappella.	In church style.
Alla Madre.	(To the Mother.) Hymns, etc., addressed to the Virgin Mary.
Alla marcia.	In the style of a march.
All' amico curagli il fico, all' inimico il persico.	Pull a fig for your friend, and a peach for your enemy.
Alla militare.	In military, marching style.
Alla moderna.	In the modern style.
All' antica.	In the ancient manner.
Alla quinta.	At the interval of a fifth.
Allargando.	Lengthening, extending the notes.
Alla rinfusa.	Helter-skelter, higgledy-piggledy.
Alla stretta.	In a compressed style.
Alla zingara.	In gipsy fashion.
Alla zoppa.	In a halting style.
Alle calende greche.	(At the Greek Calends.) When two Sundays come in a week.
Allegramente.	Cheerfully, gaily.

Allegrettino.	Rather slower than Allegro.
Allegretto (*Alltto.*).	Lively, pretty.
Allegrezza.	Cheerfulness, gaiety
Allegrissimamente.	Most cheerfully.
Allegrissimo.	Most cheerful.
Allegro (*Allo.*).	Sprightly, lively.
Allegro agitato.	Quick and in an agitated manner.
Allegro assai.	Very fast.
Allegro comodo.	Quick, but not excessively so.
Allegro con brio.	Quickly and vivaciously.
Allegro con fuoco.	Quick and in fiery style.
Allegro con moto.	Quick, with movement.
Allegro con spirito.	Quick, with spirit.
Allegro di bravura.	Quick, with brilliant execution.
Allegro di molto.	With great rapidity.
Allegro furiosc.	Quick and in a furious manner.
Allegro giusto.	Quick, but with the notes distinctly played.
Allegro ma grazioso.	Quick, but in a graceful style.
Allegro ma non presto.	Quick, but not excessively so.
Allegro ma non troppo.	Quick, but not too rapid.
Allegro risoluto.	Quick and in a bold manner.
Allegro veloce.	In a rapid, cheerful style.
Allegro vivace.	In a rapid, lively style.
Allegro vivo.	Quick and in lively style.
Allentando.	Slackening.
Allentare.	To slacken the time.
All' impossibile nessuno è tenuto.	No one is obliged to do impossibilities.
All' improvviso.	Extemporaneously.
All' inglese.	In the English style.
All' italiana.	In the Italian style.
Al loco.	To return to the original place.
All' opera si conosce il maestro.	(The master is known by his work.) The carpenter is known by his chips.
Allor che Dio sui buoni Fa cader la sventura, ei dona ancora Il cor di sostenerla.—*Manzoni*.	Even when God sends misfortune on the good, still He gives them the heart to endure it.
All' ottava.	An octave above or below.
All' ultimo del salmo si canta la gloria.	(The Gloria is sung at end of the Psalm.) He laughs best who laughs last.
All' unisono.	In unison.
Al male estremo, rimedio violento.	Desperate ills need desperate remedies.
Al molino ed alla sposa sempre manca qualche cosa.	A mill and a woman are always in want of something.
Al nemico che fugge il ponte d'oro.	A bridge of gold for the flying enemy.
Al piacere.	At pleasure.
Al più.	The most.

Al più cattivo porco vien la miglior pera.

It is the most ill-favoured pig that gets the best pear.

Al primo colpo, non cade l'albero.

The tree does not fall at the first blow.

Al rigore di tempo.

In strict time.

Al solito.

In the ordinary manner.

Alta vendetta
D'alto silenzio è figlia.—*Alfieri*.

Deep vengeance is the daughter of deep silence.

Al Tedesco.

In the German manner.

Alterezza.

Loftiness, sublimity.

Alternamente.

Alternately.

Altieramente.

In lofty style.

Altisono.

With a loud echoing sound.

Alto (A or Alt.).

The highest male, and lowest female voice.

Alto rilievo.

(High relief.) Sculpture where the figures carved stand out from the plain surface of the stone.

Altra cosa è il dire, altra il fare.

It is one thing to say, another to do.

Altra risposta, disse, non ti rendo,
Se non lo far : chè la dimanda onesta
Si dee seguir con l' opera tacendo.
　　　　　　　—*Dante*.

" I answer not,"
Said he, " but by the deed. To fair request
Silent performance maketh best return."

Altri tempi, altri costumi.

Other times—other manners.

Altro che!

Certainly; I should think so.

A Lucca ti vidi, a Pisa ti connobbi !

(I saw thee at Lucca, I knew thee at Pisa.) Once bitten, twice shy.

Alzamento di mano.

The upward beat in conducting.

Amabile.

In a gentle manner.

Amabilmente.

Gently.

Amami poco, ma continua.

Love me little, love me long.

Amante non sia chi coraggio non ha.

(Let him not be a lover, who is not courageous.) Faint heart never won fair lady.

Amaramente.

Bitterly.

Amar cosa inamabile non puossi.
　　　　　　　—*Guarini*.

One cannot love an unloveable thing.

Amarissimo.

Very bitter.

Amato non sarai, se a te solo penserai.

If you think of yourself alone, you will not be loved.

A mezza voce.

In a subdued tone.

Amicizia reconciliata piaga mal saldata.

A patched-up friendship is an unhealed wound.

Amico d' ognuno, amico di nessuno.

Everybody's friend is nobody's friend.

Amor, che al cor gentil ratto s' apprende.—*Dante*.

Love, whose lesson a gentle heart doth quickly learn.

Amor, che a nullo amato amar perdona.
　　　　　　　—*Dante*.

Love, that from the loved one takes no denial.

Amor che nella mente mi ragiona.
　　　　　　　—*Dante*.

Love, that discourses in my thoughts.
　　　　　　　—*Cary*.

Amor, ch' or cieco or Argo, ora ne veli
Di benda gli occhi, ora ce gli apri e giri ;
Tu per mille custodie entro a' più casti
Verginei alberghi il guardo altrui
portasti.—*Tasso.*

That Love who now conceals his piercing eyes,
And now, like Argus, every thing descries ;
Who bring'st to view each grace that shuns the light,
And midst a thousand guards directs the lover's sight.—*Hoole.*

Amor depose la faretra e l'arco,
Onde sempre va carco.—*Tasso.*

Love laid aside his bow and quiver, with which he is always armed.

Amore è cieco.

Love is blind.

Amor è il vero prezzo con cui si compra amore.

Love is the true price with which love is bought.

A Moresco.

In Moorish style.

Amor e signoria non vogliono compagnia.

Love and lordship like no fellowship.

Amorevole.

Tenderly ; with much feeling.

Amorevolmente.

In a loving manner.

Amor nel nostro petto
È un volontario affetto ;
Nè mai forza, o rigore
Può limitar la libertà del core.
                    —*Metastasio.*

Love is a feeling that comes into our hearts of our own choice ; for neither force nor harshness can limit the heart's freedom.

Amor non conosce travaglio.

Love never tires.

Amoroso (*Amo·*).

Tenderly, loving.

Amor regge senza legge.

Love rules without laws.

Amor, tosse, e fumo, malamente si nascondono.

Love, a cough, and smoke, are difficult to hide.

Amor tutti fa uguali.

Love makes all men equal.

Anarmonia.

Violations of the rules of harmony,

Anche il mar, che è si grande, si pacifica.

Even the sea, in spite of its vastness, is sometimes calm.

Anche la rana morderebbe se avesse denti.

(Even the frog would bite if it had teeth.) Even the worm will sometimes turn.

Anch' io sono pittore !

I too am a painter !*

Andante (*Andte.*).

Moderately slowly.

Andante affettuoso.

Slowly and in a tender style.

Andante cantabile.

Slow and in a singing style.

Andante con moto.

Slow, with movement.

Andante grazioso.

Slow and graceful.

Andante maestoso.

Slow and in majestic style.

Andante ma non troppo.

Slow, but not too much so.

Andante pastorale.

Slow, and in pastoral style.

Andantino (*Andno.*).

Somewhat livelier than *Andante.*

---

* So Correggio is said to have exclaimed when he beheld the St. Cecilia of Raphael. In his *Miscellanies of Literature,* Mr. I. Disraeli points out that ambitious youths see in the achievements of great men mainly what they feel might be accomplished by themselves. This may account for the popularity of biographies and memoirs of eminent persons, for in such books mediocrities think they read what they themselves might have done had their merits met with their due meed of approbation.

Andare stretto.

(To do business shabbily.) To spoil the ship for a ha'porth of tar.

A nemico che fugge, fa un ponte d'oro.

Make a golden bridge for a flying foe.

Animato (*Anim⁰·*).

With animation.

Animazione.

Animation.

Animosamente.

In a spirited manner.

Anno di neve, anno di bene.

A snow year, a rich year.

A padre guadagnatore, figlio spenditore.

A miserly father has a spendthrift son

Aperta ha la porta chiunque apporta.

Who brings anything finds an open door.

A piacere.

At pleasure; *ad lib.*

A poco a poco.

By little and little; by degrees.

Appassionamente.

In a passionate manner.

Appassionato.

With passion; in an impassioned manner.

Appetito non vuol salse.

Hunger is the best sauce.

Appiccare il Maio ad ogn' uscio.

(To hang the May at every door.) To pay court to every maid.

Appoggiato.

(Propped.) The notes are to be played so as to glide insensibly into each other.

Appoggiatura.

A note inserted between others to effect an easy movement.

A prima vista.

At first sight.

Aquila non mangia mosche.

An eagle does not feed upon flies. *Aquila non capit muscas.*

Arco.

The bow (of the violin, etc.).

Ardentemente.

Ardently.

Ardir, che ai forti è brando, e mente, e scudo.—*Alfieri.*

Audacity is the sword, the shield, and the intelligence of the brave.

Arditamente.

Boldly.

Aria.

An air, song.

Aria buffa.

A comic song.

Aria cantabile.

A singing melody.

Arietta.

A short air or song.

Arioso.

In light, airy manner.

A rivederci *or* A rivederla.

(Till we meet again.) *Au revoir.*

Armonizzare.

To put into correct harmony.

Arpeggio (*Arp⁰·*).

Indicating that the notes are to be struck in rapid succession, not simultaneously, but in quick sequence, as on the harp.

Asino che ha fame mangia d'ogni strame.

An ass which is hungry eats any straw.

Assai.

Enough; very.

Assai ben balla a chi Fortuna suona.

He dances well to whom Fortuna pipes.

Assai presto si fa quel che si fa bene.

What is done well, is never done too slowly.

Assai romor, e poco lana.	Much cry and little wool.
A suo arbitrio.	According to the performer's discretion.
A suo bene placito.	As the performer pleases.
A suo comodo.	According to the convenience of the performer.
A tavola rotonda non si contende del luogo.	At a round table there's no dispute about place.
A tempo.	In time.
A tempo giusto.	In strict time.
A tempo ordinario.	In ordinary time.
Attaca subito.	(Attack suddenly.)　A direction that a second movement is to be begun instantly after the close of the first.
Attorno, attorno.	Here, there, and everywhere.
Avea piacevol viso, abito onesto, Un umil volger d'occhi, un andar grave : Un parlar si benigno e si modesto, Che parea Gabriel che dicesse ; Ave. Era brutta, e diforme in tutto il resto ; Ma nascondea questa fattezze prave Con lungo abito, e largo ; e sotto quello Attossicato avea sempre il coltello. —*Ariosto.*	Her garb was decent, lovely was her face, Her eyes were bashful, sober was her pace ; With speech, whose charms might every heart assail, Like his who gave the blest salute of— Hail ! But all deform'd and brutal was the rest, Which close she covered with her ample vest, Beneath whose folds, prepar'd for bloody strife, Her hand for ever grasp'd a poison'd knife —*Hoole.**
A Venezia chi vi nasce, mal vi si pasce.	He who is born at Venice is badly fed there.
Avere sulla punta della lingua.	To have a thing at the tip of one's tongue.
Aver il diavol addosso.	To have the devil on one's back.)　To be in a rage.
Aver la pera monda.	(To have one's pear ready pared.)　To be born with a silver spoon in one's mouth.
Aver le traveggole.	To see double ;　to see one thing for another.
A vicenda.	Alternately.
A vostro comodo.	At your leisure ;　at your convenience.
Bacio di bocca spesso cuor non tocca.	A kiss of the lips often touches not the heart.
Badate a' fatti vostri.	Mind your own business !
Baldamente.	Boldly ;　in a gay fashion.
Ballatetta.	A short ballad.

---

* A description of **Fraud**, which is here personified.

Ballatore.

A male dancer.

Bambino.

An infant : a little boy.*

Bandito (*pl.* banditi).

An outlaw.

Barba bagnata è mezzo rasa.

(When the beard is lathered, it is half shaved.) *Dimidium facti, qui bene cœpit, habet.*

Barcarola.

(A melody or air sung by the gondoliers of Venice.) A piece of instrumental music in imitation of such airs.

Basso (*B*).

Bass ; the lowest male voice.

Basso rilievo.

(Low relief) ; sculpture where the figures do not stand out far.

Batti il ferro mentre è caldo.

You must strike while the iron is hot.

Battitura.

Beating time.

Battuta.

The accented part of the bar in music ; the part marked in beating time.

Beata fu mai
Gente alcuna per sangue ed oltraggio ?
Solo al vinto non toccano i guai :
Torna in pianto dell' empio il gioir.
                    —*Manzoni.*

Was ever any nation made happy by shedding blood and oppressing ? Nay, it is the conquered alone to whom ills come not, while the mirth of the evil-doer is changed into wailing.

Bella cosa far niente.

Idleness is a nice employment.

Bella cosa tosto è rapita.

A pretty thing is soon taken.

Bella donna e veste tagliuzzata sempre s'imbatte in qualche uncino.

A pretty girl and a tattered gown are sure to find some hook in the way.

Bella femmina che ride, vuol dir, borsa che piange.

When a pretty woman smiles, look to your purse.

Belle parole non pascon i gatti.

(Fine words don't feed cats.) Fine words butter no parsnips.

Bellicosamente

In a war-like manner.

Benchè la bugia sia veloce, la verità l'arriva.

Although a lie is swift, truth catches it at last.

Bene placito.

At pleasure.

Ben fiorisce negli uomini il volere ;
Ma la pioggia continua converte
In bozzacchioni le susine vere.
                    —*Dante.*

                    The will in man
Bears goodly blossoms ; but its ruddy promise
Is, by the dripping of perpetual rain, Made mere abortion.

Ben marcato.

(Well marked.) To be played with emphasis.

Ben moderato.

Very moderate.

Ben perduto è conosciuto.

A thing lost, its value is known.

Ben pronunziato.

The words or notes to be well articulated.

Ben trovato.

Well found ; very ingenious.

Berretta in mano non fece mai danno.

(Cap in hand does no harm.) Politeness costs nothing, but it goes a long way.

---

* The word is commonly used in reference to the representations of the infant Christ in sacred art.

Bersaglieri	(Sharpshooters.) Italian light infantry troops.
Biscanto.	A vocal duet.
Bisogna battere il ferro mentre è caldo.	Strike while the iron is hot.
Bisogna fa trottar la vecchia.	Need makes the old wife trot.
Bisogna tagliare secondo il panno.	You must cut your coat according to your cloth.
Bisogna voltar la vela secondo il vento.	As the wind blows, so you must set the sail.
Bisogno fa l' uomo ingegnoso.	(Necessity makes a man clever.) Necessity is the mother of the arts.
Bocca chiusa, mosca non ci entra.	A closed mouth catcheth no flies.
Bravissimo.	Exceedingly well done.
Bravo.	Well done !
Bravura.	A florid, brilliant, difficult air.
Breve orazione penetra.	God listens to short prayers.
Brillante (*Brill.*).	Brilliant ; lively.
Brio.	Fire.
Buffo.	Comic ; the comic actor in an opera.
Buona nota.	The accented note.
Buon giorno, buon' opera.	The better the day, the better the deed.
Buon principio è la metà dell' opera.	A good beginning is half the work.
Buon vino fa buon sangue.	Good wine makes good blood.
Burlescamente.	Jestingly.
Burletta.	A short comic opera.
Buttar via un vermicello, per pigliar un luccio.	(Set a worm to catch a pike.) A sprat to catch a herring.
Cadenza.	An ornamental passage introduced by a musical performer, either actually or apparently impromptu, and heralding the close.
Cader dalla padella nelle bragie.	To fall out of the frying pan into the fire.
Calando (*Cal⁰·*).	Gradually becoming slower and less vigorous.
Calmato.	Calmly.
Cambiare.	To change.
Cambio non è furto.	Exchange is no robbery.
Camera.	A small room.
Camminando.	Flowing style.
Campana.	A bell.
Campanajo.	A bell-ringer.
Campanile.	A belfry.
Can che morde non abbaja in vano.	A dog that bites does not bark at nothing.
Cane che abbaja poco morde.	Snarling curs are slow to bite.
Cane vecchio non abbaja indarno.	The old dog does not bark for nought.

Canone.	(Canon.) A musical term to indicate that the same melody is taken up by the different parts in succession, at the distance of one or more bars. In the *canone cancrizans* the melody is sung backwards in one of the parts.
Can scottato d'acqua calda ha paura, poi della fredda.	(The scalded dog dreads hot water, and afterwards cold.) The burnt child dreads the fire.
Cantabile (*Cantab.*).	In graceful, elegant, singing style.
Cantafera.	The melody.
Cantajuolo.	A street singer.
Cantando.	In a singing manner.
Cantare a aria.	Singing and improvising at the same time.
Cantare a orecchio.	Singing by ear.
Cantare di maniera.	Singing gracefully.
Cantata.	A composition for one or more voices, including recitatives and airs; now usually a short composition in oratorio form, but without dramatis personæ.
Cantatore.	A male singer.
Cantatrice.	A female singer.
Canti a cappella.	Sacred vocal music.
Canti carnevali.	Songs sung during the Carnival week.
Cantilena.	The part of a composition containing the melody or air.
Canto.	The treble, or highest part in choral music.
Canto funebre.	A funeral hymn.
Canto gregoriano.	Gregorian chant.
Canto primo.	First treble.
Can vecchio non s'avvezza a portar collare.	(An old dog cannot be taught to wear a collar.) It is hard to teach an old dog new tricks.
Canzone.	A song or melody in two or three parts.
Canzonetta.	A canzonet; a short song.
Capo.	The head; beginning.
Capo d' anno.	New Year's Day.
Capo d' opera.	A masterpiece; *chef-d'œuvre*.
Capperi !	Dear me ! Hey-day !
Cappita ! Caspita !	Wonderful !
Capriccio.	An irregular composition, in which the composer follows his fancy or caprice, rather than rule.
Capriccioso.	In free, fantastic style.
Carbonaro (*pl.* carbonari).	(A charcoal-burner.) A member of an Italian secret society; an ultra-democrat.

Carmagnola.

A dance accompanied by singing.

Casa il figlio quando vuoi, e la figlia quando puoi.

Marry your son when you please, and your daughter when you can.

Casa mia, per piccina che tu sia, tu mi pari una badia.

My home, however tiny you may be, You seem a Paradise to me.

Casino.

Club-house.

Cattiva è quella lana, che non si può tingere.

It is a bad cloth that will take no colour.

Cattivo è quel vento che a nessuno è prospero.

It is an ill wind which blows nobody any good.

Cavaliere errante.

A knight errant ; a tramp.

Cavallo che corre non ha bisogno di sproni.

Do not spur the willing horse.

Cavar la castagna dal fuoco con la zampa altrui.

(To get the chestnuts out of the fire with another's paw.) To make a cat's-paw of one.

Cavatina.

An air in one part or movement ; a short, simple air.

Cembalo.

The harpsichord.

Cento carra di pensieri non pagheranno un' oncia di debito.

(A hundred waggon-loads of thoughts will not pay one ounce of debt.) A pound of care will not pay an ounce of debt.

Cercare il pelo nell' uovo.

(To seek the hair in the egg.) To pick faults where no faults are. To find spots in the sun.

Chè cima di giudizio non s' avvalla.
—*Dante.*

(The height of judgment does not stoop.) God's justice is not diverted from its course.

Che dolce più che più giocondo stato
Saria di quel d' un amoroso core ?
Che viver più felice, e più beato
Che ritrovarsi in servitù d' Amore ?
—*Ariosto.*

What state of man such rapture can impart
As the soft passions of an amorous heart ?
What life so blest as his, decreed to prove
With pleasing chains the servitude of Love ?—*Hoole.*

Che dona, e tolle ogn' altro ben fortuna,
Sol in virtù non ha possanza alcuna.
—*Ariosto.*

Fortune, who gives and takes away all other human blessings, has no power over courage.

Che giova nelle fata dar di cozzo ?
—*Dante.*

What profits it to strive against the power of Fate ?

Chè la luce divina è penetrante
Per l' universo, secondo ch' è degno,
Si che nulla le puote essere ostante.
—*Dante.*

For, through the universe
Wherever merited, celestial light
Glides freely, and no obstacle prevents.
—*Cary.*

Chè l' antico valore
Negli Italici cuor non è ancor morto.
—*Petrarch.*

For the ancient courage in the hearts of Italians is not yet dead.

Che la pace mal finge nel volto
Chi si sente la guerra nel cor.
—*Metastasio.*

It is difficult for a man, who has war in his heart, to wear a look of peace upon his brow.

Che 'l perder tempo a chi più sa più
spiace.—*Dante.*

Che 'l sciocco volgo non gli vuol dar
fede
Se non le vede, e tocca chiare, e piane.
—*Ariosto.*

Chè l' uso de' mortali è come fronda
In ramo, che sen va, ed altra viene.
—*Dante.*

Che non men che saver, dubbiar m'
aggrata.—*Dante.*

Che non pùo far d' un cuor, c' abbia
suggetto
Questo crudele, e traditor Amore!
—*Ariosto.*

Che non pur ne' miei occhi è Paradiso.
—*Dante.*

Chè per vendetta mai non sanò piaga.
—*Guarini.*

Che sarà sarà.

　　　　　Chè, seggendo in piuma
In fama non si vien, nè sotto coltre:
Senza la qual chi sua vita consuma
Cotal vestigio in terra di sè lascia,
Qual fumo in aere od in acqua la
schiuma.—*Dante.*

Chè sovente addivien che 'l saggio e 'l
forte
Fabbro a sè stesso è di beata sorte.
—*Tasso.*

Chè spesso avvien che ne' maggior
perigli
Sono i più audaci gli ottimi consigli.
—*Tasso.*

Che talor cresce una beltà un bel
manto.—*Ariosto.*

Chi abbisogna, non abbia vergogna.

Chi ad altri scava la fossa, non di rado
vi cade il primo.

Chi al carbone s'accosta, o si tinge o si
scotta.

Chi, accecato dall' ambizione, si con-
duce in luogo, dove non può più
alto salir, è poi con massimo danno
di cadere necessitato.
—*Machiavelli.*

Chi ama, crede.

Loss of time most grieveth him who
knoweth most.

The herd unletter'd nothing will believe
But what their senses plainly can perceive.—*Hoole.*

　　　　　For, in mortals, use
Is as the leaf upon the bough: that
goes
And other comes instead.—*Cary.*

Ignorance not less than knowledge
charms.—*Cary.*

What can't he do with hearts he has
suppressed,
This cruel one, this wicked traitor Love!
— *Croker.*

These eyes of mine are not thy only
Paradise.—*Cary.**

Revenge never healed a wound.

(What is to be, will be.)   Motto of
the Duke of Bedford.

Fame cometh not by lolling on a couch
of down, or idling 'neath a canopy.
Yet he who spends his life bereft of
fame, leaves no more trace behind
him than doth the smoke in the sky,
or foam upon the sea.

The wise and bold man is often the
architect of his own good fortune.

For it often is the case that in desperate
dangers the boldest counsels are the
best.

Fine clothes often make beauty still
more beautiful.

A needy man must not be shy.

He who lays a trap for others, often is
caught himself.

You cannot play with pitch and not be
defiled.

He who, blinded by ambition, raises
himself to a position whence he cannot mount higher, must thereafter
fall with the greatest loss.

He who loves, trusts.

* This is one of the prettiest *concetti* in the Divine Comedy. Dante's eyes are distracted
from viewing the sights of Paradise to gaze upon the fair form of his beloved Beatrice, who is
conducting him through the abode of the blessed. She remonstrates with him in the words
quoted above.

Chiama gli abitator dell' ombre eterne
Il rauco suon della Tartarea tromba ;
Treman le spazïose atre caverne
E l' aër cieco a quel romor rimbomba.
Nè sì stridendo mai, dalla superne
Regïoni del cielo il folgor piomba,
Nè sì scossa giammai trema la terra
Quando i vapori in sen gravida serra.
            —*Tasso.*

The trumpet now, with hoarse-resounding breath,
Convenes the spirits in the shades of death :
The hollow caverns tremble at the sound ;
The air re-echoes to the noise around !
No louder terrors shake the distant pole,
When through the skies the rattling thunders roll :
Not greater tremors heave the labouring earth
When vapours, pent within, contend for birth !—*Hoole.*

Chi ama me, ama il mio cane.

Love me, love my dog.

Chiaramente.

Clearly.

Chiaro mi fu allor com' ogni dove
In cielo è paradiso.—*Dante.*

Then saw I clearly how each spot in heaven
Is Paradise.—*Cary.*

Chiaroscuro.

An artistic distribution of light and shade.

Chi ascolta alla porta, ode il suo danno.

A listener never hears any good of himself.

Chi asino nasce, asino muore.

He that is born an ass, is always an ass.

Chiave d' oro apre la porta di ferro.

A golden key opens an iron door.

Chiave d'oro apre ogni porta.

A golden key opens any door.

Chi ben cena ben dorme.

He that sups well, sleeps well.

Chi ben congettura, bene indovina.

The best prophet is the best guesser.

Chi ben serra, ben apre.

Safe bind, safe find.

Chi ben vive, ben muore.

A good life makes an easy death.

Chi bestia va a Roma bestia ritorna.

He that goes to Rome a fool returns a fool.

Chi biasima, vuol comprare.

He who decries the goods means to buy them.

Chi burla, vien burlato.

The jest recoils on him who makes it.

Chi cerca mal, mal trova.

He who looks for evil, generally finds it.

Chi compra ha bisogno di cent' occhi, chi vende ne ha assai di uno.

Who buys hath need of a hundred eyes ; who sells hath enough if he hath one.

Chi compra terra, compra guerra.

Who buyeth land, buyeth war.

Chi con l'occhio vede, col cuor crede.

(He that sees with the eye, believes with the heart.)   Seeing is believing.

Chi conta i colpi, o la dovuta offesa,
Mentre arde la tenzon, misura e pesa ?
            —*Tasso.*

A fool is he that comes to preach or prate,
When men with swords their right and wrong debate.—*Fairfax.*

Chi da presto raddoppia il dono.

(He gives twice who gives quickly.) He gives twice who gives in a trice.
Bis dat qui cito dat.

Chi dice i fatti suoi, mal tacerà quelli d' altrui.

He who tells his own business, is seldom silent concerning that of other people.

Chi di gallina nasce convien che raspi, o razzoli.

(What is born of hen will scrape.) What is bred in the bone never comes out of the flesh.

Chi disse popolo, disse veramente un pazzo: perchè egli è un monstro pieno di confusione e d' errore: e le sue opinioni sono tanto lontane dalla verità, quanto è, secondo Tolommeo, la Spagna dall 'Indie.
—*Guicciardini.*

He who speaks of the People, speaks of a madman; for the People is a monster full of confusion and mistakes; and the opinions of the People are as far removed from the truth, as, according to Ptolemy, the Indies are from Spain.

Chi dorme coi cani si sveglia colle pulci.

(Who sleeps with dogs gets up with fleas.) You cannot play with pitch without being defiled.

Chi due lepri caccia, l'una non piglia, e l'altra lascia.

He who hunts two hares, fails to catch either.

Chi è causa del suo mal, pianga sè stesso.

He who has been the author of his own troubles, must bewail them himself.

Chi è ferito d' amoroso strale
D' altra piaga non teme.—*Guarini.*

He who is smitten by the arrow of love, is not afraid of any other wound.

Chi è imbarcato col diavolo, ha da passar in sua compagnia.

He who ships with the devil, must finish the voyage in his company.

Chi è lontano, ha sempre torto.

(The absent are always blamed.) *Les absents ont toujours tort.*

Chi è reo, e buono è tenuto, può fare il male, e non gli è creduto.

The man who is a knave, but is considered honest, is able to do wrong without suspicion.

Chiesa libera in libero stato.

A free church in a free state.*

Chi fa a suo modo, non gli duole il capo.

He who does as he pleases, has no headache.

Chi fabbrica su quel d' altri, perde le calcina e pietre.

He who builds on another's ground loses his mortar and his stone.

Chi fa il conto senza l'oste, gli convien farlo due volte.

He who reckons without his host, must reckon twice.

Chi ferra, inchioda.

(He that shoes a horse pricks him.) It is a good horse that never stumbles, and a good wife that never grumbles.

Chi ha a fare con Tosco non convien esser losco.

He who has to deal with a Tuscan must have both eyes open.

Chi ha arte per tutto ha parte.

(He that has an art, has everywhere a part.) A good workman need never be short of work.

Chi ha denti, non ha pane ; e chi ha pane, non ha denti.

He who has teeth, has no bread ; and he who has bread, has no teeth.

Chi ha da esser impiccato, non sarà mai annegato.

He who is born to be hanged, will never be drowned.

Chi ha in sè alcuna umanità, non si può di quella vittoria interamente rallegrare, della quale tutti i suoi sudditi internamente si contristano.
—*Machiavelli.*

Any monarch, who has any feeling of humanity in him, cannot entirely rejoice in that victory which has brought secret sorrow upon all his subjects.

* The ideal of Cavour which he attempted to realise in Italy.

Chi ha l' amor nel petto, ha lo sprone a' fianchi.

He who has love in his breast, has spurs in his sides.

Chi ha pazienza, vede la sua vendetta.

The patient man sees his vengeance come at last.

Chi ha testa di vetro non vada a battaglia di sassi.

(He who has a head of glass should not fight with stones.) Those who live in glass houses should never throw stones.

Chi la dura la vince.

(Patience conquers hardship.) He that endureth overcomes.

Chi lava il capo all' asino, perde il sapone.

He who washes the head of an ass, wastes his soap.

Chi l'ha per natura, fin alla fossa dura.

That which we have by nature remains with us till death.

Chi mal comincia peggio finisce.

A bad beginning makes a worse ending.

Chi mal pensa, mal abbia.

Evil to him who evil thinks.

Chi mal semina, mal raccoglie.

(He who sows evil, reaps evil.) Sow the wind, and reap the whirlwind.

Chi mette il piè sull' amorosa pania
Cerchi ritrarlo, e non v' inveschi l'ale :
Che non è in somma Amor, se non insania
A giudicio de' savi universale.
　　　　　　　　　　—*Ariosto*.

Whoe'er his feet on Cupid's snares shall set,
Must seek t' escape, ere in th' entangling net
His wings are caught ; for sage experience tells,
In love's extreme, extreme of madness dwells.—*Hoole*.

Chi molte cose comincia, poche ne finisce.

(He that commences much, finishes little.) He has too many irons in the fire.

Chi molto pratica, molto impara.

Practice makes perfect.

Chi nasce bella nasce maritata.

She that is born handsome is born married.

Chi niente sa, di niente dubita.

The ignoramus has no doubts.

Chi non ama il vino, la donna, e il canto
Un pazzo egli sarà e mai un santo.

Who loves not Wine, Woman, and Song,
Remains a fool his whole life long.

Chi non chiede, non ottiene.

(He who asks for nothing, receives nothing.) A timid dog never gets a bone.

Chi non fa, non falla.

He who does nothing makes no blunders.

Chi non fa quando può, non fa quando vuole.

He who will not when he may,
When he will he shall have nay.

Chi non ha cervello, abbia gambe.

(He that has no brains, ought to have legs.) Who has not a good tongue, ought to have good hands.

Chi non ha cuore, abbia gambe.

(He that has no heart [courage] ought to have legs.) One pair of heels is often worth two pairs of hands.

Chi non ha danari in borsa, abbia miel in bocca.

He that has not money in his purse, must have honey in his mouth.

Chi non ha nulla, non è nulla.

He who possesses nothing, is reputed nothing.

Chi non può dimenticare può perdonare.

One may forgive yet not forget.

Chi non può fare come vuole, faccia come può.

He that canno do as he would, must do as he can.

Chi non può quel che vuol, quel che può voglia.—*Guarini.*

He who cannot do what would content him, must be content with what he can.

Chi non rompe l'uova, non fa la frittata.

(He who does not break the eggs, does not make the omelette.) No gains without pains.

Chi non sa adulare, non sa regnare.

He who knows not how to flatter, knows not how to rule.

Chi non sa niente, non dubita di niente.

He who knows nothing, doubts nothing.

Chi non s'arrischia, non guadagna. Chi non risica non rosica.

Nothing venture, nothing have.

Chi non vuol affaticarsi in questo mondo, non ci nasca.

He who will not struggle in this world, should not be born in it.

Chi parla assai, falla spesso.

(Who speaks too much is sure to blunder.) Speech is silvern, silence is golden.

Chi parla semina, chi tace raccoglie.

He who speaks sows, he who is silent gathers.

Chi parla troppo non può parlar sempre bene.—*Goldoni.*

He who speaks too much, cannot always speak well.

Chi per man d'altri s'imbocca, tardi satolla.

He that depends on another man's table often dines late.

Chi piglia leoni in assenza,
Suol temer dei topi in presenza.

He who attacks the lion that is far away, trembles in the presence of a mouse.

Chi più dura, la vince.

Patience conquers in the end.

Chi più intende, più perdona.

(Who knoweth most forgiveth most.) *Tout comprendre c'est tout pardonner.*

Chi più sa, meno parla.

He who knows most, talks least.

Chi pratica con lupi impara a urlar.

(He that keeps company with a wolf will learn to howl.) Tell me who you keep company with, and I'll tell you what you are.

Chi risponde presto, sa poco.

He who answers quickly, knows little of the matter.

Chi s' ajuta il ciel l' ajuta.

Heaven helps the man who helps himself.

Chi semina, raccoglie.

As a man sows so shall he also reap.

Chi serve comune serve nessuno.

(The servant of the public is the servant of no man.) The public rewards its benefactors with ingratitude.

Chi serve in corte muore sulla paglia.

He who serves at the Court dies on a pallet of straw.

Ch si contenta, gode.

Contentment is better than riches.

Chi si fa pecorella, i lupi la mangiano.

He who makes himself a sheep is devoured by the wolves.

Chi si loda, si lorda.

(He who praises himself, does himself no good.) Self praise is no recommendation.

Chi si marita in fretta stenta adagio.

Marry in haste and repent at leisure.

Chi si scusa, s'accusa.

He who excuses himself, accuses himself. *Qui s'excuse s'accuse.*

Chi sputa contra il vento si sputa contra il viso.

(He that spits against the wind spits in his own face.) He that blows in the dust fills his eyes.

Chi tace acconsente.

Silence gives consent.

Chi tace confessa.

(Silence is confession.) Silence gives consent.

Chi tardi arriva male alloggia.

(Who arrives late finds bad accommodation.) The sluggard never gets in time.

Chi tempo ha, e tempo aspetta, tempo perde.

He who has time, and wastes it, never regains it.

Chi t'ha offeso non ti perdona mai.

He that has offended you will never forgive you.

Chi troppo abbraccia, poco stringe.

He who grasps too much obtains little.

Chi tutto abbraccia, nulla stringe.

(He that grasps at all catches none.) Grasp all, lose all.

Chi tutto vuole, tutto perde.

He who wants everything, loses all.

Chi un soldo ti ha rubato, ti prenderà il ducato.

He who robs you of a penny to-day, would rob you of a pound to-morrow.

Chi va al mulino s' infarina.

(He who goes to the mill is covered with flour.) You cannot play with pitch and not be defiled.

Chi va lontan dalla sua patria, vede
Cose da quel, che già credea, lontane,
Che narrandole poi non se gli crede,
Estimato bugiardo ne rimane.— *Ariosto.*

Who travels into foreign climes shall find
What ne'er before was imag'd in his mind;
Which, when he tells, the hearers shall despise,
And deem his strange adventures empty lies.—*Hoole.**

Chi va piano va sano, e chi va sano va lontano.

He who goes slowly goes wisely, and he who goes wisely goes far.

Chi va piano, va sano ed anche lontano.

(He that goes gently goes safely and also far.) Fair and softly go far in a day.

Chi vuol dir mal d'altrui, pensi prima a sè stesso.

He who speaks evil of others, should first examine himself.

Chi vuole avere l'animo tranquillo, impari a comportare l'una e l'altra fortuna, cioè l' avversa e la prospera.
—*Guicciardini.*

The man who wishes to have a tranquil mind, must learn to endure Fortune in both her aspects, that is, both when she frowns and when she smiles.

Chi vuol esser mal servito, tenga assai famiglia.

He who wishes to be served ill, let him keep many servants.

* A quotation which may give comfort to explorers, whose tales of wondrous exploits fail to convince the British public.

Chi vuol gastigar un villano, lo dia a gastigar ad un altro.	(He who would chastise one rogue, should entrust the task to another.) Set a thief to catch a thief.
Chi vuol il lavoro mal fatto, paghi innanzi tratto.	He who wishes work to be badly done, should pay in advance.
Chi vuol saldar piaga non la maneggia.	He who wishes to heal a wound does not open it.
Chi vuol vada, chi non vuol mandi.	He who wishes a thing done, let him go to do it himself; he who does not wish it done, let him send another.
Cicerone.	A guide.
Cicisbèo (Pl. cicisbèi).	A gallant; a philanderer.
Ciò che Dio vuole, Io voglio.	(What God wills, I will.) Motto of Lord Dormer.
Clavicembalo.	A harpsichord.
Coda.	(Tail.) A short passage extending the conclusion of a piece of music.
Colla parte (C. P.), or Colla voce.	(With the part, or voice.) The accompanist is to keep in time with the principal part (in cases where the performer quickens or slackens his pace at pleasure).
Coll' arco. (C. A.)	(With the bow). Indicating that the player is to resume the bow, after notes played by a twitch of the fingers.
Come avviene a un disperato spesso, Che da lontan brama, e disia la morte, E l'odia poi, che se la vede appresso. —Ariosto.	As often happens to a despairing man, who longs and yearns for death when it is not near, yet hates it on its near approach.
Come buon sartore Che, com' egli ha del panno, fa la gonna.—Dante.	Like a good craftsman who cuts his coat according to his cloth.
Come canta il cappellano, così responde, il sagrestano.	As the parson chants, the clerk replies.
Come d' autunno si levan le foglie L'una appresso dell' altra, infin che il ramo Rende alla terra tutte le sue spoglie. —Dante.	As fall the leaves in autumn time, each closely following each, until at length the bough is bared of all its glories. Thick as autumnal leaves, that strew the brooks In Vallombrosa, where the Etrurian shades High over-arch'd imbower.—Milton.
Come i buoni costumi per mantenersi hanno bisogno di buone leggi, così le leggi per mantenersi hanno bisogno di buoni costumi.—Machiavelli.	As good morals need good laws to maintain them, so the laws cannot be maintained without good morals.
Come l'arbore è caduto, ognun vi corre colla scure a far legna.	When the tree has fallen, every man runs up with an axe.
Come l'oro nel foco Così la fede nel dolor s'affina.—Guarini.	As gold is purified in the furnace, so the faithful heart is purified by its afflictions.

Come t' è picciol fallo amaro morso ! — What a grievous pain a little fault doth
                              —*Dante.*   give thee !

Comodo (*Com.*). — Easy ; in comfortable style.

Compagnia d'uno, compagnia di niuno. — (The company of one is the company of none.) One man's company is no company.

Compagno allegro per cammino ti serve per ronzino. — A merry companion on the road is as good as a nag.

Comprare gatta in sacco. — (To buy a cat in a bag.) To buy a pig in a poke.

Con agevolezza. — In an easy, agile style.

Con amore. — (With love.) In an eager, enthusiastic manner.

Con anima. — With animation.

Con brio. — With spirit.

Con celerità. — With speed.

Concertante. — A piece of music, in which several principal instruments or voices take the principal part alternately, the others accompanying.

Concerto — A composition for a single principal instrument, with accompaniments for a full orchestra.

Concerto spirituale. — A sacred concert.

Concetto. — A pretty thought ; *bon mot.*

Con comodo. — At a convenient rate.

Con cura. — Carefully.

Con delicatezza. — With delicacy.

Con diligenza. — Diligently.

Con dolcezza. — With sweetness.

Con dolore. — With grief.

Conduttore. — Conductor.

Con espressione. — With expression.

Confortarsi con gli agliett — (To console oneself with garlic.) To be buoyed up with false hopes.

Con forza. — With force.

Con fuoco. — With fire or spirit.

Con gli amici è questo
Il mio costume antico, ai giusti preghi
Soddisfar tosto e lietamente, e gli altri
Apertamente refiutar.—*Manzoni.* — With friends this has been my old habit, to accede to just prayers promptly and gladly, while such requests as are not just, I openly refuse.

Con grazia. — With grace.

Con gusto. — Tastefully ; in elegant style.

Con la penna e con la spada
Nessun val quanto Torquato. — With the pen, or with the sword none is the peer of Tasso.*

Con la volpe convien volpeggiare — (With the fox we must play the fox.) Set a thief to catch a thief.

---

* Tasso was once attacked in Ferrara by two would-be assassins. He defended himself successfully, and this saying became proverbial.

Con le prevenzioni, e con le diversioni si vincono le guerre. – *Guicciardini.*

Success in war is obtained by anticipating the plans of the enemy, and by diverting their attention from our own designs.

Conoscente (*pl.* conoscenti).

A connoisseur.

Conoscere il pel nell' uovo.

(To know the hair in an egg.) To know on which side one's bread is buttered.

Con pazienza.

Patiently.

Con permesso.

By your leave ; with your permission.

Con piacere.

With pleasure.

Con scienza.

With learning ; with thorough knowledge.

Con sordini.

(With mutes.) With the mutes on the violin to diminish the sound.

Contadina.

A peasant girl.

Con tempo e la paglia, si maturan le nespole.

Time and patience make medlars ripe.

Contesa vecchia tosto si fa nuova.

An old quarrel is soon revived.

Conti chiari amici cari.

(Clear reckonings, dear friends.) Even reckoning keeps long friends.

Conto spesso è amicizia lunga.

Short reckonings make long friendships.

Contrabbasso (*C. B.*).

The double bass ; the largest of the violin class of instruments.

Contrabbandiere.

A smuggler.

Contrada dei nobili.

(The quarter of the nobles.) The fashionable end of a town.

Contra-fagotto.

The double bassoon.

Contralto (*C.*).

The lowest female voice.

Contra miglior voler, voler mal pugna. —*Dante.*

Against a stronger will one's will doth strive in vain.

Contra tenore.

Counter tenor.

Con tutta la forza.

With the full strength.

Con variazione.

With variations.

Conversazione.

A social gathering.

Convien, che ovunque sia, sempre cortese
Sia un cor gentil, ch' esser non può altramente ;
Che per natura, e per abito prese
Quel, che di mutar poi non è possente. — *Ariosto.*

A noble heart by noble deeds is known,
Sway'd by no change, no dictates but its own ;
In every lore of courtesy refin'd,
Where habit stamps what virtue had enjoin'd.—*Hoole.*

Corifeo.

The leader of a band of dancers.

Corimagistro.

The director of a choir.

Corno.

A horn.

Corno di bassetto.

The basset-horn ; a large instrument like the clarionet.

Corno di caccia.

The French hunting horn.

Corno inglese.

The English horn.

Corpo di Bacco !

(Body of Bacchus !) Good Heavens !

Corre lontano chi non torna mai.

He runs far who never turns.

Corte Romana non vuol pecora senza lana.

The Roman Court does not care for sheep without wool.

Corvi con corvi non si cavan gli occhi

Crow does not peck the eyes of crow.

Cosa ben fatta è fatta due volte.

A thing well done is doubly done.

Cosa cambiata non è rubata.

Exchange is no robbery.

Cosa fatta, capo ha.

A thing once done, there is an end.*

Così come un' malato non debbe essere curato, e maneggiato da un' medico, nel quale non ha fede o gli è sospetto : così uno stato, specialmente quando egli è perturbato, non debbe esser' curato o maneggiato da ministri ed uffizieri sospetti ed odiosi al popolo. —*Guicciardini.*

Just as a sick man ought not to be tended and controlled by a physician in whom he has no confidence, so a state, especially when it is in a disturbed condition, ought not to be tended and controlled by ministers and officials whom the people distrust and dislike.

Così fan tutte.

That is the way of all women.

Così fan tutti.

That is the way of the world.

Così trapassa al trapassar d' un giorno
Della vita mortale il fiore e 'l verde :
Nè, perchè faccia indietro april ritorno,
Si rionfiora ella mai, nè si rinverde.
Cogliam la rosa in sul mattino adorno
Di questo dì, che tosto il seren perde :
Cogliam d' amor la rosa ; amiamo or quando
Esser si puote riamato amando.—*Tasso.*

So, in the passing of a day, doth pass
The bud and blossom of the life of man,
Nor e'er doth flourish more, but like the grass
Cut down, becometh withered, pale and wan :
Oh gather then the rose while time thou hast ;
Short is the day, done when it scant began,
Gather the rose of love, while yet thou mayest,
Loving, be loved ; embracing, be embraced.—*Fairfax.*

Cospetto !

Confound it !

Cresce il dì, cresce 'l freddo, dice il pescatore.

As the day lengthens, the cold strengthens, says the fisherman.

Crescendo (*Cr. or Cresc.*).

(Increasingly.) With gradually increasing loudness, indicating that the notes it refers to are to be gradually swelled.

Cuor forte rompe cattiva sorte.

A stout heart breaks down evil fortune.

Da capo (*D. C.*).

From the beginning ; over again.

Da capo al fine.

From the beginning to the end.

Da capo senza repetizione.

From the beginning without any repetition.

Da cappella.

For the church.

Da chi mi fido, mi guardi Iddio ;
Da chi non mi fido mi guarderò io.

From those whom I trust, may God preserve me ; from those whom I trust not, I will preserve myself.

Dal detto al fatto vi è un gran tratto.

From saying to doing is a long step.

* An old proverb quoted by Dante in the *Divina Commedia.* Milton made use of it as a reply to those who warned him that his too arduous studies would destroy his sight.

Dalla rapa non si cava sangue.

(You cannot have blood from a radish.) You can't squeeze blood from a stone.

Dallo spendere assai ne resultano gravezze, dalle gravezze querele.
—*Machiavelli.*

From excessive expenditure (on the part of a Government) discontent results, and discontent provokes complaints.

Dal parlar vostro
Un novo modo di milizia imparo ;
Che i soldati comandino, e che i duci
Ubbidiscano.—*Manzoni.*

From your speech I learn of a new kind of warfare, where the soldiers command and the leaders obey.

Dal segno (*D.S.*).

Repeat from the sign 𝄋

D' amor non s' intende
Chi prudenza ed amore unir pretende.
—*Metastasio.*

He who tries to unite love with prudence knows nothing of love.

Danari fanno danari.

Money makes money.

Dar del naso dentro.

To put one's foot in it.

Dare cazzuole.

To ply with honied words ; to give false promises.

Dare in guardia la lattuga ai paperi.

(To give the lettuce to the keeping of the geese.) To give the wolf the wether to keep.

Dà retta.

I say.   Listen.

Darne consiglio
Spesso non sa chi vuole,
Spesso non vuol chi sa.—*Metastasio.*

The man who is willing to give advice often is unable to do so, while he that has the power to do so has not the will.

Da scherzo.

In a playful style.

Da stagione tutto è buono.

Everything is good in its proper time.

Da teatro.

For the theatre.

Da temersi è chi tace.—*Alfieri.*

The silent foe is he that should be feared.

Da tempo al tempo.

(To time give time.) Time and patience work wonders.

Decamerone.

A period of ten days ; a collection of ten musical compositions.*

Decrescendo. (*Decresc.*)

Decreasing the sound.

Del cuojo d'altri si fanno coregge larghe.

They cut large thongs from other people's leather.

Delle ingiurie il rimedio è lo scordarsi.

The best remedy for wrongs is to forget them.

Del senno di poi n'è piena ogni fossa.

Every ditch is full of wisdom that comes after the event.

Dentro da un orecchio e fuora dall'altro.

In at one ear, and out at the other.

De' peccati de' signori fanno penitenza i poveri.

The poor do penance for the sins of the rich.

Devotissimo suo.

Yours truly.

Di badessa tornar conversa.

(From an abbess to become a lay-sister.) To come down in the world. From horses to asses.

* This is the title of Boccaccio's most famous work. It consists of various stories which Boccaccio puts in the mouths of certain noble ladies and gentlemen who adopted this means to distract their thoughts while Florence was being devastated by the plague. One of the more familiar stories in this collection is the tale of " the patient Griselda."

Di bravura.

In a florid style; with brilliance.

Di buona terra tò la vigna, di buona madre tò la figlia.

(Take a vine of a good soil, and the daughter of a good mother.) Like father, like son.

Di buona volontà sta pieno l'inferno.

Hell is paved with good intentions.

Di buon' ora.

Early.

Di chiaro.

Clearly.

Di colto.

At once.

Diecetto.

A piece written for ten performers.

Di giovani ne muojono molti, di vecchi ne scampa nessuno.

Of young men many die, of old men not any escape.

Di Giovenezza il bel purpureo lume.
—*Tasso.*

(The beauteous purple light of youth.) The bloom of young desire, and purple light of love.—*Gray.*

Dì il vero e affronterai il diavolo.

Speak the truth and shame the devil.

Dilettante (*Pl.* dilettanti).

One that cultivates art or science only by way of amusement or recreation.

Di malvagi ogni terreno abbonda.
—*Metastasio.*

Every land has abundance of knaves.

Diminuendo (*Dim.*).

Gradually decreasing in loudness. Opposite to crescendo.

Dimmi con chi vai, e saprò quello che fai.

(Tell me who you keep company with, and I'll tell you what your character is.) A man is known by his associates.

Dimmi con chi vai, e ti dirò chi sei.

(Tell me who are your friends, and I will tell you what you are.) Birds of a feather flock together.

Di molto.

Very; e.g. *Adagio di molto*, very slow.

Di novello tutto par bello.

All things please when newly seen.

Di nuovo.

Again.

Di' oggimai che la Chiesa di Roma
  Per confondere in sè duo reggimenti
  Cade nel fango, e sè brutta e la
    soma.—*Dante.*

The Church of Rome, uniting two forms of government that ill assort (the temporal and spiritual power), falls into the mud, and defiles both herself and the burden that she carries.

Dio manda il freddo secondo i panni.

(God sends the cold according to the clothes.) He tempers the wind for the shorn lamb.

Dio non voglia

Heaven forbid.

Di padre santalotto figlio diavolotto.

A pious father has a knavish son.

Di posta.

At once.

Di questo Signor splendido ogni intento
Sarà, che 'l popol suo viva contento.
—*Ariosto.*

Of this illustrious lord the sole intent Shall be, to make his people live content.—*Croker.*

Di quieto.

Quietly.

Diretto.

Directed, conducted.

Direttore.

Director, conductor.

Disaccentato.

Unaccented.

Di salto.	By leaps and bounds.
Disarmonichissimo.	Extremely unharmonious.
Disinvolto.	Unrestrainedly.
Disinvolturato.	Free ; without constraint.
Dispicca l'impiccato, che impiccherà poi te.	Save a thief from the gallows, and he'll cut your throat.
Distonare.	To sound out of tune.
Di un dono far due amici.	(With one gift to make two friends.) To kill two birds with one stone.
Divertimento.	A short musical piece, vocal or instrumental, in a light and familiar style.
Divieni tosto vecchio, se vuoi vivere lungamente vecchio.	(You must soon become old, if you wish to live long old.) Old young and old long.
Doglia di moglie morta dura fino alla porta.	Grief for a dead wife lasts as far as the door.
Dolce (*Dol.*).	Soft and sweet (music).
Dolce far niente.	The pleasure of idleness.
Dolcemente.	Softly, with gentleness.
Dolci cose a vedere, e dolci inganni.	(Sweet to the eye and flattering to the sense.) All that glitters is not gold.
Dolente.	Doleful, plaintive.
Dolorosamente.	Sorrowfully.
Doloroso.	The melancholy style ; soft and pathetic (music).
Domanda all' osto s' egli ha buon vino.	(Ask your host if his wine be good.) Ask my companion if I be a thief.
Donne, asini e noci voglion le mani atroci.	Women, asses, and nuts need strong hands to break them.
Donne, preti, e polli non son mai satolli.	Women, priests and poultry are never satisfied.
Dono molto aspettato è venduto, non donato.	(A gift long waited for is sold, given.) He loses his thanks who promiseth and delayeth.
Dopo.	After.
Dopo il cattivo ne vien il buon tempo.	(After bad weather comes good.) After a storm comes a calm.
Dopo la morte non val medicina.	No use to send for a doctor when the patient is dead.
Doppio movimento.	(Double movement.) Exceedingly fast.
Doppio pedale (*Dopp. Ped.*).	Double pedalling in organ playing.
Doppio tempo.	Double time.
Dove entra il bere se n' esce il sapere.	When the wine is in, the wit is out.
Dov' è l'amore, là è l' occhio.	The eye turns to the place where love is.
Dove l'oro parla, ogni lingua tace.	Where gold speaks, every tongue is silent.
Dove sono donne ed oche non vi sono parole poche.	Where there are women and geese, there is plenty of gabble.
Dove sono molto cuochi, la minestra sarà troppo salata.	Too many cooks spoil the broth.

Dove una cosa per sè senza la legge
opera bene, non è necessaria la legge.
—*Machiavelli.*

Where a matter works well without the
interference of the laws, a law is unnecessary.

Dovunque il guardo io giro
Immenso Dio ti vedo :
Nelle opre tue t'ammiro,
Ti riconosco in me.
La terra, il mar, le sfere
Parlan del tuo potere.
Tu sei per tutto, e noi
Tutti viviamo in te.—*Metastasio.*

Wherever I turn my eyes I see Thee, O
omnipresent God : in Thy handi-
works I marvel at Thee, and perceive
Thy hand in mine own self. The
earth, the sea, the heavenly spheres
proclaim Thy power. Thou pervadest
all things, and all men draw their life
from Thee.

Dramma lirico.

Lyric drama.

Dramma per musica.

Musical drama.

Drammaticamente.

Dramatically.

Due.

Two.

Due cori.

Two choirs.

Due pedali.

Two pedals.

Due teste vagliano piu che una sola.

Two heads are better than one.

Duettino.

A short duet.

Duetto.

A duet ; a musical composition for two
voices or two instruments.

Due visi sotto una beretta.

(To carry) two faces under one hood.

Due volte.

Twice.

Dulcicanore.

Harmoniously.

Duolo.

Sorrow, pathos.

Duomo.

A cathedral.

Duramente.

Harshly.

Duro con duro non fa mai buon muro.

Hard with hard makes not a good wall.

E a quel giusto simíl, che fra' ladroni
Perdonando spirava ed esclamando :
Padre, padre, perchè tu m' abban-
doni ?
Per chi a morte lo tragge anch' ei
pregando,
Il popol mio, dicea, che sì delira,
E il mio spirto, Signor, ti racom-
mando.—*Vincenzo Monti.*

And like to the Righteous One, who
hanging among thieves, forgave and
cried out with His latest breath, "My
father, my father, why hast Thou
deserted me" ; so he, praying for
those who dragged him to death,
exclaimed, "My distracted people
and my spirit I commit, O Lord, to
Thee.*

È ardito il gallo sopra il suo letame.

Every cock is bold on his own dunghill.

E caddi, come corpo morto cade.
—*Dante.*

Then swooning, to the ground e'en like
a corpse I fell.†

* A quotation from Monti's *Bassvilliana*, a poem in which he denounces the execution of
Louis XVI., and describes the entry of the French monarch's soul into heaven. Bassville,
whose name is given to the poem, was the ambassador of the French Republic to the Court of
Naples. In 1793 the Romans, shocked by the excesses of the Reign of Terror, and infuriated
by Bassville's bold support of the same, killed the French envoy in the streets of Rome, and
Monti, seeing what was the popular view of the moment, wrote his *Bassvilliana*, whereby he
greatly enhanced his reputation. When, a few years after, Monti, who was a kind of poetical
Vicar of Bray, changed his views, he wrote another poem execrating Louis XVI. in the
bitterest terms, and went so far as to declare that his *Bassvilliana* was written as a jest.
† In the sluggish rhythm of this line, Dante imitates the sound produced by a body falling
to the ground.

È cattivo vento che non è buono per qualcheduno.

It is an ill wind that blows nobody good.

Eccheggiare.

To resound.

È certissimo che muove molto l'instinto dell' onore, il quale nutrisce nel petto degli uomini, l' essere nati nobilmente.—*Guicciardini.*

It is most certain that the instinct of honour, which is fostered in the breast of man, is strongly appealed to when one is conscious of being nobly born.

E chi piglia una tirannide, e non ammazza Bruto, e chi fa uno stato libero, e non ammazza i figliuoli di Bruto, si mantiene poco tempo.
—*Machiavelli.*

He who establishes a despotism, and slays not Brutus, or he who founds a free state and slays not the sons of Brutus, abides for but a little time.*

È come il cane dell' ortolano, che non mangia de' cavoli egli, e non ne lascia mangiar agli altri.

(He is like the gardener's dog, who never eats cabbages himself, nor allows others to eat them.)   He acts like the dog in the manger.

È confermato per proverbio comune, che gli uomini, quando si approssimano i loro infortuni, perdono principalmente la prudenza.
—*Guicciardini.*

A common proverb establishes the fact that, when men see misfortunes threaten them, they, first of all, lose their prudence.

È cosa in questo mondo d' importanza assai conoscer sè stesso, e saper misurare le forze dell' animo e dello stato suo.—*Machiavelli.*

To know oneself is a matter of great importance in this world, so also it is important to be able to estimate the strength of one's mental and physical powers.

È così dolce
Il perdonar quando si vince! e l' ira.
Presto si cambia in amistà ne' cori
Che batton sotto il ferro.—*Manzoni.*

It is so sweet to pardon when we conquer, and wrath is quickly changed to amity in the hearts that throb beneath a soldier's coat.

E dei saper che tutti hanno diletto,
Quanto la sua veduta si profonda
Nel vero, in che si queta ogn' intelletto.—*Dante.*

And all
Are blessed, even as their sight descends
Deeper into the truth, wherein rest is
For every mind.—*Cary.*

E del mio vaneggiar vergogna è l' frutto
E 'l pentirsi, e 'l conoscer chiaramente,
Che quanto piace al mondo è breve sogno.—*Petrarch.*

I blush for all the vanities I've sung,
And find the world's applause a fleeting dream.—*Campbell.*

Ed è sano consiglio
Tosto lasciar quel che tener non puoi.
—*Guarini.*

'Tis the wisest plan quickly to let go that which we cannot hold.

È facile far paura al toro dalla finestra.

(It is easy to frighten a bull from a window.)   All are heroes when no danger is near.

Egli beve il vino in agresto.

(He drinks his wine before it is out of the press.)   He is spending his capital ; he is out-running the constable.

---

* The reference is to the Brutus who expelled the Tarquins from Rome.   Afterwards, when the revolutionists found that his own sons were plotting the return of the exiled kings, he himself condemned them to death.   Brutus, the slayer of Julius Cæsar, claimed the founder of the Roman republic as his ancestor.

Egli è povero come un topo di chiesa.

He is as poor as a church mouse.

Egli è quello che Dio vuole ;
E sarà quello che Dio vorrà !

He is what God wills; he will be what God pleases.*

Egli fa come la volpe dell' uve.

(He acts like the fox with the grapes.) He conceals his discomfiture.

Egli ha il diavol addosso.

(He is carrying the devil on his back.) He is in a furious temper.

Egli m'ha dato un osso da rodere.

(He has given me a bone to gnaw.) A bone to pick.

Egli misura gli altri con la sua canna.

He measures other people by himself.

È gran felicità poter vivere in modo, che non si riceva, nè si faccia ingiuria ad altri ; ma chi s' adduce in grado, che sia necessitato, o a gravare, o a patire, deve per mio consiglio pigliare il tratto a vantaggio ; perchè è così giusta difesa quella, che si fa per non essere offeso, come quella, che si fa quando l' offesa è fatta.—*Guicciardini.*

It is a great happiness to be able to live in such a way that we neither suffer nor inflict wrongs ; but if one is brought to such a pass that he must either hurt another or be hurt himself, he ought, in my judgment, to take the initiative ; for that defence, which is undertaken to prevent an attack, is as just as that which is undertaken after the attack has been delivered.

Egualmente.

Equally.

Ei fu.   Siccome immobile,
Dato il mortal sospiro,
Stette la spoglia immemore
Orba di tanto spiro,
Così percossa, attonita
La terra al nunzio sta.—*Manzoni.*

He passed ; and as immovable
As, with the last sigh given,
Lay his own clay, oblivious,
From that great spirit riven,
So the world stricken and wondering
Stands at the tidings dread.†
          —*W. D. Howells.*

È istinto di natura
L'amor del patrio nido.   Aman anche esse
Le spelonche natie le fiere istesse.
          —*Metastasio.*

The love of home is a natural instinct. Even the wild beasts love their native lairs.

E la sua volontate è nostra pace.
          —*Dante.*

In doing His (God's) will we find our peace.

E la virtù verace
Quasi palma sublime
Sorge con più vigor quando s'opprime.
          —*Metastasio.*

True courage, like the lofty palm tree, rises more vigorously, the more it is pressed down.

Elegantemente.

Elegantly.

È mala cosa esser cattivo, ma è peggiore esser conosciuto.

It is a bad thing to be a knave, but it is worse to be found out.

È mal rubare a casa de' ladri.

(It is hard to rob thieves' houses.) Set a thief to catch a thief.

È meglio aver oggi un uovo, che domani una gallina.

(It is better to have an egg to-day than a hen to-morrow.) A bird in the hand is worth two in the bush.

È meglio aver poco che niente.

Better to have little than nothing.

---

* The motto of the famous soldier Castruccio Castracani.
† The opening lines of *Il Cinque Maggio,* "The Fifth of May," the famous ode that Manzoni wrote upon the death of Napoleon.

È meglio cader dalle finestre che dal tetto.

(It is better to fall from the window than from the roof.) It's never so bad but it might have been worse.

È meglio esser capo di cardella che coda di storione.

Better be the head of a sprat than the tail of a sturgeon.

È meglio esser fortunato che savio.

(It is better to be lucky than wise. Lucky men need little counsel.

È meglio esser mendicante che ignorante.

Better be a beggar than a fool.

È meglio esser solo, che mal accompagnato.

It is better to be alone than in bad company.

È meglio il cuor felice, che la borsa piena.

A contented mind is better than riches.

È meglio invidia che pietà.

It is better to be envied than pitied.

È meglio piegare, che rompere.

It is better to bend than to break.

È meglio senza cibo restar che senz' onore.

(Better be without food than without honour.) Rather death than false of faith.

È meglio tardi che mai.

Better late than never.

È meglio un uccello in gabbia, che cento fuori.

A bird in the hand is worth two in the bush.

Emozione.

With emotion.

È natura degli uomini, quando si partono da uno estremo, nel quale sono stati tenuti violentemente, correre volonterosamente, senza fermarsi nel mezzo, all' altro estremo.
—*Guicciardini.*

It is the nature of men, when they have been kept at one extreme against their will, to rush readily to the other extreme, without pausing half-way to consider.

È natural' degli uomini, d'essere benigni, e mansueti estimatori delle azioni proprie, ma severissimi censori delle azioni d'altri.—*Guicciardini.*

It is innate in men to look with a kind and gentle eye upon their own acts, but to be most severe censors of the actions of others.

Energicamente (*Energ.*).

Energetically.

Enfaticamente.

Emphatically.

Enfiatamente.

Pompously.

Eppur si muove.

Nevertheless, it does move.*

È pur troppo vero.

It is but too true.

Equabilmente.

Equality ; with smoothness.

E quale

Qual havvi affetto che pareggi, o vinca
Quel dolce fremer di pietà, che ogni alto
Cor prova in sè ? che a vendicar gli oltraggi
Val di fortuna ; e più nomar non lascia
Infelici color, che al comun duolo
Porgon sollievo di comune pianto.
—*Alfieri.*

　　　　Tell me what emotion then
Excels or equals that soft beat of pity,
Thrilling the pulses of each noble heart,
Which, of itself, suffices to avenge
The wrongs of fortune ; and no longer leaves
That heart unblest, whose comprehensive love
Embraces everywhere the cause of man.
—*C. Lloyd.*

---

* When Galileo was compelled by the Inquisition to abjure his theories concerning the motion of the earth, he is said to have uttered these words immediately after his enforced renunciation of the truth he had discovered. Unfortunately, the story appears to be a fiction, but it is one of those popular fictions which are hard to kill.

Era già l' ora che volge il disio
Ai naviganti, e intenerisce il core
Lo di ch' han detto ai dolci amici
　addio :
E che lo novo peregrin d' amore
Punge, se ode squilla di lontano
Che paia il giorno pianger che si more.
　　　　　　—*Dante*.

Now was the hour that wakens fond
　desire
In men at sea, and melts their thought-
　ful heart
Who in the morn have bid sweet friends
　farewell,
And pilgrims newly on his road with love
Thrills, if he hear the vesper bell from
　far,
That seems to mourn for the expiring
　day.—*Cary*.

Erba mala presto cresce.

An ill weed grows apace.

Esce di mano a lui che la vagheggia
Prima che sia, a guisa di fanciulla,
Che piangendo e ridendo pargoleggia,
L'anima semplicetta, che sa nulla,
Salvo che, mossa da lieto fattore
Volontier torna a ciò che la trastulla.
　　　　　　—*Dante*

Forth from his plastic hand, who
　charm'd beholds
Her image ere she yet exist, the soul
Comes like a babe, that wantons sport-
　ively,
Weeping and laughing in its wayward
　moods ;
As artless, and as ignorant of aught,
Save that her Maker, being one who
　dwells
With gladness ever willingly she turns
To whate'er yields her joy.—*Cary*.

È sempre buono aver due corde al proprio arco.

It is always well to have two strings to
one's bow.

　　　　È sempre glorioso il posto
Dove si serve la sua patria—*Manzoni*.

That position, in which a man serves
his country, is always honourable.

　　　　E son come d'amor baci baciati
Gl' incontri di due cori amanti amati.
　　　　　　—*Guarini*.

Kisses, when given in love, are, so to
speak, the meeting together of two
loving hearts.

Esornare.

To embellish.

Espressione.

With expression ; feeling.

Espressivo.

Expressively ; with expression.

Essere più di parole che di fatti.

(More talk than deeds.)　Great boast,
small roast.

Esser fortunato come un cane in chiesa.

(To have the same luck as a dog in
a church.)　To be unlucky.

Esser fuori di sè.

To be beside oneself.

Esser tra l'ancudine e il martello.

(To be between the anvil and the hammer.) To be in desperate straits. Between the devil and the deep sea.

Estrinciendo.

To play with decision.

Estro poetico.

(Poetic rage.)　The fervour of inspiration.

È un cattivo andare contro la **corren**te.

It is a bad business to row against the
stream.

È un gran diletto
D' un infido amato punir l'inganno.
　　　　　　— *Metastasio*.

It is a great delight to punish a deceitful lover.

È un gran pacier la morte.—*Manzoni*.

Death is a great peacemaker.

È un mal giuoco dove **nessun** guadagna.

'Tis a sorry game where nobody wins.

È un mal giuoco, quel che non vale la candela.

'Tis a sorry game that is not worth the candle.

Fa bene a te e ai tuoi, e poi agli altri se tu puoi.

(Do good to thyself and thine, and afterwards to others if thou canst.) Charity begins at home.

Fa bene la fortuna questo, che ella elegge un uomo, quando ella voglia condurre cose grandi, di tanto spirito e di tanta virtù che egli conosca quelle occasioni che ella gli porge.
—*Machiavelli.*

This indeed is Fortune's work ; she chooses a man, when she wishes to bring about great events, so full of mettle and merit that he is able to discern the opportunities which Fortune offers him.

Faggiolo.

A flageolet.

Fagotto.

The bassoon.

Fa il bene che dico, e non il male che faccio.

Do as I say, and not as I do.

Falotico.

Fantastic.

Falsetto.

An artificial voice.

Fanciulli piccioli, dolor di testa ; fanciulli grandi, dolor di cuore.

Little children cause the head to ache, but, grown-up, cause the heart to break.

Fantasia.

A musical composition not bound by any strict rules.

Fantastico.

Fantastic.

Fantoccino.

Doll ; puppet.

Fa quel che devi, e n'arrivi ciò che potrà.

Do your duty come what may.

Far castelli in aria.

To build castles in the air.

Far d'una mosca un elefante.

(To make an elephant out of a fly.) To make mountains out of mole-hills.

Fare almanacchi.

(To make calendars.) To build castles in the air ; *châteaux en Espagne.*

Fare le scale di Sant' Ambrogio.

(To be employed on St. Ambrose's stairs.) To spend one's time in idle gossip.*

Far fiasco.

To fail utterly.

Far furore.

To stir up enthusiasm.

Far venir l'acqua alla bocca.

To make one's mouth water.

Fede ed innocenza son reperte
  Solo nei parvoletti.—*Dante.*

Faith and innocence are found in none but babes.

Femmina è cosa garrula e fallace :
Vuole e disvuole ; è folle uom che sen fida.—*Tasso.*

A woman is ever chattering, and ever deceiving : she wills one thing, and then another. Foolish the man who trusts her.

Ferocità.

With fierceness.

Ferventemente.

Fervently.

Festivamente.

In a gay manner.

Fiacco.

In a languid style.

---

* A saying that originated from the habit of village gossips, who are wont to gather outside the church to discuss the scandal of the day.

Fiasco.	An utter failure.
Fiato.	Breath.
Ficcanaso.	Meddlesome intruder.
Ficcare carote.	To tell fibs.
Fieramente.	Proudly.
Figliuolo, il negare è il fiore del plato.	My son, the best policy in a law case is to deny everything.
Figurante.	A theatrical super.
Filar la voce.	To prolong the sound.
Finale.	The final part of a musical piece.
Fin a qui.	To this place.
Finchè la pianta è tenera, bisogna drizzarla.	(You must bend the tree while it is tender.) As the twig grows, the tree's inclined.
Finchè v' è fiato, v' è speranza	While there is life, there is hope.
Fine (*Fin.*).	The end ; finish.
Fioreggiante.	In a florid style.
Fioriture.	Flourishes (in music) ; ornamental passages introduced by a performer.
Fiume torbo guadagno de' pescatori.	It is good fishing in troubled waters.
Flauto.	The flute.
Flauto piccolo.	The small flute ; flageolet.
Flebile (*Flebe.*).	In weeping, mournful style.
Flebilmente.	Dolefully ; with sadness.
Focoso.	In a fiery style.
Foglietto.	A copy of the musical score, used by the leader of an orchestra.
Forte (*F. or For.*).	Loud.
Forte è l'aceto di vin dolce.	(Strong is the vinegar from sweet wine.) The sweetest wine makes the sharpest vinegar. *Corruptio optimi pessima.*
Forte possibile.	Playing as loudly as possible.
Fortissimo (*Ff. or Fo.*).	Very loud.
Forzando (*Forz. or Fz.*).	An emphasis upon a single note.
Fra Modesto non fu mai priore.	(Friar Modest was never a prior.) Cry your own wares if you wish to sell them.
Freddamente.	With coldness.
Fregiatura.	A musical embellishment.
Frescamente.	Freshly, with vigour.
Fretta.	With speed, haste.
Frottala.	A ballad.
Fuga.	A fugue.
Fuga doppia.	A double fugue.
Fugato.	A piece containing passages in imitation of the fugue style, but not a regular fugue.
Funhetta.	A short fugue.
Funzioni.	Masses *or* oratorios.

Furiosamente.	Furiously.
Furioso (*Fur⁰·*).	Vehemently.
Furore.	Great attraction, enthusiasm, fury, rage.

Gajo.	Gaily; merrily.
Galantemente.	In a graceful pleasing manner.
Galantuomo.	An honest man; a gentleman.
Gamma.	(The gamut.) The scale of any key.
Gatta guantata non piglia mai sorce.	(A gloved cat never catches mice.) A muffled cat is no good mouser.
Gaudioso.	Joyously.
Gavotta.	A lively dance tune; originally a French dance—*gavotte*.
Generalissimo.	Commander-in-chief.
Gettar le margherite ai porci.	To throw your pearls before swine.
Giga.	A jig.
Giochevole.	In a jocose, merry style.
Giocoso.	Humorously; in a sportive vein.
Giojoso.	Joyously.
Giorno delle ceneri.	Ash-Wednesday.
Gioviale.	Jovial.
Giovine ozioso, vecchio bisognoso.	A young man idle, an old man needy.
Giovine Santo, Diavolo vecchio.	(A young saint, an old devil.) Early piety is often deceptive.
Giubilante.	In a jubilant manner.
Giudico il mondo sempre essere stato ad un medesimo modo, ed in quello essere stato tanto di buono, quanto di tristo. —*Machiavelli*.	I judge the world to have always been alike, and to have always had as much good as evil in it.
Giulivissimo.	Very joyful.
Giuoco di mano giuoco di villano.	Horseplay is roughs' play.
Giustamente.	Strictly; with precision.
Giusto.	Exact.
Gli ambasciadori essere l' occhio, e l' orecchio degli Stati. —*Guicciardini*.	Ambassadors are the eyes and ears of the countries they represent.
Gli amici legano la borsa con un filo di ragnatelo.	(Friends fasten their purses with a spider's thread.) True friends give help unasked.
Gli assenti hanno torto.	The absent are always in the wrong.
Glissando.	(In a gliding manner.) The effect produced by gliding the fingers along the keys.
Glissato.	In a slurred style.
Gli uomini hanno gli anni che sentono, e le donne quelli che mostrano.	Men are as old as they feel, but women are as old as they look.
Gli uomini oziosi sono istrumento a chi vuole alterare.—*Machiavelli*.	Idle folk are instruments ready to the hand of a revolutionist.

Gli uomini quasi tutti naturalmente sempre preporrano, il rispetto dell' interesse loro : e sono pochissimi quelli, che conoscono quanto vaglia la gloria, e l' onore.—*Guicciardini.*

Men, for the most part, will naturally pay chief regard to their own interests ; and there are very few who know the value of glory and honour.

Goccia a goccia s' incava la pietra.

Drop by drop wears away the stone.

Gorgheggi.

Vocal exercises to be sung quickly.

Grado ascendente.

An ascending degree.

Grado descendente.

A descending degree.

Granata nuova spazza ben la casa.

New brooms sweep clean.

Grandioso.

In grand, lofty style.

Grandisonante.

Very sonorously.

Gran tamburo.

A large drum.

Grappa.

A brace or bracket connecting two or more staves.

Grassa cucina, magro testamento.

A fat kitchen, a lean will.

Grazia.

With grace.

Graziosamente.

Gracefully, in a charming manner.

Grazioso (*Graz.*).

In a flowing, graceful movement.

Gruppetto.

A small group of musical notes ; the embellishment called " a turn."

Guarda innanzi che tu salti.

Look before you leap.

Guardati d' aceto di vin dolce.

(Beware of vinegar made from sweet wine.) Beware the anger of a patient man.

Guardati da chi non ha da perdere.

Beware of him that has nothing to lose.

Gusto.

Taste, enjoyment, zest.

Gustosamente.

Tastefully.

Gustoso.

Tasteful ; expressive.

Harmonici.

Harmonics.

Ha sempre dimostrato l' esperienza, e lo dimostra la ragione, che mai succedono bene le cose, che dependono da molti.—*Guicciardini.*

Experience has always proved, and reason confirms, that things which depend upon the efforts of many for their accomplishment, are never brought to a successful issue.

I consigli che procedono da capo canuto e pieno d' esperienza, sono più utili. —*Machiavelli.*

The advice which comes from a head that is grey and full of experience, is the wisest and best.

I consigli nuovi, ed inusitati possono al primo aspetto, parere forse più gloriosi, e più magnanimi, ma riescono poi senza dubbio più pericolosi, e più fallaci di quegli, che in ogni tempo, ha appresso a tutti gli uomini approvato la ragione, e l' esperienza. —*Guicciardini.*

New and untried ideas may, at first sight, appear more splendid and nobler (than those in vogue), but afterwards they unquestionably prove more dangerous and more deceitful than those which, in every age, the reason and experience of the majority of mankind has approved of.

I danari del comune sono come l' acqua benedetta, ognun ne piglia.

Public money is like holy water, all take some as they can.

I danari fanno correre i cavalli. | It is money that makes the mare to go.

Idillio. | An idyl ; a pastoral poem.

I due contrari fan che il terzo goda. | (When two fall out, the third rejoices.) When thieves fall out, honest men come by their own.

I fatti sono maschi, le parole femmine. | (Deeds are males, words females.) Actions befit men, words befit women.

I frutti proibiti sono i più dolci. | Stolen fruit is the sweetest.

I governi ben regolati hanno canove pubbliche da mangiare e da bere, e da ardere per un anno.—*Machiavelli.* | Well-regulated governments maintain a store of provisions and fuel sufficient for one year.

I gran dolori sono muti. | Great sorrows are dumb.

I guadagni mediocri empiono la borsa. | (Moderate gains fill the purse.) Take care of the pence, and the pounds will take care of themselves.

Il buono è buono, ma il meglio vince. | Good is good, but better is better.

Il buon sangue giammai non può mentire. | (Good blood cannot lie !) True nobility always shows itself.

Il cane dell' ortolano non mangia la lattuga, e non la lascia mangiare agli altri. | (The gardener's dog does not eat the lettuce himself and does not allow others to do so.) The dog in the manger.

Il danaro è fratello del danaro. | (Money is the brother of money.) One penny earns another.

Il diavolo non è così brutto come si dipinge. | The devil is not so black as he is painted.

Il diavolo tenta tutti, ma l' ozioso tenta il diavolo. | The devil tempts everyone, but the lazy man tempts the devil.

Il fine perchè i ministri sono mandati in una città è di reggere e governare i sudditi con amore e con giustizia, e non stare a gareggiare e contendere insieme ; ma aversi a intender bene, come fratelli, e cittadini mandati da un medesimo principe.—*Machiavelli.* | The end and purpose, for which magistrates are sent to administer the affairs of a city, is that they shall govern the inhabitants in a kind and just manner ; and they ought not to wrangle and squabble among themselves, but to act as colleagues and fellow-citizens who have been appointed by the same ruler.

Il fine loda l'opera. | (The end praises the work.) The end crowns the work.

Il lupo cangia il pelo, ma non il vizio. | The wolf changes his coat, but not his nature.

Il Maestro di color che sanno.—*Dante.* | The Master of the wise.*

Il male per libra viene, va via per once. | Sorrows come in pounds, and go in ounces.

Il meglio è l' inimico del bene. | (Better is the enemy of good.) *Le mieux est l'ennemi du bien.*

Il merto d' ubbidir perde chi chiede La ragion del comando.—*Metastasio.* | He loses the merit of obedience who asks why the command is given.

Il mondo è di chi ha pazienza. | (The world belongs to the patient man.) *Tout vient à point à qui sait attendre.*

* Dante speaks in these terms of Aristotle, of whom he was a great admirer.

Il mondo è di chi se lo piglia.

(The world belongs to the bold man.) Fortune favours the brave.

Il mondo è fatto a scale ; chi le scende, e chi le sale.

The world is like a staircase, which one goes up and another comes down.

Il mondo è un bel libro, ma poco serve a chi non lo sa leggere.—*Goldoni.*

The world is a beautiful book, but it is of little use to him who cannot read it.

Il perdonare viene da animo generoso. —*Machiavelli.*

Forgiveness proceeds from a generous soul.

Il pianger noi Cosa fatta non toglie.—*Alfieri.*

Our tears will not undo what has been done.

Il più crudel tormento, Ch' hanno i malvagi, è il conservar nel core Ancora a lor dispetto, L' idea del giusto, e dell' onesto i semi.—*Metastasio.*

The most cruel torment that evil-doers suffer, is the fact that they still have the idea of righteousness and the germs of honesty in their hearts, whether they wish it or not.

Il più delle volte le avversità non vadino sole.—*Guicciardini.*

In the majority of cases misfortunes do not come alone.

Il più forte ha sempre ragione.

Right is always on the side of the strongest.

Il poco mangiar e poco parlare non fece mai male.

Eating little and speaking little have never injured anyone.

Il poter sommo Più si rafferma quanto men lo mostri. —*Alfieri.*

Despotic power is strengthened most when least displayed.

Il sangue del soldato fa grande il capitano.

(The soldier's blood makes his leader great.) The privates do the fighting and the generals gain the rewards.

Il savio udendo, più savio diventa.

(The wise man by listening becomes still wiser.) Lay your hand on your mouth and let your soul be instructed.

Il secondo pensiero è il migliore.

Second thoughts are best.

Il soccorso di Pisa, cioè che viene nel tempo.

Pisa's help ; assistance that never comes in time.

Il soldato per far male è ben pagato.

The soldier is well paid for doing mischief.

Il soverchio dolor t' ha fatto insano. —*Guarini.*

Too much grief doth make thee mad.

Il tempo non indugia per nessuno.

(Time waits for nobody.) Time and tide wait for no man.

Il timor di Dio facilita qualunque impresa che si disegna nei governi. —*Machiavelli.*

The fear of God furthers every enterprise that governments do undertake.

Il vero punge, e la bugia unge.

Truth stings, while falsehood soothes.

Il voler tutto a un tempo, a un tempo spesso Fea perder tutto.—*Alfieri.*

To wish for all at once doth often cause at once the loss of all.

Il volto sciolto ed i pensieri stretti.

(The countenance open, but the thoughts strictly reserved.) The wise keep ears open and mouths shut.

Italian	English
I matti fanno le feste, ed i savi se le godono.	Fools make feasts, and wise men enjoy them.
Imbroglio.	Confusion.
Impazientemente.	Impatiently.
Imperiosamente.	Impetuously.
Impeto.	In impetuous style.
Impetuosamente.	Impetuously.
Imponente.	Imposing.
Impresario.	Manager of an opera company; contractor.
Improvvisata.	Extemporaneous composition.
Improvvisatore.	An extemporaneous composer.
In alt.	An octave above the treble fifth line.
In altissimo.	Notes above the octave in alt.
Incertezza.	Uncertainty, with indecision.
Incognito (*incog.*).	Unknown; unrecognised; under an assumed name.
Incordamento.	The tension of the strings of instruments.
In disgrazia della giustizia.	Under the frown of justice; under a cloud.
Infinite sono le varietà delle nature, e dei pensieri degli uomini, però non si può imaginar' cosa, nè si stravagante, nè si contra ragione, che non sia secondo il cervello d' alcuno.—*Guicciardini.*	Infinite is the variety of dispositions and thoughts among men; therefore one cannot imagine anything, however extravagant or irrational it may be, that is not in accord with the ideas of somebody.
In fretta.	In haste, hurriedly.
Inganno.	A trick; deception; an unexpected transition from one chord to another.
Inglese Italianizzato, Diavolo incarnato.	An Englishman Italianized is the devil incarnate.
Innamorato.	(In love.) Lover.
Innocentemente.	Innocently; with artlessness.
In organno.	An old term for part music.
In petto.	Concealed within the breast; in reserve.*
Insensibilmente.	Imperceptibly.
Instrumento a campanella.	An instrument consisting of bells, played by means of a key-board.
Instrumento a corda.	A stringed instrument.
Instrumento da flato.	A wind instrument.
Instrumento da quilla.	A spinet.
In tempo.	In time.
Intermezzo.	A musical interlude; a short dramatic piece light and sparkling, introduced between the parts of a large work (drama, opera, etc.).

* This term is applied to those Cardinals of the Roman Church who hold no bishopric or other benefice.

In terra di ciechi, beato chi ha un occhio.

Intrada.

Introduzione.

In tutte le azioni umane, e nelle guerre massimamente, bisogna accomodare il consiglio alla necessità.
—*Guicciardini.*

In un batter d' occhio.

In un giorno non si fe' Roma.

In un governo bene istituito, le guerre, le paci, le amicizie, non per soddisfazione di pochi, ma per bene comune, si deliberano.—*Machiavelli.*

In un governo bene ist it uito, le leggi si ordinano secondo il bene pubblico, non secondo l' ambizione di pochi.
—*Machiavelli.*

In uno stato, che sta la maggior parte del tempo ozioso, non può nascere uomini nelle faccende eccellenti.
—*Machiavelli.*

Io dirò cosa incredibile e vero.—*Dante.*

Io ho considerato più volte come la cagione della trista e della buona fortuna degli uomini è riscontrare il modo del procedere suo con i tempi.
—*Machiavelli.*

Io non deludo, affronto I tiranni.—*Alfieri.*

Io sarei pronto a cercare le mutazioni degli stati, che non mi piacessero, s'io potessi sperare di mutarli da me solo : ma quando io mi ricordo, che bisogna far prima con altri ; ed il più delle volte con pazzi e con maligni, i quali non sanno tacere, nè sanno fare, non è cosa ch' io aborrisca più che il pensare a quello.—*Guicciardini.*

Io sono un cacio fra due grattugie.

I pazzi per lettera sono i maggiori pazzi.

I pensieri non pagano gabelle.

I piccoli cani trovano, ma i grandi hanno la lepre.

I popoli s' ammazzano ed i principi s' abbracciano.

Istesso tempo.

In the country of the blind the one-eyed is king.

A prelude.

The introduction ; the opening movement of a musical piece.

In all human affairs, and especially in war, we must subordinate our plans to the necessities of the case.

In the twinkling of an eye.

Rome was not built in a day.

In a well-constituted government, the consideration of war, peace and alliances is conducted, not with a view to the advantage of the few, but in the interest of the common welfare.

In a well-constituted state, the laws are made to further the interests of all the citizens, and not to serve the ambitious projects of the minority.

In a state, which remains inactive for the greater part of its existence, men distinguished in achievement cannot be produced.

A thing incredible I tell, though true.
—*Cary.*

I have often thought that the cause of the success or failure of men depends upon their way of adapting themselves to the times they live in.

I brave, but I delude not, e'en a tyrant.

I should be ready to attempt to reform institutions which do not please me, could I hope to effect these changes unaided : but when I remember that I must ask the assistance of others—men who are often fools and knaves, and who are unable to act or be silent—I shrink even from the contemplation of such an attempt.

(I am a cheese between two graters.) I am between the devil and the deep sea.

No fool's so foolish as the learned fool.

Thoughts don't pay taxes.

(The little dogs start, but the big ones catch the hare.) One sows, another reaps.

The nations slay one another while their kings embrace.

Same time.

Italia, Italia, O tu cui diè la Sorte
Dono infelice di bellezza, ond' hai
Funesta dote d' infiniti guai,
Che 'n fronte scritte per gran doglia
    porte ;
Deh fossi tu men bella, o almen più
    forte,
Ond' assai più ti paventasse, o assai
T'amasse men, chi del tuo bello a i rai
Par che si strugga, e pur ti sfida a
    morte.—*Vincenzo Filicaja.*

Italia ! oh Italia ! Thou who hast
The fatal gift of beauty, which became
A funeral dower of present woes and
    past,
On thy sweet brow is sorrow ploughed
    by shame,
And annals graved in characters of
    flame.
Oh God ! That thou wert in thy naked-
    ness
Less lovely or more powerful, and
    couldst claim
Thy right, and awe the robbers back
    who press
To shed thy blood, and drink the tears
    of thy distress.—*Lord Byron.*

Jubiloso.

Jubilant ; to be played in a lively style.

L' abito non fa il monaco.
La carta non diventa rossa.
La colpa seguirà la parte offensa
In grido, come suol.—*Dante.*

The cowl does not make the monk.
Paper does not blush.
        The common cry
Will, as 'tis ever wont, affix the blame
Unto the party injured.—*Cary.*

La comodità fa l' uomo ladro.
La conscienza vale per mille testimoni.

Opportunity makes the thief.
A good conscience is better than a thou-
    sand witnesses.

Lacrimando.
Lacrimoso.
La diversità delle opinioni fra le oneste
    persone non dee mai rompere le
    amicizie.—*Vincenzo Monti.*
La Divina Commedia.
La donna è mobile.
La fame muta le fave in mandole.

In a weeping style.
Tearful ; in a mournful style.
Difference of opinion among honest
    people ought never to sever the bonds
    of friendship.
The Divine Comedy.*
Woman is a fickle thing.†
Hunger makes a bean taste like an
    almond.

La fame non vuol legge.
La fiamma è poco lontana dal fumo.

Hunger knows no laws.
(The flame is not far from the smoke.)
    Where there is smoke there is sure to
    be fire.

La fortuna ajuta i pazzi.
La gola, e 'l sonno, e l' oziose piume
Hanno del mondo ogni virtù sbandita.
                        —*Petrarch.*
Lagrimoso.
La lingua batte dove il dente duole.

Fortune favours fools.
Gluttony, sloth, and luxurious idleness
    have banished every virtue from the
    world.
In tearful, mournful style.
The tongue always touches the aching
    tooth.

---

* The title of Dante's famous epic, which is divided into three parts, *Inferno, Purgatorio* and *Paradiso*, Hell, Purgatory, and Paradise.
† The name of a familiar air in Verdi's opera *Rigoletto.*

La lingua non ha osso, ma si fa rompere il dosso.

(The tongue lacks bone but it gains us a broken back.) The tongue is a sharp sword.

L' allegro.

The merry man ; mirth.*

La madre pietosa fa la figliuola tignosa.

(A too fond mother has a scabby daughter.) Spare the rod, and spoil the child.

La mala compagnia è quella che mena gli uomini alla forca.

Bad company is what brings men to the gallows.

La mala erba cresce presto.

Evil weeds grow apace.

La maraviglia
Dell' ignoranza è figlia
E madre del saper.—*Metastasio*.

Wonder is the daughter of ignorance and the mother of knowledge.

L' ambizione dell' onore, e della gloria è laudabile, ed utile al mondo perchè dà causa agli uomini di pensare, e far cose generose ed eccelse.
— *Guicciardini.*

The ambition of honour and glory is praiseworthy, and is advantageous to the world, since it causes men to think on, and to engage actively in noble and laudable enterprises.

La memoria delle ingiurie essere maggiore senza dubbio, e più implacabile in chi le fa, che in chi le riceve.
—*Guicciardini.*

The recollection of injuries is certainly more acute and more vivid in the mind of him who inflicts, than in the mind of him who suffers them.

Lamentabile *or* Lamentevole.

In plaintive style.

Lamentabilmente.

Sorrowfully.

Lamentando.

Lamenting.

L' amico mio, e non della ventura.
—*Dante.*

A friend, not of my fortune but myself.
—*Cary*.

L' amor che muove il sole e l' altre stelle.
—*Dante.*

Love which moves the sun and other stars of heaven.

L' Amor di Libertà, bello se stanza
In cor gentile ; e se in cuor basso e lordo
Non virtù, ma furore e sceleranza.
— *Vincenzo Monti.*

The love of Liberty finds its fitting home in a noble heart ; but in a heart base and impure it is nothing but frenzy and wickedness.

La natura dei popoli è, come è ancora dei privati, voler sempre augumentare del grado, in che si trovano ; però è prudenza, cominciare a negar loro le prime cose, che domandano : perchè, concedendoglile, non li fermi, anzi gl' inviti a domandar più, e con maggiore instanza, che non facevano da principio : perchè col dare spesso a bere, si accresce, ed augumenta tutta via la sete.—*Guicciardini.*

The nature of people collectively is like that of individuals ; they are always eager to raise themselves from the station in which they find themselves ; nevertheless, it is prudent to begin by denying them their first requests ; for by making concessions to them, you do not satisfy them, but invite them to ask for more, and with greater vigour than they employed at first ; for by frequent drinking thirst is increased and made keener.

Languendo *or* Languente.

Languishingly.

L' anima tua è da viltate offesa :
La qual molte fiate l' uomo ingombra,
Si che d' onrata impresa lo rivolve,
Come falso veder bestia, quando ombra.
—*Dante.*

Thy soul is by vile fear assail'd, which oft So overcasts a man, that he recoils From noblest resolution, like a beast, At some false semblance in the twilight gloom.—*Cary.*

---

* The title of one of Milton's shorter poems.

L' animo fermo mostra che la fortuna non ha potenza sopra di lui.
—*Machiavelli.*

A steadfast soul shows that Fortune has no power over it.

La notte è madre del consiglio.

Night is the mother of counsel.

La patria è un Nume,
A cui sacrificar tutto è permesso.
—*Metastasio.*

Our country is a god to whom we may make every sacrifice.

La pigrizia è sempre bisognosa.

(Idleness is always in want.)   He that will not work, neither shall he eat.

La più trista ruota del carro è quella che cigola.

The worst wheel in the waggon creaks the loudest.

La plebe, sicura per la povertà di non poter' perdere è sempre per sua natura cupida di cose nuove.—*Guicciardini.*

The lower orders, feeling that they themselves are unable to lose anything by reason of their poverty, are always by nature inclined to revolution.

La povertà è la madre di tutte le arti.

Necessity is the mother of invention.

La povertà guasta l' amistà.

(Poverty spoils friendship.)   When poverty comes in at the door, love flies out of the window.

La pratica val più della grammatica.

Experience is the best teacher.

La prima arte del regno
È il soffrir l'odio altrui. – *Metastasio.*

The first qualification of a ruler is the ability to endure the hatred of others.

La prima carità comincia da sè.

Charity begins at home.

La prima pioggia è quella che bagna.

(It is the first shower that wets.)   It is the first step that costs.

L' arco si rompe, se sta troppo teso.

The bow breaks if it is kept too taut.

La reputazione che si trae da' parenti e da' padri è fallace, ed in poco si consuma, quando la virtù propria non l'accompagna.—*Machiavelli.*

The reputation that is derived from the possession of noble kindred and ancestors is untrustworthy, and it quickly perishes, if it is not accompanied by personal merit.

Largamente.

In a broad style.

Larghetto (*Largh.*).

A degree faster than *largo.*

Larghissimo.

Extremely slowly.

Largo (*Larg.*).

A slow, solemn movement in music.

Lascia dir le genti;
Sta come torre fermo, che non crolla
Giammai la cima per sofflar de' venti.
Chè sempre l' uomo in cui pensier rampolla
Sovra pensier, da sè dilunga il segno
Perchè la foga l' un dell' altro insolla
—*Dante.*

To their babblings leave
The crowd.   Be as a tower, that firmly set,
Shades not its top for any blast that blows,
He in whose bosom thought on thought shoots out,
Still of his aim is wide, in that the one
Sicklies and wastes to nought the other's strength.—*Cary.*

Lascia, lascia le selve
Folle garzon, lascia le fere, ed ama.
—*Guarini.*

Leave, leave the woods, silly boy, leave thy hunting, and learn to love.

Lasciate ogni speranza, voi ch' entrate !
—*Dante.*

Abandon hope, all ye who enter here.*

* See note on *Per me si va nella città dolente* in this section.

F F

La siepe non ha occhi, ma orecchie si.

(The hedge has no eyes, but it has ears.) *Les murailles ont des oreilles.* Walls have ears.

La speranza é il pan de' miseri.

Hope is the poor man's bread.

La speranza è l'ultima ch' abbandona l'infelice.

Hope is the last friend to desert the unfortunate.

La superbia andò a cavallo, e tornò a piedi.

Pride set out on horseback, and came back on foot.

La troppa familiarità genera disprezzo.

Too much familiarity breeds contempt.

Lauda la moglie e tienti donzello.

Praise married life, but remain single.

L'avere ottenute le cose desiderate, non diminuisce, ma accresce sempre i disegni di maggior' voglie, e di maggiori concetti.—*Guicciardini.*

Success in obtaining our desires does not diminish but rather increases the extent of our aspirations, and enlarges the scope of our ideas.

La verità è figlia del Tempo.

Truth is time's daughter.

La virtù degli uomini anche al nemico è accetta, quanto la viltà e la malignità dispiace.—*Machiavelli.*

Courage and merit in men are appreciated even by their enemies, while cowardice and a base spirit are loathed.

Lazzaretto.

A pest house ; a quarantine hospital.

Lazzaroni.

Idle vagabonds.

Le armi si debbono riservare in ultimo luogo, dove, e quando gli altri modi non bastino.—*Machiavelli.*

An appeal to war ought to be resorted to last of all, when all other methods (of conciliation) have failed.

Le bestemmie ritornano donde partirono.

Curses come home to roost.

Le cattive nuove sono le prime.

Bad news comes soon enough.

Le comparazioni sono tutte odiose.

Comparisons are always odious.

Le disgrazie non vengon mai sole.

Troubles never come alone.

Legatissimo.

Exceedingly smooth.

Legato (*Leg.*).

In a smooth continuous style ; without a break between the notes.

Legatura.

A bind or tie.

Leggiero *or* Leggieramente.

Lightly.

Legno.

A wooden bow stick.

L' elefante non sente il morso della pulce.

The elephant does not feel the bite of the flea.

Le leggi fanno gli uomini buoni.
—*Machiavelli.*

It is the laws that make men good.

Le leggi senza i costumi approfittano poco.—*Guicciardini.*

Laws are of little avail where there are no morals.

Le leggi son, ma chi pon mano ad esse ?
—*Dante.*

Laws there are, but what men heed them ?

Lentando.

Gradually becoming slower.

Lento (*Lnto.*).

Slow.

L' esperienza è ottima maestra.

(There is no teacher like experience.) *Experientia docet.*

Libretto.

The words of a play or opera.

Lieti fiori, e felici e ben nate erbe,
Che Madonna passando premer sole.
—*Petrarch.*

O bright and happy flowers and herbage blest,
On which my lady treads.—*Wrottesley.*

L'ignavia nei principi, e l'infedeltà nei ministri rovinano un impero, benchè fondato sopra il sangue di molti virtuosi.—*Machiavelli*.

The sloth of monarchs and the disloyalty of ministers bring an empire to ruin, even when it has been established by the spilling of the blood of many noble men.

Lingua Franca.

The mixed language half European, half Oriental, spoken in the Levant.

Lingua volgare.

(The vulgar tongue.) Italian as opposed to local dialects.

L'invidia è tra gli artefici.

Two of a trade never agree.

L'occhio del padrone ingrassa il cavallo.

(The eye of the master fattens the horse.) *Oculus domini saginat equum.*

L'occupazione è il miglior rimedio contra la noia.

The best cure for ennui is to get something to do.

Loco.

(The place.)   To be played as written.

Lo indugiare è pericoloso.

(Delay is dangerous.)   Do not put off till to-morrow what you can do to-day.

L'onestà è la migliore politica.

Honesty is the best policy.

Lontan dagli occhi, lontan dal cuore.

Out of sight, out of mind.

L'opera loda il maestro.

(The work praises the craftsman.)   The end crowns the work.

L'ozio è il padre del vizio.

Idleness is the father of sin.

L'ultima sera.—*Dante*.

(The furthest gloom.)   Death.

Lungamente non dura eccessivo dolor. Ciascuno a' mali o cede, o s' accostuma.—*Metastasio*.

Excessive grief does not endure for long. Every one either is overcome by sorrows, or gets accustomed to them.

Lunga pausa.

A long pause.

L'uomo per la parola, e il bue per le corna.

You may hold a man by his talk, and an ox by his horn.

L'uomo propone, Dio dispone.

Man proposes, God disposes.

L'uomo virtuoso e conoscitore del mondo, si rallegra meno del bene, e si rattrista meno del male.
  —*Machiavelli*.

The man of merit, who knows the world, becomes less cheered, as time goes on, by the good, and less grieved by the evil he sees in the world.

L'uovo ne vuol saper più della gallina.

(The egg should not know more than the hen.)   Jack Sprat would teach his granny.

Lupo affamato, mangia pan muffato.

A starved wolf eats mouldy bread.

Lusingando.

In a soothing, persuasive style.

Ma Beatrice si bella e ridente
  Mi si mostrò, che tra quelle vedute
  Si vuol lasciar che non seguir la mente.
    —*Dante*.

But so fair,
So passing lovely, Beatrice show'd,
Mind cannot follow it, nor words express
Her infinite sweetness.—*Cary*.

Madonna.

The Virgin Mary.

Madrigalesco.

In madrigal style.

Maestevolissimo.

Extremely majestic.

Maestoso (*Măes.*).

With grandeur ; in a majestic style.

Maestro.

Maestro di cappella.

Magari.

Maggiore (*Mag.*).

Maggior fretta minor alto.

Ma, il provveder di capitan, che giova,
S' ei de' soldati il cor non ha ?
—*Alfieri.*

Ma il temer solo è morte vera al prode.
—*Alfieri.*

Ma le promesse sue sono pei prodi ;
E o presto o tardi essa le adempie.
—*Manzoni.*

Malinconia.

Mancando (*Man. or Manc.*).

Maniera affettata.

Manubrio.

Marcato.

Marcia funebre.

Martellato.

Marziale.

Mattinata.

Matto è chi spera che nostra ragione
Possa trascorrer l' infinita via
Che tiene una sustanzia in tre persone.
State contenti, umana gente, al quia :
Chè se potuto aveste veder tutto
Mestier non era partorir Maria.
—*Dante.*

Meglio è poco che niente.

Meno (*Men.*).

Meno erra chi si promette variazione
nelle cose del mondo, che chi se le
persuade ferme e stabili.
—*Guicciardini.*

Mentre l'erba cresce, il cavallo muore
di fame.

Messa di voce.

Mesto.

Mezza voce (*M. V.*).

Mezzo (*Mez.*).

Mezzo forte (*Mf.*).

Mezzo piano (*Mp.*).

Mezzo-soprano.

Mezzo tenore.

Mezzo tuono.

(Master.)   Composer.

The director of the choir in a church

Would to Heaven it were so.

Major key.

More haste, less speed.

But what avails a leader's careful fore-
thought, if he has not his soldiers'
hearts ?

Fear alone is real death to the brave
man.

Her (Fortune) promises are for the
valiant, to whom, soon or late, she
keeps them.

Melancholy.

Languishingly.

In an affected manner.

The handle of the draw stops in an
organ.

In a marked, distinct style.

A dead march.

With force ; hammered.

In martial style.

A morning song.

Foolish is he who thinks our reason
can traverse the infinite space which
holds three persons in one substance.
Be content, O race of man, as to the
Wherefore : for had you been able to
see everything, there would have no
need for Mary to have a son.

Half a loaf is better than no bread.

Less ; less quick.

The man who looks forward to changes
in the affairs of the world, is less
deceived than he who is convinced
that they are in a firm and stable
condition.

While the grass grows, the horse dies
of hunger.

The gradual swelling and diminishing
of the voice on a long note.

Mournfully.

Middle voice.

Medium.

Between *forte* and *piano ;* not very
loudly.

Rather softly.

A low soprano.

A low tenor voice ; baritone.

A semitone.

Mi mancherà il pane forse, non mai l'onore ; ed io reputo venerabile e magnifica la povertà di colui che non ha mai prostituito il suo ingegno al potere, nè la sua anima alle sventure.
—Ugo Foscolo.

It is possible that I may be in want of bread, but of honour—never ; and I think there is something splendid and noble in the poverty of the man who has never prostituted his intellect to power, nor his soul to misfortune.*

Minaccevolmente.

Menacingly.

Minestrone.

" Fast-day " soup of the Italian peasants.

Minore (*Min.*).

Minor key.

Minuetto (*Mitto*).

Minuet.

Mi sembrava un riso
Dell' universo.—*Dante.*

All nature seemed to wear one universal smile.

Misera la volgare e cieca gente,
Che pon qui sue speranze in cose tali,
Che 'l tempo le ne porta sì repente.
—Petrarch.

Ah ! wretched are those blind, untutored folk, who rest their hopes upon the things which Time so quickly bears away.

Miser chi mal oprando si confida,
Ch' ogn' or star debbia il maleficio occulto,
Che quando ogn' altro taccia, intorno grida
L'aria, e la terra istessa, in ch 'è sepulto :
E Dio fa spesso, che 'l peccato guida
Il peccator, poi ch' alcun di gli ha indulto,
Che se medesimo, senza altrui richiesta,
Inavvedutamente manifesta.—*Ariosto.*

Most wretched man, who hopes in long disguise
To veil his evil deeds from mortal eyes !
Though all were silent else, the sounding air,
The conscious earth his trespass shall declare ;
Th' Almighty oft in wisdom so provides,
The sin to punishment the sinner guides,
Who, whilst he strives t' elude each watchful sight,
Unheeding brings his bursting guilt to light.—*Hoole.*

Misero me ! sollievo a me non resta
Altro che il pianto, e il pianto è delitto !
—Alfieri.

Ah, wretched that I am ! No comfort remains to me save to weep, and 'twere cowardice to weep !†

Misura.

Measure.

Misurato.

In strict or measured time.

Moderato (*Mod.*).

Moderately fast.

Molto.

Very.

Molto fumo e poco arrosto.

(Much smoke and little meat.) Much cry and little wool.

Monte di pietà.

A pawnbroker's shop.

Mordente.

An ornament consisting of a turn, or transient shake on a short note.

Morendo (*Mor*).

Dying away.

Moresco.

In Moorish style.

Mormorando.

In a murmuring style.

Morta la bestia, morto il veneno.

When the beast is dead he cannot bite.

---

* Ugo Foscolo, poet and patriot, was banished from his native land on account of his political opinions. He spent his last years in London, where he died in the early years of the present century.
† When Keats arrived in Italy, on the journey that was to be his last on earth, he bought a copy of Alfieri's works. The dying man opened the book at this passage in Alfieri's *Filipo.* Having read these lines, Keats closed the book, and read no more.

Mosso.

With motion ; quicker.

Motetto.

A motet, or piece of sacred music, in harmony for several voices.

Motivo.

The theme of a piece of music.

Moto.

Energy.

Muojono le città, muojono i regni :
Copre i fasti e le pompe arena ed erba :
E l' uom d'esser mortal par che si sdegni.
Oh nostra mente cupida e superba !
— *Tasso.*

Proud cities vanish, states and realms decay,
The world's unstable glories fade away !
Yet mortals dare of certain fate complain ;
O impious folly of presuming man.
—*Hoole.*

Muor giovane colui ch' al cielo è caro.

Whom the gods love dies young.

Musica di camera.

Chamber music.

Musica di chiesa.

Church music.

Nacchere.

Kettle-drums.

Nacque vestito.

(He was born with his clothes on.) He was born with a caul.

Nascene ancora la rovina della città, per non si variar gli ordini delle repubbliche co' tempi.—*Machiavelli.*

In like manner the ruin of states is brought about, because they do not modify their institutions to suit the times.

Natura il fece, e poi roppe la stampa.
—*Ariosto.*

Nature made him, and then she broke the mould.*

Navigare secondo il vento.

(To sail before the wind.) To agree with the majority.

Ne ammazza più la gola che la spada.

Gluttony kills more than the sword.

Necessità non ha legge.

Necessity knows no law.

Nè Creator nè creatura fu senz' amore.
—*Dante.*

Neither Creator nor creature was ever without love.

Negligentemente.

Negligently ; unconstrained.

Ne' governi ove la nazione o direttamente o per via di rappesentanza entra nella discussione de' suoi interessi e nella formazione delle leggi, l' arme della parola è una potenza conservatrice dei diritti cittadini, e ajutatrice nel tempo stesso della politica potestà.—*Vincenzo Monti.*

In governments where the nation either directly, or by means of representatives, takes part in the discussion of its own interests, and in the formation of its own laws, the weapon of free speech is a safeguard of the rights of citizens, and at the same time assists in the maintenance of the constitution.

Nei costumi si deve vedere una modestia grande.—*Machiavelli.*

Great modesty ought always to be found in company with a good character.

Nei governi bene istituiti, i cittadini temono più assai rompere il giuramento, che le leggi ; perchè stimano più la potenza di Dio, che quella degli uomini.—*Machiavelli.*

In well-ordered states, the citizens are more fearful of breaking their oath than the laws ; since they respect the power of God more than that of men.

---

* A quotation commonly applied to any who have proved themselves pre-eminent in the walk of life they have chosen.

Nei lavori pubblici si trattino i lavoratori di campagna in tal modo amorevolmente, che piuttosto venghino volontari che forzati.—*Machiavelli*.

In the execution of public works we ought to treat the workmen in so kind a manner, that they will work as though willingly, and not through compulsion.

Nel concedere li gradi e dignità, deve il principe andare a trovare la virtù ovunque si trova, senza rispetto di sangue.—*Machiavelli*.

In giving rank and dignities the ruler ought to go in quest of merit, wherever it may be found, without considering the high or lowly birth of the recipient.

Nel cor più non mi sento
Brillar la gioventù.
　　　　　— *Giovanni Paesiello*.

No longer do I feel within my heart the sunshine of youth.

Nella chiesa co' santi, ed in taverna co' ghiottoni.—*Dante*.

With saints in church, and with gluttons in the tavern.

Nella corte del ciel, ond' io rivegno,
　　Si trovan molte gioie care e belle
Tanto, che non si posson trar del regno.—*Dante*.

　　　　In the celestial court
Whence I return, are many jewels found,
So dear and beautiful, they cannot brook
Transporting from that realm.— *Cary*.

Nelle imprese da prendersi, deve esservi l'onor di Dio e il contento universale della città.—*Machiavelli*.

In enterprises that are to be undertaken we ought to consider first the honour due to God, and the common welfare of the state.

Nell' esazione delle tasse si deve sopratutto aver compassione alla miseria e calamità de' popoli, per mantenerli al paese più che è possibile.
　　　　　—*Machiavelli*.

In the exaction of taxes, compassion ought to be shown to the misery and sufferings of the people, in order that they may, to the greatest possible extent, continue to be preserved in the country.

Nello stile antico.

In the ancient style.

Nel mezzo del cammin di nostra vita
　Mi ritrovai per una selva oscura,
　Chè la diritta via era smarrita.
　　　　　—*Dante*.

In the midway of this our mortal life,
I found me in a gloomy wood, astray
Gone from the path direct.*
　　　　　—*Cary*.

Nel petto di uomo facinoroso non può scender alcun pietoso rispetto.
　　　　　—*Machiavelli*.

No feeling of loyalty and veneration can enter the breast of a man who is base by nature.

Nel soldato debbesi sopratutto riguardare ai costumi.—*Machiavelli*.

The moral character of soldiers ought to be considered of the greatest importance.

Nel tempo delle avversità si suole sperimentare la fede degli amici.
　　　　　—*Machiavelli*.

In the hour of trouble we test the loyalty of our friends.

Nè mai, chi ha regno, de' suoi schiavi in mente
Lasciar cader pur dee, ch' altri il potrebbe
Assalir mai.—*Alfieri*.

He that occupies a throne should never let this thought enter his subjects' minds, that his power can be attacked by others.

---

* The opening lines of Dante's *Inferno*. The poet intends to convey that he was thirty-five at the time when he composed his epic, which fixes the date at 1300 A.D. For a similar expression *Isaiah xxxviii.*, 10, may be compared, where the words of King Hezekiah are given : "I said in the cutting off of my days, I shall go to the gates of the grave."

Nemico offenso, e non ucciso ? Oh ! quale,
Qual di triplice ferro armato petto
Può non tremarne ?—*Alfieri*.

Nessun indizio si può aver maggiore d' un uomo che le compagnie con le quali usa.—*Machiavelli*.

Nessun maggior dolore,
Che ricordarsi del tempo felice
Nella miseria.—*Dante*.

Nessun mai per fuggir, o per riposo,
Venne in altezza fama ovver in gloria.
—*Frezzi*.

Nessun sente da che parte preme la scarpa, se non chi se la calza.

Niente più tosto si secca che lacrime.

Niuna cosa di sua natura è più brieve ; niuna ha vita minore, che la memoria dei beneficii, e quanto sono maggiori, tanto più (come è in proverbio) si pagano con la ingratitudine.
—*Guicciardini*.

Niuna cosa fa morir tanto contento, quanto ricordarsi di non aver mai offeso alcuno, anzi piuttosto benefi-cato ognuno.—*Machiavelli*.

Noi leggevamo un giorno per diletto
Di Lancilotto, come amor lo strinse :
Soli eravamo e senza alcun sospetto
Per più fiate gli occhi ci sospinse
Quella lettura, e scolorocci il viso ;
Ma solo un punto fu quel che ci vinse.
Quando leggemmo il disiato riso
Esser baciato da cotanto amante,
Questi, che mai da me non fia diviso,
La bocca mi baciò tutto tremante :
Galeotto fu il libro e chi lo scrisse :
Quel giorno più non vi leggemmo avante.—*Dante*.

A foe insulted and not slain ? At that, what heart, e'en though defended with a triple coat of steel, would not tremble ?

There is no surer proof of a man, than the character of those with whom he consorts.

There is no greater sorrow than to re-member former happy days in the hour of present misery.*

None who shun toil, or cultivate idle-ness, will ever reach the topmost heights of fortune or renown.

No one knows where the shoe pinches so well as he who wears it.

Nothing dries sooner than tears.

Nothing is naturally more short-lived than the memory of benefits received ; the greater they are, the more, as the proverb says, are they repaid with ingratitude.

Nothing gives us a peaceful death so much as the thought that we have never injured anyone, but rather have been of service to all men.

One day
For our delight we read of Lancelot,
How him love thrall'd. Alone we were, and no
Suspicion near us. Oft-times by that reading
Our eyes were drawn together, and the hue
Fled from our alter'd cheek. But at one point
Alone we fell. When of that smile we read,
The wished smile so rapturously kiss'd
By one so deep in love, then he, who ne'er
From me shall separate, at once my lips
All trembling kiss'd. The book and writer both
Were love's purveyors. In its leaves that day
We read no more.—*Cary*.†

* Tennyson refers to these lines in *Locksley Hall* :—
" This is truth the poet sings
That a sorrow's crown of sorrows is remembering happier things."
† The story of Francesca da Rimini, as told by herself in Dante's *Inferno*, in a passage famous for its beauty and delicacy. Leigh Hunt's *Story of Rimini* has made the tale familiar to English readers. Francesca, daughter of Guido, the lord of Ravenna, was given in marriage to Lancilotto of Rimini, a man famous as a warrior, but repulsively deformed. After her marriage, Francesca became enamoured of Paolo, her husband's brother, who was a man of a very handsome presence. Lancilotto, having surprised the guilty pair, killed them both. Silvio Pellico, however, in his tragedy *Francesca da Rimini*, gives the story a more innocent, but not less pathetic turn.

Noi eravam lunghesso il mare ancora,
  Come gente che pensa suo cammino,
  Che va col core, e col corpo dimora.
    —*Dante.*

Meanwhile we linger'd by the water's
  brink,
Like men, who, musing on their road,
  in thought
Journey, while motionless the body
  rests.— *Cary.*

Noi non potemo avere perfetta vita
  senza amici.—*Dante.*

We cannot have a perfect life without
  friends.

Non ci è il più cattivo sordo di quel
  che non vuol udire.

None so deaf as he who will not hear.

Non come fiamma, che per forza è spenta
Ma che per sè medesma si consume,
Se n' andò in pace l' anima contenta.
A guisa d' un soave e chiaro lume,
  Cui nutrimento a poco a poco manca
Tenendo al fin il suo usato costume.
    —*Petrarch.*

As a pure flame that not by force is
  spent,
But faint and fainter softly dies away,
Pass'd gently forth in peace the soul
  content :
And as a light of clear and steady ray,
When fails the source from which its
  brightness flows,
She to the last held on her wonted way.
    —*Dacre.*

Non conosce la pace, e non la stima,
Chi provato non ha la guerra prima.
    —*Ariosto.*

Peace they esteem not, nor its blessings
  know
Who ne'er the ills of war did undergo.
    —*Croker.*

Non convien cantare il trionfo, prima
  della vittoria.

You must not shout " victory " before
  the battle.

Non credere al Santo, se non fa mira-
  coli.

(Believe not the saint who works no
  miracles.) Judge a man by his acts,
  not by his reputation.

Non dee seguir amore chi non ha valore.

Faint heart never won fair lady.

Non è bello quel che è bello, ma quel
  che piace.

(Beauty is not what is beautiful, but the
  thing that pleases us.) Every man
  to his taste.

Non è fierezza quella
Che nasce da pietate.—*Guarini.*

There is no cruelty in the act which
  springs from a pure motive.

Non è fumo senza fuoco.

No smoke without fire.

Non è guadagnare, beneficando uno,
  offender più.—*Machiavelli.*

There is no profit in offending many in
  order to do a kindness to one.

Non è il mondan romore altro che un
  fiato
  Di vento, che or vien quinci ed or
  vien quindi,
  E muta nome, perchè muta lato.
    —*Dante.*

                    The noise
Of worldly fame is but a blast of wind,
That flows from diverse points, and
  shifts its name,
Shifting the point it blows from.
    —*Cary.*

Non è male alcuno nelle cose umane che
  non abbia congiunto seco qualche
  bene.—*Guicciardini.*

There is no evil in human affairs, which
  does not also bring some advantage
  with it.

        Non è pena maggiore
Che 'n vecchie membra il pizzicor d'
  amore.—*Guarini.*

There is no greater punishment than to
  be smitten by love when one's frame
  is old.

Non era l' andar sua cosa mortale
  Ma d' angelica forma.—*Petrarch.*

There was nought mortal in her stately
  tread, but grace angelic.
    —*Wrottesley.*

Non è sana ogni gioja,
Nè mal ciò che v' annoja.
Quello è vero gioire
Che nasce da virtù dopo il soffrire.
— *Guarini.*

Not good is all that giveth joy,
Nor evil all that brings annoy,
To him true joys doth virtue bring,
Who has been taught by suffering.

Nonetto.

A composition for nine instruments.

Non è ufficio di savio Principe tirare la guerra nella casa propria, per rimoverla dalla casa d' altri.
— *Guicciardini.*

It is not the duty of a wise ruler to bring war into his own dominions in order to remove it from another's.

Non fa caso.

It is of no importance.

Non far conto dell' uovo non ancor nato.

Count not your chickens before they are hatched.

Non fidatevi dell' alchimista povero, o de medico ammalato.

Do not trust a poor alchymist, or a sick physician.

Non fu mai partito savio condurre il nemico alla disperazione.
— *Machiavelli.*

It is never a wise plan to drive an enemy to desperation.

Non furono trovati i principi per far servizio loro.—*Guicciardini.*

Kings were not invented merely for other people to wait upon them.

Non ha l' ottimo artista alcun concetto
Ch' un marmo solo in se non circoscriva
Col suo soverchio, e solo a quello arriva
La man che obbedisce all' intelletto.
— *Michael Angelo.*

The sculptor never yet conceived a thought
That yielding marble has refused to aid·
But never with a mastery he wrought—
Save when the hand the intellect obeyed.—*I. Disraeli.*

Non i titoli illustrano gli uomini, ma gli uomini i titoli.—*Machiavelli.*

Titles not adorn men, but men adorn their titles.

Non mi ricordo.

I do not remember.*

Non nella pena,
Nel delitto è la infamia.—*Alfieri.*

It is the crime, and not the punishment, that brings disgrace.

Non ogni giorno è festa.

Every day is not a holiday.

Non pianse mai uno, che non ridesse un altro.

(One man's grief is another man's joy.)
One man's meat is another man's poison.

Non puoi mal fare a nave rotta.

No hurt can be done to a ship that is wrecked.

Non quello, che prende prima le armi, è cagione degli scandoli, ma colui che è primo a dar cagione che le si prendino.—*Machiavelli.*

It is not he that first begins a war who is blameworthy, but he that has given cause for fighting.

Non ragioniam di lor, ma guarda, e passa.—*Dante.*

Speak not of them, but look, and pass them by.—*Cary.*

Non ricordar il capestro in casa dell' impiccato.

Do not talk of the halter in the house of the man who has been hanged.

Non sapere l' abbicci.

(Not to know the alphabet.) To be hopelessly ignorant.

---

* At the trial of Queen Caroline one of the witnesses was an Italian who, whenever any inconvenient question was put to him, replied *Non mi ricordo.* Hence the expression has become proverbial to indicate that a person has a conveniently weak memory, whenever it is not politic to remember unpleasant incidents.

Non sarà mai lodevole quella legge che sotto una poca comodità nasconde assai difetti.—*Machiavelli.*

That law, which conceals many evils under some slight advantage, will never be praiseworthy.

Non si può chiamare infelice una città, che, fiorita lungamente, viene in basseza; perchè questo è il fine delle cose umane : nè si può imputare infelicità l' esser sottoposto a quelle leggi, che sono comuni a tutti gl' altri : ma infelici sono quelli cittadini ai quali ha dato la sorte nascer più nella declinazione della sua patria, che nel tempo della sua buona fortuna.
—*Guicciardini.*

We cannot call a city unfortunate, which, having flourished for a long time, at last sinks into obscurity. For this is the end of human things ; nor can we say that it is unfortunate to be subject to those laws, which are common to all other men : but those citizens are unfortunate whom Chance has caused to be born during the decline, rather than in the prosperous days of their country.

Non si può far d' un pruno, un melarancio.

(You cannot turn a bramble bush into an orange tree.) You cannot make a silk purse out of a sow's ear.

Non sotto l' ombra in piaggia molle
Tra fonti e fior, tra Ninfe e tra Sirene,
Ma in cima all' erto e faticoso colle
Della virtù riposto è il nostro bene.
—*Tasso.*

Not on a couch of down set in the shade amid brooks and flowers, where Nymphs and Sirens dwell, but on the crest of Virtue's steep and toilsome hill our happiness is set.

Non troppo presto.

Not too fast.

Non valere un' acca.

(Not to be worth an H.) Not to be worth powder and shot.

Non v' è rosa senza spina.

There is no rose without a thorn.

Non v' ha, nè può esservi repubblica sicura senza costumi, senza virtù.
—*Vincenzo Monti.*

There has never been, nor can there ever be, a firmly-established state where good morals and virtue do not exist.

Non vi fu, nè vi è mai legge che proibisca, o che biasimi e danni negli uomini la pietà, la liberalità, l' amore.
—*Machiavelli.*

There has never been, nor will there ever be, a law which forbids and condemns among men the exercise of piety, liberality, and love.

Nota sensibile.

The leading note.

Notazione musicale.

Musical notation.

Notturno.

A light vocal or instrumental composition.

Novella trista arriva presto.

Bad news travels fast.

Nulla nuova, buona nuova.

No news is good news.

Obbligato (*Obl.*).

(Obligatory.) A term to those parts of a musical composition which cannot be omitted.

Oboe (*pl.* oboi).

The hautboy.

Ocarina.

A small wind instrument made of terra cotta.

Odi l'altra parte.

(Hear the other side.) *Audi alteram partem.*

Odi, vedi, e taci, se vuoi vivere in pace.

Listen, see, and keep your tongue between your teeth, if you wish to live in peace.

O dolce amor, che di riso t' ammanti
　　　—*Dante.*

O gente umana, per volar su nata,
Perchè a poco vento così cadi ?—*Dante.*

Ogni cane è leone a casa sua.
Ogni cosa ha cagione.

Ogni cuffia è buona per la notte.

Ogni debole ha sempre il suo tiranno.
Ogni erba si conosce per lo seme.
Ogni fiore vuol entrar nel mazzo.

Ogni giorno ha la sua notte.

Ogni medaglia ha il suo rovescio.

Ogni pazzo vuol dar consiglio.
Ogni promesso è debito.
Ogni pruno fa siepe.

Ogni vero non è ben detto.
Ogni volpe abbia cura della sua coda.

Ognuno è peggio all' arte sua.

　　　　　　　　　Ognuno imita
Di chi regna il costume, e si propaga
Facilmente dal trono
Il vizio, e la virtù.—*Metastasio.*
Ognuno per sè e Dio per tutti. .
Ognun sa navigar per il buon tempo.

Oh misero colui che in guerra è spento,
Non per li patrii lidi e per la pia
Consorte o i figli cari,
Ma da nemici altrui
Per altra gente, e non può dir morendo :
Alma terra natia,
La vita che desti ecco ti rendo.
　　　　　　　　　—*Leopardi.*

Onde è necessario ad un principe, volen-
dosi mantenere, impare a potere essere
non buono, ed usarlo e non usarlo
secondo la necessità.—*Machiavelli.*

Sweet heavenly love, which dost array
thyself in smiles

O race of men, why, when born to soar,
do ye suffer an adverse breeze to
check your flight ?

Every dog is a lion at home.
(Nothing happens without a cause.)
Where there is smoke there is fire.

(Any head-dress is good enough for the
night.) In the night all cats are grey.

The weak man always has his tyrant.
By its fruit each plant is known.
(Every flower wishes to be one of the
nosegay.) Do not meddle with the
concerns of others.

(Every day has its night.) Sufficient
unto the day is the evil thereof.

(Every medal has its reverse side.)
There are always two sides to every
question.

Every fool is ready with advice.
Promises are debts.
(Every bramble makes the hedge.)
Every little helps.

Every truth is not good to be told.
(Every fox should look after his own
tail.) Take care of number one.

(Everyone is worst to his own trade.)
The shoemaker's children are the
worst shod.

Every one imitates the habits of a king ;
from a throne the example of vice or
virtue is easily spread.

Everyone for himself and God for all.
Everybody can steer the ship when the
sea is calm.

Ah, wretched is the man who is slain
fighting, not for the land of his
fathers, nor for his faithful wife and
dear offspring, but is killed by the
enemies of strangers, while he battles
for a nation not his own. Such an
one cannot say with his dying breath :
" My country, dear motherland, the
life thou gavest me, behold I now
restore."

Hence it is necessary for a prince, if he
wishes to maintain his position, to
learn to be not invariably good, but
to be so or not as circumstances
dictate.

Onde si aspetta meno,
Sorge talora il defensore.—*Alfieri.*

Onorate il senno antico.

Onorate l' altissimo poeta.—*Dante.*

Onor di bocca assai giova e poco costa.

Onor si acquista
Anco talvolta in soggiacer, se a nulla
Si cede pur, che all' assoluta e cruda
Necessità.—*Alfieri.*

O occhi miei, occhi non già, ma fonti !
—*Petrarch.*

O patria, o grande
Madre antica d' eroi ! Ben è crudele
Chi del sacro tuo petto
Inasprir può le piaghe, e di catene
Quella destra gravar, che il vint̪ ̨mondo
Riverente baciò.—*Vincenzo Monti.*

Opera buffa.

Opera seria.

Operetta.

Ora e sempre.

Oratorio.

Ordinario (*Ordo.*).

Ornatamente.

Oro è che oro vale.

Oro non è tutto quel che risplende.

Or se' tu quel Virgilio, e quella fonte,
Che spande di parlar si largo fiume ?
—*Dante.*

O somma Sapienza, quanta è l' arte
Che mostri in cielo, in terra e nel mal
mondo,
E quanto giusto tua virtù comparte !
—*Dante.*

Osservate con diligenza le cose dei tempi
passati; perchè fanno lume alle future.
Ill mondo è sempre d' una medesima
sorte, e tutto quello che è, e sarà, è
stato in altro tempo; perchè le cose
medesime ritornano ma sotto diversi
nomi e colori, è però ognuno non le
riconosce ; ma solo chi è savio, e le
considera diligentemente.
—*Guicciardini.*

Often from a quarter, whence we least
expect it, a helping hand doth come.

Age commands respect.

Honour the noble bard.*

Fair words go for much and cost us but
little.

Honour sometimes
Is by submission gain'd, if we indeed
Submit to nothing but to absolute
And dire necessity.—*C. Lloyd.*

O eyes of mine, not eyes, but fountains
now.

O my country, thou great and ancient
mother of heroes ! How cruel is he
who has the heart to wound thy
sacred bosom, and place heavy chains
on that right hand of thine, which
once the conquered world did kiss in
humble reverence.

A comic opera.

A serious opera.

A short opera.

Now and ever ; for ever and a day.

A sacred musical drama.

Ordinarily ; in the usual style.

In a florid style.

That is gold which buys gold.

All is not gold that glitters.

And art thou, then, that Virgil, the
source whence spreads the bounteous
flow of noble utterance ? †

Wisdom Supreme ! how wonderful the
art,
Which thou dost manifest in heaven, in
earth,
And in the evil world, how just a meed
Allotting by thy virtue unto all.—*Cary.*

Diligently consider the history of the
past, for past events throw light upon
the future. The world is always as
it has ever been. Everything which
now is, and whatever will be in the
future, has happened also in the past ;
for the same things recur,though their
names and aspects change. Still, all
men do not recognise them, but only
he who is wise, and ponders carefully
what he beholds.

---

* The greeting given to Virgil by the other great poets of antiquity when they meet him
guiding Dante through the lower world.
† In his visit to the lower world Dante describes how he is guided through Hell and Purgatory by Virgil, a most appropriate guide, for the great epic poet of the Romans had himself in
his Æneid described a visit of his hero Æneas to Hades.

Ottava alta.

An octave higher.

Ottava bassa.

An octave lower.

Ottava rima.

The eight-lined stanza.*

Ottetto.

A musical composition in eight parts.

Ottimamente il mondo è disposto allora che in esso suprema è la giustizia. —*Dante.*

The world is in its most excellent state when justice is supreme.

Ottimo rimedio è il far cosnocere a chi pensa di offenderti, che tu sei preparato, a non pretermettere cosa alcuna per difenderti.—*Guicciardini.*

The best remedy to use against a man who is minded to attack you, is to show him that you are ready, and that you will allow nothing to hinder you from defending yourself.

Ove son leggi
Tremar non dee chi leggi non infranse. —*Alfieri.*

Where there are laws,
He need not fear who has not broken them.—*C. Lloyd.*

Padron mio.

(My master.) Your servant.

Pagar uno di sua moneta.

To pay back in the same coin.

Parla bene, ma parla poco.

Speak well, but speak little.

Parlando *or* parlante.

In a speaking or declamatory style.

Parlavan rado, con voci soavi.—*Dante.*

Seldom they spake, but their words were full of sweetness.

Parmi non sol gran mal, ma che l' uom faccia
Contra natura, e sia di Dio rebello
Che s' induce a percuotere la faccia
Di bella donna.—*Ariosto.*

Not crime alone it seems, but that men do
'Gainst nature; and to God they rebels are,
Who can be brought to give the face a blow
Of a fair maid.—*Croker.*

Parte.

A part in vocal and instrumental music.

Partitura.

The score of a piece of music, containing all the parts for voices and instruments.

Partoriscono i monti, e nasce un topo.

(The mountains are in labour and a little mouse is born.) *Parturiunt montes, nascetur ridiculus mus.*

Passacaglio.

A slow movement in triple time.

Passato il pericolo gabbato il santo.

The danger passed, the saint is mocked.

Pasticcio.

A composite opera, made up of parts by different composers.

Pastorale.

A pastoral piece, or movement.

Patetico.

Pathetic.

Peccato celato, mezzo perdonato.

(A sin concealed is half pardoned.) The worst sin is to be found out.

Pedale (*Ped.*).

A pedal of the organ pressed by the foot; a long note in the bass extending over several bars.

Pensieroso.

Melancholy.

---

* The metre of Tasso's *Gerusalemme Liberata*, and also of Ariosto's *Orlando Furioso*.

Per beato ch' elle non furon pesche !

(How lucky that they were not peaches !) It might have been worse.*

Perchè colui, che sotto duro impero
Il popolo governa
Teme color, che hanno di lui timore,
Talchè sopra il suo autor cade la tema.
—Metastasio.

The ruler, who rules with a rod of iron, fears his people whom he causes to fear him ; hence such fear recoils on its author.

Perch' egl' incontra che più volte piega
L' opinion corrente in falsa parte.
—Dante.

For it generally happens that an opinion hastily formed falls into error.

Perchè non discernea il nero dal bianco.
—Ariosto.

For he could not tell black from white.

Perdendosi (*Per., Perd.,* or *Perden.*).

Gradually losing both tone and time.

Per diventar ricco in questo mondo, non
ci vuol altro che voltar la spalle a
Dio.

In order to become rich in this world, one needs only to turn one's back on God.

Per far effetto.

(To do anything in style.) For appearance' sake.

Per me si va nella città dolente,
  Per me si va nell' eterno dolore,
  Per me si va tra la perduta gente,
Giustizia mosse il mio alto fattore :
  Fecemi la divina potestate,
  La somma sapienza e il primo amore.
Dinanzi a me non fur cose create,
  Se non eterne, ed io eterna duro :
  Lasciate ogni speranza, voi ch'
    entrate !—*Dante.*

Through me you pass into the city of woe :
Through me you pass into eternal pain :
Through me among the people lost for aye.
Justice the founder of my fabric moved :
To rear me was the task of power divine,
Supremest wisdom, and primeval love ;
Before me things create were none, save things
Eternal, and eternal I endure.
All hope abandon, ye who enter here.†
        —Cary.

Però come un principe ha più rispetto a
se, che ai popoli, non è più principe,
ma tiranno.—*Guicciardini.*

When a prince pays more regard to himself than to his subjects, he is no longer a prince, but a tyrant.

        Per ora il campo è questo,
In cui dobbiam militar noi ; cercarvi
Onore, o morte.—*Alfieri.*

This is the field in which we're called to fight ;
Here let us seek for honour or for death.
        —C. Lloyd.

      Per sentir più dilettanza
Bene operando, l'uom di giorno in
giorno,
S'accorge che la sua virtude avanza.
        —Dante.

      And, as by sense
Of new delight, the man who perseveres
In good deeds doth perceive from day to day,
His virtue growing.—*Cary.*

---

* This saying is commonly applied to pusillanimous folk who take a thrashing without resisting. According to Mr. I. Disraeli it originated as follows. The occupants of Castle Poggibonsi were in the habit of presenting some baskets of peaches to the Court of Tuscany as a kind of annual tribute. On one occasion, peaches being scarce, they sent figs instead. The pages of the Court were indignant, and pelted the messengers with the fruit. The latter, however, took the matter quietly, remarking that peaches would have hurt them more.

† These, the opening lines of Canto III. of Dante's *Inferno,* form the inscription written over the gates of Hell. The last line of this passage is perhaps the most often quoted line of the Divine Comedy.

Per te, per te, che cittadini hai prodi,
Italia mia, combatterò, se oltraggio
Ti moverà la invidia. E il più gentile
Terren non sei di quanti scalda il sole ?
D' ogni bell' arte non sei madre, o
    Italia ?
Polve d' eroi non è la polve tua ?
Agli avi miei tu valor desti e seggio,
E tutto quanto ho di più caro alberghi !
            —*Pellico.*

            O my Italy, for thee
Who valiant citizens dost rear, for thee
I will combat, when envy shall arouse
Outrage 'gainst thee. And art thou
    not of all
The lands the sun doth warm the
    gentlest still ?
Of every fine art, O my Italy,
The mother art thou not, my Italy ?
What is thy dust but heroes pulverized ?
The valour of my grandsires what but
    thou
Did rouse ? In thy fair bosom lies my
    home,
My all, my all.*
            — *J. F. Bingham.*

Per troppo dibatter, la verità si perde.
    By too much debate truth is obscured.

Pesante.
    With weight ; impressively.

Pezzi.
    Musical excerpts ; selections.

Piacere.
    Pleasure.

Piacevole.
    In a pleasing style.

Piaga per allentar d' arco non sana.
            —*Petrarch.*
           The slackening of the bow
Assuages not the wound its shaft has
    given.—*Campbell.*

Piangendo.
    Plaintively ; weepingly.

Piangevolmente.
    Dolefully.

Pianissimo (*Pp.*).
    Very soft.

Piano (*P.*).
    Soft.

Piccolo.
    Small.

Pietra mossa non fa muschio.
    A rolling stone gathers no moss.

Più. Di più in più.
    More. More and more.

Più lento.
    Slower.

Più tengono a memoria gli uomini le
    ingiurie, che li beneficii ricevuti.
            —*Guicciardini.*
    Men's memories are more tenacious of
    injuries than of benefits they have
    received.

Più tosto mendicanti che ignoranti.
    Better starve the body than the mind.

Più vede un occhio del padrone che
    quattro de' servitori.
    One eye of the master sees more than
    four of the servant's.

Pizzicato.
    (Pinched.) An indication that the vio-
    lin is to be played with the fingers
    alone, and not with the bow.

Poca favilla gran fiamma seconda.
            —*Dante.*
    A little spark produces a great flame.

Pocetta.
    A pocket fiddle.

Poco.
    A little.

Poco a poco.
    Little by little.

Poco curante.
    (Caring little.) A careless indifferent
    person.

---

* These lines are put by Silvio Pellico into the mouth of Paolo, one of the characters in the tragedy *Francesca da Rimini.* It would be difficult to find a nobler or truer expression of patriotism than is contained in these lines, or a truer patriot than the man who wrote them.

Poco fiele fa amaro molto miele.

One drop of gall spoils a pot of honey.

Poco roba, poco pensiero.

Little wealth, little care.

Podestà.

Chief magistrate.

Polenta.

Porridge made of maize-flour.

Pomposo (*Pomp.*).

In pompous style.

Portando la voce.

Sustaining the voice.

Portar la battuta.

To follow the beat.

Portato.

Sustained.

Povertà non è colpa.

Poverty is no shame.

Povertà non ha parenti.

A poor man has no relations.

Precipitando.

Hurriedly.

Prender due colombe, o piccioni con una fava.

To kill two birds with one stone.

Prestissimo.

Very quick.

Presto e bene, non si conviene.

(Quickly and well, seldom agree.) More haste less speed.

Presto maturo, presto marcio.

Soon ripe, soon rotten.

Presto o tardi.

By-and-by; sooner or later.

Pria Veneziani, poi Cristiani.

Venetian first, Christian afterwards.

Prima donna.

The principal female singer in an opera.

Prima volta.

The first time.

Primo tempo.

The first time ; the time marked at the opening of a musical piece.

Pur troppo.

It is but too true.

Quando Dio non vuole, il santo non puole.

When God will not the Saint cannot.

Quando la libertà della stampa non trova un freno interiore nella probità e nell' erubescenza d'un giornalista, un giornale non è più l' innocente e dilettevole pascolo della quotidiana curiosità, ma si cangia in vile stromento delle passioni.
— *Vincenzo Monti.*

When the freedom given to the press is not kept within bounds by a feeling of honesty and a regard for propriety in the heart of the journalist, a newspaper is no longer the innocent pasture, whence curiosity may derive its daily meal of pleasant sustenance, but becomes the instrument for the exciting of base passions.

Quando nelle consulte sono pareri contrarii, se alcuno esce fuora con qualche partito di mezzo, quasi sempre è approvato non perchè il più delle volte li partiti di mezzo non sieno peggiori che gli estremi : ma perchè i contradittori calono più volentieri a quelli, che all' oppinioni contrarie ; ed anco gli altri, o per non dispiacere, o per non esser capaci, si gettono a quelli, che par loro che abbiano manco disputa.—*Guicciardini.*

When opposite opinions are expressed in councils, if any one comes forward with some middle course of action, it is almost always adopted, not because middle courses are not often worse than extremes, but because the disputants agree to a compromise more readily than to a course they entirely oppose : moreover the others present, either from a desire not to displease or from lack of brains, readily adopt that view which seems likely to involve less dispute.

G G

Quando si parte 'l giuoco della zara,
Colui che perde si riman dolente.
—*Dante.*

When from their game of dice men
separate,
He who hath lost remains in sadness
fix'd.—*Cary.*

Quando ti verrà l'occasione di cosa, che
tu desideri, pigliala senza perder'
tempo; perchè le cose del mondo
si variano tanto spesso, che non si
può dire d' aver cosa, finchè non si ha
in mano.—*Guicciardini.*

As soon as you see an opportunity of
obtaining what you desire, grasp it
without loss of time; for the affairs
of the world change so rapidly, that
we are unable to say that we have
anything until we have it in our hand.

Quando uno è stato buon amico, ha
buoni amici ancor lui.—*Machiavelli.*

A man who has been a true friend, does
not lack true friends himself.

Quando viene la fortuna, apri le porte.

When Fortune knocks, open wide your
doors.

Quante teste, tanti cervelli.

Many men many minds.

      Quanto in servir fa dotto
La gelida vecchiezza!—Ah! se null'
altro,
Che tremare, obbedir, soffrir, tacersi,
Col più viver s'impara, acerba morte,
Pria che apparar arte sì infame, io
scelgo.—*Alfieri.*

           How propense,
Gelid old age, art thou to servitude!
Ah! if nought else by length of years is
learn'd,
But how to tremble, to obey, to endure,
In silence to endure; rather than learn
Such abject arts, I choose the bitterest
death.—*C. Lloyd.*

      Quanto la cosa è più perfetta,
Più senta il bene, e così la doglienza.
—*Dante.*

As each thing approaches nearer to perfection, it feels both pleasure and pain
more acutely.

Quanto più è grave l' importanza di
quello che si tratta, tanto si debbe
procedere più circunspetto, e fare
maturamente quelle deliberazioni, che
errate una volta non si possono più
ricorreggere, specialmente nei casi di
guerra.—*Guicciardini.*

In proportion to the importance of the
matter we have in hand, so we ought
to proceed with circumspection, and
to conduct our deliberations with due
care. For if we once commit a
blunder in affairs of this kind, it is
impossible to remedy our mistake,
especially if we are dealing with a
question of war.

Quanto più se n' ha, tanto più se ne
vorrebe.

The more one has, the more one wants.

Quantunque il simular sia le più volte
Ripreso, e dia di mala mente indici:
Si trova pur in molte cose, e molte
Aver fatti evidenti benefici.—*Ariosto.*

Altho' dissembling, most time, meets
with blame,
And is a token of an evil mind,
It has, in many cases I could name,
Done services important to mankind.
      —*Croker.*

Quartetto.

A musical composition for four voices or
instruments.

Quarto d'aspetto.

A semiquaver rest.

Quasi un dolce dormir ne suoi begli
occhi,
Sendo lo spirto già da lei diviso,
Era quel, che morir chiaman gli
sciocchi,
Morte bella parea nel suo bel viso.
—*Petrarch.*

E'en as in balmy slumbers lapt to lie
(The spirit parted from the form below),
In her appear'd what th' unwise term to
die;
And Death sate beauteous on her beau-
teous brow.—*Dacre.*

Quattri-croma.

A semi-demisemiquaver.

Quattrino risparmiato due volte guadag-
nato.

A penny saved is doubly earned.

            Quel cattivo coro
Degli Angeli, che non furon ribelli
Ne fur fedeli a Dio, ma per se foro.
                —*Dante.*

            That ill band
Of angels mix'd, who nor rebellious
  proved,
Nor yet were true to God, but for themselves.—*Cary.*

Quel ch' è fatto, è fatto.

(What is done is done.)   There is no
use in crying over spilt milk.   *Hin
ist hin.*

Quel che pare burla, ben sovente è vero.

There is many a true word spoken in
jest.

Quel dominio è solo durabile, che è
volontario.—*Machiavelli.*

That sovereignty only is lasting, which
is in harmony with the wishes of those
who are ruled.

Quella guerra è giusta, che è necessaria.
              —*Machiavelli.*

The just war is that which is undertaken
through necessity.

            Quelli studi
Ch' immortal fanno le mortal virtudi.
               —*Ariosto.*

Those studies which make mortal virtues
to be immortal.*

Quel signor dell' altissimo canto.
               —*Dante.*

The monarch of the loftiest poesy.†

Questo è il signor; di cui non so espli-
carme
Se sia maggior la gloria o in pace, o in
arme.—*Ariosto.*

Of this great prince I scarcely can relate,
Whether in peace or war he was most
great.—*Croker.*

Questo non mi calza.

That does not please me.

Questo vento non vaglia la biada.

This zephyr does not even fan the wheat.

Quieto.

Quietly; calmly.

Quintetto.

A musical piece for five voices or instruments.

Quivi sospiri, pianti ed alti guai
  Risonavan per l' aer senza stelle.
               —*Dante.*

Here sighs, and groans, and deep
laments, resounded through the star-
less air.‡

Raccomandare il lardo alla gatta.

(To entrust the bacon to the cat.)   To
set a fox to mind the chickens.

Raddolcendo (*Raddol.*).

Becoming gradually softer.

Raddoppiamento.

The doubling of a musical interval.

Rallentando (*Ral.*, *Rall.*, or *Rallo.*).

Slackening the time.

Rapidamente.

With rapidity.

Rara in amor la fedeltà si trova.
              —*Metastasio.*

Fidelity and love are seldom found
together.

Rare volte nocque il tacere, spesso il
parlare.

Silence seldom does harm, but talking
often does.

Recitativo.

Recitative.

Recitativo accompagnato.

Accompanied recitative.

---

* A fine description of the function of history.   † A description of Homer.
‡ A description of the condition of the souls in hell.

Recitativo secco.

Unaccompanied recitative.

Recitativo stromente.

Recitative orchestrally accompanied.

Rè galantuomo.

King and gentleman.*

Regola che mai, o raro falla : Non si muti dove non è difetto, perchè non è altro che disordine. Dove però tutto è disordine, meno vi rimane del vecchio, meno vi rimane del cattivo.
—*Machiavelli.*

This is a rule which never, or rarely fails : Do not make innovations where there is nothing that needs amendment, for that merely produces confusion. But where all is confusion beforehand, the less there remains of what has existed before, the less there is left to remedy.

Religiosamente.

Religiously ; with devotion.

Render pane per focaccia.

(To give back bread for a bun.) Tit for tat.

Rialto.

The name of a famous bridge in Venice.

Ride bene chi ride l' ultimo.

He laughs best who laughs last.

Ridotto.

A club ; a gambling saloon.†

Rifacimento.

A refurbishing or dressing-up.

Riffioramente.

Embellishments added by a musical performer.

Rinforzando (*Rf.* or *Rfz.*).

Laying special emphasis on some note.

Ripieno.

(That which fills up.) Voices or instruments swelling the volume of sound.

Riposatamente.

Restfully.

Risvegliato.

Awakened ; with renewed animation.

Ritardando (*Rit.* or *Ritard.*).

Retardingly.

Ritardato.

Decreased in speed.

Ritenuto (*Rit.* or *Ritten.*).

Held back ; a sudden decrease in the time.

Ritmo di tre battute.

(Rhythm of three beats.)   Triple time.

Ritornello.

An interlude between a musical theme and the variations thereon.

Rodomontata.

Rodomontade ; bluster.‡

Romanza.

A simple story or ballad.

Rondinella pellegrina
  Che ti posi in sul verone,
Ricantando ogni mattina
  Quella flebile canzone,
Che vuoi dirmi in tua favella
  Pellegrina rondinella ?—*Grossi.*

Pilgrim swallow ; pilgrim swallow
  On my grated window's sill,
Singing as the mornings follow,
  Quaint and pensive ditties still,
What would'st tell me in thy lay ?
  Prithee, pilgrim swallow, say ? §
—*W. D. Howells.*

* In these terms Victor Emmanuel described his occupation in the census list of Turin.
  † In former days these *ridotti*, or gambling-saloons, were to be found in every part of Italy, and gambling was the vice of all classes of society, as indeed, so far as lotteries are concerned, it is the besetment of the Italians of to-day. Even Manzoni was in his youth bitten by the gambling mania, and was found in one of the *ridotti* by Vincenzo Monti The older poet warned the young man that gambling would blight his prospects of poetic fame. and Manzoni took the warning so much to heart that he at once forswore play, and, to prove the strength of his resolution, he continued, for some time, to visit the *ridotti* without wagering there.
  ‡ Rodomonte is the name of one of the characters in Ariosto's *Orlando Furioso.*
  § This is the first stanza of the song in Grossi' sromance, *Marco Visconti* Mr. W. D. Howells, in his *Modern Italian Poets*, from which the above translation is taken, speaks of it as " one of the tenderest little songs in any tongue."

Rondino; rondoletto.

A short rondo.

Rondo.

A movement consisting of several parts, each ending with a repetition of the first part.

Rossor di sera buon tempo mena, rossor di mattina empie la marina.

A red sky in the evening brings fine weather, but a red sky in the morning fills the sea.

Ruvidamente.

Roughly.

Saggio fanciullo è chi conosce il suo vero padre.

He is a wise child who knows his own father.

Saggio guerriero antico
Mai non ferisce in fretta.
                    —*Metastasio.*

The experienced warrior is never in a hurry to strike a blow.

Saltarello.

An Italian dance of a lively kind.

Salve, O divino, a cui largì Natura
Il cor di Dante e del suo duca il canto :
Questo fia 'l grido dell' età ventura,
Ma l' età che fu tua te 'l dice in
    pianto.

Hail, inspired poet, on whom Nature bestowed the heart of Dante, and the poetic power of Dante's guide (Virgil). This will be the cry of the generations to come, but the generation that was thy own weeps as thus it speaks to thee.*

Sbarra doppia.

A double bar.

Sbirri.

Police officers.

Scena.

An operatic scene.

Scherzando, *or* Scherzoso (*Scherz.*).

In a playful style.

Scherzo.

A light and sportive musical movement.

Scintillante.

Bright and sparkling.

Sciolto.

In a free and open manner.

Scordatura.

A method of tuning an instrument, in order to produce unusual effects.

Scozzese.

In the Scottish style.

Sdegno.

With disdain.

Se d' alcuno s' intende, o legge, che, senza alcuno suo commodo, o interesse, ami più il male, che il bene, si deve chiamare bestia, e non uomo, poichè manca dell' appetito naturale.
                    —*Guicciardini.*

If one hears or reads of any man, who, without any idea of his own advantage or interest, prefers wickedness to goodness, such a one must be considered not a man, but a beast, for his inclinations are inhuman.

Se gli da un dito, si prende il braccio.

Give him an inch, and he will take an ell.

Segno.

A sign ; a mark.

Segreto confidato non è più segreto.

Tell a secret, and it is no longer yours.

Se la donna vuol, tutto la puol.

(What woman wills, all will.) A wilful woman must have her way.

Semplice.

In a simple style.

Sempre (*Semp.*).

Always.

---

* The epigram that Manzoni wrote on the death of Vincenzo Monti, lamenting the loss of the friend who had encouraged his own early efforts as a poet.

Sempre a quel ver ch' ha faccia di menzogna
De' l' uom chiuder le labbra quant' ei puote,
Però che senza colpa fa vergogna.
—*Dante.*

Ever to that truth
Which but the semblance of a falsehood wears,
A man, if possible, should bar his lip;
Since, although blameless, he incurs reproach.—*Cary.*

Sempre che l' inimico è più possente,
Più, chi perde, accettabile ha la scusa.
—*Ariosto.*

The stronger the enemy is, the better the excuse of him who has been defeated.

Sempre è maggior del vero
L' idea d' una sventura
Al credulo pensiero
Dipinta da timor.—*Metastasio.*

The anticipations of misfortunes, which fear arouses in a mind too prone to forebodings, are always worse than the reality.

Sempre ha torto il più debole.

(The weakest is always in the wrong.) Might goes before Right. *Macht geht vor Recht.*

Sempre natura, se fortuna trova
Discordè a sè, come ogni altra semente
Fuor di sua region, fa mala prova.
E, se il mondo laggiù ponesse mente
Al fondamento che natura pone,
Sequendo lui, avria buona la gente.
Ma voi torcete alla religione
Tal che fia nato a cingersi la spada,
E fate rè di tal ch' è da sermone
Onde la traccia vostra è fuor di strada.
—*Dante.*

Nature ever,
Finding discordant fortune, like all seed
Out of its proper climate, thrives but ill.
And were the world below content to mark
And work on the foundation nature lays,
It would not lack supply of excellence.
But ye perversely to religion strain
Him, who was born to gird on him the sword,
And of the fluent phraseman make your king:
Therefore your steps have wander'd from the path.—*Cary.*

Se non è vero, è ben trovato.

If not true, it is very ingenious.*

Senza (*Sen.*).

Without.

Senza ceremonie.

Without ceremony.

Senza complimenti!

No compliments, pray!

Senza danari, non si paga l' oste.

You cannot settle your score without money.

Senza debiti, senza pensieri.

Out of debt, out of danger.

Senza organo.

Without the organ.

Senza replica.

Without repetition.

Se occhio non mira, cuor non sospira.

What the eye does not see, the heart does not grieve for.

Se pesti un verme, ei ti si attorce al piede.

Even a worm will turn if you tread upon it.

Septetto.

A musical composition for seven instruments.

Seque.

Here follows.

Serenata.

A serenade; an evening concert in the open air.

Serrar la stalla quando sono scappati i buoi.

To lock the stable door when the horse is stolen.

* According to Büchmann, this expression first appeared in Giordano Bruno's *Gli eroìci furori.*

Sestetto.

A musical composition for six voices or instruments.

Sforzando.

With a strong musical accent.

Sforzato (*Sf.* or *Sforz.*).

With emphasis.

Siam navi all' onde algenti
  Lasciate in abbandono :
  Impetuosi venti
  I nostri affetti sono :
  Ogni diletto è scoglio :
  Tutta la vita è mar.—*Metastasio.*

We are like derelict ships, tossing on the cold, cold waves : our passions are the squalls that urge us on : every pleasure is a hidden reef, and life one boundless sea.

Siamo tutti figli d'Adamo.

(We are all sons of Adam.) A cat may look at a king.

Siciliana.

In Sicilian style.

Si deve stimare chi è, non chi può esser liberale.—*Machiavelli*

We ought to esteem the man who is liberal, not the man who is able to be so.

Si è tagliate le gambe con la propria falce.

(He has cut his leg with his own sickle.) He has brought the trouble on himself.

Simili con simili vanno.

Like goes with like.

Simpatico.

Nice, genial, jolly.

Si piace.

According to the discretion of the performer.

Si può pagar l' oro troppo caro.

Wealth may be bought at too dear a price.

Si replica.

To be repeated.

Si scriva.

As written.

Si segue.

As follows.

Sistro.

A zither.

Slentando (*Slent.*).

A gradual diminishing of musical time.

Smaniante.

With fury.

Smorzando (*Smorz.*).

A gradual diminishing of the loudness of the music.

Soave.

Sweet.

Soccorso non viene mai tardi.

Succour never comes too late.

Soggetto.

A musical subject ; theme.

Sogliono comunemente poter più negli uomini senza comparazione, gli stimoli dell' interesse proprio, che il rispetto del beneficio comune.
                    —*Guicciardini.*

Generally speaking, the stimulus of self-interest is incomparably stronger among men than consideration for the common weal.

Solco onde, e' n rena fondo, e scrivo in vento.—*Petrarch.*

I plough in water, build upon the sand, and write upon the wind.

Soldato, acqua, e fuoco, presto si fan luoco.

Soldiers, water, and fire, soon make room for themselves.

Solfeggio.

Sol-faing ; system of arranging the scale of music by the names do, re, mi, fah, soh, la, si ; a voice exercise.

Sonata.

A musical composition of several movements for a single instrument.

Sonatina.

A short sonata.

Sono pane e cacio.

(They are bread and cheese.) They are sworn friends.

Soprano (S).

The highest female voice.

Sordini.

Mutes; little instruments on the bridge of the violin, etc., deadening the sound.

Sospirando.

Sighing style.

Sostenuto (*Sos. or Sost.*).

A musical note sustained to its full length, with no break between it and the next note.

Sotto la bianca cenere, sta la brace ardente.

(Under the white ash, the flame is hidden.) Do not trust to appearances.

Sotto pena di morte.

On pain of death.

Sotto un crudel impero troppo mai non si tace.—*Metastasio*.

Under a cruel despotism one can never be too silent.

Sotto voce (*S. V.*).

In an undertone, or whisper.

Spesso da un gran male, nasce un gran bene.

(Often a great good comes from a great evil.) There is a silver lining to every cloud.

Spesso è da forte
Più che il morire, il vivere.—*Alfieri*.

Sometimes the test of courage it becomes
Rather to live than die.—*C. Lloyd*.

Spesso in poveri alberghi, e in picciol tetti,
Nelle calamitadi, e nei disagi,
Meglio s' aggiungon d' amicizia i petti,
Che fra ricchezze invidiose, ed agi
Delle piene d' insidie, e di sospetti
Corti regali, e splendidi palagi ;
Ove la caritade è in tutto estinta,
Nè si vede amicizia, se non finta.
—*Ariosto*.

Oft in poor cot, and humble mansion
Amidst distresses and calamities,
Better, within the breast, is friendship shown,
Than 'midst invidious riches, and soft ease :
With treach'ry fill'd, and with suspicion,
Are regal courts, and splendid palaces,
Where totally extinct is charity,
Nor friendship, save what's counterfeit, we see.— *Croker*.

Spesso men sa, chi troppo intender vuole.—*Guarini*.

He who would fain learn too much, often knows but little.

Spiccato.

With distinctly separated musical sounds; played in a staccato manner.

Spirito.

Spirit; animation.

Spiritoso.

Spirited.

Spogliar Pietro, per vestir Paolo.

To rob Peter, in order to pay Paul.

Staccato (*Stacc.*).

A short distinct and pointed style.

Stanza.

A verse of a song or poem.

Star accorto.

To be on the alert.

Star colle mani alla cintola.

(To stand with the hands on the hips.) To idle away the time.

Stare ne' gengheri.

To be on one's guard.

Star fra le due acque.

(To stand between two streams.) To halt between two opinions.

Stavo ben, ma per star meglio, sto qui.	I was well ; but trying to be better, I find myself here.*
Stesso.	The same.
Stinguendo.	Gradually decreasing the sound.
Strepito.	Noise.
Stretto.	The quickening of musical time.
Stringendo.	Acceleration of musical time.
Stromenti.	Instruments.
Stromenti di corda.	Stringed instruments.
Stromenti di vento.	Wind instruments.
Subiti.	Quick.
Suonar sordamente.	To be played softly.
Svegliato.	Briskly ; sprightly.

Tal padrone, tal servitore.	Like master, like man.
Tal ti ride in bocca, Che dietro te l' accocca.	Before your eyes he seems all smiles, Behind your back he's full of wiles.
T' annoia il tuo vicino ! Prestagli uno zecchino.	Does your neighbour's presence annoy you ? Lend him money.
Tanti paesi, tanti usanze.	So many countries, so many customs.
Tanto.	So much.
Tanto buono che val niente.	It is so very good that it's good for nothing.
Tanto è possente Amore Quanto dai nostri cor forza riceve.— —*Guarini*.	The power of Love over us is determined by the strength that our own hearts give it.
Tanto ne va a chi ruba, quanto a quel che tiene il sacco.	(The thief never gets so much as he who holds the bag.) The receiver is worse than the thief.
Tanto tonó ch' alfin piovve.	(So long it thundered that at last it rained.) Long looked for come at last.
Tardando.	Lingering.
Tedesco furor.—*Petrarch*.	The wild fury of the Germans.
Tempo.	Time.
Tempo era dal principio del mattino ; E il Sol montava in su con quelle stelle Ch' eran con lui, quando l' amor divino Mosse da prima quelle cose belle. —*Dante*.	The hour was morning's prime, and on his way Aloft the sun ascended with those stars, That with him rose when Love divine first moved Those its fair works.—*Cary*.
Tempo giusto.	In correct time.
Tempo primo.	In the time of the first movement.
Tempo rubato.	(Robbed time.) When some notes of a bar are prolonged, robbing others of their proper length.
Tenendo il canto.	The melody sustained.

* An old epitaph quoted by Addison in the *Spectator*.

Teneramente.	Tenderly.
Tenore (*T.* or *Ten.*).	Tenor.
Tenore buffo.	The tenor comic singer in an opera.
Tenore robusto.	Powerful tenor voice.
Tenuto (*Ten.*).	A note to be sustained during its whole length.
Terra cotta.	Baked clay.
Terzetto.	A trio, or musical piece for three voices or instruments.
Thema, Tema.	A theme ; musical subject.
Timorosamente.	In a timid style.
Timpani.	Kettle drums.
Timpani coperti.	Muffled drums.
Torso.	The trunk of a statue.
Traduttore, traditore.	Translators are traitors.
Tra la bocca ed il boccone, mille cose accadono.	There's many a slip 'twixt the cup and the lip.
Tranquillamente.	Tranquilly.
Tre cose belle in questo mondo : prete parato, cavaliere armato, e donna ornata.	Three things are beautiful in this world : a priest in his vestments, a knight in armour, and a woman in her ornaments.
Tremando Tremolo (*Tr.* or *Trem.*).	Tremulous vibration of a note.
Trillo.	A trill *or* shake.
Triole.	A triplet ; a group of three notes of equal length.
Tristo è quef barbiere che ha un sol pettine.	Ill fares the barber who has only one comb.
Tromba.	A trumpet.
Troppo cara è la vendetta, Quando costa una viltà.—*Metastasio.*	Vengeance, purchased by an act of infamy, is purchased at too dear a price.
Troppo disputare la verità fa errare.	Discussing truth too much leads to error.
Tu proverai si come sa di sale Lo pane altrui, e com' e' duro calle Lo scender e' l salir per l' altrui scale. —*Dante.*	Thou shalt prove How salt the savour is of other's bread : How hard the passage, to descend and climb By other's stairs.* —*Cary.*
Tutta forza.	With all the force.
Tutte le strade conducono a Roma.	All roads lead to Rome.
Tutti (*T.*).	All together.
Tutti a tutti Siam necessari ; e il più felice spesso Nel più misero trova Che sperar che temer.—*Metastasio.*	We are all necessary one to one another ; and the happiest man often finds something to hope for, or to fear in the most wretched.

* In these words Cacciaguida predicts the exile of Dante from Florence. This event took place in the year 1302.

Tutti fatti a sembianza d' un Solo,
Figli tutti d' un solo Riscatto,
In qual ora, in qual parte del suolo
Trascorriamo quest' aura vital,
Siam fratelli ; siam stretti ad un patto :
Maledetto colui che l' infrange,
Che s' innalza sul fiacco che piange,
Che contrista uno spirto immortal !
                              —*Manzoni*.

We are all made in one Likeness holy,
    Ransomed all by one only redemp-
        tion ;
Near or far, rich or poor, high or lowly,
    Wherever we breathe in life's air.
We are brothers, by one great preëmp-
    tion
    Bound all ; and accursed be its
        wronger,
    Who would ruin by right of the
        stronger,
Wring the hearts of the weak with
    despair.—*W. D. Howells*.

Tutti gli uomini naturalmente sono buoni ; cioè, che, dove non cavano piacere o utilità del male, piace più loro il bene, che' l male. Ma sono varie le corruttele del mondo, e fragilità loro ; che facilmente, e spesso per interesse proprio inclinano al male. Però da savi legislatori fu per fondamento delle repubbliche trovato il premio, e la pena, non per violentare gli uomini a far o l' uno, o l' altro ; ma, perchè seguitino l' inclinazione naturale.— *Guicciardini*.

All men are naturally virtuous ; that is to say, that where they do not derive any pleasure or advantage from wicked courses, virtue pleases them more than vice. But so various are the corruptions of the world, and such is the frailty of men, that they often, for their own interest, incline to vice. For this reason wise legis-lators have made a system of rewards and punishments to be the basis of states, not to force men into one course of conduct or the other, but in order that all should follow their natural bent.

Tutti i gusti son gusti.

(All tastes are tastes.)   There is no accounting for taste.

Tutti quanti.

Every one.

Tutto è bene che riesce bene.

All's well that ends well.

Tutto il frutto del vincere consiste nel usar la vittoria bene.—*Guicciardini*.

All the good results of conquest depend upon the right use of the victory obtained.

Tutto il male non vien per nuocere.

(Every evil comes not to hurt.)   Some evils are blessings in disguise.

Tutto quello, che ha il principe, gli è dato per uso, e beneficio d' altri : e però retenendolo a se, frauda gli uomini di quel che deve loro con molta sua infamia.—*Guicciardini*.

All that a prince possesses is given him for the use and benefit of others ; by keeping these things for himself alone, he defrauds others of that which he owes them, and this to his own exceeding shame.

Una corda.

One string.

       Un alma grande
È teatro a se stessa.   Ella in segreto
S' approva, e si condanna.—*Metastasio*.

A noble soul is, as it were, its own theatre, and there, in secret, it ap-proves or condemns its own acting.

Una mano lava l' altra, e tutte due lavano il viso.

One hand washes the other, and both wash the face.

Una rondina non fa primavera.

One swallow does not make a summer.

Una scopa nuova spazza bene.

A new broom sweeps clean.

Una volta furfante, e sempre furfante.

(Once a rogue, always a rogue.) What's bred in the bone will come out in the flesh.

Un bel morir tutta la vita onora.

A noble death is an honour to the whole life.

Un buon cittadino, per amore del ben pubblico, deve dimenticare le ingiurie private.—*Machiavelli*.

A good citizen ought to forget his own private wrongs when the interests of the common good are concerned.

Un buono o savio principe deve amare la pace e fuggire la guerra.
—*Machiavelli*.

A good and wise ruler ought to love peace and shun war.

Un freddo amico è mal sicuro amante.
—*Metastasio*.

A cold friend makes an untrustworthy lover.

Un governo, che ama dominar uomini e non armenti, non solo non pone ostacolo ai progressi dell' intelletto, ma con ogni guisa di scuole li promuove.—*Vincenzo Monti*.

A government, which desires to rule men and not beasts, not only does not place any barrier in the way of intellectual progress, but promotes it by establishing schools of every kind.

Unisoni.

(Unisons.) Two or more parts played in unison.

Un mal chiama l' altro.

(One evil summons another.) It never rains but it pours.

Un ministro estero deve esser grato a chi è mandato, pratico, prudente, sollicito, e amorevole di suo sovrano e della sua patria.—*Machiavelli*.

An ambassador ought to be acceptable to those to whom he is sent, as well as experienced, prudent, diligent, and devoted to his sovereign and his country.

Uno stato ingrandisce con esser l'asilo della gente cacciata e dispersa.
—*Machiavelli*.

A country waxes great through being the refuge of persecuted and exiled people.

Un principio tristo deve partorire altre simili cose.—*Machiavelli*.

An evil principle is sure to produce results of a similar character.

Uomo amante, uomo zelante.

(A loving man, a jealous man.) No love without jealousy.

Uomo avvisato è mezzo salvato.

Forewarned is forearmed.

Uomo condennato e mezzo impiccato.

Give a dog a bad name, and hang him.

Uso fa legge.

Custom makes the law.

Val più un asino vivo, che un dottore morto.

A living donkey is better than a dead professor.

Variazoni (*Var.*).

Variations on a musical air.

Vaso che va spesso al fonte, ci lascia il manico o la fronte.

The pitcher that goes often to the well is broken at last.

Vaso vuoto suona meglio.

An empty barrel gives the loudest sound.

Vedi Napoli e poi mori.

(See Naples, and then die.) You have seen the best the world can show, so that there is nothing left to live for.

Veloce.

With great rapidity.

Vender il miele a chi ha le api.

(To sell honey to a bee-keeper.) To carry coals to Newcastle.

Vengo di Cosmopoli.	(I come from Cosmopolis.) I am a citizen not of any one country, but of the world.
Vermicelli.	Thin rolls of paste made with flour, cheese, yolks of eggs, and saffron.
Vettura.	Carriage; hackney coach.
Vetturino.	The driver of a vettura.
V' ha patria dove Sol uno vuole, e l' obbediscon tutti ? 　　　　　—*Alfieri*.	Callest thou *that* a country, where one man rules, and all the rest obey ?
Via il gatto ballano i sorci.	When the cat's away the mice will play.
Vibrato.	Strongly vibrating.
Vicino alla chiesa, lontan da Dio.	The nearer to church, the farther from God.
Vigoroso (*Vig.*).	Energetically.
Villanella.	An Italian dance, in which dancing and singing are combined.
Viola (*Va.*).	The tenor violin.
Viola da gamba.	A six-stringed violoncello.
Viola pomposa.	An instrument resembling a violoncello having five strings instead of four.
Violone.	The double bass.
Virtuoso.	A skilful performer.
Vivace (*Viv.*).	Brisk, lively.
Viva il rè.	Long live the king !
Viver insieme come cane e gatto.	(To live like dog and cat.)　To be constantly quarrelling.
Voce di compositore.	A composer's voice.*
Voce di petto.	Chest voice (the natural voice).
Voce di popolo, voce di Dio.	The people's voice is the voice of God. *Vox populi, vox Dei.*
Voce di testa.	Head voice (falsetto).
Volante.	Very fast.
Volata.	A rapid series of musical notes.
Voler bene.	To wish one well.
Voler male.	To wish one ill.
Volesse Iddio !	Would to God !
Volontieri.	Willingly; delighted.
Volteggiando.	Crossing the hands when performing on the pianoforte.
Volti (*V.*).	Turn over.
Volti subito (*V.S.*).	Turn over quickly.
Zampogna.	A bagpipe.
Zelosamente.	Zealously.
Zingaro.	A gipsy.

* The inferior quality of the voices of musical composers has become proverbial among the Italians. on much the same principle that a shoemaker's children are the worst shod.

Spanish.

Abad avariento por un bodigo pierde ciento.

A greedy rector in gaining one loaf loses a hundred.*

Abajanse los adarves, y alzanse los muladares.

(High walls sink, and dunghills rise.) Humility is the mark of the truly great, as bumptiousness proves the ill-bred man.

A' barba de necio aprenden todos á rapar.

On a fool's chin all learn to shave.

A' barba muerta, poca vergüenza.

(To a dead beard little respect.) The dead are soon forgotten.

A' bestia loca, recuero modorro.

To a mad beast, a stupid driver.

Abrenuncio Satanas! Mala capa llevarás.

I renounce thee, Satan! Then thou shalt wear a shabby cloak.†

Abril frio, mucho pan y poco vino.

(A cold April, much bread and little wine.) A cold April is good for the corn, and bad for the vine.

Abril y Mayo, la llave de todo el año.

April and May are the key of the whole year.

A' buen adquiridor, buen espendedor.

(To a good gatherer a good spender.) A miserly father and a spendthrift son.

A' buen bocado, buen grito.

(For a toothsome morsel, a deep groan.) Dyspepsia waits upon the epicure.‡

A' buen Capellán, mejor Sacristán.

To a good priest, a better sacristan.§

A' buen entendedor, breve hablador.

To a good hearer a brief speaker.

A' buen entendedor, pocas palabras.

(To a good listener a few words.) A word to the wise is sufficient. *Verbum sap.*

---

* The *bodigo* is a loaf offered by the people to the priest of their church. Nuñez explains this proverb, saying that in the villages the priest abuses the man who fails to bring his offering, so that the latter is so offended that he ceases to offer anything at all.

† A cynical saying to indicate that, although honesty is the best policy, those who practise it will not become rich.

‡ Collins, in his *Spanish Proverbs*, says that this proverb is also used to express that we should not be too careful of the expense and labour of an undertaking when its object is useful. Χαλεπὰ τὰ καλά.

§ A saying that is commonly applied to a cute man who has found his match. There is an amusing account of the origin of this saying in a very old work, entitled *Alivio de Caminantes*, "Travellers' Comfort." A priest was dining in an inn off a roast pigeon. Seeing a peasant sitting there, he invited him to share his repast, hoping thereby to save his own pocket. The peasant, however, replied that the pleasant smell alone of the pigeon served him as a dinner. "Then you ought to pay for the pleasure," said the priest. A dispute arose, and the village sacristan was called as arbitrator, and decided that the peasant must pay. But the wily sacristan, having received the coin, merely rang it on the table, remarking that, as the priest had demanded pay for a smell, he should be paid with a sound.

A' buey viejo, no le cates abrigo.

(Do not seek shelter for an old ox.) Jack Sprat would teach his granny to suck eggs.

A' caballo nuevo, caballero viejo.

An old rider for a young horse.

A' caballo presentado no hay que mirarle diente.

Do not look a gift horse in the mouth.

A' cabo de cien años los reyes son villanos,
A' cabo de ciento y diez los villanos son reyes.

At the end of a hundred years the kings are peasants,
At the end of a hundred and ten the peasants are kings.

A' cada necio agrada su porrada.

(Every fool is pleased with his bauble.) Every man has his hobby. *A chaque fou plaît sa marotte.*

A' cada puerco su San Martin.

(Every pig has its St. Martin's Day.) Every dog has its day. *

A' canas honradas no hay puertas cerradas.

To honoured gray hairs there are no closed doors.

A' carne de lobo, diente de perro.

(For flesh of wolf, tooth of dog.) Diamond cut diamond ; set a thief to catch a thief.

A' casa de tu tia, mas no cada dia.

(Go to your aunt's house, but not every day.) Familiarity breeds contempt.

A' celada de bellacos, mejor es el hombre por los pies que por las manos.

(Against rogues in ambush 'twere better for a man to use his feet than hands.) Discretion is the better part of valour.

Achacoso como Judio en Sabado.

(As ill as a Jew on a Saturday.) Malingering.†

A' chico pajarillo, chico nidillo.

(A little bird, a little nest.) Every man in his proper station.

Acierta errando.

He blunders into the right.

Acogerse á fidelium.

(To have recourse to the Fidelium.) Any port in a storm.‡

Acometa quien quiera, el fuerte espera.

(Let him attack who pleases, the strong man waits.) The weak man is impetuous, the strong is patient.

A' cuentas viejas, barajas nuevas.

(Old reckonings, new quarrels.) Short reckonings make long friends.

A' cuerdos, necios e locos
Veo heredar las riquezas
De sus padres, e muy pocos
Las virtudes e proezas.
—*F. Perez de Guzman.*

I see men—both wise and fools—inherit the riches of their fathers, but very few of them, however, inherit their merits and prowess.

Adelante está la casa del abad.

The parson's house is farther on.§

A' dineros pagados, brazados quebrados.

When the money is paid the arms are broken.‖

* The Spanish peasant generally kills his pig on St. Martin's Day, i.e., in November.
† In the days of persecution, a Jew, fearing to observe the rules of his Sabbath by abstaining from work, used to sham illness on Saturday to escape detection.
‡ *Fidelium Deus* are the first words of a familiar prayer. When a priest forgets the collect proper for some special occasion he says the *Fidelium Deus* as a makeshift.
§ The typical reply made to a beggar by the person whose charity both begins and ends at home.
‖ The celerity with which a workman ceases work when pay-time comes is notorious.

Adiós, que esquilan.

Good-day! I am in a desperate hurry.*

A' Dios rogando y con el mazo dando.

Praying to God and plying the hammer.†

A' do ira el buey que no are?

(Where will the ox go and not be made to plough?) Idleness is nowhere possible.

A' dos pardales en una espiga nunca hay liga.

Two sparrows upon one ear of wheat cannot agree.

A' do te quieren mucho, no entres á menudo.

(Where you are often invited, don't go frequently.) Intimacy breeds contempt.

A' espaldas vueltas, memorias muertas.

Out of sight, out of mind.

A' falta de hombres buenos, le hacen á mi padre alcalde.

(Through lack of good men, they made my father magistrate.) Hobson's choice.

A' falta de pan, buenas son tortas.

(When bread is lacking, oatcakes are good.) Half a loaf is better than no bread.

A' fuer de Aragon, buen servicio mal galardon.

According to the custom of Arragon, good work and poor pay.‡

A' grande mal, gran remedio.

Desperate ills need desperate remedies.

Agua de Mayo, pan para todo el año.

Rain in May brings bread for the year.

Agua pasada no muele molino.

Water that has flowed past will not turn the mill.

A' hija casada, salen nos yernos.

(When the daughter is wed the sons-in-law appear.) Help is always to be had except when it is needed.

Ahora que tengo oveja y borrego, todos me dicen, En hora buena estéis Pedro?

Now that I own a sheep and a lamb, everybody says, "How do you do, Peter?"

A' Idos de mi casa, y, Qué quereis con mi mujer, no hay responder.

To "Out of my house," and "What do you want with my wife?" there is no replying.

A' ira de Dios no hay casa fuerte.

Against God's anger no house is strong.

Alabate cesto, que venderte quiero.

(Praise thyself, basket, for I wish to sell thee.) A good article sells itself.

A' la buena mujer poco freno basta.

For a good woman a small bridle is enough.

A' la burla dejarla, cuando más agrada.

Leave the jest when 'tis at its best.

Al agradecido más de lo pedido.

To the grateful man give more than he asked.

A' la hija mala, dineros y casarla.

A dowry and marriage, the cure for a bad daughter.

A' la larga el galgo á la liebre mata.

(In the end the greyhound kills the hare.) Time and patience work wonders.

---

* According to the dictionaries the literal meaning of this saying is, "Good-day—they are shearing sheep," but Sbarbi considers that this explanation is absurd. He connects *esquilan* with *esquila*, "a bell," and says that originally the saying probably originated with members of religious houses. presbyteries, &c., who would naturally be in a desperate hurry when the bell was rung for the performance of one of the offices of the church.

† Cromwell's somewhat similar maxim was, "Trust in God and keep your powder dry."

‡ This custom may be said to be common to the whole world.

Al aldeano dale el pié, y tomarte ha la mano.

(If you give a boor your foot, he will take your hand.) Give him an inch, and he'll take an ell.

Al amigo, manda el higo, al enemigo, el prisco.

Send the fig to your friend, and the peach to your enemy.

Al amigo su vicio.

(To a friend his faults.) Make allowance for a friend's fads.

Al amo imprudente, el mozo negligente.

(A reckless master has a feckless man. Like master like man.

Al amor el remedio es tierra en medio.

(The cure for love is land between. Absence does *not* make the heart grow fonder.

A' la mujer barbuda, de lejos la saluda.

A woman with a beard salute from a distance.*

A' la mujer casta, Dios le basta.

(For the chaste woman God suffices.) A good woman is virtuous for virtue's sake.

A' la mujer mala, poco le aprovecha guardarla.

It is useless to watch a bad woman.

Al asno muerto, la cebada al rabo.

(When the ass is dead, barley at his tail.) After death the doctor.

A' la viña guarda el miedo, y no viña-dero.

Fear, and not the vine-dresser, protects the vineyard.

Al borracho fino, no le basta agua ni vino.

(The inveterate drunkard is not sated with water or wine.) Ever drunk, ever dry.

Al buen callar llaman Santo.

(To wise silence men give the name of saint.) Speech is silvern, silence is golden.†

Al buen pagador no le duelen prendas.

(A good paymaster is not troubled about pledges.) A good paymaster may build St. Paul's.

Al buen varon, tierras agenas patria le son.

(To the stout heart foreign lands are a fatherland.) *Omne solum forti patria est.*

Al cabo de los años mil, tornó el agua á su cubil.

(At the end of a thousand years the water returns to its cask.) We always return to our old loves.

Alcalde de aldea, el que lo quiere ése lo sea.

(Let him who pleases be mayor of a village.) Petty dignities are not worth acquiring.

Al dejar este mundo y meternos la tierra adentro, por tan estrecha senda va el principe como el jornalero.
                                    —*Cervantes.*

When we quit this world and are placed in the earth, the prince walks along as narrow a path as the journeyman.

Al desdichado, poco le vale ser esforzado.

(Courage is of little use to the unlucky man.) It is better to be born lucky than rich.

* The Spaniards consider that hair on a woman's chin indicates a very passionate disposition. Such a person is best avoided.
† In *Don Quixote* Sancho Panza changes the form of this proverb to give credit to himself, *Al buen callar llaman Sancho,* "To silence men give the name of Sancho." Mr. Ulick Burke, however, says that this latter form of the proverb was known before Cervantes' time.

Alegrias, antruejo, que mañana serás ceniza.

(Rejoice, Carnival, for to-morrow thou wilt be ashes.) Eat, drink, and be merry, for to-morrow we die.*

Al enemigo que huye, la puente de plata.

(To the flying foe, a bridge of silver.) Make terms with an enemy when you can.

Al fin es debido el honor.

(To the end is the honour due.)   All's well that ends well.

Al fin se canta la gloria.

(The Gloria is sung at the end of the psalm.) Don't halloa till you are out of the wood.

Al freir de los huevos lo verá.

(It will be seen when the eggs are fried.) Time will show.†

Algo ageno, no hace heredero.

(Another's property leaves no heir.) Ill-gotten gains do not prosper. *Male parta male dilabuntur.*

Algo ó nada.

(Something or nothing.) Neck or nothing.

Alguacil.

A constable; an inferior officer of justice.

Alguacil descuidado, ladrones cada mercado.

(A negligent constable, thieves every market-day.) When the cat's away, the mice will play.

Al gusto dañado lo dulce le es amargo.

To a debased palate the sweet tastes bitter.

Al hijo de tu vecino, límpiale las narices y métele en tu casa.

(Wipe your neighbour's son's nose, and take him into your house.)   Seek a husband for your daughter among the people whose characters you know.

Al hijo y al mulo en el culo.

For a son and a mule a blow behind.

Al hombre bueno no le busques abolengo.

Do not trouble about the ancestors of a good man.

Al hombre desnudo, más valen dos camisones que no uno.

For the naked man, two shirts are better than one.

Al hombre inocente, Dios le endereza la simiente.

(God makes the seed of the good man to grow.) "Yet saw I never the righteous forsaken, nor his seed begging their bread."

Al hombre mayor, darle honor.

(To the greater man give honour.) Honour to whom honour is due.

Al hombre osado, la fortuna le da la mano.

(To the bold man Fortune offers her hand.) Fortune favours the brave. *Audaces Fortuna juvat.*

Al hombre venturero, la hija le nace primero.

A lucky man's first child is a daughter.‡

* Antruejo is the name given to the carnival time, the three days that precede Lent. *Ceniza* refers to the *Dia de ceniza*, i.e., Ash Wednesday.

† A man, having entered another's house, walks off with the frying-pan. The owner meets him as he departs and asks what he has under his cloak. *Al freir de los huevos lo verá*, replied the thief as he ran off.

‡ Because as Nunez quaintly explains, if the eldest child is a daughter, Nature provides the man with a nurse for the male children that follow.

Al huesped, por ruin que sea, siempre se le da el primer lugar.	To the guest, however poor he be, the best place is always given.
Al invierno lluvioso, verano abundoso.	A rainy winter brings a summer of plenty.
Allá se me ponga el sol, do tengo el amor.	(May the sun set for me where I keep my love.) May I end my days with her I love.
Allá van leyes do quieren reyes.	(Laws follow the roads that kings wish them to take.) *Macht geht vor Recht.**
Allegador de la ceniza y derramador de la harina.	(A niggard with the ashes, and a spendthrift with the flour.) Penny wise and pound foolish.
Al loco y al toro darles corro.	To the fool and the bull give a wide berth.
Al mozo mal mandado, ponle la mesa, y envia le al recado.	If your servant loiters, set his meal on the table, and send him on an errand.
A' los osados ayuda la fortuna.	Fortune favours the brave. *Audaces Fortuna juvat.*
Al perro flaco, todas son pulgas.	(The starved dog is covered with fleas.) The poorer the man is, the more he is neglected.
Al peso de los años Lo eminente se rinde ; Que á lo fácil del tiempo No hay conquista difícil.—*Calderon.*	Age does not respect The fair or the sublime ; Nothing stands erect Before the face of time. —*D. F. MacCarthy.*
Al pobre no es provechoso acompañarse con el poderoso.	It is not an advantage for a poor man to consort with the rich.
Al que mal hicieres no le creas.	Trust not the man whom you have injured.
Al que tiene mujer hermosa, ó castillo en frontera, ó viña en carrera, nunca le falta guerra.	He that hath a pretty wife, a castle on the frontier, or a vineyard by the highway, never lacks warfare.
Al que tiene suegra, cedo se la muera.	May he who has a mother-in-law see her die soon.
Alquimia probada, tener renta y no gastar nada.	It is proved alchemy, to have an income and to spend nothing.
Al raton que no tiene más que un agujero, presto le cogen.	(The rat who has only one hole is speedily caught.) It is always well to have two strings to one's bow.
Al ruin lugar, la horca al ojo.	(In a poor town the gallows meet the eye.) The unfortunate man wears a shabby coat.†

* This is one of the best-known, as well as one of the oldest, Spanish proverbs. It arose from the action of Alfonso VI., who, at the beginning of the twelfth century, decided whether the Gothic or Roman Missals should be used in his country. The King resolved to leave the matter to chance, and threw both into the flames, saying the one which came out unburnt should be chosen. But when the Gothic Missal survived the ordeal, he threw it back into the flames, and decided in favour of the Roman. From this act, *Allá van leyes do quieren reyes*, became a popular saying in Spain.

† Collins says that the gibbets for malefactors were usually erected on a hill adjoining small towns, presumably as a warning to all who approached the place. Mr. Disraeli says that this saying is applied to those persons who, when asked a favour, make a pretence of refusing before granting it.

Al sastre pobre, la aguja que se doble.

(To a poor tailor a needle that will bend.) The poor must adapt themselves to circumstances.

Al villano con la vara de avellano.

For a sturdy rogue a sturdy rod.

Al yerno y al cochino, una vez el camino.

To a son-in-law and the pig, once is often enough to show the road.

A' malas hadas, malas bragas.

Bad fortune goes badly breeched.

A' mal capellan, mal sacristan.

(A knavish parson has a knavish clerk.) Like master, like man.

A' manos lavadas Dios les dá que coman.

(God puts food into clean hands.) Honesty is the best policy.

A' maravedi de pleito, real de papel.

A pennyworth of lawsuit costs half-a-crown's worth of paper.

Amar y saber, no puede todo ser.

Love and prudence cannot go together.

Amen, amen, al cielo llega.

(Amen, amen, reaches heaven.) More things are wrought by prayer than this world dreams of.— *Tennyson.*

Amigo del buen tiempo,
Múdase con el viento.

A fine-weather friend changes with the wind.

Amigo de pleitos, poco dinero; amigo de médicos, poca salud; amigo de frailes, poca honra.

Friend of lawsuits, little wealth; friend of doctors, little health; friend of friars, little honour.

Amigo reconciliado enemigo doblado.

(A friend reconciled is twice a foe.) Offended love never forgives.

Amigos deste siglo, rostros humanos, corazones de fieras.—*A. Perez.*

Friends nowadays have human faces, but hearts of beasts.

Amigo viejo, tocino y vino añejo.

A friend, bacon, and wine, are all the better for keeping.

A' mi padre llaman hogaza, y yo muero de hambre.

My father's name is Baker, yet I die for lack of bread.*

A' mocedad ociosa vejez trabajosa.

An idle youth brings a laborious age.

Amor de asno, coz y bocado.

(The love of an ass is a kick and a bite.) Rustic lovers are given to horseplay.

Amor de niño, agua en cestillo.

A boy's love is water in a basket.

Amores nuevos, olvidan viejos.

(New loves, the old forgot.) The new love, the true love; the old love, the cold love.

Amor mio; mis amores.

My love; my darling.

A' moro muerto gran lanzada.

(Great stabbing of a dead Moor.) Even hares can insult a dead lion.

A' mucho hablar, mucho errar.

(Much talking, many blunders.) Silence is wisdom for the fool.

A' muertos y á idos, pocos amigos.

(The dead and the departed have few friends.) *Les absents ont toujours tort.*

A' mula vieja, cabezadas nuevas.

(To an old mule new trappings.) Fine feathers make fine birds.

Anda el gato en el palomar.

(The cat is in the dovecot.) There is a man among the maids.

* Literally, " My father's name is Loaf," &c., but I do not think that Loaf is to be found among British names of persons.

Andando y hablando, marido á la horca.

Walking and talking, husband to the gallows.*

Andar á caza con huron muerto.

(To go after rabbits with a dead ferret.) To pursue a quest without proper means.

Andar á caza de gangas.

(To go a-hunting wild-fowl.)   To go on a wild-goose chase ; to wait expect· ing something to turn up.

Andar de zocos en colodros.

(To go from clogs to buskins.)   Out of the frying-pan into the fire.

Andar entre la cruz y el agua bendita.

To walk between the cross and the holy water.†

Ante la puerta del rezador, nunca eches tu trigo al sol.

Before the door of a man who is always praying, never leave your corn to dry.

Antes al ruiseñor que cantar, que á la mujer que parlar.

The nightingale will cease singing ere a woman ceases chattering.

Antes di que digan.

(Tell before they tell.)   Have the first word; one tale is good until another's told.

Antes moral tardío, que almendro florido.

Better a late mulberry than an almond-tree in flower.‡

Antes que conozcas, ni alabes, ni cohondas.

Neither praise nor blame until you know.

Antes que te cases, mira que lo haces.

Look before you ere you wed.

Antigua contienda entre la Fortuna y la Naturaleza.—*Antonio Perez.*

(There is an old quarrel between Fortune and Nature.)   *Honores mutant mores.*

A' otro perro con ese hueso.

(Give that bone to another dog.)   No tricks upon strangers.

A' padre guardador, hijo gastador.

After a miserly father comes a spendthrift son.

A' palabras locas orejas sordas.

To foolish words turn deaf ears.

A' perro viejo nunca cuz, cuz.

To an old dog never say cuz, cuz.§

Aplicacion y Minerva.   No hay eminencia sin entrambas, y si concurren excesso.   Mas consegue una mediana con aplicacion que una superioridad sin ella.   Comprase la reputacion á precio de trabajo ; poco vale que poco cuesta.—*Gracian.*

Application and natural ability.   Without both these it is impossible to attain eminence ; and, when they are both united, the highest eminence is reached.   A moderate intellect, combined with application, succeeds better that mere genius.   Work is the coin that purchases a reputation, and that which costs us little is of little value.

A' pobreza no hay vergüenza.

Poverty has no shame.

* The story is told of a woman whose husband was condemned to death.   He wished to linger in order to give his wife his last instructions, but the good woman, impatient of the delay, said, *Andando y hablando, marido.*
† That is, to be at the last gasp.   A crucifix and holy water are brought to the death-bed of the dying Catholic.
‡ The almond-tree blooms early, so is liable to be blighted by severe weather.   Hence the proverb is used of precocious children, who seldom fulfil their early promise.
§ Cuz, the word used by Spaniards for calling a dog.   Nuñez explains that it would be needless to call an old dog, as it would follow close to its master's heel.   But the saying appears to be equivalent to the English, " You cannot catch an old bird with chaff."

A' poco pan, tomar primero.

(When bread is scarce take the first slice.) Every man for himself, and the devil catch the hindmost.

Aprendiz de Portugal, no sabe coser y quiere cortar.

An apprentice from Portugal, he does not know how to sew, but wishes to cut out.*

A' puñadas entran las buenas hadas.

(Good fortune comes by punching.) The timid dog gets no bone; no gains without pains.

Aquellos son amigos que hacen amistades. —*Gracian.*

Those are friends who do friendly acts.

Aquellos son ricos que tienen amigos.

Those who possess good friends are truly rich.

A' quien dan, no escoge.

Beggars must not be choosers.

A' quien dices poridad, á ese tu das la libertad.

You surrender your liberty to him to whom you tell your secret.

A' quien Dios quiere, bien en Sevilla le dan de comer.

He whom God loves is fed well in Seville.

A' quien Dios quiere bien, la casa le sabe.

To him to whom God wishes well, his house is sweet.

A' quien Dios quiso bien, en Granada le dió de comer.

He to whom God has wished well, in Granada gets plenty to eat.

A' quien está en su tienda, no le achacan que se hallo en la contienda.

He who stays in his own shop, is not accused of being mixed up in the brawl.

A' quien madruga, Dios le ayuda.

(God helps him who rises betimes.) Heaven helps him who helps himself; the early bird catches the worm.

A' quien miedo han, lo suyo le dan.

He who is feared receives his own.

A' quien no mata puerco, no le dan morcilla.

No black pudding is given to him who kills no pig.

A' quien no tiene nada, nada espanta.

He who has nothing, has nothing to fear.

A' quien se humilla, Dios le ensalza.

God exalts him who humbles himself.

A' quien te da el capon, dale la pierna y el alon.

(To him who gives the capon, give the leg and the wing.) One good turn deserves another.

A' quien tiene buena mujer ningun mal le puede venir, que no sea de sufrir.

To him who has a good wife no sorrow comes that he is unable to endure.

Ara bien hondo, cogerás pan en abondo.

(Plough a deep furrow, and you will reap an abundance of corn.) Spend, and God will send.

Arboles son amores desdichados A' quien el hielo marchitó floridos.
              —*Lope de Vega.*

Like a tree by hoar-frost blighted Is lovers' love when unrequited.

Arde verde por seco, y pagan justos por pecadores.

Green burns for dry, and the righteous pay for sinners.

Ares, no ares, renta me pagues.

Plough, or plough not, pay me the rent.

A' rio revuelto ganancia de pescadores.

It is good fishing in troubled waters.

---

* This saying illustrates the antipathy of the Spaniards towards the Portuguese.

Armas y dineros buenas manos quieren.

Weapons and money should have good hands to hold them.

Asi es el marido sin hecho, como casa sin techo.

A husband without experience is like a house without a roof.

Asna con pollino, no vá derecha al molino.

(An ass, when with her colt, does not go straight to the mill.) A mind full of cares, a field full of tares.

Asno cojo, mas habias de madrugar.

(Lame ass, you ought to rise earlier.) Dull wits need more labour to polish them.

Asno cojo, y hombre rojo y el demonio, todo es uno.

A lame ass, a red-haired man, and the devil, are one and the same thing.

Asno con oro, alcanzalo todo.

(An ass laden with gold overtakes everything.) It is money that makes the mare to go ; the rich fool is accounted wise.

Asno de muchos, lobos le comen.

(The ass with many owners is devoured by the wolves.) Everyone's business is nobody's work.

A' suegras beodas, tinajas llenas.

To drunken mothers-in-law give brimming jugs.*

A' tí lo digo, hijuela, entendedlo vos, mi nuera.

(I tell it to you, daughter ; hear it, daughter-in-law.) I speak to the post that the gate may hear.

A' tu hijo, buen nombre y oficio.

To thy son leave a good name and a profession.

A' un asno, bastale una albarda.

(One load is enough for one ass.) His own troubles are enough for every man.

Aun no asamos, y ya empringamos.

(We are not yet roasting, but already we baste the meat.) We are counting our chickens before they are hatched.

Aunque fortuna es mudable,
Al trabajo es favorable.

Although Fortune is fickle, she smiles on work.

Aunque la mona se vista de seda, mona se queda.

A monkey is still a monkey, though it is dressed in silk.

Aunque manso tu sabueso, no le muerdas en el bezo.

(Though your bloodhound be tame, do not bite him on the lip.) Beware the anger of a patient man.

Aunque seas prudente, viejo, no desdeñes el consejo.

(Although you are prudent, old man, disdain not advice.) None are so wise that they need not to learn.

A' un traidor, dos alevosos.

(To one traitor two treacherous comrades.) Set a thief to catch a thief.

Ausencia enemiga de amor, quan lejos de ojo, tan lejos de corazon.

(Absence is love's enemy ; far from the eyes is far from the heart.) Out of sight, out of mind.

A' veces lleva el hombre á su casa, con que llore.

Sometimes a man takes home what may cause him to weep.†

---

* That is, in order that they may speedily kill themselves. The unpopularity of mothers-in-law appears to be almost universal.
† The records of the Divorce Court show that it is often the friend of the husband who leads the wife astray.

Averigüelo Vargas.

(Let Vargas decide it.) The matter is too deep for ordinary mortals.*

A' virgo perdido, y cabeza quebrada, nunca faltan rogadores.

(Lost virginity, and a broken head, are never without sympathisers.) Those who have ruined a maid or assaulted a man are always ready to effect a compromise, in order to avoid trouble.

A' vuelta del sol, caga el buey en el timon.

(Towards sunset the ox befouls the plough.) The diligent relax when their work is done.

A' vuestra salud.

Your good health.

Ayer vaquero, hoy caballero.

(Yesterday cowherd, to-day a gentleman.) The progress of the *nouveau riche*.

Barro y cal encubren mucho mal.

Brick and lime conceal much crime.†

Beber los vientos.

(To drink in the winds.) To be in a state of anxious expectation.

Beber vino como puerco suero.

(To drink wine as a sow does whey.) To drink by the pailful.

Becerrilla mansa todas vacas mama.

The gentle calf sucks the teats of every cow.

Bel hombre no es todo pobre.

A handsome man is not utterly poor.

Bien está cada piedra en su agujero.

(Every stone is well in its own crevice.) A place for everything, and everything in its place.

Bien hace quien su critica modera;
Pero usarla conviene más severa
Contra censura injusta y ofensiva,
Cuando no hablar con sincero denuedo
Poca razon arguye, ó mucho miedo.
   —*Yriarte*.

He who restrains his criticism does well; but the severest criticism ought to be used against unjust and brutal censure. For then, not to speak out with frank boldness convicts one of little sense, or else of great timidity.

Bien hay, amén mil veces,
Quien sirve á señor discreto!
   —*Lope de Vega*.

Happy, happy is that servant who is to a wise lord bound.

Bien predica quien bien vive.

(He preacheth best who liveth best.) Example is better than precept.

Bien sabe el asno en cuya cara rebuzna.

(The ass knows well in whose face he brays.) The boorish person knows to whom he dare be rude.

Bien sabe el sabio que no sabe, el necio piensa que sabe.

The wise man knows that he is not wise, but the fool imagines that he himself is wise.

Bien engas, mal, si vienes solo.

Welcome, sorrow, if you come alone.

Bobos van al mercado, cada cual con su asno.

(Fools go to market, each on his own ass.) *A chaque fou plaît sa marotte.*

Bocado comido no gana amigo.

A morsel eaten gains no friend.

* Vargas was a contemporary of Ferdinand and Isabella, and enjoyed a great reputation for profound learning and wisdom.
+ A suitable motto for the jerry-builder.

Boca que dice de sí, dice de no.

(The mouth which says yes, says no.) Every medal has its reverse.

Boda de negros.

(A wedding of negroes.) A noisy frolic ; an Irish wake.

Bofeton amagado nunca bien dado.

(A threatened blow is never well given.) Cowards are often loudest in their threats.

Bonete y almete hacen casas de copete.

The student's cap and the helmet make houses great.*

Buen abogado mal vecino.

A good lawyer is a bad neighbour.

Buena de mejores, por mengua de seguidores.

Virtuous of the virtuous, through lack of followers.†

Buena es misa misar, y casa guardar.

(It is good to hear Mass and good to look after one's house.) Religious duties should be attended to, but domestic ones should not be neglected.

Buena fama hurto encubre.

A good reputation conceals theft.‡

Buena vida, padre y madre olvida.

(Prosperity forgets father and mother.) The man who has " got on " does not remember his poor relations.

Buen corazón quebranta mala ventura.

A stout heart overcomes bad fortune.

Buen jubon me tengo en Francia.

I have a good jacket in France.§

Bueno, bueno, bueno, mas guarde Dios mi burra de su centeno.

Good, good, good, but God keep my ass out of his rye.‖

Buenos dineros, son casa con pucheros.

(A house and a stock of provisions are good money.) The man whose necessities are satisfied does not feel the lack of money.

Buen principio, la mitad es hecha.

Well begun is half done.

Buey viejo surco derecho.

An old ox makes a straight furrow.

Burla burlando vase el lobo al asno.

All in the way of fun the wolf attacks the ass.

Burláos con el asno daros ha en la cara con el rabo.

(Jest with an ass, and he will flap his tail in your face.) Too much familiarity breeds contempt.

Burláos con el loco en casa, burlará con vos en plaza.

Jest with the fool at home, and he'll jest with thee in the market.

Buscais cinco pies al gato.

(You are looking for five feet on a cat.) You are on a vain quest ; you hope for the impossible.

Buscar á Marica por Rabena, ó al bachiller en Salamanca.

(To look for Mary in Ravenna, or for the bachelor in Salamanca.) To look for a needle in a bundle of hay.

---

* Scholarship and skill in war make men famous.
† A gibe at those women who plume themselves on their virtue, though their lack of looks exposes them to few temptations.
‡ Perhaps this explains why titled directors were so much sought after by promoters of shaky companies.
§ A saying of the boaster who can lie fearlessly about his possessions in a distant land. We used to have a pleasantry, " He has large estates in Russia," derived, I believe, from a music-hall song that took the town some years ago.
‖ A hit at those " unco' guid " folk who, though they scorn the things of this world, have a very keen eye when their own interests are threatened.

Caballero.	A gentleman.
Caballo que vuela, no quiere espuela.	Do not spur a free horse.
Cada buhonero alaba sus agujas.	(Every hawker praises his own needles.) Every man cries up his own wares.
Cada cosa en su tiempo, y nabos en adviento.	Everything in season, and turnips in Advent.*
Cada dia gallina amarga la cocina.	Fowl every day makes bitter fare.*
Cada gallo canta en su muladar.	Every cock crows on his own dunghill.
Cada semana tiene su disanto.	(Every week has its Sunday.) The blackest cloud has a silver lining.
Cada uno alega en derecho de su dedo.	(Every man claims his right to his own finger.) Every man has a right to his own.
Cada uno case con su igual.	Let each marry with his equal.
Cada uno en su casa, y Dios en la de todos.	(Every one in his own house and God in all of them.) Every man for himself and God for us all.
Cada uno es como Dios le hijó, y aun peor muchas veces.—Cervantes.	Every one is as God made him, and frequently much worse.
Cada uno es hijo de sus obras. —Cervantes.	(Every man is the child of his own works.) A man is the architect of his own fortunes.
Cada uno estornuda como Dios le ayuda.	(Every one sneezes as God pleases.) A man's heart deviseth his ways; but the Lord directeth his steps. —Proverbs xvi., 9.
Cada uno mire por el virote.	(Let each man look out for the arrow.) Let every man mind his own business.†
Cada uno sabe adonde le aprieta el zapato.	Every one knows best where the shoe pinches him.
Cada uno se entiende, y trastejaba de noche, y hurtaba las tejas á su vecino.	Every one knows what he is about, mends his own roof at night, and steals his neighbour's tiles.
Cada uno tiene su alguacil.	(Every man has his constable.) All are subject to the laws.
Callar como negra en baño.	(Silent as a negress in a bath.) Silent as the grave.‡
Callate y callemos, que sendas nos tenemos.	(Be mum, let us both be mum, for we both have means.) Silence is good counsel for thieves.
Calle el que dió, hable el que tomó.	Let the giver be silent, let the receiver speak.
Callen barbas, y hablen cartas.	(Let beards be silent, let writings speak.) Documentary evidence is always the best.

* We learn from one of the characters in Gilbert and Sullivan's opera, *Patience*, that even toffee palls when it is eaten at every meal.

† This saying is said to have been first uttered by a general in command of a Spanish town. This town was constantly attacked by the Moors. When the general quitted his command, the burghers asked him how they should act in his absence if the Moors attacked them. *Cada uno mire por el virote*, he replied, meaning that, as the Moors were noted archers, every man would do well to be on his guard against exposing himself to unnecessary risks.

‡ A negress making use of her master's bath, would naturally be as quiet as possible, in order to avoid detection and punishment.

Canónigo del Salvador, y Abad de Olivares, todo es aire.	Canon of Salvador, and Abbot of Olivares, are nothing but air.*
Canta la rana y no tiene pelo ni lana.	(The frog croaks though it has neither hair nor wool.) Contentment is better than riches.
Cantarillo que muchas veces va á la fuente ó deja el asa ó la frente.	The pitcher which goes often to the well loses either its handle or its spout.
Cara de beato, y uñas de gato.	(A saint's face, and the claws of a cat.) A pious knave.
Caro cuesta el arrepentir.	Repentance costs dear.
Cartas, sospiros del alma ausente enamorada.—*A. Perez.*	Letters are the sighs of the heart that loves in spite of absence
Casa hospedada, comida y denostada.	A house given to hospitality, is devoured and reviled.
Casarás y amansarás.	(Marry and be tamed.) Marry in haste and repent at leisure.
Casar, casar, suena bien y sabe mal.	Marry! Marry! sounds well but has a bad taste.
Castillo apercebido, no es decebido.	(A castle prepared is not surprised.) Forewarned is forearmed.
Ciencia es locura si buen seso no la cura.	Knowledge is folly if not controlled by good sense.
Ciencia es para pobres riqueza, para ricos primor, y para viejos contentamiento.	Learning is wealth to the poor, an adornment to the rich, and contentment to the aged.
Cierra tu puerta, y harás tu vecina buena.	(Keep your door shut, and you will make your neighbour a good woman.) Opportunity makes the thief.
Cobra buena fama, y echate á dormir.	Acquire a good name and go to sleep.
Cochino fiado, buen invierno, y mal verano.	A pig bought on trust, good in winter, bad in the summer.†
Come poco y cena mas Duerme en alto y vivirás.	Lunch lightly, and dine well; sleep high up, and you will live.
Comida hecha, compañia deshecha.	When good cheer is lacking friends will be packing.
Como canta el abad, asi responde el sacristan.	As the parson chants, the clerk responds.
Como se vive, se muere.	(As one lives, one dies.) A good beginning makes a good ending.
Compañia de dos, compañia de Dios.	(Two in company is God's company.) Two's company, three is none.
Comprar en feria, y vender en casa.	Buy at a fair, and sell at home.
Comunicado el dolor Se aplaca si no se vence.—*Calderon.*	Sorrow, when told to another, is appeased if 'tis not cured.
Con agena mano sacar la culebra del horado.	(To draw the snake from the hole with another's hand.) To make a cat's-paw of another.
Con buen trage, se encubre ruin linage.	Fine clothes conceal a bad ancestry.

---

* These two ecclesiastical posts had no pay attached to them, so that the names were used as a proverbial illustration of an empty honour.

† Because a pig is usually killed in the winter, but must be paid for when the summer comes round again.

Con el rey y la inquisicion, chiton !

With the King and the Inquisition—mum's the word!

Con facilidad se piensa y se acomete una empresa, pero con dificultad las mas veces se sale de ella.—*Cervantes*.

With ease we plan and attempt an enterprise, but very often we have difficulty in quitting it.

Con hijo de gato ne se burlan los ratones.

Mice do not play with the son of the cat.

Con la distancia la pasion se agranda, Como la sombra cuando el sol se aleja. —*R. de Campoamor*.

Passion is increased by distance, as the shadows lengthen when the sun declines.

Con latin, rocin y florin andarás el mundo.

With Latin, a nag, and money you can traverse the world.

Con lo que Sancha sana, Marta cae mala.

(What cures Sancha makes Martha sick.) One man's meat is another man's poison.

Con mala persona el remedio mucha tierra en medio.

In dealing with a knave, the remedy is to give him a wide berth.

Conocer los afortunados, para la eleccion, y los desdichados para la fuga. —*Gracian*.

Observe the fortunate, in order to select them, and the unfortunate, in order to avoid them.*

Conocidos muchos, amigos pocos.

Many acquaintances, few friends.

Con su pan se lo coman.

(May they eat it with their bread.) May the evil recoil on the head of the doers.

Continuada felicidad fué siempre sospechosa; mas segura es la interpolada, y que tenga algo de agridulce.—*Gracian*.

An unbroken course of good fortune is always suspicious ; prosperity is more secure when it is sometimes interrupted, and when it is on occasions bitter-sweet.

Contra fortuna no vale arte ninguna.

There is no fighting against fate.

Contra gusto no hay disputa.

About tastes there is no disputing. *De gustibus non est disputandum*.

Contra peon hecho dama no para pieza en tabla.

(Against a pawn become a queen, no piece can stay on the board.) The worst tyrant is he that is risen from the lowest rank.

Corazon del alma, la confianza en Dios. —*Antonio Perez*.

The heart of the soul is trust in God.

Corregidor.

A magistrate.

Cortes de principes, sepultura de vivos. —*A. Perez*.

Courts of princes, burial alive.

Cortesia de boca mucho vale y poco cuesta.

Politeness is worth much and costs little.

Cortesia es el mayor hechizo politico de grandes personages.—*Gracian*.

Courtesy is the subtle fascination that great personages employ.

Cortesias engendran cortesias.

Politeness begets politeness.

Cosa mala nunca muere.

An evil thing never dies.

Coz de yegua no hace daño al potro.

A kick from the mare does not hurt the colt.

* This saying is quoted by Addison in his essay in No. 293 of the *Spectator*. The habit of always selecting the lucky as employés is said to be an important factor in the success of the Rothschilds.

Cria cuervos y te sacarán los ojos.

(Rear crows and they will peck out your eyes.)   Save a thief from the gallows and he will cut your throat.

Cual el cuervo,
Tal su huevo.

(As the crow, so the egg.)   Like father, like son.

Cuando Dios amanece, para todos amanece.

When God sends the day, He sends it for all.

Cuando en las obras del sabio
No encuentra defectos,
Contra la persona cargos
Suele hacer el necio.—*Yriarte*.

When no faults are found in the works of the wise man, the fool is wont to make attacks upon his person.

Cuando la miseria está muy extendida, la immoralidad es general.—*R. de Campoamor*.

When misery is widespread, immorality is general.

Cuando nace la escoba, nace el asno.

(When the broom grows, the ass is born.)   With the disease comes the cure.

Cuando no han los campos, no han los Santos.

(When the fields yield not, the Saints receive not.)   With an empty purse you cannot give.

Cuando no puede uno vestirse la piel del leon, vestase de la vulpeja.
— *Gracian*.

When you cannot clothe yourself in the lion's skin, put on that of the fox.

Cuando pierde de su punto
La justicia, no se acierta
En admitir la piedad.—*Lope de Vega*.

It is never right to allow pity to turn justice from its rightful course.

Cuando una sospecha es perpetua, es una verdad eterna.—*R. de Campoamor*.

When a suspicion endures, it becomes an eternal truth.

Cuando viene el bien, metelo en tu casa.
—*Cervantes*.

When a blessing comes to thee, take it into thy house.

Cuentaselo á tu abuela.

(Tell it to your granny.)   Tell that to the marines.

Cuidado ageno de pelo cuelga.

Another's sorrow hangs by a hair.

Cuidados agenos matan el asno.

Other folks' troubles kill the ass.

Culpa no tiene quien hace lo que puede.

He is not blamed who does his best.

Cuñados y perros bermejos, pocos buenos.

Of brothers-in-law and red-haired dogs few are good.

Da Dios almendras á quien no tiene muelas.

God gives almonds to him who has no teeth.

Da Dios habas á quien no tiene quijadas.

God gives beans to him who is toothless

Dádivas quebrantan peñas.

(Gifts break rocks.)   A golden key will open any door.

Dando gracias por agravios, negocian los hombres sabios.

Repaying injury with kindness is the way that prudent men act.

Dar gato por liebre.

(To give cat for hare.)   To give chalk for cheese.

Dar voces al lobo.

(To shout after the wolf.)   To cry over spilt milk.

Da ventura á tu hijo, y echalo en el mar.

(Give your son luck, and throw him into the sea.) It is better to be born lucky than rich.*

De aquí para allí.

This way and that; to and fro.

De *Arte amandi* escribió Ovidio,
Pero todo es falsedad;
Que el amor y la poesia
Por arte no satisfacen,
Porque los poetas nacen
Y el amor amantes cria.
—*Tirso de Molina.*

Ovid wrote an *Art of Love*, but it is all untrue. Love and poetry do not satisfy by their art, for poets are born, and lovers are made by love.

Debajo del buen sayo, está el hombre malo.

(Under a good cloak there may be a bad man.) A man may smile and smile, and be a villain.

Debajo de una mala capa, hay un buen bebedor.

(Under a ragged cloak there may be a fine tippler.) Many an honest man is clothed in rags.†

De buena planta, planta tu viña,
Y de buena madre toma la hija.

For thy vineyard take a cutting from a good vine, and for thy wife the daughter of a good mother.

Decir y hacer no comen á una mesa.

(Saying and doing do not eat at the same table.) Between saying and doing a man may marry his daughter.

De cualquier manera que vaya vestido seré Sancho Panza.

(However I am dressed, I shall still be Sancho Panza.) I shall be neither more nor less meritorious.

De curiosos es callar por aprender.
—*A. Perez.*

Curious folk should be silent in order to learn.

De dineros y bondad, siempre quita la mitad.

In talking of money and goodness, always halve what is told you.

De fisico experimentador y de asno bramador, "libera nos."

From a doctor who experiments on his patients, and from a braying ass— Good Lord deliver us.

De gran subida gran caida.

The greater the rise the greater the fall.

De hombre seco y no de hambre, huye del como del landre.

From a man who is lean and has no lack of food, flee as from the plague.

De hombres es errar, de bestias perseverar en el error.

To err is human, to persist in error the part of a beast.

Del agua mansa me guarde Dios, que de la brava yo me guardaré.

(God protect me from still water, from the rough I will protect myself.) Heaven keep me from a treacherous enemy.

De la honra es breve atajo
El estudio que el cuerdo ama,
Porque al templo de la fama
Se entra por el del trabajo.
—*Tirso de Molina.*

Study, which the wise man loves, is the shortest path to honour. Into the Temple of Fame we enter by the gate of Work.

---

* A proverb quoted by Schopenhauer in his *Parerga et Paralipomena.* For a similar idea compare *Fortuna te dé Dios, hijo*, &c.

† Another version of this proverb says, *Hay un buen vividor*, i.e., "Under a ragged cloak there may be a well-living man." The common opinion that a tippler is a fine fellow betrays a lamentable ignorance of the real selfishness of that class of people

Del alcalde al verdugo, ved como subo. | (From magistrate to hangman, see how he rises.) From horses to asses.

De la mano á la boca, se pierde la sopa. | (From the hand to the mouth the soup is spilt.) There's many a slip 'twixt the cup and the lip.

De la mar la sal, y de la mujer mucho mal. | From the sea comes salt, from woman comes evil.

Del dicho al hecho hay gran trecho. | From saying to doing is a long way.

Del fraile toma el consejo y no el ejemplo. | Follow the friar's advice but not his example.

Del hombre arraigado no te verás vengado. | You will never be avenged on the man of property.

De los enemigos los menos. | The fewer enemies, the better.*

De los hijos el que muere es mas amado. | Of children the one that dies is most dearly loved.

De los hombres letrados se hacen los obispos. | (Bishops are chosen from the learned.) Schoolmaster bishops.

De los ingratos esta lleno el infierno. | Hell is full of the ungrateful.

De los leales se hinchen los hospitales. | The workhouses are full of honest folk.

De luengas vias, luengas mentiras. | From long journeys, long lies.†

De Madrid al cielo. | (From Madrid to Heaven.) Madrid is the next place to Heaven, in the opinion of the proud Madrilenos.

De mis amigos me libre Dios, que de mis contrarios me guardaré yo. | God preserve me from my friends; from my foes I will preserve myself.

De mis viñas vengo, no sé nada. | (I come from my vineyard, and know nothing.) I am a simple fellow, and have no head for great matters.

De moza adivina, y de mujer Latina, "libera nos." | From a girl who tells fortunes, and from a woman who knows Latin—Good Lord deliver us.

De noche todos los gatos son pardos. | (At night all cats are grey.) Joan's as fair as my lady in the dark.

De pequeña centella, gran hoguera. | A little spark kindles a great fire.

De piel agena larga la correa. | Of another's leather cut large thongs.

De pobre á rico, dos palmos ; De rico á pobre, dos dedos. | From poverty to wealth, the breadth of two hands : from wealth to poverty, the breadth of two fingers.

De potro sarnoso buen caballo hermoso. | A ragged colt may turn out a fine horse.

De puerta cerrada el diablo se torna. | The devil turns away from a closed door.

De qué sirve la hermosura,
(Cuando lo fuese la mia)
Si me falta la alegria ?
Si me falta la ventura ?—*Calderon.* | What does loveliness avail me,
(If, indeed, 'tis mine to vaunt it)
If my joy of heart be wanted ?
If life's happiest feelings' fail me ?
—*D. F. MacCarthy.*

---

* According to Mr. Ormsby, the proverb originated in the following manner. Philip II. was anxious to exterminate the Moriscos of Southern Spain, but being fearful lest in so doing he should be acting in a manner not befitting a Christian monarch, he consulted the Church, and received the above reply.

† A useful motto for a book of travellers' tales.

De ruin paño nunca buen sayo.

(From bad cloth a good coat is never made.) You cannot make a silk purse of a sow's ear.

De sabios es mudar de consejo.

The wise man may change his opinion, but the fool never.

Desaire comun es de afortunados, tener muy favorables los principios, y muy tragicos los fines.—*Gracian.*

This is commonly the ill turn that Fortune does to the unlucky; a pleasing entrance, but a tragic exit from the stage of life.

De oldado que no tiene capa, guarda la vaca.

From a soldier who has no cloak keep thy cow.

D' espacio piensa, y obra á priesa.

Consider slowly and act promptly.

Despues de comer, dormir, y de cenar pasos mil.

After dinner rest a while; After supper walk a mile.

Despues de vendimias cuébanos.

(After the vintage, baskets.) Help that comes too late.

Déte Dios, hijo, ventura,
Que ella traerá lo demás.
    —*Tirso de Molina.*

God give thee luck, my son; with that the rest will come.

De todos los caminos de la vida
El más corto y mejor es el del cielo.
    —*R. de Campoamor.*

Of all the roads of life the shortest and the best is that which leads to Heaven.

De tu mujer y de tu amigo experto, no creas sino lo que supieres cierto.

About your wife and your tried friend, believe nothing except what you know for certain.

De un hombre necio á veces buen consejo.

Sometimes a fool gives good counsel.

Dicen los niños en el solejar lo que oyen á sus padres en el hogar.

Children say in the sunshine what they hear their parents speak of by the fire.

Dicente que eres bueno, mete la mano en tu seno.

(When they say you are good put your hand on your heart.) Ask yourself whether your reputation is deserved.

Dichoso es, no él que lo parece á otros, mas á si.

The happy is not he who seems so to others, but he who seems so to himself.

Dijo la sarten á la caldera, quitate allá ojinegra.

(The frying-pan said to the kettle, "Go away, black face.") The pot calling the kettle black.

Dime con quien andas, decirte he quien eres.

Tell me what company you keep, and I will tell you what you are.

Dineros y no consejos.

(Money and not advice.) Sermons are cheap, but help costs something.

Dios consiente y no para siempre.

God suffers us, but not for ever.

Dios desavenga, quien nos mantenga.

(God send quarrels that I may live.) The prayer of a lawyer.

Dios es el que sana, y el medico lleva la plata.

God effects the cure, and the doctor takes the fee.

Dios hará merced. Y aun tres dias sin comer.

"God will provide." "Another three days without food."*

* The first part of this proverb is the remark of a person from whom alms have been solicited. The rest is the comment of the unsuccessful supplicant.

Dios me libre de hombre de un libro.

Dios proveerá, mas buen haz de paja se querrá.

Dios que dá la llaga, dá la medicina.

Dios sabe la verdad de todo.

Dios va abriendo su mano.

Do fuerza viene, derecho se pierde.

Donde está la verdad está Dios.
—*Cervantes.*

Donde fuego se hace humo sale.

Donde hay gana hay maña.

Donde hay mucho amor no suele haber demasiada desenvoltura.

Donde las dan las toman.

Donde no hay tocinos no hay estacas.

Donde no se piensa salta la liebre.

Donde perdió la niña su honor ? Donde habló mal y oyó peor.

Donde una puerta se cierra, otra se abre.

Do no hay vergüenza, no hay virtud.

Dos amigos con una bolsa, el uno canta, el otro llora.

Dos dias tienen de gusto
Las mujeres (sino yerran
Los que sus acciones tasan)
Y son en él que se casan,
Y el que á su marido entierran.
—*Tirso de Molina.*

Dos linages solos hay en el mundo, el "Tener" y el "No Tener."

Dos pocos, y un mucho hacen á un hombre.

Duelos con pan son menos.

God deliver me from a man of one book.

God will provide, but a good bundle of straw will be useful.

God who sends the wound, sends the medicine.

(God knows the truth in everything.) " God is not mocked."

God is always opening his hand.

When Force comes on the scene, Right goes packing.

Where truth is, there is God.

There is no fire without some smoke.

Where there's a will there's a way.

Where there is much love, there is seldom great boldness.

One good turn deserves another.

Where there is no hook, there will hang no bacon.

The hare leaps from the bush where we least expect her.

(Where did the girl lose her virtue ? Where she spoke ill, and heard worse.) Evil communications corrupt good manners.

Where one door closes, another opens.

Where there is no shame, there is no virtue.

Two friends with one purse, one sings, the other weeps.

Unless the people who study feminine ways err, there are two blissful days in a woman's life. The first, the day on which she is married ; the second, the day she buries her husband.

There are but two families in the world, the Haves and the Have-nots.

(Two littles and one much make a man rich.) Little shame, little conscience, and much impudence are necessary.

(Sorrows with bread are lessened.) Fat sorrow is better than lean sorrow.

Echar el alma á las espaldas.

(To throw one's soul over one's shoulders.) To say good-bye to honour and conscience.

I I

Echar la capa al toro.

(To throw one's cloak at the bull.) To use desperate means to save one's life.*

Echar margaritas á puercos.

To throw pearls before swine.

El abad de lo que canta yanta.

The abbot dines by his chanting.

El agua como buey, y vino como ey.

(Treat water like an ox, and wine like a king.) Drink water freely, wine sparingly.

El agua ni enferma, ni adeuda, ni enviuda.

Water causes neither sickness, debt, nor widowhood.

El amigo ha de ser como la sangre, que acude luego á la herida sin esperar que la llamen.—*A. Perez.*

A friend ought to be like the blood, which runs quickly to the wound without waiting to be called.

El amor á la patria es la ley de gravedad del alma.—*R. de Campoamor.*

Love of one's country is the soul's law of gravity.

El amor de los que de veras aman cresce con la ausencia.—*Antonio Perez.*

Love in those who truly love increases with absence.

El amor es atrevido: el respeto medroso.—*A. Perez.*

Love is bold; Respect is timid.

El amor favorable ó contrario causa melancolia.—*Antonio Perez.*

Love, requited or unrequited, produces melancholy.

El amor iguala á todos estados.—*A. Perez.*

Love makes all positions equal

El amor mira con unos anteojos que hacen parecer oro al cobre, á la pobreza riqueza, y á las lagañas perlas. --*Cervantes.*

Love looks through spectacles which make copper appear gold, poverty appear wealth, and sore eyes seem to drop pearls.†

El amor quiere el *cuerpo,* y la amistad el *alma.*—*R. de Campoamor.*

Love desires the body, Friendship the soul.

El amor sustento de la vida humana. —*A. Perez.*

Love is the support of human life.

El amor y la fe en las obras se ve.

Love and faith in deeds are seen.

El ansar de Cantinpalo, que salió al lobo al camino.

The goose of Cantinpalo, that went out on the road to meet the wolf.

El asno á la vihuela.

(The ass at the guitar.) *Asinus ad lyram.*

El asno sufre la carga, mas no la sobrecarga.

(The ass endures its proper load, but not the excessive load.) It is the last straw that breaks the camel's back.

El barato de Juan del Carpio.

John Carpio's reward.‡

El Bien nunca muere.
　　　　—*Don Juan Manuel.*

Goodness never dies.

El bobo, si es callado, por sesudo es reputado.

The fool, if he is silent, is accounted wise.

---

* An expression borrowed from the practice of the bull-fighters, who throw their cloak aside in order to divert the bull from themselves.

† *Lagañas* are the specks of coagulated matter which are often seen in the eyes of people with weak sight.

‡ Juan del Carpio is said to have been an unfortunate fellow who undertook to wait upon a party of merry-makers at a dinner. When the wine had mounted to the heads of the guests, they began to quarrel and throw the candlesticks about. In the darkness poor Juan's head was broken, and—unkindest cut of all—he received no pay.

El buen pagador señor es de lo ageno.

A good paymaster is master of another's wealth.

El buen paño en el arca se vende.

(Good cloth sells itself in the box.) Good wine needs no bush.

El buen soldado, sacalo del arado.

The good soldier, take from the plough.*

El buey que me acornó, en buen lugar me echó.

(The bull that tossed me, pitched me into a good place.) Misfortunes are sometimes blessings in disguise.

El buey sin cencerro, piérdese presto.

The ox without a bell is quickly lost.

El caballero de la Triste Figura.

The Knight of the Woeful Countenance.†

El ciego mal juzgará de colores.

A blind man is a bad judge of colours.

El comer y el rascar todo es empezar.

To eat and to scratch, a man need but begin.

El consejo de la mujer es poco, y quien no le toma es loco.

The advice of a wife is a little thing, and he who does not take it is a fool.

El Constante Principe.

The Constant Prince.‡

El cuitádo del maravedi hace cornado, y el liberal, del maravedi real.

The covetous man turns a farthing into a penny, but the generous man turns it into a sixpence.

El dar limosna nunca mengua la bolsa.

Almsgiving never lightens the purse.

El dar y el tener, seso ha menester.

To give and to keep need a wise head.

El deseo hace hermoso lo feo.

Desire makes beautiful what is ugly.

El Diablo está en Cantillana.

The Devil is in Cantillana.§

El dinero hace al hombre entero.

Money makes the man.

El Dorado.

The Golden Land.

El encarecer es ramo de mentir.
—*Gracian.*

Exaggeration is a branch of lying.

El escusarse antes de ocasion es culparse.—*Gracian.*

To excuse oneself beforehand is to accuse oneself. *Qui s'excuse, s'accuse.*

El golpe de la sarten, aunque no duele, tizna.

(The blow from a frying-pan blackens, even though it does not hurt.) If you throw plenty of mud some of it is bound to stick.

El habito no hace el monge.

The cowl does not make the monk. *Cucullus non facit monachum.*

El hacer bien á villanos es echar agua en la mar.

(To do a good turn to a knave is like throwing water in the sea.) Nurse a viper in your bosom, and it will sting you.

---

* The plan followed by the Romans, as Nuñez is careful to mention. However, although the country districts produced the best soldiers in the days of Cincinnatus, the contrary to this saying appears to be true in modern times, when the best soldiers, in intelligence if not in physique, are drawn from the towns.

† The title that the gallant Don Quixote, Knight de la Mancha, gives himself when he writes to the fair Dulcinea del Toboso.

‡ The title of one of Calderon's best-known plays. The hero, Don Ferdinand, Intante of Portugal, was taken captive by the Moors, and remained their prisoner from 1438 to 1443, when he died in captivity.

§ This expression is said to have been applied to one Juan Tenorio, a brigand whose depredations made him the terror of his countrymen during the reign of Alfonso XI.

El hacer bien nunca se pierde. — A good deed is never lost.

El hacerse immortal cuesta la vida!
—*R. de Campoamor.* — Making ourselves immortal costs us life.

El hijo muerto y el apio en el huerto. — (The son dead, and the celery in the garden.) After death, the doctor; after meat, mustard.

El hilo por lo mas delgado quiebra. — (The thread breaks where it is thinnest.) The chain breaks at its weakest link.

El hombre es el fuego, la mujer la estopa, viene el diablo y sopla. — Man is the fire, woman the tow, and the devil comes and fans the flame.

El hombre perezoso, en la fiesta es acucioso. — The lazy man is energetic at the feast.

El hombre propone, y Dios dispone. — Man proposes, God disposes.

El hombre propone, Dios dispone, y viene la mujer y lo descompone. — Man proposes, God disposes, then woman comes and discomposes.

El huello descubre el natural del hombre.—*Antonio Perez.* — His deportment reveals a man's nature.

El huesped, y el pez, á tres dias huele. — A guest and a fish stink after three days.

El Judio azotó su hijo porque ganó la primera. — The Jew thrashed his son because he won the first game.*

El ladrón. de la aguja al huevo; del huevo al buey; del buey á la horca. — The thief's progress : from a needle to an egg; from an egg to an ox; from an ox to the halter.

El mal de milano, las alas quebradas y el pico sano. — The kite's misfortune, its wings broken, and its bill sound.†

El malo siempre piensa engaño. — The knave always suspects knavery.

El marido antes con un ojo que con un hijo. — The husband with one eye rather than with a son.

El mayor bien gozado
Jamás es grande hasta que ya es pasado.
—*R. de Campoamor.* — Our greatest joys are never great until they have left us.

El melon y la mujer malos son de conocer. — (A melon and a woman are difficult to know.) Only an expert knows a good one by their exterior.

El mentir no tiene alcabala. — There is no tax on telling lies.‡

El mónstruo de la naturaleza. — The prodigy of Nature.§

El mozo perezoso por no dar un paso dá ocho. — The lazy varlet takes eight steps to save one.

El muerto á la fosada, y el vivo á la hogaza. — The dead to the grave, and the living to the table.

El olvido, la muerte de la muerte!
—*R. de Campoamor.* — To be forgotten is the death of death.

---

* It is a familiar trick of professional gamblers to lose at first. Rawdon Crawley, as readers of *Vanity Fair* will remember, was singularly unskilful at the commencement of a game of billiards.

† This saying is applied to braggarts who, like Falstaff, are very bold until they meet " men in buckram."

‡ *Y por eso lo usan todos tanto.* "And for that reason all men use it so much," adds Nuñez.

§ This was the title given by his admiring compatriots to Lope de Vega, whose amazing skill was equalled only by the prolific nature of his writings.

El órden nace, la anarquía se hace.
     —*R. de Campoamor.*

(Order is born, anarchy is made.) Men are naturally law-abiding, but misrule breeds revolutionaries.

El pan comido y la compañia deshecha.

(The bread eaten and the company dispersed.) When poverty comes our friends go packing.

El perro del hortelano, ni come las berzas, ni las deja comer al estraño.

The gardener's dog neither eats the cabbages, nor lets another eat them.*

El poco hablar es oro, y el mucho es lodo.

Little speaking is gold, much speaking is mud.

El poder de la tierra no tiene poder en os ánimos.—*Antonio Perez.*

(Authority over the world holds no authority over the mind.) Though a man is enslaved, still his thoughts are free.

El podrá ser, es la esperanza de los necios.

" It may happen " is the hope of fools.

El principio de la salud está en conocer la enfermedad.—*Cervantes.*

To understand the disease is the first step to the cure.

El puerco sarnoso revuelve la pocilga.

(The pig with the itch upsets the whole pig-sty.) One rotten sheep mars the whole flock.

El puerto de las miserias es la paciencia.

(Patience is the haven of sorrows.) Time heals all things.

El que callar no puede, hablar no sabe.

He who cannot be silent, knows not how to speak.

El que ha ovejas, ha pellejas.

He who has sheep, has fleeces.

El que hoy cae puede levantarse mañana.

He who falls to-day may rise to-morrow.

El que merca y miente su bolsa lo siente.

He who trades and lies, his purse feels it.

El que muere pobre, no muere ántes de tiempo.

(He that dies a poor man, dies not prematurely.) It is better for a man to die than suffer want.

El que no sabe gozar de la ventura cuando le viene, que no se debe quejar si se le pasa.—*Cervantes.*

He that does not know how to enjoy prosperity when it comes to him, ought not to complain when it passes him by.

El que tiene el padre alcalde seguro va á juicio.

He whose father is the magistrate goes fearlessly to trial.

El que tiene tejados de vidro, no tire piedras al de su vecino.

Those who have their house tiled with glass, should not throw stones at their neighbour's.

El rey es mi gallo.

(The king is my cock.) The strongest is the side for me.†

El rey va hasta do puede, y no hasta do quiere.

The king goes as far as he can, not as far as he would.

El rio pasado, el santo olvidado.

The river crossed, the saint forgotten.

---

* The gardener's dog corresponds to our " dog in the manger." Calderon wrote a comedy with the title *El perro del Ortelano.* In this play a noble lady acts the part of the dog in the manger, for, being enamoured of one of her servants, she will not allow him to marry, nor will she, until love proves too strong for her, wed him herself.
† Cock-fighting is a popular sport in Spain.

El saber y el valor alternan grandeza ;
porque lo son hacen immortales; tanto
es uno quanto sabe, y el sabio todo
lo puede.   Hombre sin noticias,
mundo á escuras. Consejos, y fuerzas,
ojos, y manos ; sin valor es esteril la
sabiduria.—*Gracian.*

Knowledge and courage go together to
the making of greatness ; for they
cause it to be immortal ; a man is
what his knowledge is, and to the
wise man all is possible.   A man
without knowledge, a world in darkness. Counsel and strength, eyes and
hands. Without courage knowledge
is a barren possession.

El santo enojado, con no rezarle está
pagado.

To the angry saint no prayers are paid.

El sastre del Campillo, coser de balde,
y poner el hilo.

The tailor of Campillo, who sewed for
nothing, and found his own thread.

El secreto de Anchuelos.

(The secret of Anchuelos.)   A secret
that every one knows.*

El sentir es libre, no se puede, ni deve
violentar.—*Gracian.*

Thought is free ; it neither can, nor
ought it to, suffer violence.

El socorro de Escalona, cuando llega el
agua, es quemada la villa toda.

The help of Escalon ; when the water
arrives, the town is burnt.†

El sueño es alivio de las miserias de los
que las tienen despiertas. — *Cervantes.*

Sleep is a healing balm to those whose
sorrows sleep not.

El tiempo es el descubridor de todas
las cosas.

Time is the discoverer of all things.

El tiempo, y yo á otros dos.

Time and I against any other two.‡

El usar saca oficial.

Practice makes the craftsman.

El viejo en su tierra, y el mozo en la
agena, mienten de una manera.

The old man in his own land, and the
youth abroad, both lie in the same
manner.

El vino no trae bragas, ni de paño, ni
de leño.

(Wine wears neither linen nor woollen
breeches.)   When wine's in wit's out.

En batallas tales
Los que vencen son leales,
Los vencidos los traidores.—*Calderon.*

In contests of this kind (civil war) the
victors are considered the loyalists,
the vanquished, traitors.

En boca cerrada no entra mosca.

(A fly does not enter a shut mouth.) A
still tongue shows a wise head.

En buen dia, buenas obras.

(On a good day, good deeds.)   The
better the day, the better the deed.

En casa del bueno el ruin cabe el fuego.

(In a good man's house the beggar sits
by the fire.)   The poor man has the
best place in the house.

En casa del herrero cuchillo mangorrero.

In the house of the smith a haftless
knife. §

---

* Anchuelos is situated between two hills. The proverb is said to have arisen from the
habit of an amorous shepherd and shepherdess, who, tradition declares, were wont to shout
loving messages to one another from hill to hill, oblivious of the listeners below.
† Escalona is a small town situated some eight miles from Toledo. It is situated on the
crest of a hill, and, according to Collins, when a fire broke out in the place it was impossible
to bring water from the bottom of the hill soon enough to prevent the flames from taking a
firm hold.
‡ This saying is commonly attributed to Charles V., although Schopenhauer gives the credit
of it to Philip II.
§ This is the old form of the proverb. *Mangorrero* is given in the dictionaries as meaning
"hafted," but, as Don José Sbarbi points out in his *Monografia* on Spanish proverbs, such a
sense makes the proverb pointless. In its correct sense, the proverb is equivalent to our
" Who goes worse shod than the cobbler's wife ? "

En casa del mezquino manda más la mujer que el marido.

In the poor man's cottage the wife rules more than the husband.

En casa del moro no hables algarabia.

(Do not speak Arabic in the house of the Moor.) Don't talk Latin before the learned.

En cueros.

Stark naked.

En el mejor paño cae la raza.

In the best cloth the thread is rough.

En España se empieza tarde, y se acaba nunca.

In Spain they begin late and finish never.

En invierno no hay amigo como una capa.

In winter time there is no friend like a good cloak.

En la creacion no importa tanto el *cómo* y el *cuando*, como el *por qué* y el *para qué.—R. de Campoamor.*

In (considering) the Creation, the How and the When does not matter so much as the Why and the Wherefore.

En la tardanza está el peligro.

Delays are dangerous.

En lo justo
Dice el cielo que obedezca
El esclavo á su señor ;
Porque si el señor dijera
A' su esclavo que pecara,
Obligacion no tuviera
De obedecerle ; porque
Quien peca mandado, peca.—*Calderon.*

In all things just,
Heaven, no doubt, commands obedience,
And no slave should fail therein ;
But, if it should chance, the master
Should command the slave to sin
Then there is no obligation
To obey him : he who sins
When commanded, no less sinneth.
—*D. F. MacCarthy.*

En los casos raros un solo exemplo hace experiencia.—*A. Perez.*

In rare cases does one occurrence give experience.[*]

En los nidos de antaño, no hay pajaros hogaño.

(In last year's nests there are no birds of this year.) Gather the roses while ye may. *Carpe diem.*

En ménos que se dice el Credo.

(In less time than it takes to say the Creed.) More quickly than you can say Jack Robinson.

En puerta abierta el justo peca.

At an open door the just man sins.

En tiempo del rey Vamba.

(In the time of King Wamba.) In the dim, forgotten past.[†]

En tierra de ciegos, el tuerto es rey.

In the country of the blind, the one-eyed is king.

Entre dos muelas cordales nunca pongas tus pulgares.

(Between two double teeth never put your fingers.) Do not interfere between husband and wife.

Entre hermano y hermano, dos testigos, y un notario.

Between brother and brother, two witnesses and a lawyer.

Entre padres y hermanos,
No metas tus manos.

Between fathers and brothers put not your hands.

En un momento se cae la casa.

In a twinkling down falls the house.

En vino y ni en toro, no eches tu tesoro.

Do not invest in wine or bulls.[‡]

Esa es buena y honrada que es muerta y sepultada.

She is a good and honoured woman who is dead and buried.

* We, on the contrary, say of a painful experience "Once bitten, twice shy."
† Wamba is said to have ruled in the 7th century, A.D.
‡ In Spain, the land of the bull-fight, bulls sometimes fetch fabulous prices.

Esa es harina de otro costal.

(That is flour from a different sack.) That is quite another pair of shoes.

Esa es la herencia de Adan.
—*Calderon.*

That (Misery) is the heritage of the sons of Adam.

Es amarga más que fiel
La justicia á los viciosos,
Pero dulce más que miel
A' los nobles virtuosos.
—*Fernán Perez de Guzman.*

Justice is more bitter than gall to the wicked, but sweeter than honey to the noble and the good.

Es bueno mandar, aunque sea á un hato de ganado.—*Cervantes.*

It is fine thing to command, even if it be only a herd of cattle.

Es bueno vivir para ver.

It is good to live in order to see.) The longer you live, the more you learn.

Escritura, buena memoria.

(Writing, the best memory.) Writing makes the exact man.

Es de Lope.

It is Lope's.*

Es de vidrio la mujer.

(Of glass is woman made.) Chastity once lost can never be regained.

Es duro el alcacel para zampoñas.

'Tis hard to make a bag-pipe out of a green corn-stalk.

Ese es tu enemigo, el que es de tu oficio.

(He is your enemy who is of your trade.) Two of a trade never agree.

Ese te quiere bien que te hace llorar.

(He loves thee well who makes thee weep.) For whom the Lord loveth he chasteneth, and scourgeth every son whom he receiveth.
—*Hebrews* xii. 6.

Es grande y noble
Convertir en virtudes
Imperfecciones.—*J. E. Hartzenbusch.*

It is a great and noble task to change one's failings into virtues.

Es la virtud del hombre
La que le inclina á los ilustres hechos.
—*Lope de Vega.*

Virtue in a man is that which inclines him to noble acts.

Es soberbia la hermosura.
—*Lope de Vega.*

(Beauty is haughtiness.) Beauty and pride go hand in hand.

Estar como el diablo apareció á San Benito.

(To be as the devil appeared to St. Benedict.) *In puris naturalibus.*

Esta sola es la ventaja del mandar, poder hacer mas bien que todos.
—*Gracian.*

This is the unique advantage of being a ruler—that one is able to do more good than anyone else.

Estiman algunos los libros por la corpulencia, como si le escriviessen para exercitar los brazos, que los ingenios.
—*Gracian.*

Some folk estimate the value of books by their thickness, as though they were written to exercise the arms rather than the brains.

Estómago hambriento no escucha razones.

There is no arguing with an empty stomach.

Es valiente como la espada del Cid.

(He is as brave as the sword of the Cid.) The bravest of the brave.

Exaltado progresista.

An advanced progressist ; a Radical.

* So great was the fame of **Lope de Vega** among his countrymen, that the expression *Es de Lope* was commonly applied to any smart saying.

Excusar victorias del patron. Todo vencimiento es odioso, y del dueño, ó necio, ó fatal. Siempre la superioridad fué aborrecida, quanto mas de la misma superioridad.—*Gracian.*

Avoid victories over one's superior. All victories are invidious things, and one gained over one's master is foolish, if not fatal. Superiority is always abhorred, and much more so superiority established over superiority.

Fandango.

A lively dance.

Fiel, pero desdichado.

Faithful, but unlucky.

Fonda.

An hotel.

Fortuna te dé Dios, hijo, Que el saber, poco te basta.

God give thee luck, my son ; as for wisdom, a little sufficeth thee.

Fortuna y Fama. Lo que tiene de inconstante la una, tiene de firme la otra. La primera para vivir, la segunda para despues : aquella contra la invidia, esta contra el olvido : la fortuna se desea, y tal vez se ayuda, la fama se diligencia. Deseo de reputacion nace de la virtud : fue y es hermana de Gigantes la Fama, anda siempre por extremos, ó monstruos, ó prodigios, de abominacion, de aplauso.—*Gracian.*

Fortune and Reputation. While the former is inconstant, the latter abides; while Fortune concerns the present life, Reputation affects the after time; the one is a bulwark against Envy, the other against Oblivion. We desire Fortune, and sometimes can assist it ; but Reputation we must earn. The desire for Reputation is the child of a virtuous instinct ; it was, and is, the sister of giants, for it always runs to extremes, producing either monsters that excite our loathing, or prodigies that gain our applause.

Frutos del trabajo justo Son honra, provecho y gusto.

The fruits of honest toil are honour, profit, and enjoyment.

Fueron mis esperanzas Como el almendro : Florecieron temprano, Cayeron presto.

My hopes were like the almond-tree ; they bloomed soon and were as quickly blighted.*

Gato escaldado del agua fria há miedo.

A scalded cat is afraid of cold water.

Gato maullador nunca buen cazador.

A mewing cat is not a good mouser.

Gemidos y lagrimas de opprimidos, memoriales á Dios.—*Antonio Perez.*

The sighs and tears of the oppressed are petitions sent to God.

Gente de costa todos ladrones.

The people of the sea-coast are all thieves.†

Gitano.

A gipsy.

Goza tu del poco mientras busca mas el loco.

(Enjoy thy little while the fool seeks for more.)   Contentment is better than riches.

Grande arma es la necessidad.

(Necessity is a strong arm.)   Necessity is the mother of invention.

---

* The almond-tree is typical of disappointed hopes.   See note on *Antes moral tardío,* &c. in this section.

† A saying that was old long before the habit of taking an annual trip to the sea-coast made the rapacity of the hotel-keepers, &c., known unto all men.

Grandeza verdadera, la bondad de cada uno.—*A. Perez.*

(True greatness in every man is goodness.)
Kind hearts are more than coronets,
And simple faith than Norman blood.
—*Tennyson.*

Gran dote cama de rencillas.

A great dowry is a bed of thorns.

Gran placer comer y no escotar.

It is a great pleasure to dine without paying the bill.

Gran victoria es la que sin sangre se alcanza.

Great is the victory that is won without bloodshed.

Guardate de amigo reconciliado,
Y de viento que entra por horado.

Beware of a friend reconciled, and of wind that comes through a hole.

Guardate, moza, de promesa de hombre que como cangrejo corre.

Beware, maiden, of a man's promise, for it goes crab-fashion.

Guerra al cuchillo.

War to the knife.

Guerra, caza, y amores, por un placer mil dolores.

War, hunting, and love, for one pleasure bring a thousand pains.

Guerrilla.

An irregular petty war; an armed mountaineer, member of an independent band harassing the enemy by irregular attacks.

Haber moros y cristianos.

(Moors and Christians together.) Donnybrook Fair.

Habiendo pregonado vino, vende vinagre.

After having advertised wine he sells vinegar.

Habla poco, escucha mucho, y no errarás.

Speak little, hearken much, and thou wilt not be deceived.

Hablar poco y bien, tenerte han por alguien.

Speak little and well, and people wil take you for somebody.

Hablar sin pensar es tirar sin encarar.

To speak without thinking is to shoot without taking aim.

Habló el buey y dijo "Mu."

(The ox spoke and said "Moo.") Silence is the wisdom of the fool.

Hacer Angulemas.

(To act in Angoulême fashion.) To be impertinent.*

Hacer castillos en el aire.

(To build castles in the air.) *Bâtir des châteaux en Espagne.*

Hacer de la gata de Juan Hurtado.

(To play the part of John Hurtado's cat.) To dissemble; to act treacherously.†

Hacer la cuenta con la almohada.

(To reckon with one's pillow.) To ponder before acting.

Hacer la cuenta sin la huespeda.

To reckon without one's host.

Hacienda.

A country estate.

Hambre y frio, entregan al hombre á su enemigo.

Hunger and cold deliver a man up to his enemy.

---

* The inhabitants of Angoulême were an object of great detestation to their neighbours, the Spaniards.
† John Hurtado's cat feigned death in order to deceive its prey.

Hase de guardar y estimar la mujer buena, como se guarda y estima un hermoso jardin que está lleno de flores y rosas.—*Cervantes*.

A good woman ought to be protected and prized like a beautiful garden which is full of flowers and roses.

Hasta el cuarenta de Mayo
No te quites el sayo.

Don't cast your clout
Till May is out.

Hasta la muerte todo es vida.
—*Cervantes*.

(Until death comes, all is life.) While there is life, there is hope.

Hay diferentes opiniones, como hay diferentes gustos.—*Cervantes*.

There are differences of opinion just as there are differences of taste.

Hay más estacas que tocino.

(There are more hooks than bacon) There are more mouths than loaves to fill them.

Hay una cosa más alta que los deberes públicos, y es el honor individual.
—*R. de Campoamor*.

There is one thing higher than public duties—it is private honour.

Haz bien y no cates á quien, haz mal y guarte.

Do well and fear no one; do ill, and be on your guard.

Hazme la barba, y hacerte he el copete.

(Shave me, and I will brush your hair.) Scratch my back, and I'll scratch thine.

Hermosa es por cierto la que es buena de su cuerpo.

She is truly beautiful who is chaste in body.

Herradura que chacotea clavo le falta.

The horseshoe that clatters needs a nail.*

Hidalgo.

A gentleman belonging by birth to the inferior nobility.

Hidalguia.

Nobility.

Hija desposada hija enagenada.

A daughter married is a daughter lost.

Hijo fuiste, padre serás,
Cual hiciste, tal habrás.

A son thou wert, and father shall be; And what thou didst shall be done to thee.†

Hijos del entendimiento, los escritos.
—*Antonio Perez*.

Writings are the children of the understanding.

Hijo sin dolor, madre sin amor.

(A son without pain, a mother without love.) A mother's love goes out most to those children who have caused most pain and anxiety.

Hombre de un libro.

A man of one book.

Hombre harto no es comedor.

(A man replete is no eater.) Enough is as good as a feast.

Hombre juicioso y notante. Señorease él de los objetos, no los objetos dél.
—*Gracian*.

A man of judgment and observation is master of things, and not things of him.

Hombre pobre todo estrazas.

A poor man is all schemes.

Honra y provecho no caben en un saco.

Honour and lucre do not keep in the same bag.

---

* Schopenhauer quotes this proverb, with approval, in his *Parerga et Paralipomena*. His explanation of it is that men always boast most of possessing that quality which they really lack. Thus the man who declares to men that women cannot resist him is generally timidity itself in the presence of the other sex.
† An old saying used to point the moral that unfilial conduct brings its own punishment.

Huerto y tuerto, y mozo y potro, y mujer que mira mal, quiérense saber tratar.

A garden and a squinting man, a lad and a colt, a wife who has a leering eye—all these require skilful management.

Hurtar el puerco, y dar los pies por Dios.

(To steal a hog, and give away the feet in alms to God.)   To be liberal at another's expense.

Huye amigos afectados
Cuando lisonja te ofrezcan ;
Que aunque fieles te parezcan,
En vez de oro son dorados.
        —*Tirso de Molina.*

Flee from pretended friends when they offer you flattery; however true such may appear, they are not real gold, but only metal gilded.

Huyendo del toro, cayó en el arroyo.

(Flying from the bull, he fell into the brook.)   From Scylla to Charybdis; out of the frying-pan into the fire.

Iglesia, ó mar, ó casa real, quien quiere medrar.

The church, the sea, or the king's household for him who would thrive.*

Il sabio muda conscio, il necio, no.

The wise man changes his mind, the fool, never.

Ingenio sin prudencia, loco con espada

Wit without discretion is a fool with a sword.

Ir á la guerra ni casar, no se ha de aconsejar.

Never advise a man to go to the wars, nor to marry.

Ir por lana y volver trasquilado

To go for wool and to return shorn.

Ir por las sierras de Ubeda.

(To go by the mountains of Ubeda.) To deliver a rambling discourse ; to wander from the point.

Italia para nacer, Francia para vivir, España para morir.

Italy to be born in, France to live in, and Spain to die in.

Jo que te estriego, burra de mi suegro.

Whoa ! while I dress you down, my father-in-law's ass. †

Juego de manos, juego de villanos.

Practical jokes belong only to the vulgar.

Junta.

A congress ; assembly.

Juntate á los buenos y serás uno de ellos.

Seek the company of the good and you will be one of them.

Justicia, y nó por mi casa.

Let justice be done, but not in my house.

La alabanza propia envilece.

Self-praise is no recommendation.

La ausencia es al amor, lo que al fuego el aire; que apaga el pequeño, y aviva el grande.

Absence is to love what the wind is to fire; it quenches the weak and increases great affections.

La boca sin muela es como molino sin piedra.

A mouth without teeth is like a mill without a grindstone.

---

* These were the three professions open to a man of birth in medieval times.
+ The remark of a peasant when giving his wife a little salutary correction.

La buena fama segundo es patrimonio.

A good reputation is a second inheritance.

La buena y mala Fortuna, los dos sculptores de la Naturaleza para el pulimento de la materia humana.
—*Antonio Perez.*

Good and ill fortune are Nature's two sculptors, employed to polish the stone—Man.

La caridad bien ordenada empieza por sí.

Charity begins at home.

La casa quemada acudir con el agua.

(To run up with water when the house is burnt.) To shut the stable door when the horse is stolen.

La eminencia en los hechos dura, en los dichos passa.—*Gracian.*

Eminent deeds endure, but words, however eminent, pass away.

La esperanza es la última hez que apuramos en el fondo del cáliz de la amargura.—*R. de Campoamor.*

Hope is the last of the dregs that we strain out of the bottom of the cup of sorrows.

La esperanza, viatico de la vida humana.
—*A. Perez.*

Hope is the viaticum of the life of man.

La experiencia afina las reglas de cada arte.—*A. Perez.*

Experience modifies the rules of every art.

La experiencia es madre de la ciencia.
—*Cervantes.*

(Experience is the mother of knowledge.) Experience is good if not bought too dear. *Experientia docet.*

La fortuna de las feas, las bonitas la desean.

Pretty women desire the luck of the ugly ones.

La Fortuna señoréa en animos bajos, y no en los nobles y altos.
—*Antonio Perez.*

Fortune lords it over baseborn souls, but not over the noble and the great.

La gloria de cien Bayardos franceses no bastaria á compensar la deshonra de un solo Robespierre.
—*R. de Campoamor.*

The glory of a hundred French Bayards would not suffice to counterbalance the disgrace of a single Robespierre.

La gotera dando hace señal en la piedra.

Continual dropping wears away the stone.

La hermosura de los ánimos cresce con la edad, como se disminuye con la misma la corporal.—*A. Perez.*

The beauty of the mind increases with age, just as physical beauty decreases from the same cause.

La justicia de Peralvillo.

(Peralvillo justice.) Lynch law.

La lengua del mal amigo,
Mas corta que cuchillo.

The tongue of a false friend is sharper than a knife.

La lengua y las palabras, rama y hojas del corazon ; y testimonio dan si está seco ó verde el corazon.
—*Antonio Perez.*

The tongue and the words are the branch and leaves of the heart, and indicate whether it is dried up or full of sap.

Le latra con sangre entra.—*Cervantes.*

(Learning comes with blood.) Learning can only be acquired by painful striving.

La libertad no consiste en hacer lo que se quiere, sino en hacer lo que se debe.—*R. de Campoamor.*

Liberty consists not in doing what one wishes, but in doing what one ought.

La mala educación de la juventud es la ruína de las naciones.

The neglected education of the young is the ruin of nations.

La mala llaga sana, la mala fama mata.

A bad wound heals ; a bad name kills.

La máxima es trillada,
Mas repetirse debe :
Si al pleno acierto aspiras,
Une la utilidad con el deleite.—*Yriarte.*

The maxim is a little trite, but ought to be repeated : if you desire to obtain the greatest success (in writing), mingle what is useful with what is pleasing.*

La mentira tiene las piernas cortas.

A lie has short legs.

La misa dígala el cura.

(Let the Priest say the Mass.) Every man to his trade.

La mujer del ciego, para quién se afeita ?

For whom does the blind man's wife adorn herself ?

La mujer que mucho bebe, tarde paga lo que debe.

The woman who drinks much is slow in paying her debts.

La mujer y el huerto no quieren más de un dueño.

A woman and a garden require only one master.

La mujer y el vidrio siempre están en peligro.

Women and glass are always in danger.

La mujer y la gallina por andar se pierden aina.

A woman and a hen are soon lost by gadding about.

La mula y la mujer por halagos hacen el mandado.

A mule and a woman must be coaxed into obedience.

La noche es capa de pecadores.

The night is a cloak for sinners.

La ocasion hace el ladron.

Opportunity makes the thief.

La pasion no tiene ojos.—*A. Perez.*

(Passion has no eyes.) Love is blind.

La piedad es la virtud favorita de Dios.
—*A. Perez.*

Charity is the virtue beloved of God.

La planta muchas traspuesta ni crece, ni medra.

The plant often transplanted neither grows, nor thrives.

La pluma corta más que espadas afiladas.—*Antonio Perez.*

The pen is a keener weapon than sharpened swords.

La pobreza no es vileza, mas inconveniencia.

Poverty is no shame, but an inconvenience.

La prenda de Pedro Macho.

Peter Macho's security.†

La primera mujer escoba, la segunda señora.

(The first wife is a broom, the second a lady.) A man usually treats a second wife better than his first.

La rueda de la fortuna anda más lista que una rueda de molino.

Fortune's wheel turns faster than a mill-wheel.

Las avecitas del campo tienen á Dios por su proveedor y despensero.
—*Cervantes.*

The little birds of the field have God as the provider and dispenser of their food.

Las canas de Don Diego Osorio.

The white hairs of Don Diego Osorio.‡

Las cosas que son más para olvidadas son las más acordadas.—*Gracian.*

The things we remember best are those it were best to forget.

Las gracias pierde quien promete y se detiene.

He loses his thanks who promises and dallies.

---

* Evidently a reference to Horace's line *Omne tulit punctum qui miscuit utile dulci.*
+ Pedro Macho is said to have been a person who wished to borrow a sum of money on security already hypothecated.
‡ The saying is common to those whose hair has become white prematurely through sorrow, &c. Don Diego Osorio was sentenced to death by the King, and when he heard the sentence read out his hair turned white.

SPANISH] LA VERDE

Las grandes hazañas para los grandes hombres estan guardadas.
—*Cervantes.*

Great exploits are reserved for great men.

Las hazañas son la sustancia del vivir, y las sentencias el ornato.—*Gracian.*

Actions are the real substance of life; words are merely its adornment.

Las malas nuevas siempre son ciertas.

Bad news is always true.

Las más veces son buenas las razones del pueblo, y juicios ciertos.
—*Antonio Perez.*

Very often the arguments of the people are good, and their judgments true.*

Las necedades del rico por sentencias pasan en el mundo.—*Cervantes.*

The silly platitudes of the rich man are considered to be axioms by the world of fashion.

La sospecha commueve los animos, como el veneno los estomagos.
—*Antonio Perez.*

Suspicion affects the mind, as poison the stomach.

Las palabras son sombra de los hechos; son aquellas las hembras, estos los varones.—*Gracian.*

Words are the shadow of deeds; the former are feminine, the latter masculine.

Las primeras hacen los primeros hombres.—*Gracian.*

Eminent deeds make eminent men.

Las repúblicas son sublimes concepciones malogradas : las engendra la fraternidad, las amamanta la anarquía, y el despotismo las ahoga.
—*R. de Campoamor.*

Republics are sublime conceptions disappointed : fraternity breeds them, anarchy suckles them, and despotism drowns them.

Las riquezas son bagajes de la fortuna.

Riches are the sumpter mules of fortune.

Las virtudes sin prudencia son hermosura sin ojos.

Virtue without discretion is beauty without eyes.

La Traicion aplace, mas no él que la hace.

The treason pleases, but not the traitor.

La verdad adelgaza, y no quiebra.

Truth can be stretched, but it does not break.

La verdad es hija de Dios.

Truth is God's daughter.

La verdad está en el vino.

(Truth is in wine.)   *In vino veritas.*

La verdad siempre anda sobre la mentira como el aceite sobre el agua.
—*Cervantes.*

Truth always rises above falsehood, as oil above water.

La verde primavera
De mis floridos años
Pasé cautivo, amor, en tus prisiones,
Y en la cadena fiera
Cantando mis engaños,
Lloré con mi razon tus sinrazones;
Amargas confusiones
Del tiempo, que ha tenido
Ciega mi alma, y loco mi sentido !
—*Lope de Vega.*

In the green season of my flowering years,
I lived, O love ! a captive in thy chains ;
Sang of delusive hopes and idle fears,
And wept thy follies in my wisest strains :
Sad sport of time when under thy control,
So wild was grown my wit, so blind my soul.—*Lord Holland.*

---

* A comment on the familiar saying *Vox populi, vox Dei*. Perez, however, gives an unusual interpretation of the Latin phrase. He says that "the voice of the people is the voice of God" refers to the oppressed people, whose cry for succour, when it reaches the ears of God, evokes a prompt response.

La Vida, navegacion, la Muerte, puerto.
—*A. Perez.*

Life is a voyage, and Death its port of arrival.

La voz del pueblo es voz de Dios.

(The voice of the people is the voice of God.) *Vox populi, vox Dei.*

Letras sin virtud, son perlas en el muladar.—*Cervantes.*

Learning without virtue is like pearls on a dunghill.

Libro cerrado no saca letrado.

A closed book never makes a scholar.

Libros y amigos pocos y buenos.

Books and friends should be few and good.

Llorar he, agüelo, que ahora no puedo.

(I will mourn for you, grandfather; at present I have no time.) A fat legacy is a great consolation to the bereaved.

Locos y niños, dicen la verdad.

Children and fools speak truth.

Lo facil se ha de emprender como dificultoso, y lo dificultoso como facil.
—*Gracian.*

One ought to attempt easy tasks as though they were difficult, and difficult tasks as though they were easy.

Lo que á unos no agrada á otros contenta.

(What displeases some delights others.) *De gustibus non est disputandum.*

Lo que cuesta poco, se estima en menos.
—*Cervantes.*

That which costs little is little esteemed.

Lo que luego se hace, luego se deshace, mas lo que ha de durar una eternidad, ha de tardar otra en hacerse.
—*Gracian.*

That which is quickly done, is quickly undone; but that which is to endure for an eternity, requires an eternity in the making of it.

Lo que mucho vale, mucho cuesta.

What is much valued, costs much.

Lo que se aprende en la cuna siempre dura.

(What is learnt in the cradle always lasts.) What is bred in the bone comes out in the flesh.

Lo que te dijére el espejo, no te lo dirán en consejo.

(The mirror will tell thee of that thy friends will never say.) The mirror is no flatterer.

Los amigos verdaderos, fuerte guarda, y consuelo grande su memoria.
—*A. Perez.*

True friends are a strong protection, and the memory of them is a great consolation.

Los ánimos que ejercitan de su natural las virtudes, no buscan gracias por ellas.—*Antonio Perez.*

People who practise virtues through the impulse of their innate goodness, do not look for thanks.

Los dichos en nos, y los hechos en Dios.

(Words are our part, works are God's.) Man proposes, God disposes.

Los dineros del sacristan cantando se vienen y cantando se van.

(The sacristan's money comes with singing, and with singing departs.) Easy come, easy go.

Los dineros hacen dueñas y escuderos.

Money makes ladies and esquires.

Los dolores grandes, veneno de la vida.
—*A. Perez.*

Great sorrows are the poison of life.

Los gustos y los pesares alternan.

Pleasures and pains come by turns.

Los hijos de Maria Rabidilla,
Cada uno en su escudilla.

The children of Mary Rabidilla, each in his own corner.*

* The family of Mary Rabidilla is the type of those families in which all the members are at daggers drawn.

Los jueces, en vez de ser unos tortura-
dores del cuerpo, deben ser unos médicos del alma.—*R. de Campoamor.*

(Judges, instead of being punishers of
the body, ought to be physicians of
the mind.)   All punishment should
be remedial in its character.

Los locos hacen los banquetes, y los
sabios los comen.

Fools make feasts, and wise men eat
them.

Los materialistas piensan con los ojos, y
los idealistas ven con el entendimiento.—*R. de Campoamor.*

Materialists think with their eyes, and
idealists see with their mind.

Los primeros movimientos no son en
mano del hombre.—*Cervantes.*

(The first movements are not under the
control of man.)   Man is not the
master of his impulses.

Los ricos temen á las zorras en propor-
cion al número de sus gallinas.
            —*R. de Campoamor.*

The rich fear rogues in proportion to
the number of their fowls.

Los sujetos eminentemente raros de-
penden de los tiempos.   No todos
tuvieron el que merecian, y muchos
aunque le tuvieron no acertaron á
lograrle.   Fueron dignos algunos de
mejor siglo, que no todo lo bueno
triunfa siempre; tienen las cosas su
vez, hasta las eminencias son al uso;
pero lleva una ventaja lo sabio, que
es eterno; y si este no es su siglo,
muchos otros lo serán.—*Gracian.*

Men of the rarest parts depend upon
the times in which they live.   All
have not found the time they deserved,
and many, though they have found it,
have not succeeded in making use of
it.   Some have been worthy of a
better age, for the good does not
always triumph.   Things have their
season, and even talents are subject
to fashion.   However, the wise man
has one advantage,—he is for all
time.   If the present is not his proper
century, many others will be so.

Madre, que cosa es casar?   Hija hilar
parir, y llorar.

Mother, what is marriage?   My child, it
is to spin, bear children, and weep.

Mal de muchos, consuelo de tontos.

(The sorrow of many is fools' consolation.)   "We are all mortal" is poor
comfort for the dying man.

Mal de muchos, consuelo es.

(Misfortunes of many console.)   Trouble
is lightened when others share it.

Mal de muchos, gozo es.

The misfortunes of many afford pleasure.*

Mal haya el vientre, que del pan comido
no le viene miente.

Plague on the belly that forgets the
bread it has eaten.

Mal me quieren mis comadres, porque
les digo las verdades.

My gossips love me not, because I speak
truths to them.

Malo es errar, y peor perseverar.

It is an evil thing to sin, and worse to
persevere in it.

Mandad y haced, y sereis bien servido.

Give the order and do the work yourself,
and you will be well served.

Manos blancas no ofenden.

The hands of Beauty do not hurt.

Más aguada alegria es la que los hijos
dan.

Much tempered is the joy that children
give.

---

* In his *Innocents Abroad* Mark Twain describes the unholy joy that a good sailor feels
when he sees his fellow-passengers suffering from *mal de mer.*

Más cuesta mal hacer, que bien hacer.

It is more costly to do evil than to do good.

Más cura la dieta que la lanceta.

Diet cures more than the lancet.

Más mató la cena que curó Avicena.

Gluttony kills more people than Avicena cured.*

Más produce el año que el campo bien labrado.

(The year produces more than the well-worked field.) Fine weather is a better cultivator than careful tillage.

Más quiero asno que me lleve, que caballo que me dermeque.

I prefer an ass that carries me to a horse that throws me.

Más sabe el loco en su casa que el cuerdo en la agena.

The fool knows more in his own house than the wise man in another's.

Más vale algo que nada.

(Better something than nothing.) Half a loaf is better than no bread.

Más vale al que Dios ayuda, que al que mucho madruga.

He prospers more whom God helps, than he who is up betimes.

Más vale buena esperanza que ruin posesion.—*Cervantes*.

(Good hope is better than bad possessions.) It is hope for the future that makes present suffering endurable.

Más vale el buen nombre que las muchas riquezas.—*Cervantes*.

A good name is worth more than great riches.

Más vale ir solo, que mal acompañado.

Better alone than in bad company.

Más vale mala composicion que buen pleito.

A bad compromise is better than a good verdict.

Más vale maña que fuerza.

Dexterity is better than strength.

Más vale migaja de Rey que zatico de Caballero.

(Better the crumbs of the king than the crust of a lord.) The king's favour is better than that of the most powerful of his subjects.

Más vale pájaro en mano que buitre volando.

(A sparrow in the hand is better than a bustard flying.) A bird in the hand is worth two in the bush.

Más vale saber que haber.

(Better to know than to have.) Knowledge is better than wealth.

Más vale salto de mata que ruego de buenos hombres.

(Better a leap over the hedge than the prayers of good men.) Better to take no risks than trust to Providence to escape from danger.

Más vale ser cabeza de ratón, que cola de león.

Better be the head of a mouse than the tail of a lion.

Más vale ser necio que porfiado.

Better be ignorant than obstinate.

Mas vale tarde que nunca.

Better late than never.

Más vale tuerto que ciego.

A man had better be half blind than have both his eyes out.

Más vale un amigo que pariente primo.

A friend is worth more than the nearest kinsman.

Más vale un *toma* que dos *te daré*.

One "Take this," is worth more than two "I will give you."

Más ven cuatro ojos que dos.

(Four eyes see more than two.) Two heads are better than one.

* Avicena was a famous physician, the Abernethy of Spain.

Mejor curada está herida que no se dió,
que la que se cura bien.

The wound which is not given is better
healed, than that which, however
well cured, has been inflicted.

Mejor es doblar, que quebrar.

Better bend than break.

Menea la cola el can, nó por ti, sino por
el pan.

The dog wags his tail, not for you, but
for the crust.

Ménos camino hay de virtud á vicios
que de vicios á virtud.

The road from virtue to vice is shorter
than that from vice to virtue.

Miedo guarda la viña.

Fear protects the vineyard.

Mientras en mi casa estoy, Rey soy.

(When in my own house I am a king.)
A man's house is his castle.

Mientras la grande se abaja, la chica
barre la casa.

While the tall maid is stooping, the
little one sweeps the house.

Mientras piensa el cuerdo obra el loco.

(While the prudent ponders, the foolish
works.)   More haste, less speed.

Mientras se duerme todos son iguales.

We are all equal when we are asleep.

Milicia es la vida del hombre contra la
malicia del hombre.—*Gracian.*

A man's life is one long warfare against
the malice of his fellow-man.

Mirar las cosas con anteojos de larga
vista.

(To look at things through strong
glasses.)   To look always on the
sunny side of life.

Moderado.

A conservative.

Muchas hay muy buenas mujeres ; es
verdad : las que están enterradas.

There is an abundance of good women;
yes—but they are in their graves.

Muchas pocos hacen un mucho.

Many littles make a mickle.

Mucho en el suelo, poco en el cielo.

Rich here, poor hereafter.

Mucho es conseguir la admiracion
comun ; pero mas la aficion.
                    —*Gracian.*

It is a great thing to win the admiration
of the people, but a greater to gain
their love.

Muchos por faltos de sentido, no le
pierden. – *Gracian.*

Many people never lose their senses,
because they possess none.

Muchos s n los caminos por donde lleva
Dios á los suyos al cielo.—*Cervantes.*

Many are the roads whereby God lead
his own to heaven.

Muchos van por lana, y vuelven tras-
quilados.

(Many go for wool, and return shorn.)
The biter is sometimes bitten.

Mucho tienen los reyes del invierno,
Que hacen temblar los hombres.
                    —*Lope de Vega.*

Kings and the winter have much in
common ; both make men tremble in
their presence.

Mudanza de tiempos, bordon de necios.

(Change of weather, talk of fools.) The
weather is the one topic that never
fails.

Muy buenos somos cuando enfermamos.

(We are very good when we are sick.)
The Devil was sick, the Devil a saint
would be.

Muy dificil conocer el corazon del
hombre por palabras.—*A. Perez.*

It is very difficult to know a man's
heart from his words.

Necios y porfiados, hacen ricos los
letrados.

Fools and stubborn folk enrich the
lawyers.

Ni de estopa buena camisa, ni de puta
buena amiga.

You cannot make a good shirt out of
tow, nor a trusty mistress of a harlot.

Ni fea que espante, ni hermosa que mate.

(Not ugly enough to frighten, nor so beautiful as to kill.) A woman whose appearance is, as the Americans say, homely.

Ni fies de villano, ni bebas agua de charco.

Neither trust a knave, nor drink stagnant water.

Ni firmes carta que no leas, ni bebas agua que no veas.

Neither sign a paper you have not read, nor drink water you have not seen.

Ni hay bien sin galardon, ni mal sin punicion.

No good act goes unrewarded, nor evil act unpunished.

Ninguna esperanza es buena
Que está en voluntad agena.

No hope is good which depends upon another's will.

Ninguno cierre las puertas ;
Si amor viniese á llamar,
Que no le ha aprovechar.
— *Juan de la Enzina.*

Let no man shut his doors :
If Love should come to call,
'Twill do no good at all.— *G. Ticknor.*

Ni quito Rey, ni pongo Rey.

I do not oppose the king, nor do I establish the king.*

No ando á buscar pan de trastrigo por las casas agenas.

(I do not look for better than fine wheaten bread in other folk's houses.) The best is good enough for me.

No aventures mucho tu riqueza
Por consejo de ome que ha pobreza.
— *Don Juan Manuel.*

Do not risk much money on the advice of a man who is poor.

No basta lo entendido, desease lo genial.
— *Gracian.*

It is not sufficient to possess intellect, character also is required.

Nobles desgracias
Defiendan les hombres nobles.
— *Calderon.*

Noble men should ward off misfortunes from the noble.

Nobleza consiste en la virtud.
— *Cervantes.*

(Nobleness consists in virtue.) 'Tis only noble to be good.— *Tennyson.*

Noche tinta, blanco el dia.

(The night is dark, the day is clear.) Night increases our fears, day drives them away.

No dice más la lengua que lo que siente el corazon.

(The tongue says no more than the heart feels.) " Out of the abundance of the heart the mouth speaketh."

No entra en misa la campana y á todos llama.

(The bell does not go to Mass, but calls every one thither.) Example is better than precept.

No es cada dia Pascua ni vendimia.

(Every day is not Easter nor vintage.) Christmas comes but once a year. Be merry while you may.

No es el bien conocido hasta que es perdido.

The blessing is not known until it is lost.

---

* As to the origin of this proverb, I derive the following information from Mr. Ulick Ralph Burke's admirable work, *Sancho Panza's Proverbs.* Pedro the Cruel engaged in a fight with his brother Don Enrique. Both brothers fell to the ground. The page of Don Enrique assisted his master to rise, with the words *Ni quito Rey, ni pongo Rey, pero ayudo á mi señor.* " I oppose not the King, nor do I set him up, but help my master."

No es menester que digais
Cúyas sois, mis alegrias ;
Que bien se ve que sois mias
En lo poco que durais.—*Calderon.*

There is little need to say
Whose thou art, sweet joy divine,
Since 'tis plain thou must be mine
By the shortness of thy stay.
                —*D. F. MacCarthy.*

No es oro todo lo que reluce.

All is not gold that glitters.

No es un hombre mas que otro, si no
hace mas que otro.—*Cervantes.*

No man is greater than another, unless
he does greater things.

No hace el numen el que lo dora, sino
el que lo adora.—*Gracian.*

It is not he who adorns, but he who
adores that makes the divinity.

No ha de quejarse de su suerte un
noble.—*Calderon.*

A noble man should ne'er rail at his
fate.

No hay cerradura, si es de ora la ganzúa

(There is no lock if the pick is of gold.)
A golden key will open any door.

No hay grillos honrosos.—*A. Perez.*

There are no such things as honourable
bonds.*

No hay leona más fiera, ni fiera más
cruel, que una linda dama ; como de
tal se ha de huir.—*Antonio Perez.*

There is no lioness more savage, nor
any beast more cruel, than a beautiful
woman : from such one must flee.

No hay libro tan malo, que no tenga
alguna cosa buena. –*Cervantes.*

No book is so bad that it contains no
good in it.

No hay mal que por bien no venga.

There is no evil which may not turn out
well.

No hay mejor bocado, que el hurtado.

(No morsel so sweet as that which is
stolen.)   Stolen fruit is sweetest.

No hay mejor cirujano que el bien
acuchillado.

There is no better surgeon than he who
is experienced.

No hay memoria á quien el tiempo no
acabe, ni dolor que muerte no le
consuma.—*Cervantes.*

There is no memory which time does
not blot out, nor grief which death
does not destroy.

No hay mujer posible que no sea una
posible Eva ?—*R. de Campoamor.*

Is there any woman possible who is not
a possible Eve ?

No hay pariente pobre.– *Cervantes.*

A poor relation has no existence.†

No hay sugeto en que no imprima
El fuego de amor su llama ;
Pues vive mas donde ama
El hombre, que donde anima.
Amor solamente estima
Cuanto tener vida sabe
El tronco, la flor y el ave :
Luego es la gloria mayor
Desta vida—amor, amor.—*Calderon.*

No creature lives on which love's flame
Has not impressed its burning seal ;
The man feels more who love doth feel
Than when Love's breath first warmed
his frame.
Love owns one universal claim—
To Love, it only needs To Be,—
Whether a bird, a flower, a tree :
Then the chief glory, far above
All else in life must be Love, Love,
                —*D. F. MacCarthy.*

No hay tal razon como la del baston.

(There is no argument better than that
of the rod.)   Spare the rod and spoil
the child.

---

* He is careful to add that there is an exception to this rule when one is suffering for
Christ's sake.
 † In Tom Robertson's play *Caste* there is a somewhat similar remark made by the mother
of George D'Alroy. When introduced to the bibulous Eccles and his daughters, she denies
that a family bearing the name Eccles has any existence.

No huye el que se retira.

No nos queda otra señal
De nuestro rey soberano,
Que en nada pone la mano
Que no le suceda mal.
No ocupa mas pies de tierra el cuerpo
del Papa que el del sacristan.
—*Cervantes.*
No oyen los reyes quando no quieren,
ni ven lo que no quieren.
—*Antonio Perez.*
No pensando se pierden todos los necios.
—*Gracian.*
No perdona el vulgo tacha de ninguno.

No perecer de desdicha agena.—Es
menester gran tiento con los que se
ahogan, para acudir al remedio sin
peligro.—*Gracian.*
No puede el hijo de Adán
Sin trabajo comer pan.
No puede haber Heroe que no tenga
algun extremo sublime.—*Gracian.*

No puede ser el cuervo más negro que
las alas.

No puede ser entendido el que no fuere
bien entendedor.—*Gracian.*

No sabe mandar el que no sabe
disimular.
No saber de la Misa la media.

No saber el Christus.

No se acuerda el cura de cuando fué
sacristan.

No se acuerda la suegra que fué nuera.

No se agradece al pequeño
Lo que se admira en el grande.
—*J. E. Hartzenbusch.*
No seas perezoso, y no serás deseoso.

(He who retreats does not flee.)
He that fights and runs away,
May live to fight another day.
This token have we of our king,
Who rules according to his will,
To whatsoe'er he puts his hand,
'Tis always sure to turn out—ill.*
The dead body of the Pope does not
occupy more feet of ground than that
of the sacristan.
Kings are deaf when they please, and
blind to all they *will* not see.

All fools fail because they do not think.

The vulgar never forgive the fault of
anyone.
Do not die of another's misfortune.—
There is need of much care in helping the drowning, in order to give
help without endangering oneself.
A son of Adam cannot eat bread without labour.
There can be no hero without a touch
of something unique and sublime in
his nature.
(The crow cannot be blacker than its
wings.) There is nothing gained by
exaggerating a trouble.
He who cannot readily understand
another's meaning, cannot readily
make himself understood.
He who knows not how to dissimulate,
knows not how to rule.
(Not to know half the Mass.) To be
utterly ignorant; not to know
chalk from cheese.
(Not to know the alphabet.) To be an
absolute ignoramus.†
(The curate does not remember the time
when he was sacristan.) *Honores
mutant mores.*
The mother-in-law forgets that she was
a daughter-in-law.
What is admired in the great, in the
petty displeases.

Shun idleness, and you will avoid need.

---

* This epigram, written by an unknown hand, was published in the reign of Philip IV. The King was so incensed by it that, when Quevedo was falsely accused of being its author, he sentenced the famous but unlucky writer to a long term of imprisonment.
† The *Christus* here refers to the cross marked on the back of the book, from which the young Spaniard learns his alphabet.

No se conoce el bien hasta que se ha perdido.—*Cervantes.*

We never know the value of a thing until we have thrown it away.

No se ganó Zamora en una hora.

Zamora was not captured in an hour.*

No se mueve la hoja en el árbol sin la voluntad de Dios.

The leaf on the tree does not quiver without the will of God.

No se puede repicar y andar en la procesion.

(It is impossible to toll the bell and walk in the procession.) You cannot be in two places at once. One cannot have a cake and eat it too.

No se toman truchas á bragas enjutas.

(Trout are not caught with dry breeches.) No gains without pains.

No tenga dias de descuido ; gusta la suerte de pegar una burla, y atropellará todas las contingencias para coger desapercebido.—*Gracian.*

Have no careless days, for Fate loves to play tricks, and will upset all probabilities in order to catch a man unprepared.

No todo lo que es brillante
Riqueza al avaro ofrece,
Oro, la alquimia parece,
Vidrio hay que imita al diamante.
— *Tirso de Molina.*

Not everything that glitters promises wealth to him who covets it ; for gold the alchemist may imitate, and diamonds sometimes are made of— glass.

No vale un bledo.

It is not worth a rush.

No vendas la piel del oso antes de haber lo muerto.

Do not sell the bearskin before you have killed the bear.

Nunca buena olla con agua sola.

A good stew can never be made with water alone.

Nunca el discreto
Mujer ni vidrio probó.—*Lope de Vega.*

A wise man puts neither a woman nor glass to a severe test.

Nunca el juglar de la tierra tañe bien en la fiesta.

(The mountebank of the district is never honoured at the feast.) A prophet is without honour in his own country.

Nunca el sabio dice, no pensé.

The wise man never says, "I did not think."

Nunca lo bueno fué mucho.--*Cervantes.*

The good was never plentiful.

Obra de comun, obra de ningun.
Obra empezada medio acabada.
Obrar bien, que Dios es Dios.
Obrar con buenos instrumentos.
— *Gracian.*

What is everybody's work is nobody's.
Well begun is half done.
Do right, for God is God.
(Work with good instruments.) Employ the best assistance if you wish to achieve anything.

Obras son amores, que no buenas razones.

Deeds, and not fine speeches, are the proof of love.

Ofrecer mucho especie es de negar.

To offer too much is a kind of denial.

* Mr. U. R. Burke says of this proverb, "Zamora is a very ancient fortified city in Leon, whose very name, says Ford, awakes a thousand recollections of mediæval chivalry. An important frontier town on the Douro, it was recovered from the Moors by Alonso el Catolico, in 748 ; and stood a long and bloody siege by Abdurrahman in 939, when 40,000 Moors are said to have been slain. Finally, it was taken in 985 by Al Mansúr. Zamora was again besieged in 1072, by Sancho II., of Castile, who failed, in spite of the assistance of the Cid himself, to take the city—and was killed outside the walls. Zamora is at the present day a city of some 12,000 inhabitants, and of little modern interest."

Oh cómo premian sin cuesta
Principes que honrando premian.
—*Calderon.*

Oh ! at what a little cost
Princes can reward brave actions !
By a word of praise 'tis done !
—*D. F. MacCarthy.*

Ojo del amo engorda el caballo.

The master's eye makes the horse fat.

Ojos que no ven, corazon no quebrantan.

What the eyes do not see, the heart does not grieve for.

Olla podrida.

A dish of meat and vegetables boiled together ; a hash.

Oracion breve sube al cielo.

Short prayers mount to heaven.

Oveja que mucho bala, bocado pierde.

The sheep that bleats much, loses a mouthful.

Paga adelantada, paga viciosa.

(Payment beforehand is bad payment.) Lazy folk will not work when the incentive of gain is gone.

Paga lo que debes y sabrás lo que tienes.

Pay what you owe, and you will know what you are worth.

Pagan justos por pecadores.

The righteous pay for sinners.

Palabras hembras son hechos machos.

Words are feminine, deeds are masculine.

Palabras señaladas no quieren testigo.
Palabras sin verdad, paja sin grano.
—*A. Perez.*

Noble words need no witnesses.
Words without truth, corn without grain.

Palabras y plumas el viento las lleva.

Words and feathers are borne away by the wind.

Para los desgraciados se hizo la horca.

(For the unfortunate the gallows are erected.) Give a dog a bad name and hang him.

Para puertas de celos
Tiene amor llave maestra.
—*Lope de Vega.*

Love holds the master-key of the doors that jealousy closes.

Para todo hay comentario.

There is a reason for everything.

Para todo hay remedio sino para la muerte.

There is a remedy for everything save death.

Pareceme, Sancho, que no hay refran que no sea verdadero, porque todos son sentencias sacadas de la misma esperiencia, madre de las ciencias todas.—*Cervantes.*

It seems to me, Sancho, that there is no proverb which is not true, for they are all opinions formed from the same experience, which is the mother of all knowledge.

Pasan
Los años con tanta furia,
Que parece que con cartas
Van por la posta á la muerte,
Y que una breve posada
Tiene la vida á la noche,
Y la muerte á la mañana.
—*Lope de Vega.*

The years hasten on so quickly, that we seem to post along the road to Death; our life is only a brief sojourn in an inn ; birth brings us there in the evening, and in the morning Death takes us away.

Paso á paso van lejos.

(Step by step goes far.) *Chi va piano va sano, e chi va sano va lontano.*

Pedir peras al olmo.

(To look for pears on the elm.) To seek impossibilities.

Pedro por qué atiza ? Por gozar de la ceniza.

Why does Peter stir the fire ? In order to enjoy the heat.

Peor es ocuparse en lo impertinente, qua hacer nada.—*Gracian.*

To be busy about things that do not concern us, is worse than doing nothing at all.

Perdida es lejia en la cabeza del asno.

Wasted is soap on the head of an ass.

Pereza llave de pobreza.

Idleness is the key to Poverty's door.

Perro ladrador nunca es buen mordedor.

A barking dog is never a good biter.

Perro viejo.

(An old dog.) A cute customer; a knowing old bird.

Picado de la tarantula.

(Bitten by the tarantula.) A victim of a moral or physical disease.

Piedra movediza nunca la cubre moho.

A rolling stone gathers no moss.

Piensa el ladron que todos son de su condicion.

The thief thinks that all are of his profession.

Pisando la tierra dura
De continuo el hombre está,
Y cada paso que da
Es sobre su sepultura.
Triste ley, sentencia dura,
Es saber que en cualquier caso
Cada paso (gran fracaso !)
Es para andar adelante,
Y Dios no es á hacer bastante
Que no haya dado aquel paso.
　　　　　　—Calderon.

On the hard earth, year by year,
Man is treading, hopeless, brave,
But each step is o'er his grave,
Daily drawing near and near.
Mournful sentence—law severe—
But which cannot be mistaken,
Every step (what fears awaken !)
Is to that dark goal commissioned,
So that God is not sufficient
To prevent that step being taken.
　　　　　　—D. F. MacCarthy

Poco te importa el ser sabio
Si no fueres venturoso.
　　　　　— Tirso de Molina.

It is of little importance to be wise, if you are not also lucky.

Por demas es la citola en el molino cuando el molinero es sordo.

Useless is the clapper in the mill when the miller is deaf.

Por el hilo se saca el ovillo.

(By the thread we unwind the skein.) A straw shows which way the wind blows.

Por gozar lo mio en mis dias, y despues herédeme quien quisiere.

So that I enjoy my own while I'm alive, he that wills may be my heir.

Por la muestra se conoce el paño.

The cloth is known by the pattern.

Porque al fin
Hacer bien nunca se pierde.
　　　　　—Calderon.

For in the end a good action is never lost.

Porque dígan, que es amor
Homicida del ingenio.— *Calderon.*

For men say they often find
Love's the slayer of their mind.

Porque dijo un sabio un dia
Que á los sastres se debia
La mitad de la hermosura.
　　　　　—Lope de Vega.

For it was a wise man who said, that beauties owed half their good looks to their dressmakers.

Porque hay penas y congojas
Que la dicen los afectos
Mucho mejor, que la boca.—*Calderon.*

For there are some pains and sorrows
That by feelings are expressed
Better than when words are spoken.
　　　　　—D. F. MacCarthy.

Por sol que haga ne dejes tu capa en casa.

Although it be sunny, do not leave your cloak indoors.

Por su mal nacen las alas á la hormiga.

The ant grows wings to its own hurt.

Posada.

A dwelling; lodging-house.

Presto maduro, presto podrido.

Soon ripe, soon rotten.

Pronunciamiento.

A public declaration; an announcement of revolution.

Pues asi llegué á saber,
Que toda la dicha humana
En fin pasa como sueño.—*Calderon.*

Thus have I learned that all human happiness at last passes away like a dream.

Pues el rosario tomais,
   No dudo que le receis
   Por mi, que muerto me habeis,
O' por vos, que me matais.—*Rebolledo.*

Fair lady, when your beads you take,
   No doubt your prayer is still
Either for my poor murdered sake,
   Or else for yours that kill.
                              —*G. Ticknor.*

   Pues no hay lugar
Para la muerte secreto.—*Calderon.*

There is no hiding-place from death.

   Pues tan parecidas
A' los sueños son las glorias,
Que las verdaderas son
Tenidas por mentirosas,
Y las fingidas por ciertas?—*Calderon.*

                    So like to dreams
Are then all the world's chief glories
That the true are oft rejected
As the false, the false too often
Are mistaken for the true?
                              —*D. F. MacCarthy.*

   Pues vence mas
Aquel que sin sangre vence.
                              —*Calderon.*

He conquers best who conquers without bloodshed.

Que amor no es mas que porfia :
No son piedras las mujeres.
                              —*Lope de Vega.*

A lover's part is to be persistent, for women never have a heart of stone.

Que el traidor no es menester,
Siendo la traicion pasada.—*Calderon.*

There is no need for the traitor when once the treacherous act is done.

Qué es la vida?   Un frenesi
Qué es la vida?   Una ilusion
Una sombra, una ficcion,
Y el mayor bien es pequeño ;
Que toda la vida es sueño,
Y los sueños sueño son.—*Calderon.*

What is life?   'Tis but a madness.
What is life?   A mere illusion,
Fleeting shadow, fond delusion,
Short-lived joy that ends in sadness ;
Whose most steadfast substance seems
But the dream of other dreams.

Que genero de pena puede darla
   Mas pena que las penas en que vive
A' quien solo pudiera consolarla
   La muerte que la vida apercibe ?
La muerte es menos pena que espe-
   rarla ;
   Una vez quien la sufre la recibe ;
Pero por mucho que en valor se extreme
Muchas veces le passa quien la teme.
                              —*Lope de Vega.*

Ah! what have I in dying to bemoan ?
   What punishment in death can they
      devise
For her who living only lives to groan,
   And see continual death before her
      eyes ?
Comfort's in death, where 'tis in life
   unknown ;
   Who death expects feels more than
      he who dies :—
Though too much valour may our for-
   tune try,
To live in fear of death is many times
to die.—*J. Oxenford.*

Que hace el loco á la postre, hace el
   sábio al principio.

What the fool does in the end, the
   wise does at the beginning.

Que hacer bien
Es tesoro que se guarda
Para quando es menester.—*Calderon.*

A good action is a treasure stored up
   until the day of the doer's need.

Que las guardas con el oro
Son fáciles de romper.—*Calderon.*

It is easy to break through prison bars
   when you have gold in your hand.

Que no el tener cofres llenas
La riqueza en pie mantiene;
Que no es rico el que más tiene,
Sino el que ha menester menos.
         — *Tirso de Molina.*

It is not the possession of overflowing
   coffers that is the support of riches.
   The rich man is not he who owns
   most, but he who needs the least.

Que no hay cosa que no sea
Difícil al comenzar.—*Tirso de Molina.*

There is nothing which is not difficult
   at the commencement.

Que perezoso es el dia
De una esperanza.—*Calderon.*

How slowly doth hope's day depart.

Querida; querido mio.

Darling ; my sweetheart.

Que salió á veces mejor el aviso en un
   chiste, que en el mas grave magis-
   terio.—*Gracian.*

Counsel given in a jesting tone is often
   more effectual than the most serious
   discourse.

Que siempre es consejo sabio,
Ni pleitos con poderosos
Ni amistades con criados.
        —*Lope de Vega.*

It is always a wise plan not to have
   squabbles with the great, nor friendships with their servants.

Que son raros los deseados.—*Gracian.*

(Few men are missed.) Death rarely
   makes a gap that cannot be filled.

Quien á buen arbol se arrima, buena
   sombra le cobija.

(He who leans against a good tree, enjoys good shade.) The man who has
   a powerful patron is free from care.

Quien á los veinte no puede, y á los
   treinta no sabe, y á los cuarenta no
   tiene, y á los cincuenta no reposa, no
   sé qué mas le espere.

He who is not vigorous at twenty, nor
   wise at thirty, nor rich at forty, nor
   resting at fifty, let him abandon hope.

Quien á uno castiga, á ciento hostiga.

He who chastises one, threatens a
   hundred.

Quien bien ama tarde olvida.

Who loves truly forgets slowly.

Quien bien ama, teme.

He who loves much, fears much

Quien bien see, non se lieve.
        —*Don Juan Manuel.*

(He that hath a good seat should not
   move.) *Le mieux est l'ennemi du
   bien.*

Quien busca el peligro perece en el.
        —*Cervantes.*

He who seeks for danger, perishes
   therein.

Quien calla no dice nada.

(He who is silent does not say nothing.)
   Silence is sometimes eloquent.

Quien calla otorga.

Silence gives consent.

Quien canta sus males espanta.

(He who sings drives away his sorrows.)
   In sweet music is such art
   Healing pain and grief of heart.

Quien da pan á perro ajeno,
Pierde pan y pierde perro.

Whoever gives a crust to another's dog,
   loses both crust and dog.

Quien determina de se casar á sus
   vecinos ha de mirar.

He who is determined to marry ought
   to look at his neighbours.

Quien dineros tiene, alcanza lo que quiere.

He who has money obtains what he wants.

Quien dineros tiene, hace lo que quiere

He who has money acts as he pleases.

Quien duerme bien, no le pican las pulgas.

He who sleeps soundly is not bitten by fleas.

Quien en l'arenal sembra, non trilla pegujares.

He that sows in the sand reaps no crops.

Quien es amigo del vino, enemigo es de sí mismo.

(He who is a friend of wine, is his own enemy.)
" Oh! that men should put an enemy into their mouths,
To steal away their brains."

Quien escucha, su mal oye.

Listeners never hear good of themselves.

Quien esposa una viuda tendrà cada rato la cabeza de un muerto echada en su plato.

Whoso marries a widow will often have the head of a dead man thrown upon his plate.

Quien está ausente todos los males tiene y teme.

(He who is absent suffers and fears every ill.) *Les absents ont toujours tort*.

Quien feo ama, hermoso le parece.

She who loves an ugly man, thinks that he is comely.

Quien hace por comun, hace por ningun.

Who works for the public, works for nobody.

Quien haga aplicaciones,
Con su pan se lo coma.—*Yriarte*.

(He who makes applications, let him eat it with his bread.) Plague take the fellow who thinks my writings are directed against individuals.*

Quien larga vida vive mucho mal vide.

He who lives a long life sees much sorrow.

Quien mala cama hace,
En ella se yace.

(He who doth ill make his bed
Must needs upon it rest his head.)
As you make your bed, so you must lie.

Quien mal enhorna, saca los panes tuertos.

(He who puts the bread carelessly in the oven, draws out crooked loaves.)
As the twig's bent, the tree's inclined.

Quien mucho abarca poco aprieta.

(Over-reaching cheats itself.) Grasp all, lose all. Grasp no more than thy hand will hold.

Quien mucho duerme. poco aprende.

Who sleeps much, learns little.

Quien neciamente peca, neciamente se va al Infierno.

He who sins foolishly, foolishly goes to hell.

Quien no adoba gotera, hace casa entera.

(He who does not repair his gutter, repairs the whole house.) A stitch in time saves nine.

Quien no ha visto á Granada,
No ha visto nada.

He who has not seen Granada, has seen nothing.†

* These words, which form part of Yriarte's introduction to his Fables, have become proverbial in Spain in the same sense as we use *Honi soit qui mal y pense*.
† There is more reason in this saying than in most of the kind, for Granada owns the ruins of the Alhambra.

Quien no há visto á Sevilla
No há visto maravilla.
Quien no sabe, no vale.

Quien no sabe qué es honra no la
estima.—*Lope de Vega.*
Quien no tiene mujer, mil ojos ha
menester.
Quién por vanagloria humana
Pierde una divina gloria?
Que pasado bien no es sueño?
Quién tuvo dichas heróicas,
Que entre sí no diga, cuando
Las revuelve en su memoria,
Sin duda que fue soñado
Cuanto vi?—*Calderon.*
Quien pregunta, no yerra.
Quien promete en deude se mete.

Quien quiere tomar, convienele dar.
Quien siembra abrojos no ande descalzo.

Quien su tiempo gasta en cosas vanas,
no ve la muerte que está sobre sus
espaldas.
Quien te alabare con lo que non has
en ti,
Sabe, que quiere relever lo que has de
ti.—*Don Juan Manuel.*
Quien te conseja encobrir de tus amigos,
Engañar te quiere assaz, y sin testigos.
　　　　　—Don Juan Manuel.
Quien teme la muerte, no goza la vida.

Quien tiene tienda, que atienda.
Quien todo lo quiere, todo lo pierde.

Quien yerra y se enmienda, á Dios se
encomienda.
Quieres hacer del ladron, fiate del.

Quitada la causa, se quita el pecado.
　　　　　—Cervantes.

Raiz de la Fe y del Amor, el corazon.
　　　　　—Antonio Perez.

Who to Seville has never been,
Has never yet true wonders seen.*
(Who knows nothing is worth nothing.)
Worthless is the witless man.
Whoso knows not what honour is, does
not value it.
He who has no wife, has need of a
thousand eyes.
Who for human vanities
Would forego celestial glory?
What past bliss is not a dream?
Who has had his happy fortunes
Who hath said not to himself
As his memory ran o'er them,
"All I saw, beyond a doubt,
Was a dream.'—*D. F. MacCarthy.*
Nothing lost for lack of asking.
(He who promises makes himself a
debtor.)　An honest man's word is
his bond.
He who would receive, must give.
He who sows thistles should not go
barefoot.
He who wastes his time in vain pursuits,
perceives not Death, who leans over
his shoulders.
He that praises you for that which you
have not, wishes to take from you
that which you have.

He who counsels you to keep a secret
from your friends, desires to cheat
you without witnesses.
He who fears death, gains no joy from
life.
If one has a shop let him tend it.
(He who would have all, loses all.)
Grasp all, lose all.
He who sins and amends, commends
himself to God.
If you wish to make the thief honest,
trust him.
Remove the cause, and you remove the
sin.†

The heart is the root whence grow
Faith and Love.‡

* The people of Seville are very proud of their town.　Similarly the Italians say *Vedi
Napoli e poi mori.*
† Similarly Bacon declares that the best means of curing seditions is to remove the causes
of them.
‡ This is very like the famous *Les grandes pensées viennent du cœur* of Vauvenargues.

Recoje tu heno mientras que el sol lu-
ciere.

Make hay while the sun shines.

Reglas hay de ventura, que no toda es
acasos para el sabio ; puede ser ayu-
dada de la industria. Contentanse
algunos con ponerse de buen aire á
las puertas de la fortuna, y esperan á
que ella obre ; mejor otros passan
adelante, y valense de la cuerda auda-
cia, que en alas de su virtud, y valor,
puede dar alcance á la dicha, y lison-
jearla eficazmente.—*Gracian.*

There are rules of success, which is not
merely a matter of luck with the wise
man ; for success can be assisted by
care. Some folk are content to plant
themselves with a cheerful smile at the
gates of Fortune, and hope that she
will open to them. Others act more
wisely in pressing onward, and they
profit by their wise audacity; for borne
along on the wings of their courage
and boldness, they overtake Fortune,
and coax her to favour them.

Remuda de pasturage hace bicerros
gordos.

Goats get fat by change of pastures.

Rostro ledo, y el perdon, gran ven-
ganza es del baldon.

A smiling face, and forgiveness, are the
best way to avenge an insult.

Ruegos de grande fuerza es que te hace.

The request of a lord coerces thee to
act.

Ruin consuelo el aplauso de los muchos.

Poor comfort is the mob's applause.

Saber secretos de Principes muy más
peligroso que tener muy obligado á
un Principe.—*A. Perez.*

To know a prince's secrets is much more
dangerous than to put him under an
obligation.

Saberse dejar ganando con la fortuna.
       —*Gracian.*

Know how to leave your luck when
winning.

Sacar fuerza de flaqueza.

(To draw strength from weakness.) To
attempt a task beyond one's powers.

Santa Maria la más léjos es la más
devota.

The most distant St. Mary's is the
holiest shrine.*

Sea uno primero señor de si, y lo serás
despues de los otros.—*Gracian.*

Be master of yourself, first of all, and
afterwards you will be the master of
others.

Se há de usar de esta vida como cosa
agena.

We ought to use this life as a thing not
our own.

Señal mortal de un Principe que no pide
consejo.—*Antonio Perez.*

'Tis a bad symptom in a prince when he
does not ask advice.

Sentir con los menos, y hablar con los
mas.—*Gracian.*

Think with the Few, speak with the
Many.

Servicios pasados son como deudas
viejas, que se cobran pocas.
       —*Antonio Perez.*

Past services are like old debts, for few
are ever paid.

Siempre cree en Dios quien cruza el
Océano.—*R. de Campoamor.*

Whoso crosses the Ocean, believes in
God.

Siempre el año pasado fué mejor.

(The past year was always best.) "The
good old times," says the *laudator
temporis acti.*

Siempre favorece el cielo los buenos de-
seos.—*Cervantes.*

Heaven always favours good desires.

* **A proverb applied to those people who are always inclined to praise all things but those
at their own door.**

Sierra.

A chain of mountains with jagged ridges like the teeth of a saw.

Siesta.

The hottest part of the day, when most Spaniards take a nap.

Si no va el otero á Mahoma, que vaya Mahoma al otero.

If the mountain will not come to Mahomet, Mahomet must come to the mountain.

Sin reglas del arte
Borriquitos hay
Que una vez aciertan
Por casualidad.— *Yriarte*.

Without any rules of literary art, there are asses who sometimes attain success by accident.

Sobre gustos no hay nada escrito.

There's no accounting for tastes.

Sobre un buen cimiento se puede levantar un buen edificio, y el mejor cimiento en el mundo es el dinero.
— *Cervantes*.

On a good foundation a good edifice can be built, and the best foundation in the world is money.

Socorros de España, tarde ó nunca.

Spanish succour comes late or never.*

Solamente es rico el que lo sabe ser.

He alone has wealth, who knows how to use it.

Sólo Dios hace lo que *quiere*. El hombre hace lo que *puede*.
—*R. de Campoamor*.

God alone does what he *wishes*. Man does what he *can*.

Sólo se vence la pasion amorosa con huirla.—*Cervantes*.

Flight is the only cure for the passion of love.

Somos todos hijos de Adan.

(We are all Adam's sons.)
The gardener Adam and his wife
Smile at the claims of long descent.
— *Tennyson*.

Sonó la flauta
Por casualidad.— *Yriarte*.

He played the flute by accident.†

Sufre por saber, y trabaja por tener.

Suffer in order to know, and toil in order to have.

Tal amo, tal criado.

Like master, like man.

Tan grande es el yerro, como él que yerra.

The greatness of the sinner is the measure of the sin.

Tan présto va el cordero como el carnero.

(The lamb goes as soon as the sheep.) Death threatens old and young alike.

Tanto vales como has.

(You are worth what you have.) Money makes the man.

Tenemos hijo ó hija ?

(Have we a son or a daughter ?) Is the business likely to turn out well or ill ?

Tener al padre alcalde.

(To have the judge as one's father.) To be under the protection of the great.

Tener es temer.—*R. de Campoamor*.

(To have is to fear.) Wealth spells anxiety.‡

* The truth of this proverb was abundantly illustrated during the recent Hispano-American War.
† These lines from one of Yriarte's Fables have become proverbial. They are generally applied to those who become successful through luck rather than from any merits of their own.
‡ On the other hand, *Cantabit vacuus coram latrone viator.*

Portuguese.

A affeição é principio de aprender.

Inclination is the first step to knowledge.

A agua o dá, a agua o leva.

(The water gives it, the water takes it.) Lightly come, lightly go.

A cão mordido todos o mordem.

(All bite the dog that is bitten.) Give a dog a bad name, and hang him.

A caridade bem entendida principia por casa.

Charity begins at home.

A casa do amigo rico irás sendo requerido, e á casa do necessitado sem ser chamado.

Go to the house of a rich friend when you are invited; to the house of a needy friend go without being summoned.

Achar fôrma para o sapato.

(To find a last for the shoe.) To meet one's match.

A Deus poderás mentir, mas não pódes enganar a Deus.

You may lie to God, but you cannot deceive Him.

A experiencia é o fructo, que se colhe dos erros.

Experience is the fruit which is culled from the tree of errors.

A fé não tem olhos, quem quer ver não tem fé.

Faith has no eyes; he has no faith who wishes to see.

Agosto e vindima não é cada dia.

August and vintage come not every day.

Agosto tem a culpa, Setembro leva a fructa.

August gets the blame, September takes the fruit.

Agua molle em pedra dura, tanto dá, até que fura.

Soft water falling on a hard rock at length wears it away.

A homem farto as cerejas amargam.

To a cloyed man cherries taste bitter.

A homem ventureiro a filha lhe nasce primeiro.

The lucky man has a daughter for his first child.*

Ainda que somos negros, gente somos, e alma temos.

Though our skins are black, we are men, and have souls.†

A India é praça de cavalleiros.

India is the mart of gentlemen.‡

* In poor families the eldest daughter is the family drudge.
† The Portuguese do not appear to have taken this saying to heart, if we can trust the tales of their treatment of the natives in Africa.
‡ The Portuguese, as is natural, considering that Portugal was the home of Vasco da Gama and Camoens, have several proverbialisms dealing with India. Most of these sayings are not very flattering to the country in question.

A India é sepultura de homens honrados.

India is the tomb of honoured men.

A India mais vão do que tornam.

To India more go than return.

A ingratidão é sepultura do amor.

Ingratitude is the sepulchre of love.

A injustiça e tyrannia, ainda que maltratam, não affrontam.

Injustice and tyranny, although the injure, do not dismay.

Alcança quem não cança.

Success comes to him who faints not.

A lingua do maldizente, e o ouvido do que o ouve, são irmãos.

The tongue of him who utters slander, and the ear of him who hearkens to it, are brothers.

A mais refinada malicia é a que se disfarça com apparencias de virtude.

The most refined wickedness is that which is covered with the appearance of virtue.

A mãos lavadas Deus lhes dá que comam.

God puts food into clean hands.

Amar a Deus é a maior das virtudes, ser amado de Deus, é a maior das felicidades.

To love God is the greatest of virtues; to be loved of God is the greatest of blessings.

Amar e saber não póde ser.

Love and prudence go not together.

Ama-se a traição, aborrece-se o traidor.

Treason is loved, the traitor abhorred.

Amigo anojado, inimigo dobrado.

A friend offended is twice a foe.

Amigo de bom tempo, muda-se com o vento.

Fine-weather friends change with the wind.

Amigos e mulas falecem a duras.

Friends and mules fail us on the roughest ground.

Amigo velho mais vale que dinheiro.

An old friend is worth more than money.

Amor e senhoria não quer companhia.

Love and lordship like no fellowship.

Amor não tem lei.

Love has no law.

A mortos e a idos, não ha amigos.

The dead and the absent have no friends.

A mulher de boa vida não teme ao homem de má lingua.

The woman who leads a good life, does not fear the slanderous tongue of man.

A mulher que a dous ama, a ambos engana.

The woman who loves two, deceives both.

Antes bom Rei, que boa lei.

(Better is a good king than a good law.) The letter of the law is nothing, the administration is everything.

Antes dobrar que quebrar.

Better to bend than break.

Antes só, que mal acompanhado.

Better be alone than in bad company.

Ao bom amigo com teu pão, e com teu vinho.

To a good friend with thy bread and with thy wine.

Ao bom calar chamam santo.

Good silence is called saintliness.

Ao medico, ao advogado, e ao abbade fallar verdade.

To your doctor, your lawyer, and your priest, speak the truth.

Aonde o ouro falla, tudo calla.

Where money speaks all else is silent.

Aos senhores, que mandam cousas injustas, não obedecem os subditos em cousas justas.

Rulers who order what is unjust, are disobeyed by their subjects even in what is just.

A palavra é prata, o silencio é ouro.

Speech is silvern, silence is golden.

A pobreza não é vileza.

Poverty is no shame.

Aquelles são ricos, que tem amigos.

They are rich who have friends.

A quem has de rogar, não has de assanhar.

You must not vex the man from whom you have to ask a favour.

As aguas do mar ao mar, e todas as cousas ao seu natural.

Sea-water to the sea, and all things in their proper place.

As cousas arduas e lustrosas
Se alcançam com trabalho e com fadiga ;
Faz as pessoas altas e famosas
A vida que se perde e que periga.
—*Camoens.*

Deeds of difficulty and of fame are achieved by toil and struggle ; it is the life which is endangered, or lost, that makes men famous and of high renown.

As cousas humildes não são tão sujeitas á mudança ; as raizes, e os troncos sentem mais raras vezes as violencias.

Humble things are never very liable to change, just as the roots and trunks of trees rarely feel the violence of the storms.

Asno de muitos, lobos o comem.

(The wolves eat the ass which many folk own.)   What is every man's business is no man's business.

Asno que tem fome, cardos come.

The hungry ass eats thistles.

As obras, e não a duração, são a medida certa da vida humana.

The true measure of human life is not its length, but how much we accomplish therein.

As paredes tem ouvidos.

Walls have ears.

A um ruim ruim e meio.

(To one knave a knave and a-half.) Set a thief to catch a thief.

Auto da fé

Act of the Faith.*

A vestidura que a muitos ha de cobrir, a contentamento de todos se ha de cortar.

The coat which has to cover many, must be cut so as to please all.

Azeite, vinho e amigo, o mais antigo.

Of oil, wine, and friends, the oldest is the best.

Bem sabe o gato cujas barbas lambe.

The cat knows well whose cheek she licks.

Boa é a tardança que assegura.

Good is the delay which renders more secure.

Boca de mel, coração de fel.

A mouth of honey and a heart of gall.

Bocado comido não ganha amigo.

A morsel eaten gains no friend.

Bolsa vazia, e casa acabada, faz o homem sisudo, mas tarde.

An empty purse, and a house completed, make a man wise, but the wisdom comes too late.

Bom coração quebranta má ventura.

A stout heart overcomes ill fortune.

Bom entendedor, poucas palavras.

(A good listener, few words.)   A word to the wise is enough.

Bom é o que Deus dá.

Good is that which God gives.

Bom principio é a metade.

A good beginning is half the battle.

---

* The name given to the burning of a heretic by the Inquisition. On such occasions a declaration of the reasons of the condemnation, etc.—the *auto da fé*—was publicly read out. The words are now commonly applied to any conflagration.

Bom saber é calar até ser tempo de fallar.

It is prudence to be silent until it is time to speak.

Buscar agua em fonte secca.

(To seek water in a dry fountain.) To look for a needle in a bundle of hay.

Cada carneiro por seu pé pende.

(Every sheep should hang by its own foot.) Every tub must stand on its own bottom.

Cada porco tem seu S. Martinho.

(Every pig has its Martinmas.) Every dog has his day.

Cada qual com seu egual.

(Every man with his equal.) Birds of a feather flock together.

Cada qual por si, e Deus por todos.

Every man for himself, and God for us all.

Cada terra com seu uso, cada roca com seu fuso.

Every land its own customs; every distaff its own spindle.

Cada um canta, como tem graça, e casa como tem ventura.

Every man sings according to his pleasure, and marries according to his luck.

Cada um colhe segundo semeia.

As a man sows, so shall he reap.

Cada um é senhor em sua casa.

(Every man is lord in his own house.) Every man's house is his castle.

Cada um sabe onde lhe aperta o sapato.

Every man knows where the shoe pinches him.

Cahir da frigideira nas brasas.

To fall out of the frying-pan into the fire.

Caldeira de Pedro Botelho.

Peter Botelho's cauldron.*

Caminho da virtude alto e fragoso,
Mas no fim doce, alegre e deleitoso.
    —Camoens.

The path of virtue is steep and rugged, but in the end it is sweet, joyous, and delightsome.

Canta Martha depois de farta.

(Martha sings when she has had her fill.) A full stomach, the heart merry.

Cão ladrador nunca bom mordedor.

A barking dog is ne'er a good biter.

Casar, casar, sôa bem, e sabe mal.

Marriage sounds well, but tastes bitter.

Castiga o bom, melhorará; castiga o máo, peorará.

Chastise the good, and he will amend; chastise the wicked, and he will become worse.

Cobra boa fama, faze o que quizeres.

Gain a good name, and do as you please.

Com agua passada não moe o moinho.

Water that has flowed past does not turn the mill.

Com a mulher e o dinheiro, não zombes, companheiro.

No jests with my wife or my money, comrade!

Com arte e com engano se vive meio anno; com engano e com arte se vive a outra parte.

With craft and trickery one may live half a year; with trickery and craft one may live the other half.

Com El Rei, e com a Inquisição chiton!

With the King and the Inquisition—hush!

* A slang term for hell.

Comer a custa da barba longa.	(To eat at the expense of the long beard.) To live at another's charge; to toady for a livelihood.
Com o olho, e com a Fé, não zombarei.	I will not jest with my eye, nor with the Faith.*
Coração que suspira não tem o que deseja.	The heart which sighs lacks what it longs for.
Corvos a corvos não se tiram os olhos.	Crows do not peck out the eyes of crows.
Curtas tem as pernas a mentira, e apanha-se azinha.	A lie has short legs and is soon overtaken.
Cutelo máo corta o dedo, e não córta o pão	A bad knife cuts the finger and not the bread.

Da ma mulher te guarda, e da boa não fies nada.	Beware of a bad woman, and do not trust a good one.
Da mão á boca se perde a sopa.	(From hand to mouth the soup is lost.) There is many a slip 'twixt the cup and the lip.
Debaixo de boa palavra, ahi está o engano.	(Under fine words is cheating hid.) Fine words butter no parsnips.
De bons propositos está o Inferno cheio, e o Ceo de boas obras.	Hell is full of good intentions, and Heaven is full of good works.
De noite todos os gatos são pardos.	In the night all cats are grey.
Despertar o cão que dorme.	(To awaken the sleeping dog.) To stir up the mud; to open old sores.
De tal arvore, tal fructo.	Like tree, like fruit.
Deus ajuda aos que trabalham.	God helps those who help themselves.
Do mal o menos.	Of evils choose the least.
Dos pequenos as culpas se chamam grandes, e as dos grandes pequenas.	The sins of the petty are called great, and the sins of the great are called petty.
Dous olhos não bastam para chorar grandes males.	Two eyes are not enough to weep for great sorrows.

Em almas não ha Rei que mande.	(Over the mind no king has sway.) Thought is free.
Em boca cerrada não entra mosca.	A fly does not enter a closed mouth.
Em cada terra seu uso.	Every land has its own customs.
Em casa de Mouro, não falles algaravia.	(Do not speak Arabic in the house of a Moor.) Do not talk Latin before the learned.
Em quanto ha vida, ha esperança.	While there is life there is hope.
Em salvo está o que repica.	He who rings the alarm bell is himself in safety.†

* The eyes are always too precious to trifle with, and the Faith, especially in the days of the Inquisition, was a dangerous thing for scoffers to sharpen their wits on.
† A saying that is applied to those people who, while running no risk themselves, advocate a strenuous course of action for other people.

Em tempo de figos não ha amigos.

(At the time of figs there are no friends.) None think of their friends' interests when their own are involved.

Em uma hora não se ganhou Zamora.

(Zamora was not captured in an hour.) Rome was not built in a day.

Ensaboar a cabeça do asno, perda do sabão.

It is waste of soap to wash the head of an ass.

Estar na aldeia, e não ver as casas.

(To be in the village, and not see the houses.) Not to see the wood for the trees.

Esmolou S. Matheus, esmolou para os seus.

(St. Matthew begged for alms, he begged for his friends.) Charity begins at home.

Este é meu amigo, que moe no meu moinho.

He is my friend who grinds at my mill.

Fallar sem cuidar, é atirar sem apontar.

To speak without thinking is like shooting without taking aim.

Fazer bem a velhacos, é deitar agua no mar.

To do a kindness to knaves is to throw water in the sea.

Fazer d'uma via dous mandados.

(To perform two errands on one journey.) To kill two birds with one stone.

Gato escaldado d'agua fria tem medo.

The scalded cat is afraid of cold water.

Guarde-vos Deus de amigo reconciliado.

God keep you from a friend who was once your foe.

Guarde-vos Deus de physico experimentador, e de asno ornejador.

God keep you from a doctor who tries experiments, and from an ass that brays.

Guar-te dos azos, e guar-te-ha Deus dos peccados.

Keep thyself from the occasions, and God will keep thee from sin.

Homem apercebido, meio combatido.

A man prepared, is half the battle.

Homem farto não é comedor.

(The sated man is not an eater.) Enough is as good as a feast.

Homem morto não falla.

Dead men tell no tales.

Homem põe, e Deos dispõe.

Man proposes, God disposes.

Homem, que madruga, de algo tem cura.

The man who rises early has something on his mind.

Ira de irmãos, ira de diabos.

The wrath of brothers, the wrath of devils.

Isto é outro cantar.

(That is another song.) That is quite another pair of shoes.

Lançar o gato ás barbas de outrem.

(To throw the cat on the face of another.) Escaping from a difficulty by implicating another.

Lá vão leis onde querem cruzados. | Laws go where dollars please.

Lá vão os pés onde quer o coração. | The feet go where the heart wills.

Leis em favor do Rei se estabelecem, As em favor do povo só perecem.
— *Camoens*. | Laws in the king's favour stand unchanged ; those in favour of the poor are annulled.

Levar agua ao mar. | (To carry water to the sea.) Coals to Newcastle.

Longe da vista, longe do coração. | Out of sight, out of mind.

Mãe, casai-me logo, que se me arruga o rosto. | Mother, marry me soon for my face is wrinkling.*

Mais leve cousa é padecer qualquer tormento que esperal-o. | It is easier to suffer any woe, than to expect it.

Mais valem amigos na praça, que dinheiros na arca. | Friends in the market are worth more than money in the chest.

Mais vale um passaro na mão, que dous que voando vão. | A bird in the hand is worth two flying.

Mal vae ao fuso quando a barba não anda em cima. | (It goes ill with the spindle when the beard is not over it.) Women are ships and must be manned.

Matar dous coelhos de uma cajadada. | (To kill two rabbits with one crook.) To kill two birds with one stone.

Melhor é o anno tardio, que vazio. | (Better a late year than an empty one.) Better late than never.

Melhor é uma casa na villa, que duas no arrabalde. | One house in the town is better than two in the country.

Melhor é um pão com Deus, que dous com o demo. | Better one loaf with God than two with the devil.

Melhor he merecel-os, sem os ter, Que possuil-os, sem os merecer.
— *Camoens*. | It is better to merit blessings without possessing them, than to possess them without meriting them.

Mentiras de caçadores são as maiores. | Sportsmen's lies are the greatest.†

Merenda comida, companhia desfeita. | (The meal eaten, the company dispersed.) Friendship thrives while the pot boils.

Miguel, Miguel, não tens abelhas, e vendes mel. | Michael, Michael, you have no bees, still you sell honey.

Muita palha, e pouco grão. | (Much straw and little grain.) Great cry and little wool.

Muito sabe o rato, mas mais sabe o gato. | The mouse knows much, but the cat knows more.

Mulher, vento, e ventura, azinha se muda. | Woman, wind, and fortune, change quickly.

Na agua envolta pesca o pescador. | The fisher catches fish in troubled waters.

---

* The cry of the spinster whose face is her only fortune.
† In England it is the angler who is considered apt to ignore the truth, so long as he can give " verisimilitude to an otherwise bald and unconvincing narrative."

Na arca aberta o justo pecca.

(At an open chest the just man sins.) Opportunity makes the thief.

Na India os mais vivem de esperança, e o commum morre sem paga.

In India most folk live on hope, and the greater number die without reward.

Na India todos são ricos, porque lhes basta pouco.

In India all men are rich, for a little suffices them.

Não bebas cousa que não vejas, nem assignes carta que não leias.

Drink nothing you have not seen, sign nothing you have not read.

Não corta as bainhas.

(He does not cut the scabbard.) In his case the blade will never wear out the sheath.

Não é honra acabar cousas pequenas.

There is no honour in petty achievements.

Não é maior entre os doutos o mais nobre, senão o mais sciente.

Among the learned the most highly-born is not the greatest, but he who knows the most.

Não é o bom bocado para a boca de asno.

(The tasty morsel is not for the ass's mouth.) Cast not pearls before swine.

Não é o diabo tão feio como o pintam.

The devil is not so black as he is painted.

Não ha atalho sem trabalho.

(There is no short road without toil.) No gains without pains.

Não ha cousa mais cara, que a que custa vergonha.

Nothing is so expensive as that which costs us shame.

Não ha melhor espelho que o amigo velho.

There is no better mirror than an old friend.

Não ha peior zombaria que a verdade.

Truth is the worst kind of jest.

Não louves até que proves.

(Praise not until you prove.) If you trust before you try, you may repent before you die.

Não saber ler.

(Not to know reading.) Not to know black from white.

Não se póde viver sem amigos.

Without friends life is impossible.

Não se vence perigo sem perigo.

Danger is not overcome without danger.

Não vive mais o leal, que quanto quer o traidor.

The loyal man lives no longer than the traitor wills.

Nas barbas do homem astroso se ensina o barbeiro novo.

On the beard of the unlucky man the novice learns to shave.

Na terra dos cegos o torto é rei.

In the country of the blind the one-eyed is king.

Nem por muito madrugar, amanhece mais asinha.

The dawn comes no sooner for all one's early rising.

Nem todos os que estudam são lettrados
Nem todos os que vão á guerra são soldados.

(All who study are not learned, nor all who go to war soldiers.) All are not huntsmen that blow the horn.

Nem tudo o que luz é ouro.

All is not gold that glitters.

Nem um dedo faz mão, nem uma andorinha verão.

One finger does not make a hand, nor one swallow a summer.

No mar tanta tormenta e tanto dano,
Tantas vezes a morte apercebida!
Na terra tanta guerra, tanto engano,
Tanta necessidade aborrecida!
Onde pode acolher-se hum fraco
  humano,
Onde terá segura a curta vida?
Que não se arme e se indigne o Ceo
  sereno
Contra hum bicho da terra tão pequeno!
                    —*Camoens*.

At sea, so many storms and loss so
  great,
So often death arrayed and seeming
  sure,
On land, so many wars, so much deceit,
And so much wretched misery to endure!
Where shall weak man discover a retreat,
Where may he deem his short life's
  hour secure?
That calm Heaven's might and anger
  may not fall
Upon a worm of earth so weak and
  small.—*J. J. Aubertin*.

Nos trabalhos se vêem os amigos.

A friend in need is a friend indeed.

Nunca de rabo de porco bom virote.

(A good arrow is never made of a sow's
tail.)   You cannot make a silk purse
out of a sow's ear.

O avarento por um real perde cento.

The miser loses a hundred pence to
  gain one.

O bom dia, mette-o em casa.

(Take the fine day into thine house.)
Seize the golden opportunity.

O bom ganhar faz o bom gastar.

The good earner makes the good
  spender.

Obra começada, meia acabada.

A work begun is half done.

O fim corôa a obra.

The end crowns the work.

Oh grandes e gravissimos perigos!
Oh caminho de vida nunca certo!
Que aonde a gente põe sua esperança
Tenha a vida pouca segurança!
                    —*Camoens*.

Oh dangers great and dire!   Oh path
of life that is always obscure!   Where-
so'er men set their hopes, life affords
but little security.

O homem feliz sempre deve temer,
sempre deve esperar o infeliz.

The fortunate man ought always to fear;
  the unfortunate ought always to hope.

O homem tendo a mulher feia, tem a
fama segura.

The man who has an ugly wife, holds
  his reputation safe.

Oh quanto deve o Rei, que bem
governa,
De olhar que os conselheiros ou privados
De consciencia e de virtude interna
E de sincero amor sejam dotados!
Porque, como está posto na superna
Cadeira, pode mal dos apartados
Negocios ter noticia mais inteira
Do que lhe der a lingua conselheira.
                    —*Camoens*.

Oh, how a king who governs well
  should see
That counsellors, and those more in-
  timate,
With love sincere and true endowed
  should be,
With conscience and with purity innate!
For, as he thronèd sits in majesty,
Of matters far removed, affairs of state,
But little more can he be made aware
Than what the official tongue may
  choose declare.—*J. J. Aubertin*.

O magnanimo tem a honra dos outros
por sua.

The high-souled man holds the honour
  of others as dear as his own.

O maior dos infortunios é quando póde pouco, e quer muito ; e a maior das fortunas é quando o homem quer pouco, e póde muito.

O mal ganhado, leva-o o diabo.

O monte pariu um rato.

Onde não ha el rei o perde.

O peior porco come a melhor lande.

O primeiro bem do mundo, que o homem ha de procurar, é bom nome ; só deste nome temos a propriedade ; de todos os mais temos o uso.

Ouro é o que ouro vale.

Ouve, vê, e cala, se queres viver em paz.

Paga o justo pelo peccador.
Palavras não enchem barriga.

Pão e vinho anda caminho.

Para os entendidos acenos bastam.

Peccado confessado é meio perdoado.
Pela boca morre o peixe.

Perdoar é vencer.
Pouco se estima o que tem cada vizinha.

Quando em casa não está o gato, estende-se o rato.
Quanto, no rico assi como no pobre, Póde o vil interesse e sêde imiga
Do dinheiro, que a tudo nos obriga.
            —*Camoens*.
Quantos mais medicos, mais molestias.
Que inimiga não ha tão dura e fera
Como a virtude falsa da siñ cera.
            —*Camoens*.

The greatest misfortune is to have many wants and little power ; the greatest good fortune is to have much power and few wants.

(Evil gains, the devil takes them.)
Male parta, male dilabuntur.

(The mountain gave birth to a mouse.)
Parturiunt montes nascetur ridiculus mus.

(Where there is nothing the king loses his own.) The penniless man can pay no taxes.

(The worst pig eats the best acorn.)
The worst pig often gets the best pear.

The first blessing in the world which a man ought to seek is a good reputation. This alone is our permanent possession ; of the rest we are only tenants.

(Gold is that which is worth gold.) A thing is worth what it will fetch.

Listen, see, and be silent, if you wish to live in peace.

The just man pays for the sinner.
(Words do not fill the belly.) Help is the best consolation.

With bread and wine we may travel well.

(A nod is enough for the wise.) *Verbum sat sapienti.*

A sin confessed is half forgiven.

(The fish dies by its mouth.) Silence seldom doth harm.

To forgive is to conquer.

What all districts own is but little esteemed.

When the cat is away the mice will play.

How powerful, in the rich as in the poor, is vile self-interest, and the hateful lust of gold which enchains us all.

The more doctors, the more diseases.

There is no enemy so fierce and cruel as is simulated virtue to that which is sincere.

Quem a boa arvore se acolhe, boa sombra o cobre.

(He who leans on a good tree is well protected by the shade.) The poor man thrives if he has a good patron.

Quem ama a Beltrão, ama o seu cão.

(He who loves Bertrand, loves his dog.) Love me, love my dog.

Quem ama o perigo n' elle perecerá.

He who loves danger will perish in it.

Quem ameaça, e não dá, medo ha.

He who threatens, and strikes not, is himself afraid.

Quem anda em demanda, com o demo anda.

He who goes to law, goes with the devil.

Quem cala consente.

Silence gives consent.

Quem canta, seus males espanta.

He who sings drives away his grief.

Quem cerca em derredor este rotundo
Globo, e sua superficie tão limada,
He Deos: mas o que he Deos ninguem
o entende;
Que a tanto o engenho humano não se
estende —*Camoens.*

He who encircles the smooth, round surface of this world, is God. But what God is no man knoweth, for that knowledge passes the wit of man.

Quem com máo vizinho ha de vizinhar com um olho ha de dormir, e com outro vigiar.

He who has to live with bad neighbours must sleep with one eye shut and the other open.

Quem deve cento, e tem cento e um não teme a nenhum.

(He who owes a hundred and owns a hundred-and-one is afraid of nobody.) Out of debt, out of danger.

Quem é amigo de vinho, de si mesmo é inimigo.

A friend of wine is an enemy to himself.

Quem espera por sapatos de defuncto toda a vida anda descalço.

He who hopes for a dead man's shoes walks all his life unshod.

Quem faz bem ao astroso não perde parte, mas perde todo.

He who does a service to the unlucky wastes not half, but all his pains.

Quem faz casa na praça, uns dizem que é alta, outros que é baixa.

He who builds a house in the market-place, is told by some that it is too high, and by others that it is too low.

Quem faz injuria vil e sem razão,
Com forças e poder em que está posto,
Não vence; que a victoria verdadeira
He saber ter justiça nua e inteira.
       —*Camoens.*

He who inflicts vile, unreasoning wrong, using the means that his station gives him, is not a conqueror. True conquest consists in knowing how to maintain pure and absolute justice.

Quem mostra temor, dá ousadia a seu contrario.

He who shows fear, gives courage to his adversary.

Quem muito abarca, pouco abraça.

(He who grasps much, gains little.) Grasp all, lose all.

Quem muito estima as couzas pequenas, nunca faz nenhuma grande.

He who highly esteems pretty things, never does anything great.

Quem não espera, não obra.

He who has no hope, does no work.

Quem o feio ama, bonito lhe parece.

She who loves an ugly man, thinks him handsome.

Quem pouco sabe, asinha o reza.

The man with a little knowledge soon displays it.

Quem quando pode não quer, quando quer não pode.

He that will not when he may,
When he will he shall have nay.

Quem ruim é em sua terra ruim é fóra d' ella.

(He who is knavish in his own land is knavish abroad.) *Cælum non animum mutant qui trans mare currunt.*

Quem se muda Deus ajuda.

He who amends is helped by God.

Quem só come seu gallo, só sella seu cavallo.

He who eats his fowl alone, alone must saddle his nag.

Quem te faz festa, não soendo fazer, ou te quer enganar, ou te ha mister.

He that makes a fuss of you when not wont to do so, either desires to cheat you, or has some need of you.

Quem tem boca vae a Roma.

He who has a tongue goes to Rome.

Quem tem bom ninho, tem bom amigo.

(He who has a good nest, has a good friend.) In prosperity we have plenty of friends.

Quem teme o perigo não se mette n' elle.

(He who fears danger should not run into it.) He that hath a head of wax must not walk in the sun.

Quem tem quatro e gasta cinco, não ha mister bolsa, nem bolsinho.

He who has four and spends five, needs neither purse nor pocket.

Rogos de Rei mandados são.

Kings' requests are commands.

Se queres bom conselho, pede-o ao velho.

If you wish good advice, consult the aged.

Se queres saber quem é o villão, mette-lhe a vara na mão.

(If you wish to know which is the knavish fellow, put the stick in his hand.) Office proves the man.

Se te fizeres mel, comer-te-hão as moscas.

If you make yourself honey, the flies will eat you.

Siso em prosperidade, amigo em necessidade, e mulher rogada casta, raramente se acha.

Wisdom in prosperity, a friend in need, a woman tempted yet chaste, are rarely seen.

Sobre dinheiro não ha companheiro.

In a question of money there are no comrades.

Tal ha de ser quem quer co' o dom de Marte
Imitar os illustres e igualal-os :
Voar co' o pensamento a toda parte,
Adivinhar perigos e evital-os :
Com militar engenho e subtil arte
Entender os imigos e enganal-os
Crer tudo em fim ; que nunca louvarei
O capitão que diga : " Não cuidei."
　　　　　　　　　　—Camoens.

Such must he be who with a martial heart
The illustrious equal would, and emulate :
Must fly with thoughtfulness to every part,
Dangers avoid and e'en anticipate ;
With military genius, subtle art
The foe must understand and lure to fate ;
In fine, mark all ; ne'er will I praise, indeed,
The Captain who could say, " I did not heed."—*J. J. Aubertin.*

Tanto morre o Papa, como o que não tem capa.

The Pope is as liable to death as the man who has no coat.

Tarde dar e negar estão a par.

To give tardily and to refuse are near akin.

Tarde ou cedo dá o tempo a cada um o que merece.

Soon or late Time gives to every man what he deserves.

Tornar á vacca fria.

(To return to the cold beef.) *Revenir à nos moutons.*

Tres irmãos, tres fortalezas.

Three brothers, three fortresses.

Tudo consiste em ser homem de bem.

To be an honest man is the all in all.

Uma mão lava a outra, e ambas o rosto.

One hand washes the other, and both the face.

Um aspide não mata outro.

(One asp slays not another.) Dog does not eat dog.

Velho amador, Inverno com flor.

An old man in love is like a flower in winter.

Vender gato por lebre.

(To sell the cat for hare.) To give chalk for cheese.

Vento e ventura pouco dura.

Wind and fortune quickly change.

Viuva rica com um olho chora, e com outro repica.

A rich widow weeps with one eye and laughs with the other.

Viva quem vence.

(Hurrah for the conqueror!) It is always best to be on the winning side.

Voz do povo, voz de Deus.

(The voice of the people is the voice of God.) *Vox populi, vox Dei.*

Zombai com o doudo em casa, zombará comvosco na praça.

Jest with the boor in the house, he will jest with you in the market.

AUTHORS QUOTED.

The dates given are invariably A.D., *unless otherwise indicated.*

Dumouriez, French Statesman and General, 1739—1823
Dupin, French Jurist, 1782—1865

Emeric David, French Archæologist, 1755—1839
Ennius, Latin Poet, 239—169 B.C.
Enzina, Juan de la, Spanish Poet, 15th century
Epicharmus, Greek Poet, flourished 5th century B.C.
Epictetus, Greek Philosopher, died about 120
Epicurus, Greek Philosopher, 337—270 B.C.
Erasmus, Latin Scholar, 1467—1536
Esternod, French Poet, 1590—1640
Eupolis, Greek Comic Poet, 446—411 B.C.
Euripides, Greek Dramatist, 480—407
Evers, J. L., Goldsmith of Hamburg

Favre, Jules, French Politician, 1809—1880
Fénelon, French Litterateur, etc., 1651—1715
Ferrier, Louis, French Dramatic Poet, 1652—1721
Fichte, German Philosopher, 1762—1814
Filicaja, Vincenzo, Italian Poet, 1642—1707
Flahaut, Madame de, French Novelist, 1761—1836
Flammarion, Camille, French Astronomer and Author, 1842—
Fléchier, French Preacher, etc., 1632—1710
Flemming, Paul, German Poet, 1609—1640
Florian, French Fabulist, 1755—1794
Fontenelle, French Philosopher, 1657—1757
Forster, George, German Philosopher, 1754—1794
Foscolo, Ugo, Italian Writer, 1777—1827
Fournier, Edouard, French Litterateur, 1819—1880
Francis I., King of France, 1494—1547
François de Neufchâteau, French Poet, etc., 1750—1828
Frank, Félix, French Critic, etc., 1837—
Frederick II., the Great, King of Prussia, 1712—1786
Frederick III., German Emperor, 1831—1888
Frezzi, Bishop of Foligno, died 1416

Gambetta, French Politician, 1838—1882
Gaucher de Châtillon, Constable of France, 1250—1328
Gaudin, French Statesman, 1756—1844
Gautier, Théophile, French Poet, etc., 1811—1872
Gavarni (Paul Chevallier), French Caricaturist, 1801—1866
Geibel, German Poet, 1815—
Gellert, German Poet, 1715—1769
Gerfaut (Madame de la Grangerie), French Journalist, 1847—
Gessner, German Poet, 1730—1788
Girardin, Madame de, French Authoress, 1804—1855
Girardin, St. Marc, French Statesman, etc., 1801—1873
Gleim, German Poet, 1719—1803
Gobet, French Poet, 18th century
Goethe, German Poet, etc., 1749—1832
Goldoni, Italian Dramatist, 1707—1793
Gosse, French Litterateur, 1773—1834
Gracian, Spanish Writer of Maxims, etc., 1584—1658

Grécourt, French Poet, 1684—1743
Grégoire, Bishop of Blois, 1750—1831
Gresset, French Poet, 1709—1777
Grévy, Jules, President of the French Republic, 1807—1891
Grimwald, Duke of Benevento, 7th century
Grossi, Italian Poet, etc., 1791—1853
Guarini, Italian Poet, 1537—1612
Guibert, French Strategist and Litterateur, 1743—1790
Guicciardini, Italian Historian and Diplomatist, 1482—1540
Guizot, French Historian, etc., 1787—1874
Guzman, F. Perez de, Spanish Poet, 15th century

Halm (Baron de Münch-Bellinghausen), German Dramatist, etc., 1806—1871
Hartzenbusch, J. E., Spanish Poet, etc., 1806—1880
Hegel, German Philosopher, 1770—1831
Heine, German Poet, 1799—1856
Heliodorus, Greek Writer, 1st century
Henry IV., King of France, 1553—assassinated, 1610
Heraclitus, Greek Philosopher, flourished 500 B.C.
Herder, German Philosopher, 1744—1803
Herodotus, Greek Historian, 484—406 B.C.
Hesiod, Greek Poet, 9th century B.C.
Hierocles, Greek Philosopher, flourished 5th century
Hippocrates, Greek Physician, etc., about 460—about 357 B.C.
Hipponax, Greek Satirist, flourished 540 B.C.
Hippothoon, Greek Poet, flourished 4th century B.C.
Hoffmann, H. von Fallersleben, German Poet, etc., 1798—1874
Hölty, Chr., German Poet, 1748—1776
Homer, Greek Poet, flourished probably about 1000 B.C.
Horace, Latin Poet, 65—8 B.C.
Houssaye, Arsène, French Poet, 1815—
Hugo, General, French Writer and Strategist, 1774—1827
Hugo, Victor, French Poet, Novelist, etc., 1802—1885
Humboldt, W. von, German Philosopher, 1767—1835

Isocrates, Greek Orator, 436—338 B.C.

Jeanne d'Arc, The "Maid of Orleans," 1412—1431
Joubert, French Moralist, 1734—1824
Jouffroy, French Philosopher, 1796—1842
Jouy, French Dramatist, died 1846
Juvenal, Latin Satirist, about 40—about 128

Karr, Alphonse, French Novelist, 1808—1890
Kock, Paul de, French Novelist, 1794—1871
Körner, German Poet, 1788—1812

Laberius, Latin Dramatist, 107—43 B.C.
Labiche, French Dramatist, etc., 1815—1888
La Bruyère, French Writer of Maxims, Moralist, 1639—1696
Lachaud, G., French Publicist, 1846—
La Chaussée, French Dramatist and Poet, 1692—1754